PLAYING FOR A WINNER

Playing for a Winner

*How Baseball Teams' Success
Raises Players' Reputations*

Brandon Isleib

Foreword by Craig Calcaterra

McFarland & Company, Inc., Publishers
Jefferson, North Carolina

LIBRARY OF CONGRESS CATALOGUING-IN-PUBLICATION DATA

Names: Isleib, Brandon, 1985– author.
Title: Playing for a winner : how baseball teams' success raises players' reputations / Brandon Isleib ; foreword by Craig Calcaterra.
Description: Jefferson, North Carolina : McFarland & Company, Inc., Publishers, 2016. | Includes bibliographical references and index.
Identifiers: LCCN 2016047151 | ISBN 9781476665382 (softcover : acid free paper) ∞
Subjects: LCSH: Baseball—Economic aspects—United States. | Baseball players—Rating of—United States. | Baseball teams—Evaluation—United States. | Mass media and sports—United States.
Classification: LCC GV880 .I75 2016 | DDC 331.2817963570973—dc23
LC record available at https://lccn.loc.gov/2016047151

BRITISH LIBRARY CATALOGUING DATA ARE AVAILABLE

ISBN (print) 978-1-4766-6538-2
ISBN (ebook) 978-1-4766-2701-4

© 2017 Brandon Isleib. All rights reserved

No part of this book may be reproduced or transmitted in any form or by any means, electronic or mechanical, including photocopying or recording, or by any information storage and retrieval system, without permission in writing from the publisher.

Front cover: Opening game of the 2013 World Series in Fenway Park (photograph by Rick Berry)

Printed in the United States of America

*McFarland & Company, Inc., Publishers
Box 611, Jefferson, North Carolina 28640
www.mcfarlandpub.com*

Table of Contents

Acknowledgments   vii
Foreword by Craig Calcaterra   1
Preface   5
Introduction   7

— **PART I** —
MOMENTUM, STATISTICS AND NUMBERS

1. Bird, Plane or Dynasty?   9
2. The Math of Perception   11
3. Momentum, Spotlight and SpWAR   17
4. SpWAR and the Hall of Fame   24
5. The Most Famous Players   35
6. Baseball in the Dark: The Best Players Outside the Spotlight   66

— **PART II** —
MOMENTUM, SEASONS AND NARRATIVES

7. The Early Narrative, 1871–1900   76
8. A Permanent Rival Emerges, 1901–1917   100
9. A Call to Arms and an Arms Race, 1918–1934   128
10. The Post-Ruth Era, 1935–1951   155
11. The Yankees and Dodgers, 1952–1968   183
12. Divisions of Labor, 1969–1981   212
13. A Post-Strike World, 1982–1993   243
14. Playing Your Wild Cards Right, 1994–2002   276

15. No Change but Steroids, 2003–2011	304
16. The Last (?) Changes, 2012–2015	335
17. Modern Playoffs: Better for Fans, Worse for Everyone Else	351
Chapter Notes	355
Index	367

Acknowledgments

Around 2011, I developed the basic concepts behind Momentum, my statistic to measure relative team reputations. This book initially was going to talk about it only in that context, a continuation of my work in the *2013 Hardball Times Annual* on the most surprising seasons in baseball history.

But Craig Calcaterra's articles on the retiring Derek Jeter as the "Face of Baseball"[1] got me thinking about player fame. As I was writing my initial book concept, the stats I derive from Momentum in this book—Spotlight, SpWAR, and Fame—came together to measure what Craig was talking about.

So besides Craig, who also was one of the most enthusiastic early discussers of the ideas, there are loads of other people to thank. First is everyone with whom I discussed these concepts. I checked in with many baseball fans, but I also talked to non-fans about fame and spotlight, and their comprehending my ideas gave me a lot more confidence to take those ideas to their conclusion. (That includes you, Mom—hi there.) Beyond that, I'd like to thank the following people.

Twins' PR director Dustin Morse sent my 2008 article "Sir Bert the Obscure,"[2] which discusses attendance records for Hall of Famers' teams similar to how this book uses Spotlight, to Bert Blyleven; Bert's e-mail response to that article contained the quote that starts the introduction. In August 2015 I asked for permission to repurpose the quote, and through Dustin Bert graciously agreed.

Nate Silver, Joe Sheehan, and Christina Kahrl gave me my first article on anything anywhere on Baseball Prospectus in 2007. Steve Treder found me there, and in 2008, at the urging of the late and hugely missed John Brattain, I started writing for Dave Studenmund at the *Hardball Times*. While there, I met Geoff Young, an incredibly dear friend who edited the first draft and gave input at several critical stages, Anna McDonald, the first person to tell me I should write a book one day, and Chris Jaffe, whose positive experiences with McFarland motivated me to send them a query letter.

Others revitalized me mid-project. When I met Rob Neyer, he got where

I was going and wanted to see more; his interest helped me resume my writing speed. After a throwaway Twitter exchange, British comedian, writer, and actress Carrie Quinlan surprised me with a fun voiceover advertisement for my book. And Brent Gold rescued me from self-made delays with proofing and editing of the second draft.

Lastly, my wife Amber patiently listened to all these concepts for years, patiently let me write this book for a year, and patiently read and edited it.

I hope you have people as amazing in your life as I've been blessed to have in mine.

Foreword
by Craig Calcaterra

Each November the Baseball Writers Association of America releases its annual Hall of Fame ballot. Each January the BBWAA announces which of the former players on that ballot received 75 percent of the vote and will be inducted into Cooperstown the following July. In between November and January baseball writers, analysts and unusually invested fans engage in open warfare regarding who is and who isn't a worthy choice for baseball's highest honor. For people like me who like to argue with anyone and about anything it's just another holiday gift. Sometimes the best one under the tree.

I would be lying, however, if I said that any of this arguing has made much of a difference over the years. With a few random exceptions I don't think anyone's mind has ever been truly changed. Sure, eventually a voter may throw his support behind someone he didn't initially think worthy or withdraw his support from someone he once did, but no single exchange on Twitter or angry blog post is the reason. Even if it was, the voter will usually not admit it, as there is too much bad blood and political nonsense between the two broadly warring camps on the matter: voters and members of the mainstream media who got their start covering baseball in the pre-internet age on the one hand and younger, more analytically-inclined baseball fans and writers who make up the online baseball commentariat on the other.

The legacy media contingent has, historically and by virtue of its journalism training, explained the game through stories, anecdotes and references to real or imagined character traits of the players involved, pumping up those they perceive to be heroes and slamming those they perceive to be villains. Such arguments can be described—much to the chagrin of those making them—as arguments from "narrative." Arguments in which the writer observes or researches what happened on the field and distills it into stories. Sometimes they're wonderful stories such as the ones about Pedro Martinez's competitive nature which shine a new and revealing light on his obvious on-the-field greatness. Sometimes they're, well, fictional, such as stories about how Jim Rice was allegedly "the most feared batter of his time" despite there being no evidence for the proposition whatsoever.

The analytical crowd has, historically, strived to distill baseball down to its objective and, hopefully, quantifiable essence. They've tried to push out subjective factors like character, heroism and villainy in their assessment of players. They've also tried to push out media and market bias as best they could, making the case that, say, Bert Blyleven was every bit as good and in fact significantly better than Jack Morris despite the fact that the former played for a lot of losing teams in smaller cities and the latter performed an amazing feat or two on baseball's largest stage. Of course this group has its own blind spots at times. It often tends to unduly discount the notion of a player's fame, however subjective that concept can be, and forgets that the Hall of Fame is not merely an institution which validates achievements but, likewise, a museum which strives to tell the story of baseball and its history. I mean, maybe Jim Rice *wasn't* feared, but is anyone harmed by him having a plaque on a wall that a lot of baseball fans of a certain age are happy to see?

No matter the strengths and faults of each camp's approach, each camp routinely accuses the other of *only* caring about its narratives or its numbers and each camp has accused the other of not truly enjoying baseball as much as they enjoy establishing their primacy as gatekeepers for how the game is perceived. And so we fight on. And on. Indeed, after all of these years it's become a pretty rote exercise in which people talk past one another more than anything. Even a guy like me who enjoys fighting about things has begun to grow a little tired of it all.

Which is why I was utterly gobsmacked when I met up with Brandon in Seattle last year and he told me about this book. A book which attempts to actually *quantify narrative*. To place an actual numerical value on a player's fame and public profile and to understand how much the team he played for and the success it had impacted that player's legacy. To answer questions such as "Why is Jim Rice in the Hall of Fame and Dwight Evans *not* in the Hall of Fame?" without the first answer being "Because the voters are stupid!" Maybe—just maybe—the voters were no more stupid than anyone else but something else was actually going on that we've never really noticed with Evans, Rice, and their various Red Sox teams. Something that impacted their Hall of Fame case and is a bit more complicated and makes their disparate voting results that much more understandable. Maybe it's a similar something to the phenomenon of why everyone is convinced that an East Coast Bias exists which has caused harm to the legacy of Lou Whitaker while the comparable Willie Randolph—a Yankee for the vast majority of his career—has likewise been historically underrated. Did they move New York further away from the East Coast between 1976 and 1988, or is something else going on?

There most certainly is something else going on. Or at least there was when these guys played: games. Games with wins and losses and daily changes in the standings which, as the season progresses, turn into pennant races. The analytical among us talk so much about the results of any one game and the numbers which players aggregate over the course of a season. The reporters talk so much about the storylines that spin out of any one season or group of seasons. We argue about which is more important, the numbers or the stories, but in reality they've always been working in concert when it comes to the business of building a player's legacy. The great objective performances of players necessarily result in a pennant race and every pennant race turns into a story. Those stories are inexplicable without the performances. We talk about numbers and narratives being separate things all the time but, in reality, they are inextricable from one another.

Inextricable, but not *inexplicable*. Indeed, this book is a revelation when it comes to explaining how those performances interact with the results of games and pennant races to create legacies. I don't know that anyone has ever tried to do this before and, if they have, they certainly didn't succeed. Brandon has succeeded wildly and in such a way that, if there is any justice in the world, the analytics crew and the ink-stained wretches will stop having the same old arguments every December.

Giving us time for new ones that, in a few years, Brandon can resolve again. He's pretty useful that way.

Craig Calcaterra is a lead writer and editor at NBC's MLB website, having written for the site since 2009. Before that, he wrote for the Hardball Times, *maintained the Shysterball blog, and spent 11 years as an attorney.*

Preface

This book's primary subject is measuring relative team reputations and their impact on team and player fame. Like a spotlight illuminates or a microscope magnifies, a team's consistent success illuminates and magnifies its most important players and achievements. Using daily playoff contention to measure relative team reputations creates an objective, quantifiable base to start the inquiry—the more days a team is successful, the more articles will be written in praise of it and the more that team will be paid attention to—and once those relative team reputations are determined, they can be used as multipliers on player productivity to get an idea of how players were looked at as they were playing.

This approach lends itself to a few applications. Of my two main applications in this book, Hall of Fame voting is the one more discussed in culture. Despite the reams of statistics of everyone on a Hall of Fame ballot, the idea of "feeling like a Hall of Famer" persists. That feel has to come from somewhere, and it is my assertion that adjusting productivity with a team spotlight multiplier approximates what voters, all writers, are actually voting on—a combination of statistics and story.

The less discussed application is no less important: understanding how the rise and fall of teams affects how the story of baseball has been told through the years. I discuss every year's playoff races in this book, but not from a strict win-loss perspective or from an *ex post facto* look at end-of-season totals. Instead, I look more at how teams famous in a particular moment were performing. Did a famous team entering the season significantly underperform? If so, that underperformance framed the narrative differently than if they succeeded. Nobody living through history waits until the end of the story to determine how they processed it; that history is lived a day at a time. Sports seasons are no different, and understanding relative team reputations helps restore baseball's narrative to how it was experienced as it unfolded.

As far as I am aware, this material is the first of its kind. Countless writers over the years have discussed concepts of fame and high-profile teams, but the idea of quantifying it appears to be new. Certainly, quantifying based on something that always exists and is directly comparable with like items—days of playoff contention—rather than taking an approach based more in media studies, like using newspaper circulation or television viewing figures, takes this work in a different direction than Q Scores or similar measures. Types of media come and go, but sports always have a first place to aim for; a fame measurement centered around first place, which always exists and always highlights whoever's in it, allows for direct historical comparisons.

The bulk of this material is data-crunching after years of refining my approach's particulars. As my work involves formulas to re-assess existing public data (for which I primarily used baseball-reference.com, whose version of Wins Above Replacement [WAR] I use in this book for convenience), most of the work was filtering the data through the formulas and tweaking the formulas to best capture general understandings of baseball's narrative. As far as the narratives themselves are concerned, daily standings, primarily obtained from the now defunct baseballrace.com and compiled by hand otherwise, and team schedules were critical to telling those narratives as they happened in real time. When comparing one year's performances to a previous year's, the Society for American Baseball Research (SABR) BioProject biographies on those players shed light on what happened. As much as I love finding historical nuggets, this material is not made of the type of research that uncovers them. This in no way implies a reduction of material investigated and processed for this book. To augment the thousands of web pages of data and biographies, I have sourced my historical facts with contemporary newspapers, primarily from wire/Associated Press reports, as these tended to circulate the day after an important event. It is surprising how many baseball facts are passed down through the years and the books without sourcing primary materials; anchoring history with sources from the time yields a wealth of resources to learn baseball from the ground up.

As this book would be an unreasonable size if I included everything I wanted to include, I have started baseballspotlight.com to host data and discuss related material. That website is intended to be a living extension of this book, a continuation of what this book starts—a deep investigation into where the story of baseball comes from and how it affects what we pay attention to.

Introduction

"Would Derek Jeter be as big as he is if he came up with the Tampa Bay Rays or the Washington Nationals? Who knows but he is loved in New York. And he should be because he's a great player but the bigger market helps make him BIGGER."—Bert Blyleven[1]

The difference Bert is talking about—from great player to mythical, from baseball famous to pop culture famous—is widely recognized, from debates at the bar to talk radio to Hall of Fame arguing season. But what drives that difference? Why are some players less famous than others while being as good by the numbers?

It's easy to say that playing in a large media center is the main difference, but that leaves a lot of things unexplained. Stump Merrill's 1991 Yankees were in New York, but they were 11th in league attendance, and until writing this introduction I couldn't have told you who their best pitcher was. It was Scott Sanderson, who pitched six of his 19 seasons in Chicago and two in New York but whose Wikipedia entry is wispy.[2] On the flipside, loads of people know who Pete Rose is from his years of play in Cincinnati, a traditionally small media market even as the team's games were reasonably well attended while he played there. If Derek Jeter (whose middle name, incidentally, is Sanderson) had been part of the Big Red Machine, he would have been far more famous than if he'd been part of the Scott Sanderson Experience. Size of the market is one thing, but how much that market—or the nation—wants to pay attention is another.

Is attendance the main difference? If so, it doesn't explain the '70s A's, who in their three straight world championship seasons were below average in league attendance in two of those years and below the Yankees in all three. Yet cursory talk about early '70s baseball invokes Catfish Hunter, Rollie Fingers, and Charlie Finley long before Roy White or Bobby Murcer.

If playing in New York or being a well-drawing team doesn't guarantee that a great performance will be ingrained into mass consciousness, does anything come closer? It's my view that the markets, the narrative, and the spotlight of baseball—what makes everybody pay attention—are made from daily contention for the postseason. Seasons are experienced by the day, days are summarized by writers, and the headlines and attention will gravitate to successful teams. Put Derek Jeter on the 1930s Cardinals, 1950s Dodgers, or 1970s A's and you get the same basic narrative—greatness on a team whose exploits are good enough to write about every day. Put him on the 1930s Dodgers, 1950s A's, or 1970s Cardinals and the perception changes. Contention drives narrative; narrative drives writers; writers drive fame.

That sequence is simplistic, but it has two major advantages. First, it's objectively measurable. There's always a first place, and there are always teams in it and others fighting for it; you can look at daily standings and get an idea of who is receiving increased coverage. Second, it's measurable across all time. It's easier to be in first place now than in the past—each league has three first places instead of one—but apart from that, daily contention is directly comparable across eras. If daily contention creates the spotlight that magnifies teams and their players' relative quality, then directly comparing team spotlights opens up several areas of inquiry.

In this book, I focus on two inquiries. First, I use these concepts to discuss baseball history as it was experienced—looking at baseball from the perspective of teams most involved in the conversation. Babe Ruth debuted in 1914 and Lou Gehrig started his consecutive games streak in 1925, but those facts were more significant in 1935 than when they happened, and 1914's and 1925's storylines had little to do with them. Quantifying team reputations daily and looking at pennant races instead of end-of-season records puts the narrative back where it belongs: a day-to-day retelling that helps us experience seasons moving forward instead of backward.

Second, I use relative team reputations as a multiplier on player productivity to quantify the spotlight put on certain players and how much that spotlight overrates them (and in so doing underrates others). I have real measurements to answer questions like "What if he'd played in New York?" and suggest why certain players are in the Hall of Fame while others have had difficulty getting in. Just as there are ways to translate a player's statistics in his actual environment (e.g., 2015 in Fenway Park) to another (e.g., 1935 in Wrigley Field), my methods can translate a player's reputation from his actual team to another.

Due to what I'm measuring, the measurements never can be exactly right. But using simple data to show where the spotlight was at any given time is a leap forward from musings and speculations. If at the end of this book I've given you the concepts and vocabulary to tell me why I'm wrong, then this material still will have been a success.

PART I
MOMENTUM, STATISTICS AND NUMBERS

1. Bird, Plane or Dynasty?

Team reputations don't spring from myths or preseason predictions; they're earned, rising and falling through the years. The Giants rose and fell every other year in the first half of the 2010s, so despite winning three championships in five years, the Cardinals were still the team to beat in those years because they were consistently good every year. At any given time, there's a pecking order with top dogs and underdogs, and daily contention seems to drive the perception more than win-loss record or postseason victories.

A day's standings gives us two sets of information. Wins and losses give an **absolute** position for every team—this team is 97–65 while this other team is 92–70. But how much better is a 97–65 team than a 92–70 team? What's the frame of reference for that? The gap looks big on paper, but there's nothing to measure it against; given the length of the season, we can't even compare it with other sports.

So the standings are more intuitively used to process the playoff races—**relative** team positions over time. Much like in the old joke where I don't have to outrun the bear chasing us—I just have to outrun you—standings tell us who's outrunning whom. I can't conceive of the qualitative differences between a .600 and a .550 team, but I can conceive of a team outrunning another.

Given enough time as a fan, that running, that jockeying for position, will be the season's lasting impression, because we experience those races daily over about 180 days a year, not as an end-of-year summary. The 2014 Athletics were a decent 88–74 and made the playoffs, but they will be remembered as a largely dominant team that wilted at the end. The 2014 Royals were 89–73 and also made the playoffs, but they came from far behind, got hot late, and played a higher level of ball through game seven of the World Series. Over 180 days, they got virtually the same result, but how they got there affects our perception of their strengths and our expectations that they'd win a random game, say, in August.

The Athletics had built their reputation, their winning tradition, over several years of strong records. The Royals had not. We could look at the few games' difference at season's end and make some predictions, but at the time those predictions were informed largely by the Royals having been closer to the bear than the Athletics since 2012.[1]

Win-loss records help us grasp broad levels of quality, but first place versus second or third is much easier to grasp. There isn't always a 100-win team to look at, but there **is** always a first-place team. So it is intuitive and natural to place our focus and attention on first place and measure everybody else relative to them. Games Behind isn't much of an analytical tool, but it captures what we experience as daily baseball observers. Team B is three games behind Team A. That becomes intriguing if they're playing a three-game series this weekend, as B could force a tie with A—this is the foundation for excitement. And the more we observe teams in or around that first-place spotlight, the more we expect them to be there, the more we think their moves matter, and in general the more **relevant** we consider a team.

At heart, then, team perception is a function of days spent in a pennant race; the more a team is involved, the more the public observes that team. A team in the race day-in and day-out will be discussed day-in and day-out. The recent Giants didn't sustain a season-long run until 2014, so even though 2014's team by win-loss record was closer to 2011's than that of the 2010 and 2012 championship teams, the shape of their season gave them a stronger reputation going into the playoffs than in the other years.

If this makes sense to you, then you and this book will get along great. Although I have specifics that I believe make a lot of sense in measuring team perception, they are less important than the principles of how teams are perceived. In the next chapter I outline my specifics and why/how I arrived at them.

2. The Math of Perception

I call my statistic for relative team perception Momentum, because there is a sense of momentum and inertia to perceptions. Although team performances can drop suddenly, observers don't immediately avert their gaze; they will watch the team ship sink if it's sinking, just because they've already been looking in that team's direction. And winning reputations don't come instantly; they come through sustained success.

If teams are worth talking about relative to their being in first place, then excitement will be driven by whether first place is realistic for a team. The easiest block of time to discuss how realistic that possibility is in advance is one of baseball's units of measure: a series. If two teams enter a head-to-head series and the victor will take over first place, that's as exciting as a series gets, and it means both teams will be in the spotlight. Baseball doesn't have the same sort of titan-clash feel that football can hype for a week; the closest approximation is pre-series chatter. So if a team is in first place or a series (by which I mean the typical three-game series) away, that team will be discussed as part of the season's narrative for however long they're that close.

So a team gains Momentum when it is in first place or within three games of it, and it loses Momentum when it isn't. More specifically, a team gains Momentum when it is

- at least two games over .500 **and**
- within three games of first place, within two games of the first wild card, or (for 2012 and later) leading the second wild card.

As these goals have varying levels of difficulty depending on how many divisions and wild cards there are (i.e., how many "first places" there are), different eras gain different amounts of Momentum per day:

1871–1968: 4 points
1969–1993: 3 points
1994–present: 2 points

If a team isn't gaining Momentum, it loses 1 point per day, down to a floor of 0.

Because the measurements involve Games Behind and records over .500, and because early season results are skewed heavily by strength of schedule, I don't start measuring Momentum for a league-season until a team that would gain Momentum has played 20 games. In 2014, that date was April 27 for the AL and April 26 for the NL. Conveniently, thanks to in-season off days, starting 20 games in normally makes my measuring period about 162 days every year.

An easy example of how this works: on June 21, 1961, the Yankees, Tigers, and Indians were all within three games of first place. As first place is rarefied air in a league without divisions, that's a big deal. All three teams received 4 points for that achievement. The Orioles and White Sox had Momentum at the time but didn't have good enough records (in fact, neither team gained Momentum all year); therefore, on June 21, they lost 1 point each. The Athletics, Red Sox, Twins, Angels, and Senators had no Momentum entering June 21; they stayed at 0. On June 22, the Indians fell off the pace; they would lose 1 point every day for the rest of the season, but it took until September 6 for that loss to offset the Momentum they had at the start of the 1961 season. The Tigers and Yankees, meanwhile, continued to gain 4 points per day through most of the season.

That's how to measure Momentum during a season. The offseason gets a different type of adjustment based on how close team reputations were entering the offseason. The offseason shifts perceptions through the hot stove league, the hype surrounding various trades and signings. I simulate that through a measure of league balance, with the premise that the offseason can't **increase** excitement since it has no games, but it can **preserve** excitement depending on how close the teams were entering the offseason.

The offseason is more interesting when teams' moves are expected to matter, and they are expected to matter the more teams are involved. If the Yankees have won everything for years, what does it matter who the Browns sign? But if several teams are discussed, they all matter more—more of their Momentum carries over to the next year. So teams in a league carry over anywhere from half (the offseason preserved no excitement) to all their Momentum (the offseason preserved all the excitement) off the formula

$$\text{Next April} = \text{October}/(2-x)$$

where x is a league's "Median" team Momentum divided by mean team Momentum. If the mean is greater than the "median"—which has happened nine times—then the league maintains all its Momentum in the offseason, and October's and the next April's Momentum are equal.

2. The Math of Perception

"Median" is in quotation marks because it's not a true median in every case; it's a fulcrum relative to how many playoff teams are in the league (because that is the minimum number of teams gaining Momentum every day, assuming teams are sufficiently above .500). Here are the "medians" for each era:

1871–1993: Actual median
1994–2011 AL, 1994–1997 NL: 8th
1998–2011 NL: 9th
2012 AL: Mean of 8th and 9th
2012 NL: Mean of 9th and 10th
2013–present: 9th

It's a lot harder to explain than in-season Momentum, but this example should help. At the end of 1958, here is the list of all AL teams with Momentum:

| Yankees | 1062 |
| The other teams | 0 |

The Yankees had so dominated the pennant races—since August 1957, non-Yankee AL teams had gained 20 points of Momentum **total**—that nobody else was involved. So you'd expect the Yankees to be contenders again and nobody else to matter, regardless of player acquisitions. The x derived by median/mean is 0, meaning the Yankees had half that Momentum (1062/[2–0]), or 531, on Opening Day 1959. Because of how dull the pennant races had been, **any** movement by a 0-point team was inherently more interesting than it would be other years, so the Yankees' adjustment is harsher to bring them closer to the pack.

Similarly, at the end of 1999—amid rumors of league contraction—here's how the AL looked:

Indians	642
Yankees	626
Rangers	549
Red Sox	444
Athletics	32
Blue Jays	27
The other teams	0

That's not a balanced league either, given that four teams were gaining Momentum every day. X is again 0, so all the teams' points are cut in half by the dull 1999 offseason.

On the other hand, the late '50s and early '60s NL involved several teams each year, and 1961 was a four-team race. Here's NL Momentum at the end of 1961:

Reds	592
Dodgers	542
Giants	381
Pirates	363
Braves	270
The other teams	0

The Pirates and Braves were riding largely on previous years' glories, but they had enough reputation to matter in 1961. In an eight-team league, it's hard to have five teams matter fairly equally. The NL's median was higher than the mean, so x was 1.18. Rather than saying those teams **gained** Momentum in the offseason, I say that those teams entered Opening Day 1962 with the same Momentum with which they ended 1961. Any move could upset that balance quickly, so the offseason was more exciting than an all-Yankeesfest or the AL monopoly of 1999. This means that 0-point teams from 1961—the Cardinals, Cubs, and Phillies—had farther to go to pass the other five, but that makes sense: the five teams with points had strong reputations, so there was much less reason to observe the also-rans. If the Reds were to stumble in 1962, the assumption would be that one of the other four close teams would pick up the slack. Conversely, if the Yankees stumbled in 1959—and they did—it would be an unknown leading the way.

A harsher adjustment for more dominance may seem counterintuitive, but when we get to the season summaries where I display month-to-month Momentum totals, it will make more sense. Without an offseason adjustment of this type, the tail end of a dynasty is too long. And while offseasons can be exciting, they can't be exciting without some expectation that any of the moves **matter**, and parity is necessary to feel like a move or three can put a team over the top.

Narrative isn't just driven by dominance; it's driven by the writers thinking something is worth talking about, and after a boring season, new contenders, even if short-lived, are worth discussing.

I handle 1892's and 1981's split seasons as having two starting points for measuring 20 games into the season, with teams losing Momentum in between. For 1892, that in-between is July 13–August 5; for 1981, it's June 12–August 28 (AL) and June 11–August 29 (NL). My understanding of both seasons is that the split format was a drag on overall interest, so that's why I've chosen that way. For 1994, I stop the season on August 12 like it was the true end of the season and carry Momentum over as normal; this shortchanges teams on the rise that would normally get an extra six weeks—like the Expos and Indians of those years.

Why Don't You Factor in the Playoffs?

Great question; glad you asked. First off, playoff impact is hard to measure. You could say teams still in the playoffs gain Momentum but nobody else loses it in that time; that approach is defensible. But generally, by the time the next Opening Day rolls around, expectations surrounding that team aren't tied to a postseason victory or defeat. It doesn't affect preseason power rankings or any of the type of spotlight available to teams for most of the offseason; the playoffs are acknowledged to be a crapshoot that doesn't reflect on team quality anyway.

The Reds lost to the Yankees quickly in the 1961 World Series. Did their appearance in the World Series raise their Momentum? Did their quick exit lower it again? Does winning a wild-card game or an LDS raise profile that much? (Having been a baseball fan almost entirely in the wild-card era, I have a hard time even remembering who won an LDS.) With too many of those questions unanswerable, I've chosen to omit the playoffs from Momentum. Playoffs definitely matter for the season they're in, so later concepts in this book take them into account. But as far as I'm concerned, they shouldn't go into Momentum.

Putting All This into Recent Examples

The 2014 NL was a lot more boring than the AL in terms of pennant races and therefore Momentum. The NL had several teams battling, but they were mostly the same ones as in 2013; the battles were fine but the war was dull. The ninth-place "median" team in the NL at season's end had 0 points. By contrast, the AL's ninth-place team was the Mariners with 104 points, just ahead of the Rays and Blue Jays. So the AL got a softer adjustment than the NL; the AL simply had more teams with recent contention and therefore intrigue entering 2015. Going into 2016, here was each league's ranking team-by-team, with the previous seasons' starts for some context, the leader in each division bolded, and playoff teams from the previous season italicized:

AL	2014	2015	2016		2014	2015	2016		2014	2015	2016
BAL	178	*284*	174	CHI	23			HOU			265
BOS	278	79		CLE	117			LA		188	184
NY	331	238	**451**	DET	**330**	**431**	360	OAK	206	354	160
TB	219	39	41	KC		*71*	**323**	SEA		70	
TOR		51	127	MIN				TEX	**461**	*235*	**220**

Even without wins and losses, Momentum gives a feel for how each team fared and how they stacked up against each other. Ending 2014 and starting

2015, the AL for the first time since 1992 had a top three without the Yankees or Red Sox. The Athletics finally broke through after years of late runs, just in time to have the public watch a collapse and a sort of fire sale—not what you want to be doing that publicly. Meanwhile, the Tigers' consistency put them in the AL lead entering 2015, for the first time since 1969. And the Astros' surge from doormat to contender looks as sudden in this chart as it felt.

NL	2014	2015	2016		2014	2015	2016		2014	2015	2016
ATL	*452*	307	73	CHI			126	AZ	*77*		
MIA				CIN	329	105		COL	2		
NY			*137*	MIL		128		LA	175	*235*	*277*
PHI	72			PIT	236	129	177	SD			
WAS	51	*159*	*137*	STL	*471*	*356*	*336*	SF	*213*	*266*	180

The Cardinals and Braves have been the only first place teams in the NL overall since April 2003, except for a brief reign by the Phillies from September 2011 to May 2012. The Giants had been the team to beat in the West, but their inconsistency in 2015 made the Dodgers the team to beat entering 2016. The Pirates kept contending late in the year, so their reputation suffered compared to fast-starting teams, despite three straight years in the playoffs.

That's a lot of explanation for what's supposed to be intuitive, but I wanted to show every knob I tweak so you can agree or re-tweak. Most tweaks will change a team's "era"—what years we think of as a run of contention—by no more than a year on either end, so conclusions generally will hold up regardless.

I'll use Momentum more thoroughly in the season summaries, but for now I want to take Momentum's estimates of team reputations into the world of player reputations.

3. Momentum, Spotlight and SpWAR

You've seen some of how Momentum tracks a season and how it portrays relative team rankings through a time frame. Various factors affect team fame and reputation, but Momentum at least serves as a quantifiable core.

And since that core is quantifiable, we can use it as a numerical proxy for related concepts. One of the biggest applications is to an eternal debate: how much might someone's Hall of Fame chances be influenced by playing for one team over another? Since baseball writers, specifically the BBWAA, elect (or **don't** elect) players to the Hall of Fame, players' Hall of Fame chances will be partly narrative-driven. Saying a player doesn't **feel like** a Hall of Famer is code for not matching a narrative. And with a tool to measure narrative, we can approximate who **feels like** a Hall of Famer beyond their stats.

As with Momentum, I'm most concerned about demonstrating the utility of concepts and approach; numbers can't fully explain the BBWAA. Contour my premises to your liking.

What Is Reputation?

I propose this basic equation for life generally and baseball specifically:

Productivity × Spotlight = Reputation

How the spotlight works varies dramatically from subject to subject, and it's most predictable in sports, but in general famous people have produced something and gotten noticed for it. Some musicians get very popular off a single album and loads of sales and media appearances; some others build a reputation primarily off relentless touring. They often get to the same place in terms of revenue and fans, but the former **feel** more famous because the spotlight's on them more. Being the New Hot Thing can't ordinarily turn someone into a star if they haven't produced **anything**, but it can magnify that something into looking quite big. You can become a star by lots of production, but your narrative won't be the same.

For baseball, once there's an idea for measuring Momentum, we can plug numbers into the formula above and get somewhere. In baseball terms, the formula is:

WAR × Spotlight = SpWAR

I'm saying the same thing as the fame equation but with new terms:

WAR = Wins Above Replacement, a comprehensive statistic that estimates how many wins a player was worth to his team over freely available talent, such as a minor leaguer.[1] Historically, WAR is not always the best proxy of estimated productivity, because people cared about different statistics at different times. I'm tempted to use offensive WAR only for hitters, but as there are plenty of players (including Hall of Famers) renowned for their defense, it gets too pointillist to figure out who should have their defense counted and who shouldn't. You could count defensive contributions only for certain positions (up-the-middle and third base, for instance), but then players switching positions becomes a problem. Was Pete Rose's defense only important some years and not others? It's not worth parsing. WAR is good enough as a proxy of productivity for our purposes, and it's at least consistent and comparable over time.

Spotlight = How much a player's team Momentum kept him in the public eye. Rather than using Momentum's numbers to create Spotlight, I'm using a team's league Momentum **ranking** every day through a season to create a weighted average of daily ranking for that season. Since Momentum starts accumulating 20 games into a season, I start counting the daily ranking 20 days before Momentum starts accumulating; in other words, the relative order of teams remains intact the first 20 days of the season and then can change afterward.

SpWAR = Spotlight WAR, the WAR that it **feels** like a player accumulated.

How much can the spotlight improve a player's perception? I am working with the assumption that constant daily contention can make a 4-win player—1 win south of the All-Star line—look like a 6-win player—1 win north of the All-Star line, and a magnification of 50 percent. While it's unclear to what extent the 1990s Yankees are more famous than their Royals contemporaries, it's uncontroversial to state that being on the 1990s Yankees turned some productive players into stars they wouldn't be otherwise. Spotlight doesn't generally confuse bad players with good ones, but it can make good ones look great, and using a basic maximum of 50 percent accomplishes that well enough.

I have chosen to measure spotlight as a multiplier on WAR rather than an additive. It may be that every player on a team gets an equal benefit from the spotlight, but thinking through the recent Braves stints of Melvin Upton, Jr., and Dan Uggla, it's clear that players with negative WAR seem **worse** than they actually are, which is what spotlight multiplied by a negative WAR will show. Jonathan Singleton struggled mightily as a rookie in 2014, and his WAR was quite negative (-0.8), but he had the sense to do it quietly in Houston rather than loudly in Atlanta.

So if we say a 4-win player can look like a 6-win player, we can create a basic percentage spotlight based on a team's daily ranking in the regular season and a Spotlight of 1.0 to 1.5:

1st place in Momentum = 50% spotlight (multiply WAR by 1.5)
2nd place in Momentum = 40% spotlight (multiply WAR by 1.4)
3rd place in Momentum = 30% spotlight (multiply WAR by 1.3)
4th place in Momentum = 20% spotlight (multiply WAR by 1.2)
5th place in Momentum = 10% spotlight (multiply WAR by 1.1)
Everybody else = 0% spotlight (WAR stays the same)

So if a player's team was first in Momentum all season, I multiply that player's WAR by 50 percent. If the player's team was second, I multiply by 40 percent. If the team was in first for half the season but second the other half, I multiply by 45 percent. A weighted average allows for a range of Spotlight multipliers, giving the most credit to teams who were the alpha team the longest.

With large leagues and several playoff spots, this method doesn't capture the teams in the middle too well, so up to that 10 percent I'll give a team credit for the weighted average of Momentum **percentage** in a season. If a team was in fifth place half the time and sixth place the other half (1.05 Spotlight), but averaged to 6 percent of the league points, I give 1.06 instead of 1.05. Most teams adjusted this way have similarly small tweaks.

What About the Playoffs?

There you are asking questions again. You are persistent ... here, unlike with Momentum, the playoffs are an active factor. Playoff teams have a few things uniquely true for them:

1. They play more games than other teams;
2. They play to a more concentrated audience, whether it's fans shifting focus to playoff teams from their favorite teams or the public who only gets interested at the end; and
3. They have a chance to pull off major upsets while everybody's watching.

The first two items are covered by adding Spotlight to the regular season score. I add 0.10 for the World Series, 0.05 for other playoff series, and 0.02 for the wild card game; the World Series has more exposure and also indicates that the team in question has played longer than other teams. This means that teams leading in Momentum all year that also go to the World Series would achieve a maximum possible Spotlight of 1.60. The regular season can only provide up to 1.50; the playoffs have extra fame to give.

For item three, consider how upsets become famous. "Miracle" teams aren't famous before their miracle; nobody watched them all season like they did with other teams. If a "miracle" team loses to the alpha team, the alpha team doesn't gain anything from that; Goliath was expected to win. But if a "miracle" team wins, then that team has effectively stolen the spotlight in which they were guests.

In that sense, people don't see the underdog win so much as they see the famous team lose. The 1969 Mets are famous not from their regular season results because they were in the race for so little time; they are famous from beating the powerhouse Orioles.[2] So instead of counting the Mets' regular season Spotlight for 1969, it's more representative to give them the exact same Spotlight as the highest regular season Spotlight of a team they beat in a playoff series (note that the modern wild-card game is not a series). The Mets' regular season was at 1.00–they entered the narrative very late—but they beat the Braves (1.25 in the regular season) and the Orioles (1.41 in the regular season). The 1969 Mets' season Spotlight is 1.41.

Because that extra spotlight comes from a specific result rather than the daily narrative, that 1.41 has no weight on the next season; the 1.00 regular-season figure is what carries over. The Mets weren't necessarily expected to romp through 1970 just because they won the 1969 World Series; the entirety of 1969 performance and reputation would be a bigger factor.[3] Similarly, the 2014 Royals weren't the class of the AL just because they went to the World Series; they were viewed as an okay team that derived their fame from the playoffs and so weren't rated highly going into 2015.[4]

This playoff adjustment neatly dovetails the Spotlight rating extending multipliers down to five teams per league. Only occasionally are leagues five deep in positive-Momentum teams before divisional play; as more playoff rounds exist, more Spotlight is up for grabs in the postseason rather than the regular season.

Enough explanation ... here are all the World Series where the teams' combined Spotlight (without playoff adjustment) was 3.0, i.e., the maximum 1.5 on each side:

1913 (Athletics–Giants)
1923 (Yankees–Giants)
1937 (Yankees–Giants)
1952 (Yankees–Dodgers)
1953 (Yankees–Dodgers)
1955 (Yankees–Dodgers)
1956 (Yankees–Dodgers)
1958 (Yankees–Braves)
1963 (Yankees–Dodgers)

And here are all the World Series where the teams' combined Spotlight (without playoff adjustment) was 2.3 or less:

1967 (Red Sox 1.05–Cardinals 1.23)
1979 (Orioles 1.17–Pirates 1.03)
1982 (Brewers 1.09–Cardinals 1.16)
1985 (Royals 1.15–Cardinals 1.08)
1991 (Twins 1.11–Braves 1.02)
2002 (Angels 1.04–Giants 1.26)
2005 (White Sox 1.10–Astros 1.06)
2008 (Rays 1.06–Phillies 1.07)
2010 (Rangers 1.12–Giants 1.05)
2014 (Royals 1.01–Giants 1.25)
2015 (Royals 1.12–Mets 1.05)

When various media members complain that nobody watches the World Series, this is a mathematical estimate of what they mean—there isn't a famous team involved like those Yankees-Dodgers matchups from the 1950s.[5] And the current playoffs system is set up to deliver medium-spotlight matchups in the World Series, so the media ought to adjust—perhaps most of all the Hall of Fame voters, whose narrative is increasingly fractured the longer and deeper divisional play goes.

To Recap:

A team's Spotlight for a season is a weighted average of league Momentum ranking for each day of the season, awarding 10 percent for fifth place, 50 percent for first, and 10 percent increments in between. This makes a team's regular-season Spotlight anything from 1.00 (normal team) to 1.50 (first in Momentum all season). If a team's weighted average of league Momentum percentage is higher than the ranking, the percentage will be the base instead.

Teams making the World Series get 0.10 added to their regular-season Spotlight; teams making other playoff series get 0.05 added. If, after adding that amount, that Spotlight is less than the regular-season Spotlight of an opponent in a playoff series, and the opponent is defeated, the opponent's regular-season Spotlight will be used instead. Making the wild card game gets 0.03 added, but no Spotlight upsets are available for a single game; the reward for winning it is moving from 0.02 added to 0.05 added for making a playoff series.

So what does that look like for a given year? Here are my 2015 Spotlights—multiply a player's WAR by the Spotlight below to determine SpWAR.

Team	Spotlight	Method Obtained
Cardinals	1.55	Ranking + Playoffs
Cubs	1.50	Beating Cardinals in Playoffs
Tigers	1.48	Ranking
Dodgers	1.41	Ranking + Playoffs
Yankees	1.39	Ranking + Wild Card Game
Mets	1.36	Beating Dodgers in Playoffs
Giants	1.29	Ranking
Athletics	1.24	Ranking
Royals	1.22	Ranking + World Series
Orioles	1.19	Ranking
Braves	1.16	Ranking
Nationals	1.14	Ranking
Rangers	1.14	Points Share + Playoffs
Pirates	1.11	Points Share + Wild Card Game
Astros	1.10	Points Share + Playoffs
Blue Jays	1.09	Beating Rangers in Playoffs
Angels	1.08	Points Share
Twins	1.04	Points Share
Brewers	1.03	Points Share
Rays	1.03	Points Share
Reds	1.02	Points Share
Mariners	1.01	Points Share
Red Sox	1.01	Points Share
Indians	1.00	
White Sox	1.00	
D-backs	1.00	
Marlins	1.00	
Padres	1.00	
Phillies	1.00	
Rockies	1.00	

That's the typical spread of a modern season—teams that are famous for being on top, a couple teams that are famous for winning in October, flux in the middle, and several moribund teams at the end. It doesn't mean the teams were good while in the Spotlight, but a good performance was more likely to get noticed on high-Spotlight teams.

So how does that affect perceptions of player seasons? Here's a 20-player roster for 2015. One's ranked by WAR; the other's ranked by SpWAR. I've bolded the players who are on one team but not the other.

WAR Team	SpWAR Team
C: Buster Posey (6.1)	C: Buster Posey (7.9)
1B: Paul Goldschmidt (8.8)	**1B: Anthony Rizzo (9.5)**
2B: Ian Kinsler (6.0)	2B: Ian Kinsler (8.9)
SS: Brandon Crawford (5.6)	SS: Brandon Crawford (7.2)
3B: Josh Donaldson (8.8)	3B: Josh Donaldson (9.6)
LF: Yoenis Cespedes (6.3)	LF: Yoenis Cespedes (9.0)
CF: Mike Trout (9.4)	CF: Mike Trout (10.2)
RF: Bryce Harper (9.9)	RF: Bryce Harper (11.3)
IF: Joey Votto (7.6)	**IF: Kris Bryant (8.9)**
IF: Manny Machado (7.1)	IF: Paul Goldschmidt (8.8)
OF: Kevin Kiermaier (7.4)	**OF: Jason Heyward (10.1)**
OF: A.J. Pollock (7.4)	**OF: Lorenzo Cain (8.8)**
SP: Zack Greinke (9.3)	SP: Zack Greinke (13.1)
SP: Jake Arrieta (8.6)	SP: Jake Arrieta (12.9)
SP: Clayton Kershaw (7.5)	SP: Clayton Kershaw (10.6)
SP: Dallas Keuchel (7.2)	SP: John Lackey (8.7)
SP: Max Scherzer (7.0)	SP: Max Scherzer (8.0)
P: David Price (6.0)	P: Dallas Keuchel (7.9)
P: Sonny Gray (5.8)	P: David Price (7.8)
P: John Lackey (5.6)	P: Sonny Gray (7.2)

These are minor changes compared to most years—it's incredibly rare for the best pitchers to all be on famous teams—but it makes the changes you'd expect. The Cubs' playoff success makes them more remembered than they otherwise would be, and Jason Heyward's and John Lackey's years look much better when Spotlight is factored in. A.J. Pollock had a significantly more productive year than Jason Heyward, but Heyward's year will be a lot easier to remember because he was on the Cardinals and Pollock was on the Diamondbacks. Pollock led WAR 7.4–6.5, but Heyward led SpWAR 10.1–7.4.

While the system isn't perfect, it gets the point across—some good players look great based on where they play, and others get pushed down in the pecking order for toiling in obscurity. Spotlight and SpWAR let us translate player-seasons across teams to get a sense of how fame affects perception of talent. And that lets us evaluate fame's most famous use—Hall of Fame voting.

4. SpWAR and the Hall of Fame

Obviously, the Hall of Fame is meant for great players. Just as obviously, it has some good-not-great players who were on great teams and omits some great players who were on good-not-great teams. Using WAR and SpWAR as we did with the 2015 All-Star teams last chapter, we can chart a player's entire career and measure not just SpWAR but what percentage pure fame "inflates" a player's reputation, i.e., how much a player's SpWAR is over his WAR. There are several statistical efforts that focus on whether a player is above median standards for the Hall of Fame. Based on my age, I most easily think of Jay Jaffe's JAWS system, the first system I knew that blended peak and career performances into a single metric.[1] When talking with him for this book, he pointed to Bill James as the originator of the peak/career duality, even as Jaffe's work made the metric that framed my thoughts on the analysis. So my approach owes primary inspiration to Jaffe and secondary inspiration to any others taking a dual approach or using median Hall of Fame statistics as a frame of reference.

My dual approach is WAR v. SpWAR. For frame of reference, here are some WAR figures for the Hall of Fame:

BBWAA median WAR: 70.2 (Frankie Frisch and Barry Larkin)
BBWAA 25th percentile: 59.9 (in between Joe McGinnity and Yogi Berra)
All HOF median WAR: 63.5 (Billy Hamilton)
All HOF 25th percentile: 49.9 (Hoyt Wilhelm)

Players right around that BBWAA median include Larry Walker (72.6), Alan Trammell (70.7), Tim Raines (68.9), and Edgar Martinez (68.3). All of them have had trouble getting in quickly; their stats say they should be pretty easy Hall of Famers.

The trouble is that the BBWAA is made of W(riters). And while many writers value stats, they don't **have** to for their jobs. They can use narrative, and as writers there's some pull to a good narrative. Not all great seasons are noticed as great at the time because the eye naturally is drawn to the famous teams.

That's what SpWAR describes. If we measure Hall of Famers and candidates by SpWAR instead of WAR, we should get a better sense on how the writers as a group are likely to see the candidates. Running the same calculations as above but for SpWAR:

BBWAA median SpWAR: 90.9 (in between Ozzie Smith and Al Simmons)
BBWAA 25th percentile: 73.1 (in between Joe Medwick and Willie Keeler)
All HOF median SpWAR: 78.1 (Craig Biggio)
All HOF 25th percentile: 63.9 (between Nellie Fox and Phil Rizzuto)

Those figures give a pretty wide swing based on our assumptions. A player with 90.9 WAR on terrible teams will still look pretty good to the BBWAA, because the player will still have 90.9 SpWAR (90.9 × 1). But those players are rare. Players with around 60 WAR are much more common, and if they play for a perennially famous team, they can get up to 91.4 SpWAR as well. Drop down to the BBWAA 25th percentile mark, and a player with 46 WAR—a notch below Bernie Williams (49.4)–can get a Hall of Fame conversation based on the teams for which he played. (Bernie's career inflates 44.7 percent—a high inflation percentage—to 71.2 SpWAR, but that's still below standard for a Hall of Famer.)

The median inflation of a BBWAA-elected Hall of Famer is 27.2 percent above actual WAR–the average of Eddie Mathews and Pedro Martinez. So a typical BBWAA Hall of Famer was on the third- or fourth-most-famous team in his league—not necessarily a contender every year but frequently in the mix.

Dennis Eckersley is right above that median—27.6 percent—from a career WAR of 62.4 and SpWAR of 79.6. The table below shows how he got there. (Rounding errors might exist season-to-season in the numbers below. You'll live.) The Fame column is SpWAR minus WAR.

Year	Tm	Spt	WAR	SpW	Fame
1975	CLE	1.01	5.3	5.4	0.1
1976	CLE	1.00	2.9	2.9	0.0
1977	CLE	1.00	5.1	5.1	0.0
1978	BOS	1.45	7.3	10.6	3.3
1979	BOS	1.49	7.3	10.9	3.6
1980	BOS	1.25	2.1	2.6	0.5
1981	BOS	1.06	0.8	0.8	0.0
1982	BOS	1.24	4.5	5.6	1.1
1983	BOS	1.16	-0.4	-0.5	-0.1
1984	BOS	1.04	0.3	0.3	0.0
1984	CHC	1.11	3.9	4.3	0.4
1985	CHC	1.27	4.6	5.8	1.2
1986	CHC	1.10	1.9	2.1	0.2
1987	OAK	1.04	3.0	3.1	0.1

Year	Tm	Spt	WAR	SpW	Fame
1988	OAK	1.38	2.2	3.0	0.8
1989	OAK	1.60	2.6	4.2	1.6
1990	OAK	1.60	3.3	5.3	2.0
1991	OAK	1.49	1.5	2.2	0.7
1992	OAK	1.45	2.9	4.2	1.3
1993	OAK	1.35	0.7	0.9	0.2
1994	OAK	1.08	-0.2	-0.2	-0.0
1995	OAK	1.02	0.0	0.0	0.0
1996	STL	1.07	0.4	0.4	0.0
1997	STL	1.04	0.2	0.2	0.0
1998	BOS	1.15	0.2	0.2	0.0

Cleveland aside, Eckersley's best seasons generally were when his teams were at their most famous. His narrative syncs pretty well. But let's take it a step further. Here are his teams ranked by WAR:

BOS 22.1
OAK 16.0
CLE 13.3
CHC 10.4
STL 0.6

And his teams by SpWAR:

BOS 30.6
OAK 22.8
CLE 13.4
CHC 12.3
STL 0.6

Not much difference there. But ... let's isolate Fame:

BOS 8.5
OAK 6.8
CHC 1.9
CLE 0.1
STL 0.0

Eckersley's years as a starter with the Indians are an important part of his resume, but they seem far less important if you look at the narrative. His Cubs tenure feels almost as productive even though it wasn't. And his closer days in Oakland get a major boost from his team's success.

To see how much worse we can make his career look, let's put all his good years in inverse order to his teams' Spotlights—his best years with the Indians and his worst years with the Red Sox and A's. What do we get?

4. SpWAR and the Hall of Fame

Spt	WAR	SpW	Fame
1.00	7.3	7.3	0.0
1.00	7.3	7.3	0.0
1.01	5.3	5.4	0.1
1.02	5.1	5.2	0.1
1.04	4.6	4.8	0.2
1.04	4.5	4.7	0.2
1.04	3.9	4.1	0.2
1.06	3.3	3.5	0.2
1.07	3	3.2	0.2
1.08	2.9	3.1	0.2
1.10	2.9	3.2	0.3
1.11	2.6	2.9	0.3
1.15	2.2	2.5	0.3
1.16	2.1	2.4	0.3
1.24	1.9	2.4	0.5
1.25	1.5	1.9	0.4
1.27	0.8	1.0	0.2
1.35	0.7	0.9	0.2
1.38	0.4	0.6	0.2
1.45	0.3	0.4	0.1
1.45	0.2	0.3	0.1
1.49	0.2	0.3	0.1
1.49	0.0	0.0	0.0
1.60	-0.2	-0.3	-0.1
1.60	-0.4	-0.6	-0.2

It's the same WAR of 62.4. But unfavorably distributed, Eckersley's SpWAR is 66.4–an inflation of only 6.1 percent and well below even 25th percentile BBWAA SpWAR. The Veterans Committee isn't necessarily interested in 66.2 SpWAR either, and it seems likely that the Hall would pass Eckersley by altogether.

While several players can make it on their productivity alone—WAR is still the primary component of SpWAR, after all—most need a bit of help to improve their case. Here are the 16 BBWAA Hall of Famers as of 2015 with inflation over 40 percent (again, with the rounding caveat):

Name	WAR	SpWAR	Inflation
Yogi Berra	59.4	93.6	57.6%
Roy Campanella	34.1	53.3	56.3%
Whitey Ford	53.9	84.2	56.2%
Jackie Robinson	61.5	95.6	55.5%
Joe DiMaggio	78.3	120.8	54.3%
Mickey Mantle	109.7	168.4	53.5%
Duke Snider	66.5	101.2	52.2%
Bill Dickey	55.8	84.9	52.2%
Lou Gehrig	112.3	169.3	50.8%
Sandy Koufax	53.2	79.4	49.3%
Babe Ruth	183.9	272.2	48.0%
Frankie Frisch	70.2	103.7	47.7%

Name	WAR	SpWAR	Inflation
Herb Pennock	44.3	64.5	45.6%
John Smoltz	66.6	95.7	43.7%
Red Ruffing	70.7	101.1	43.0%
Don Drysdale	61.3	87.2	42.3%

Whitey Ford is particularly instructive. Ford's WAR is a bit below even the 25th percentile for the BBWAA. But he was famous enough to be about 40th percentile for SpWAR. Being on the Yankees for that long makes him **feel** like a Hall of Famer a lot more than others of similar output. Tim Hudson out produced him (57.2 WAR), but his best year in Atlanta was 2010, at only a 1.10 Spotlight, and the Athletics usually were made of late surges rather than early dominance, lowering their Spotlight from what you might expect. So his career SpWAR was 68.2—a 19.23 percent inflation, but an SpWAR only slightly above the BBWAA's bottom tenth. It's a hard sell without a hook of some kind, like a round number or postseason dominance.

And that brings us to the bottom of the list—the 18 BBWAA Hall of Famers with under 11 percent inflation:

Name	WAR	SpWAR	Inflation
Dave Winfield	63.8	70.6	10.6%
Paul Molitor	75.7	83.7	10.6%
Nolan Ryan	83.7	92.5	10.5%
Billy Williams	63.6	70.2	10.4%
Bert Blyleven	96.4	106.2	10.2%
Harry Heilmann	72.2	79.0	9.4%
Walter Johnson	165.8	179.6	8.3%
Ryne Sandberg	67.7	72.8	7.5%
Dazzy Vance	62.6	67.3	7.5%
Bruce Sutter	24.5	26.3	7.4%
Robin Yount	77.0	82.3	6.9%
Ted Lyons	67.2	71.5	6.4%
Ken Griffey	83.4	88.1	5.6%
Luke Appling	74.4	77.8	4.6%
Phil Niekro	97.3	101.4	4.2%
George Sisler	56.7	58.8	3.7%
Ralph Kiner	49.4	50.1	1.4%
Ernie Banks	67.6	67.1	-0.7%

(Yes, Ernie Banks's SpWAR is lower than his WAR, due to his negative WAR in 1969–71. We'll revisit Banks shortly.)

The list divides into a few groups. There's the group that could get in on productivity alone; this includes Blyleven, Johnson, and Niekro. Johnson and Niekro also hint that lifelong association with a team gives an alternative narrative to being on winning teams. Unless you're on a dynasty, spending 20 years with the same team will give you less spotlight overall, because your team will have a natural rise and fall. Roberto Alomar kept signing with winning teams in his prime; his inflation is 37.0 percent. If he had stayed with the Blue Jays, Orioles, or Indians longer than he did, his reputation would have fallen with them. On the flipside, if Bert Blyleven had stayed with one team for his career, maybe he would have had an easier time getting in.

Then there's the magic number group—3000 hits or 300 wins. Johnson and Niekro are in this group as well, and we can add Winfield (a Yankee in the wrong decade to be one), Molitor, Ryan, and Yount. Any of these could have played for the least-watched team every year and it wouldn't matter; they had the magic induction number, so in they went. Griffey had 600 home runs and had fame outside his terrible teams by having a father from the Big Red Machine—the most famous team of his day—and a starring role in a video game baseball franchise because Nintendo owned his team.

There's also the 20-years-later group—Heilmann, Vance, and Kiner. All three took a gazillion ballots to get in; under modern rules, they would have fallen off the ballot after a couple of years. These were not darlings of the BBWAA, and I think it's safe to consider them anomalies. Vance and Kiner also had amazing peaks, a Hall of Fame group founded by George Sisler. (Heilmann hitting at least .393 four times is pretty good too.)

So you have two well-recognized ways of getting in the Hall despite low Spotlight—productivity and round numbers—and a meld of late selections and bright/short flames. That leaves:

Billy Williams
Ryne Sandberg
Bruce Sutter
Ted Lyons
Luke Appling
Ernie Banks

Well, that's not a hard group to figure out. Uniquely among cities, if you play in Chicago and its press thinks you should be a Hall of Famer, then forget round numbers or winning—you've got a good chance.

New York has inflated a lot of records, but it's almost always from winning teams. Don Mattingly's SpWAR inflation is low—like Winfield, he was on the wrong Yankees—and his BBWAA support never cleared 30 percent. Ron Guidry and Willie Randolph were on some more famous Yankee teams; they didn't get close either. But Chicago has had bad teams for so long that its press has dissociated Spotlight from winning. As a result, Chicago has a list of players whose SpWAR profiles look like nobody else the BBWAA has ever elected.

Granted, there are other arguments for several of them. At time of retirement, Lyons and Appling were among the top five active WAR leaders, albeit not particularly impressive ones (and it didn't help Arky Vaughan, who had the same claim). If 500 home runs was a magic number for induction once upon a time, then Ernie Banks (and fellow Chicagoan Frank Thomas) qualifies on that front. Regardless, it appears Chicago stands alone in its constant signal boost. In Sandberg's case, playing on WGN regularly helped his fame.²

Here are all the Hall of Famers elected by the BBWAA or the Veterans Committee in its various incarnations, sorted by SpWAR.

Name	WAR	SpWAR	Fame	Inflation
Babe Ruth	183.9	272.2	88.3	48.0%
Willie Mays	156.0	207.8	51.8	33.2%
Cy Young	170.1	206.1	36.0	21.2%
Ty Cobb	151.1	191.8	40.7	26.9%
Walter Johnson	165.8	179.6	13.8	8.3%
Stan Musial	128.2	171.5	43.3	33.8%
Hank Aaron	142.5	170.8	28.3	19.9%
Eddie Collins	124.0	169.5	45.5	36.7%
Lou Gehrig	112.3	169.3	57.0	50.8%
Honus Wagner	130.9	169.1	38.2	29.2%
Mickey Mantle	109.7	168.4	58.7	53.5%
Tris Speaker	133.8	168.0	34.2	25.6%
Kid Nichols	116.8	161.7	44.9	38.4%
Pete Alexander	116.9	151.0	34.1	29.2%
Ted Williams	123.1	148.0	24.9	20.2%
Lefty Grove	110.0	142.7	32.7	29.7%
Mel Ott	107.6	141.0	33.4	31.0%
Rogers Hornsby	126.9	140.9	14.0	11.0%
Greg Maddux	104.8	140.9	36.1	34.4%
Frank Robinson	107.4	139.6	32.2	30.0%
Mike Schmidt	106.6	138.0	31.4	29.5%
Rickey Henderson	110.8	134.4	23.6	21.3%
Christy Mathewson	95.4	133.0	37.6	39.4%
Joe Morgan	100.4	130.8	30.4	30.3%
Randy Johnson	104.1	128.3	24.2	23.2%
Tom Seaver	106.1	125.3	19.2	18.1%
Cap Anson	94.0	125.0	31.0	33.0%
Nap Lajoie	107.4	123.6	16.2	15.1%
Jimmie Foxx	96.3	123.5	27.2	28.2%
Eddie Mathews	96.2	122.4	26.2	27.2%
Joe DiMaggio	78.3	120.8	42.5	54.3%
Warren Spahn	92.9	119.9	27.0	29.1%
John Clarkson	85.8	119.1	33.3	38.8%
Eddie Plank	86.5	115.8	29.3	33.9%
George Brett	88.3	112.5	24.2	27.4%
Roberto Clemente	94.6	110.5	15.9	16.8%
Cal Ripken	95.6	109.7	14.1	14.7%
Pedro Martinez	85.9	109.2	23.3	27.1%
Wade Boggs	91.1	108.7	17.6	19.3%
Brooks Robinson	78.5	108.0	29.5	37.6%
Steve Carlton	84.0	108.0	24.0	28.6%

4. SpWAR and the Hall of Fame

Name	WAR	SpWAR	Fame	Inflation
Carl Yastrzemski	96.2	107.5	11.3	11.7%
Gaylord Perry	93.6	107.0	13.4	14.3%
Bert Blyleven	96.4	106.2	9.8	10.2%
Al Kaline	92.3	103.9	11.6	12.6%
Frankie Frisch	70.2	103.7	33.5	47.7%
Old Hoss Radbourn	73.5	102.3	28.8	39.2%
Johnny Bench	74.9	102.0	27.1	36.2%
Tom Glavine	74.0	101.9	27.9	37.7%
Tim Keefe	88.8	101.8	13.0	14.6%
Phil Niekro	97.3	101.4	4.1	4.2%
Dan Brouthers	79.5	101.3	21.8	27.4%
Pee Wee Reese	66.4	101.2	34.8	52.4%
Duke Snider	66.5	101.2	34.7	52.2%
Red Ruffing	70.7	101.1	30.4	43.0%
George Davis	84.8	100.5	15.7	18.5%
Bob Gibson	81.9	99.3	17.4	21.2%
Reggie Jackson	73.7	99.1	25.4	34.5%
Roger Connor	84.2	96.1	11.9	14.1%
Charlie Gehringer	80.4	95.7	15.3	19.0%
Robin Roberts	83.0	95.7	12.7	15.3%
John Smoltz	66.6	95.7	29.1	43.7%
Jackie Robinson	61.5	95.6	34.1	55.4%
Paul Waner	72.6	95.0	22.4	30.9%
Fergie Jenkins	82.7	93.8	11.1	13.4%
Yogi Berra	59.4	93.6	34.2	57.6%
Rod Carew	81.1	93.6	12.5	15.4%
Carl Hubbell	67.8	92.5	24.7	36.4%
Nolan Ryan	83.7	92.5	8.8	10.5%
Sam Crawford	74.9	92.2	17.3	23.1%
Roberto Alomar	66.7	91.4	24.7	37.0%
Ozzie Smith	76.6	91.3	14.7	19.2%
Arky Vaughan	72.8	91.0	18.2	25.0%
Al Simmons	68.8	90.5	21.7	31.5%
Jim Palmer	67.9	90.4	22.5	33.1%
Frank Baker	62.7	89.4	26.7	42.6%
Stan Coveleski	65.1	88.1	23.0	35.3%
Ken Griffey	83.4	88.1	4.7	5.6%
Don Sutton	68.8	87.9	19.1	27.8%
Pud Galvin	83.4	87.4	4.0	4.8%
Don Drysdale	61.3	87.2	25.9	42.3%
Ed Walsh	63.2	86.5	23.3	36.9%
Juan Marichal	61.8	85.2	23.4	37.9%
Fred Clarke	67.9	85.0	17.1	25.2%
Bill Dickey	55.8	84.9	29.1	52.2%
Willie McCovey	64.8	84.5	20.1	31.2%
Johnny Mize	70.9	84.4	13.5	19.0%
Whitey Ford	53.9	84.2	30.3	56.2%
Goose Goslin	66.3	84.2	17.9	27.0%
Gary Carter	69.8	84.0	14.2	20.3%
Paul Molitor	75.7	83.7	8.0	10.6%

Name	WAR	SpWAR	Fame	Inflation
Barry Larkin	70.2	83.6	13.4	19.1%
Frank Thomas	73.4	83.5	10.1	13.8%
Bobby Wallace	76.4	83.0	6.6	8.6%
Joe Gordon	57.1	82.9	25.8	45.2%
Joe Cronin	66.3	82.8	16.5	24.9%
Bob Feller	65.2	82.5	17.3	26.5%
Robin Yount	77.0	82.3	5.3	6.9%
Eddie Murray	68.0	82.2	14.2	20.9%
Red Faber	68.3	81.6	13.3	19.5%
Vic Willis	66.9	81.0	14.1	21.1%
Carlton Fisk	68.3	79.7	11.4	16.7%
Dennis Eckersley	62.4	79.6	17.2	27.6%
Sandy Koufax	53.2	79.4	26.2	49.2%
Harry Heilmann	72.2	79.0	6.8	9.4%
Lou Boudreau	62.9	78.7	15.8	25.1%
Rube Waddell	61.1	78.4	17.3	28.3%
Mordecai Brown	55.0	78.2	23.2	42.2%
Craig Biggio	65.2	78.1	12.9	19.8%
Luke Appling	74.4	77.8	3.4	4.6%
Billy Hamilton	63.5	77.3	13.8	21.7%
Joe McGinnity	60.3	77.3	17.0	28.2%
Hal Newhouser	60.4	77.2	16.8	27.8%
Andre Dawson	64.6	77.1	12.5	19.3%
Tony Gwynn	68.9	77.1	8.2	11.9%
Billy Herman	54.6	77.1	22.5	41.2%
Monte Ward	64.2	76.5	12.3	19.2%
Ed Delahanty	69.7	76.3	6.6	9.5%
Amos Rusie	68.5	75.8	7.3	10.7%
Waite Hoyt	53.4	75.7	22.3	41.8%
Ron Santo	70.6	75.5	4.9	6.9%
Tony Lazzeri	49.9	74.3	24.4	48.9%
Mickey Welch	63.9	74.3	10.4	16.3%
Hank Greenberg	57.5	74.1	16.6	28.9%
Harmon Killebrew	60.5	74.0	13.5	22.3%
Jimmy Collins	53.5	73.8	20.7	39.0%
Joe Tinker	53.3	73.7	20.4	38.3%
Enos Slaughter	55.0	73.5	18.5	33.6%
Joe Medwick	55.6	73.3	17.7	31.8%
Mickey Cochrane	52.1	72.9	20.8	39.9%
Willie Keeler	53.8	72.9	19.1	35.5%
Ryne Sandberg	67.7	72.8	5.1	7.5%
Willie Stargell	57.4	72.3	14.9	26.0%
Gabby Hartnett	53.4	72.0	18.6	34.8%
Luis Aparicio	55.7	71.9	16.2	29.1%
Ted Lyons	67.2	71.5	4.3	6.4%
Richie Ashburn	63.3	70.8	7.5	11.8%
Dave Winfield	63.8	70.6	6.8	10.6%
Eppa Rixey	56.8	70.3	13.5	23.8%
Billy Williams	63.6	70.2	6.6	10.4%
Zack Wheat	60.0	70.1	10.1	16.8%

4. SpWAR and the Hall of Fame

Name	WAR	SpWAR	Fame	Inflation
Jesse Burkett	60.3	69.6	9.3	15.4%
Tony Perez	53.8	69.6	15.8	29.4%
Bill Terry	54.2	69.5	15.3	28.2%
Early Wynn	51.6	69.5	17.9	34.7%
Johnny Evers	47.4	68.5	21.1	44.5%
Mike Piazza	59.3	68.5	9.2	15.5%
Jim Bunning	60.5	67.8	7.3	12.1%
Harry Hooper	53.1	67.8	14.7	27.7%
Orlando Cepeda	50.2	67.4	17.2	34.3%
Joe Kelley	50.4	67.3	16.9	33.5%
Dazzy Vance	62.6	67.3	4.7	7.5%
Jake Beckley	61.8	67.1	5.3	8.6%
Ernie Banks	67.6	67.1	-0.5	-0.7%
Larry Doby	49.7	66.9	17.2	34.6%
Dave Bancroft	48.7	65.7	17.0	34.9%
Chief Bender	43.9	65.5	21.6	49.2%
Joe Sewell	53.8	65.5	11.7	21.7%
Bob Lemon	48.5	65.4	16.9	34.8%
Lefty Gomez	43.0	65.2	22.2	51.6%
Jim O'Rourke	51.2	64.8	13.6	26.5%
Herb Pennock	44.3	64.5	20.2	45.6%
Nellie Fox	49.0	63.9	14.9	30.4%
Phil Rizzuto	40.6	63.8	23.2	57.1%
Max Carey	54.1	63.6	9.5	17.6%
Bobby Doerr	51.5	63.6	12.1	23.5%
Kiki Cuyler	46.7	63.4	16.7	35.8%
Earle Combs	42.5	63.1	20.6	48.5%
Jim Rice	47.3	62.8	15.5	32.8%
Sam Rice	53.0	62.8	9.8	18.5%
Burleigh Grimes	47.0	62.4	15.4	32.8%
Hoyt Wilhelm	49.9	62.2	12.3	24.6%
Elmer Flick	53.1	62.1	9.0	16.9%
Frank Chance	45.8	61.1	15.3	33.4%
Hugh Duffy	43.1	60.8	17.7	41.1%
King Kelly	44.3	59.9	15.6	35.2%
Hughie Jennings	42.5	59.7	17.2	40.5%
Dizzy Dean	42.7	59.3	16.6	38.9%
George Sisler	56.7	58.8	2.1	3.7%
Bid McPhee	52.2	57.9	5.7	10.9%
Travis Jackson	44.0	57.8	13.8	31.4%
Deacon White	45.2	57.5	12.3	27.2%
Kirby Puckett	50.9	57.3	6.4	12.6%
Lou Brock	45.1	56.6	11.5	25.5%
Red Schoendienst	42.4	56.0	13.6	32.1%
Edd Roush	45.1	55.6	10.5	23.3%
Buck Ewing	47.7	55.5	7.8	16.4%
Addie Joss	45.8	54.7	8.9	19.4%
Roger Bresnahan	42.0	54.6	12.6	30.0%
Heinie Manush	45.7	54.3	8.6	18.8%
Earl Averill	48.0	54.2	6.2	12.9%

Name	WAR	SpWAR	Fame	Inflation
Roy Campanella	34.1	53.3	19.2	56.3%
Sam Thompson	44.4	53.1	8.7	19.6%
Ernie Lombardi	46.0	51.6	5.6	12.2%
Rabbit Maranville	42.8	51.1	8.3	19.4%
Jack Chesbro	41.3	50.4	9.1	22.0%
Ralph Kiner	49.4	50.1	0.7	1.4%
Pie Traynor	36.1	49.7	13.6	37.7%
Goose Gossage	41.9	49.2	7.3	17.5%
Rube Marquard	34.4	48.9	14.5	42.2%
Hack Wilson	39.0	48.8	9.8	25.1%
Ross Youngs	32.2	48.3	16.1	50.0%
Catfish Hunter	36.5	48.0	11.5	31.5%
Chuck Klein	43.7	47.2	3.5	8.0%
Jesse Haines	35.7	46.9	11.2	31.4%
George Kell	37.6	45.8	8.2	21.8%
Jim Bottomley	35.3	45.7	10.4	29.5%
Chick Hafey	30.0	40.1	10.1	33.7%
Bill Mazeroski	36.1	39.7	3.6	10.0%
George Kelly	25.2	37.8	12.6	50.0%
Ray Schalk	28.4	36.3	7.9	27.8%
Freddie Lindstrom	28.2	34.8	6.6	23.4%
Rollie Fingers	25.1	32.0	6.9	27.5%
Lloyd Waner	24.2	31.7	7.5	31.0%
Rick Ferrell	29.7	31.3	1.6	5.4%
Tommy McCarthy	17.2	26.3	9.1	52.9%
Bruce Sutter	24.5	26.3	1.8	7.3%

5. The Most Famous Players

There are three primary relationships to baseball (as with any hobby or pursuit):

1. A non-fan;
2. A moderate fan; and
3. An invested fan.

We've been investigating how the narrative might influence a writer or fan paying a little less attention to the game than a fully invested fan does. The same measurements allow us to estimate what lives in the ring of non-investment. SpWAR lets us estimate the most famous players at any given time—the blind guesses on *Jeopardy!* or who shows up in Simon and Garfunkel songs (it's hard to imagine "our nation turn[ing] its lonely eyes to" Ted Williams, and not just because Joe DiMaggio is a more lyrical name).[1]

If Productivity (WAR) × Spotlight (Spotlight!) = Reputation (SpWAR), then SpWAR - WAR = raw Fame. For example, a 6-WAR player on a 1.50-Spotlight team has 3 points of his reputation made entirely of Fame (6 × 1.50 = 9; 9 - 6 = 3). As you might guess from those figures, three points of Fame from a single season is high and rare. Most players will generate no Fame because they're on 1.00-Spotlight teams; there is no amount of value they can produce to force their accomplishments into, say, my mom's consciousness.

So Fame is tied to WAR but not directly—you can be a legend within the sport and have no mass popularity, while you can be pretty good and a Yankee and become an icon. There **has** to be some Spotlight before a player's existence will cross from baseball into pop culture.

While Fame, as measure of the non-fan, might not seem to affect Hall of Fame voting, it does if a good chunk of the membership stops following baseball regularly (as the BBWAA's policy of lifetime memberships, only changed in 2015, can lead to).[2] Consider Jim Rice and Dwight Evans. Jim Rice is in the Hall of Fame off a 47.3 WAR and 62.8 SpWAR. Dwight Evans, Rice's teammate his entire career, is not in the Hall of Fame off a 67.2 WAR and 82.2 SpWAR.

Even to the casual observer, it should have been clear that Evans was better than Rice. But tracking their Fame reveals a surprising difference. Listing the year, the Red Sox Spotlight for every year (except for 1991, when Evans was an Oriole), and how much career Fame Rice and Evans each had accumulated—and we'll throw in Fred Lynn's Red Sox tenure for good measure:

1972 (1.04): Evans 0.0
1973 (1.04): Evans 0.1
1974 (1.14): Evans 0.7, Lynn 0.1, Rice 0.0
1975 (1.50): Lynn 3.8, Evans 3.2, Rice 1.5
1976 (1.31): Lynn 5.2, Evans 4.4, Rice 2.2
1977 (1.32): Lynn 5.7, Evans 5.1, Rice 3.9
1978 (1.45): Lynn 7.7, Rice 7.3, Evans 6.4
1979 (1.49): Lynn 12.0, Rice 10.3, Evans 8.3
1980 (1.25): Lynn 13.1, Rice 10.8, Evans 9
1981 (1.06): Rice 11.0, Evans 9.4
1982 (1.24): Rice 11.7, Evans 10.9
1983 (1.16): Rice 12.6, Evans 11.1
1984 (1.04): Rice 12.7, Evans 11.4
1985 (1.00): Rice 12.7, Evans 11.4
1986 (1.50): Rice 15.5, Evans 13.6
1987 (1.19): Rice 15.5, Evans 14.5
1988 (1.08): Rice 15.6, Evans 14.7
1989 (1.04): Rice 15.5, Evans 14.8
1990 (1.22): Evans 15.0
1991 (1.00): Evans 15.0

So while they were teammates, here's who looked the best every year by WAR and Fame:

	WAR	Fame
1974:	Evans	Evans
1975–78:	Evans	Lynn
1979–80:	Lynn	Lynn
1981–89:	Evans	Rice

Despite leading the trio in WAR pretty much their entire careers, Dwight Evans always came up less famous despite the same Spotlight. This is because Evans's best seasons came when the Red Sox weren't as important, like 1981 and 1982, while Rice's best seasons coincided with a surge in Red Sox reputation, like 1978 and 1979. To the untrained eye, Rice **appeared** superior to Evans for 12 straight seasons. If Rice's big years were swapped with Evans's—1978–79 and 1981–82, respectively—Evans would have been more famous than Rice. Rice's career worked **with** the team narrative, and Evans's worked **against** the team narrative. And it's in measuring Fame that it's most clearly seen.[3]

So to link the type of person with their metric of choice:

1. A non-fan uses something like Fame;
2. A moderate fan uses something like SpWAR; and
3. An invested fan uses something like WAR.

I can name football players and Hollywood stars only when they're famous; I can't tell you who's respected for a lifetime body of work in either one unless they've pierced my awareness with something major. This is how most people are with baseball, and isolating the Fame component of SpWAR lets us estimate how the non-fan—and the BBWAA's apathetic edges—view baseball players.

What follows is a yearly top-five list of career WAR and Fame. I'll pause for comment when it makes sense to—or at least when I want to say something. First names are given for a player's debut on a particular list or as necessary to distinguish between players of the same last name.

1871	*WAR*	*Fame*
	George Zettlein, 4.9	Dick McBride, 1.5
	Rynie Wolters, 4.3	George Zettlein, 1.3
	Dick McBride, 4.0	Levi Meyerle, 0.6
	Al Spalding, 3.3	Al Spalding, 0.5
	Cherokee Fisher, 2.2	Jimmy Wood, 0.5
1872	*WAR*	*Fame*
	Spalding, 15.4	Spalding, 6.3
	Zettlein, 11.3	McBride, 3.5
	McBride, 8.8	Ross Barnes, 2.4
	Candy Cummings, 8.7	George Wright, 1.6
	Bobby Mathews, 8.1	Zettlein, 1.3
1873	*WAR*	*Fame*
	Spalding, 24.3	Spalding, 10.3
	Zettlein, 19.8	Zettlein, 4.6
	Mathews, 18.1	Barnes, 4.6
	Cummings, 16.5	McBride, 4.1
	McBride, 15.1	Wright, 3.1
1874	*WAR*	*Fame*
	Spalding, 34.8	Spalding, 14.5
	Mathews 31.6	Barnes, 5.6
	Zettlein, 23.7	Zettlein, 4.6
	Cummings, 23.1	Wright, 4.4
	McBride, 21.8	McBride, 4.1
1875	*WAR*	*Fame*
	Spalding, 49.0	Spalding, 20.9
	Mathews, 39.7	Barnes, 8.1

1875	WAR	Fame
	Cummings, 35.6	Wright, 6.5
	Zettlein, 32.2	Zettlein, 4.9
	McBride, 31.0	Cal McVey, 4.8

The National Association is in the one-man "rotation" era, meaning all the most productive players are pitchers. But only one of them could play for Boston, so the fame as MLB headed into the National League was 80 percent Red Stockings (most of whom were moving to Chicago).

1876	WAR	Fame
	Spalding, 58.7	Spalding, 24.6
	Mathews, 43.1	Barnes, 10.3
	Cummings, 39.9	Wright, 8.0
	Zettlein, 31.3	McVey, 6.2
	McBride, 30.2	Deacon White, 5.4

This was the first year that only one name overlapped in the top five; it's happened 14 other times. Given that WAR/Fame split indicates a divergence between baseball's players and narrative, seven of those 14 predating annual World Series is important:

Seasons with only one player on both the top five WAR and Fame lists, grouped by decade

1876
1883, 1885, 1886, 1887
1900, 1902, 1903
1980, 1981, 1982, 1983
1994, 1999
2008

The chasm between 1903 and 1980 was made largely by competitive imbalance. The best players were on the winning teams more often because there were only a few functioning teams in several of those years. The amateur draft and free agency increased parity and competition, while expansion lowered the odds of a single team having all the talent; this increases the odds of WAR/Fame disagreement.

1877	WAR	Fame
	Spalding, 58.4	Spalding, 24.7
	Mathews, 41.2	Barnes, 10.4
	Cummings, 38.5	Wright, 8.6
	Jim Devlin, 33.9	Tommy Bond, 8.1
	Tommy Bond, 33.2	McVey, 7.1

Devlin was banned from baseball after the season for his role in the Louisville gambling scandal.[4] He achieved the bulk of his WAR in 1876 and 1877. Bond achieved his WAR over four seasons, his Fame coming from Hartford in 1876 and Boston in 1877. Spalding's career was winding down, and Bond was the new ace on his former and still highly reputed team.

1878	WAR	Fame
	Spalding, 58.4	Spalding, 24.7
	Bond, 47.0	Bond, 14.9
	Deacon White, 19.9	Wright, 8.9
	Wright, 19.4	White, 7.7
	McVey, 18.6	McVey, 7.6

This is the only season where these lists completely align. Bobby Mathews didn't play in the NL in 1878 and neither did Ross Barnes.

1879	WAR	Fame
	Bond, 61.4	Bond, 21.6
	Mathews, 43.8	Barnes, 10.6
	Barnes, 26.6	Wright, 9.7
	Wright, 23.7	White, 8.1
	White, 23.6	McVey, 7.7

1880	WAR	Fame
	Bond, 62.9	Bond, 22.2
	Cap Anson, 24.3	Wright, 9.7
	White, 24.1	White, 8.1
	Wright, 23.8	Jim O'Rourke, 7.8
	Jim McCormick, 22.3	Cap Anson, 7.6

Although Cap Anson played from 1871 to 1897, you don't hear of him much in stories about the 1870s. That's because, as these charts show, he wasn't much of a factor in them. The Rockford Forest City team of 1871 was far away from the Chicago team he'd be known for (in fame, not in geographical location).

1881	WAR	Fame
	Bond, 62.9	Bond, 22.2
	Mathews, 43.1	Barnes, 10.7
	Anson, 30.1	Anson, 10.5
	McCormick, 29.7	Wright, 9.7
	Barnes, 27.9	White, 8.6

1882	WAR	Fame
	Bond, 62.6	Bond, 22.2
	Mathews, 47.2	Anson, 12.7
	McCormick, 40.0	Wright, 10.2
	Anson, 34.5	White, 8.6
	White, 26.5	O'Rourke, 8.5

1883	WAR	Fame
	Mathews, 52.4	Anson, 13.6
	McCormick, 48.4	Larry Corcoran, 10.4
	Pud Galvin, 37.2	Will White, 10.0
	Anson, 36.8	Old Hoss Radbourn, 8.7
	Tim Keefe, 31.8	Deacon White, 8.6

1884	WAR	Fame
	Bond, 61.0	Bond, 22.2
	Galvin, 57.7	Radbourn, 18.3
	Mathews, 56.7	Anson, 15.4
	McCormick, 55.1	Corcoran, 12.6
	Old Hoss Radbourn, 44.8	Will White, 10.8

The American Association gave a chance for Fame if you didn't play for Chicago or Providence. Corcoran was the ace in Chicago, Radbourn was the ace in Providence, and Deacon White's brother Will was the ace for the AA contenders in Cincinnati.

Tim Keefe set the single-season record for WAR in 1883 at 20.0; it was 19.7 without his hitting. Radbourn's 1884 is the second-highest WAR at 19.3; it was 19.1 without his hitting (I exclude hitting from pitchers' records unless hitting was a significant part of their value, like Walter Johnson, Wes Ferrell, or Red Ruffing). Keefe played for the then anonymous New York Metropolitans, while Radbourn played for the quite famous Providence Grays. So Keefe's season has an SpWAR of 19.7 (and Fame of 0), while Radbourn's has an SpWAR of 28.7 and Fame of 9.6–unbeatable unless the game changes dramatically. Pud Galvin's pitching in 1884 by itself would be the single-season WAR record at 20.5, but his hitting was awful and he played for the Buffalo Bisons, so his season is more obscure than Radbourn's.

(Relevant to Jim McCormick and Tommy Bond's comeback: I don't count Union Association statistics for WAR or Fame, as its schedule and strength are too irregular to quantify.)

1885	WAR	Fame
	Mathews, 63.3	Radbourn, 21.7
	Galvin, 58.9	Anson, 16.9
	Radbourn, 52.0	Corcoran, 12.6
	McCormick, 57.8	Ned Williamson, 11.8
	Keefe, 46.3	Will White, 11.3
1886	WAR	Fame
	McCormick, 65.0	Radbourn, 22.1
	Galvin, 63.2	Anson, 20.3
	Mathews, 63.2	Williamson, 12.9
	Radbourn, 56.6	George Gore, 12.8
	Keefe, 56.4	Corcoran, 12.6

Until Barry Bonds, Jim McCormick is the last WAR leader not in the Hall of Fame; Zettlein, Mathews, and Tommy Bond are the others in that list. The list of Fame leaders not in the Hall until Barry is Dick McBride, Tommy Bond, and Pete Rose.

5. The Most Famous Players

1887	WAR	Fame
	Galvin, 70.5	Anson, 22.5
	McCormick, 67.6	Radbourn, 22.5
	Keefe, 63.5	Bob Caruthers, 16.5
	Mathews, 62.2	John Clarkson, 15.6
	Radbourn, 58.4	Williamson, 14.2

1888	WAR	Fame
	Galvin, 77.2	Anson, 25.3
	Keefe, 73.8	Radbourn, 22.8
	Anson, 64.7	Caruthers, 18.8
	Radbourn, 59.8	Clarkson, 16.5
	Mickey Welch, 53.9	Williamson, 15.7

1889	WAR	Fame
	Galvin, 78.2	Anson, 27.8
	Keefe, 78.0	Radbourn, 24.7
	Anson, 71.1	Clarkson, 22.9
	Radbourn, 64.4	Caruthers, 22.2
	Welch, 60.6	Williamson, 15.7

1890	WAR	Fame
	Keefe, 83.0	Radbourn, 28.8
	Galvin, 77.1	Anson, 28.0
	Anson, 76.5	Clarkson, 26.8
	Radbourn, 72.9	Caruthers, 24.0
	Welch, 66.1	Silver King, 17.7

King's career is unusual. Three straight years as young ace for the St. Louis Browns (ages 19–21) and then in the Players League for Chicago got him into this top five. But he'd achieved 83 percent of his career WAR and 97 percent of his career Fame by this point; he'd leave the majors after 1893 and come back for two okay seasons in 1896–97. It's like a 19th-century version of Dwight Gooden's career arc.

1891	WAR	Fame
	Keefe, 81.9	Clarkson, 30.7
	Galvin, 80.3	Anson, 28.9
	Anson, 80.3	Radbourn, 28.8
	Clarkson, 75.5	Caruthers, 25.8
	Radbourn, 73.3	King, 17.7

1892	WAR	Fame
	Keefe, 87.7	Clarkson, 32.4
	Galvin, 83.6	Anson, 30.3
	Anson, 83.6	Caruthers, 26.0
	Clarkson, 81.3	Dan Brouthers, 19.3
	Roger Connor, 69.8	King, 18.3

Connor and Brouthers make for an interesting contrast. They are each other's most similar batter and put up spectacular numbers in roughly the same time period, but Brouthers played for Detroit and the Boston Reds in his prime while Connor stayed with the less famous New York Giants. Brouthers was elected to the Hall of Fame in 1945, while Connor was elected in 1976.

John Clarkson was elected in between them in 1963; I don't know why it took that long given his level of Fame. It could be that his comparatively early death (1909 versus 1922 for Anson and 1932 for Brouthers) left him more unknown to the Hall of Fame voters by the time of the Hall's founding; a Hall of Fame established in 1915 almost certainly would have voted him in on the first ballot.[5]

1893	WAR	Fame
	Keefe, 88.9	Clarkson, 32.7
	Anson, 85.8	Anson, 30.6
	Clarkson, 82.8	Caruthers, 26.0
	Connor, 74.2	Brouthers, 20.7
	Brouthers, 73.2	Kid Nichols, 20.1
1894	WAR	Fame
	Anson, 88.7	Clarkson, 33.3
	Clarkson, 85.7	Anson, 30.7
	Connor, 77.8	Nichols, 24.1
	Brouthers, 77.1	Brouthers, 21.8
	Jack Glasscock, 61.7	Jack Stivetts, 19.2

In a one-league world, there were fewer long careers to go around, so WAR figures started to drop off. The highest Spotlight for any team Glasscock was on was 1.29 (1890 Giants). He won the batting title that year and gained 2.1 points of Fame—almost half his lifetime total of 4.6.

Stivetts, on the other hand, was the second starter behind Kid Nichols for the famed Boston Beaneaters and had cleared 4.5 Fame by the end of his second season (he started with the equally famous St. Louis Browns). He was 26 by 1894 but wouldn't pitch after 31; early burnout is a common theme among pitchers of the era. Helping Stivetts's totals was that he could hit; he was a backup corner outfielder on several of his teams and slugged .367/.417/.533 in 1897. His career was too short to merit serious Hall of Fame consideration, but he had a fine career, magnified by playing almost entirely for the Browns and Beaneaters.

1895	WAR	Fame
	Anson, 90.8	Anson, 30.9
	Connor, 81.4	Nichols, 28.9
	Brouthers, 77.6	Brouthers, 21.8
	Glasscock, 61.9	Stivetts, 20.2
	Kid Nichols, 61.9	Hugh Duffy, 13.6

5. The Most Famous Players

1896	WAR	Fame
	Anson, 93.0	Nichols, 31.1
	Connor, 84.3	Anson, 31.0
	Brouthers, 79.5	Stivetts, 21.9
	Nichols, 69.0	Brouthers, 21.9
	Cy Young, 67.1	King, 18.3
1897	WAR	Fame
	Anson, 93.9	Nichols, 34.7
	Connor, 84.1	Anson, 31.0
	Nichols, 79.9	Stivetts, 23.0
	Young, 74.7	King, 18.3
	Amos Rusie, 64.8	Duffy, 15.4

Anson's retirement and King's re-retirement combined with the one-league era to create a dip in the fame of baseball players. This dip was mostly filled by Baltimore Orioles.

1898	WAR	Fame
	Nichols, 90.6	Nichols, 39.8
	Young, 81.6	Stivetts, 22.9
	Rusie, 69.2	Duffy, 17.0
	Billy Hamilton, 54.7	Hughie Jennings, 15.5
	Jack Stivetts, 51.5	Cy Young, 13.8

Nichols and Young weren't far apart by WAR, but Nichols's Beaneaters were significantly more famous than the Cleveland Spiders.

1899	WAR	Fame
	Nichols, 98.0	Nichols, 43.3
	Young, 90.1	Stivetts, 22.8
	Hamilton, 56.7	Duffy, 17.5
	Bid McPhee, 52.4	Jennings, 16.0
	Ed Delahanty, 52.0	Young, 14.2
1900	WAR	Fame
	Nichols, 102.7	Nichols, 44.8
	Young, 97.6	Duffy, 17.7
	Hamilton, 60.9	Jennings, 16.5
	Delahanty, 55.0	Joe Kelley, 14.9
	Ted Breitenstein, 53.0	Willie Keeler, 14.6

Only one period in baseball history has had second-place Fame be this low since Duffy and later Keeler attained it: the early 1990s. Remember that when we get to there.

1901	WAR	Fame
	Young, 110.2	Nichols, 45.0
	Nichols, 108.5	Young, 18.0
	Rusie, 68.4	Duffy, 17.7
	Hamilton, 63.3	Jennings, 16.8
	Delahanty, 61.6	Kelley, 16.4

1902	WAR	Fame
	Young, 120.2	Young, 22.0
	Delahanty, 68.3	Keeler, 17.7
	George Davis, 57.5	Jennings, 17.2
	Jesse Burkett, 53.7	Kelley, 16.4
	Jake Beckley, 53.3	Herman Long, 13.8
1903	WAR	Fame
	Young, 127.4	Young, 25.5
	Delahanty, 69.5	Keeler, 17.7
	Davis, 57.4	Jennings, 17.2
	Burkett, 56.4	Kelley, 16.4
	Beckley, 56.0	Jimmy Collins, 14.7

Kid Nichols's brief retirement left a Fame void. Collins was the lowest fifth-place finish until 1993–95.

1904	WAR	Fame
	Young, 136.9	Nichols, 45.0
	Nichols, 116.1	Young, 30.3
	Davis, 64.6	Keeler, 18.5
	Burkett, 60.3	Duffy, 17.7
	Beckley, 60.2	Collins, 17.4

Dan Brouthers (21.8 Fame) and Jim O'Rourke (13.6 Fame) played briefly as a stunt for the Giants, their first games since 1896 and 1893, respectively.

1905	WAR	Fame
	Young, 144.5	Nichols, 45.0
	Nichols, 117.5	Young, 33.8
	Davis, 71.8	Collins, 19.5
	Bill Dahlen, 65.7	Honus Wagner, 19.2
	Burkett, 62.9	Keeler, 19.0
1906	WAR	Fame
	Young, 146.6	Nichols, 44.9
	Nichols, 116.6	Young, 34.2
	Davis, 78.8	Wagner, 22.0
	Dahlen, 68.9	Collins, 19.7
	Honus Wagner, 66.9	Keeler, 19.3
1907	WAR	Fame
	Young, 154.2	Young, 34.7
	Davis, 82.7	Wagner, 22.8
	Wagner, 75.8	Collins, 20.7
	Dahlen, 69.4	Bill Dahlen, 19.0
	Nap Lajoie, 68.4	Keeler, 19.0

Bill Dahlen not being in the Hall of Fame is similar to Bobby Grich not being in the Hall of Fame. WAR and Fame generally indicate that both should be in, but they haven't gotten the love you'd expect.[6] It took George Davis a long time to get in as well.

5. The Most Famous Players   45

1908	WAR	Fame
	Young, 163.8	Young, 34.7
	Wagner, 87.3	Wagner, 25.6
	Davis, 84.3	Christy Mathewson, 21.0
	Lajoie, 76.3	Collins, 20.7
	Dahlen, 74.7	Dahlen, 19.1
1909	WAR	Fame
	Young, 167.0	Young, 35.6
	Wagner, 96.5	Wagner, 30.5
	Davis, 84.7	Mathewson, 23.9
	Lajoie, 82.7	Keeler, 19.1
	Dahlen, 75.4	Dahlen, 19.1
1910	WAR	Fame
	Young, 169.4	Young, 36.0
	Wagner, 101.7	Wagner, 32.8
	Lajoie, 92.5	Mathewson, 26.1
	Dahlen, 75.3	Eddie Plank, 19.9
	Christy Mathewson, 74.7	Mordecai Brown, 19.2

For the first time, none of the top five famous players in baseball had ever been each other's teammates. This would also be true in 1911 and 1912. It has never happened since.

1911	WAR	Fame
	Young, 170.3	Young, 36.0
	Wagner, 108.2	Wagner, 34.9
	Lajoie, 95.2	Mathewson, 29.5
	Mathewson, 82.1	Plank, 23.7
	Dahlen, 75.2	Brown, 20.9
1912	WAR	Fame
	Wagner, 116.3	Wagner, 37.3
	Lajoie, 100.6	Mathewson, 33.7
	Mathewson, 89.4	Plank, 26.0
	Bobby Wallace, 76.4	Ed Walsh, 22.7
	Eddie Plank, 68.9	Brown, 21.5
1913	WAR	Fame
	Wagner, 119.3	Mathewson, 37.9
	Lajoie, 105.9	Wagner, 37.6
	Mathewson, 96.3	Plank, 27.7
	Plank, 71.8	Eddie Collins, 23.1
	Wallace, 76.8	Walsh, 23.0
1914	WAR	Fame
	Wagner, 122.9	Wagner, 38.2
	Lajoie, 106.0	Mathewson, 38.2
	Mathewson, 96.9	Plank, 28.8
	Wallace, 76.8	Collins, 28.6
	Walter Johnson, 75.6	Ty Cobb, 23.9

1914 was also Johnson's first year of obtaining any sizable Fame, with 3.0 points of it. He would end his career with 13.2, most of it coming after he turned 34.

Most career WAR for players who never were top five in Fame
Walter Johnson, 165.8
Rogers Hornsby, 126.9
Nap Lajoie, 107.4
Tom Seaver, 106.1
Phil Niekro, 97.3
Bert Blyleven, 96.4
Carl Yastrzemski, 96.2
Cal Ripken, 95.6
Roberto Clemente, 94.6
Gaylord Perry, 93.6

	1915	*WAR*	*Fame*
		Wagner, 128.5	Wagner, 38.2
		Lajoie, 107.6	Mathewson, 37.6
		Mathewson, 95.7	Collins, 30.9
		Johnson, 87.7	Plank, 29.3
		Plank, 80.0	Cobb, 28.0
	1916	*WAR*	*Fame*
		Wagner, 131.0	Wagner, 38.2
		Lajoie, 107.4	Mathewson, 37.6
		Johnson, 98.4	Collins, 32.1
		Mathewson, 95.3	Cobb, 31.8
		Cobb, 86.3	Plank, 29.3
	1917	*WAR*	*Fame*
		Wagner, 131.0	Wagner, 38.2
		Johnson, 106.4	Cobb, 35.5
		Cobb, 97.6	Collins, 34.5
		Plank, 86.5	Plank, 29.3
		Wallace, 77.0	Walsh, 23.3
	1918	*WAR*	*Fame*
		Johnson, 118.0	Cobb, 36.7
		Cobb, 104.2	Collins, 35.8
		Eddie Collins, 79.5	Frank Baker, 24.2
		Tris Speaker, 77.5	Pete Alexander, 21.0
		Wallace, 76.3	Art Fletcher, 17.3

I was not expecting Fletcher to show up on this list. Fletcher provided a ridiculous amount of defensive value as the Giants' shortstop; that's enough to get him on this list for two years. In general, 30 seems to be the amount of Fame that makes someone a household name; only 36 players have reached that level.

17's a far cry from 30, but plenty of people outside baseball fandom presumably were able to name Art Fletcher as the Giants' shortstop.

1919	WAR	Fame
	Johnson, 128.8	Collins, 38.5
	Cobb, 110.7	Cobb, 37.0
	Collins, 84.6	Baker, 25.0
	Speaker, 82.4	Alexander, 23.6
	Alexander, 69.0	Fletcher, 20.0
1920	WAR	Fame
	Johnson, 131.7	Collins, 42.2
	Cobb, 113.1	Cobb, 37.0
	Collins, 92.4	Alexander, 26.4
	Speaker, 90.9	Speaker, 22.5
	Alexander, 81.1	Babe Ruth, 22.4

These six players would rule both lists for most of the 1920s. Part of baseball's nostalgia is a sense that giants (not the Art Fletcher kind) used to roam the earth in a simpler time, and this period of WAR and Fame stability is largely why. It's a pretty easy period to understand for the non-fan and dedicated fan alike.

1921	WAR	Fame
	Johnson, 137.1	Collins, 43.7
	Cobb, 119.7	Cobb, 37.0
	Speaker, 97.3	Ruth, 28.4
	Collins, 96.9	Alexander, 26.7
	Alexander, 85.8	Baker, 26.1
1922	WAR	Fame
	Johnson, 142.6	Collins, 44.7
	Cobb, 126.4	Cobb, 37.0
	Speaker, 104.2	Ruth, 32.0
	Collins, 100.8	Speaker, 28.5
	Alexander, 90.4	Alexander, 26.7
1923	WAR	Fame
	Johnson, 147.3	Collins, 44.8
	Cobb, 131.9	Ruth, 40.5
	Speaker, 113.2	Cobb, 37.1
	Collins, 107.1	Speaker, 32.0
	Alexander, 95.6	Alexander, 26.7
1924	WAR	Fame
	Johnson, 154.8	Ruth, 46.3
	Cobb, 137.3	Collins, 44.8
	Speaker, 117.7	Cobb, 38.7
	Collins, 112.3	Speaker, 32.5
	Babe Ruth, 97.8	Alexander, 27.4

Ruth broke the Fame record held by Kid Nichols (Ruth being filmed and on the radio made him more famous than Nichols anyway). Nobody has ever cleared 60 points of Fame, except for Ruth—who retired with 88.3. Ruth has more career Fame than Stan Musial and Joe DiMaggio combined.

1925	WAR	Fame
	Johnson, 161.7	Ruth, 48.0
	Cobb, 143.1	Collins, 45.0
	Speaker, 124.2	Cobb, 40.0
	Collins, 117.4	Speaker, 32.5
	Alexander, 102.2	Alexander, 27.9
1926	WAR	Fame
	Johnson, 165.5	Ruth, 54.4
	Cobb, 144.7	Collins, 45.3
	Speaker, 129.6	Cobb, 40.0
	Collins, 121.5	Speaker, 32.7
	Ruth, 112.8	Alexander, 29.3
1927	WAR	Fame
	Johnson, 165.6	Ruth, 61.8
	Cobb, 149.1	Collins, 45.5
	Speaker, 133.2	Cobb, 40.5
	Ruth, 125.2	Speaker, 34.2
	Collins, 123.8	Alexander, 31.1
1928	WAR	Fame
	Cobb, 151.0	Ruth, 67.9
	Ruth, 135.3	Collins, 45.6
	Speaker, 133.7	Cobb, 40.7
	Collins, 124.0	Speaker, 34.2
	Alexander, 115.0	Alexander, 32.9
1929	WAR	Fame
	Ruth, 143.3	Ruth, 71.7
	Collins, 123.9	Collins, 45.5
	Rogers Hornsby, 119.6	Alexander, 34.1
	Alexander, 117.5	Frankie Frisch, 26.0
	Harry Heilmann, 67.6	Lou Gehrig, 21.9
1930	WAR	Fame
	Ruth, 153.6	Ruth, 75.3
	Collins, 123.9	Collins, 45.5
	Hornsby, 120.0	Alexander, 34.1
	Alexander, 117.0	Frisch, 28.6
	Heilmann, 72.2	Gehrig, 25.2
1931	WAR	Fame
	Ruth, 163.9	Ruth, 78.6
	Hornsby, 125.2	Frisch, 30.6
	Red Faber, 65.3	Gehrig, 28.0
	Frankie Frisch, 62.8	Herb Pennock, 20.3
	Dazzy Vance, 60.1	Waite Hoyt, 19.8

Frankie Frisch became the NL's Babe Ruth with the retirement of Pete Alexander. Frankie Frisch is considered to have gotten many of his teammates elected to the Hall of Fame when on the Veterans Committee.[7] Had Babe Ruth ever been on the Veterans Committee, I bet he would have been considered authoritative about the caliber of his teammates.

1932	WAR	Fame
	Ruth, 172.2	Ruth, 82.5
	Hornsby, 125.3	Gehrig, 31.8
	Heilmann, 72.1	Frisch, 31.0
	Faber, 66.6	Lefty Grove, 23.6
	Lou Gehrig, 65.5	Pennock, 20.4
1933	WAR	Fame
	Ruth, 178.6	Ruth, 85.7
	Hornsby, 126.5	Gehrig, 35.3
	Gehrig, 72.4	Frisch, 32.0
	Faber, 68.4	Grove, 26.2
	Frisch, 66.3	Hoyt, 20.3
1934	WAR	Fame
	Ruth, 183.7	Ruth, 88.3
	Hornsby, 126.8	Gehrig, 40.5
	Gehrig, 82.8	Frisch, 33.0
	Frisch, 68.8	Grove, 26.2
	Lefty Grove, 64.9	Hoyt, 21.3
1935	WAR	Fame
	Ruth, 183.7	Ruth, 88.3
	Hornsby, 126.8	Gehrig, 44.7
	Gehrig, 91.5	Frisch, 33.5
	Grove, 74.4	Grove, 26.3
	Frisch, 70.3	Hoyt, 21.9
1936	WAR	Fame
	Hornsby, 126.8	Gehrig, 50.0
	Gehrig, 100.6	Frisch, 33.5
	Grove, 85.4	Grove, 29.1
	Frisch, 70.5	Tony Lazzeri, 22.8
	Jimmie Foxx, 68.4	Hoyt, 22.3

The most famous player ever retired and gave Fame lead to the third most famous player ever.

1937	WAR	Fame
	Hornsby, 127.0	Gehrig, 54.6
	Gehrig, 108.3	Frisch, 33.5
	Grove, 95.0	Grove, 29.7
	Foxx, 72.2	Lazzeri, 23.9
	Frisch, 70.4	Mel Ott, 23.1
1938	WAR	Fame
	Gehrig, 112.6	Gehrig, 57.2
	Grove, 100.2	Grove, 31.0
	Foxx, 79.7	Ott, 27.5

1938	WAR	Fame
	Mel Ott, 74.4	Lazzeri, 24.4
	Charlie Gehringer, 71.3	Jimmie Foxx, 24.2
1939	WAR	Fame
	Gehrig, 112.4	Gehrig, 57.0
	Grove, 107.2	Grove, 32.0
	Foxx, 86.6	Ott, 30.1
	Ott, 80.1	Red Ruffing, 25.5
	Gehringer, 76.2	Foxx, 25.1

Although Lou Gehrig and Joe DiMaggio were teammates, the eras in which people think of them are not connected. Red Ruffing bridges the gap between them.

The Yankees had a top-five player in Fame every year from 1918 to 1954. New York teams had such a streak from 1900 to 1916 and again from 1918 to 1968.

1940	WAR	Fame
	Grove, 110.0	Grove, 32.7
	Foxx, 91.7	Ott, 31.9
	Ott, 85.3	Ruffing, 26.8
	Gehringer, 80.0	Foxx, 26.4
	Al Simmons, 69.8	Carl Hubbell, 24.4
1941	WAR	Fame
	Grove, 109.9	Grove, 32.7
	Foxx, 96.0	Ott, 32.4
	Ott, 89.9	Ruffing, 27.9
	Gehringer, 80.5	Foxx, 27.1
	Simmons, 69.4	Bill Dickey, 25.5
1942	WAR	Fame
	Ott, 96.2	Ott, 32.4
	Foxx, 96.1	Ruffing, 29.2
	Gehringer, 80.6	Joe DiMaggio, 27.5
	Paul Waner, 70.5	Foxx, 27.1
	Red Ruffing, 68.5	Dickey, 26.4
1943	WAR	Fame
	Ott, 99.0	Ott, 32.4
	Waner, 72.2	Dickey, 28.8
	Arky Vaughan, 70.9	Hubbell, 24.7
	Simmons, 68.6	Paul Waner, 22.2
	Carl Hubbell, 67.8	Lefty Gomez, 22.2

These charts go weird due to World War II, as Ruffing was gone in 1943–44, Foxx in 1943, DiMaggio in 1943–45, and Dickey in 1944–45. In their place are Gomez and Waner. Gomez was perennially in the World Series with the Yankees, while Waner was only in one postseason. But the Pirates hung around several pennant races through the '20s and '30s—their Spotlight never fell below 1.14 in that time—and Waner was highly productive in those years.

1944	WAR	Fame
	Ott, 104.3	Ott, 32.4
	Foxx, 95.8	Foxx, 27.1
	Waner, 72.7	Waner, 22.4
	Simmons, 68.7	Al Simmons, 21.7
	Joe Cronin, 66.1	Joe Medwick, 17.0

17.0 was the lowest fifth place from 1904 to 1988.

1945	WAR	Fame
	Ott, 108.8	Ott, 33.4
	Foxx, 96.4	Ruffing, 29.8
	Waner, 72.8	Foxx, 27.1
	Ruffing, 69.7	Waner, 22.4
	Cronin, 66.4	Charlie Keller, 18.0

1946	WAR	Fame
	Ott, 107.9	Ott, 33.4
	Ruffing, 71.5	Ruffing, 30.4
	Ted Lyons, 67.2	DiMaggio, 29.4
	Luke Appling, 61.3	Dickey, 29.1
	Bill Dickey, 55.8	Billy Herman, 22.5

Dickey's 55.8 is the lowest fifth-place WAR from 1903 to 2015. Ruffing's 71.5 is the lowest second-place WAR in that same time period. After Joe DiMaggio's retirement, second place has been 80 WAR or higher every year except 2014, when Alex Rodriguez was suspended.

1947	WAR	Fame
	Ott, 107.8	Ott, 33.3
	Vaughan, 72.4	DiMaggio, 31.7
	Ruffing, 70.4	Ruffing, 30.4
	Appling, 66.0	Herman, 22.5
	Joe DiMaggio, 58.6	Keller, 21.1

1948	WAR	Fame
	Vaughan, 72.9	DiMaggio, 35.1
	Appling, 69.4	Stan Musial, 24.0
	DiMaggio, 65.5	Joe Gordon, 23.7
	Johnny Mize, 65.0	Keller, 21.6
	Ted Williams, 63.4	Arky Vaughan, 18.2

Give DiMaggio back the three wartime seasons and it's reasonable to believe he would have had another ten points of Fame, which would put him in the top five all-time with Ruth/Mantle/Gehrig/Mays. It appears society has filled in those seasons like they existed and accorded him top-five status instead of the top-ten my formulas say he has. Or maybe marrying Marilyn Monroe accomplished that.

1949	WAR	Fame
	Appling, 74.4	DiMaggio, 37.8
	Williams, 72.6	Musial, 27.0
	DiMaggio, 69.9	Gordon, 25.3
	Mize, 67.4	Keller, 21.8
	Lou Boudreau, 60.7	Ted Williams, 19.1
1950	WAR	Fame
	Williams, 76.5	DiMaggio, 40.9
	DiMaggio, 75.2	Musial, 30.0
	Appling, 74.5	Gordon, 25.8
	Mize, 69.4	Keller, 22.0
	Stan Musial, 64.9	Williams, 20.4
1951	WAR	Fame
	Williams, 83.7	DiMaggio, 42.7
	DiMaggio, 78.1	Musial, 33.6
	Musial, 74.0	Williams, 22.4
	Mize, 70.3	Keller, 22.2
	Bob Feller, 65.0	Pee Wee Reese, 21.8

Reese taking as long as he did to make the Hall of Fame is surprising. The BBWAA's record with shortstop valuation is pretty terrible.

1952	WAR	Fame
	Williams, 84.0	Musial, 36.8
	Musial, 82.0	Reese, 24.3
	Mize, 70.8	Jackie Robinson, 23.7
	Boudreau, 63.0	Williams, 22.5
	Feller, 62.1	Keller, 22.2

DiMaggio and Robinson are similar in having missing seasons and an external fame connection. That Robinson could crack the list in just six seasons is a Ruth/Gehrig/DiMaggio-type pace.

Musial taking the Fame lead when there wasn't a Yankee around connects to Mel Ott, as both were NL stalwarts and chronic nice guys. Musial is the only Fame leader between Eddie Collins and Frank Robinson not to have played for a New York team.

1953	WAR	Fame
	Musial, 89.7	Musial, 39.4
	Williams, 86.0	Robinson, 27.9
	Mize, 71.0	Reese, 27.4
	Feller, 63.2	Williams, 23.1
	Hal Newhouser, 59.0	Phil Rizzuto, 22.7
1954	WAR	Fame
	Musial, 96.6	Musial, 40.4
	Williams, 93.7	Reese, 30.4
	Feller, 64.8	Robinson, 29.7
	Newhouser, 60.2	Williams, 23.5
	Pee Wee Reese, 58.8	Rizzuto, 22.7

1955	WAR	Fame
	Musial, 102.7	Musial, 40.4
	Williams, 100.6	Reese, 32.9
	Feller, 65.2	Robinson, 31.3
	Reese, 63.0	Duke Snider, 25.3
	Newhouser, 60.4	Williams, 24.1

Snider joining Reese and Robinson is a reminder that Casey Stengel's Yankees operated with comparatively few megastars and a furiously rotating cast. Stengel's stars would get their due a few years later, but in 1955, individual fame belonged to Dodgers.

1956	WAR	Fame
	Musial, 108.2	Musial, 41.5
	Williams, 106.7	Reese, 34.5
	Reese, 65.7	Robinson, 34.0
	Feller, 65.2	Snider, 29.9
	Warren Spahn, 63.2	Yogi Berra, 25.2

1957	WAR	Fame
	Williams, 116.3	Musial, 42.6
	Musial, 114.3	Reese, 34.7
	Spahn, 67.9	Snider, 32.3
	Reese, 66.1	Mickey Mantle, 30.6
	Robin Roberts, 58.3	Berra, 27.0

Robin Roberts and Fergie Jenkins have similar profiles in WAR and SpWAR (and therefore in Fame). Both started around 50 percent Hall of Fame support and took a few ballots to get in (four for Roberts and three for Jenkins). Falling just short of 300 wins, I wonder whether they'd get voted in by the current BBWAA membership, which seems to overvalue Fame.

1958	WAR	Fame
	Williams, 120.3	Musial, 43.1
	Musial, 118.4	Mantle, 35.8
	Spahn, 72.0	Reese, 34.8
	Reese, 66.4	Snider, 32.5
	Roberts, 64.5	Berra, 29.0

Yankees, Dodgers, and Musial. That's 1950s baseball to a non-fan.

1959	WAR	Fame
	Williams, 120.1	Musial, 43.1
	Musial, 118.7	Mantle, 39.0
	Spahn, 77.5	Snider, 33.3
	Mantle, 67.5	Berra, 30.8
	Roberts, 66.9	Williams, 24.8

1960	WAR	Fame
	Williams, 123.1	Musial, 43.1
	Musial, 120.6	Mantle, 42.0

1960	*WAR*	*Fame*
	Spahn, 80.2	Snider, 33.6
	Mantle, 73.8	Berra, 31.9
	Roberts, 70.7	Warren Spahn, 25.0
1961	*WAR*	*Fame*
	Musial, 123.2	Mantle, 48.3
	Spahn, 84.3	Musial, 43.1
	Mantle, 84.3	Snider, 34.4
	Willie Mays, 76.9	Berra, 33.2
	Roberts, 69.7	Spahn, 26.1

Fame entering the 1961 home run chase:

Mickey Mantle, 42.0
Roger Maris, 3.6

People care about records when famous people hold them. It's less jarring to the public if records go from a famous person to another famous person, so Mantle seemed more "worthy" than Maris to take Ruth's record.[8] Babe Ruth's fame looms so large over everybody else that the non-fan gets involved when anything involves him. And as the 1961 home run chase and other records discussed later show, it is often counterproductive when the non-fan has a Fame-based opinion on how baseball should be.

1962	*WAR*	*Fame*
	Musial, 126.8	Mantle, 51.8
	Mantle, 90.2	Musial, 43.1
	Spahn, 89.9	Snider, 35.0
	Mays, 87.4	Berra, 33.3
	Roberts, 74.1	Spahn, 26.6
1963	*WAR*	*Fame*
	Musial, 128.1	Mantle, 53.6
	Mays, 98.0	Musial, 43.3
	Spahn, 93.9	Snider, 35.0
	Mantle, 93.0	Berra, 34.0
	Eddie Mathews, 81.7	Willie Mays, 30.0

Until 2006, this was the high water mark since the Cobb/Collins/Alexander/Speaker/Ruth days for having several famous players.

1964	*WAR*	*Fame*
	Mays, 109.0	Mantle, 56.4
	Mantle, 97.9	Mays, 35.0
	Spahn, 92.0	Snider, 34.7
	Mathews, 86.3	Whitey Ford, 28.2
	Roberts, 80.7	Spahn, 26.7

5. The Most Famous Players

1965	WAR	Fame
	Mays, 120.3	Mantle, 57.3
	Mantle, 99.6	Mays, 39.8
	Spahn, 92.6	Ford, 30.1
	Mathews, 91.7	Spahn, 27.0
	Hank Aaron, 88.1	Eddie Mathews, 25.7

After managing in 1964, Yogi Berra (34.0) played four games while coaching.

1966	WAR	Fame
	Mays, 129.2	Mantle, 58.5
	Mantle, 103.1	Mays, 44.0
	Aaron, 95.9	Ford, 30.2
	Mathews, 94.4	Sandy Koufax, 26.2
	Roberts, 83.1	Mathews, 25.8

Koufax made the Fame list right before he had to retire...

1967	WAR	Fame
	Mays, 133.6	Mantle, 58.8
	Mantle, 107.0	Mays, 46.0
	Aaron, 104.4	Ford, 30.3
	Mathews, 96.2	Mathews, 26.1
	Frank Robinson, 76.9	Don Drysdale, 24.6

...replaced by Drysdale, of course.

1968	WAR	Fame
	Mays, 139.8	Mantle, 58.8
	Aaron, 111.3	Mays, 48.5
	Mantle, 109.7	Mathews, 26.2
	Mathews, 96.4	Drysdale, 25.9
	Robinson, 80.6	Hank Aaron, 23.9

1969	WAR	Fame
	Mays, 142.9	Mays, 49.2
	Aaron, 119.2	Frank Robinson, 27.0
	Robinson, 88.1	Aaron, 26.3
	Al Kaline, 82.1	Drysdale, 25.9
	Roberto Clemente, 76.9	Juan Marichal, 22.2

1970	WAR	Fame
	Mays, 148.1	Mays, 49.7
	Aaron, 124.2	Frank Robinson, 29.9
	Frank Robinson, 92.9	Aaron, 28.0
	Kaline, 85.3	Marichal, 22.5
	Clemente, 82.4	Brooks Robinson, 19.3

Fifth-place Willie Mays's 30.0 Fame in 1963 is very different from fifth-place Brooks Robinson's 19.3 in 1970. The WAR in fifth is slightly higher, but the Fame is much lower. And that extra Fame is how baseball seems "better" in the 1950s and 1960s than in 1970.

1971	WAR	Fame
	Mays, 154.4	Mays, 51.4
	Aaron, 131.5	Frank Robinson, 31.8
	Frank Robinson, 96.2	Aaron, 28.2
	Clemente, 89.7	Marichal, 23.3
	Kaline, 88.5	Brooks Robinson, 22.9
1972	WAR	Fame
	Mays, 156.2	Mays, 51.9
	Aaron, 135.4	Frank Robinson, 32.0
	Frank Robinson, 98.1	Aaron, 28.2
	Clemente, 94.5	Brooks Robinson, 24.6
	Kaline, 91.1	Marichal, 23.4
1973	WAR	Fame
	Mays, 156.2	Mays, 51.9
	Aaron, 140.0	Frank Robinson, 32.1
	Frank Robinson, 102.9	Aaron, 28.2
	Kaline, 91.6	Brooks Robinson, 26.5
	Bob Gibson, 80.6	Marichal, 23.6
1974	WAR	Fame
	Aaron, 142.1	Frank Robinson, 32.1
	Frank Robinson, 106.2	Brooks Robinson, 28.9
	Kaline, 92.5	Aaron, 28.2
	Gibson, 82.2	Marichal, 23.6
	Carl Yastrzemski, 78.5	Willie McCovey, 20.3

Dropoffs of more than 20 points of the highest Fame from one year to the next:

1901–1902, Kid Nichols to Cy Young (45.0–22.0);

1935–1936, Babe Ruth to Lou Gehrig (88.3–50.0);

1939–1940, Lou Gehrig to Lefty Grove (57.0–32.7); and very nearly 1973–1974, Willie Mays to Frank Robinson (51.9–32.1).

Of course, 1974 invoked Ruth again, as Hank Aaron broke Ruth's career home run record. As with Maris-Mantle v. Ruth, the public was involved again, and it was negative again, this time with racism instead of homerism.

1975	WAR	Fame
	Aaron, 142.1	Frank Robinson, 32.2
	Frank Robinson, 107.1	Brooks Robinson, 29.5
	Gibson, 81.9	Aaron, 28.2
	Yastrzemski, 81.3	Marichal, 23.4
	Brooks Robinson, 79.0	Pete Rose, 20.6
1976	WAR	Fame
	Aaron, 142.6	Frank Robinson, 32.2
	Frank Robinson, 107.2	Brooks Robinson, 29.5
	Yastrzemski, 84.3	Aaron, 28.2
	Brooks Robinson, 78.5	Rose, 24.7
	Gaylord Perry, 76.1	Joe Morgan, 23.4

5. The Most Famous Players

1977	WAR	Fame
	Yastrzemski, 89.4	Brooks Robinson, 29.5
	Joe Morgan, 80.5	Rose, 25.8
	Tom Seaver, 79.2	Morgan, 25.7
	Perry, 79.0	Johnny Bench, 22.9
	Brooks Robinson, 78.4	Paul Blair, 20.7

The Fame figures support the Big Red Machine as the most famous team of its day.

1978	WAR	Fame
	Yastrzemski, 91.4	Rose, 26.8
	Seaver, 83.9	Morgan, 26.1
	Perry, 83.3	Bench, 24.2
	Morgan, 82.1	Reggie Jackson, 22.1
	Pete Rose, 77.4	Jim Palmer, 20.9

And here's Pete Rose as the face of baseball. This is why random people have opinions on his lifetime ban. Had it been a baseball-famous player rather than a famous-famous player, the whole thing would have been kept in-house, so to speak. Not that Carl Yastrzemski would have bet on baseball, but banning him would not have been part of popular culture the way Rose's has. The fame aspect has complicated the Rose ban from its inception, the same way it has complicated Barry Bonds's, Roger Clemens's, and Alex Rodriguez's woes. Any move Rob Manfred would take with them affects baseball's **public** image; that's tough to deal with.

1979	WAR	Fame
	Yastrzemski, 93.7	Rose, 28.2
	Seaver, 87.3	Morgan, 27.1
	Perry, 86.5	Bench, 26.3
	Morgan, 84.8	Jackson, 22.5
	Rose, 80.4	Palmer, 21.6

1980	WAR	Fame
	Yastrzemski, 94.5	Morgan, 29.1
	Seaver, 89.0	Rose, 28.0
	Perry, 88.8	Bench, 27.0
	Morgan, 88.4	Jackson, 23.9
	Phil Niekro, 82.7	Palmer, 21.9

1981	WAR	Fame
	Yastrzemski, 95.0	Morgan, 29.1
	Seaver, 93.0	Rose, 28.4
	Morgan, 90.4	Bench, 27.1
	Perry, 90.1	Jackson, 24.4
	Niekro, 84.4	Palmer, 22.3

The Money Store employed Phil Rizzuto and then Jim Palmer as pitchmen.[9] Both reached fifth in Fame. Should the Money Store ever be its own entity again, the fifth-most famous player in baseball should get ready.

1982	WAR	Fame
	Yastrzemski, 96.3	Morgan, 29.1
	Morgan, 95.5	Rose, 28.1
	Perry, 92.4	Bench, 27.1
	Seaver, 92.2	Jackson, 25.2
	Niekro, 87.5	Mike Schmidt, 23.8
1983	WAR	Fame
	Morgan, 98.7	Morgan, 30.5
	Yastrzemski, 96.1	Rose, 27.2
	Seaver, 94.7	Bench, 27.1
	Perry, 93.7	Schmidt, 26.7
	Niekro, 90.2	Jackson, 24.3
1984	WAR	Fame
	Morgan, 100.3	Morgan, 30.5
	Seaver, 98.7	Schmidt, 29.7
	Niekro, 94.8	Rose, 27.2
	Mike Schmidt, 87.8	Jackson, 24.2
	Steve Carlton, 86.3	Steve Carlton, 24.2

Steve Carlton and Nolan Ryan fighting for the career strikeout record was captivating for baseball fans because it was Walter Johnson's record. It was not as relevant as a home run record to general culture because it was Walter Johnson's record.

1985	WAR	Fame
	Seaver, 103.7	Schmidt, 30.7
	Niekro, 96.5	Rose, 27.2
	Schmidt, 92.9	Jackson, 24.7
	Carlton, 87.3	Bobby Grich, 24.5
	Bert Blyleven, 82.4	Carlton, 24.4

The main problem with using WAR as the starting point of Fame is that the non-fan might not value defense, walks, and other things that made Grich's WAR what it was. Rather than say that player X (like Grich) wasn't valued for some skills but player Y (like Ozzie Smith) was, I'd rather use a consistent measurement like WAR, understanding that some results might not look right. Grich might not be right, but then again he might be—California was the closest thing to a dynasty in the '80s American League, and the Orioles were a powerhouse before that. In any event, Grich is one of the first players in the Fame list that looks incorrect to me. Andruw Jones doesn't look right for his era either. All of them have high defensive value in common.

If a measurement is invented that captures what was valued in a given season better than WAR does, multiplying that value by Spotlight will be more accurate than my process.

1986	WAR	Fame
	Seaver, 106.3	Schmidt, 31.2
	Schmidt, 99.0	Rose, 27.2
	Niekro, 97.5	Grich, 25.6
	Blyleven, 86.6	Jackson, 25.4
	Carlton, 85.6	Carlton, 24.2
1987	WAR	Fame
	Schmidt, 105.1	Schmidt, 31.4
	Niekro, 97.4	Jackson, 25.4
	Blyleven, 91.4	Carlton, 24.1
	Carlton, 85.0	George Brett, 24.0
	George Brett, 76.8	Don Sutton, 19.2

The retirements of Rose and Grich started a decline in Fame that would end in a historic low.

1988	WAR	Fame
	Schmidt, 106.9	Schmidt, 31.4
	Blyleven, 90.4	Brett, 24.1
	Carlton, 84.1	Carlton, 24.0
	Brett, 82.0	Sutton, 19.1
	Don Sutton, 68.7	Tommy John, 17.7
1989	WAR	Fame
	Schmidt, 106.5	Schmidt, 31.4
	Blyleven, 96.4	Brett, 24.2
	Brett, 83.7	Fred Lynn, 17.8
	Nolan Ryan, 73.7	John, 17.5
	Rickey Henderson, 69.9	Bob Welch, 15.7

Where did all the Fame go? In a nutshell, it got swallowed up by parity. The highest regular season Spotlight in the 1988 AL was 1.36; that is the lowest leader of any major league between 1890 and 1990. The next-lowest leaders are the 1961 NL (1.37/Giants), the 1982 NL (1.38/Expos), and the 1980 AL (1.41/Royals), and the only lower figure ever is the 1995 AL (1.33/Indians). Two of those figures are affected by the previous season not playing out in full.

Any league leader below a 1.45 regular season Spotlight is rare, as it implies that no one held the Momentum lead for even half the season. It had happened 18 times to a league before 1980. From 1981 to 1986, the NL had five such seasons; it's had only one since (1994).

When the narrative is decentralized, it will lead to fewer players standing out in the minds of the non-fan and even to the casual fan, as Fame and SpWAR are distributed less predictably than they otherwise would be. The 1990 WAR leaders were plenty good, but they weren't truly famous; Brett's first-place Fame of 24.3 was the lowest lead since 1902.

So what replaces it appears to be anecdote-level samples, a fixation on round numbers, and other oddities. The Cubs and White Sox were on WGN, which might have impacted Bruce Sutter's, Ryne Sandberg's, and Frank Thomas's Hall of Fame cases and even Andre Dawson's MVP. The Braves were on TBS, and that extra visibility appears to have deified the 1991 World Series and therefore impacted the fame of Jack Morris, Kirby Puckett, and John Smoltz. (Morris was in back-to-back World Series against the Braves; this extra media coverage is what separates him from Alan Trammell and Lou Whitaker.) The 1982 Braves-Cardinals NLCS might have given similar extra visibility to the 1982 Cardinals as well, although KMOX wasn't exactly a UHF station. Whitey Herzog is in the Hall of Fame off a decent but ultimately thin resume; the extra visibility was bound to help.

While productivity hasn't correlated with Hall of Fame votes, maybe we should be more grateful that the BBWAA hasn't messed up the other way and voted in all the Bob Welches.

1990	*WAR*	*Fame*
	Blyleven, 96.2	Brett, 24.2
	Brett, 87.7	Lynn, 17.7
	Henderson, 79.8	Welch, 17.5
	Ryan, 77.3	Willie Randolph, 16.6
	Robin Yount, 72.4	Rickey Henderson, 16.0
1991	*WAR*	*Fame*
	Brett, 88.1	Brett, 24.2
	Henderson, 84.4	Henderson, 18.3
	Ryan, 82.5	Welch, 17.4
	Yount, 73.3	Randolph, 16.6
	Gary Carter, 69.8	Dennis Eckersley, 15.6
1992	*WAR*	*Fame*
	Blyleven, 96.5	Brett, 24.2
	Henderson, 90.0	Henderson, 20.8
	Brett, 88.6	Welch, 18.5
	Ryan, 84.4	Randolph, 17.0
	Yount, 74.9	Eckersley, 16.9
1993	*WAR*	*Fame*
	Henderson, 95.0	Brett, 24.2
	Brett, 88.4	Henderson, 22.7
	Ryan, 83.8	Welch, 18.7
	Yount, 77.0	Eckersley, 17.2
	Cal Ripken, 76.7	Devon White, 16.3

Teams with at least 1.50 Spotlight for five or more consecutive years:

1886–90 Browns
1910–14 A's
1942–46 Cardinals
1947–56 Dodgers

1948–58 Yankees
1969–73 Orioles
1986–91 Mets
1995–01 Braves
1998–04 Yankees
2006–13 Cardinals

Every one of those has at least one incredibly famous player on them. Bob Caruthers, Plank/Baker/Collins, Musial, DiMaggio/Mantle/Berra/Ford, Reese/Robinson/Snider, and the Robinsons were just some of the legends from the teams above.

And then there's the Mets, with Darryl Strawberry's 14.6 Fame missing the top five in one of the weakest-ever years for Fame. By all expectations, the 1993 list should have had Strawberry and Dwight Gooden on it, but drugs and injuries combined to derail the legacy of one of history's biggest dynasties. Eventually, the most famous player from the dynasty would be David Cone as a hybrid Met-Yankee. But the list by 1993 is less about the abundance of A's as it is the absence of Mets. The team won loads of games but had neither the pennants nor famous players expected of it.

1994	WAR	Fame
	Henderson, 98.6	Henderson, 23.0
	Ripken, 80.7	Welch, 18.6
	Wade Boggs, 80.3	White, 17.5
	Ozzie Smith, 75.6	Eckersley, 17.1
	Lou Whitaker, 73.4	Willie Wilson, 15.5

Wilson's 15.5 Fame is the lowest fifth-place finish since 1886.

1995	WAR	Fame
	Henderson, 101.4	Henderson, 23.0
	Ripken, 84.6	White, 17.7
	Boggs, 80.3	Eckersley, 17.1
	Smith, 74.9	Orel Hershiser, 15.9
	Whitaker, 74.9	Barry Bonds, 15.3

And White's 17.7 Fame is the lowest second-place finish since 1885.

A note about Cal Ripken's consecutive games streak: as discussed with various records in previous years, one of the big reasons it captivated the public is that it was Lou Gehrig's record. Gehrig was not famous for playing more consecutive games than Everett Scott; he was famous for being an amazing player who was also on the Yankees. As part of his lore, the consecutive games record was given cultural meaning. Ripken breaking Gehrig's record is the player version of a team stealing the spotlight. Unlike with Babe Ruth's records breaking, the public was eager to see Ripken break it. But it wasn't Ripken's or baseball's fame driving the interest—baseball was at a low point in individual Fame—it was Lou Gehrig's enduring legacy, and Ripken invoked it with game 2,131. If Everett Scott (the record holder before Gehrig) or Steve Garvey (the closest challenger before Ripken) held it and Gehrig never had, it wouldn't be as prestigious.

1996	*WAR*	*Fame*
	Henderson, 103.3	Henderson, 23.2
	Ripken, 88.4	White, 17.7
	Boggs, 87.9	Hershiser, 17.4
	Barry Bonds, 83.4	Eckersley, 17.2
	Roger Clemens, 81.3	Boggs, 16.8
1997	*WAR*	*Fame*
	Henderson, 104.9	Henderson, 23.3
	Clemens, 93.2	Greg Maddux, 19.3
	Bonds, 91.5	Hershiser, 18.8
	Ripken, 90.2	White, 18.3
	Boggs, 89.9	Boggs, 17.6
1998	*WAR*	*Fame*
	Henderson, 107.2	Henderson, 23.3
	Clemens, 101.4	Maddux, 22.9
	Bonds, 99.6	David Cone, 19.2
	Ripken, 92.1	Hershiser, 19.1
	Boggs, 91.3	Tom Glavine, 18.6

Neither Mark McGwire nor Sammy Sosa were at the level of Babe Ruth's accomplishments—joining everybody else ever.

1999	*WAR*	*Fame*
	Henderson, 109.0	Maddux, 24.8
	Clemens, 104.3	Henderson, 23.7
	Bonds, 103.4	Cone, 21.8
	Ripken, 94.8	Glavine, 20.3
	Boggs, 91.1	Bonds, 19.6
2000	*WAR*	*Fame*
	Bonds, 111.1	Maddux, 28.4
	Henderson, 109.7	Henderson, 23.5
	Clemens, 108.9	Glavine, 23.0
	Ripken, 96.1	Roberto Alomar, 21.4
	Maddux, 81.7	Cone, 21.3

Maybe chicks dug pitching, stolen bases, and defensive play at second base.[10] If baseball felt like it was in a resurgence in the late '90s, it wasn't just post-strike talk; the continued success of the Yankees and Braves, as well as the invocation of old Ruth/Gehrig records, let baseball stars back into the national conversation.

5. The Most Famous Players

2001	WAR	Fame
	Bonds, 122.9	Maddux, 31.2
	Clemens, 114.5	Glavine, 25.0
	Henderson, 110.2	Alomar, 24.7
	Ripken, 95.5	Henderson, 23.5
	Maddux, 86.7	Roger Clemens, 22.3
2002	WAR	Fame
	Bonds, 134.7	Maddux, 33.4
	Clemens, 117.1	Bonds, 26.9
	Henderson, 110.6	Glavine, 26.9
	Maddux, 91.1	Alomar, 24.7
	Randy Johnson, 81.8	Chipper Jones, 24.6
2003	WAR	Fame
	Bonds, 143.9	Maddux, 34.1
	Clemens, 121.1	Bonds, 30.6
	Henderson, 110.8	Jones, 26.9
	Maddux, 92.4	Glavine, 26.9
	Johnson, 83.4	Clemens, 26.2
2004	WAR	Fame
	Bonds, 154.5	Bonds, 34.9
	Clemens, 126.6	Maddux, 34.4
	Maddux, 95.6	Jones, 29.1
	Johnson, 92.0	Clemens, 28.9
	Jeff Bagwell, 79.3	Glavine, 26.9

And here's where Bonds, already part of the Babe Ruth spotlight from 2001, becomes the face of baseball. He was not everyone's favorite face of baseball.

2005	WAR	Fame
	Bonds, 155.1	Bonds, 35.0
	Clemens, 134.3	Maddux, 34.7
	Maddux, 98.4	Clemens, 32.8
	Johnson, 97.7	Chipper Jones, 31.3
	Pedro Martinez, 84.1	Andruw Jones, 28.7
2006	WAR	Fame
	Bonds, 159.1	Maddux, 35.3
	Clemens, 137.9	Bonds, 35.3
	Maddux, 101.6	Clemens, 33.1
	Johnson, 99.4	Chipper Jones, 32.8
	Pedro Martinez, 85.1	Andruw Jones, 31.0
2007	WAR	Fame
	Bonds, 162.4	Maddux, 35.9
	Clemens, 139.4	Chipper Jones, 35.8
	Maddux, 104.1	Bonds, 35.5
	Johnson, 100.7	Clemens, 33.7
	Alex Rodriguez, 94.3	Andruw Jones, 32.1

Andruw Jones's 32.1 is the highest fifth-place since Pete Alexander in 1928. That high level can't last long—and it didn't, with Bonds and Clemens leaving the majors—and when Fame declines, people feel like baseball is on a downward trajectory. Yes, 2016 baseball doesn't have a collection of venerated stars like Bonds/Maddux/Clemens/Chipper. Also yes, that many players of their fame rarely play at the same time.

2008	WAR	Fame
	Maddux, 104.6	Chipper Jones, 37.8
	Johnson, 104.0	Maddux, 36.1
	Rodriguez, 101.1	Andruw Jones, 31.9
	Martinez, 85.3	Derek Jeter, 29.5
	Ken Griffey, 83.8	John Smoltz, 29.3
2009	WAR	Fame
	Rodriguez, 105.2	Chipper Jones, 37.9
	Johnson, 104.3	Albert Pujols, 32.3
	Martinez, 86.0	Jeter, 32.1
	Griffey, 84.3	Andruw Jones, 31.9
	Chipper Jones, 77.3	Manny Ramirez, 30.3
2010	WAR	Fame
	Rodriguez, 109.4	Chipper Jones, 38.1
	Griffey, 83.6	Pujols, 36.1
	Albert Pujols, 81.2	Jeter, 32.8
	Jones, 79.7	Andruw Jones, 31.9
	Jim Thome, 70.9	Ramirez, 30.5

Thome's fifth-place WAR was the lowest fifth-place since 1990. There wasn't yet a Fame void, but there was starting to be a relative productivity void.

2011	WAR	Fame
	Rodriguez, 113.3	Pujols, 39.2
	Pujols, 86.4	Chipper Jones, 38.5
	Jones, 82.2	Jeter, 33.4
	Thome, 72.4	Andruw Jones, 32.4
	Derek Jeter, 70.1	Ramirez, 30.5
2012	WAR	Fame
	Rodriguez, 115.5	Chipper Jones, 39.5
	Pujols, 91.2	Pujols, 39.4
	Jones, 85.0	Jeter, 34.6
	Thome, 72.9	Andruw Jones, 32.6
	Jeter, 72.3	Andy Pettitte, 26.8

At the time, it struck me as odd that Chipper Jones would be feted so heavily on retirement, but given these numbers I suppose it was to be expected.[11]

Also, Andy Pettitte had the good sense to address his entire PED controversy **before** being quite so famous. At the time of Pettitte's admission in 2008, his career Fame was 22.9–still pretty good in many years, but nowhere close to breaking the top five.[12] Thanks to retirements, he stood out more from the crowd after he had rehabilitated his reputation. Shrewd move, Andy.

2013	WAR	Fame
	Rodriguez, 115.8	Pujols, 39.4
	Pujols, 92.7	Jeter, 34.3
	Jeter, 71.6	Pettitte, 27.9
	Adrian Beltre, 70.9	Mariano Rivera, 26.3
	Carlos Beltran, 67.6	Alex Rodriguez, 25.1

Albert Pujols and four Yankees. Rivera and Dennis Eckersley are the only relievers to crack the Fame list.

2014	WAR	Fame
	Pujols, 96.6	Pujols, 39.7
	Beltre, 77.9	Jeter, 34.3
	Jeter, 71.8	Robinson Cano, 20.6
	Beltran, 67.4	David Ortiz, 19.9
	Chase Utley, 62.0	Rafael Furcal, 17.9

2015	WAR	Fame
	Rodriguez, 118.8	Pujols, 40.0
	Pujols, 99.7	Rodriguez, 26.3
	Beltre, 83.8	Cano, 20.6
	Beltran, 68.3	Ortiz, 20.0
	Miguel Cabrera, 64.7	Miguel Cabrera, 18.7

Going forward, it looks like Albert Pujols will be the face of baseball for however long he plays. While Robinson Cano might be productive enough to climb the chart, the Mariners don't look like they'll be the new Yankees soon. Adrian Beltre, Dustin Pedroia, and current NL leader Adam Wainwright are about a year behind this list, Yadier Molina and Justin Verlander are about two years behind, and Jon Lester's about three years behind.

Probably the most interesting names moving forward are the younger guys who have been on some famous teams and still have upward trajectory available. The Dodgers look primed to increase their Spotlight as the Braves fade, making Clayton Kershaw a prime candidate to leap forward in Fame. Buster Posey is in a similar spot with the Giants, assuming the team and his catching hold up. Max Scherzer isn't markedly famous, but his time with Detroit was productive, and the Nationals are trying to stay in the spotlight. Jason Heyward entered 2016 with 11.2 points of Fame; at his age, he's got a long time to get on the list.

Conclusion

Fame is related to productivity, but it accumulates in its own pile. What your neighbor knows about baseball players might only be Fame, which is frustrating in discussions. Still, it's progress to measure who the non-fan is likely to have heard of and to be able to separate it from career value.

6. Baseball in the Dark: The Best Players Outside the Spotlight

Every once and again, you hear about players who have the most games played without making the playoffs or the World Series. It was a sort of big deal when Adam Dunn was on the playoff-bound A's in 2014. It was a big deal when Craig Biggio finally got to play in a World Series. Ernie Banks had decent chances of the playoffs in 1969 and 1970 but never got there. Luke Appling didn't even have that good a chance.

But all of them at least got to play for a team in the spotlight, even briefly. Of the four, Dunn had the worst of it; his 25 games in a 1.28 Spotlight for the A's was his only exposure over 1.10. Back when Dunn was on the Reds, I tended to think of Ryan Howard as a more popular Adam Dunn, as their skill sets were similar but one was in the spotlight. Dunn and Howard were born 10 days apart. Neither of them aged particularly well, and both gave back most of their value when they had to wear a glove. Howard has two World Series appearances and six top-ten MVP finishes; Dunn has neither. Put Adam Dunn on those successful Phillies teams, and I imagine he'd be remembered a bit like Ryan Howard from that era.

Who were the best players comparable to pre–2014 Dunn? Who played their entire careers outside the spotlight? I'll define "outside the spotlight" as never being on a team with at least 1.20 Spotlight. Appling was on a 1.25 once (the 1935 White Sox); Dunn was on a 1.28 once. We're looking for a 20-man team of retired players more in the dark than them. So here's the team with the highest WAR completely in the dark, with career WAR and highest Spotlight listed in parentheses:

Catchers—Jason Kendall (41.5, 1.15) and **Fred Carroll** (22.4, 1.13)

Kendall and Carroll are linked by similarity of surname, long tenures in Pittsburgh, and a good batting eye. Kendall had some fine offensive years but played forever due to defense; Carroll only played eight years, didn't stick behind the plate, and left the majors at age 27 when his offense disappeared.

Kendall was on several low-Spotlight teams but made the playoffs three straight years with three different teams (A's, Cubs, and Brewers); Carroll's highest Spotlight was similar (for Columbus as a 19-year-old) but there were no playoffs to go to.

First base—Todd Helton (61.5, 1.10)

That 1.10 comes from the 2007 World Series. The rest of the time, Helton was putting up numbers made ridiculous by Coors Field but with an offensive profile that played anywhere. Helton is right around the career rank for his position that Kendall is for his. That aside, Helton has a reasonable Hall of Fame case, but his time in obscurity will not help.

Second base—Miller Huggins (35.4, 1.18)

Huggins is similar to Mike Hargrove, who qualified for the second-string version of this team, in that they were patient hitters on anonymous teams who made up for it in their managing careers. His rookie year with the 1904 Reds was his most visible.

Shortstop—Miguel Tejada (47.1, 1.18)

Momentum and Spotlight differ from award voting narratives because they emphasize opposite ends of the season. If you want to look at MVP voting under an SpWAR-style microscope, it's better to multiply by the team ranking at the **end** of the season rather than using Spotlight, which tracks it through a **whole** season (and therefore feels like it overemphasizes the beginning). As the A's had an unusual string of playoff appearances borne entirely from late runs, Tejada's Spotlight is low—that 1.18 is from the 2011 Giants—but his MVP support was good, including an MVP that came primarily for his role in the 2002 winning streak that brought the A's a division title. He's therefore an anomaly on this list, but his A's were an anomalous team, so what can I say?

Third base—Toby Harrah (51.2, 1.11)

His final year, with the 1986 Rangers, was his greatest Spotlight; his WAR in it was negative. He hit 20 homers in five seasons, stole 20 bases in five seasons, and walked more than he struck out for his career. These are all marks of a star, but playing for the '70s Rangers and '80s Indians was the AL's equivalent of a witness protection program.

Infield—Scott Fletcher (32.0, 1.11)

On more famous teams Fletcher would have been one of those players written about as the "glue" to the team, something written only about middle infielders and catchers with low power. He was on two very good teams, the 1983 White Sox and the 1992 Brewers, but they made late runs to the playoffs. His highest Spotlight comes from Harrah's 1986 Rangers. He hit .300 that year and got some downballot MVP voting, slightly ahead of Rookie of the Year Jose Canseco. It was his only year with an above-average OPS, but it presumably was one of many years in which he was a nicer man than Jose Canseco. He also had a presidential dog named after him.[1]

Left field—Carlos Lee (28.2, 1.17)

His highest Spotlight was the 2000 White Sox that scrubbed out in the ALDS. He was traded to the Brewers the year before the White Sox won the World Series and joined the Astros as they were about to decline. By raw numbers, his most similar batter is Orlando Cepeda. As they both posted positive defensive WAR in only two seasons, Cepeda might be Lee's most similar fielder as well.

Center field—Burt Shotton (23.6, 1.16)

Another high-walk (713, versus 228 extra-base hits) St. Louis player who became a famous manager in New York. His only year out of St. Louis as a player was 1918, when his Senators caught fire in the last half of the season but ran out of games due to World War I. Despite a decent year, he was waived, and Branch Rickey picked him up for the Cardinals after managing him with the Browns. He wasn't a build-around player by any means, but in his prime he was a premier table setter.

Right field—Jim Fogarty (15.2, 1.05)

Playing seven seasons for some 19th-century Philadelphia teams, Fogarty could take a walk and was fast enough to play center field regularly. In 1889, he led the NL with 99 steals—31 ahead of King Kelly in second place. It was the largest gap between first and second place for 26 years, broken when Ty Cobb stole 45 more bases than Fritz Maisel (96 to 51) in 1915. Fogarty died at age 27; he was not much of a hitter, but he had several good seasons.

Outfield—Bobby Higginson (23.0, —)

That's right—Bobby Higginson played his career completely in the dark, between the end of the Sparky Anderson Tigers and the 2006 World Series Tigers. He had three very good seasons and some okay ones, and my recollection of him is that he was considered the poster boy for an inept franchise. In addition to his lack of Spotlight, he made no All-Star teams and gained no votes in any awards while he played. He did get put on the 2011 Hall of Fame ballot, but he didn't even get a pity vote (joining Carlos Baerga, Lenny Harris, Charles Johnson, Raul Mondesi, and Kirk Rueter). Bobby Higginson's career was anonymity personified.

Pitcher—Ed Morris (42.5, 1.13)

Pitching for various Columbus and Pittsburgh teams in the 1880s, Cannonball Ed won a league-leading 41 games in 1886. Like many pitchers of that era, he was done early, his last season coming at age 27. But in seven years he went 171-122. Dude knew how to pack a lot into a few years.

Pitcher—Ned Garver (38.7, 1.10)

Known somewhat for being on sad-sack teams due to his 20 wins for the 1951 Browns—a feat that nearly got him the MVP—Garver's 1.10 Spotlight was for a single start with the Tigers in 1952. Otherwise, his highest mark was the next year, at 1.05. It's easy to forget how bad the Tigers were in the mid-'50s; that 1952 Tigers team he was traded to lost more games than the 1951 Browns did. By the time they got good again, he had aged some, and he played out the string with the Kansas City A's and expansion Angels. He had a great career given the circumstances.

Pitcher—Larry Dierker (34.2, 1.06)

Dierker was a key member of the 1969 Astros rotation that set the MLB team record for pitcher strikeouts; he was 22 and was in his sixth year in the majors. The 1969 and 1972 editions of the team contended a little—the 1.06 mark is from 1972-and Dierker played key roles on both teams. His most similar pitchers from ages 21 to 27 include Chief Bender, Don Drysdale, and Felix Hernandez, but he was unable to pitch past 30. He did become a successful manager of the Biggio-Bagwell Astros, however—I did not expect so many managers to be on this randomly assembled team.

Pitcher—Ken Raffensberger (33.5, 1.13)

Raffensberger came up with the Cardinals as the Reds became dominant, was traded to the Cubs as they tailed off, went to the Phillies a few years later, then spent eight years with the Reds as the Cardinals were dominant. Raffensberger's career looks a lot like contemporary Ned Garver's, except that Raffensberger was a lefty in the National League. He had excellent control and led the league in shutouts in 1949 and 1952, and that's about the only way he could get a win with a punchless Reds lineup.

Pitcher—Russ Ford (31.3, 1.12)

When your biggest spotlight comes from a Federal League team, that's a big old asterisk. Ford's 1910 season is one of the best rookie seasons of all time—26-6, 1.65, 11.0 WAR—but he didn't last beyond 1915 in part because the rules changed and banned his emery ball. He happened to pitch in one of the only sustained stretches where playing for the Yankees wasn't a ticket to fame.

Pitcher—Teddy Higuera (30.6, 1.02)

Like Ford, Teddy wasn't from the United States (Ford was Canadian,

Higuera Mexican), had his first full season at age 27, dazzled early (1986, losing the Cy Young Award to Roger Clemens), then declined rapidly. He was hurt from 1991 to 1994, missing all of 1992 and posting ERAs over 7.00 in 1993–94. Even with all that, he remains the Brewers' career pitching WAR leader, five higher than Ben Sheets and 13 higher than Chris Bosio.

Pitcher—Bob Ewing (30.5, 1.19)

Ewing had a little more Spotlight than the other pitchers on this list; the Reds he spent eight years with at the beginning of the 20th century were occasionally competitive. In every year but one he was between two games under .500 and two games over .500 despite above-average ERAs; his 20–11, 2.51 campaign was the exception. He was a high-strikeout pitcher early in his career, which didn't get started until age 29. His career reminds me a lot of the Andy Benes/Todd Stottlemyre mold—if your rotation is deep enough that he'd be your third starter, you feel good about your postseason chances.

Pitcher—Ed Brandt (27.8, 1.19)

Brandt started his career 21–45 with an ERA over 5.00 for the Boston Braves of the late 1920s. When the offensive environment calmed down, Brandt reversed course, from a 4–11, 5.01 line in 1930 to 18–11, 2.92 in 1931, posting similarly positive lines most of the rest of his career. He was a fine swingman on the 1938 Pirates, his final season and his highest Spotlight as they nearly won the pennant.

Troy Tulowitzki (IF), Ryan Braun (LF), Andrew McCutchen (CF), Jose Bautista (RF), and Felix Hernandez (P) would make this list on WAR if they retired right now. They each have many years left to get off this list, though. It's a weird list that many players of higher WAR nearly made except for a Yankees cameo or an end-of-career, veteran-presence reserve role. If you're a pretty good player, chances are you will lead a team to prominence or a prominent team will acquire you. For this group, it didn't come together. Here's hoping the active players above get more exposure to match their prodigious feats.

Part II
Momentum: Seasons and Narratives

7. The Early Narrative, 1871–1900

Most of the rest of this book tells season stories through the lens of Momentum, starting with the first major league, the National Association, and going forward to 2015. For each season, I will give team Momentum at the beginning of a season, at the end of a season, and each first of the month sandwiched between the endpoints (with leaders **bolded**) to give the sense of relative rising and falling that characterizes season perception. This team is rising from nothing; are they for real, or will the slow-starting juggernaut heat up and overtake them? If the reputation gap is large, we'll expect the juggernaut to find its usual tricks; as it closes, we increasingly believe the new team is a winner.

The biggest obstacle to telling the 19th century's story is league instability, as teams showed up and left or switched leagues or some other oddity. When a team switched leagues, I calculated its offseason adjustment with the league it was coming **from**, not the league it was going **to**. In the archetypal league switch—a team has dominated the lesser league and wants a more stable/profitable league—it is correct to assume they are not the best team in their new league, meaning the likely harsher adjustment from dominating their old league makes more sense.

I start each season's table with who entered it with Momentum (with their team initials **bolded**), then listing the rest in alphabetical order. (For teams that folded after a season in which they had Momentum, I calculate them in the "median." This doesn't matter often.) At the bottom of each table, I underline that team's Spotlight for the year, **bolding** first-place and/or playoff teams and putting an asterisk where Spotlight was increased by a playoff upset. I also include other tables to list the league or division leaders in WAR, SpWAR, and Fame, ranked in the opposite order to list together the important players on well-lit teams.

My essay form in these summaries owes a debt to the Neft/Cohen *Sports Encyclopedia: Baseball* series, on which I raised myself as a kid.

1871: Well, It's a Start

	BOS	CHI	PHA	WAS
Start	(Formless and void)			
8/1				27
9/1		68	104	
10/1	108	188	224	
End	224	304	340	
Spt.	1.15	1.27	1.37	1.19

Name	Tm	Pos	WAR	SpW	Fame
McBride	PHA	P	**4.0**	5.5	1.5
Zettlein	CHI	P	**4.9**	6.2	1.3
Meyerle	PHA	3B	**1.7**	2.3	0.6
Spalding	BOS	P	**3.4**	3.9	0.5
Wolters	NY	P	**3.0**	3.0	

July 10, 1871, is the beginning of Momentum, as on that date the Washington Olympics were 12–8, 2.5 games behind the 11–2 (and therefore unqualifying so far) Philadelphia Athletics. Once the Olympics fell too far behind, that was it; they ended the season 15–15, went 2–7 in 1872, and left the league.

A lot of Momentum in this era is generated not by actual games—teams barely played 30 games a season—but by great records sustained in long periods between games. Still, it is the closest thing available, and in that brief window the Washington Olympics were the first and only team to gain Momentum. They had plenty of players from Harry Wright's legendary Cincinnati Red Stockings and a great core led by shortstop Davy Force, but pitcher Asa Brainard was more famous than good.[1] The Philadelphia Athletics didn't pitch much better, but Levi Meyerle hit .492/.500/.700.

The Chicago White Stockings' great year was undone by the Great Chicago Fire; they would not play again until 1874.[2]

1872: A Theme Asserts Itself

	BOS	PHA
Start	112	170
7/1	116	169
8/1	240	138
9/1	364	107
10/1	484	77
End	604	47
Spt.	1.48	1.42

Name	Tm	Pos	WAR	SpW	Fame
Spalding	BOS	P	10.9	16.1	5.2
Barnes	BOS	2B	4.3	6.4	2.1
McBride	PHA	P	4.8	6.8	2.0
Wright	BOS	SS	3.0	4.4	1.4
Cummings	NY	P	8.7	8.7	
Zettlein	2 TM	P	6.4	6.4	
Mathews	BAL	P	6.3	6.3	

The Athletics were 30–14, but it never mattered against Boston's 39–8. Boston scored 521 runs (over 10 runs per game) and gave up 224. Ross Barnes's .430/.452/.583 led the hitters; Al Spalding posted a 1.85 ERA (though nearly five runs per game due to the era's defense) and batted .353/.363/.447.

1873: The Other Philadelphia

	BOS	PHA	BAL	PWS
Start	302	24		
7/1	288	10		52
8/1	257			176
9/1	226		63	300
10/1	276		43	420
End	400		52	484
Spt.	1.45	1.10	1.15	1.39

Name	Tm	Pos	WAR	SpW	Fame
Spalding	BOS	P	7.6	11.0	3.4
Zettlein	PWS	P	8.5	11.8	3.3
Barnes	BOS	2B	4.9	7.1	2.2
Wright	BOS	SS	3.3	4.8	1.5
Cummings	BAL	P	7.8	9.0	1.2
Mathews	NY	P	10.0	10.0	

Across town from the Athletics, the new Philadelphia Whites had more talent, and they not only reached 20 games much faster than the Red Stockings (the benefits of making your own schedule), they started 27–3. They would go 9–14 the rest of the way, however; as they faded, they were first challenged by the Baltimore Canaries, a high-offense team led by erstwhile Boston catcher Cal McVey, Davy Force, Lip Pike, and new pitching sensation Candy Cummings. The Red Stockings started 17–11 but finished 26–5 and four games ahead of the second-place Whites. Deacon White came from the defunct Cleveland Forest Citys to replace McVey in Boston; he proved to be McVey's equal at bat and a fine complement to the still-slugging Ross Barnes (.431/.465/.616).

1874: Mutual Respect

	BAL	BOS	PWS	NY
Start	26	200	242	
7/1		304	216	
8/1		428	185	
9/1		552	154	
10/1		672	124	44
End		788	95	85
Spt.	1.08	1.48	1.42	1.07

Name	Tm	Pos	WAR	SpW	Fame
Spalding	BOS	P	8.7	12.9	4.2
Cummings	PWS	P	6.6	9.4	2.8
McVey	BOS	RF	3.0	4.4	1.4
Wright	BOS	SS	2.7	4.0	1.3
Mathews	NY	P	13.5	14.5	1.0
McBride	PHA	P	6.7	6.7	

The Whites lost several players to the re-formed Chicago team. Only the Red Stockings and Mutuals gained Momentum, the latter's coming from a 16-win streak (August 8–October 2) that included beating the Red Stockings back-to-back in Boston. But it wasn't enough to overcome a deeper and stronger team; New York ended in second place, 7.5 games back.

Boston had an above-average OPS+ at every position but third base. Deacon White's presence pushed the returning Cal McVey to the outfield. Shortstop and manager's brother George Wright was the team's steadiest star.

1875: No Contest

	BOS	NY	PWS
Start	394	43	48
6/1	438	32	37
7/1	558	2	7
8/1	682		
9/1	806		
10/1	926		
End	1046		
Spt.	1.50	1.10	1.15

Name	Tm	Pos	WAR	SpW	Fame
Spalding	BOS	P	12.8	19.2	6.4
Barnes	BOS	2B	5.1	7.7	2.6
McVey	BOS	1B	4.6	6.9	2.3
White	BOS	C	4.4	6.6	2.2
Fisher	PWS	P	8.2	9.4	1.2
Cummings	HAR	P	12.6	12.6	
Bond	HAR	P	11.0	11.0	
McBride	PHA	P	9.2	9.2	

The chaos of a $10 league entry fee finally met the chaos of free-range scheduling. The Brooklyn Atlantics were 2–42 and the Keokuk Westerns 1–12, their win coming from the 4–15 St. Louis Red Stockings. Boston started 26–0, finishing 71–8 overall (.899), and scored more than twice what they allowed, highlighted by a series against Washington that they won 8–2, 22–5, and 24–0. They could have won with me playing leftfield.

One team having all the Momentum spoke ill of the league's health—something had to give. Less Keokuk and more competition were necessary.[3]

1876: Less Keokuk

		BOS	CHI	HAR
Start		523		
7/1		499	96	76
8/1		468	220	110
9/1		437	344	79
10/1		407	464	49
End		387	544	29
Spt.		1.48	1.37	1.25

Name	Tm	Pos	WAR	SpW	Fame
Spalding	CHI	P	9.2	12.6	3.4
Bond	HAR	P	10.3	12.9	2.6
Barnes	CHI	2B	6.0	8.2	2.2
Wright	BOS	SS	3.1	4.6	1.5
Devlin	LOU	P	18.0	18.0	
Bradley	STL	P	8.6	8.6	

Deacon White, Cal McVey, Ross Barnes, and Al Spalding went to Chicago in the new National League, where as new White Stockings they fought off an early challenge from the Hartford Dark Blues and ended at .788. Boston only went 7–23 against teams above .500, finishing at .557. But you can't fault manager Harry Wright, as he had to find half a new team. Imagine if the dispersed 1994 Expos had all signed with the Yankees; that's more or less what happened between Boston and Chicago in 1876.

1877: Fixed That Right Up

	BOS	CHI	HAR	LOU	STL
Start	194	272	15		
7/1	198	266	34	20	24
8/1	322	235	103	144	143
9/1	401	204	72	263	152
End	541	169	37	228	117
Spt.	1.47	1.39	1.18	1.26	1.15

Name	Tm	Pos	WAR	SpW	Fame
Bond	BOS	P	11.6	17.1	5.5
Devlin	LOU	P	13.3	16.8	3.5
White	BOS	1B	3.3	4.9	1.6
O'Rourke	BOS	CF	2.6	3.8	1.2
Nichols	STL	P	4.1	4.7	0.6

Al Spalding moved to first base, Ross Barnes fell ill, and Boston acquired Tommy Bond; this was enough to move Boston back in front of Chicago. Through mid–July, the six-team league had an exciting four-team race among Boston, Louisville, St. Louis (who had tied for second in 1876 but without any stretch of Momentum) and Hartford, who played in Brooklyn before the Los Angeles Angels of Anaheim made such moves cool. Game-fixing in Louisville and St. Louis marred the end of the season, and both teams folded along with Hartford-Brooklyn. Given gamblers' early inroads, it's possible having few good pennant races in surrounding years preserved the game's health by giving the gamblers little chance to influence pennant races.

1878: Red and White

	BOS	CHI	CIN
Start	271	85	
7/1	279	83	68
8/1	403	142	112
9/1	527	116	81
End	643	87	52
Spt.	**1.50**	**1.38**	**1.27**

Name	Tm	Pos	WAR	SpW	Fame
Bond	BOS	P	13.8	20.7	6.9
Larkin	CHI	P	4.0	5.5	1.5
Ferguson	CHI	SS	3.1	4.3	1.2
Start	CHI	1B	2.4	3.3	0.9
Weaver	MIL	P	10.3	10.3	
Ward	PRO	P	4.8	4.8	

Only the Red Stockings, White Stockings, and Reds returned from 1877, and the Reds reaped the benefits. Cal McVey came from Chicago to manage and play third base, Deacon White came from Boston and brought his brother Will to pitch, and slugging leftfielder Charley Jones stayed put; the new Reds rode a fast start through mid–July. Chicago started 26–15 but ended 4–15; they were the last challenge to Boston that year. Boston had a below-average offense, but they allowed a run fewer per game than anyone else thanks to Tommy Bond.

1879: A New Challenger

	BOS	CHI	CIN	BUF	PRO
Start	322	44	26		
7/1	301	128	5		
8/1	270	252			
9/1	299	376		7	96
End	380	367			212
Spt.	1.46	1.44	1.10	1.04	**1.18**

Name	Tm	Pos	WAR	SpW	Fame
Bond	BOS	P	**14.4**	**21.0**	**6.6**
Larkin	CHI	P	5.0	7.2	2.2
Jones	BOS	LF	4.5	6.6	2.1
Williamson	CHI	3B	4.2	6.1	1.9
Ward	PRO	P	**7.4**	**8.7**	1.3
Galvin	BUF	P	**9.0**	**9.4**	0.4
McCormick	CLE	P	**9.6**	**9.6**	

Once again, Chicago didn't know how to finish a season, starting 30–8 behind Ned Williamson, Cap Anson, and Silver Flint but ending 16–25; they scuffled in August and dropped out in early September. When they faded, the second-year Providence Grays entered the picture. Managed and shortstopped by George Wright and full of league stalwarts—Joe Start, Paul Hines, and Jim O'Rourke—they also had 19-year-old phenom Monte Ward as primary moundsman (teams now generally used multiple pitchers).

The Buffalo Bisons showed up briefly as well but gave way to Boston, who had a real offense with Charley Jones and John O'Rourke (Jim's brother). The Grays, however, went 15–4 in September and secured the pennant. They were the first team to capture a pennant while being third or lower in Momentum.

1880: Chicago Runs Unopposed

	BOS	CHI	PRO
Start	190	184	106
7/1	163	**292**	79
8/1	132	**416**	48
9/1	101	**540**	17
End	71	**660**	
Spt.	1.40	**1.50**	1.27

Name	Tm	Pos	WAR	SpW	Fame
Corcoran	CHI	P	7.1	10.7	3.6
Anson	CHI	1B	5.0	7.5	2.5
Gore	CHI	CF	4.6	6.9	2.3
Ward	PRO	P	6.6	8.4	1.8
McCormick	CLE	P	**10.4**	**10.4**	
Richmond	WOR	P	8.1	8.1	

Tommy Bond lost his effectiveness and Providence lost some offense, so in Chicago Cap Anson and a stellar outfield of Abner Dalrymple, George Gore, and Cincinnati import King Kelly joined rookie and near-rookie pitchers Larry Corcoran and Fred Goldsmith for an easy pennant.

1881: Chicago Is the New Boston

	BOS	CHI	BUF	CLE	WOR
Start	36	330			
7/1	5	454	89		
8/1		578	68		
9/1		702	37		
End		818	8		
Spt.	**1.14**	**1.50**	1.34	1.02	1.01

Name	Tm	Pos	WAR	SpW	Fame
Anson	CHI	1B	5.8	**8.7**	**2.9**
Galvin	BUF	P	**8.4**	**11.3**	**2.9**
Williamson	CHI	3B	3.2	4.8	**1.6**
Kelly	CHI	RF	2.8	4.2	**1.4**
Whitney	BOS	P	**7.8**	**8.9**	**1.2**
Derby	DET	P	**8.8**	8.8	
McCormick	CLE	P	**6.4**	6.4	

Chicago kept the same team and held steady as the Bisons faded after July. The Worcester Ruby Legs started 8–0 but finished in last place; the Cleveland Blues' trajectory was similar.

Once again, a single dominant team gave an opening, as did the NL's sometimes strict league policies. The American Association formed at the end of 1881, broadening major league geography and upping the potential number of famous teams.[4]

1882: Time to Associate

NL	BOS	CHI	BUF	DET	PRO	TRO
Start		409	4			
7/1	5	404		108	120	5
8/1		528		232	244	
9/1		642		241	368	
End		766		210	492	
Spt.	1.02	**1.50**	1.06	1.25	1.34	1.04

Name	Tm	Pos	WAR	SpW	Fame
Corcoran	CHI	P	**6.0**	**9.0**	**3.0**
Radbourn	PRO	P	**7.8**	**10.5**	**2.7**

Name	Tm	Pos	WAR	SpW	Fame
Weidman	DET	P	**10.2**	**12.8**	**2.6**
Goldsmith	CHI	P	4.9	7.4	**2.5**
McCormick	CLE	P	**11.2**	**11.2**	

AA	CIN	LOU	PHI	STL
Start				
7/1	100	45	59	**104**
8/1	**224**	34	113	108
9/1	**348**	3	82	77
End	**472**		51	46
Spt.	1.46	1.13	1.38	1.37

Name	Tm	Pos	WAR	SpW	Fame
W. White	CIN	P	**10.9**	**15.9**	**5.0**
Weaver	PHI	P	**6.6**	**9.1**	**2.5**
McCormick	CIN	P	3.7	**5.4**	1.7
Carpenter	CIN	3B	3.2	4.7	1.5
Mullane	LOU	P	**5.3**	**6.0**	0.7
Driscoll	PIT	P	**5.2**	5.2	

Harry Wright left Boston to join his brother George in Providence. With Old Hoss Radbourn an emerging ace, the Grays stayed in the race with Chicago until the end of the season, although Chicago's core was still strong enough to win. The Detroit Wolverines, with ace Stump Weidman, catcher Charlie Bennett, and little else, contended from June to August but faded to sixth place.

The American Association was a four-team race in a six-team league. The St. Louis Brown Stockings, led by hometown brothers Bill and Jack Gleason on the left side of the infield, got half their wins by the end of June and ended in fifth. The Philadelphia Athletics were led by catcher Jack O'Brien and pitcher Sam Weaver, while the Louisville Eclipse featured ace Tony Mullane and Pete Browning, whose .378/.430/.510 line led the league in all three categories.

But it was Pop Snyder's Reds who won the league by 13 games. Snyder, who had replaced Deacon White as catcher in Boston, oversaw a team that allowed 3.4 runs/game against the league average of 5.2. The offense was also strong, led by Hick Carpenter, who hit .342/.360/.422 after a three-year career line of .220/.226/.267.

1883: Sneaky Beans

NL	CHI	DET	PRO	BOS	CLE
Start	383	105	246		
6/1	395	107	253		4
7/1	435	122	373		69
8/1	404	91	**497**		193

NL	CHI	DET	PRO	BOS	CLE
9/1	473	60	621	36	317
End	529	31	717	152	388
Spt.	1.45	1.23	1.45	1.05	1.23

Name	Tm	Pos	WAR	SpW	Fame
Radbourn	PRO	P	13.4	19.4	6.0
Corcoran	CHI	P	6.5	9.4	2.9
Farrell	PRO	2B	5.2	7.5	2.3
McCormick	CLE	P	8.5	10.5	2.0
Whitney	BOS	P	11.0	11.6	0.6
Galvin	BUF	P	11.0	11.0	

AA	CIN	PHI	STL	LOU
Start	269	29	26	
6/1	266	41	23	
7/1	276	161	83	60
8/1	265	285	207	89
9/1	269	409	331	58
End	240	525	412	29
Spt.	1.43	1.45	1.33	1.15

Name	Tm	Pos	WAR	SpW	Fame
W. White	CIN	P	8.9	12.7	3.8
Mathews	PHI	P	5.2	7.5	2.3
Mullane	STL	P	6.4	8.5	2.1
McGinnis	STL	P	6.2	8.2	2.0
Keefe	NY	P	19.7	19.7	

The 1883 season might be the first great season in MLB history. A four-team race in the AA ended with the Athletics on top by a game over St. Louis. The Athletics were offense-driven, led by Jack O'Brien, Harry Stovey, and one-year wonder Mike Moynahan. The pitching featured standout seasons from National Association veterans Bobby Mathews and George Bradley. Cincinnati's core stayed the same and was fine, but was just one good team among several; St. Louis was similar.

The NL started off as a four-team scramble with 1882's leaders, Chicago, Detroit, and Providence, joined by Cleveland, who finally gave longtime ace Jim McCormick some help in Hugh "One-Arm" Daily on the mound and Fred Dunlap at the plate. Detroit couldn't keep up past June and ended in seventh.

But what looked like a Cleveland-Providence battle over the summer—Providence relied heavily on Old Hoss Radbourn, Paul Hines, and their up-the-middle combo of Jack Farrell and Arthur Irwin—let Chicago back in (same players as ever). A couple weeks later, the Boston Beaneaters, who had changed managers (from second baseman Jack Burdock to first baseman John Morrill), forced themselves into the conversation; 32–28 on July 28, they would finish 31–7 to steal the pennant.

As Momentum measures it, this was the first "stolen" pennant, where a team with comparatively little reputation came out on top. Certainly, Old Hoss Radbourn, King Kelly, and Cap Anson are better known to baseball fans than Boston's Burdock, Morrill, Ezra Sutton, Grasshopper Jim Whitney, and Charlie Buffinton.

1884: Consolidation and Upheaval

NL	BOS	CHI	CLE	DET	PRO	NY
Start	95	331	243	19	449	
6/1	131	322	234	10	480	26
7/1	251	292	204		595	16
8/1	375	261	173		719	
9/1	394	230	142		843	
End	346	182	94		1035	
Spt.	1.33	1.34	1.23	1.01	1.50	1.03

Name	Tm	Pos	WAR	SpW	Fame
Radbourn	PRO	P	**19.1**	**28.7**	**9.6**
Buffinton	BOS	P	**14.9**	**19.8**	**4.9**
Sweeney	PRO	P	6.3	9.5	**3.2**
Whitney	BOS	P	7.4	9.8	**2.4**
Welch	NY	P	**12.1**	**12.5**	0.4
Galvin	BUF	P	**20.5**	**20.5**	

AA	CIN	LOU	PHI	STL	BAL	COL	NY
Start	120	15	**263**	206			
6/1	115	35	**278**	201		1	16
7/1	145	150	**273**	236	24	24	136
8/1	234	254	242	**325**	3	148	260
9/1	203	268	211	294		272	**384**
End	155	250	163	246		289	**576**
Spt.	1.14	1.26	1.30	**1.38**	1.00	1.13	**1.28**

Name	Tm	Pos	WAR	SpW	Fame
Hecker	LOU	P	**15.5**	**19.5**	**4.0**
Keefe	NY	P	7.5	9.6	**2.1**
Orr	NY	1B	5.8	7.4	**1.6**
Taylor	PHI	P	5.2	6.8	**1.6**
Morris	COL	P	**8.6**	**9.7**	1.1
Mullane	TOL	P	**11.6**	**11.6**	

The Grays' two-man rotation of Old Hoss Radbourn and Charlie Sweeney became one-man when Sweeney defected to the Union Association. The Grays allowed 3.4 runs/game in a league averaging 5.5; with a passable offense led by Paul Hines, it was good enough to outlast the Beaneaters, who hung in through August.

The American Association weirdly expanded to 12 teams for a year.[5] The new teams generally were terrible, and with no obviously good team to leverage all the free wins, it was like few things before or since. On June 28, half the teams were over .640 and within two games of first place. Indicating the chaos, Momentum lead changed twice, from the still-respectable Athletics to the Browns, with great seasons from a young Arlie Latham and surprise Fred Lewis, then to the New York Metropolitans, who won by having the deepest team: dual aces in Tim Keefe and Jack Lynch; a 190 OPS+ from rookie Dave Orr; and more infield offense from Dude Esterbrook and 35-year-old shortstop Candy Nelson.

The Columbus Buckeyes, second in AA Momentum, folded in the offseason; so did the NL's Cleveland Blues. Contention had a less direct relationship to finances than it does today.

1885: The Browns Stand Alone ...

NL	BOS	CHI	PRO	NY	
Start	195	103	**584**		
6/1	192	115	**581**	12	
7/1	162	235	**606**	132	
8/1	131	359	**575**	256	
9/1	100	483	**544**	380	
End	61	**639**	505	491	
Spt.	1.26	1.39	1.48	1.24	

Name	Tm	Pos	WAR	SpW	Fame
Clarkson	CHI	P	**13.1**	**18.2**	**5.1**
Radbourn	PRO	P	7.2	10.7	3.5
Welch	NY	P	10.5	13.0	2.5
Connor	NY	1B	8.1	10.0	1.9

AA	CIN	LOU	NY	PHI	STL
Start	125	201	**464**	131	198
6/1	151	182	**445**	112	259
7/1	121	152	**415**	82	379
8/1	90	121	384	51	**503**
9/1	59	90	353	20	**627**
End	20	51	314		**783**
Spt.	1.19	1.31	1.44	1.10	1.44

Name	Tm	Pos	WAR	SpW	Fame
Caruthers	STL	P/RF	10.0	14.4	4.4
Hecker	LOU	P	7.5	9.8	2.3
Orr	NY	1B	5.0	7.2	2.2
Foutz	STL	P/1B	5.0	7.2	2.2
Morris	PIT	P	**13.6**	**13.6**	
Henderson	BAL	P	7.2	7.2	

Only four teams finished at least three games over .500. The Grays started 19–7 but ended 34–50 and disbanded. The New York Giants imported Dude Esterbrook and Tim Keefe from the crosstown Metropolitans. Keefe joined Mickey Welch to form the majors' best pitching staff, and while Keefe didn't have Dave Orr's run support anymore, he had Roger Connor's; both New York first basemen cleared 200 OPS+.

The Giants competed with the White Stockings all year, but the latter pulled away in the end. Surprisingly, the important parts of the lineup remained the same as ever: Cap Anson; the Dalrymple-Gore-Kelly outfield; and third baseman Ned Williamson. The difference was rookie John Clarkson, who threw ten shutouts in a brilliant season.

In the AA, nobody challenged the Browns after May. No Browns position player cleared 3 WAR, but Bob Caruthers and Dave Foutz combined for 14 WAR as pitchers and 1 as hitters. Crucially, no single player was a hole on defense; in an era where unearned runs were nearly as frequent as earned runs, the Browns were the league's stingiest in both categories.

1886: ... and Stay Alone

NL	BOS	CHI	NY	DET
Start	31	319	246	
6/1	22	335	237	36
7/1		445	212	156
8/1		524	181	280
9/1		628	195	404
End		804	151	470
Spt.	1.08	**1.50**	1.34	1.32

Name	Tm	Pos	WAR	SpW	Fame
Kelly	CHI	RF/C	7.3	**11.0**	**3.7**
McCormick	CHI	P	7.2	**10.8**	**3.6**
Clarkson	CHI	P	7.1	**10.7**	**3.6**
Baldwin	DET	P	**10.8**	**14.3**	**3.5**
Anson	CHI	1B	6.9	**10.4**	**3.5**
Keefe	NYG	P	**10.1**	**13.5**	3.4
Brouthers	DET	1B	**8.2**	**10.8**	2.6
Ferguson	PHI	P/RF	**11.8**	**11.8**	

AA	CIN	LOU	NY	STL	BAL	BRO	PHI	PIT
Start	10	27	162	**405**				
6/1		5	140	**493**	1	42	48	40
7/1			110	**613**		127	83	80
8/1			79	**737**		96	52	49
9/1			48	**861**		65	21	18

AA	CIN	LOU	NY	STL	BAL	BRO	PHI	PIT
End			4	1037		4		
Spt.	1.03	1.06	1.34	1.50	1.00	1.30	1.14	1.07

Name	Tm	Pos	WAR	SpW	Fame
Caruthers	STL	P/RF	11.9	17.9	6.0
Foutz	STL	P/RF	11.4	17.1	5.7
O'Neill	STL	LF	4.9	7.4	2.5
Latham	STL	3B	4.3	6.5	2.2
Ramsey	LOU	P	12.6	13.4	0.8
Morris	PIT	P	11.0	11.8	0.8

The Detroit Wolverines bought the Buffalo Bisons (as in the whole team), and with the reinforcements they gave the White Stockings a run for their money.[6] But Anson's men, led by his own standout season, won 14 straight in August/September to stay in front.

The Browns started 26–19, but a 67–27 finish meant nobody else gained Momentum past June 26. The offense thrived with the emergence of Tip O'Neill and Yank Robinson and a turnaround from Arlie Latham, and by WAR Bob Caruthers was the AA's fifth-best hitter and fourth-best pitcher.

1887: Triumph of Money

NL	CHI	DET	NY	BOS
Start	402	235	75	
7/1	359	407	32	117
8/1	413	531	11	141
9/1	522	655		110
End	483	811		71
Spt.	1.43	1.47	1.15	1.25

Name	Tm	Pos	WAR	SpW	Fame
Clarkson	CHI	P	14.9	21.3	6.4
Baldwin	CHI	P	6.0	8.6	2.6
Thompson	DET	RF	5.3	7.8	2.5
Brouthers	DET	1B	5.3	7.8	2.5
Casey	PHI	P	10.4	10.4	
Ferguson	PHI	P/2B	10.4	10.4	
Whitney	WAS	P	7.6	7.6	

AA	BRO	NY	STL
Start	11	2	519
7/1			707
8/1			831
9/1			955
End			1111
Spt.	1.07	1.04	1.50

Name	Tm	Pos	WAR	SpW	Fame
Caruthers	STL	RF/P	**11.0**	**16.5**	**5.5**
O'Neill	STL	LF	6.9	10.4	**3.5**
King	STL	P	6.2	9.3	**3.1**
Foutz	STL	RF/P	4.2	6.3	**2.1**
Kilroy	BAL	P	**10.8**	10.8	
Smith	CIN	P	**10.1**	10.1	
Ramsey	LOU	P	**8.2**	8.2	

The pennant-winning Wolverines scored 7.6 runs/game; the league averaged 6.1. Dan Brouthers and Sam Thompson are the only teammates ever to hit at least 20 doubles, 20 triples, and 10 homers each; one more Thompson double would have made it 30/20/10. The White Stockings fell from the top due to turnover; that offensive core had been together a long time, and while Marty Sullivan and Jimmy Ryan were serviceable, they weren't Kelly/Gore revisited. Philadelphia ended 3.5 back off a 16-win streak at the end; they gained no Momentum in 1887.

And neither did anyone in the AA other than the Browns, who returned most of the 1886 team. Tip O'Neill batted .435/.490/.691 for a team that scored 8.2 runs/game. As teams moved to three-man rotations, 19-year-old rookie Silver King joined Caruthers and Foutz and led the team in wins.

1888: Three Strikes and Detroit's Out

NL	BOS	CHI	DET	NY
Start	36	242	**406**	
6/1	83	304	**388**	
7/1	73	424	**473**	
8/1	42	538	**597**	54
9/1	11	507	**571**	178
End		461	**525**	362
Spt.	1.21	1.40	1.50	**1.18**

Name	Tm	Pos	WAR	SpW	Fame
Brouthers	DET	1B	6.6	**9.9**	**3.3**
Conway	DET	P	5.6	8.4	**2.8**
Krock	CHI	P	6.8	**9.5**	**2.7**
Ryan	CHI	CF	5.7	8.0	**2.3**
Keefe	NY	P	**10.3**	**12.2**	1.9
Welch	NY	P	**8.0**	9.4	1.4
Buffinton	PHI	P	**12.1**	**12.1**	
Sanders	PHI	P	**7.8**	7.8	

AA	STL	BRO	CIN	PHI
Start	**555**			
6/1	**614**	70	84	

AA	STL	BRO	CIN	PHI
7/1	674	190	69	
8/1	753	314	78	
9/1	877	338	57	
End	1061	292	11	
Spt.	1.50	1.34	1.33	1.03

Name	Tm	Pos	WAR	SpW	Fame
King	STL	P	14.5	21.8	7.3
Caruthers	BRO	RF/P	6.8	9.1	2.3
O'Neill	STL	LF	4.1	6.2	2.1
Hudson	STL	P	4.0	6.0	2.0
Hughes	BRO	P	5.2	7.0	1.8
Reilly	CIN	1B	5.2	6.9	1.7
Seward	PHI	P	9.9	10.2	0.3
Stovey	PHI	LF	5.4	5.6	0.2

On July 16, the NL had its expected White Stockings-Wolverines race. Three weeks later, the Giants were in front to stay, as the Wolverines lost 16 straight and Chicago couldn't put anything together. In the year when rules finally settled on a three-strike strikeout, Detroit's pitching was too thin to support its robust offense.[7] Chicago had sent John Clarkson to Boston, so they too were thin despite Jimmy Ryan's breakout; the ace was rookie Gus Krock, who would start 20 more games in the majors after 1888.

The evolution of a three-man rotation affected some teams worse than others; the Giants, who already had Tim Keefe and Mickey Welch, won by finding a third starter in Cannonball Titcomb (who would leave the majors the same time as Krock). Roger Connor, Buck Ewing, and Mike Tiernan anchored a good-not-great lineup.

The Browns created their own competition when they sold Bob Caruthers and Dave Foutz to the Brooklyn Bridegrooms. But Brooklyn's offense was only so-so, leaving the Browns alone after August apart from a small effort by the Athletics. Manager Charlie Comiskey pitched Silver King half the time to great effect; in September, the Browns purchased Ice Box Chamberlain from Louisville, and he gave them 14 fantastic starts. On offense, Tommy McCarthy was a nice find, but the O'Neill/Robinson/Latham core remained the heart of the batters.

The Wolverines folded while leading the NL in Momentum; this left the top to the White Stockings, although they had not won a pennant in two years.[8]

1889: Not What You Think

NL	CHI	NY	BOS	CLE	PHI
Start	230	181			
6/1	212	183	44		34

NL	CHI	NY	BOS	CLE	PHI
7/1	**182**	153	164	14	4
8/1	151	202	**288**	68	
9/1	120	306	**412**	37	
End	76	482	**588**		
Spt.	1.39	1.39	1.38	1.14	1.05

Name	Tm	Pos	WAR	SpW	Fame
Clarkson	BOS	P	**16.7**	23.1	6.4
Welch	NY	P	**6.7**	9.3	2.6
Anson	CHI	1B	6.4	8.9	2.5
Brouthers	BOS	1B	6.2	8.6	2.4
Buffinton	PHI	P	**11.3**	11.9	0.6
Sanders	PHI	P	**6.9**	7.2	0.3
Glasscock	IND	SS	**6.7**	6.7	

AA	BRO	CIN	STL	PHI	KC
Start	146	6	531		
6/1	120		635		
7/1	100		755	55	
8/1	94		879	24	
9/1	208		1003		
End	384		1074		
Spt.	1.40	1.04	1.50	1.12	1.01

Name	Tm	Pos	WAR	SpW	Fame
Chamberlain	STL	P	9.4	14.1	4.7
King	STL	P	8.4	12.6	4.2
Caruthers	BRO	P	8.7	12.2	3.5
Stivetts	STL	P	5.7	8.6	2.9
Duryea	CIN	P	8.3	8.6	0.3

While the Giants won consecutive pennants, Momentum lead didn't pass to them due to a slow start. The White Stockings' fade—they did not adequately replace Gus Krock when he faltered—turned the NL over to the Beaneaters, who took Dan Brouthers and Hardy Richardson from the defunct Wolverines to lead an otherwise shaky offense and got rebounds from John Clarkson and Old Hoss Radbourn. The Giants' 17–4 stretch in June/July and 12 straight wins in September were enough to win the pennant by a single game, with 1888's standouts joined by former Chicago stalwart George Gore.

In the AA, the Browns led in Momentum all year, but they also narrowly lost the pennant to the Bridegrooms. 1889 was the first year both league Momentum leaders missed the playoffs (the others are 1921, 1934, 1948, 1954, 1982, 1984, and 1987). Brooklyn's famous duo of Caruthers and Foutz were backed capably by Oyster Burns and Darby O'Brien in the outfield. The Browns had last year's pitching trio for a full season, but Yank Robinson and Arlie Latham's downturns at the plate left Tip O'Neill and catcher Jocko Milligan carrying too much responsibility.

St. Louis remained the team to beat in the American Association when Brooklyn jumped to the National League. But that wasn't the only wrench of the offseason. The players chafed against the reserve clause and formed their own league.[9]

1890: The Players' League

NL	BOS	BRO	CHI	NY	CIN	PHI
Start	**294**	192	38	241		
6/1	**280**	238	44	257	31	56
7/1	**250**	238	14	227	151	101
8/1	309	**332**		196	195	190
9/1	398	**456**		165	164	239
End	359	**632**		121	120	195
Spt.	1.44	1.43	1.04	1.29	1.11	1.19

Name	Tm	Pos	WAR	SpW	Fame
Nichols	BOS	P	**13.1**	18.9	5.8
Clarkson	BOS	P	**8.8**	12.7	3.9
Rusie	NY	P	7.8	10.1	2.3
Gleason	PHI	P	**11.9**	14.2	2.3
Rhines	CIN	P	**11.4**	12.7	1.3

AA	STL	LOU	PHI	ROC
Start	**537**			
6/1	**519**	15	60	72
7/1	**489**		180	137
8/1	**463**	96	254	106
9/1	**432**	220	223	75
End	388	396	179	31
Spt.	1.50	1.22	1.31	1.24

Name	Tm	Pos	WAR	SpW	Fame
Stivetts	STL	P/CF	7.8	11.7	3.9
McMahon	2 TM	P	**10.0**	12.3	2.3
McCarthy	STL	RF	4.6	6.9	2.3
Stratton	LOU	P	9.7	11.8	2.1
Healy	TOL	P	7.3	7.3	

PL	BOS	BRO	CHI	NY	PHI
Start					
6/1	**68**	68	8	16	
7/1	**188**	108	4	31	
8/1	**312**	167	73	25	
9/1	**436**	256	77	29	
End	**612**	227	33		
Spt.	1.50	1.42	1.23	1.21	1.01

7. The Early Narrative

Name	Tm	Pos	WAR	SpW	Fame
Radbourn	BOS	P	8.2	12.3	4.1
Weyhing	BRO	P	8.0	11.4	3.4
King	CHI	P	13.8	17.0	3.2
Baldwin	CHI	P	8.5	10.5	2.0

The Players' League took several marquee names from top teams, shuffling the established leagues' talent dramatically. The Brooklyn Bridegrooms entered the NL, kept most of their core—Caruthers/Foutz/O'Brien/Burns were supported by Hub Collins and George Pinkney—and won the NL easier than they had the AA. The Beaneaters' rotation—rookie Kid Nichols, holdover John Clarkson, and a resurgent Pretzels Getzien—got them in the race late, but they faded after September 11 and finished fifth.

In the AA, St. Louis gained Momentum only on July 30; the bulk of the team had gone to the PL's Chicago Pirates. The new Rochester Broncos were the first to lead the pennant race, but they bowed out in late June, leaving a race between the Louisville Colonels and Philadelphia Athletics. The Athletics ran out of money in midseason and scrapped its team; having started 37–17, they ended 17–61.[10] Without any remaining challengers, the Colonels cruised to victory, taking Momentum lead on the second-to-last day of the season.

The Colonels had gone 27–111 the previous year, so the Players' League left them alone, allowing Chicken Wolf, Phil Tomney, rookie standout Harry Taylor, and pitchers Scott Stratton and Red Ehret to jell. While they were a fluke team, A) improving over 60 games is still a lot, and B) they took the Bridegrooms to a 3–3–1 tie in the postseason before it got too cold to keep playing.[11]

The PL race saw the Boston Reds outlast the Brooklyn Ward's Wonders and New York Giants in September. No team was stellar, but the Reds' lineup ran five deep (the always-together Dan Brouthers and Hardy Richardson, Harry Stovey, King Kelly, and Billy Nash) to Brooklyn's three (namesake Monte Ward, Dave Orr, and Lou Bierbauer).

After the season, the PL folded, and its Boston and Philadelphia entries replaced Rochester and Philadelphia in the AA. 1890's chaos had plenty left over for 1891.

1891: The End of Viability

NL	BOS	BRO	CIN	NY	PHI	CHI	CLE	PIT
Start	271	477	91	91	147			
6/1	272	458	72	72	148	72	9	3
7/1	282	428	42	192	128	177		

NL	BOS	BRO	CIN	NY	PHI	CHI	CLE	PIT
8/1	361	397	11	301	97	301		
9/1	430	366		345	66	425		
End	485	331		310	31	540		
Spt.	1.41	1.44	1.03	1.23	1.17	1.23	1.00	1.00

Name	Tm	Pos	WAR	SpW	Fame
Nichols	BOS	P	9.6	13.5	3.9
Clarkson	BOS	P	9.6	13.5	3.9
Staley	2 TM	P	7.9	11.0	3.1
Hutchinson	CHI	P	10.5	12.9	2.4
Rusie	NY	P	8.6	10.6	2.0

AA	BOS	LOU	STL	BAL
Start	309	198	194	
6/1	416	220	236	94
7/1	536	190	356	159
8/1	660	159	475	128
9/1	784	128	474	97
End	924	93	439	62
Spt.	1.50	1.32	1.38	1.17

Name	Tm	Pos	WAR	SpW	Fame
Buffinton	BOS	P	8.1	12.2	4.1
Haddock	BOS	P	7.2	10.8	3.6
Stivetts	STL	P/RF	9.4	13.0	3.6
Brouthers	BOS	1B	5.6	8.4	2.8
McMahon	BAL	P	9.4	11.0	1.6
Weyhing	PHI	P	9.5	9.5	

At almost any point in time, at least one of the three highest ranked teams in a league will be gaining Momentum. But 1889–1891 was an unusual time, and for nearly a full month over May/June, the National League was upside down. The Phillies were involved for a couple days, but early on it was a (Chicago) Colts-Giants race. Defending champion Brooklyn—now just the Grooms—gained Monte Ward at shortstop and manager, but Bob Caruthers was the only halfway reliable pitcher. The Beaneaters took the last two games of a series with the Colts in June, starting a nine-win streak for the former and a seven-loss streak for the latter; by June 19 Boston had joined Chicago and New York near the top.

On August 12, the Beaneaters took Momentum lead, but they dropped from the race 11 days later, allowing the Colts, who entered the season with no points, to take Momentum lead on September 3. The established teams are dead; long live the Colts! But on September 16, the Beaneaters started an 18-win streak that won them the pennant. The Colts went from nobodies to the alpha team to disappointments in one season.

The Colts had an ace in Bill Hutchinson and an excellent infield of Cap

Anson, Fred Pfeffer, Jimmy Cooney, and rookie Bill Dahlen. But while the Colts had one good pitcher, the Beaneaters still had three. John Clarkson and Kid Nichols were as good as ever, but as Pretzels Getzien went back to mediocrity, Boston found Harry Staley, a 24-year-old released by Pittsburgh nine starts into the season. The offense was led by a breakout performance from young shortstop Herman Long and the acquisition of longtime star Harry Stovey when the Boston Reds moved to the AA.

Speaking of the Reds, they entered the AA as the alpha team and were the only team to gain Momentum after August 7. Hardy Richardson was declining, but Dan Brouthers was still in top form, joining Hugh Duffy and Duke Farrell, who came over from the Chicago PL entry and each had a league-leading 110 RBI, and veteran Paul Radford, who moved from outfielder to shortstop capably. Like the Beaneaters, the Reds used the scrap heap to complement veteran Charlie Buffinton on the mound; George Haddock (who doesn't even have the best name on his own staff thanks to Cinders O'Brien), 9–26, 5.76 in 1890 and 11–21 before that, was 34–11/2.49 for the Reds.

Louisville started 12–4 but went 3–12 right after; they fell to seventh place as none of their important players lived up to their billing. St. Louis got Charlie Comiskey and Tip O'Neill back, but not Silver King, leaving them thin.

After the season, the AA initially was going to downsize to eight teams and put a new team in Chicago; but in early November, a new plan to make a 12-team league with only one team in each city (to avoid financial instability) arose. On December 18, the leagues merged, with the Boston Reds disbanding and the other AA teams with Momentum—St. Louis, Louisville, and Baltimore—joining the NL along with Washington.[12]

1892: Nobody Likes Split Seasons

Because this season had two pennant races,[13] I restart Momentum 20 games into the second pennant race; nobody generated Momentum from July 13 to August 5.

	BAL	BOS	BRO	CHI	LOU	NY	PHI	STL	CLE
Start	34	406	277	**452**	51	260	26	239	
6/1	11	**498**	304	429	38	237	3	216	
7/1		**618**	314	399	8	207		186	
8/1		**642**	303	368		176		155	
9/1		**641**	297	337		175	30	124	100
End		**607**	253	293		131		80	276
Spt.	1.00	**1.48**	1.30	1.42	1.01	1.18	1.01	1.10	**1.04**

Name	Tm	Pos	WAR	SpW	Fame
Nichols	BOS	P	9.3	13.8	4.5
Stivetts	BOS	P/LF	7.6	11.2	3.6
Hutchinson	CHI	P	8.6	12.2	3.6
Staley	BOS	P	5.7	8.4	2.7
Brouthers	BRO	1B	8.8	11.4	2.6
Stein	BRO	P	7.2	9.4	2.2
Rusie	NY	P	7.8	9.2	1.4

The new teams from the AA promptly took the new ninth- through twelfth-place spots in the NL. Then again, it isn't fair to assume team continuity, as a lot of player reshuffling occurred. The Browns were not their 1891 selves, as Charlie Comiskey and Tip O'Neill went to Cincinnati. The Colts weren't themselves, either; Fred Pfeffer was gone and his replacement Jim Canavan hit .166/.248/.239. His double-play partner Jimmy Cooney hit similarly and lost his job. Even as Bill Dahlen blossomed, the bottom of the lineup doomed the Colts to seventh.

The Beaneaters added Hugh Duffy from the other Boston and Jack Stivetts from St. Louis. Although Harry Stovey was so bad that he was released in June, Boston had little trouble winning the first half, although Brooklyn, who'd imported Dan Brouthers, George Haddock, and third baseman Bill Joyce from Boston and rescued former Colt Ed Stein from the scrap heap, challenged them.

The second half was almost entirely about the Cleveland Spiders, who'd never had a winning season and who hadn't imported much talent. John Clarkson, who'd been released in Boston as a cost-cutting measure, joined Cleveland for the second half, but the rest had short resumes. Cy Young led the pitching, with rookie Nig Cuppy not too far behind, and standout second baseman Cupid Childs was supported by first baseman Jake Virtue and catcher Chief Zimmer. As great a story as the Spiders were, the Beaneaters had more Momentum by far, won nine more games than them, nearly won the second half, and beat them in the postseason 5–0–1. It was still very much Boston's league.

1893: Farther Away

	BOS	BRO	CHI	CLE	NY	STL	PHI	PIT
Start	355	148	172	162	77	47		
6/1	379	182	161	156	66	66	26	36
7/1	499	287	131	156	51	36	136	91
8/1	623	281	100	125	20	5	250	60
9/1	747	250	69	94			219	29
End	863	221	40	65			190	
Spt.	**1.50**	1.39	1.17	1.22	1.03	1.02	1.19	1.04

Name	Tm	Pos	WAR	SpW	Fame
Nichols	BOS	P	11.8	17.7	5.9
Young	CLE	P	11.7	14.3	2.6
Stivetts	BOS	P/RF	4.6	6.9	2.3
Kennedy	BRO	P	5.7	7.9	2.2
Delahanty	PHI	LF	6.9	8.2	1.3
Rusie	NY	P	11.6	11.9	0.3
Killen	PIT	P	7.4	7.7	0.3
Breitenstein	STL	P	11.2	11.4	0.2

It was more chaos in 1893, not from leagues but from the rules, as the pitcher's box was replaced with a rubber and moved from 50 feet from home plate to 60 feet 6 inches.[14] Although it was a six-team race into mid–June, by July it came down to the defending Beaneaters, the Grooms, and the surprising Phillies. The Grooms exited with a 1–15 streak in July and the Beaneaters went 27–3 over July/August, leaving the pitching-poor Phillies no chance to catch up. The Grooms' pitching was headlined by Ed Stein and an emerging Brickyard Kennedy, while Dan Brouthers continued slugging. The Phillies were built around their outfield of Ed Delahanty, Billy Hamilton, and former Detroit standout Sam Thompson; as good as they were, the Phillies didn't need too much else to be at least competitive. The Beaneaters were not as good a team as their record indicated, but Kid Nichols showed no ill effects from the new pitching distance, and Jack Stivetts, Hugh Duffy, Tommy McCarthy, Billy Nash, and Herman Long were a deep support cast.

Contention from surprise teams tends to elongate the spotlight of formerly strong teams, since it takes longer for a team from the bottom than a team with similar reputation to pass them. The Colts started the year second in Momentum but finished ninth in the standings, famous if not good.

1894: Silent Lineup Assembly

	BOS	BRO	CHI	CLE	PHI	BAL	NY	PIT
Start	432	111	20	32	95			
6/1	448	92	1	98	166	76		72
7/1	568	77		133	211	196		92
8/1	692	46		102	180	300	4	61
9/1	816	15			71	149	424	98	30
End	822				42	120	540	169	1
Spt.	1.50	1.09	1.01	1.19	1.32	1.28	1.06	1.05

Name	Tm	Pos	WAR	SpW	Fame
Nichols	BOS	P	8.0	12.0	4.0
Duffy	BOS	CF	6.8	10.2	3.4

Name	Tm	Pos	WAR	SpW	Fame
Stivetts	BOS	P/LF	6.0	9.0	**3.0**
Hamilton	PHI	CF	**8.2**	**10.8**	**2.6**
Delahanty	PHI	LF	6.0	7.9	**1.9**
Young	CLE	P	**10.1**	**12.0**	**1.9**
Rusie	NY	P	**14.2**	**15.1**	0.9
Meekin	NY	P	**11.3**	**12.0**	0.7
Breitenstein	STL	P	**9.7**	9.7	

The Beaneaters contended through the entire season, but the team wasn't nearly as deep; Kid Nichols and Jack Stivetts still anchored the pitching admirably, and Hugh Duffy was outstanding (hitting a record .440), but that was about it. The Phillies contended early; their batting average is also famous, as four outfielders hit .400.

But the question over the summer was whether the revitalized Giants or Ned Hanlon's surprising Orioles could outlast the Beaneaters. Although the Giants had the long-famous Monte Ward at shortstop, he was much more important as a manager. Their offense, carried by former Spiders George Davis and Jack Doyle, was below-average, but they had two aces in Amos Rusie, who lowered his ERA while offense went up, and Jouett Meekin, who had scuffled in trials with Louisville and Washington.

While Rusie, Meekin, and a 31–7 finish to the season were nearly enough, the Orioles' deep offense and 20–3 September won the pennant. The most famous Oriole entering 1894 was Dan Brouthers, acquired with promising youngster Willie Keeler from Brooklyn in the offseason for some role players. Midseason pickups in 1893–shortstop Hughie Jennings, who had been inconsistent for Louisville, came by trade, and outfielder Steve Brodie, purchased from St. Louis—provided depth. Joining young holdovers Joe Kelley and John McGraw, every spot in the lineup produced at least 2 WAR and had an above-average OPS+. With minimum 474 plate appearances (C Wilbert Robinson's total), only three other teams have been that deep—the 1931 Yankees, 1976 Reds, and 2011 Angels. Ned Hanlon had with little fanfare built the deepest offense in history. And like the 1976 Reds, it made up for a lack of ace pitching; Sadie McMahon was good, but the other main pitchers were Kid Gleason, who by 1896 would be a full-time infielder, and Duke Esper, who improved after his July purchase from Washington but entered Baltimore 5–12 with a 7.45 ERA.

So while the Beaneaters remained the class of the league, the Orioles were the next-best thing. The Orioles had hitting, the Giants had pitching, and the Beaneaters had the resume. The battle lines looked pretty well drawn for 1895.

1895: Erasing the Battle Lines

	BAL	BOS	CLE	NY	PHI	PIT	CHI	CIN
Start	270	412	21	85	60	1		
6/1	256	398	47	66	51	68	71	76
7/1	346	493	137	36	26	188	171	56
8/1	435	552	261	5	5	312	225	120
9/1	544	521	385			366	199	89
End	660	492	491			337	170	60
Spt.	1.42	1.48	1.15	1.07	1.04	1.20	1.12	1.04

Name	Tm	Pos	WAR	SpW	Fame
Nichols	BOS	P	10.1	15.0	4.9
Hoffer	BAL	P	8.7	12.4	3.7
Jennings	BAL	SS	7.5	10.7	3.2
Kelley	BAL	LF	5.9	8.4	2.5
Keeler	BAL	RF	5.3	7.5	2.2
Hawley	PIT	P	9.8	11.8	2.0
Young	CLE	P	12.1	13.9	1.8
Breitenstein	STL	P	8.4	8.4	

Jouett Meekin turned back into a pumpkin and Amos Rusie regressed to being "just" a good pitcher. Boston still had a deep team behind Kid Nichols and Hugh Duffy, but they disappeared after July. So while the Orioles dominated the narrative and won the pennant, the rest is a lot more complex, as seven teams were still gaining Momentum in July. The Giants, Reds, Colts, Pirates, and Spiders were all third in Momentum at some point during the season.

For the Orioles, Dan Brouthers aged and Wilbert Robinson regressed, but the lineup remained full of stars, and rookie Bill Hoffer provided a front to the rotation. The rest of the pitching was about as good as in 1895, but with Hoffer's dominance, those somewhat interchangeable pitchers became depth, as Sadie McMahon, Duke Esper, Dad Clarkson (John's brother), and George Hemming turned in decent performances.

1896: More-ioles

	BAL	BOS	CHI	CIN	CLE	PIT	PHI
Start	360	268	93	33	267	183	
6/1	438	351	126	121	340	246	44
7/1	558	441	96	241	460	216	99
8/1	657	410	65	365	539	185	68
9/1	781	379	34	459	508	154	37
End	881	354	9	434	483	129	12
Spt.	1.50	1.31	1.04	1.16	1.36	1.14	1.02

Name	Tm	Pos	WAR	SpW	Fame
Jennings	BAL	SS	8.3	12.5	4.2
Young	CLE	P	10.1	13.7	3.6
Hoffer	BAL	P	7.1	10.7	3.6
Cuppy	CLE	P	9.8	13.3	3.5
Kelley	BAL	LF	7.0	10.5	3.5
Hawley	PIT	P	8.0	9.1	1.1
Killen	PIT	P	7.5	8.6	1.1

On June 15, the Orioles were 28–18–certainly fine, but it was about as good as five other teams. (That day is the only day the Washington NL franchise ever gained Momentum.) But Baltimore's 35–9 followup obliterated Philadelphia, Boston, and Cleveland, leaving only the Reds, whose deep starting pitching (Frank Dwyer, Billy Rhines, and former Louisville standout Red Ehret) kept them alive through September. The Orioles were closer to 1894's sluggers than 1895's balance; Hughie Jennings played a great shortstop while hitting .401, and Joe Kelley slugged .543. The important teams' rosters changed little.

1897: Hanlon v. Selee

	BAL	BOS	CHI	CIN	CLE	PHI	PIT
Start	452	182	4	223	248	6	66
6/1	516	166		272	232		80
7/1	621	281		282	202		50
8/1	630	405		296	171		19
9/1	714	529		295	140		
End	842	657		263	108		
Spt.	1.50	1.33	1.00	1.32	1.25	1.00	1.07

Name	Tm	Pos	WAR	SpW	Fame
Jennings	BAL	SS	7.3	11.0	3.7
Nichols	BOS	P	10.9	14.5	3.6
Keeler	BAL	RF	7.1	10.7	3.6
Kelley	BAL	LF	5.1	7.7	2.6
Breitenstein	CIN	P	7.8	10.3	2.5
Young	CLE	P	7.5	9.4	1.9
Rusie	NY	P	8.4	8.4	

Cincinnati contended intermittently until August, and Baltimore and Boston fought it out until the end, with Boston upstaging the narrative by winning the pennant. Frank Selee's Beaneaters still had Kid Nichols, but the offense improved and scored .5 runs/game more than even the Orioles, primarily through depth; Hugh Duffy, former Phillie Billy Hamilton, and rookie Chick Stahl formed a solid outfield, and breakout third baseman Jimmy Collins handled both sides of the ball well. Fred Tenney, new to full-time play at first base, was as competent as veterans Bobby Lowe and Herman Long up the middle.

For the Orioles, Jennings/Keeler/Kelley/McGraw remained the heart of the offense, aided by Heinie Reitz, Jack Doyle, and Pittsburgh acquisition and doubles leader Jake Stenzel. The rotation was deep, including rookies Jerry Nops and Joe Corbett, but none of the pitchers were nearly as good as Boston's Nichols. For the Reds, aces Frank Dwyer and Billy Rhines were joined by veteran lefty Ted Breitenstein, purchased from the Cardinals after a down year. Each of them was better than any Orioles pitcher, but the team had almost no hitting.

1898: Not Massively Different

	BAL	BOS	CIN	CLE
Start	421	328	131	54
6/1	400	337	205	123
7/1	395	427	325	218
8/1	364	491	449	192
9/1	373	585	563	166
End	404	761	579	122
Spt.	1.38	1.47	1.35	1.20

Name	Tm	Pos	WAR	SpW	Fame
Nichols	BOS	P	10.8	15.9	5.1
Collins	BOS	3B	6.9	10.1	3.2
McJames	BAL	P	8.1	11.2	3.1
Lewis	BOS	P	6.3	9.3	3.0
Jennings	BAL	SS	7.5	10.4	2.9
Maul	BAL	P	7.4	10.2	2.8
Griffith	CHI	P	10.6	10.6	

The Beaneaters' key contributors were as good in 1898 as in 1897, and Ted Lewis and rookie Vic Willis became reliable sidekicks to Kid Nichols. The Orioles had the better Pythagorean record, as they finally found some pitching with a rebound season from Al Maul. More importantly, a trade with Washington—first baseman Jack Doyle, second baseman Heinie Reitz, and pitcher Doc Amole for first baseman Dan McGann, second baseman Gene DeMontreville, and pitcher Doc McJames—was about a 17 WAR advantage in 1898 and hedged against slight declines from Willie Keeler and Joe Kelley.

The Reds' 27–7 start kept them in contention through mid–September and the Orioles back until August. Billy Rhines had been traded for a package including pitcher Pink Hawley, who rebounded from a down year, and veteran slugger Mike Smith, a fine leader for a thin offense. But the Beaneaters still took the NL flag comfortably.

1899: Gone into Syndication

	BAL	BOS	CIN	CLE	BRO	CHI	PHI	STL
Start	202	381	290	61				
6/1	177	416	315	36	100	65	61	78
7/1	147	411	285	6	220	35	31	48
8/1	116	380	254		344	4		17
9/1	85	399	223		468			
End	41	355	179		644			
Spt.	1.23	1.47	1.35	1.04	1.32	1.02	1.01	1.05

Name	Tm	Pos	WAR	SpW	Fame
Willis	BOS	P	10.5	15.4	4.9
Nichols	BOS	P	7.4	10.9	3.5
Hahn	CIN	P	8.5	11.5	3.0
Stahl	BOS	RF	5.6	8.2	2.6
Tenney	BOS	1B	5.3	7.8	2.5
McGinnity	BAL	P	8.6	10.6	2.0
Kitson	BAL	P	8.0	9.8	1.8
McGraw	BAL	3B	8.0	9.8	1.8
Young	STL	P	8.5	8.9	0.4
Delahanty	PHI	LF	8.0	8.1	0.1

Brooklyn's success didn't come out of nowhere; it came out of Baltimore. Syndicate ownership—owning two teams at the same time—transferred Ned Hanlon, Dan McGann, Willie Keeler, Joe Kelley, Hughie Jennings, and Doc McJames from Baltimore to Brooklyn and the newly-named Superbas. St. Louis pulled the same trick, importing Cleveland's Bobby Wallace, Jesse Burkett, Cupid Childs, Patsy Tebeau, Cy Young, and Nig Cuppy and rebranding as the Perfectos, but they only contended through May. Meanwhile, Cleveland, fourth in Momentum entering 1899, finished 20–134, their spotlight somehow making the season seem worse.

The Superbas left Boston and Cincinnati in a rough spot. The Reds held on as long as the Perfectos did; rookie Noodles Hahn was exceptional and first baseman Jake Beckley had his best season in years, but nobody else was good enough. Boston contended into August; the core was unchanged, but Vic Willis became as good as Kid Nichols, while Fred Tenney's development compensated for lineup aging.

The Superbas won with Baltimore talent—Jim Hughes, a 3-WAR rookie in 1898, posted a 7.6 mark in 1899, and Willie Keeler and Joe Kelley helped drive the offense. Bill Dahlen had been traded from Chicago to Baltimore at the beginning of 1899 and then transferred to Brooklyn; he was as good as ever. But existing Brooklyn talent was crucial as well; veterans second baseman Tom Daly and pitcher Brickyard Kennedy, who had been around the last time Brooklyn was famous, did their part, and Jack Dunn was a fine third starter.

In December, in anticipation of his team getting cut from the league,

Louisville owner Barney Dreyfuss sold his share in the team, bought into Pittsburgh, and acquired his best former players for his new team.[15] After league decisions on cutting teams—Louisville and Cleveland were near-definites[16]—dragged for months, the final decision was made in March to drop them along with Baltimore and Washington.[17]

1900: Superbas as Superb

	BOS	BRO	CIN	CHI	PHI	PIT	STL
Start	176	321	88				
6/1	158	378	70	43	72	27	6
7/1	128	478	40	13	177	7	
8/1	97	602	9		146		
9/1	66	726			115		
End	23	898			72	25	
Spt.	1.32	1.50	1.15	1.03	1.32	1.06	1.00

Name	Tm	Pos	WAR	SpW	Fame
McGinnity	BRO	P	5.7	8.6	2.9
Kennedy	BRO	P	4.2	6.3	2.1
Dinneen	BOS	P	6.5	8.6	2.1
Flick	PHI	RF	5.9	7.8	1.9
Kelley	BRO	LF	3.5	5.3	1.8
Hahn	CIN	P	6.4	7.4	1.0
Wagner	PIT	RF	6.5	6.9	0.4
Young	STL	P	7.5	7.5	

The Beaneaters acquired Bill Dinneen from the defunct Washington team, but Vic Willis fell off a cliff and the team continued to age. The Reds weakened at the margins; both they and the Beaneaters were nonfactors. The summer fight was between the Superbas, who imported second-year ace Joe McGinnity from Baltimore and brought back a developing Jimmy Sheckard (he'd played in Baltimore in 1899 like it was a farm team), and the Phillies, who still had Ed Delahanty but were led by young stars Nap Lajoie and Elmer Flick.

Whereas the Phillies rode a 14–5 start a long way, the Superbas started 21–16. But their 14–1 stretch in June wrapped up as the Phillies were in a downturn, and Brooklyn was alone at the top in July and August. On August 5, the Superbas were eight games ahead of the Phillies and ten ahead of the Pirates.

The Superbas went 8–10 over the rest of August while the Pirates went 14–8, including taking two of three from the Superbas. With Honus Wagner, a reasonable rotation, and little else, the Pirates started September 11–1, and it looked like the Pirates-nee-Colonels could upset the mighty Superbas-nee-Orioles, but the Superbas had seven straight scheduled games against the Beaneaters (home, then away) and went 6–1 in them to take the pennant.

8. A Permanent Rival Emerges, 1901–1917

Superteams had left the fewest major league cities for 20 years. American League president Ban Johnson took advantage of the 1899 contraction chaos by sticking a team in Chicago in 1900 with Charlie Comiskey's involvement,[1] then moved eastward and declared the American League a major league before the 1901 season.[2] The league got enough stars and quality baseball to stick, and even in those early days team narratives were being built.

Since I hadn't yet explicitly stated it: **Momentum is not directly comparable across leagues**, because levels of competition often differ significantly between leagues. Spotlight is directly comparable across leagues; Momentum is only comparable within a league.

1901: Don't Mind Us

AL	BOS	CHI	DET	WAS
Start				
6/1		68	53	14
7/1	60	188	63	
8/1	144	312	32	
9/1	188	436	1	
End	168	576		
Spt.	1.30	1.50	1.27	1.07

Name	Tm	Pos	WAR	SpW	Fame
Young	BOS	P	12.6	16.4	3.8
Callahan	CHI	P/3B	5.8	8.7	2.9
Griffith	CHI	P	5.7	8.6	2.9
Hoy	CHI	CF	4.1	6.2	2.1
Collins	BOS	3B	6.7	8.7	2.0
Miller	DET	P	7.1	9.0	1.9
Lajoie	PHI	2B	8.4	8.4	
McGinnity	BAL	P	7.6	7.6	

8. A Permanent Rival Emerges

NL	BOS	BRO	PHI	PIT	CIN	NY	STL
Start	11	449	36	12			
6/1		432	79	45	68	36	
7/1		457	109	165	103	116	24
8/1		431	133	289	72	105	98
9/1		425	227	413	41	74	117
End		390	202	**553**	6	39	82
Spt.	1.03	1.48	1.29	**1.38**	1.10	1.13	1.08

Name	Tm	Pos	WAR	SpW	Fame
Sheckard	BRO	LF	6.4	**9.5**	3.1
Donovan	BRO	P	5.9	8.7	2.8
Wagner	PIT	SS/RF	**7.1**	**9.8**	2.7
Chesbro	PIT	P	5.5	7.6	2.1
Orth	PHI	P	6.8	**8.8**	2.0
Mathewson	NY	P	**9.1**	**10.3**	1.2
Hahn	CIN	P	**7.8**	8.6	0.8
Wallace	STL	SS	**7.7**	8.3	0.6
Willis	BOS	P	**8.8**	**9.1**	0.3

Assuming the AL succeeded because of the marquee names it lured is an oversimplification. Of 1900's top ten in WAR, four of them jumped to the AL: Cy Young and Bill Dinneen to Boston and Joe McGinnity and John McGraw to Baltimore. Nap Lajoie had been a star in the NL but hadn't played a full season since 1898, while Boston shortstop Freddy Parent, Philadelphia pitcher Eddie Plank, and Detroit pitcher Roscoe Miller were rookies. Pitcher-manager Clark Griffith guided the White Sox to the first AL pennant, fighting only Boston from July to early September.

On June 27, first and sixth in the NL were separated by only three games. The Reds had been contending a couple weeks earlier, but they fell so hard that they ended the season in last; the Giants joined them with a .297 record after June 27. The all-offense Cardinals hung in until mid–August, when the Superbas rejoined the Phillies-Pirates race. The Pirates took over first in Momentum on September 4, the same day the other NL teams stopped gaining any.

1902: Now It Gets Ugly

AL	BOS	CHI	DET	PHI	STL
Start	84	288			
6/1	152	346	46	64	28
7/1	177	466	16	104	
8/1	206	590		133	46
9/1	330	669		217	125
End	356	640		353	136
Spt.	1.40	1.50	1.07	**1.26**	1.12

Name	Tm	Pos	WAR	SpW	Fame
Young	BOS	P	10.0	14.0	4.0
Davis	CHI	SS	5.7	8.6	2.9
Dinneen	BOS	P	7.0	9.8	2.8
Waddell	PHI	P	9.7	12.2	2.5
Patterson	CHI	P	4.5	6.8	2.3
Plank	PHI	P	5.8	7.3	1.5
Bradley	CLE	3B	6.7	6.7	
Delahanty	WAS	LF	6.7	6.7	

NL	BRO	CIN	NY	PHI	PIT	STL
Start	241	4	24	125	342	51
6/1	218		1	102	434	28
7/1	188			72	554	
8/1	157			41	678	
9/1	126			10	802	
End	92				938	
Spt.	1.40	1.00	1.03	1.26	1.50	1.08

Name	Tm	Pos	WAR	SpW	Fame
Wagner	PIT	RF/SS	7.3	11.0	3.7
Leach	PIT	3B	5.9	8.9	3.0
Chesbro	PIT	P	5.5	8.3	2.8
Beaumont	PIT	CF	5.1	7.7	2.6
Clarke	PIT	LF	5.0	7.5	2.5
Taylor	CHI	P	9.3	9.3	
Hahn	CIN	P	8.9	8.9	
Willis	BOS	P	8.4	8.4	
Pittinger	BOS	P	7.5	7.5	

The NL race is easy to describe—nobody gained Momentum except the Pirates. But 1902 is far from an easy narrative. The Milwaukee Brewers moved to St. Louis,[3] became the Browns, and poached six of the best Cardinals. The Phillies also lost several stars, including Elmer Flick to the A's. But a Pennsylvania court injunction ruled several A's were Phillies property,[4] so AL president Ban Johnson sent Flick, Nap Lajoie, and Bill Bernhard out of Pennsylvania's jurisdiction to Cleveland.[5] For the second straight season, Brooklyn star Jimmy Sheckard jumped to Baltimore and back again.[6] Baltimore's John McGraw got suspended indefinitely in the AL,[7] signed with the Giants, and acquired as many great Orioles as possible (a few, like fellow suspendee Joe Kelley and Cy Seymour, went to Cincinnati).[8]

On the field, the White Sox seemed to fend off all opponents by mid-July, but a six-loss streak let the superteam Browns, A's, and (Boston) Americans back in. The A's went 16–1 at one point in August, starting the run 4.5 games back and ending it three up, and they survived a Browns sweep and nine-win streak to stay at the top. The A's were 24–21 when they acquired former Chicago Orphan Rube Waddell from Los Angeles in the California League.

8. *A Permanent Rival Emerges*   103

After that, they were 35–25 when he wasn't the pitcher of record and 24–7 when he was.

Waddell started his Hall of Fame path compensating for a team that lost two Hall of Famers to a court injunction. That chaos was baseball in 1902.

1903: Pax New Yorka

AL	BOS	CHI	PHI	STL	CLE	DET
Start	218	392	216	83		
6/1	217	471	295	77	13	33
7/1	337	461	415	102	13	3
8/1	461	430	419	71		
9/1	585	399	403	40		
End	697	371	375	12		
Spt.	1.50	1.42	1.38	1.20	1.02	1.01

Name	Tm	Pos	WAR	SpW	Fame
Young	BOS	P	7.1	10.7	3.6
Waddell	PHI	P	8.8	12.1	3.3
Dinneen	BOS	P	6.6	9.9	3.3
Parent	BOS	SS	6.4	9.6	3.2
Plank	PHI	P	7.2	9.9	2.7
Collins	BOS	3B	5.3	8.0	2.7
Lajoie	CLE	2B	8.0	8.2	0.2
Bradley	CLE	3B	7.1	7.2	0.1

NL	BRO	PIT	CHI	NY
Start	46	469		
6/1	21	519	96	80
7/1		619	191	195
8/1		743	160	174
9/1		867	129	143
End		979	101	115
Spt.	1.12	1.60	1.29	1.30

Name	Tm	Pos	WAR	SpW	Fame
Wagner	PIT	SS	7.6	12.2	4.6
Leever	PIT	P	6.5	10.4	3.9
McGinnity	NY	P	11.6	15.1	3.5
Mathewson	NY	P	9.9	12.9	3.0
Phillippe	PIT	P	4.9	7.8	2.9
Sheckard	BRO	LF	7.0	7.8	0.8
Hahn	CIN	P	7.8	7.8	

Just before the leagues signed a peace agreement,[9] there were some final reminders of their war. The husk of Baltimore's assets moved to New York to become the Highlanders and compete directly with the Giants who had poached half their team. Instead of poaching right back, however, the Highlanders got potentially better prizes in Jack Chesbro, Jesse Tannehill, and three other Pirates, plus Willie Keeler from crosstown Brooklyn.[10] But for all the fame, the team never got going; instead, Chicago and Philadelphia fought most of the early battle, with Boston replacing Chicago in the scrum in early June and pulling away from Philadelphia in August. For the White Sox, who eventually ended in seventh, the pitching was a letdown past Doc White. For the Americans, second-year Patsy Dougherty joined the core by leading the league in hits and runs.

The Pirates didn't adequately replace Chesbro and Tannehill, but they had plenty of talent on hand to end the race by July 4. The Cubs, Giants, and Pirates all had two good pitchers—Jake Weimer/Jack Taylor, Christy Mathewson/Joe McGinnity, and Deacon Phillippe/Sam Leever, respectively—but the Cubs and Giants could only produce one major batsman each (Frank Chance and Roger Bresnahan), while the Pirates' lineup, still built around the Louisville core, was as deep as ever.

The new World Series brought thrills and heralded peace between the leagues. But the freeze on player movement that new peace brought meant that teams that hadn't thrived in player raids now would have to build on whatever they happened to have.

1904: East Coast Bias

AL	BOS	CHI	PHI	STL	CLE	NY
Start	354	189	191	6		
6/1	441	171	213		8	
7/1	561	181	183			32
8/1	685	215	152			56
9/1	809	304	181			180
End	965	280	142			336
Spt.	**1.50**	1.35	1.32	1.03	1.02	1.16

Name	Tm	Pos	WAR	SpW	Fame
Young	BOS	P	9.5	14.3	4.8
Waddell	PHI	P	10.5	13.9	3.4
Parent	BOS	SS	6.2	9.3	3.1
Plank	PHI	P	**8.5**	11.2	2.7
Collins	BOS	3B	5.3	8.0	2.7
Tannehill	BOS	P	5.3	8.0	2.7
Davis	CHI	SS	7.2	9.7	2.5
Chesbro	NY	P	**10.2**	11.8	1.6
Lajoie	CLE	2B	8.6	8.7	0.1

NL	CHI	NY	PIT	CIN
Start	51	58	**489**	
6/1	115	137	**463**	104
7/1	180	257	**433**	174
8/1	149	381	**402**	143
9/1	118	**505**	371	112
End	79	**661**	332	73
Spt.	1.30	**1.44**	1.46	1.18

Name	Tm	Pos	WAR	SpW	Fame
McGinnity	NY	P	**9.8**	14.1	4.3
Wagner	PIT	SS	8.3	12.1	3.8
Dahlen	NY	SS	5.6	**8.1**	2.5
Mathewson	NY	P	5.5	7.9	2.4
Leever	PIT	P	4.7	6.9	2.2
Weimer	CHI	P	**6.1**	7.9	1.8
Hahn	CIN	P	**6.5**	7.7	1.2
Nichols	STL	P	**7.6**	7.6	

The Americans started the year 18–5, and through most of June they stood without competition. But the Highlanders, fueled by Willie Keeler's and Jack Chesbro's return to form, started making noise at the end of June, as did the White Sox, and the A's rode a 16–3 streak into contention in mid–August. The Americans and Highlanders re-separated themselves and were neck-and-neck through September, with the White Sox joining them at the end (the season now being 154 games instead of 140 gave extra time). Ultimately, the Americans won it as their reputation anticipated. The Americans were thinner than in 1903, but the pitching was deep and strong enough to need only five pitchers all year—Young, Dinneen, trade pickup Jesse Tannehill, Norwood Gibson, and George Winter.

In the NL, the Pirates finally felt the effect of losing players to the Highlanders; Deacon Phillippe aged suddenly, and while June purchase Patsy Flaherty (11–25 the previous year) was a surprisingly competent replacement, the staff remained thin. Pittsburgh gained no Momentum in 1904; instead, the Giants, Cubs, and Reds fought through mid–June, after which the Giants took control.

The Cubs were still led by Frank Chance and Jake Weimer, while the Reds had veteran hitters Joe Kelley and Cy Seymour to support young pitchers Noodles Hahn, Jack Harper, and Tom Walker. The Giants' pitching now had an offense behind it, as veteran shortstop Bill Dahlen, a trade acquisition from Brooklyn, joined rookie third baseman Art Devlin in excellence on the left side of the diamond. Augmented by Dan McGann and Sam Mertes, the Giants had as balanced a lineup as the Pirates had been for years. The Giants had no chance to add to their glory in the postseason because their owner refused to play the rival American League. The incident remains one of the only times a sports owner has refused both more money and more spotlight.

1905: Chaos and Its Opposite

AL	BOS	CHI	NY	PHI	CLE	WAS
Start	578	167	201	85		
6/1	553	227	176	135	80	15
7/1	523	287	146	205	200	
8/1	492	411	115	289	324	
9/1	461	490	84	413	373	
End	424	558	47	561	336	
Spt.	1.46	1.39	1.19	**1.38**	1.17	1.01

Name	Tm	Pos	WAR	SpW	Fame
C. Young	BOS	P	7.6	11.1	3.5
Waddell	PHI	P	9.2	12.7	3.5
Davis	CHI	SS	7.2	10.0	2.8
Tannehill	BOS	P	5.5	8.0	2.5
Plank	PHI	P	6.6	9.1	2.5
Killian	DET	P	6.8	6.8	

NL	CHI	CIN	NY	PIT
Start	45	42	379	191
6/1	39	16	468	190
7/1	9		588	160
8/1			712	129
9/1			836	98
End			984	61
Spt.	1.14	1.07	**1.60**	1.40

Name	Tm	Pos	WAR	SpW	Fame
Mathewson	NY	P	9.1	14.6	5.5
Wagner	PIT	SS	10.1	14.1	4.0
Donlin	NY	CF	6.5	10.4	3.9
Dahlen	NY	SS	5.5	8.8	3.3
McGann	NY	1B	4.9	7.9	3.0
Reulbach	CHI	P	8.3	9.5	1.2
Seymour	CIN	CF	8.0	8.6	0.6
I. Young	BOS	P	9.2	9.2	

The AL Momentum lead changed twice—the only such time in the AL until 1960. The Senators, 38–113 the year before, went 6–1 against Boston in April, and Boston never recovered, with Freddy Parent and their pitching depth vanishing. The Highlanders started 7–3 but went 6–19 right after; they never entered the race either, mostly receding to 1903's level of play. The Cleveland Naps pulled out in front of the White Sox and A's in June, but a five-loss streak dropped them back into the race, and their 23–47 finish took them out of it. The now two-team race went down to the end, but the A's stayed slightly ahead thanks in part to a series win over the White Sox in late September.

The White Sox had the deep rotation similar to the 1904 Americans, headlined by Doc White and Nick Altrock, and a decent lineup that also played great defense, led by outfielder-manager Fielder Jones and an infield of Jiggs Donahue, Frank Isbell/Gus Dundon, George Davis, and Lee Tannehill. The A's weren't as deep or as defensively minded, but Rube Waddell and Eddie Plank were dual aces and Harry Davis, Danny Murphy, Topsy Hartsel, and Socks Seybold helped the A's to a league-leading .338 SLG.

The NL race was basically just the Giants, as they started 32–9. The Giants had a team OPS+ of 112–high enough that the rest of the league was below-average. Mike Donlin played his first season of at least 130 games and led the league in runs from a .356/.413/.495 line that only Honus Wagner and Cy Seymour approached. Christy Mathewson compensated for a weakening pitching staff with a 31–9, 1.28 record produced in part by his third straight strikeout title and his fewest walks and wild pitches to that point (he had led the latter category in his first three full years).

1906: Chicaugust

AL	BOS	CHI	CLE	NY	PHI	DET
Start	352	464	279	39	466	
6/1	328	440	315	30	562	
7/1	298	410	435	150	682	4
8/1	267	389	514	274	806	
9/1	236	478	498	333	865	
End	200	622	462	432	829	
Spt.	1.19	1.46	1.32	1.14	1.50	1.00

Name	Tm	Pos	WAR	SpW	Fame
Lajoie	CLE	2B	10.0	13.2	3.2
Turner	CLE	SS	9.4	12.4	3.0
Davis	CHI	SS	6.3	9.2	2.9
Waddell	PHI	P	5.7	8.6	2.9
White	CHI	P	6.2	9.1	2.9
Flick	CLE	CF/RF	6.5	8.6	2.1
Orth	NY	P	7.7	8.8	1.1
Stone	STL	LF	8.7	8.7	

NL	NY	PIT	CHI	PHI
Start	492	30		
6/1	604	32	112	14
7/1	699	147	232	
8/1	668	126	356	
9/1	637	95	480	
End	601	59	624	
Spt.	1.50	1.31	1.45	1.05

Name	Tm	Pos	WAR	SpW	Fame
Devlin	NY	3B	8.0	12.0	4.0
Chance	CHI	1B	7.3	10.6	3.3
Brown	CHI	P	7.1	10.3	3.2
Steinfeldt	CHI	3B	7.0	10.2	3.2
Wagner	PIT	SS	9.3	12.2	2.9
Willis	PIT	P	8.2	10.7	2.5

Although the Cubs had played nearly .600 ball in previous seasons, they hadn't mattered to pennant races as much as the White Sox entering 1906. .600 had never won a pennant, and on June 29 the Cubs, Pirates, and Giants were all at .650. But the exceptionally deep Cubs went 71–16 after that and didn't lose consecutive games after July. Harry Steinfeldt, coming off two down years in Cincinnati, was obtained for the older, more reliable Jake Weimer. With Joe Tinker and Johnny Evers playing great up the middle, Tinker to Evers to Chance became a nightmare, as the team gave up 2.5 runs per game. Contrary to their resultant fame, they were only third in double plays turned, but the pitching staff, headlined by Brown, Jack Pfiester, and Ed Reulbach, was stingy enough that a double play spelled doom like few things could.

As for the Giants, nobody can keep up with 71–16, but Mike Donlin's May injury[11] and Christy Mathewson's tumble from a 230 ERA+ to 88 didn't help.

The Pirates had a legitimate ace again in acquisition Vic Willis, but he and Honus Wagner couldn't do everything.

The AL was typically chaotic through July. The A's were still as good as in 1905, the Naps had a reasonable rotation featuring Addie Joss, Bob Rhoads, and Otto Hess to match their top hitters, and the Highlanders went 16–1 near the end of May to enter the conversation, riding a fantastic year from Al Orth, rebounds from Jimmy Williams and Kid Elberfeld, and a sophomore improvement from first baseman Hal Chase.

When the A's and White Sox met for a five-game series on August 5, the A's were 2.5 up on the Highlanders, seven up on the Naps they had just swept, and 7.5 up on the White Sox. The White Sox won all five games of the series by a combined 25–6, then swept the Highlanders, then won seven more games as part of a 19-win streak, leaving them 5.5 games up on everybody. The Highlanders forced themselves back in, but it wasn't enough.

As in 1905, the White Sox were not loads better than the A's outside defense, but Ed Walsh became an excellent second starter behind Doc White.

Each AL team had Momentum from May 12–14, the first such occurrence in any league (and the only one until 1958).

1907: Goliath Wins

AL	BOS	CHI	CLE	NY	PHI	DET
Start	199	618	459	429	823	
6/1	173	722	538	413	797	35
7/1	143	842	643	383	772	30
8/1	112	966	732	352	781	39
9/1	81	1090	801	321	905	163
End	46	1195	781	286	1045	303
Spt.	1.07	1.46	1.30	1.20	1.44	**1.13**

Name	Tm	Pos	WAR	SpW	Fame
Walsh	CHI	P	7.7	**11.2**	3.5
Plank	PHI	P	6.2	**8.9**	2.7
Lajoie	CLE	2B	7.6	**9.9**	2.3
Davis	CHI	SS	4.6	**6.7**	2.1
Bender	PHI	P	4.8	**6.9**	2.1
Joss	CLE	P	6.3	**8.2**	1.9
Cobb	DET	RF	**6.8**	7.7	0.9
Killian	DET	P	**6.6**	7.5	0.9
Young	BOS	P	**7.6**	8.1	0.5

NL	CHI	NY	PIT
Start	**312**	300	30
6/1	397	**400**	5
7/1	**517**	385	
8/1	**641**	354	
9/1	**765**	323	
End	**905**	288	
Spt.	**1.58**	1.42	1.09

Name	Tm	Pos	WAR	SpW	Fame
Overall	CHI	P	5.6	**8.8**	3.2
Mathewson	NY	P	7.6	**10.8**	3.2
Brown	CHI	P	5.3	**8.4**	3.1
Evers	CHI	2B	5.3	**8.4**	3.1
Lundgren	CHI	P	5.2	8.2	3.0
Wagner	PIT	SS	**8.9**	9.7	0.8
Magee	PHI	LF	**6.9**	6.9	
Karger	STL	P	**6.7**	6.7	
Ewing	CIN	P	**6.5**	6.5	

In the three World Series to date, every participant was leading its league in Momentum apart from the 1906 White Sox, who entered at number two. So imagine the surprise when number four Detroit showed up to face the Cubs, who'd seen Orval Overall and Carl Lundgren step up to compensate for regression from Jack Pfiester, Frank Chance, and Harry Steinfeldt. The Cubs hadn't been challenged since the beginning of June, as the Giants were thin and the rest of the league wasn't good. The Pirates and Phillies finished with respectable records, but they were nonfactors.

The Tigers were part of an early race with the White Sox and the Naps. The White Sox were the most consistent and stood alone in mid–July. Right-fielder Ed Hahn, an old rookie in 1905, was having an excellent third season, while Ed Walsh continued to dominate the league on his way to pitching 422 innings.

But in a reverse of 1906, the White Sox lost four of five to the A's at the end of July, which brought the A's into the race; on July 26, fourth place was two games behind first. The Naps held on until September 5, while the other three stayed relevant through the final week. The Tigers had the softest remaining schedule, with series against Boston, Washington, and St. Louis, and they won ten straight to steal the pennant. Each outfielder—sluggers Ty Cobb, Sam Crawford, and Davy Jones—created more WAR than the infield and catcher combined, and veteran starters Bill Donovan, Ed Killian, and Ed Siever had great years.

1908: Could Have Gone on Forever

AL	BOS	CHI	CLE	DET	NY	PHI	STL
Start	34	**882**	576	224	211	771	
6/1	9	857	651	229	296	**871**	16
7/1		**952**	771	239	291	876	131
8/1		**1016**	825	358	260	845	255
9/1		**1000**	799	482	229	814	339
End		**1133**	892	630	192	777	352
Spt.	1.00	1.49	1.31	**1.27**	1.10	1.40	1.05

Name	Tm	Pos	WAR	SpW	Fame
Walsh	CHI	P	**10.1**	15.1	5.0
Plank	PHI	P	7.1	9.9	2.8
Joss	CLE	P	**8.1**	10.6	2.5
Lajoie	CLE	2B	7.9	10.3	2.4
Vickers	PHI	P	6.0	8.4	2.4
Jones	CHI	CF	4.8	7.2	2.4
Young	BOS	P	**9.6**	9.6	

NL	CHI	NY	CIN	PHI	PIT	BOS
Start	453	144				
6/1	521	157	14	39	32	
7/1	641	157	49	19	132	
8/1	765	281	18		256	
9/1	799	405			375	
End	932	553			508	
Spt.	**1.60**	1.40	1.09	1.07	1.24	1.01

8. A Permanent Rival Emerges   111

Name	Tm	Pos	WAR	SpW	Fame
Brown	CHI	P	**8.2**	**13.1**	**4.9**
Tinker	CHI	SS	**7.9**	**12.6**	**4.7**
Mathewson	NY	P	**11.1**	**15.5**	**4.4**
Evers	CHI	2B	5.6	9.0	**3.4**
Reulbach	CHI	P	4.9	7.8	**2.9**
Wagner	PIT	SS	**11.5**	**14.3**	2.8
McQuillan	PHI	P	**9.4**	**10.1**	0.7

You can measure a pennant race's chaos by how many days of Momentum a league's teams gained. A two-team race all year would have twice as many days gained as a one-team "race," and so on. Before divisional play, any number over 400 signaled historical chaos. The 1908 NL race came in at 403. But the AL race had 446, 4th-best in the era:

1915 FL 507
1895 NL 474
1956 NL 448
1908 AL 446

So why has the NL story been told more regularly? First, the NL race involved the three teams that tended to matter in that era. 1908 is an important part of all their narratives, whereas the AL race involved teams without larger relevance. Second, the NL hadn't had a pennant race go into September since 1901, so 1908 was surprising, whereas the AL looked like this seemingly every year. Third, the AL teams weren't very good. The standings on June 8:

CHI 23–20
STL 24–21
CLE 24–21
NY 22–20
PHI 23–21
DET 22–22
BOS 21–26
WAS 18–26

That's standingese for "nothing's happened." The A's were in the middle of losing 11 out of 12 and they never got back in the race thanks to the league's worst offense. And the Highlanders, who had started 16–8 (.667), revealed that start to be one of the falsest in history, going 35–95 (.269) the rest of the way.

Through July, the White Sox, Naps, Tigers, and Browns were in the race. The Tigers and Browns pulled ahead for a month before the other two came back in. The Browns played the first half of September entirely against the other three contenders and went 6–11; they gained Momentum as late as September 25, but that stretch doomed them. The Tigers benefited from a soft schedule again, won 10 straight in their final 13 games, and took their second straight pennant while remaining the league's fourth-ranked team by Momentum. The Tigers punted defense and got offensive help for Ty Cobb and Sam Crawford with resurgences from Matty McIntyre and Claude Rossman, while the pitching tried to be adequate. The White Sox were led by Ed Walsh and an aging lineup featuring Fielder Jones, Patsy Dougherty, and Freddy Parent.

The NL's story was simpler, as the Giants, Cubs, and Pirates stuck it out nearly from beginning to end, pulling away from the Phillies and Reds in June. The Cubs came out on top, but add any number of games to the end of the schedule and it might have come out differently. For the Cubs, Johnny Evers and Joe Tinker hit to match their defensive reputations, while Mordecai Brown was better than usual. The Giants benefited from the return of Mike Donlin from acting[12] and Hooks Wiltse ably backing Christy Mathewson. The Pirates were the thinnest team, but Honus Wagner's .354/.415/.542 line was 20 points better on AVG, 13 points better on OBP, and a ridiculous 90 points better on SLG than second place (Donlin/Evers/Donlin, respectively).

1909: The Tigers Get Their Due

AL	CHI	CLE	DET	NY	PHI	STL	BOS
Start	1119	881	622	190	768	348	
6/1	1097	859	710	243	831	326	55
7/1	1067	829	830	218	846	296	25
8/1	1036	798	954	187	865	265	4
9/1	1005	767	1078	156	974	234	62
End	969	731	1222	120	1013	198	26
Spt.	1.46	1.27	1.44	1.05	1.32	1.10	1.01

Name	Tm	Pos	WAR	SpW	Fame
Cobb	DET	RF	9.8	14.1	4.3
Collins	PHI	2B	9.7	12.8	3.1
Smith	CHI	P	6.5	9.5	3.0
Bush	DET	SS	6.4	9.2	2.8
Walsh	CHI	P	6.1	8.9	2.8
Morgan	2 TM	P	6.8	8.6	1.8
Lajoie	CLE	2B	6.4	8.1	1.7

NL	CHI	NY	PIT	PHI
Start	466	277	254	
6/1	565	251	353	15
7/1	565	221	473	
8/1	534	190	597	

8. A Permanent Rival Emerges

NL	CHI	NY	PIT	PHI
9/1	518	159	721	
End	482	123	865	
Spt.	1.45	1.31	1.53	1.04

Name	Tm	Pos	WAR	SpW	Fame
Wagner	PIT	SS	**9.2**	14.1	**4.9**
Brown	CHI	P	**8.7**	12.6	**3.9**
Overall	CHI	P	**7.2**	10.4	**3.2**
Mathewson	NY	P	**9.2**	12.1	**2.9**
Camnitz	PIT	P	**5.4**	8.3	**2.9**
Reulbach	CHI	P	**5.4**	7.8	**2.4**
Rucker	BRO	P	**7.8**	7.8	

One of the biggest assumptions of Momentum is that teams at the top have to stop contending for anyone to pass them. For the Tigers, 1909 was finally the year teams in front stopped contending, as the Naps were thin and the White Sox, led by player-manager Billy Sullivan and his .162/.226/.174 line, hit so badly that pitcher Doc White was mostly an outfielder.

This turned the season into a Tigers lead with sporadic A's contention that intensified as the season went on and surprise interjections from the Red Sox, with good offense and literally no rotation (only one pitcher started 20 games; only five even started ten). The Tigers swept them both in a 14-win streak starting August 19 and took over first for good.

The A's found most of their reinforcements in second-year standout Eddie Collins and rookies Frank Baker and Harry Krause; their deep rotation was unusual for the normal A's build. But while Collins and Baker were performing at the level of Cobb and Crawford, they didn't have anyone like the Tigers' rookie Donie Bush, who played a fine shortstop and led the league in sacrifice hits by 11 and walks by 26. Bush's complementary skill set made the Tigers' offense formidable, sufficient for pitchers George Mullin, Ed Killian, and Ed Summers to win with.

In the NL, the Cubs and Pirates were the main competitors. The Pirates' 20–1 streak in June and 16–0 streak in September were enough to clear even the 104-win Cubs out of the playoff picture. The Cubs threw 32 shutouts, and while the lineup was average, it at least was deep. The Giants won 92 games but gained no Momentum, as Christy Mathewson's rotation mates Red Ames and rookie Rube Marquard had rough seasons.

Honus Wagner had experienced an insufficient supporting cast, but in 1909, he and pitchers Howie Camnitz and Vic Willis were joined on the mound by rookie Babe Adams. If Wagner and Fred Clarke were the Pirates' Cobb and Crawford, then their Donie Bush was Dots Miller, a rookie second baseman who hit the league's third-most doubles.

1910: Pennant Races Made Easy

AL	BOS	CHI	CLE	DET	NY	PHI	STL
Start	23	856	646	**1080**	106	895	175
6/1		833	628	**1087**	138	957	152
7/1		803	598	**1182**	253	1077	122
8/1		772	567	1151	222	**1201**	91
9/1		741	536	1120	191	**1325**	60
End		697	492	1076	147	**1501**	16
Spt.	1.00	1.30	1.20	1.45	1.07	**1.55**	1.03

Name	*Tm*	*Pos*	WAR	SpW	*Fame*
Collins	PHI	2B	**10.5**	16.3	5.8
Coombs	PHI	P	9.7	15.0	5.3
Cobb	DET	CF	**10.5**	15.2	4.7
Walsh	CHI	P	**10.9**	14.2	3.3
Bender	PHI	P	5.3	8.2	**2.9**
Ford	NY	P	**11.0**	11.8	0.8
Johnson	WAS	P	**11.4**	11.4	

NL	CHI	NY	PIT	CIN	PHI
Start	241	61	**433**		
6/1	308	153	**480**	57	1
7/1	428	228	**450**	27	
8/1	**552**	267	419		
9/1	**676**	236	388		
End	**852**	192	344		
Spt.	**1.56**	1.30	1.44	1.08	1.01

Name	*Tm*	*Pos*	WAR	SpW	*Fame*
Cole	CHI	P	**5.6**	8.7	3.1
Hofman	CHI	CF/1B	5.3	8.3	3.0
Wagner	PIT	SS	5.2	7.5	2.3
Brown	CHI	P	4.8	7.5	2.7
Tinker	CHI	SS	4.0	6.2	2.2
Mathewson	NY	P	7.3	9.5	2.2
Magee	PHI	LF	6.7	6.8	0.1
Moore	PHI	P	**5.7**	5.8	0.1
Rucker	BRO	P	7.2	7.2	

After July 15, the A's and Cubs were the only teams that gained Momentum. The A's swept consecutive doubleheaders against the Highlanders July 1–2 as part of a 17–3 run. The Cubs started 11–11, had a 25–5 tear, and let the Giants back in by going 8–12. But the up-and-down season went up again with a 33–7 run that sealed the deal.

For the Pirates, Dots Miller tanked and Honus Wagner and Fred Clarke finally started to age; their declines offset Bobby Byrne's and Babe Adams's fine seasons. The Giants and Cubs each had a lineup without weaknesses and a rookie starter impressively backing a Hall of Famer (Christy Mathewson/

8. A Permanent Rival Emerges

Louis Drucke and Mordecai Brown/King Cole respectively), but the Cubs' defense was the league's best, while the Giants were competent at best. For the Cubs, Frank Schulte was in his prime and Joe Tinker and Johnny Evers continued to star up the middle.

In the AL, the Tigers' pitching had been on the right side of passable in 1909; it switched sides in 1910. The A's had the league's best pitching, as Chief Bender and Jack Coombs combined for a 54–14 record and Coombs's pitching WAR (9.7) nearly eclipsed the entire Tigers' staff (11.8). The lineup was deep; Eddie Collins and Frank Baker were supported by young players Rube Oldring and Jack Barry and the continued success of veteran Danny Murphy.

1911: All's Well That Ends Well

AL	CHI	CLE	DET	NY	PHI	STL
Start	517	365	797	109	**1113**	12
6/1	490	338	905	82	**1086**	
7/1	460	308	1025	52	**1141**	
8/1	429	277	1149	21	**1190**	
9/1	398	246	1193		**1314**	
End	357	205	1152		**1478**	
Spt.	1.30	1.20	1.40	1.07	**1.60**	1.00

Name	Tm	Pos	WAR	SpW	Fame
Cobb	DET	CF	**10.7**	**15.0**	4.3
Collins	PHI	2B	6.5	**10.4**	3.9
Baker	PHI	3B	6.4	**10.2**	3.8
Plank	PHI	P	6.3	**10.1**	3.8
Bender	PHI	P	6.0	9.8	3.6
Walsh	CHI	P	**9.0**	**11.7**	2.7
Jackson	CLE	RF	**9.2**	**11.0**	1.8
Gregg	CLE	P	**9.1**	**10.9**	1.8
Johnson	WAS	P	**8.8**	8.8	

NL	CHI	NY	PIT	PHI	STL
Start	426	96	172		
6/1	454	149	240	108	
7/1	**574**	269	270	218	
8/1	**698**	388	289	342	19
9/1	**817**	507	393	336	
End	**821**	671	352	295	
Spt.	**1.50**	**1.46**	1.33	1.19	1.02

Name	Tm	Pos	WAR	SpW	Fame
Mathewson	NY	P	7.4	**10.8**	3.4
Marquard	NY	P	6.1	8.9	2.8
Schulte	CHI	RF	5.3	8.0	2.7
Doyle	NY	2B	5.5	8.0	**2.5**
Sheckard	CHI	LF	5.0	7.5	**2.5**
Wagner	PIT	SS/1B	**6.5**	8.6	2.1

Name	Tm	Pos	WAR	SpW	Fame
Adams	PIT	P	**6.4**	8.5	2.1
Alexander	PHI	P	**8.4**	10.0	1.6
Rucker	BRO	P	**8.7**	8.7	

The Tigers started 1911 21–2, scoring over six runs a game in that stretch. But George Mullin turned out to be the only reliable pitcher as manager Hughie Jennings tried several interchangeably mediocre youngsters. The A's went 36–9 from the end of May to the middle of July, pulled away in August, and ended 13.5 games up. For the A's, Jack Coombs fell to earth, but Eddie Plank made a fine comeback, 20-year-old Stuffy McInnis took over first base from Harry Davis and was roughly his equal, while centerfielder Rube Oldring's decline was compensated for by good work from leftfielder Bris Lord. Catchers Ira Thomas and Jack Lapp combined for 4.5 WAR, with the latter posting a .435 OBP.

Although the final NL standings showed clear stratification—the Giants were 7.5 ahead of the Cubs, who were seven ahead of the Pirates, who were five ahead of the Phillies—the race involved all of them through early August, with a July cameo from the Cardinals. The Phillies started 21–6, with even better offense than the Tigers'. But Fred Luderus, Hans Lobert, and Sherry Magee were no Sam Crawfords and certainly no Ty Cobbs, and while rookie Pete Alexander and Earl Moore were great pitchers, there wasn't enough talent after them. The Pirates stayed in the race through August 28, largely off Honus Wagner's and Fred Clarke's returns to form and starting pitcher Lefty Leifield's best season in five years. But catcher George Gibson's missing only 27 games in the last three years showed up in his .209/.281/.260 line.

That left the Cubs and Giants. The Cubs got 30 2B, 21 3B, and 21 HR from leftfielder Frank Schulte and good batting from Heinie Zimmerman, who replaced Johnny Evers after his nervous breakdown.[13] But the Cubs lineup was effectively five deep—Schulte, Zimmerman, Joe Tinker, Jimmy Sheckard, and Jim Doyle—while the Giants' eleventh-best position player, Art Wilson, produced more than the Cubs' sixth-best. Like the A's setup, Wilson teamed with Chief Meyers for 4.8 WAR at catcher. On the mound, Rube Marquard, a major letdown in 1909, was nearly Christy Mathewson's equal, while Red Ames was a creditable third starter and Doc Crandall provided value as a swingman, pinch-hitter, and emergency middle infielder.

1912: You Must Have at Least Two Pitchers to Ride This Ride

AL	CHI	CLE	DET	PHI	BOS	WAS
Start	205	118	661	**848**		
6/1	309	92	635	**822**	16	

8. A Permanent Rival Emerges 117

AL	CHI	CLE	DET	PHI	BOS	WAS
7/1	359	62	605	792	136	24
8/1	328	31	574	761	260	
9/1	297		543	730	384	
End	262		508	695	524	
Spt.	1.27	1.11	1.40	1.50	1.48*	1.00

Name	Tm	Pos	WAR	SpW	Fame
Wood	BOS	P	10.4	15.4	5.0
Speaker	BOS	CF	10.1	15.0	4.9
Baker	PHI	3B	9.5	14.3	4.8
Collins	PHI	2B	8.8	13.2	4.4
Cobb	DET	CF	9.2	12.9	3.7
Walsh	CHI	P	11.4	14.5	3.1
Jackson	CLE	RF	9.6	10.7	1.1
Johnson	WAS	P	14.6	14.6	

NL	CHI	NY	PHI	PIT	CIN
Start	567	463	204	243	
6/1	543	554	180	219	61
7/1	513	674	150	189	31
8/1	482	798	119	158	
9/1	451	922	88	127	
End	416	1062	53	92	
Spt.	1.42	1.58	1.20	1.30	1.05

Name	Tm	Pos	WAR	SpW	Fame
Mathewson	NY	P	7.3	11.5	4.2
Marquard	NY	P	5.8	9.2	3.4
Zimmerman	CHI	3B/1B	7.0	9.9	2.9
Doyle	NY	2B	5.0	7.9	2.9
Tesreau	NY	P	5.0	7.9	2.9
Evers	CHI	2B	5.9	8.4	2.5
Wagner	PIT	SS	8.1	10.5	2.4
Alexander	PHI	P	6.4	7.7	1.3
Rucker	BRO	P	8.2	8.2	

On June 13, the Giants held a 12-game lead with a 37–8 record, and the lead held up. Larry Doyle and Chief Meyers were the only fearsome hitters, but the lineup was deep, as John McGraw expertly kept bad performances off the team. More importantly, the Giants became the first NL team to have three 5 WAR pitchers. The Cubs got Johnny Evers back, but the pitching, forever their mainstay, deserted them. While rookie Larry Cheney led the league in wins, King Cole's ERA was 10.89 before he was traded, Ed Reulbach flopped, and Mordecai Brown's July knee injury was thought to be career-ending.[14]

In the AL, the A's and Tigers mimicked the Cubs in having one good pitcher each (Eddie Plank and Jean Dubuc); neither gained Momentum all year. Into the breach stepped the White Sox, Senators, and Red Sox. The Senators won 17 straight over May/June, but the Red Sox went 14–1 around the same time, and afterwards they had losing streaks of **any** length only twice. They matched the Giants' feat of three 5-WAR pitchers, but theirs were even more impressive, as Smoky Joe Wood went 34–5 and 30-year-old near-rookie Buck O'Brien and Ray Collins backed him up. The fourth starter, rookie Hugh Bedient, was as good as Plank and Dubuc. The offense was only two deep, but Tris Speaker rivaled Ty Cobb and Eddie Collins in excellence, while Larry Gardner starred at third base.

The pennant races themselves might not have been amazing, but the surprise of who wasn't involved at the top—in every case due to pitching woes—provided plenty of intrigue.

1913: Maybe You Don't Need Any Pitchers

AL	BOS	CHI	DET	PHI	CLE	WAS
Start	356	178	345	**471**		
6/1	325	222	314	**555**	104	43
7/1	295	192	284	**675**	119	13
8/1	264	161	253	**799**	88	
9/1	233	130	222	**923**	57	
End	199	96	188	**1059**	23	
Spt.	1.40	1.20	1.30	**1.60**	1.09	1.01

Name	*Tm*	*Pos*	**WAR**	*SpW*	*Fame*
Collins	PHI	2B	**9.0**	14.4	**5.4**
Baker	PHI	3B	**7.9**	12.6	**4.7**
Speaker	BOS	CF	**8.3**	11.6	**3.3**
McInnis	PHI	1B	5.3	8.5	**3.2**
Barry	PHI	SS	4.7	7.5	**2.8**
Russell	CHI	P	**8.8**	10.6	1.8
Johnson	WAS	P	**16.0**	16.2	0.2

NL	CHI	NY	PHI	PIT	BRO	STL
Start	222	**568**	28	49		
6/1	248	**549**	99	20	65	18
7/1	218	**574**	219		35	
8/1	187	**698**	193		4	
9/1	156	**822**	162			
End	122	**958**	128			
Spt.	1.34	**1.60**	1.33	1.08	1.10	1.01

Name	*Tm*	*Pos*	**WAR**	*SpW*	*Fame*
Mathewson	NY	P	**6.9**	11.0	**4.1**
Marquard	NY	P	5.1	8.2	**3.1**
Tesreau	NY	P	5.0	8.0	**3.0**
Fletcher	NY	SS	4.6	7.4	**2.8**
Alexander	PHI	P	**6.8**	9.0	2.2
Seaton	PHI	P	**6.5**	8.6	2.1

Name	Tm	Pos	WAR	SpW	Fame
Adams	PIT	P	**7.8**	**8.4**	0.6
Sallee	STL	P	**5.9**	6.0	0.1

Tigers' pitchers had a collective 86 ERA+, well below average. The Tigers won 66 games.

Athletics' pitchers had a collective 88 ERA+. The Athletics won 96 games, the pennant, and the World Series. Riding a 37–10 start to the flag, the difference for the A's was their historically great infield; only the 1898 Orioles and 1913 A's have gotten 4.7 WAR from each infielder. Combined with rookie catcher Wally Schang's top-ten MVP performance, the A's scored 5.2 runs/game; the next best in the AL was the Red Sox at 4.2.

On June 10, right around when AL opponents stopped bothering the A's, the crosstown Phillies had a six-game lead off a 29–12 record. 32-year-old Gavvy Cravath, in only his third full year, was a slugging sensation, and Pete Alexander had help on the mound from sophomore Tom Seaton and Ad Brennan. But the Giants went 41–8 immediately after that point, and sweeping the Phillies June 30–July 3 sent them and everybody else packing. The Giants' rotation remained deep, with Mathewson/Marquard/Tesreau joined by 28-year-old rookie Al Demaree, and John McGraw again helped his team by recognizing who **not** to play.

1914: A League Begins ...

AL	BOS	CHI	CLE	DET	PHI	STL	WAS
Start	117	56	14	111	**624**		
6/1	90	29		219	**677**		56
7/1	60			339	**797**	31	111
8/1	39	11		393	**921**	5	150
9/1	8			362	**1045**		119
End				326	**1189**		83
Spt.	1.21	1.07	1.02	1.39	**1.60**	1.02	1.23

Name	Tm	Pos	WAR	SpW	Fame
Collins	PHI	2B	**9.1**	**14.6**	**5.5**
Baker	PHI	3B	7.3	11.7	**4.4**
Johnson	WAS	P	**13.0**	**16.0**	**3.0**
Barry	PHI	SS	4.3	6.9	**2.6**
Crawford	DET	RF	6.2	8.6	**2.4**
Speaker	BOS	CF	**9.9**	**12.0**	2.1
Leonard	BOS	P	**9.3**	**11.3**	2.0

NL	CHI	NY	PHI	BOS	CIN	PIT	STL
Start	61	**479**	64				
6/1	42	**525**	50		53	76	

NL	CHI	NY	PHI	BOS	CIN	PIT	STL
7/1	12	645	20		123	86	
8/1	56	769			92	55	
9/1	50	893		64	61	24	48
End	24	937		208	25		12
Spt.	1.21	1.50	1.15	1.50*	1.29	1.18	1.02

Name	Tm	Pos	WAR	SpW	Fame
James	BOS	P	8.2	12.3	4.1
Rudolph	BOS	P	6.5	9.8	3.3
Burns	NY	LF	6.4	9.6	3.2
Maranville	BOS	SS	5.0	7.5	2.5
Evers	BOS	2B	4.9	7.4	2.5
Alexander	PHI	P	8.4	9.7	1.3
Pfeffer	BRO	P	7.7	7.7	

FL	BAL	BRO	BUF	CHI	IND	STL
Start 6/1	68			4		25
7/1	188		76	124	68	
8/1	207		45	248	137	
9/1	281	26	14	372	226	
End	267			528	382	
Spt.	1.40	1.07	1.12	1.43	1.26	1.11

Name	Tm	Pos	WAR	SpW	Fame
Hendrix	CHI	P	6.9	9.9	3.0
Quinn	BAL	P	5.8	8.1	2.3
Suggs	BAL	P	5.7	8.0	2.3
Zwilling	CHI	CF	5.1	7.3	2.2
Wilson	CHI	C	5.0	7.2	2.2
Falkenberg	IND	P	7.9	10.0	2.1
Kauff	IND	RF/CF	7.8	9.8	2.0
Ford	BUF	P	7.0	7.8	0.8

The new Federal League took talent from both leagues, waving loads of money around and generally recreating the chaos of 1901–1902. For awhile, the established leagues seemed normal. On June 9, the A's narrowly led the Senators, Tigers, and Browns, while the Giants narrowly led the surprising Reds and Pirates. But the Pirates went tanked immediately after and the Reds played under .300 the rest of the way; both finished in the cellar.

Just when the Giants looked competition-free around July, the Cubs sprang from 26–30 to contention while the Giants spun their wheels. But the Cubs sank after losing two to the Braves, who'd started 12–28. The Braves kept winning after that series, sweeping the Cardinals (who'd sneaked into third place) and Giants. On August 17, the Braves started gaining Momentum, only the sixth day in the 20th century they had gained any. The Giants kept scuffling, losing to the Pirates and Reds and letting the Cardinals and Cubs back into the conversation. The Braves ended that conversation with a 25–5 finish.

The Giants' pitching problems were masked by their home field; Jeff Tesreau was the only starter worth anything. Every member of the lineup had an above-average OPS+–only the 1894 Orioles had achieved that before—but George Burns was the sole standout. The Braves had no hitting to speak of outside outfielder Joe Connolly, but the team's 2.09 ERA in the second half didn't need much support.

The AL hadn't been quite so dramatic, but it was a four-team race of sort-of-okay teams in June and July, with the A's, Tigers, Senators, and White Sox all relatively equal and the Red Sox peeking in. On July 15, sixth place was only 4.5 behind first—but the A's had just started a 39–6 run, that removed any doubt from the outcome. The team was still built around its infield, but there was a little bit more pitching, as Chief Bender and 19-year-old sensation Rube Bressler covered for flagging veterans (Eddie Plank) and growing youngsters (Bob Shawkey, Bullet Joe Bush, Weldon Wyckoff, and Herb Pennock).

In the inaugural Federal League race, the Baltimore Terrapins were 22–11 through May 30 while 1.5 games separated second from last. But Baltimore's hitting was nothing special, and the Chicago Chi-Feds found enough pitching (if not a creative name) and the Indianapolis Hoosiers found enough hitting to outclass Baltimore on both fronts. The Terrapins still had a shot in mid–September, but the Hoosiers finished 8–0 to win the pennant by 1.5 games.

The Hoosiers had Cleveland veteran Cy Falkenberg on the mound, Benny Kauff at the plate, and little else. Claude Hendrix jumped from the Pirates to the Chi-Feds and led the league in wins; the extreme pitchers' park obscured hitters' contributions, but Joe Tinker and Art Wilson provided name-brand offense while outfielders Dutch Zwilling and Al Wickland deepened the lineup. For the Terrapins, besides aces Jack Quinn and George Suggs, 38-year-old catcher Fred Jacklitsch, an occasional NL backup who hadn't been seen in the majors since 1910, received full-time play and turned in a .376 OBP.

As those names show, the Federal League wasn't yet top-shelf, but the pennant race was good. Perhaps if it hadn't gone up against one of the greatest pennant races of all time in the National League, it would have mattered more. Regardless, 1915 was another chance to attract big names.

1915: ... *A League Ends*

AL	DET	PHI	WAS	BOS	CHI	NY
Start	163	**595**	42			
6/1	279	**566**	13	17	98	39

AL	DET	PHI	WAS	BOS	CHI	NY
7/1	339	**536**		22	218	9
8/1	448	**505**		131	342	
9/1	**557**	474		255	331	
End	**636**	438		399	295	
Spt.	1.43	1.47	1.06	**1.31***	1.25	1.05

Name	Tm	Pos	WAR	SpW	Fame
Cobb	DET	CF	**9.5**	**13.6**	**4.1**
Collins	CHI	2B	**9.4**	**11.8**	2.4
Speaker	BOS	CF	7.1	9.3	2.2
Dauss	DET	P	5.1	7.3	**2.2**
Veach	DET	LF	4.9	7.0	**2.1**
Scott	CHI	P	6.3	7.9	1.6
Johnson	WAS	P/PH	**12.1**	**12.8**	0.7
Morton	CLE	P	**7.2**	7.2	

NL	BOS	CHI	CIN	NY	STL	BRO	PHI	PIT
Start	111	13	13	**498**	6			
6/1	137	109		**474**			92	
7/1	117	229		**444**	44		187	4
8/1	86	298		**413**	48	87	311	
9/1	80	317		392	17	206	**435**	
End	54	281		356		200	**579**	
Spt.	1.22	1.32	1.04	1.47	1.03	1.09	**1.41**	1.00

Name	Tm	Pos	WAR	SpW	Fame
Alexander	PHI	P	**10.9**	**15.4**	**4.5**
Cravath	PHI	RF	7.0	9.9	2.9
Tesreau	NY	P	5.1	7.5	2.4
Luderus	PHI	1B	5.7	**8.0**	2.3
Doyle	NY	2B	4.5	6.7	**2.1**
Pfeffer	BRO	P	**5.8**	6.3	0.5
Toney	CIN	P	**7.9**	**8.2**	0.3
Mamaux	PIT	P	**6.1**	6.1	

FL	BAL	CHI	NEW	BRO	KC	PIT	STL
Start	134	**264**	191				
6/1	107	**362**	294	8	73	108	
7/1	77	**377**	309	18	193	138	96
8/1	46	**501**	278		317	182	200
9/1	15	**615**	372		431	296	214
End		**693**	370		399	424	307
Spt.	1.10	**1.50**	1.35	1.01	1.25	1.19	1.07

Name	Tm	Pos	WAR	SpW	Fame
Zwilling	CHI	CF	4.1	**6.2**	**2.1**
Wilson	CHI	C	3.9	**5.9**	**2.0**
Mann	CHI	LF/RF	3.2	4.8	1.6
Fischer	CHI	C	3.1	4.7	1.6
Flack	CHI	RF/LF	3.1	4.7	1.6
Konetchy	PIT	1B	**4.8**	5.7	0.9

Name	Tm	Pos	WAR	SpW	Fame
Allen	PIT	P	**4.7**	5.6	0.9
Davenport	STL	P	**8.4**	9.0	0.6
Plank	STL	P	**6.3**	6.7	0.4
Kauff	BRO	CF	**6.8**	6.9	0.1

Without money to compete with the Federal League, Connie Mack sold his best remaining A's.[15] Eddie Collins went to the White Sox and Frank Baker went home; in midseason, Bob Shawkey, Jack Barry, and Eddie Murphy went to the Yankees, Red Sox, and White Sox, respectively. The A's were 28–48 (.368) in the first half; the midseason sales led them to a 15–61 (.197) second half.

Having abdicated, the A's watched the Tigers, White Sox, and Red Sox fight through August. The Tigers still had Ty Cobb, Sam Crawford, and Donie Bush, but Bobby Veach led the league in doubles, third baseman Ossie Vitt was a Donie Bush clone in his first full season as a regular, and Hooks Dauss and Harry Coveleski gave the Tigers pitching for once. The White Sox had hitting for once, adding Eddie Collins to slugging first baseman Jack Fournier, but their pitching faltered, and they blew a six-game lead with a .500 July and August. In those months, the Red Sox went 43–16, adding a 20–7 September, including taking three of four from the Tigers, to narrowly win the pennant. Tris Speaker and Smoky Joe Wood remained the stars, but the team had many contributors, as Ernie Shore, Rube Foster, and Dutch Leonard filled out the rotation; rookie Babe Ruth was a 2.7-WAR pitcher and slugged .576.

The Giants echoed the A's by starting 3–10, including 0–5 against the Phillies; trades for Cardinals pitcher Pol Perritt and Phillies third baseman Hans Lobert couldn't stop Christy Mathewson and Rube Marquard from being below-replacement (the replacement in this case being 30-year-old Sailor Stroud, a washout with the Tigers five years prior). The Braves also traded for a Phillie, slugger Sherry Magee, but Bill James could only provide 68 innings after 1914's heavy workload.

The Phillies and Cubs fought most of the summer but no team was very good; on August 10, sixth place (.505) was 3.5 games behind first (.541). The Dodgers (who on August 19 were tied for first **and** outscored on the season), Phillies, and Braves separated themselves from the quintet; the Phillies went 5–1 against the Braves in August and September and took the flag. The Phillies were not a deep team, but rookie shortstop Dave Bancroft proved adept on both sides of the ball, first baseman Fred Luderus had his best season to date, Gavvy Cravath led the league in most offensive categories, and Pete Alexander led in most pitching categories.

The Federal League as late as August 20 was still a five-team race, with the Newark Peppers (formerly defending champion Indianapolis), Kansas City Packers, Chicago Whales, and Pittsburgh Rebels separated by a half-game and the St. Louis Terriers threatening behind them. The Terriers then took consecutive series from Chicago, Kansas City, and Pittsburgh. The Rebels were the only team gaining Momentum by September 8, but they did not leverage their soft September schedule, while the Terriers won nine straight and the Whales finished 16–4 off roughly the same opponents. When the dust settled, the Whales had the highest win percentage, the Terriers had an extra win and loss to finish second, and the Rebels were in third, a half-game back.

For the champion Whales, Dutch Zwilling and Art Wilson continued to lead the offense, while Mordecai Brown made a triumphant return to Chicago for the thin pitching staff. George McConnell was the other decent starter; at age 37, he went 25–10 after a career record of 12–29. The Rebels were named for their manager, former Cardinals outfielder Rebel Oakes, whose main offensive contribution was getting Pirates first baseman Ed Konetchy to play for him.[16]

As finances brought the Federal League to an end, it ended just like league battles and joint ownership from previous decades, as the Whales merged with the Cubs and the Terriers merged with the Browns.[17]

1916: Free Wins for Everybody!

AL	BOS	CHI	DET	PHI	CLE	NY	WAS
Start	299	221	**477**	328			
6/1	282	194	**450**	301	108	23	96
7/1	297	164	**475**	271	228	108	171
8/1	371	203	**449**	240	332	232	140
9/1	**495**	262	433	209	366	201	109
End	**631**	383	509	175	332	167	75
Spt.	**1.49**	1.16	1.47	1.26	1.20	1.06	1.05

Name	*Tm*	*Pos*	*WAR*	*SpW*	*Fame*
Ruth	BOS	P/PH	**10.4**	**15.5**	**5.1**
Cobb	DET	CF	8.0	11.8	3.8
Coveleski	DET	P	6.4	**9.4**	**3.0**
Leonard	BOS	P	5.0	7.5	**2.5**
Veach	DET	LF	5.0	7.4	**2.4**
Speaker	CLE	CF	8.6	10.3	1.7
Jackson	CHI	LF/RF	7.0	8.1	1.1
Johnson	WAS	P/PH	**10.7**	11.2	0.5

NL	BOS	BRO	CHI	NY	PHI
Start	41	153	214	272	**442**
6/1	69	211	222	290	**500**

NL	BOS	BRO	CHI	NY	PHI
7/1	44	331	192	315	**595**
8/1	78	455	161	284	**604**
9/1	132	579	130	253	**613**
End	188	715	96	219	**749**
Spt.	1.12	**1.43**	1.21	1.34	1.50

Name	Tm	Pos	WAR	SpW	Fame
Alexander	PHI	P	**10.6**	**15.9**	**5.3**
Pfeffer	BRO	P	6.3	9.0	2.7
Wheat	BRO	LF	6.0	8.6	2.6
Rixey	PHI	P	4.3	6.5	2.2
Fletcher	NY	SS	6.3	8.4	2.1
Vaughn	CHI	P	6.5	7.9	1.4

Jack Nabors was 12–1 for D-ball teams in Talladega and Newnan, including a 13-inning no-hitter, when the A's purchased him in 1915 for $500. In the majors, he was 0–5 in 1915 and 1–20 in 1916. His career problems mirrored his team's; the A's started 13–18, tied for fifth, but went 23–99 after that.

So playing the A's was basically a free win. And in the final standings, seventh place was a game under .500 while the six teams above were all at least .500. Because of this and the lack of a dominant team, it was hard to be out of contention for long. The early going had the Indians, Senators, and Yankees at the top, giving way to a Red Sox–White Sox matchup. The Tigers' strong August made it a three-team race nearly to the end, but the Red Sox swept the Tigers in mid–September and won the pennant by two games. Tris Speaker was traded to Cleveland because he wouldn't take a pay cut.[18] Speaker's production was replaced by Babe Ruth becoming the second-best pitcher in the league and best slugger on the team. The Tigers were hurt by Sam Crawford finally aging and Hooks Dauss's inability to replicate 1915.

In the NL, the Cubs-nee-Whales didn't take over the league, and the Giants were on-again, off-again as they tried to find pitching. After June, the race was primarily between the Phillies and the Brooklyn Robins, with intermittent contention from the Braves. The Phillies beat the Robins consistently down the stretch, but they couldn't get more than 1.5 ahead, and the Robins took three of four from the Giants at season's end—impressive given that the Giants had just won 26 straight—to lock up the pennant.

For the Phillies, Pete Alexander threw 16 shutouts and Eppa Rixey became a reliable second starter, but import Chief Bender was awful and the offense declined across the board, something the thin roster couldn't take. The Robins got a career year out of Zack Wheat to join 1913 MVP Jake Daubert, and they rediscovered the good Rube Marquard after two years of Giants' frustration, backing up ace Jeff Pfeffer.

So nothing went as expected except for the A's losing. The Red Sox sent their best players to Cleveland and still won a pennant, while the Browns and Cubs couldn't win with two teams' worth of talent.

1917: Refreshingly Normal

AL	BOS	CHI	CLE	DET	NY	PHI	WAS
Start	**570**	346	300	460	151	158	68
6/1	**650**	441	285	435	201	133	43
7/1	**755**	561	255	405	171	103	13
8/1	**849**	685	224	374	140	72	
9/1	**933**	809	193	343	109	41	
End	900	**941**	160	310	76	8	
Spt.	1.49	**1.48**	1.20	1.33	1.09	1.04	1.01

Name	Tm	Pos	WAR	SpW	Fame
Cicotte	CHI	P	**11.4**	16.9	5.5
Ruth	BOS	P/PH	**8.6**	12.8	4.2
Cobb	DET	CF	**11.3**	15.0	3.7
Mays	BOS	P	**5.8**	8.6	2.8
Jackson	CHI	LF/RF	**5.8**	8.6	2.8
Coveleski	CLE	P	**8.3**	10.0	1.7
Bagby	CLE	P	**8.3**	10.0	1.7

NL	BOS	BRO	CHI	NY	PHI	STL
Start	132	503	68	154	527	
6/1	104	474	184	215	**583**	12
7/1	74	444	244	335	**703**	
8/1	43	413	213	459	**682**	
9/1	12	382	182	583	**651**	
End		349	149	**715**	618	
Spt.	1.11	1.36	1.18	**1.45**	1.49	1.00

Name	Tm	Pos	WAR	SpW	Fame
Alexander	PHI	P	**9.3**	13.9	4.6
Fletcher	NY	SS	**7.4**	10.7	3.3
Burns	NY	LF	**6.0**	8.7	2.7
Zimmerman	NY	3B	**5.3**	7.7	2.4
Cravath	PHI	RF	**4.4**	6.6	2.2
Vaughn	CHI	P	**6.8**	8.0	1.2
Hornsby	STL	SS	**9.9**	9.9	
Groh	CIN	3B	**7.0**	7.0	
Cooper	PIT	P	**6.9**	6.9	

On May 17, the Cubs were 22–9 and had outscored other teams in the league by over a run per game, thanks in part to a hitter-friendly stadium. The Giants were three games behind them giving up the fewest runs in the league, thanks in part to a pitcher-friendly stadium. The Phillies had no extremes but still had

Pete Alexander. After May 17, the Cubs scored the second-fewest runs in the league, while the Giants scored the most and allowed the fewest, and after July 4 only the Giants gained Momentum. (The Robins started 5–14 and never gained Momentum; the development of rookie pitcher Leon Cadore didn't offset his teammates' return to career norms.)

Gavvy Cravath and Dave Bancroft bounced back for the Phillies with support from Eppa Rixey, Chief Bender, and Milt Stock. For the Giants, only Art Fletcher, George Burns, and Jeff Tesreau were around from the previous great Giants teams, as ex-Cub Heinie Zimmerman and ex-Federal Leaguer Benny Kauff thrived. Ferdie Schupp made good on a full season after his 0.90 ERA in 1916, and Fred Anderson, another Federal League survivor, turned 1916's -2.5 WAR into an ERA title in 1917.

In the AL, the Tigers gained no Momentum; Ty Cobb, Bobby Veach, and a bunch of third starters weren't enough. The race was almost exclusively between the Red Sox and White Sox, with the latter's 30–10 finish wrapping it up by September. The Red Sox continued to have a lineup that was more good than great; Larry Gardner turned in another fine year and outfielders Duffy Lewis and Harry Hooper contributed at the plate. Babe Ruth continued to lead the pitching, winning four starts thanks to his own RBIs; Carl Mays and Dutch Leonard were also good.

But that core wasn't as strong as Chicago's, who had acquired Shoeless Joe Jackson to supplement Eddie Collins and slugging centerfielder Happy Felsch. On the mound, veteran and occasional standout Eddie Cicotte led the league in ERA while pitching 20 more innings than anyone else. With the rest of the rotation still pretty deep—Reb Russell, Red Faber, and Jim Scott were all competent—and lefty Dave Danforth providing nine starts and 122 quality relief innings, the White Sox had plenty of talent.

9. A Call to Arms and an Arms Race, 1918–1934

The Federal League's aftermath was mostly over, but a world war and gambling scandals delayed the return to "normal baseball." Once those massive events were over, however, baseball achieved new levels of stability in terms of franchise locations and external threats.

1918: No Cubs Were Harmed in the Making of This Race

AL	BOS	CHI	CLE	DET	NY	PHI	WAS
Start	560	**586**	100	193	47	5	
6/1	**660**	601	145	168	132		
7/1	**780**	596	190	138	252		10
8/1	**904**	565	219	107	276		4
9/1	**1028**	534	268	76	245		
End	**1032**	533	272	75	244		
Spt.	**1.58**	1.42	1.20	1.18	1.22	1.00	1.00

Name	Tm	Pos	WAR	SpW	Fame
Ruth	BOS	LF/P	7.4	11.7	**4.3**
Hooper	BOS	RF	4.9	7.7	**2.8**
Mays	BOS	P	3.5	5.5	**2.0**
Bush	BOS	P	3.4	5.4	**2.0**
Coveleski	CLE	P	**9.7**	**11.6**	1.9
Cobb	DET	CF	6.6	7.8	1.2
Johnson	WAS	P/PH	**11.6**	**11.6**	
Perry	PHI	P	**8.5**	**8.5**	
Sisler	STL	1B	6.8	6.8	

NL	BRO	CHI	NY	PHI
Start	208	89	**427**	369
6/1	185	106	**519**	346
7/1	155	226	**639**	316
8/1	124	350	**658**	285
9/1	93	474	**627**	254

NL	BRO	CHI	NY	PHI
End	92	478	626	253
Spt.	1.24	1.39	1.50	1.37

Name	Tm	Pos	WAR	SpW	Fame
Vaughn	CHI	P	7.8	10.8	3.0
Tyler	CHI	P	6.9	9.6	2.7
Fletcher	NY	SS	4.6	6.9	2.3
Burns	NY	LF/CF	4.3	6.5	2.2
Hollocher	CHI	SS	5.0	7.0	2.0
Grimes	BRO	P	4.7	5.8	1.1
Hornsby	STL	SS	5.4	5.4	

World War I cut the season short by a month and about 28 games.[1] For the NL, this didn't matter; the race was over after the Giants, who'd started 18–1, lost four of five to the Cubs in an 8–16 freefall in August. The Giants saw a great debut from rightfielder Ross Youngs, but Ferdie Schupp was worth -1.8 WAR in only 33 innings, leaving the pitching thin again. The Cubs, meanwhile, had three of the league's four best ERAs in Hippo Vaughn, Lefty Tyler, and Phil Douglas (imagine if offseason purchase Pete Alexander hadn't been off in the war). On offense, rookie shortstop Charlie Hollocher led the league in hits.

The AL started messily. For seven weeks the Red Sox were in front, but never by more than three games. The White Sox started contending in May, but they sank into mediocrity, expedited by Joe Jackson's entering the war's civilian work force. The Indians heated up when the White Sox cooled off, and although the Red Sox fought them and the Yankees off for awhile, they returned in mid-August. The Senators had the best record in the league after May and were four games back when the season ended; they or the Indians might have overtaken the Red Sox had the season gone its normal length.

The Red Sox were helped tremendously by the half-purchase/half-trade for Joe Bush, Wally Schang, and Amos Strunk from the A's. The best performance, however, belonged to Babe Ruth, whose bat made him primarily a position player. Ruth's 1918 remains the only time a player has reached 26 doubles, 11 triples, and 11 home runs in under 100 games. And along with George Sisler (and Andy Sonnanstine by accident[2]), Ruth is the only player since batting order data exists (1914) to bat in the top half of the lineup while being the game's starting pitcher.

1919: If Only They Hadn't Cut 14 Games

AL	BOS	CHI	CLE	DET	NY
Start	733	379	193	53	173
6/1	717	443	232	37	157
7/1	687	558	342	7	262

AL	BOS	CHI	CLE	DET	NY
8/1	656	682	311		291
9/1	625	806	280		260
End	597	918	252		232
Spt.	1.46	1.54	1.30	1.05	1.20

Name	Tm	Pos	WAR	SpW	Fame
Cicotte	CHI	P	9.5	14.6	5.1
Ruth	BOS	LF/P	10.2	14.9	4.7
Jackson	CHI	LF/RF	5.8	8.9	3.1
Williams	CHI	P	5.4	8.3	2.9
Collins	CHI	2B	5.1	7.9	2.8
Coveleski	CLE	P	6.5	7.8	1.3
Veach	DET	LF	6.6	7.8	1.2
Johnson	WAS	P/PH	10.8	10.8	

NL	BRO	CHI	NY	PHI	CIN
Start	53	274	359	145	
6/1	73	259	394	130	45
7/1	43	229	514	100	100
8/1	12	198	638	69	224
9/1		167	637	38	348
End		139	609	10	460
Spt.	1.10	1.36	1.50	1.24	1.44*

Name	Tm	Pos	WAR	SpW	Fame
Alexander	CHI	P	7.4	10.1	2.7
Fletcher	NY	SS	5.3	8.0	2.7
Vaughn	CHI	P	7.3	9.9	2.6
Burns	NY	LF	5.1	7.7	2.6
Groh	CIN	3B	5.4	7.8	2.4
Cadore	BRO	P	6.0	6.6	0.6
Adams	PIT	P	7.2	7.2	
Hornsby	STL	3B/SS	6.7	6.7	

Without shortening the season to 140 games,[3] the Black Sox scandal might not have happened. The White Sox had been gaining Momentum alone since July 14, but the Indians won ten straight in September, while the White Sox lost their last four games, so the gap between them was 3.5 games at the season's premature end. The Indians, Yankees, and White Sox were the only AL teams to gain Momentum, in large part because the White Sox started 24–7. Shoeless Joe Jackson was back, Eddie Cicotte had another monstrous year, and Lefty Williams developed from a fourth starter into a co-ace; together Cicotte and Williams started over half of Chicago's games. The Red Sox had little frontline talent outside the amazing Babe Ruth; Joe Bush was only able to make two starts.[4]

The Cubs didn't gain any Momentum, leaving the race to the Giants and Reds; the Reds' 22–8 August gained them seven games, putting them ahead for good. The Cubs got Pete Alexander back to add to a great staff, but they scored the fewest runs in the league. The Giants had some reasonable starting pitching in Jesse Barnes and Fred Toney, but Art Fletcher, George Burns, Ross Youngs, and Larry Doyle's best season in four years were the main reasons the team contended. The Reds could match Fletcher/Burns/Youngs with third baseman Heinie Groh, second baseman Morrie Rath, and centerfielder Edd Roush. Pat Moran found the Reds a rotation where previous manager Christy Mathewson had not, and their rotation was about 0.5 of WAR better than the Giants' at each spot, headlined by veteran Slim Sallee's 21 wins and 20 walks.

The offseason was filled with discussion about how honestly the World Series was played,[5] as well as the sale of Babe Ruth to the Yankees, the third such sale between the teams in the past year. Unlike the previous two, the Red Sox received no players back.[6] A thin team got thinner.

1920: Everything

AL	BOS	CHI	CLE	NY
Start	389	598	164	151
6/1	470	584	260	137
7/1	440	559	380	257
8/1	409	533	504	381
9/1	378	617	623	455
End	346	745	751	573
Spt.	1.32	1.47	**1.48**	1.23

Name	Tm	Pos	WAR	SpW	Fame
Speaker	CLE	CF	8.5	12.6	4.1
Coveleski	CLE	P	8.5	12.6	4.1
Bagby	CLE	P	8.4	12.4	4.0
Collins	CHI	2B	7.9	11.6	3.7
Jackson	CHI	LF	7.6	11.2	3.6
Ruth	NY	RF/LF	11.9	14.6	2.7
Sisler	STL	1B	9.8	9.8	

NL	CHI	CIN	NY	PHI	BRO	PIT	STL
Start	71	234	309	5			
6/1	111	334	284		76	64	
7/1	166	454	254		191	39	80
8/1	140	573	223		315	8	64
9/1	109	697	322		439		33
End	77	715	335		567		1
Spt.	1.23	1.48	1.37	1.03	**1.38**	1.03	1.06

Name	Tm	Pos	WAR	SpW	Fame
Roush	CIN	CF	5.9	8.7	**2.8**
Alexander	CHI	P	**12.1**	**14.9**	**2.8**

Name	Tm	Pos	WAR	SpW	Fame
Grimes	BRO	P	6.8	9.4	2.6
Youngs	NY	RF	6.4	8.8	2.4
Ruether	CIN	P	4.6	6.8	2.2
Bancroft	2 TM	SS	6.8	8.9	2.1
Hornsby	STL	2B	9.6	10.2	0.6

The NL was competitive early; on May 30 the Reds, Cubs, Pirates, and Robins all gained Momentum. A month later, the Pirates mostly had fallen out, and the Cardinals, off a 17–9 June, had replaced them. A 10–20 July took them right back out, and the Cubs weren't much better, leaving July to the Reds and Robins, mostly because other teams were struggling to pass .500.

The Giants climbed out of a deep hole by beating the Reds frequently in July and August; the Giants were 16–6 against the Reds in 1920, the team's best head-to-head record. But the Giants' worst record was against the Robins, and Brooklyn's ten-win streak in mid–September took them from a tie for first to five games up in just a week.

The Reds were still fine, but most of the stars trailed off slightly and Slim Sallee was ineffective. The Giants traded Art Fletcher and money for the Phillies' Dave Bancroft, which worked out great, but shortstop upgrades were not pitching upgrades, and while the staff had three 20-game winners in Fred Toney, Art Nehf, and Jesse Barnes, that had a lot to do with their run support. The Robins had ace Burleigh Grimes (who also hit .303/.358/.432) at the front of a deep staff that Wilbert Robinson mixed and matched all year. They also had the league's oldest lineup, with two top hitters in outfielders Zack Wheat and Hi Myers and two top fielders in second baseman Pete Kilduff and shortstop Ivy Olson.

In the AL, the Red Sox rode great pitching to a 21–9 start, with the Indians a half-game behind. But the Sox's lack of offense caught up with them, and the Yankees swept them at the end of May in the middle of a 18–2 run that lifted them into season-long contention. Babe Ruth (who broke his single-season home run record from 1919 on **July 19**),[7] Carl Mays, and Bob Shawkey were the Yankees' best players; all three were purchases in an era when player purchases were the nearest thing to free agent signings.

The White Sox joined the race with a five-game sweep of the Senators in mid–August. The team construction hadn't changed, and pitcher Red Faber had his best season in years. But the Indians had even better frontline talent. Eddie Collins, Joe Jackson, and Happy Felsch were great, but Tris Speaker was as good as Collins, and Jim Bagby and Stan Coveleski were the league's best pitchers. They also had standout shortstop Ray Chapman, but immeasurable tragedy struck when Carl Mays hit him with a pitch on August 16 and Chapman died the next day.⁸ The Indians went into a tailspin as they picked up the pieces; they regrouped to a strong finish.

On September 27, the Yankees were eliminated from winning the pennant, and the White Sox were a half-game behind the Indians; Buck Weaver, Joe Jackson each got a hit to help win a low-scoring game against the Tigers. Four days later, when the White Sox played their final series, Weaver and Jackson, and five other players were no longer on the team due to their role in fixing the 1919 World Series.⁹ Understandably, the White Sox lost that final series, cementing Cleveland's pennant.

1921: First Place to Second Seeds

AL	BOS	CHI	CLE	NY	DET	WAS
Start	243	522	**526**	402		
6/1	242	496	**630**	471	27	12
7/1	212	466	**750**	556		37
8/1	181	435	**874**	665		6
9/1	150	404	**998**	789		
End	119	373	**1112**	913		
Spt.	1.20	1.33	1.50	**1.47**	1.01	1.04

Name	Tm	Pos	WAR	SpW	Fame
Ruth	NY	LF/CF	**12.9**	19.0	6.1
Faber	CHI	P	**11.3**	15.0	3.7
Coveleski	CLE	P	7.0	10.5	3.5
Speaker	CLE	CF	6.4	9.6	3.2
Sewell	CLE	SS	4.8	7.2	2.4
Jones	BOS	P	6.7	8.0	1.3
Mogridge	WAS	P	**6.9**	7.2	0.3
Shocker	STL	P	7.8	7.8	

NL	BRO	CHI	CIN	NY	STL	PIT
Start	312	42	**393**	185	1	
6/1	322	17	**368**	225		100
7/1	292		**338**	260		220
8/1	261		307	309		**344**
9/1	230		276	343		**468**
End	199		245	467		**522**
Spt.	1.31	1.05	1.42	**1.43**	1.01	1.31

Name	Tm	Pos	WAR	SpW	Fame
Bancroft	NY	SS	7.4	10.6	3.2
Frisch	NY	3B/2B	6.9	9.9	3.0
Grimes	BRO	P	7.8	10.2	2.4
Rixey	CIN	P	4.8	6.8	2.0
Luque	CIN	P	4.3	6.1	1.8
Glazner	PIT	P	**5.1**	6.7	1.6
Hornsby	STL	2B	10.8	10.9	0.1

The AL race consolidated after mid–June to the Indians and Yankees, with the Yankees usually slightly behind. A six-game sweep of the Senators from August 30–September 3 put them on top, and taking three of four from the Indians with a week to go, including a 21–7 thrashing, sealed it. The Yankees went 14–8 against the Indians for the season, a major part of their victory.

The Indians were about as good in 1921 as they were in 1920. Jim Bagby was a little overworked in 1920 and couldn't maintain the pace, but George Uhle and Duster Mails completed their first full seasons creditably, while Allan Sothoron, bouncing around the league the last couple years, found his groove after joining Cleveland. The Yankees had traded (actually traded this time) with the Red Sox for veteran catcher Wally Schang and young pitcher Waite Hoyt and got vital contributions from both. Hoyt and Carl Mays were the only standout pitchers and were ridden hard. Bob Meusel provided extra slugging for the unstoppable Babe Ruth, who broke his single-season home run record for the third straight year and became the second player after John McGraw with back-to-back OBPs of over .500 (only Barry Bonds has joined them).

In the NL, the Reds started 11–24. Their first six losses were against the Pirates, who started 16–3 and were in the race through September. But the Giants swept them in five games in August and capped a ten-win streak in September by beating the Pirates twice. The Giants were 16–6 against the Pirates and won the league by four games.

The Reds had run out of hitters; neither Heinie Groh nor Edd Roush played the entire season due to holding out, and the replacements were inadequate.[10] The Pirates' lineup wasn't miles better—defense-first shortstop Rabbit Maranville batted third most of the year—but Max Carey was good, and nobody was terrible. Most importantly, manager and ex-catcher George Gibson's rotation was far and away the league's best. Babe Adams and Wilbur Cooper were longtime standouts and Earl Hamilton had been a successful reclamation project; with rookies Whitey Glazner, who gave up the fewest hits/inning in the league, and Johnny Morrison, the Pirates gave up 3.86 runs/game in a league that allowed 4.59. The Giants still were about workhorse pitching that got generous run support and good defense at key positions. In addition to Dave Bancroft's great year and Frankie Frisch's development, Ross Youngs, George Kelly, and the catching platoon of Earl Smith and Frank Snyder were key contributors.

For the first time, the World Series didn't contain a top seed by Momentum, which seems odd as an all-New York series, but the history that makes it seem odd hadn't been written yet.

1922: St. Louis and New York

AL	BOS	CHI	CLE	NY	STL
Start	65	206	**614**	504	
6/1	37	178	591	**616**	107
7/1	7	148	561	**731**	207
8/1		117	530	**855**	331
9/1		86	499	**979**	455
End		56	469	**1099**	535
Spt.	1.07	1.24	1.41	**1.57**	1.24

Name	Tm	Pos	WAR	SpW	Fame
Shawkey	NY	P	7.0	**11.0**	**4.0**
Ruth	NY	LF/RF	6.3	**9.9**	**3.6**
Speaker	CLE	CF	6.9	**9.7**	**2.8**
Coveleski	CLE	P	6.3	**8.9**	**2.6**
Bush	NY	P	4.6	**7.2**	**2.6**
Faber	CHI	P	**9.6**	**11.9**	2.3
Sisler	STL	1B	**8.7**	**10.8**	2.1
Williams	STL	LF	**7.9**	**9.8**	1.9
Shocker	STL	P	**7.3**	**9.1**	1.8
Rommel	PHI	P	**7.4**	7.4	

NL	BRO	CIN	NY	PIT	STL
Start	138	170	323	**361**	
6/1	112	144	**427**	390	25
7/1	102	114	**547**	415	30
8/1	71	83	**671**	384	104
9/1	40	52	**795**	353	148
End	10	22	**915**	323	118
Spt.	1.16	1.26	**1.58**	1.42	1.16

Name	Tm	Pos	WAR	SpW	Fame
Bancroft	NY	SS	**6.0**	**9.5**	**3.5**
Cooper	PIT	P	**6.3**	**9.0**	**2.7**
Morrison	PIT	P	**6.1**	**8.7**	**2.6**
Frisch	NY	2B/3B	4.4	7.0	**2.6**
Kelly	NY	1B	3.8	**6.0**	**2.2**
Carey	PIT	CF	5.1	**7.2**	2.1
Hornsby	STL	2B	**10.0**	**11.6**	1.6
Grimes	CHI	1B	**5.6**	5.6	

In both leagues, after June only St. Louis and New York gained Momentum. The Cardinals were a thin team kept in contention by Rogers Hornsby's dominance. Losing 11 of 14 in an August stretch, including a sweep by the Giants, sealed the Cardinals' fate. The Pirates finished with an identical record, but their 7–21 record from June 11–July 12 left too much ground to make up. The Pirates had found more offense to back Max Carey, with a breakout from Carson Bigbee and a .368/.423/.668 line in part-time outfield work for former

White Sox pitcher Reb Russell, but Whitey Glazner stumbled and there wasn't enough talent elsewhere to compensate.

By contrast, the Giants had talent seemingly everywhere. With Dave Bancroft leading off and Frankie Frisch usually batting third, there were loads of RBI opportunities for Irish Meusel, Ross Youngs, and George Kelly. Phil Douglas led the pitching until his life spiraled out of control in ways that would get him banned from baseball.[11] Rosy Ryan, in and out of the rotation most of the year, led the league in ERA with 3.01.

In the AL, the Indians' depth of role players ran out, and Babe Ruth was suspended until May 20.[12] Thus, the Browns found themselves with league's two best hitters in .420-hitting George Sisler and Ken Williams and the best pitcher in Urban Shocker. The Browns stayed competitive with the Yankees all year. The Yankees took three of four from the Browns on August 25–28—the same stretch in which the Giants swept the Cardinals—and two of three in mid–September to provide the margin of victory. The usual middle of the order hitters, Babe Ruth, Wally Pipp, Bob Meusel, and Wally Schang, all contributed, and the pitching improved with the acquisition of Bullet Joe Bush and Bob Shawkey's return to form.

1923: Triumph

AL	CHI	CLE	NY	STL	DET	PHI
Start	29	247	**579**	282		
6/1	3	271	**668**	256	4	24
7/1		241	**788**	226		14
8/1		210	**912**	195		
9/1		179	**1036**	164		
End		143	**1180**	128		
Spt.	1.03	1.39	**1.60**	1.31	1.02	1.07

Name	*Tm*	*Pos*	*WAR*	*SpW*	*Fame*
Ruth	NY	RF/LF	**14.1**	22.6	8.5
Speaker	CLE	CF	**9.0**	12.5	3.5
Pennock	NY	P	**5.8**	9.3	3.5
Uhle	CLE	P	**7.5**	10.4	2.9
Sewell	CLE	SS	**7.5**	10.4	2.9
Bush	NY	P	**4.8**	7.7	**2.9**
Williams	STL	LF	**7.6**	10.0	2.4
Heilmann	DET	RF	**9.3**	9.5	0.2

NL	BRO	CIN	NY	PIT	STL
Start	5	11	479	169	62
6/1			583	143	36
7/1			703	133	6

NL	BRO	CIN	NY	PIT	STL
8/1		24	**827**	137	
9/1		28	**951**	106	
End		2	**1095**	70	
Spt.	1.01	1.18	**1.60**	1.40	1.14

Name	Tm	Pos	WAR	Spw	*Fame*
Frisch	NY	2B	**7.1**	**11.4**	**4.3**
Bancroft	NY	SS	3.7	5.9	**2.2**
Youngs	NY	RF	3.6	5.8	**2.2**
Carey	PIT	CF	4.9	6.9	**2.0**
Luque	CIN	P	**10.6**	**12.5**	1.9
Rixey	CIN	P	**6.0**	**7.1**	1.1
Hornsby	STL	2B	**6.7**	**7.6**	0.9
Ring	PHI	P	**7.7**	**7.7**	

With Babe Ruth back for a full year and George Sisler out for the year, the Yankees had no challengers after May and won the pennant by 16 games. Despite Ruth's .393/.545/.764 line, the Yankees were only third in runs scored, but they allowed 97 fewer runs than any other AL team, as starting pitchers Bullet Joe Bush, Waite Hoyt, and Bob Shawkey were joined by former A's and Red Sox youngster Herb Pennock's best season to date.

The Giants had some resistance from the Pirates and Reds, but from May on they were always at least two games ahead. The pitching slumped to normal Giants levels—Reds ace Dolf Luque produced more WAR than the entire Giants' staff, and no Giant pitcher placed even tenth in the league in wins. But with a lineup running seven deep and Frankie Frisch, Dave Bancroft, Heinie Groh, and teenager Travis Jackson producing four of the top ten defensive WARs in the league—despite playing only three positions among them—it barely mattered who pitched.

1924: Are We Too Late?

AL	CLE	NY	STL	BOS	DET	WAS
Start	72	**590**	64			
6/1	49	**682**	111	71	47	
7/1	19	**802**	86	171	167	44
8/1		**916**	55	140	281	168
9/1		**1040**	24	109	345	292
End		**1156**		80	316	408
Spt.	1.10	1.50	1.20	1.22	1.28	**1.50***

Name	Tm	Pos	WAR	Spw	*Fame*
Ruth	NY	RF/LF	**11.7**	**17.6**	**5.9**
Pennock	NY	P	**7.9**	**11.9**	**4.0**
Johnson	WAS	P	**7.4**	**11.1**	**3.7**

Name	Tm	Pos	WAR	SpW	Fame
Goslin	WAS	LF	6.4	9.6	3.2
Zachary	WAS	P	4.7	7.1	2.4
Ehmke	BOS	P	8.3	10.0	1.7

NL	CIN	NY	PIT	BRO	CHI
Start	1	548	35		
6/1	53	640	12	24	92
7/1	23	760			182
8/1		884			151
9/1		1008	8		120
End		1124	74	116	91
Spt.	1.17	1.60	1.13	1.09	1.34

Name	Tm	Pos	WAR	SpW	Fame
Frisch	NY	2B	7.4	11.8	4.4
Youngs	NY	RF	5.9	9.4	3.5
Kelly	NY	1B	4.8	7.7	2.9
Jackson	NY	SS	4.0	6.4	2.4
Groh	NY	3B	3.4	5.4	2.0
Vance	BRO	P	10.4	11.3	0.9
Wheat	BRO	LF	6.7	7.3	0.6
Fournier	BRO	1B	6.3	6.9	0.6
Hornsby	STL	2B	12.1	12.1	

On June 24, both leagues had unfamiliar teams vying for the pennant. The Giants, with their normal formula, were trying to shake off the Cubs, a young team (over half the lineup was under 25) with major improvements from sophomores George Grantham and Gabby Hartnett. In the AL, sixth place was only three games behind first, as the Yankees had scored the second-fewest runs in the league.

The Giants, managed by Hughie Jennings while John McGraw was away, pulled away as the Cubs faded, including sweeping the Cubs on July 12–15, and found themselves alone through September. Jennings installed rookie Hack Wilson in centerfield for an injured Billy Southworth (who'd been acquired in sending Dave Bancroft to Boston); Wilson hit .378/.434/.631 with Jennings managing, helping keep the team afloat.[13]

Meanwhile, the AL was a fight among the Yankees, Tigers, and Senators. The Yankees had stabilized their offense around the usual suspects—Babe Ruth and complementary pieces—while the pitching core remained the team's strength. The Tigers were winning with their old strategy: Ty Cobb and another outfielder driving in a waterbug, high-OBP middle infielder (Harry Heilmann and Topper Rigney, respectively). Catcher Johnny Bassler and first baseman Lu Blue rounded out a lineup with five players over .400 OBP. For the Senators, Goose Goslin, Sam Rice, and Joe Judge were all excellent hitters, Roger Peckinpaugh fielded everything at shortstop, and longtime ace Walter Johnson was in top form.

The Senators came to New York and took three of four, and first place, from the Yankees at the end of August. At the same time, the Robins swept the Giants in Brooklyn, compounding the Giants' problems from getting swept by the Pirates earlier in August—events that cut the Giants' lead from seven games to two and let the Robins and Pirates breathe down the Giants' neck. But the Giants and Senators held their narrow leads, capping exciting and unexpected races.

1925: Old York

AL	BOS	DET	NY	WAS	CHI	CLE	PHI
Start	44	172	630	222			
6/1	18	146	604	306	24	3	88
7/1		116	574	426			208
8/1		85	543	550			312
9/1		54	512	674			421
End		21	479	806			388
Spt.	1.04	1.23	1.46	**1.54**	1.03	1.00	1.23

Name	Tm	Pos	WAR	SpW	Fame
Johnson	WAS	P	6.9	**10.6**	**3.7**
Goslin	WAS	LF/CF	6.5	10.0	3.5
Coveleski	WAS	P	6.5	10.0	3.5
Pennock	NY	P	6.6	9.6	3.0
Shocker	NY	P	5.7	8.3	2.6
Heilmann	DET	RF	6.9	8.5	1.6

NL	BRO	CHI	NY	PIT
Start	65	51	628	41
6/1	42	28	720	18
7/1	12		840	68
8/1			964	192
9/1			983	316
End			950	448
Spt.	1.19	1.12	**1.50**	1.44*

Name	Tm	Pos	WAR	SpW	Fame
Cuyler	PIT	RF	6.9	9.5	**2.9**
Scott	NY	P	5.4	8.1	2.7
Frisch	NY	3B/2B	4.0	6.0	2.0
Kelly	NY	2B/1B	3.7	5.6	1.9
Carey	PIT	CF	4.2	6.0	1.8
Hornsby	STL	2B	**10.2**	**10.2**	
Rixey	CIN	P	6.1	6.1	
Vance	BRO	P	6.1	6.1	
Luque	CIN	P	6.0	6.0	

The Senators started the season 7–3, 6–2 of it against the Yankees. Babe Ruth didn't play until June, and he came back to a 15–25 team; it wasn't until August that the Yankees even won three straight. The A's filled the void by starting

20–5, receiving simultaneous development from pitchers Slim Harriss and Sam Gray and outfielder Al Simmons to join the continued quality work of Eddie Rommel. The race stayed tight between the A's and Senators until the A's lost 11 straight from August 24 to September 7, the last two against the Senators. They righted the ship, but they had given up eight games in the standings, which was the final margin of victory. The Senators' hitting had aged a bit, making Goose Goslin more clearly the leader of the lineup, but the rebound acquisitions of pitchers Stan Coveleski and Dutch Ruether gave 38 more wins to complement Walter Johnson. As Coveleski was 35 years old and Johnson 37–and no rotation had ever relied so much on aging talent—manager and second baseman Bucky Harris used young Firpo Marberry exclusively in relief, giving him more important roles as the season progressed.[14]

The Giants started off as hot as the A's with, of all things, pitching. Jacks Scott and Bentley headlined as the offense figured to catch up soon, and on May 23 the team was 6.5 games ahead of the second-place Robins. But Travis Jackson and Ross Youngs struggled, and a 13–14 June, headlined by Bentley's 0–3, 9.38 showing, included losing four straight to the Pirates. The Giants were a .500 team after a 24–8 start, and while the Pirates and Giants fought it out most of the season, the Pirates won nine straight heading into September to stay comfortably ahead. The Pirates were built around the same offensive core as in 1924, with Glenn Wright and Kiki Cuyler continuing to excel alongside Max Carey. An offseason trade with the Cubs—Rabbit Maranville, Charlie Grimm, and Wilbur Cooper for primarily George Grantham and Vic Aldridge—paid immediate dividends. Cooper and Maranville were coming off great seasons but started aging in 1925, while Grantham moved from second base to first base competently to replace Grimm and Aldridge joined Lee Meadows and Ray Kremer as dependable, if unspectacular, starters.

1926: Easy Mode and Hard Mode

AL	DET	NY	PHI	WAS	CLE	CHI
Start	11	245	199	413		
6/1		350	204	458	22	30
7/1		470	174	428		
8/1		594	143	397		
9/1		718	112	366		
End		830	84	338	33	
Spt.	1.03	1.56	1.30	1.44	1.04	1.07

Name	*Tm*	*Pos*	*WAR*	*SpW*	*Fame*
Ruth	NY	LF/RF	11.5	17.9	6.4
Gehrig	NY	1B	6.8	10.6	3.8

Name	Tm	Pos	WAR	SpW	Fame
Goslin	WAS	LF/CF	**6.8**	9.8	3.0
Shocker	NY	P	4.7	7.3	2.6
Grove	PHI	P	**7.4**	9.6	2.2
Uhle	CLE	P/PH	**8.7**	9.0	0.3

NL	NY	PIT	BRO	CHI	CIN	STL
Start	475	224				
6/1	453	197	39	80	108	
7/1	423	287	9	80	228	72
8/1	392	371		79	352	106
9/1	361	**495**		48	471	205
End	333	502	20		**583**	317
Spt.	1.44	1.42	1.03	1.12	1.31	1.46*

Name	Tm	Pos	WAR	SpW	Fame
Kremer	PIT	P	**5.9**	8.4	2.5
Waner	PIT	RF	5.3	7.5	2.2
Frisch	NY	2B	4.6	6.6	2.0
Hornsby	STL	2B	4.4	6.4	2.0
Bell	STL	3B	4.4	6.4	2.0
Wilson	CHI	CF	5.2	5.8	0.6
Root	CHI	P	5.2	5.8	0.6
Petty	BRO	P	5.3	5.5	
Carlson	PHI	P	**8.3**	8.3	0.2

The Yankees started 30–9, including a 16-win streak in May; by its end, they were up by 8.5 games and had staved off all challengers. Although losing four of six to the Indians in September gave Cleveland a small chance, the Yankees were always ahead. The Senators were still good but saw slight declines from their oldest stars, while the Yankees found their offense again—their pitching WAR declined from their seventh-place 1925 team but they won 22 more games.

The NL champion Cardinals only ended two games worse than the Yankees, but the race was chaotic. Even with the Giants' pitching disappearing and Ross Youngs's illness ending his season in August, the Giants were occasionally within view of the top, still only 4.5 back on July 18 because no team was particularly good. The Reds had looked the best through most of the year, and they alone were gaining Momentum around July 4, led by exceptional depth— they would become the first team with eight hitters at 2.5 WAR or above. Hughie Critz was an outstanding defensive 2B, and Bubbles Hargrave, Curt Walker, and the leftfield platoon of rookie Cuckoo Christensen and former A's pitcher Rube Bressler helped the team to an absurd .815 mark (22–5) against left-handed pitching. But the Giants swept the Reds July 9–11 over four games, and so a few weeks later everybody but the Braves and Phillies had a legitimate chance at getting hot and taking first place.

By August, the race was between the Reds, Cardinals, and Pirates. In September, the Pirates' offense ran out, and the Reds won eight straight and then lost six straight, giving the pennant to the Cardinals. The Cardinals were similarly deep to the Reds, but instead of the Reds' black hole at shortstop, they had Tommy Thevenow, whose deadball-esque .256/.291/.311 was more than offset by his defense, and MVP catcher Bob O'Farrell. Rogers Hornsby's .317/.388/.463 was down from 1925's .403/.489/.756, but it was still plenty good; young corner infielders Les Bell and Jim Bottomley rounded out the offensive core.

The World Series, ending with Babe Ruth caught stealing,[15] was an instant classic and a fittingly weird end to a fundamentally weird season.

1927: Palette Swap

AL	CLE	NY	PHI	WAS	CHI
Start	17	438	44	178	
6/1		544	30	159	86
7/1		664		129	96
8/1		788		98	65
9/1		912		67	34
End		1036		36	3
Spt.	1.03	**1.60**	1.11	1.40	1.26

Name	Tm	Pos	WAR	SpW	Fame
Ruth	NY	RF/LF	**12.4**	19.8	7.4
Gehrig	NY	1B	**11.8**	18.9	7.1
Combs	NY	CF	6.8	10.9	4.1
Lazzeri	NY	2B	6.3	10.1	3.8
Hoyt	NY	P	5.7	9.1	3.4
Moore	NY	P	5.6	9.0	3.4
Thomas	CHI	P	**8.4**	10.6	2.2
Lyons	CHI	P	**7.4**	9.3	1.9
Heilmann	DET	RF	**7.2**	7.2	

NL	CHI	CIN	NY	PIT	STL	PHI
Start	16	473	270	408	257	
6/1	58	445	352	**485**	324	10
7/1	123	415	322	**605**	364	
8/1	247	384	291	**729**	393	
9/1	371	353	275	**788**	392	
End	390	322	349	**912**	471	
Spt.	1.15	1.36	1.21	**1.58**	1.30	1.00

Name	Tm	Pos	WAR	SpW	Fame
P. Waner	PIT	RF	6.9	10.9	4.0
Kremer	PIT	P	6.7	10.6	3.9
Meadows	PIT	P	5.3	8.4	3.1
Frisch	STL	2B	**9.2**	12.0	2.8

9. *A Call to Arms and an Arms Race* 143

Name	Tm	Pos	WAR	SpW	Fame
Hill	PIT	P	4.6	7.3	**2.7**
Hornsby	NY	2B	**10.1**	**12.2**	2.1
Vance	BRO	P	**7.8**	7.8	

The story wasn't much different in the AL than it was in 1926. Going into June, the Yankees were trying to fight off the surprising White Sox under rookie manager and veteran catcher Ray Schalk. The Yankees took three of four from the Sox June 7–10, after which the Yankees played .731 ball and the White Sox .376. Besides their robust hitting—they remain the only team with 6.3+ WAR from four hitters—Waite Hoyt and 30-year-old rookie swingman Wilcy Moore made big contributions. The team scored 6.3 runs/game in a league averaging 4.9.

The NL was down to the wire again with several teams, but the Reds weren't one of them after starting 7–20. Red Lucas became a frontline talent on the mound and at the plate, but the 1926 Reds had been built on depth and that depth mostly took a step back. The Cardinals had traded Rogers Hornsby for Frankie Frisch[16] and now had a full season of Pete Alexander, but they fell a little behind the Pirates early.

First place belonged to the Pirates in June and the Cubs in July and August. At the end of August, Hornsby's hard-hitting Giants swept Hack Wilson's Cubs and entered the picture, while the Cubs started a 1–10 freefall. But they and everyone else fell to the Pirates' 19–3 run that took them from two back to 4.5 up, enough to survive a stumble in the final two weeks and win the pennant.

Similar to the Yankees, the Pirates had a near-rookie, wrong-side-of-30 righthander providing a lot of value, as Carmen Hill, who had scrubbed out of the 1915–1919 Pirates and hadn't been seen much in the majors since then, won 22 games. On offense, slugger Paul Waner, his rookie brother Lloyd, and 36-year-old waiver pickup Joe Harris were all top-10 in AVG and OBP.

1928: Two-Year Reunion

AL	CHI	NY	WAS	CLE	PHI	STL
Start	2	518	18			
6/1		611		29		
7/1		731				
8/1		855				
9/1		979			31	
End		1095			147	
Spt.	1.04	1.60	1.07	1.13	1.09	1.03

Name	Tm	Pos	WAR	SpW	Fame
Ruth	NY	RF/LF	**10.1**	**16.2**	**6.1**
Gehrig	NY	1B	9.4	15.0	5.6

Name	Tm	Pos	WAR	SpW	Fame
Pennock	NY	P	5.8	**9.3**	3.5
Pipgras	NY	P	4.8	**7.7**	2.9
Hoyt	NY	P	4.7	7.5	2.8
Grove	PHI	P	**6.9**	7.5	0.6
Goslin	WAS	LF	**7.5**	**8.0**	0.5
Manush	STL	LF	**7.3**	7.5	0.2

NL	**CHI**	**CIN**	**NY**	**PIT**	**STL**	**BRO**
Start	390	322	349	**912**	471	
6/1	471	438	435	**903**	537	24
7/1	456	498	450	**873**	647	
8/1	425	467	444	**842**	771	
9/1	394	436	478	811	**895**	
End	395	407	554	782	**1011**	
Spt.	1.18	1.23	1.19	1.47	**1.53**	1.00

Name	Tm	Pos	WAR	SpW	Fame
P. Waner	PIT	RF	6.8	**10.0**	3.2
Sherdel	STL	P	5.5	**8.4**	2.9
Bottomley	STL	1B	5.3	**8.1**	2.8
Hafey	STL	LF	5.0	7.7	2.7
Grimes	PIT	P	5.5	**8.1**	2.6
Benton	NY	P	**6.6**	7.9	1.3
Lindstrom	NY	3B	**6.3**	7.5	1.2
Vance	BRO	P	**10.0**	**10.0**	
Hornsby	BOS	2B	**8.8**	**8.8**	

The Yankees started 39–8, holding a 13.5-game lead on July 1 after beating the A's in a doubleheader. But the pitching declined in the second half enough that they were merely good the rest of the way; meanwhile, the A's had found their offense and went 44–17 over July and August. They hadn't had to face the Yankees in that time, but their tear against the rest of the league put them up by a half-game for the next meeting, a doubleheader on September 8 to start a four-game series. The Yankees swept the doubleheader and took the series, and that was almost the entire margin of victory at season's end. Most of the league's best hitters were on one team or the other and the A's rotation was deeper, but the A's went 6–16 against the Yankees.

In the NL, everybody but the Braves and Phillies finished over .500. The Pirates started well, and getting Burleigh Grimes from the Giants worked out great, but Lee Meadows was hurt and Ray Kremer aged. The Cardinals' 20–6 June left them largely unopposed through July and August, but their offense struggled in August, and much like in 1927, the Giants put themselves back into the race by sweeping the Cardinals August 17–19.

With two weeks to go, the Cardinals had the Giants and Cubs hot on their heels; all three gained Momentum as late as September 14. The Giants won four straight doubleheaders against the Braves but then had no more games against the Braves or Phillies. The Cubs still had seven against them and would win five; the Cardinals won all eight of theirs and narrowly stayed on top. The Cardinals were 8–14 against the Giants and 11–11 against the Cubs, but unlike the A's, bowing to their closest competition didn't hurt them, since they went 20–2 against the Phillies.

The Giants and Cubs were revitalized by ace pitching. For the Giants, Larry Benton was backed by a superb defensive infield. For the Cubs, breakout Sheriff Blake and rookie Pat Malone were a fine mound duo to support Hack Wilson's and Gabby Hartnett's slugging. But the Cardinals had the best overall rotation, with Pete Alexander and Jesse Haines getting great support from Bill Sherdel and 37-year-old Clarence Mitchell, the latter of whom had been cut by the Phillies early in the year.

1929: Midsummer Slumpers

AL	NY	PHI	DET	STL
Start	**547**	74		
6/1	**566**	148	39	57
7/1	**536**	268	9	27
8/1	**505**	392		
9/1	474	**516**		
End	439	**656**		
Spt.	1.47	**1.53**	1.08	1.13

Name	Tm	Pos	WAR	SpW	Fame
Simmons	PHI	LF	**7.9**	**12.1**	**4.2**
Foxx	PHI	1B	**7.9**	**12.1**	**4.2**
Grove	PHI	P	7.1	10.9	3.8
Ruth	NY	RF/LF	**8.0**	11.8	3.8
Lazzeri	NY	2B	7.8	11.5	3.7
Gehrig	NY	1B	7.6	11.2	3.6
Walberg	PHI	P	6.0	9.2	3.2

NL	CHI	CIN	NY	PIT	STL	BOS
Start	395	407	554	782	**1011**	
6/1	483	385	532	835	**1099**	1
7/1	598	355	532	955	**1204**	
8/1	722	324	501	1059	**1173**	
9/1	846	293	470	1028	**1142**	
End	986	258	435	993	**1107**	
Spt.	1.36	1.11	1.23	1.40	**1.50**	1.00

Name	Tm	Pos	WAR	SpW	Fame
Hornsby	CHI	2B	**10.4**	**14.1**	3.7
Hafey	STL	LF	4.3	6.5	2.2

Name	Tm	Pos	WAR	SpW	Fame
Wilson	CHI	CF	6.1	8.3	2.2
Grimes	PIT	P	5.3	7.4	2.1
P. Waner	PIT	RF	4.8	6.7	1.9
Mitchell	STL	P	3.8	5.7	1.9
Ott	NY	RF	7.4	9.1	1.7
Lucas	CIN	PH/P	6.9	7.6	0.7
O'Doul	PHI	LF	7.4	7.4	

Like in 1928, the top AL hitters were Yankees and A's, with nearly identical heroes for both teams and fantastic catchers (rookie Bill Dickey for the Yankees and 1928 MVP Mickey Cochrane for the A's). But the Yankees' pitching slumped terribly, with only spot starter Tom Zachary as a reliable arm; eight AL pitchers outproduced the Yankees' team pitching WAR. Three of those pitchers—Lefty Grove, Rube Walberg, and George Earnshaw—were A's, and their production explained almost the entire 18-game gap between the two clubs at season's end.

On June 15, while the A's were nine games up, the Cardinals were 1.5 up on the Cubs and Pirates and five up on the Giants. But they went 6–23 between June 15 and July 15, including 0–4 against the Pirates and 1–8 against the Cubs, that left them 14 games back. Rookie manager Billy Southworth was fired soon after, replaced by Bill McKechnie, who had managed them the previous year.[17] Much of the decline was due to Bill Sherdel's and Jesse Haines's collapses, though with an average age of 34 in the 1928 rotation, it wasn't hard to see happening to **someone**.

On July 15, the Pirates were 2.5 games in front of the Cubs. But while the Pirates had a rough August that led to the firing of the Pirates' rough August as part of an 11–21 stretch (after which manager Donie Bush resigned in disgust),[18] the Cubs went 33–9 right after July 15 to enter September 11.5 games up and coast to the pennant.

The Pirates were led by the Waner brothers and George Grantham on offense while continuing to receive great pitching from Burleigh Grimes and a bounceback season from Ray Kremer. The Cubs were three pitchers and four hitters deep behind Pat Malone, Charlie Root, and Guy Bush on the mound and Rogers Hornsby, Hack Wilson, Riggs Stephenson, and Kiki Cuyler at the plate. Hornsby had his sixth 10-WAR season; at the time, Honus Wagner was the only other NL batsman to have had even one.

1930: Last-Minute Cardinals, First-Minute A's

AL	NY	PHI	CLE	WAS
Start	220	328		
6/1	195	398	17	100

9. A Call to Arms and an Arms Race   147

AL	NY	PHI	CLE	WAS
7/1	260	**518**	37	215
8/1	234	**642**	6	264
9/1	203	**766**		233
End	176	**874**		206
Spt.	1.35	**1.60**	1.11	1.31

Name	Tm	Pos	WAR	SpW	Fame
Grove	PHI	P	9.5	**15.2**	5.7
Simmons	PHI	LF	7.8	**12.5**	4.7
Foxx	PHI	1B	7.1	**11.4**	4.3
Ruth	NY	RF/LF	**10.3**	13.9	3.6
Gehrig	NY	1B	9.6	13.0	3.4
Cochrane	PHI	C	5.5	8.8	3.3
Cronin	WAS	SS	**8.4**	11.0	2.6
Ferrell	CLE	P/PH	**9.1**	10.1	1.0

NL	CHI	CIN	NY	PIT	STL	BRO
Start	779	204	344	784	875	
6/1	847	177	377	817	938	78
7/1	922	147	347	787	908	198
8/1	1046	116	316	756	877	322
9/1	1155	85	315	725	846	371
End	1263	58	303	698	929	404
Spt.	1.44	1.04	1.16	1.31	**1.54**	1.10

Name	Tm	Pos	WAR	SpW	Fame
Wilson	CHI	CF	**7.4**	10.7	3.3
Cuyler	CHI	RF/LF	5.9	**8.5**	2.6
Frisch	STL	2B	4.7	7.2	2.5
English	CHI	3B/SS	5.5	**7.9**	2.4
Hartnett	CHI	C	5.4	**7.8**	2.4
Terry	NY	1B	**7.6**	8.8	1.2
Vance	BRO	P	**7.1**	7.8	0.7
Herman	BRO	RF	**6.9**	7.6	0.7
Klein	PHI	RF	**6.5**	6.5	

The Cardinals started 23–13; on May 26, this left them a half-game ahead of the Robins. But the ascending Cubs swept them on the way up, and the Cardinals bottomed out. The Cubs lost Rogers Hornsby to injury but received Gabby Hartnett back from injury, and although Guy Bush's 6.20 ERA wasn't helpful, Hack Wilson drove in runs at a record pace and Woody English developed into an on-base machine. In June, July, and August, the Cubs and Robins were alone at the top, with the Cubs pulling ahead as September arrived.

The Robins swept the Cubs September 9–11 as part of a ten-win streak, leaving them in first with ten games left. But the next three were against the Cardinals, who'd recovered from a .500 record with a 29–8 rush, and the Cardinals swept to gain narrow but permanent control of first place. The Cardinals had no standouts, but Frankie Frisch and Chick Hafey were productive, and all ten primary pitchers had better-than-average ERAs, highlighted by June pickup Burleigh Grimes.

The AL was a four-team race in mid–June, featuring the expected A's and Yankees and the unexpected Senators and Indians. Neither the Indians nor the Yankees had the pitching to keep up, leaving the race to the A's and Senators. The A's won eight straight July 10–18, outscoring opponents 97–38, pulling away from the Senators to win easily.

For the Senators, 23-year-old Joe Cronin became baseball's best shortstop, while old hands Sam Rice and Joe Judge provided more offense. A June trade with the Browns that swapped star outfielders—Goose Goslin for Heinie Manush—also netted General Crowder, who joined young Bump Hadley, 6–16 the previous year, as the heads of a six-deep staff. But the A's were deep too, and their staff was led by Lefty Grove, who went 28–5 and posted an ERA 0.77 better than the nearest pitcher. And Al Simmons, Jimmie Foxx, Mickey Cochrane, and Max Bishop were all outstanding hitters that only the Yankees had the talent to match.

1931: Oh, So It's Just Them Again

AL	NY	PHI	WAS	CLE	DET
Start	88	**437**	103		
6/1	138	**507**	128		
7/1	108	**627**	163		
8/1	77	**751**	132		
9/1	46	**875**	101		
End	20	**979**	75		
Spt.	1.32	**1.60**	1.38	1.03	1.03

Name	Tm	Pos	WAR	SpW	Fame
Grove	PHI	P	**10.1**	16.2	6.1
Simmons	PHI	LF	7.5	12.0	4.5
Bishop	PHI	2B	5.8	9.3	3.5
Walberg	PHI	P	5.7	9.1	3.4
Ruth	NY	RF/LF	**10.3**	13.6	3.3
Cochrane	PHI	C	5.4	8.6	3.2
Earnshaw	PHI	P	5.0	8.0	3.0
Gehrig	NY	1B	**8.8**	11.6	2.8
Cronin	WAS	SS	6.8	**9.4**	2.6
Ferrell	CLE	P	**8.0**	8.2	0.2

NL	BRO	CHI	CIN	NY	PIT	STL	BOS
Start	329	**1030**	47	247	569	757	
6/1	306	**1012**	24	339	546	814	58
7/1	276	**992**		399	516	934	28
8/1	245	961		383	485	**1058**	

NL	BRO	CHI	CIN	NY	PIT	STL	BOS
9/1	214	930		352	454	1182	
End	188	904		326	428	1286	
Spt.	1.12	1.45	1.00	1.18	1.30	**1.55**	1.00

Name	Tm	Pos	WAR	SpW	Fame
Hornsby	CHI	2B	5.2	**7.5**	**2.3**
Hafey	STL	LF	4.2	**6.5**	**2.3**
Hallahan	STL	P	4.2	**6.5**	**2.3**
English	CHI	SS	4.9	**7.1**	**2.2**
Gelbert	STL	SS	3.6	5.6	**2.0**
Terry	NY	1B	6.1	**7.2**	1.1
Ott	NY	RF	**5.6**	6.6	1.0
Benge	PHI	P	**6.2**	6.2	
Clark	BRO	P	**5.8**	5.8	
Berger	BOS	CF	**5.7**	5.7	

Thanks to the NL, the World Series hadn't been a complete repeat since 1923. And with the defending champion Cardinals threatened in late May by the Giants and Braves, and with the Cubs getting Rogers Hornsby back, anything was possible. But the Braves collapsed to their usual record, and the Cubs had neither back end pitching nor a way to replace Hack Wilson's sudden drop in production. The Giants had more pitching than usual, but a rough July, including a series loss to the Cardinals, sent them far enough back that the Cardinals spent the last half of the season alone. The Cardinals again relied on Chick Hafey, Frankie Frisch, and an interchangeably good pitching staff; rookie Paul Derringer was placed into the rotation in June and excelled.

In the AL, it looked like the A's were going to be unchallenged after winning 20 of 21, including five of six against the Yankees, in May. But a week later the Senators started a 12-win streak of their own, resulting in the absurdity of the Senators playing .696 ball but remaining 2.5 games behind the .755 A's. The Senators' offense couldn't keep up, and the A's 13-win streak in mid–July created an impassable gulf. For the A's, Lefty Grove's 31–4 record obscured that he only gave up six runs total in the first three losses. Meanwhile, George Earnshaw and Rube Walberg were aces in their own right, and Al Simmons, Jimmie Foxx, Mickey Cochrane, and Max Bishop were more than enough offensive talent to support such great pitching.

1932: Three Arms to One

AL	NY	PHI	WAS	CLE
Start	10	**489**	38	
6/1	90	**459**	118	30
7/1	210	**429**	98	

150   PART II. MOMENTUM: SEASONS AND NARRATIVES

AL	NY	PHI	WAS	CLE
8/1	334	398	67	
9/1	458	367	36	
End	554	343	12	
Spt.	1.48	1.47	1.33	1.08

Name	Tm	Pos	WAR	SpW	Fame
Foxx	PHI	1B	10.5	15.4	4.9
Grove	PHI	P	9.0	13.2	4.2
Ruth	NY	RF/LF	8.3	12.3	4.0
Gehrig	NY	1B	7.9	11.7	3.8
Ruffing	NY	P/PH	7.9	11.7	3.8

NL	BRO	CHI	NY	PIT	STL	BOS	CIN	PHI
Start	140	673	243	319	958			
6/1	113	781	216	292	931	100	4	
7/1	83	901	186	307	901	220		8
8/1	52	960	155	431	875	229		
9/1	71	1064	124	495	844	208		
End	47	1160	100	471	820	184		
Spt.	1.04	1.55	1.14	1.30	1.45	1.13	1.00	1.00

Name	Tm	Pos	WAR	SpW	Fame
Warneke	CHI	P	6.9	10.7	3.8
D. Dean	STL	P	6.0	8.7	2.7
Bi. Herman	CHI	2B	3.5	5.4	1.9
Stephenson	CHI	LF	3.3	5.1	1.8
P. Waner	PIT	RF	5.5	7.2	1.7
Ott	NY	RF	7.9	9.0	1.1
Terry	NY	1B	7.2	8.2	1.0
Hubbell	NY	P	6.7	7.6	0.9
Ba. Herman	CIN	RF	6.6	6.6	

Apart from one game, the A's April schedule was entirely Yankees and Senators. When the calendar turned to May, the A's were 4–10, having given up the most runs in the league. From there, they scored the most runs in the league and allowed the fewest, finishing with 94 wins, but the damage had been done. Rube Walberg aged and George Earnshaw had a home run problem to go with his chronic wildness, making the A's pitching Lefty Grove and fourth starters.

That would have been enough against recent Yankee teams, but the Yankees finally found a rotation to complement Babe Ruth, Lou Gehrig, Tony Lazzeri, Earle Combs, and young star Ben Chapman. Red Ruffing was great, Lefty Gomez won 24 games, and rookie Johnny Allen gave up the fewest hits/inning in the league (barely beating out Ruffing). The Senators kept up through the beginning of June, but after that it was the Yankees all the way.

The NL race was as chaotic as in 1926. May and June was primarily between the Cubs and Braves. But many Braves hitters were playing above their heads, so entering July 4 the newly named Dodgers' seventh place losing record was only 4.5 games out of first. Something had to give, and it turned out to be both season-long contenders, as the Pirates surged past both of them to be up 5.5 games at the end of July. But the Pirates went 2–16 from July 30 to August 19, letting the Braves back into the race by losing four of five to them. More importantly, it gave first place back to the Cubs, who'd fired manager Rogers Hornsby in August, replaced him with first baseman Charlie Grimm,[19] and won 14 straight starting August 20, shaking off the Pirates and Robins.

The Cardinals gained Momentum only on July 2. While rookie Dizzy Dean fortified the rotation, the lineup gave out. The sale/trade of Chick Hafey to the Reds worked out so terribly that the two players the Cardinals received played just 30 games total before the Reds re-purchased them. The Cubs won with a sturdy, if average, lineup, the league's best pitcher in Lon Warneke, and great infield defense from second baseman Billy Herman, shortstop Billy Jurges, and third baseman Woody English.

On the first day of the World Series, Connie Mack sold Al Simmons, Jimmie Dykes, and Mule Haas to the White Sox.[20] It was the only sale the A's made that offseason, but it was ominous.

1933: The Fatal Tenth Inning

AL	NY	PHI	WAS	CHI	CLE
Start	277	172	6		
6/1	381	166	105	79	69
7/1	501	136	170	49	39
8/1	615	105	294	18	8
9/1	619	74	418		
End	589	44	538		
Spt.	1.50	1.34	**1.46**	1.12	1.07

Name	Tm	Pos	WAR	SpW	Fame
Gehrig	NY	1B	6.9	**10.4**	3.5
Cronin	WAS	SS	7.2	**10.5**	3.3
Ruth	NY	RF/LF	6.4	**9.6**	3.2
Foxx	PHI	1B	9.2	**12.3**	3.1
Grove	PHI	P	7.7	**10.3**	2.6
Gehringer	DET	2B	**7.2**	7.2	
Hadley	STL	P	**7.2**	7.2	

NL	BOS	BRO	CHI	NY	PIT	STL
Start	116	30	**729**	63	296	515
6/1	94	8	**707**	151	384	548
7/1	64		**682**	271	414	648
8/1	33		**696**	395	393	622
9/1	2		**665**	519	382	591

NL	BOS	BRO	CHI	NY	PIT	STL
End			635	639	352	561
Spt.	1.10	1.00	1.50	1.36*	1.26	1.39

Name	Tm	Pos	WAR	SpW	Fame
Warneke	CHI	P	**6.5**	9.8	3.3
Hubbell	NY	P	**8.8**	12.0	3.2
D. Dean	STL	P	5.6	7.8	2.2
Jurges	CHI	SS	4.2	6.3	**2.1**
Martin	STL	3B	5.2	7.2	2.0
Ott	NY	RF/CF	5.5	**7.5**	**2.0**
Vaughan	PIT	SS	**7.0**	8.8	1.8
Berger	BOS	CF	**6.8**	7.5	0.7
Klein	PHI	RF	**7.5**	7.5	

The AL started out slowly, with the Yankees, Senators, Indians, talent-infused White Sox, and talent-defused A's viable at the end of May, narrowing to just the Senators and Yankees. The Senators had been lucky through early June, scoring as many runs as they allowed but going 27–21. That luck turned to thrashing when the Senators went on a 23–4 tear that left them four games up on July 9. The Yankees responded with a nine-win streak, but a rough August took them out of the pennant picture.

The Yankees' offense was still second to none, but Lefty Gomez was the only reliable pitcher and the bullpen was so bad that the Yankees went 1–9 in extra-inning games. On the flipside, the Senators went 13–6 in games that went past nine innings and were the most balanced team in the league. Double-play combo Buddy Myer and Joe Cronin (the latter of whom was also the manager) were good on both sides of the ball, General Crowder won 24 games, and trades with the Tigers for pitcher Earl Whitehill and the Browns for pitcher Lefty Stewart, outfielder Fred Schulte, and the returning Goose Goslin paid off handsomely.

In winning the NL, the Giants were challenged almost in sequence by the teams ahead of them in Momentum. The Pirates were easiest to fend off, as they were giving up as many runs as they scored. The Cardinals were revitalized by Pepper Martin's resurgence, rookie leftfielder Joe Medwick's bat, and the development of pitcher Tex Carleton behind ace Dizzy Dean. But a 10–22 slide took them out of contention and resulted in second baseman Frankie Frisch becoming the manager.[21]

Next were the Cubs, who swept the Giants July 7–9 as part of a 15–2 run. Trading for Babe Herman put some thump back in the lineup; otherwise, the team was virtually unchanged. After their 15–2 stretch, they lost six straight to the Pirates and Cardinals and bowed out of the race. The series win put the Pirates back in the race, but their 5–13 slump in August left the Giants unopposed. The Giants stayed consistent all year thanks largely to Carl Hubbell's 1.66 ERA, the lowest for any pitcher since 1919. 22-year-old Hal Schumacher blossomed from a mediocre rookie into a second ace. Patient slugger Mel Ott was followed in the lineup by corner infielders Johnny Vergez and Bill Terry (and, after a June trade, Lefty O'Doul) to good effect; Terry was also the rookie manager after John McGraw's retirement.

1934: Momentum to New York, Pennants Elsewhere

AL	NY	PHI	WAS	CLE	DET	STL
Start	294	22	269			
6/1	385	3	265	48	25	
7/1	505		270	88	145	
8/1	629		239	57	269	
9/1	643		208	26	393	
End	614		179		509	
Spt.	1.50	1.07	1.36	1.17	1.36	1.01

Name	Tm	Pos	WAR	SpW	Fame
Gehrig	NY	1B	10.4	15.6	5.2
Gomez	NY	P	8.2	12.3	4.1
Gehringer	DET	2B	8.4	11.4	3.0
Rowe	DET	P	7.1	9.7	2.6
Ruth	NY	RF/LF	5.1	7.7	2.6
Harder	CLE	P	7.4	8.7	1.3
Foxx	PHI	1B	8.9	9.5	0.6

NL	CHI	NY	PIT	STL	BOS
Start	468	471	259	413	
6/1	568	556	339	508	4
7/1	643	676	349	603	
8/1	737	800	318	582	
9/1	741	924	287	551	
End	712	1040	258	572	
Spt.	1.42	1.48	1.20	1.40	1.01

Name	Tm	Pos	WAR	SpW	Fame
Ott	NY	RF	7.3	10.8	3.5
Hubbell	NY	P	7.2	10.7	3.5
D. Dean	STL	P	8.5	11.9	3.4
Terry	NY	1B	5.8	8.6	2.8
Collins	STL	1B	6.3	8.8	2.5
Vaughan	PIT	SS	6.6	7.9	1.3
Davis	PHI	P	8.3	8.3	

In mid–June, both leagues had four teams near the top. The Senators were starting to catch up to the Yankees, Indians, and Tigers, while the Giants had competition from usual suspects St. Louis, Chicago, and Pittsburgh. The Giants shook off the Pirates with a sweep June 16–19 and the Cubs with a hot August. The Cubs still had Gabby Hartnett and Lon Warneke as a premier battery, and acquiring Chuck Klein from the Phillies created a slugging outfield with Babe Herman and Kiki Cuyler, but a midseason trade with those same Phillies for first baseman Don Hurst was disastrous.[22]

The Giants, returning 1933's squad while getting Travis Jackson back from injury, had a seven-game lead in September but stopped hitting. On September 13–16, the Cardinals took three of four from the Giants; from there they stayed hot and overtook the Giants in the last few games of the season for a surprise pennant. Ripper Collins had a career year at the plate and Joe Medwick was decent support, but the team's true strength was the Dean brothers; Dizzy won 30 games and Paul would have been the staff ace almost anywhere else.

The AL settled much easier than the NL after June. Although the Yankees never slumped, the Tigers started August 13–0 to stay ahead the rest of the year. The Yankees still had Lou Gehrig, Babe Ruth, and Lefty Gomez as premier players, joined by rookie Johnny Murphy. But the Tigers, aided by their home park, scored a lot more runs, as catcher-manager Mickey Cochrane, acquired from the financially-challenged A's,[23] joined a core of ace Tommy Bridges and double-play combo Charlie Gehringer and Billy Rogell. Cochrane also guided the sophomore seasons of first baseman Hank Greenberg and pitcher Schoolboy Rowe into major contributions.

10. The Post-Ruth Era, 1935–1951

Babe Ruth initially retired at the end of 1934, and when he wasn't going to replace Joe McCarthy as Yankees' manager, he left, eventually going to the Boston Braves.[1] From May 15, 1915, to the end of 1934, he had been on a team with Momentum, and in 15 of his 21 seasons his team had the Momentum lead for at least part of the season. He retired midway through the 1935 season,[2] and baseball started a new phase.

1935: Déjà Sorta

AL	DET	NY	WAS	BOS	CHI	CLE
Start	255	307	89			
6/1	258	375	82	29	88	68
7/1	253	495	52		118	118
8/1	377	614	21		87	87
9/1	501	588			56	56
End	613	565			28	28
Spt.	**1.51**	1.49	1.13	1.01	1.25	1.21

Name	Tm	Pos	WAR	SpW	Fame
Gehrig	NY	1B	8.6	12.8	4.2
Gehringer	DET	2B	7.8	11.8	4.0
Greenberg	DET	1B	7.7	11.6	3.9
Rogell	DET	SS	5.1	7.7	2.6
Cochrane	DET	C	5.0	7.6	2.6
Ferrell	BOS	P/PH	11.0	11.1	0.1
Grove	BOS	P	9.5	9.6	0.1
Foxx	PHI	1B	8.3	8.3	

NL	CHI	NY	PIT	STL	BRO
Start	445	650	161	358	
6/1	463	718	139	346	48
7/1	433	838	114	321	18
8/1	452	962	83	310	
9/1	536	1086	52	389	
End	648	1093	24	466	
Spt.	1.50	1.50	1.20	1.30	1.04

Name	Tm	Pos	WAR	SpW	Fame
Ott	NY	RF	**7.1**	10.7	3.6
Herman	CHI	2B	6.9	10.4	3.5
Leiber	NY	CF	5.1	7.7	2.6
Galan	CHI	LF	5.1	7.7	2.6
Hartnett	CHI	C	5.0	7.5	**2.5**
D. Dean	STL	P	6.7	**8.7**	2.0
Vaughan	PIT	SS	**9.2**	**11.0**	1.8
Blanton	PIT	P	**7.2**	**8.6**	1.4
Davis	PHI	P	6.9	6.9	

The 1935 AL pennant race was similar to 1934's; the first half of the season had several teams, but July forward was all about the Tigers and Yankees. The Tigers started July 8–0 to bring themselves into the race, then started August 8–0 to pull ahead. For the Yankees, George Selkirk replaced Babe Ruth well, Red Rolfe excelled as the new third baseman, Lou Gehrig was fantastic, and Lefty Gomez gave quality innings even if 12–15 wasn't as good as 1934's 26–5. But the Tigers' core was superior. With outfielder and leadoff hitter Pete Fox jumping from 35 extra-base hits in 1934 to 61, the top of the order—Fox-Cochrane-Gehringer-Greenberg-Goslin—was intimidating; Greenberg's 168 RBI were 48 more than runner-up Gehrig's tally.

The Giants were again the leading team by Momentum while blowing a large lead, in this case a nine-game lead in July. The Giants had been mostly unchallenged to that point, starting June 26–9. Mel Ott and Bill Terry led them on offense with a great full-season debut from Hank Leiber. But only Carl Hubbell was reliable on the mound after June, leaving them a .500 team after that.

While the Cardinals' second half featured winning streaks of 14, eight, eight, and seven (in that order), the Cubs went 24–4 from July 6–31 and clinched the pennant amid winning 21 straight in September. While the Dean brothers were still the best mound tandem in the league and Joe Medwick and Ripper Collins struck fear into opposing pitchers, the Cardinals' lineup fell off sharply after them. The Cubs won in large part by trading Babe Herman and pitchers to the Pirates for Larry French; French became the number two pitcher to ace Lon Warneke, and Augie Galan, getting his first opportunity through Herman's absence, led the league in runs and stolen bases. The infield was great defensively, and Gabby Hartnett was the league's best catcher.

1936: Fashionably Late

AL	CHI	CLE	DET	NY	BOS
Start	15	15	**321**	296	
6/1		50	296	**401**	97

AL	CHI	CLE	DET	NY	BOS
7/1		20	266	**521**	132
8/1			235	**645**	101
9/1			204	**769**	70
End			178	**873**	44
Spt.	1.05	1.14	1.42	**1.58**	1.25

Name	Tm	Pos	WAR	SpW	Fame
Gehrig	NY	1B	9.1	14.4	5.3
Gehringer	DET	2B	7.4	10.5	3.1
Ruffing	NY	P/PH	5.3	8.4	3.1
Dickey	NY	C	5.1	8.1	3.0
Rolfe	NY	3B	4.8	7.6	2.8
Grove	BOS	P	11.1	13.9	2.8
Ferrell	BOS	P/PH	8.1	10.1	2.0
Allen	CLE	P	7.0	8.0	1.0

NL	CHI	NY	PIT	STL
Start	331	**559**	13	238
6/1	326	**644**	38	333
7/1	376	**639**	38	453
8/1	500	**608**	7	577
9/1	569	677		**681**
End	543	**781**		670
Spt.	1.33	1.58	1.14	1.39

Name	Tm	Pos	WAR	SpW	Fame
Hubbell	NY	P	9.6	15.2	5.6
Ott	NY	RF	7.8	12.3	4.5
Bartell	NY	SS	6.3	10.0	3.7
Medwick	STL	LF	7.1	9.9	2.8
D. Dean	STL	P	6.9	9.6	2.7
Vaughan	PIT	SS	7.6	8.7	1.1

Injuries and ailments limited Hank Greenberg to 12 games and Mickey Cochrane to 44; the rest of the team was as good as in 1935, but the two stars were too much to replace. The Yankees saw Lefty Gomez decline but got excellent work from Red Ruffing and Monte Pearson, who was acquired from the Indians for Johnny Allen. The lineup was nearly 200 runs above league average (1065 to 876), becoming only the second lineup (after the 1931 Yankees) with six 4+-WAR players in Bill Dickey, Lou Gehrig, Tony Lazzeri, Frankie Crosetti, Red Rolfe, and rookie Joe DiMaggio. They and the 1977 Rangers are the only teams ever with 4 WAR from their catcher and each infielder.

The Giants were finally the beneficiaries of a late dash to the pennant. The Giants' low point came on July 14 when, after losing three of four to the Cubs (putting the Cubs in a tie for first), they were 40–40 and ten back. The Cubs' core was augmented by a major season from outfielder Frank Demaree, and a 15-win streak in June was reminiscent of 1935's September drive.

The Cardinals had the league's best offense, headlined by Joe Medwick and rookie first baseman Johnny Mize, who supplanted another slugger in Ripper Collins. But the Cardinals couldn't find a second pitcher when Paul Dean got hurt, and they were a .500 team after June, even as they held first through August 23. The Giants won 15 straight in a 24–3 August; paired with the Cubs and Cardinals stalling, they gained 10.5 games in August and stayed on top until the end. The Giants won through the hitting of Mel Ott, the up-the-middle fielding of Dick Bartell and Burgess Whitehead, and the continued dominance of Carl Hubbell, whose 304 innings with a 2.31 ERA (while only one other pitcher in the league was under 3.00) stood out from a workmanlike staff.

1937: Stop Me If You've Heard This One

AL	BOS	DET	NY	CHI	CLE	PHI
Start	22	89	437			
6/1	5	127	505		28	36
7/1		192	625	54	63	6
8/1		161	749	23	32	
9/1		130	873		1	
End		98	1001			
Spt.	1.06	1.40	1.60	1.09	1.18	1.05

Name	Tm	Pos	WAR	SpW	Fame
Gomez	NY	P	9.4	15.0	5.6
DiMaggio	NY	CF	8.2	13.1	4.9
Gehrig	NY	1B	7.7	12.3	4.6
Ruffing	NY	P/PH	6.6	10.6	4.0
Dickey	NY	C	6.2	9.9	3.7
Greenberg	DET	1B	7.7	10.8	3.1
Grove	BOS	P	9.6	10.2	0.6

NL	CHI	NY	STL	PIT
Start	272	390	335	
6/1	264	417	342	72
7/1	384	537	392	112
8/1	508	646	361	81
9/1	632	680	330	50
End	715	808	298	18
Spt.	1.36	1.60	1.34	1.18

Name	Tm	Pos	WAR	SpW	Fame
Bartell	NY	SS	6.6	10.6	4.0
Ott	NY	RF/3B	6.4	10.2	3.8
Medwick	STL	LF	8.5	11.4	2.9
Melton	NY	P	4.8	7.7	2.9
Hubbell	NY	P	4.0	6.4	2.4
Mize	STL	1B	6.6	8.8	2.2

Name	Tm	Pos	WAR	SpW	Fame
Herman	CHI	2B	5.7	**7.8**	2.1
Camilli	PHI	1B	**6.3**	6.3	

At the end of June, the Tigers and White Sox were challenging the Yankees in the AL, while the Cubs, Giants, Cardinals, and Pirates were competitive in the NL. The Yankees and Cubs each won 20 games in July to pull ahead, and on August 3 both had leads of seven games. But while the Yankees continued to win in August and eventually won the pennant by 13.5 games, the Cubs were .500 in August, while the Giants went 41–18, including 4–1 against the Cubs, over the final third of the season to win the pennant by three games.

The Cubs succeeded primarily on the depth of their lineup and bench, which had six hitters between 100 and 105 OPS+ to complement Gabby Hartnett, Billy Herman, and Frank Demaree. The Giants won with the same key personnel as in 1936; Carl Hubbell's return to "normal" ace levels was offset by rookie Cliff Melton's 20 wins. For the Yankees, many younger players took a slight step back, but Joe DiMaggio led the league in home runs, joining Lou Gehrig and Bill Dickey as an offensive force, Lefty Gomez returned to form, leading the league in most pitching categories, and Red Ruffing was as good as ever.

1938: Only the Yankees Can Hold Huge Leads

AL	DET	NY	BOS	CLE	WAS
Start	49	**500**			
6/1	24	**580**	81	96	50
7/1		**645**	106	216	30
8/1		**769**	160	340	
9/1		**893**	129	324	
End		**1017**	98	293	
Spt.	1.09	**1.60**	1.26	1.34	1.11

Name	Tm	Pos	WAR	SpW	Fame
Ruffing	NY	P/PH	**6.2**	**9.9**	3.7
DiMaggio	NY	CF	5.4	**8.6**	3.2
Dickey	NY	C	5.1	**8.2**	3.1
Gomez	NY	P	4.5	7.2	2.7
Gehrig	NY	1B	4.3	6.9	2.6
Foxx	BOS	1B	7.6	**9.6**	2.0
Cronin	BOS	SS	**6.2**	**7.8**	1.6
Greenberg	DET	1B	**7.0**	7.6	0.6
Clift	STL	3B	**6.1**	6.1	

NL	CHI	NY	PIT	STL	CIN	BOS
Start	364	**412**	9	152		
6/1	391	**504**		129		

NL	CHI	NY	PIT	STL	CIN	BOS
7/1	491	624	19	99	33	
8/1	460	703	108	68	2	
9/1	429	672	232	37		
End	468	641	356	6		
Spt.	**1.50**	**1.50**	**1.19**	**1.26**	**1.04**	**1.01**

Name	Tm	Pos	WAR	SpW	Fame
Ott	NY	3B/RF	**8.9**	13.4	4.5
Lee	CHI	P	**7.7**	10.8	3.1
Hack	CHI	3B	**5.3**	7.4	2.1
Bartell	NY	SS	**4.1**	6.2	2.1
Bryant	CHI	P	**4.9**	6.9	2.0
Mize	STL	1B	**6.8**	8.6	1.8
Vaughan	PIT	SS	**8.6**	10.2	1.6
Goodman	CIN	RF	**5.9**	6.1	0.2

The early AL race featured the Indians, led by Earl Averill, Mel Harder, and 19-year-old Bob Feller, the Red Sox, led by Joe Cronin, Jimmie Foxx, and Lefty Grove, and the Yankees. Losing the first three games of their series with the Indians in late June put the Yankees 4.5 back, but a 20–5 July and 28–8 August put them back into first place for keeps. In addition to the normal mainstays, Tommy Henrich became a regular, and rookie Joe Gordon replaced Tony Lazzeri at second base, teaming with Frankie Crosetti to be the best defensive middle infield in the league.

The Giants started 18–3, leaving them 5.5 games up on May 11, but monthly winning percentages worsened until September. At the end of June, the Cubs, Pirates, and even the Reds looked like they might take the race over. The Pirates won 13 straight against the Reds, Cubs, and Cardinals, then took over first by winning their series against the Giants July 16–19. The Giants never got back in the race, and the Pirates took a 6.5-game lead into September.

The Cubs won their doubleheader against the Pirates on September 5 to cut their distance to five back, still in third place with the Reds in between. When the Cubs swept the Pirates again September on 27–29 as the tail end of a ten-win streak, highlighted by catcher-manager Gabby Hartnett's "Homer in the Gloamin'" on September 28, it put them 1.5 up with only three days left in the season, and the Reds finished off the Pirates in the final series to give the pennant to the Cubs.

The Giants' decline was due mainly to their pitching stars, as Cliff Melton was a .500 pitcher and Carl Hubbell's season ended in mid–August.[3] The Pirates were similarly built around their stars—Arky Vaughan's bat was fantastic, and he teamed with Pep Young for the league's best defense up the middle—but their lineup ran a little deeper with veteran first baseman Gus Suhr and rookie leftfielder Johnny Rizzo. The collection of serviceable pitching—reliever Mace Brown led the team with 15 wins—looked much better thanks to the defense.

The Cubs didn't have quite as much offensive talent, but they had similar double-play defense in their longtime combo of Billy Jurges and Billy Herman, and they had dual aces in Bill Lee and Clay Bryant, the latter of whom harnessed his wildness just enough (he led the league in walks and strikeouts) to win 19 games to Lee's 22. 39-year-old Cubs institution Charlie Root was highly effective, finishing 20 games and starting 11 others; Dizzy Dean only made ten starts but was superb in most of them.[4]

1939: Now the Reds Can Hold Leads Too

AL	BOS	CLE	NY	CHI
Start	49	147	509	
6/1	38	126	578	
7/1	8	96	698	
8/1		65	822	
9/1		34	946	
End		4	1066	
Spt.	1.14	1.40	1.60	1.02

Name	Tm	Pos	WAR	SpW	Fame
DiMaggio	NY	CF	**8.1**	**13.0**	**4.9**
Gordon	NY	2B	6.3	**10.1**	**3.8**
Feller	CLE	P	**9.3**	**13.0**	**3.7**
Rolfe	NY	3B	5.9	**9.4**	**3.5**
Selkirk	NY	LF/RF	5.4	**8.6**	**3.2**
Ruffing	NY	P/PH	5.3	8.5	**3.2**
Dickey	NY	C	5.1	8.2	**3.1**
Grove	BOS	P	**7.0**	8.0	1.0
Foxx	BOS	1B	6.8	7.8	1.0
Newsom	2 TM	P	**8.3**	8.3	

NL	CHI	NY	PIT	STL	CIN	BOS
Start	236	**323**	179	3		
6/1	221	**303**	159	78	70	
7/1	191	**273**	129	58	190	
8/1	160	242	98	27	**314**	
9/1	129	211	67		**438**	
End	99	181	37	12	**558**	
Spt.	1.34	1.45	1.24	1.11	**1.43**	1.01

Name	Tm	Pos	WAR	SpW	Fame
Walters	CIN	P	**9.8**	**14.0**	**4.2**
Ott	NY	RF/3B	5.7	8.3	2.6
Frey	CIN	2B	5.9	8.4	2.5
McCormick	CIN	1B	5.3	7.6	2.3
Goodman	CIN	RF	5.2	7.4	**2.2**
Passeau	2 TM	P	5.9	7.7	1.8

Name	Tm	Pos	WAR	SpW	Fame
Mize	STL	1B	**7.9**	**8.8**	0.9
Camilli	BRO	1B	**6.4**	**6.4**	

The Yankees didn't lose their tenth game until June 14. They were the only AL team to score over six runs a game or allow under four, and their 106–45 record was five games **under** their Pythagorean projection. Red Ruffing headed a deep staff, but it barely mattered who was pitching with Joe DiMaggio in center field and Joe Gordon, Frankie Crosetti, and Red Rolfe in the infield catching everything. Lou Gehrig had to retire due to illness, but DiMaggio, Rolfe, Bill Dickey, and George Selkirk provided plenty of offense. The 1939 Yankees, 1972 A's, and 1976 Yankees are the only teams to receive at least 5 WAR from five position players. For all intents and purposes, the Yankees were invincible.

In the NL, the Giants continued their mediocrity from the last half of 1938. The Giants had traded Dick Bartell, Hank Leiber, and catcher Gus Mancuso to the Cubs for Billy Jurges, Frank Demaree, and catcher Ken O'Dea[5]; the trade turned out well for the Giants in the short term but was mostly a wash. It certainly didn't help the Giants' thin pitching or give the Cubs enough hitting to support the deep rotation. The Pirates lost Arky Vaughan, the Waner brothers, and starting pitching to long injuries.

So apart from the Boston Bees for three days and the Cubs for one, only the Cardinals and Reds gained Momentum. The Reds won 12 straight in May and found themselves atop the league at the end of it, nearly without a challenger. The Cardinals went 19–2 from July 30 to August 20, including a 4–1 record against the Reds, and both teams were hot in September. They played the second-to-last series of the year against each other, and a Cardinals sweep would have put them in first; a series split gave the pennant to the Reds.

The Reds' 1938 core, including pitcher Paul Derringer, infielders Frank McCormick, Lonny Frey, and Billy Myers, rightfielder Ival Goodman, and catcher Ernie Lombardi received help from a new player and a nearly-new one. Third baseman Billy Werber was purchased from the A's and became the leadoff hitter, moving Frey to the second spot; both contributed high OBP and doubles power. On the mound, Bucky Walters, acquired from the Phillies in the middle of 1938, conquered his control enough to win the pitching Triple Crown and an easy MVP award.

1940: *The Yankees Stop Hitting; the Reds Need No Hitting*

AL	CLE	NYY	BOS	DET
Start	2	**533**		
6/1	89	**510**	92	

AL	CLE	NYY	BOS	DET
7/1	209	**490**	182	116
8/1	333	**459**	196	240
9/1	**457**	428	165	329
End	**569**	460	137	431
Spt.	1.39	1.48	1.25	**1.29**

Name	Tm	Pos	WAR	SpW	Fame
Feller	CLE	P	**9.9**	**13.8**	**3.9**
DiMaggio	NY	CF	**7.2**	**10.7**	**3.5**
Gordon	NY	2B	**5.8**	**8.6**	**2.8**
Keller	NY	RF/LF	**5.4**	**8.0**	**2.6**
Boudreau	CLE	SS	**6.0**	**8.3**	**2.3**
Newsom	DET	P	**7.6**	**9.8**	2.2
Greenberg	DET	LF	**7.1**	**9.2**	2.1
Rigney	CHI	P	**6.6**	6.6	

NL	CHI	CIN	NY	PIT	STL	BRO
Start	56	314	102	21	7	
6/1	47	**390**	108	2		72
7/1	17	**510**	193			192
8/1		**634**	172			241
9/1		**758**	141			210
End		**870**	113			182
Spt.	1.13	**1.60**	1.34	1.04	1.01	1.31

Name	Tm	Pos	WAR	SpW	Fame
Walters	CIN	P	**6.7**	**10.7**	**4.0**
Frey	CIN	2B	**5.9**	**9.4**	**3.5**
McCormick	CIN	1B	**5.7**	**9.1**	**3.4**
Werber	CIN	3B	**4.5**	**7.2**	**2.7**
Lombardi	CIN	C	**3.9**	**6.2**	**2.3**
Passeau	CHI	P	**6.4**	**7.2**	0.8
Vaughan	PIT	SS	**6.3**	6.6	0.3
Mize	STL	1B	**7.4**	**7.5**	0.1

The Dodgers started the season 9–0 with a three-game lead. The Reds caught up, helped by terrible starts from the Bees, Cardinals, and Pirates, and on June 1 the Giants' .613 winning percentage, enough to lead the league in several seasons, was 4.5 games back. The Dodgers, Reds, and Giants were good in June, but the Giants stopped hitting and the Dodgers went 1–5 against the Reds in July. Meanwhile, the Reds had an 18–2 stretch in July that left them 8.5 games up, and another 18–2 stretch in September erased any doubts about the pennant. While the Reds had only an average lineup, the team played outstanding defense—so outstanding that **both** shortstops, Billy Myers and Eddie Joost, were in the top ten defensive WAR for the year. All the defense meant that any halfway decent pitcher could thrive, and led by ace Bucky Walters the Reds allowed a run fewer per game than the league average and a half-run fewer than the nearest team (the Dodgers).

The Dodgers' early mojo was inverse to the shockingly punchless team in the Bronx, as the Yankees started 6–14 and 9.5 back. The Indians, Red Sox, and Tigers had the best April/May/June, respectively, and all three contended in July. The Yankees had even come back to gain Momentum for two days in June, but their offense still wasn't clicking, as Bill Dickey, Red Rolfe, and Frankie Crosetti (.194/.299/.273!) all had terrible seasons. Coupled with Lefty Gomez's absence for most of the season, the Yankees left the summer to the other three teams.

The Red Sox, led by Ted Williams and the Cronin/Foxx/Grove core, were swept by the Indians on July 20–21 as part of an eight-loss streak, virtually knocking them out. In late August, the Yankees found their offense and went on a 14–1 tear that included a sweep of the Indians; that brought the slumping Tigers back into the race. Down the stretch, the Tigers scored at least ten runs seven times in September while the Indians didn't even score seven runs that often. The Indians went 3–6 against the Tigers in September, directly handing the Tigers most of their one-game margin of victory.

The Indians had high-end talent. Lou Boudreau and Ray Mack were in their first full seasons up the middle; both contributed with the glove, and Boudreau hit well enough that he moved from leadoff to the middle of the lineup midseason, joining first baseman Hal Trosky. But after them and pitchers Bob Feller and Al Milnar, the team quality petered out.

The Tigers had a deep veteran rotation led by Bobo Newsom, Tommy Bridges, and Schoolboy Rowe, who hadn't been both healthy and effective since 1936. While the Tigers couldn't field much—Charlie Gehringer was 37, and first baseman Hank Greenberg moved to left field, which he hadn't even played in the minors, to move catcher Rudy York to first base—they could hit, with that trio joined by Barney McCosky.

1941: Headaches

AL	BOS	CLE	DET	NY	CHI
Start	83	343	260	278	
6/1	60	455	237	275	28
7/1	60	575	207	340	28
8/1	29	564	176	464	
9/1		533	145	588	
End		506	118	696	
Spt.	1.16	1.48	1.30	1.52	1.05

Name	Tm	Pos	WAR	SpW	Fame
DiMaggio	NY	CF	9.1	13.8	4.7
Feller	CLE	P	8.1	12.0	3.9

Name	Tm	Pos	WAR	SpW	Fame
Keller	NY	LF	**6.6**	10.0	3.4
Gordon	NY	2B	5.2	7.9	2.7
Heath	CLE	RF/LF	5.2	7.7	**2.5**
Williams	BOS	LF	**10.6**	**12.3**	1.7
Lee	CHI	P	**8.7**	**9.1**	0.4

NL	BRO	CIN	NY	STL
Start	91	**435**	56	
6/1	211	**405**	26	104
7/1	331	**375**		224
8/1	**455**	344		328
9/1	**579**	313		452
End	**687**	286		560
Spt.	**1.55**	1.42	1.11	1.28

Name	Tm	Pos	WAR	SpW	Fame
Reiser	BRO	CF	**7.4**	**11.5**	**4.1**
Camilli	BRO	1B	**6.8**	**10.5**	**3.7**
Wyatt	BRO	P	**6.7**	**10.4**	**3.7**
Walker	BRO	RF/CF	5.5	8.5	**3.0**
Walters	CIN	P	**7.0**	9.9	2.9
Riddle	CIN	P	**5.8**	8.2	2.4

The Indians built a five-game lead by mid–May, having started the season 16–4. But the hitting dried up after May, and the Yankees, who had given up 6.4 runs/game in May, cut that number to 3.8 in June. The Yankees went from seven games back on May 25 to tied for first a month later, including a sweep of the Indians June 14–16. While the Indians continued to play .500 ball after their good start, the Yankees went 29–3 from June 22 to July 26 and built up a lead so large that they clinched the pennant on September 4.

The Indians fell even further when Hal Trosky's headaches prevented him from taking the field regularly[6]; Cleveland finished the season under .500. Bob Feller and Lou Boudreau got great support work from Jeff Heath and Ken Keltner, but the rest of the team was slightly worse player-by-player than in 1940.

The Yankees were not as all-world as their huge lead implied—no pitcher cleared 15 wins or 3 WAR—but all four up-the-middle players were top ten in defensive WAR, leading to the fewest runs allowed even with that awful May. Rookie Phil Rizzuto took over shortstop permanently when Frankie Crosetti got hurt and was a major reason the Yankees continued their midseason surge. Meanwhile, Bill Dickey, Joe Gordon, and Joe DiMaggio hit hard and fielded great, and Charlie Keller and Tommy Henrich completed an outfield where every member hit at least 30 home runs.

In the NL, the Reds started 10–17. The Reds easily had the best rotation in the league, with Bucky Walters and Paul Derringer joined by Johnny Vander

Meer and rookie and ERA leader Elmer Riddle. But the hitting was among the league's worst—only Frank and Mike McCormick (no relation) were even above-average—and the fielding wasn't quite as strong as in 1940.

With the Reds out, only the Cardinals and Dodgers gained Momentum. Neither team was more than four games ahead or behind all year; the season's end was less a declaration of victory than an arbitrary cutoff for who'd get the headache of facing the Yankees in the postseason. The Dodgers had the better frontline talent, with Pete Reiser leading the league in AVG, SLG, runs, doubles, and triples in his first full season, joined by veteran hitters Dolph Camilli, Dixie Walker, former Cardinal Joe Medwick, and former Cub Billy Herman. For the Cardinals, Johnny Mize, Jimmy Brown, and rookie Ernie White led a group as deep as their huge farm system could produce. Brown, Marty Marion, and Creepy Crespi provided a good defensive infield for White, Lon Warneke, and the rest of the pitchers.

1942: Sneaking Up in Broad Daylight

AL	CLE	DET	NY	BOS
Start	253	59	348	
6/1	322	108	462	17
7/1	292	78	582	4
8/1	261	47	706	
9/1	230	16	830	
End	204		934	
Spt.	1.40	1.28	**1.60**	1.06

Name	Tm	Pos	WAR	SpW	Fame
Gordon	NY	2B	**8.2**	**13.1**	4.9
Keller	NY	LF	**6.7**	**10.7**	4.0
DiMaggio	NY	CF	**6.1**	**9.8**	3.7
Rizzuto	NY	SS	5.7	**9.1**	3.4
Bonham	NY	P	4.2	6.7	2.5
Williams	BOS	LF	**10.6**	**11.2**	0.6
Hughson	BOS	P	**6.2**	6.6	0.4

NL	BRO	CIN	STL	PIT
Start	344	143	280	
6/1	464	113	265	21
7/1	584	83	235	
8/1	708	52	204	
9/1	832	21	178	
End	936		267	
Spt.	1.50	1.29	**1.50**	1.06

Name	Tm	Pos	WAR	SpW	Fame
M. Cooper	STL	P	**8.4**	**12.6**	4.2
Slaughter	STL	RF	**6.2**	9.3	3.1

Name	Tm	Pos	WAR	SpW	Fame
Reese	BRO	SS	5.7	**8.6**	**2.9**
Musial	STL	LF	5.3	**8.0**	**2.7**
Camilli	BRO	1B	4.9	**7.4**	**2.5**
Ott	NY	RF	**6.3**	6.3	
Mize	NY	1B	**6.0**	6.0	
Nicholson	CHI	RF	**5.8**	5.8	

After May, the Red Sox gained Momentum for two days and the Yankees gained Momentum every day, building a league big enough to withstand Boston's 33–9 finish. The Sox had the league's best position player in Ted Williams, but the Yankees had the next four, and as usual the stellar defense made the pitching look good. Tiny Bonham went 21–5, while Spud Chandler and rookie Hank Borowy had sterling ERAs.

The NL race was similar to 1941's. The Dodgers were playing .700 ball into August, while the Cardinals were over .600 but still ten games back, although their Pythagorean records were nearly identical. The Cardinals closed the season with a 38–6 rush, including winning five of six against the Dodgers by limiting them to eight runs, to win the pennant by two games—sneaking up on a team winning over two-thirds of its games.

Once again, distinguishing the teams was difficult. Pete Reiser got hurt in July, but all the Dodgers' top performers in 1941 were as good in 1942, aided by aged starters Larry French, Curt Davis, and Johnny Allen. The Cardinals made their mark with new faces, as the war began to sap talent from the major leagues. Fifth-year veteran Mort Cooper posted a 1.78 ERA to the league's 3.31; rookie Johnny Beazley wasn't too far behind, and Max Lanier provided quality innings as well. Marty Marion continued to anchor the defense, and while Johnny Mize had been half-traded, half-sold to the Giants and Jimmy Brown declined, Enos Slaughter and rookie Stan Musial picked up the slack.

Wartime hadn't affected the Yankees much; the Dodgers had the best veterans, while the Cardinals had the best replacements. For now, the alpha teams seemed best-suited to weather the difficulties—especially as the Dodgers hired the Cardinals' Branch Rickey to run the team after general manager Larry MacPhail went to war.[7]

1943: No Overnight Success

AL	CLE	NY	DET	PHI	WAS	CHI
Start	102	**467**				
6/1	158	**543**	4	7	66	
7/1	128	**663**			176	
8/1	97	**787**			170	

AL	CLE	NY	DET	PHI	WAS	CHI
9/1	66	911			139	
End	34	1039			107	
Spt.	1.34	**1.60**	1.05	1.01	1.33	1.01

Name	Tm	Pos	WAR	SpW	Fame
Keller	NY	LF	**6.7**	**10.7**	4.0
Gordon	NY	2B	**6.7**	**10.7**	4.0
Chandler	NY	P	**6.5**	**10.4**	3.9
Bonham	NY	P	4.9	7.8	2.9
Boudreau	CLE	SS	7.9	10.6	2.7
Appling	CHI	SS	7.6	7.7	0.1

NL	BRO	STL	BOS	CIN	PIT
Start	**468**	134			
6/1	**544**	190	20		
7/1	**664**	310			
8/1	**668**	434			
9/1	**637**	558			
End	605	**686**			
Spt.	1.49	**1.51**	1.06	1.01	1.01

Name	Tm	Pos	WAR	SpW	Fame
Musial	STL	RF/LF	**9.4**	**14.2**	4.8
M. Cooper	STL	P	**5.9**	**8.9**	3.0
Klein	STL	2B	**5.8**	**8.8**	3.0
Galan	BRO	CF/LF	5.4	8.1	2.7
Herman	BRO	2B	4.7	7.0	2.3
Nicholson	CHI	RF	**6.9**	6.9	
Rowe	PHI	PH/P	**6.1**	6.1	

Branch Rickey inherited a talented team in Brooklyn, but the war was taking his talent away. Pee Wee Reese, Pete Reiser, and Larry French all went to war, and although Augie Galan and Arky Vaughan stepped up their games to combine with Billy Herman for a great offense, the pitching was Whit Wyatt and a wishing well. The Dodgers started July 1.5 games up, but a 10–19 month left them 11.5 games back, as the Cardinals went 24–7 in the same time frame and eventually won the pennant by 18 games.

The Cardinals lost Enos Slaughter and Johnny Beazley to war, but Stan Musial led the league in AVG, OBP, and SLG, rookie second baseman Lou Klein was dynamite at the top of the order, and the pitching combined for a 2.57 ERA behind Mort Cooper, Max Lanier, and a wealth of role players.

The AL race started as a fight between the Senators and Yankees. The Senators' pitching abandoned them in July as the Yankees were heating up, and the Yankees had no trouble the rest of the year. Phil Rizzuto, Joe DiMaggio, Tommy Henrich, and Red Ruffing served in war efforts, but there was talent to spare. Spud Chandler, who didn't make the majors until age 29, gave up one or no runs in the majority of his starts, went 20–4, and was named MVP.

1944: Pitching Depth in St. Louis

AL	CLE	NY	WAS	BOS	DET	PHI	STL
Start	17	**519**	54				
6/1		**582**	92		4	7	83
7/1		**607**	62	50	9		203
8/1		**626**	31	104			327
9/1		**605**		78	8		451
End		**690**		113	128		571
Spt.	1.05	**1.50**	1.23	1.19	1.07	1.02	**1.44**

Name	Tm	Pos	WAR	SpW	Fame
Stirnweiss	NY	2B	**8.5**	**12.8**	**4.3**
Lindell	NY	CF	5.4	8.1	**2.7**
Etten	NY	1B	5.4	8.1	**2.7**
Potter	STL	P	5.7	**8.2**	**2.5**
Kramer	STL	P	5.2	7.5	**2.3**
Stephens	STL	SS	5.2	7.5	**2.3**
Johnson	BOS	LF	**6.3**	7.5	1.2
Trout	DET	P	**9.6**	**10.3**	0.7
Newhouser	DET	P	**8.0**	**8.6**	0.6
Boudreau	CLE	SS	**7.9**	**8.3**	0.4

NL		BRO	STL	CIN		PIT
Start		302	**343**			
6/1		281	**427**	49		1
7/1		251	**547**	19		
8/1		220	**671**			
9/1		189	**795**			
End		159	**915**			
Spt.		1.40	**1.60**	1.12		1.01

Nsame	Tm	Pos	WAR	SpW	Fame
Musial	STL	RF/CF	**8.8**	**14.1**	**5.3**
Hopp	STL	CF	5.5	**8.8**	**3.3**
M. Cooper	STL	P	5.3	**8.5**	**3.2**
Marion	STL	SS	4.7	7.5	**2.8**
Wilks	STL	P	4.5	7.2	**2.7**
Galan	BRO	LF/CF	**6.0**	8.4	2.4
Walker	BRO	RF	5.7	**8.0**	2.3
McCormick	CIN	1B	**6.1**	7.5	1.4
Sewell	PIT	P	**6.1**	6.4	0.3
Nicholson	CHI	RF	**6.0**	6.0	

The Dodgers lost even more pitching and finished seventh with an average offense because they played kids like Hal Gregg (9–16, 5.46) and Cal McLish (3–10, 7.82). With their primary competition gone, the Cardinals were the only team to gain Momentum in the NL after June 1. 28-year-old rookie Ted Wilks went 17–4, joining a staff with a 2.67 ERA aided by the deadball-like conditions of wartime play. Catcher Walker Cooper, ace Mort's brother, provided extra thump to the lineup, joining Stan Musial and Johnny Hopp, and shortstop Marty Marion was MVP.

The Yankees lost Joe Gordon, Charlie Keller, and Spud Chandler to the war, leaving them competitive but not dominating. They started 20–11 but went 5–17 over the next three weeks, and the Tigers and Red Sox entered the picture by sweeping them in that period. The steady Browns took first, even as last place was only 6.5 games behind first on June 15.

A good July and a ten-win streak starting July 28 gave the Browns a 6.5-game lead over second place instead of 6.5 over last. But the Browns lost six out of eight games against the Tigers from August 25 to September 3, resurrecting the Tigers, Red Sox, and Yankees. On September 16, with two weeks to go, all four teams were still contending, bunched from .532 to .554 winning percentages.

The Red Sox took themselves out with a ten-loss streak, losing six of those to the Tigers and Browns. The Tigers carried a one-game lead into the final series, facing the Senators, while the Yankees, still in the mix after sweeping the White Sox, were to face the Browns. The Tigers split their series; the Browns swept theirs and won the pennant on the final day of the season.

Of the contenders, the Tigers had the best pitchers and the Yankees the best hitters. The Browns couldn't compete on either front, but shortstop Vern Stephens led the league in RBI and the rotation was five deep, led by Nels Potter and Jack Kramer. The offense was largely aided by playing in Sportsman's Park rather than being independently competent—other than Stephens, first baseman George McQuinn was the only hitter to exceed six home runs—but it scored enough at home to go 54–23 there, seven games better than any other AL team.

1945: You Can't Tell the Players Without a Program

AL	BOS	DET	NY	STL	CHI	WAS
Start	67	75	**406**	336		
6/1	47	125	**486**	356	31	
7/1	57	245	**601**	336	1	
8/1	31	369	**575**	305		45
9/1		493	**569**	274		154
End		**609**	540	245		270
Spt.	1.14	**1.45**	1.49	1.35	1.03	1.10

Name	Tm	Pos	WAR	SpW	Fame
Newhouser	DET	P	**11.2**	**16.2**	**5.0**
Stirnweiss	NY	2B	8.7	13.0	4.3
Potter	STL	P	7.0	9.5	2.5

Name	Tm	Pos	WAR	SpW	Fame
Cullenbine	2 TM	RF	5.5	**7.9**	**2.4**
Mayo	DET	2B	4.6	6.7	**2.1**
Lake	BOS	SS	**6.8**	**7.8**	1.0
Wolff	WAS	P	**5.9**	6.5	0.6

NL	BRO	STL	CHI	NY	PIT
Start	80	**457**			
6/1	90	**437**		80	
7/1	165	**522**	33	140	33
8/1	199	**566**	147	109	2
9/1	168	**565**	271	78	
End	139	**651**	387	49	
Spt.	1.35	1.50	**1.31**	1.23	1.05

Name	Tm	Pos	WAR	SpW	Fame
Barrett	2 TM	P	5.4	**8.2**	**2.8**
Kurowski	STL	3B	4.8	7.2	**2.4**
Burkhart	STL	P	4.7	7.1	**2.4**
Brecheen	STL	P	4.6	6.9	**2.3**
Galan	BRO	1B/LF	5.4	7.3	1.9
Cavarretta	CHI	1B	6.0	**7.9**	1.9
Hack	CHI	3B	6.0	**7.9**	1.9
Roe	PIT	P	7.3	7.7	0.4
Holmes	BOS	RF/LF	**8.0**	**8.0**	

As the war depleted rosters even further, fandom was rooting for laundry and anonymities. The Giants' recognizable players—manager-rightfielder Mel Ott, catcher Ernie Lombardi, and pitcher Van Mungo—put the Giants 6.5 games up on May 26. But Lombardi's .365/.472/.743 May turned to .233/.303/.289 in June, and the rest of the team wasn't good. Six teams gained Momentum on June 13; the Giants were in first on June 16, but June 19 was the last day they gained Momentum.

The Dodgers, led by hitters Augie Galan, Eddie Stanky, Dixie Walker, and Goody Rosen, led by four games on July 1. But two weeks later, **they** stopped gaining Momentum, losing three of four to the Cardinals and still lacking pitching. The final half of the season was a fight between the Cardinals and the Cubs, whose 26–6 July put them in first. The Cubs were 3–9 against the Cardinals down the stretch but 21–6 against everyone else, and they won their last five games to stay on top.

The Cardinals' pitching was led by Harry Brecheen, Ken Burkhart, and Red Barrett. Barrett was the only player received from the Braves in a sale/trade when Mort Cooper was unhappy; he'd been 26–37 in his career but went 21–9 for the Cardinals.[8] For the Cubs, veteran Claude Passeau was joined by Hank Wyse and Ray Prim, a wartime addition who had failed to stick in the majors from 1933 to 1935. Hank Borowy, purchased from the Yankees in late July, managed the ninth-best pitching WAR in the NL in only 14 starts. As the Cubs' lineup was already a player deeper than the Cardinals'–MVP Phil Cavarretta, Stan Hack, and young Andy Pafko versus Whitey Kurowski and Buster Adams—Borowy gave enough depth to beat every non–Cardinal team. If Stan Musial hadn't gone to war, the Cardinals might have won handily.

The White Sox led the AL on May 1 and the Yankees led on June 1; neither's Momentum carried over the month after. The Yankees resurfaced in early August, but a nine-loss streak, including a Tigers' sweep, sent them below .500 temporarily and out of the race permanently. Johnny Lindell went into the Army in June, and while Snuffy Stirnweiss, Nick Etten, and third baseman Oscar Grimes were good offensive players, the pitching was thin enough that coach Paul Schreiber pitched two September games—22 years after his last major-league action.[9]

The Tigers led from June 12 to the end of the season. The Senators entered the race in July and won their first seven games in August, eventually reaching a half-game back. But they were on the wrong side of a five-game split with the Tigers in mid–September, giving the Tigers enough of a cushion to win by 1.5 games.

While the Browns finished third with the same strengths and weaknesses as in 1944, the Senators contended off improvements from 39-year-old first baseman Joe Kuhel and pitcher Roger Wolff (4–15, 4.99 in 1944 but 20–10, 2.12 in 1945), complementing Dutch Leonard in the rotation. The Tigers got back Hank Greenberg on July 1; although he started slowly, he carried the team in August. Roy Cullenbine, acquired in late April from the Indians, was second in OBP and third in SLG, and 35-year-old second baseman Eddie Mayo was second in MVP voting. But the MVP for the second straight year was Hal Newhouser, following his 29–9, 2.22 campaign with a 25–9, 1.81 effort in which he threw eight shutouts and led the league in most strikeouts and fewest hits per inning.

1946: Call It a Comeback

AL	DET	NY	STL	WAS	BOS
Start	**432**	383	174	191	
6/1	**405**	361	147	164	108
7/1	**375**	331	117	134	228
8/1	344	300	86	103	**352**
9/1	313	269	55	72	**476**
End	281	237	23	40	**604**
Spt.	1.46	1.36	1.13	1.23	**1.40**

Name	Tm	Pos	WAR	Spw	Fame
Newhouser	DET	P	9.5	13.9	4.4
Williams	BOS	LF	10.9	15.3	4.4
Trout	DET	P	7.4	10.8	3.4
Greenberg	DET	1B	6.5	9.5	3.0
Pesky	BOS	SS	6.5	9.1	2.6
Feller	CLE	P	9.9	9.9	

NL	BRO	CHI	NY	STL	BOS	CIN
Start	75	210	27	354		
6/1	163	233	5	437	40	2
7/1	283	208		497	10	
8/1	407	177		556		
9/1	531	146		680		
End	659	114		808		
Spt.	1.37	1.33	1.04	1.60	1.07	1.00

Name	Tm	Pos	WAR	Spw	Fame
Musial	STL	1B/LF	8.6	13.8	5.2
Pollet	STL	P	6.6	10.6	4.0
Brecheen	STL	P	5.4	8.6	3.2
Kurowski	STL	3B	4.9	7.8	2.9
Slaughter	STL	RF	4.4	7.0	2.6
Reese	BRO	SS	6.0	8.2	2.2
Stanky	BRO	2B	5.8	7.9	2.1
Sain	BOS	P	7.0	7.5	0.5
Mize	NY	1B	6.3	6.6	0.3

It was expected that the return of the players from war would shake things up; what was unexpected was who benefited.[10] In the AL, the Red Sox started 21–3; the Yankees gained Momentum on May 6, the only day anyone but the Red Sox had any.

The Tigers improved on 1945's record, getting Hank Greenberg and Virgil Trucks back from the war and Dizzy Trout back from a down year, although the lineup never jelled. The Yankees got Joe DiMaggio, Charlie Keller, and Spud Chandler back and gave up the fewest runs in the league, but several other of their returning stars had entered the war old; Bill Dickey was ineffective while Red Ruffing got hurt in June and was out for the season. The Red Sox got back Ted Williams, standout centerfielder Dom DiMaggio, 1944's slugging leader Bobby Doerr, 1942's hits leader Johnny Pesky, and 1942's win leader Tex Hughson. All of them returned as good as they had been and were the top contributors on the team. Williams's OBP of .497 was the highest mark since Rogers Hornsby in 1928 ... apart from Williams himself in 1941–42.

In the NL, the Cubs didn't get back anyone with high enough impact to contend past mid–June. In their place, the Cardinals and Dodgers re-enacted 1941. The Dodgers held a 7.5-game lead on July 2, but the Cardinals swept the

Dodgers July 14–16 over four games to force themselves back in the picture; they ended the season tied, and the Cardinals won a best-of-three playoff to take the pennant.

The Dodgers blended returning players (Pee Wee Reese, Pete Reiser, Kirby Higbe, Hugh Casey) with 1945 standouts (Dixie Walker, Eddie Stanky, Vic Lombardi) and good rookies (Carl Furillo, Joe Hatten). But the Cardinals got back Stan Musial, Enos Slaughter, and 1943 pitching sensation Howie Pollet, who teamed with Whitey Kurowski, Harry Brecheen, and Ted Wilks to provide the heart of the new Cardinals. (Max Lanier also returned from service and started 6-0, but he jumped to the Mexican League with several others, largely Cardinals, Dodgers, and Giants.)[11] It wasn't quite the Red Sox's haul, but as the Cardinals had nearly won five straight pennants, getting the stars back was enough.

1947: Defending Champion's Lapse Is New York Team's Gain

AL	BOS	DET	NY	STL	WAS	CLE	PHI
Start	338	157	133	13	23		
6/1	391	235	131		1	26	
7/1	441	300	251				
8/1	410	269	375				
9/1	379	238	499				
End	352	211	607				
Spt.	1.47	1.35	1.48	1.02	1.04	1.04	1.01

Name	Tm	Pos	WAR	SpW	Fame
Williams	BOS	LF	9.9	14.6	4.7
DiMaggio	NY	CF	4.8	7.1	2.3
Henrich	NY	RF	4.6	6.8	2.2
McQuinn	NY	1B	4.4	6.5	2.1
Dobson	BOS	P	4.4	6.5	2.1
Newhouser	DET	P	5.9	8.0	2.1
Boudreau	CLE	SS	7.5	7.8	0.3
Gordon	CLE	2B	7.0	7.3	0.3
Lopat	CHI	P	5.4	5.4	

NL	BRO	CHI	STL	BOS	NY
Start	330	57	404		
6/1	403	145	382	88	58
7/1	523	230	352	208	178
8/1	647	199	321	262	212
9/1	771	168	300	231	181
End	879	141	273	204	154
Spt.	1.58	1.20	1.42	1.23	1.13

Name	Tm	Pos	WAR	SpW	Fame
Branca	BRO	P	6.9	10.9	4.0
Reese	BRO	SS	6.2	9.8	3.6
Kurowski	STL	3B	5.9	8.4	2.5
Walker	BRO	RF	3.9	6.2	2.3
Spahn	BOS	P	9.5	11.7	2.2
Mize	NY	1B	7.1	8.0	0.9
Blackwell	CIN	P	9.5	9.5	
Kiner	PIT	LF	8.3	8.3	

The AL took awhile to get going; the Tigers and Red Sox were on top early, joined by the Yankees and even the A's in June. On June 14, the Yankees beat the Browns 12–4 as the beginning of a 31–3 run in which they outscored their opponents 200–92. The run took them from 1.5 games back to 11.5 up, and they stayed that far up the rest of the season.

The stars-and-scrubs Red Sox didn't star quite as hard as in 1946, outside Ted Williams. Joe Dobson made up for Tex Hughson's regression, but the rotating cast at third base and the back of the pitching staff did no favors. On the flipside, the Yankees succeeded largely from a lack of weak spots in the lineup. Reliever Joe Page won 14 games, finishing fourth in MVP voting; his was the best performance among a sea of second and third starters.

The NL, with the Cardinals starting 3–11, was an early scramble among the Giants, led by Johnny Mize and rookie pitcher Larry Jansen, the Braves, led by eventual MVP Bob Elliott and near-rookie pitcher Warren Spahn, the Cubs, and the Dodgers. The Cubs didn't have the top talent to keep up and were sub–.500 every month after May, and the Dodgers shook the Braves and Giants off with 13 straight wins to end July. A rough August let the Cardinals, whose offense had awoken in June, into the race, but the early hole was too much, and the Dodgers splitting their two series with them down the stretch was enough for Brooklyn to win the pennant.

The Cardinals' lineup was thin after Stan Musial, Whitey Kurowski, and Enos Slaughter, but the pitching was deep; Harry Brecheen, Murry Dickson, Red Munger, Al Brazle, and rookie Jim Hearn compensated for Howie Pollet's falloff after 1946's heavy workload. The Dodgers were the opposite: good frontline pitching, a thin staff, and a deep lineup. 21-year-old veteran Ralph Branca won 21 games; 28-year-old rookie Harry Taylor gave up the league's fewest hits per inning. Dodgers' hitters outwalked the nearest NL team by 120, led by Dixie Walker and outstanding double play combo Pee Wee Reese and Eddie Stanky. First baseman Jackie Robinson was Rookie of the Year, and young catcher Bruce Edwards received several MVP votes for his offense and defense.[12]

1948: Complications

AL	BOS	DET	NY	CLE	PHI
Start	176	106	303		
6/1	157	87	349	60	76
7/1	127	57	399	180	161
8/1	151	26	493	304	285
9/1	270		577	428	369
End	402		699	515	336
Spt.	**1.28**	**1.13**	**1.50**	**1.39**	**1.24**

Name	Tm	Pos	WAR	SpW	Fame
Boudreau	CLE	SS	**10.4**	**14.5**	**4.1**
DiMaggio	NY	CF	**7.1**	**10.7**	**3.6**
Henrich	NY	RF/1B	**5.4**	**8.1**	**2.7**
Gordon	CLE	2B	**6.6**	**9.2**	**2.6**
Lemon	CLE	P	**6.5**	**9.0**	**2.5**
Williams	BOS	LF	**8.4**	**10.8**	**2.4**

NL	BOS	BRO	CHI	NY	STL	PIT
Start	159	**684**	110	120	212	
6/1	154	**664**	90	190	277	25
7/1	249	**634**	60	260	392	145
8/1	373	**603**	29	229	381	134
9/1	497	**662**		198	430	128
End	629	**649**		165	417	130
Spt.	**1.41**	1.50	1.03	1.22	1.36	1.07

Name	Tm	Pos	WAR	SpW	Fame
Musial	STL	RF/CF	**11.1**	**15.1**	**4.0**
Sain	BOS	P	**8.4**	**11.8**	**3.4**
Brecheen	STL	P	**8.9**	**12.1**	**3.2**
Robinson	BRO	2B/1B	**5.4**	**8.1**	**2.7**
Elliott	BOS	3B	**6.4**	**9.0**	**2.6**
Mize	NY	1B	**6.6**	**8.1**	**1.5**

In a wild year, both leagues had four teams chasing the pennant in September. In the AL, they were the Yankees, Red Sox, Indians, and A's, with the Red Sox joining in late July via a 13-game winning streak. In the NL, it was the Dodgers, Cardinals, Braves, and Pirates. The Dodgers were the latest entrant; they fell to seventh place in early July, then manager Leo Durocher, suspended in 1947, signed with the rival Giants, with 1947's interim manager Burt Shotton replacing him permanently.[13] The Braves were running away in July but fell down in August; an 18–6 September, including series wins against all three competitors, gave them the pennant.

The Dodgers had traded Eddie Stanky to the Braves before the season; Stanky fueled the Braves' first half before going down to injury. Stanky's trade let Jackie Robinson move to second base; Dixie Walker, who didn't want to play with Robinson,[14] was traded to the Pirates for Preacher Roe, who became the staff ace after going 7–22 the previous two seasons.

Stan Musial and Harry Brecheen dragged a thin Cardinals team into contention. The Pirates were built around Ralph Kiner, who led the league in home runs for the third straight year (also his third season in the majors), and infield defense. The Braves had acquired Stanky and purchased Jeff Heath from the Browns; Heath, Bob Elliott, and Rookie of the Year shortstop Al Dark provided a diverse offensive profile. On the mound, Johnny Sain got support down the stretch from Warren Spahn.

In the AL's September action, the A's, who had succeeded primarily with pitching in a 21–7 May, bowed out first with an eight-loss streak ending September 6, mostly to other contenders; the Yankees went 2–5 against the Red Sox in the final ten days and ended a few games back. The Indians and Red Sox finished tied; the Indians won the tiebreaker game to face the Braves in the World Series.

The Yankees were as good as ever, although only Joe DiMaggio and Tommy Henrich were in the lineup regularly and all year. Yogi Berra and Bobby Brown made the lineup and showed promise, while the pitching, made over by trading with the White Sox for Eddie Lopat and giving a larger role to Vic Raschi, was deep if not exciting.

The Red Sox, now managed by longtime Yankees manager Joe McCarthy, reloaded with trade-sales, acquiring shortstop Vern Stephens and pitchers from the Browns. Johnny Pesky filled the third base hole by moving to accommodate Stephens, while Stephens, Bobby Doerr, and Ted Williams were an imposing heart of the order. Joe Dobson's pitching excellence was joined by Mel Parnell, who harnessed his stuff after a disappointing debut in 1947.

The Indians were led by manager-shortstop Lou Boudreau; the defense of him, Joe Gordon at second base, Ken Keltner at third base, and rookie Larry Doby in center field helped the Indians toss 26 shutouts. Converted third baseman Bob Lemon had ten shutouts and rookie left-handed knuckleballer Gene Bearden had another six; they each won 20 games, with Bob Feller winning 19. The bullpen was tough, with Negro League standout Satchel Paige making his major league debut at 41 and leading the pen in strikeouts per inning.

1949: 97–57 and 96–58

AL	BOS	CLE	NY	PHI	DET
Start	306	393	**533**	256	
6/1	282	369	**629**	257	20
7/1	252	339	**749**	227	10

AL	BOS	CLE	NY	PHI	DET
8/1	221	323	873	196	
9/1	260	302	997	165	
End	384	271	1121	134	
Spt.	1.31	1.39	**1.60**	1.20	1.04

Name	Tm	Pos	WAR	SpW	Fame
Williams	BOS	LF	**9.1**	11.9	2.8
Lemon	CLE	P/PH	7.2	10.0	2.8
DiMaggio	NY	CF	4.4	7.0	2.6
Henrich	NY	RF	4.2	6.7	2.5
Page	NY	P	4.2	6.7	2.5
Parnell	BOS	P	7.9	10.4	2.5
Stephens	BOS	SS	6.9	9.0	2.1
Joost	PHI	SS	6.9	8.3	1.4
Trucks	DET	P	6.9	7.2	0.3

NL	BOS	BRO	NY	PIT	STL	CIN	PHI
Start	447	**461**	117	92	297		
6/1	547	516	212	67	277	30	
7/1	627	**636**	222	37	397		46
8/1	596	**760**	191	6	516		15
9/1	565	**884**	160		640		
End	534	**1008**	129		764		
Spt.	1.40	**1.57**	1.20	1.04	1.33	1.00	1.03

Name	Tm	Pos	WAR	SpW	Fame
Robinson	BRO	2B	9.6	15.1	5.5
Reese	BRO	SS	7.0	11.0	4.0
Roe	BRO	P	5.9	9.3	3.4
Newcombe	BRO	P	5.8	9.1	3.3
Musial	STL	RF/CF	**9.2**	12.2	3.0
Snider	BRO	CF	5.2	8.2	3.0
Pollet	STL	P	6.6	8.8	2.2
Kiner	PIT	LF	**8.1**	8.4	0.3

Both leagues were won by a New York team winning 97 games, trailed by a team that won 96. In the NL, the Braves, Dodgers, and Giants led early. Going 1–5 against the Cardinals in June took the Braves out of the race permanently, and the Giants' bad June left the race to the Dodgers and Cardinals the rest of the way. Like always, it went to the last day between them; the Cardinals lost four of their last five to give the pennant to the Dodgers.

For the Braves, nobody made up for Al Dark's and Johnny Sain's declines or Jeff Heath's difficulties after a broken leg suffered in 1948.[15] The Cardinals were built on their usual formula of Stan Musial, Enos Slaughter, and loads of pitching, led by Howie Pollet, Gerry Staley, and Al Brazle. The Dodgers were finally Branch Rickey's full legacy. Jackie Robinson led the league in AVG and placed second in OBP and third in SLG. Besides him, Pee Wee Reese, and

Preacher Roe, the farm system and further integration brought the Dodgers over the top, as Duke Snider, Roy Campanella, and Don Newcombe played their first full seasons to good effect.

In the AL, the Yankees had led the entire year with occasional contention from the Tigers and Indians (who went 18–1 in extra-inning games). But a sweep by the Red Sox on September 24–26 put the Red Sox a game ahead with less than a week to go. The Sox were 35–36 on July 4, but between then and the September series they had gone 56–19. In one of those glorious rarities when the season's last series involves the remaining contenders, the Yankees won both games, the only outcome that would give them the pennant.

For the Red Sox, the 1946 core—Doerr/Williams/Pesky/DiMaggio, supplemented by Vern Stephens—was all in top form. Mel Parnell and Ellis Kinder were dual aces, winning 25 and 23 games respectively. For the Yankees, only Phil Rizzuto played even 130 games, as injuries limited Joe DiMaggio's and Tommy Henrich's games played if not productivity. Reliever Joe Page was the team's best pitcher, while Vic Raschi won 21 games.

1950: Attempts at Upheaval

AL	BOS	CLE	NY	PHI	DET	WAS
Start	224	157	**652**	78		
6/1	288	151	**731**	52	57	20
7/1	258	121	**821**	22	177	
8/1	227	130	**885**		301	
9/1	216	189	**964**		425	
End	276	159	**1084**		535	
Spt.	1.35	1.24	**1.60**	1.08	1.26	1.01

Name	Tm	Pos	WAR	SpW	Fame
Rizzuto	NY	SS	6.7	**10.7**	4.0
Berra	NY	C	5.6	**9.0**	3.4
DiMaggio	NY	CF	5.3	**8.5**	3.2
Parnell	BOS	P	5.7	**7.7**	2.0
Reynolds	NY	P	3.3	**5.3**	2.0
Doby	CLE	CF	6.7	**8.3**	1.6
Houtteman	DET	P	6.1	**7.7**	1.6
Rosen	CLE	3B	5.9	7.3	1.4
Garver	STL	P	7.3	7.3	

NL	BOS	BRO	NY	STL	PHI
Start	299	**564**	72	427	
6/1	304	**639**	47	492	100
7/1	334	**749**	17	612	205
8/1	423	**793**		731	329

NL	BOS	BRO	NY	STL	PHI
9/1	407	**762**		700	453
End	377	**752**		670	573
Spt.	1.28	1.50	1.08	1.40	**1.29**

Name	*Tm*	*Pos*	*WAR*	*SpW*	*Fame*
Robinson	BRO	2B	7.5	**11.3**	3.8
Snider	BRO	CF	5.9	**8.9**	3.0
Musial	STL	1B/LF	7.3	**10.2**	2.9
Roe	BRO	P	5.4	8.1	2.7
Newcombe	BRO	P	4.3	6.5	2.2
Roberts	PHI	P	7.3	**9.4**	2.1
Stanky	NY	2B	**8.0**	8.6	0.6
Blackwell	CIN	P	7.2	7.2	

The Yankees had Joe DiMaggio the entire season, got 151 games out of Yogi Berra and fantastic play from Phil Rizzuto, and defended their AL title. Sounds simple! But the Yankees' weak June put the Tigers in front behind 22-year-old Art Houtteman, who'd been 2–16 in 1948, and a patient lineup headlined by George Kell and Vic Wertz. Larry Doby and Al Rosen brought the Indians close in July and August, but the Red Sox swapped with them on a tear similar to 1949's, a 24–3 run in August and September.

Rookie Whitey Ford's pitching helped the Yankees re-enter the race, while the Red Sox got Ted Williams back from injury in September, joining 1949's core and eventual Rookie of the Year Walt Dropo. The Tigers lost four of five to the Yankees and Red Sox from September 14–18, then lost five of six to the Indians in the last ten games of the season; the Yankees took three of four from the Red Sox in the final ten to eke out the pennant.

On July 17–halfway through the season—the Dodgers, Cardinals, Braves, and Phillies were separated by a half-game. In August, the bottom fell out of the Cardinals' thin offense—young third baseman Tommy Glaviano picked up some of the slack for Enos Slaughter's slight down year, but they and Stan Musial were it, and Gerry Staley's off-year left the pitching merely good. Boston fell off the pace as well, sunk by having only three reliable pitchers; when the hitting left in August, so did the Momentum.

The Dodgers still received excellent production from Roy Campanella, Jackie Robinson, Pee Wee Reese, and Duke Snider. But like the Braves, the Dodgers' mound crew was untrustworthy past a trio (in this case Don Newcombe, Preacher Roe, and Erv Palica). The Phillies couldn't hit much—right-fielder Del Ennis and catcher Andy Seminick at least had power—but their pitching was the league's best, led by youngsters Robin Roberts and Curt Simmons and journeyman Jim Konstanty, who won a surprise MVP for his relief work.[16] Their hot August put them far out in front—far enough that even going 1–6 against the Dodgers in September didn't shake the lead.

1951: The Stealthiest Team in 80 Years

AL	BOS	CLE	DET	NY	CHI	WAS
Start	163	94	317	642		
6/1	158	74	327	742	84	9
7/1	153	44	297	802	204	
8/1	267	98	266	926	283	
9/1	251	222	235	1050	252	
End	239	320	203	1178	220	
Spt.	1.27	1.18	1.30	**1.60**	1.24	1.00

Name	Tm	Pos	WAR	SpW	Fame
Berra	NY	C	4.8	7.7	2.9
McDougald	NY	3B/2B	4.6	7.4	2.8
Reynolds	NY	P	3.7	5.9	2.2
Lopat	NY	P	3.7	5.9	2.2
Rizzuto	NY	SS	3.6	5.8	2.2
Williams	BOS	LF	7.2	9.1	1.9
Minoso	2 TM	3B/RF	5.5	6.8	1.3
Doby	CLE	CF	6.4	7.6	1.2
Joost	PHI	SS	6.0	6.0	
Garver	STL	P	5.6	5.6	

NL	BOS	BRO	PHI	STL	CHI	NY
Start	276	551	420	491		
6/1	343	648	392	513	40	
7/1	313	768	362	488	10	
8/1	282	892	331	457		
9/1	251	1016	300	426		
End	219	1144	268	394		49
Spt.	1.20	1.50	1.30	1.40	1.03	**1.11**

Name	Tm	Pos	WAR	SpW	Fame
Robinson	BRO	2B	9.7	14.6	4.9
Musial	STL	LF/1B	9.1	12.7	3.6
Campanella	BRO	C	6.7	10.1	3.4
Hodges	BRO	1B	5.7	8.6	2.9
Roe	BRO	P	5.2	7.8	2.6
Roberts	PHI	P	8.0	10.4	2.4
Spahn	BOS	P	7.8	9.4	1.6
Kiner	PIT	LF/1B	8.1	8.1	

Apart from the 2007 Rockies, no team has gone to the playoffs with lower Momentum than the 1951 Giants. The Giants' 3–12 April, including five losses to the Dodgers, dug an early and helped put the Dodgers in front. The Giants managed a distant second by mid–June, but it looked like the Dodgers would go unchallenged the rest of the season. Enos Slaughter and the Cardinals' pitching continued to age, the Braves were rebuilding their pitching staff, and the Phillies lost Curt Simmons to the military. For the mighty Dodgers, Roy Campanella, Jackie Robinson, and Gil Hodges had three of the NL's top six slugging percentages, and Pee Wee Reese, Duke Snider, and Carl Furillo lengthened the lineup. The pitching was still thin, but Preacher Roe, Don Newcombe, and Ralph Branca were all good, and the back end wasn't quite as awful as in 1950.

On August 14–16, the Giants swept the Dodgers as part of a 16-win streak that gained them eight games in the standings. They were still six back on September 13, but they won 12 of their last 13 to force a tie with the Dodgers and a three-game playoff, which they won behind a dramatic home run by Bobby Thomson.[17] Thomson had a fine season overall, joined by Monte Irvin, rookie Willie Mays, and double-play tandem Eddie Stanky and Al Dark. The pitching was even more top-heavy than the Dodgers, topped by Larry Jansen and Sal Maglie.

In the AL, the White Sox put pressure on the Yankees with a 26–9 start behind the emergence of ace Billy Pierce, second baseman Nellie Fox, and rookie Minnie Minoso, who had started the season on the Indians. The Yankees mostly kept pace, and an 11–21 July put the White Sox out of the race, allowing the Indians and Red Sox, who had most of the same strengths as in 1950, to join in.

The Indians won 13 straight in August to narrowly take first. It was a virtual tie down to the last two weeks of the season, when the Indians lost two to the Yankees and four of five to the Tigers while the Yankees won seven of eight against the Red Sox. The Yankees won again with depth around a core of Yogi Berra and Phil Rizzuto. Vic Raschi won 21 games for the third straight year. Rookie of the Year Gil McDougald's power, patience, and versatility provided stability to manager Casey Stengel's cast of platoon players.

11. The Yankees and Dodgers, 1952–1968

If 1935–1951 was the post–Ruth era, then 1952–1968 was the post–DiMaggio era, as Joltin' Joe retired after a decline in 1951.[1] The Yankees still had plenty of talent to contend without him, just as the 1935 Yankees did without Ruth. In terms of Momentum, the Yankees and Dodgers towered over their respective leagues. As it turned out, that would be true for many more years.

1952: Not This Time

AL	BOS	CHI	CLE	DET	NY	WAS
Start	196	181	263	166	**968**	
6/1	284	169	371	139	**946**	92
7/1	374	194	451	109	**1066**	92
8/1	343	208	470	78	**1190**	61
9/1	317	177	584	47	**1314**	30
End	290	150	677	20	**1422**	3
Spt.	1.30	1.20	1.40	1.10	**1.60**	1.02

Name	Tm	Pos	WAR	SpW	Fame
Mantle	NY	CF	**6.5**	**10.4**	3.9
Berra	NY	C	5.6	**9.0**	3.4
Rizzuto	NY	SS	5.3	**8.5**	3.2
Reynolds	NY	P	4.8	7.7	2.9
Doby	CLE	CF	**7.1**	**9.9**	2.8
Rosen	CLE	3B	**6.0**	8.4	2.4
Pierce	CHI	P	**7.1**	**8.5**	1.7
Shantz	PHI	P	**9.1**	**9.1**	

NL	BOS	BRO	STL	NY	PHI	CHI	CIN
Start	148	**771**	266	33	181		
6/1	122	**855**	240	122	155	5	4
7/1	92	**975**	210	122	125		
8/1	61	**1099**	179	106	94		
9/1	30	**1223**	148	75	63		

NL	BOS	BRO	STL	NY	PHI	CHI	CIN
End	3	1331	121	73	36		
Spt.	1.13	**1.60**	1.40	1.23	1.25	1.00	1.00

Name	Tm	Pos	WAR	SpW	Fame
Robinson	BRO	2B	**8.5**	13.6	**5.1**
Hodges	BRO	1B	5.5	8.8	3.3
Musial	STL	CF/1B	8.0	11.2	3.2
Reese	BRO	SS	5.0	8.0	**3.0**
Snider	BRO	CF	4.6	7.4	2.8
Hemus	STL	2B	6.7	9.4	2.7
Roberts	PHI	P	8.3	10.4	2.1
Spahn	BOS	P	6.7	7.6	0.9

The Dodgers moved ahead after July, heading into September with a nine-game lead. They stumbled while the Giants got hot; the Dodgers averted 1951's outcome by sweeping the Braves September 19–21 while the Phillies swept the Giants. The Giants lost Willie Mays to the military early in the season; the Dodgers lost Don Newcombe as well. But the Dodgers' important hitters were firing on all cylinders, and Newcombe's absence and Preacher Roe's aging were compensated with Carl Erskine blossoming and the great work of two rookies, starter Billy Loes and reliever Joe Black. Black led the team in wins despite only starting two games, a testament not only to Black's pitching but the offense's potency.

In the AL, the Yankees, Indians, Red Sox, White Sox, and Senators were bunched at the start of June. The Yankees' 21–9 June shook off everyone other than the White Sox, but the White Sox slumped offensively in July while the Indians recovered. The Indians were only a game behind the Yankees with a week to go, but they couldn't close the gap.

The Indians had sensational frontline offense in Larry Doby, Al Rosen, and Bobby Avila, while the rotation had a trio of 20-game winners in Bob Lemon, Mike Garcia, and Early Wynn. They spent far too long giving Bob Feller a chance to turn around, however; with anyone remotely better, they likely would have won the pennant.[2]

As with many Yankees teams, the pitching, led by Allie Reynolds, looked good from the run support and great defense. Gil McDougald, Phil Rizzuto, and new full-timer Billy Martin were tight around the infield. Yogi Berra anchored the defense and offense, while outfielders Gene Woodling and Hank Bauer had standout seasons. But the jewel in the Yankees' offense was 20-year-old Mickey Mantle in his first full season; his .530 SLG was second-best in the league.

After the season, the Braves moved to Milwaukee, no longer able to compete with their crosstown rivals or the National League.[3]

1953: The Powers That Be

AL	BOS	CHI	CLE	DET	NY	WAS
Start	167	86	390	12	820	2
6/1	175	154	418		918	
7/1	145	124	388		1038	
8/1	114	93	357		1162	
9/1	83	62	326		1286	
End	57	36	300		1390	
Spt.	1.30	1.20	1.40	1.02	1.60	1.00

Name	Tm	Pos	WAR	SpW	Fame
Rosen	CLE	3B	**10.1**	**14.1**	**4.0**
Mantle	NY	CF	5.3	**8.5**	**3.2**
Berra	NY	C	4.9	**7.8**	**2.9**
Bauer	NY	RF	4.8	**7.7**	**2.9**
Woodling	NY	LF	4.1	**6.6**	**2.5**
Pierce	CHI	P	**6.3**	**7.6**	1.3
Trucks	2 TM	P	**6.1**	6.9	0.8
Boone	2 TM	3B/SS	**5.9**	6.5	0.6
Vernon	WAS	1B	**5.4**	5.4	

NL	BRO	MIL	NY	PHI	STL
Start	**700**	1	38	19	63
6/1	**796**	80	29	95	134
7/1	**916**	200		85	139
8/1	**1040**	254		54	123
9/1	**1164**	223		23	92
End	**1268**	197			66
Spt.	**1.60**	1.32	1.08	1.21	1.33

Name	Tm	Pos	WAR	SpW	Fame
Snider	BRO	CF	**9.3**	**14.9**	**5.6**
Campanella	BRO	C	7.1	**11.4**	**4.3**
Robinson	BRO	LF/3B	7.0	**11.2**	**4.2**
Reese	BRO	SS	5.1	8.2	**3.1**
Spahn	MIL	P	**8.9**	**11.8**	**2.9**
Mathews	MIL	3B	**8.3**	11.0	2.7
Musial	STL	LF/RF	**7.8**	10.4	2.6
Roberts	PHI	P	**9.8**	**11.9**	2.1

As the second half started, it looked like the Cardinals, Dodgers, and relocated Braves would have a great fight for the pennant. The Braves had the pitching edge, the Cardinals had a balanced team, and the Dodgers had their usual hitting edge.

The Dodgers started the second half sweeping the Cardinals 9–2, 14–0, 7–4, and 14–6; they swept them again at the end of August with 20–4, 6–3, and 12–5 scores. These games were part of a 55–18 second half that ended the race and an offense that scored 6.2 runs/game in a league where nobody else even scored five. Roy Campanella led the league in RBI and Duke Snider in runs, while Carl Furillo won the batting title. Jackie Robinson moved off second baseman to accommodate Jim Gilliam, who was Rookie of the Year as a leadoff hitter and great fielder. Pee Wee Reese teamed with Gilliam up the middle to steady a rotation thin outside Carl Erskine. A deep bullpen led by Clem Labine took up the slack for Joe Black's slump.

In the AL, only the Yankees gained Momentum after May. Eddie Lopat, Whitey Ford, Johnny Sain, and Vic Raschi were all top ten in ERA. Ford was the only one under 34, returning from the military to go 18–6 in his first full season. Phil Rizzuto continued his outstanding defense at shortstop, while Yogi Berra and the outfielders, Gene Woodling, Mickey Mantle, and Hank Bauer, were potent offensive threats.

1954: You Would Think That ...

AL	BOS	CHI	CLE	NY	DET
Start	30	19	157	724	
6/1	2	131	249	796	26
7/1		236	369	816	
8/1		225	493	905	
9/1		194	617	954	
End		169	717	929	
Spt.	1.06	1.29	**1.50**	1.50	1.05

Name	Tm	Pos	WAR	SpW	Fame
Mantle	NY	CF	6.9	10.4	3.5
Avila	CLE	2B	7.0	10.5	3.3
Doby	CLE	CF	5.7	8.6	2.9
Berra	NY	C	5.3	8.0	2.7
Wynn	CLE	P	5.2	7.8	2.6
Minoso	CHI	LF	8.2	10.6	2.4
Williams	BOS	LF	7.8	8.3	0.5

NL	BRO	MIL	STL	CIN	NY	PHI
Start	634	99	33			
6/1	732	132	91	28	64	76
7/1	847	127	71		184	96
8/1	841	96	40		308	65
9/1	875	65	9		432	34
End	865	40			532	9
Spt.	1.50	1.34	1.15	1.02	**1.40***	1.17

Name	Tm	Pos	WAR	SpW	Fame
Mays	NY	CF	10.6	14.8	4.2
Snider	BRO	CF	8.4	12.6	4.2
Hodges	BRO	1B	6.2	9.3	3.1
Reese	BRO	SS	6.0	9.0	3.0

Name	Tm	Pos	WAR	SpW	Fame
Antonelli	NY	P	7.5	10.5	3.0
Mathews	MIL	3B	7.8	10.5	2.7
Roberts	PHI	P	9.0	10.5	1.5
Kluszewski	CIN	1B	7.9	8.1	0.2

… winning 111 games was enough to cruise to a pennant, but the bottom of the AL, including the relocated Baltimore Orioles (formerly Browns) and soon-to-relocate Athletics (to Kansas City), was so bad that 111 didn't mean as much as usual. On July 14, the Yankees and White Sox were still gaining Momentum, even as the Indians had played .675 ball. The Indians pulled ahead by going 55–16 the rest of the way.

Besides the usual cast, the Yankees got new production from Irv Noren (compensating for Gene Woodling's decline) and rookies at first base (Bill Skowron, in a platoon), third base (Andy Carey), and the mound (Bob Grim, who won 20 games). The Yankees had great hitting and good pitching; the Indians had good hitting and great pitching. The top of the lineup—Al Smith playing his first full season, Bobby Avila, Larry Doby, and Al Rosen—all contributed. The pitching had a 2.78 ERA, led by starters Early Wynn, Mike Garcia, and Bob Lemon and rookie relievers, lefty Don Mossi and righty Ray Narleski. The Yankees were the best against teams over .500 (the Indians and White Sox), but the Indians thrashed the bottom teams, including a 20–2 record against the Red Sox.

You also would think that the Dodgers could win pennants forevermore. And like the Yankees, they had enough offense and wins to contend. But Roy Campanella dropped from a 1.006 OPS to .686, Preacher Roe emphatically was done, and Don Newcombe's return from military service was rough. The Giants got Willie Mays back from the military as well; he led the NL in AVG, SLG, and even triples while dazzling in center field and was an easy MVP. Third baseman Hank Thompson was a solid bat behind him, and the Giants got breakout pitching performances from trade acquisition Johnny Antonelli and sophomore Ruben Gomez to match Sal Maglie in the rotation, with late bloomers Marv Grissom and Hoyt Wilhelm providing an even better bullpen than the Indians'. With such great pitching, the Giants stayed in first place from June on, although the Dodgers made it close with a mid–August sweep that put them a half-game back.

1955: The National League Gets to Sleep In

AL	CHI	CLE	NY	BOS	DET
Start	84	358	**465**		
6/1	155	474	**561**		2

AL	CHI	CLE	NY	BOS	DET
7/1	205	479	**681**		
8/1	254	518	**805**	25	
9/1	378	642	**929**	34	
End	389	723	**1025**	20	
Spt.	1.30	1.40	**1.60**	1.08	1.04

Name	Tm	Pos	WAR	SpW	Fame
Mantle	NY	CF	**9.5**	**15.2**	5.7
Bauer	NY	RF	5.3	**8.5**	3.2
McDougald	NY	2B	5.2	8.3	3.1
Berra	NY	C	4.5	7.2	2.7
Wynn	CLE	P	**6.1**	**8.5**	2.4
Pierce	CHI	P	**6.9**	**9.0**	2.1
Williams	BOS	LF	**6.9**	7.5	0.6
Kaline	DET	RF	**8.2**	**8.5**	0.3

NL	BRO	MIL	NY	PHI
Start	438	20	269	5
6/1	**550**		241	
7/1	**670**		211	
8/1	**794**		180	
9/1	**918**		149	
End	**1014**		125	
Spt.	**1.60**	1.08	1.40	1.03

Name	Tm	Pos	WAR	SpW	Fame
Snider	BRO	CF	**8.6**	**13.8**	5.2
Mays	NY	CF	**9.0**	**12.6**	3.6
Newcombe	BRO	P/PH	5.4	**8.6**	3.2
Campanella	BRO	C	5.2	8.3	3.1
Furillo	BRO	RF	5.1	**8.2**	3.1
Mathews	MIL	3B	**7.3**	7.9	0.6
Ashburn	PHI	CF	**6.3**	6.5	0.2
Banks	CHI	SS	**8.1**	8.1	

The Dodgers were the only NL team to gain Momentum because they started 22–2. They were so dominant that the second-place Giants were 9.5 back ... at 12–11. While the Giants' starting pitchers took a step backwards in unison, Don Newcombe, Roy Campanella, and Carl Furillo rebounded to join the mainstays, and the infield was the best defensive unit in the league when Don Hoak started at third base, joining Jim Gilliam and Pee Wee Reese up the middle. The offense had long been tremendous, but in 1955 the Dodgers allowed the fewest runs in the league as well.

For the Indians, Al Rosen and the rotation aged (except fantastic rookie Herb Score), but going down from 111 wins was still enough to keep up with the Yankees and White Sox in the first half. The Yankees started to pull ahead, but a 12–17 July let the Indians, White Sox, and surging Red Sox into a race involving each of them intermittently through the first week of September. The

Yankees swept the Red Sox (who finished the season 4–14) September 16–18 to reclaim the lead from the Indians, who were being swept by the Tigers, for good.

The White Sox had the league's best pitcher in Billy Pierce and a great double-play combo in Nellie Fox and Chico Carrasquel. But the Yankees, bolstered by a 17-player trade with the Orioles in the offseason, reinforced their defense with shortstop Billy Hunter and pitching with Bob Turley and Don Larsen backing up Whitey Ford. The strength of the team was still its two-way position players, as Gil McDougald, MVP Yogi Berra, and Mickey Mantle had outstanding seasons up the middle.

1956: You Read My Story and I'll Read Yours

AL	BOS	CHI	CLE	NY
Start	10	198	368	522
6/1	6	184	414	618
7/1		194	389	738
8/1		163	358	862
9/1		132	327	986
End		103	298	1102
Spt.	1.06	1.30	1.40	1.60

Name	Tm	Pos	WAR	SpW	Fame
Mantle	NY	CF	11.2	17.9	6.7
Berra	NY	C	6.3	10.1	3.8
Ford	NY	P	5.2	8.3	3.1
Wynn	CLE	P	7.8	10.9	3.1
McDougald	NY	SS/2B	5.1	8.2	3.1
Score	CLE	P	7.3	10.2	2.9
Lemon	CLE	P	5.9	8.3	2.4
Kaline	DET	RF	6.5	6.5	

NL	BRO	NY	CIN	MIL	PIT	STL
Start	507	63				
6/1	590	41	88	52	47	84
7/1	685	11	208	167	122	169
8/1	714		307	291	91	138
9/1	838		381	415	60	107
End	949		462	531	31	78
Spt.	1.60	1.09	1.32	1.24	1.08	1.20

Name	Tm	Pos	WAR	SpW	Fame
Snider	BRO	CF	7.6	12.2	4.6
Gilliam	BRO	2B/LF	6.1	9.8	3.7
Newcombe	BRO	P/PH	5.4	8.6	3.2
Maglie	2 TM	P	5.2	8.2	3.0
J. Robinson	BRO	3B/2B	4.5	7.2	2.7

Name	Tm	Pos	WAR	SpW	Fame
F. Robinson	CIN	LF	**6.5**	**8.6**	2.1
Aaron	MIL	RF	**7.1**	**8.8**	1.7
Boyer	STL	3B	**6.4**	7.7	1.3
Mays	NY	CF	**7.6**	8.3	0.7

It wasn't quite the romp of the 1955 NL, but after May the 1956 AL had only nine days of Momentum other than the Yankees: the Indians on June 9 and the White Sox from June 23 to 30. Mickey Mantle won the Triple Crown, winning the home run title by 20 (52 to 32) and scoring 23 more runs than anyone else. With Bill Skowron blossoming in increased playing time, Mantle and the usual suspects had no trouble plating runs. Whitey Ford was a legitimate ace atop a rotation more young (27 and under) than good. Bob Turley took a major step backward, but Don Larsen and Tom Sturdivant were serviceable, and Johnny Kucks won 18 games.

While the AL was boring, the NL had five teams contending at the end of June. In the second half the Dodgers, Braves, and Reds[4] were never separated by more than six games and ended the season two games apart. The Reds had four of the league's top ten home run hitters in Rookie of the Year Frank Robinson, Wally Post, Ted Kluszewski, and Gus Bell; Ed Bailey was a home run away from joining them. The Braves saw pitcher Lew Burdette rebound to support Warren Spahn while Hank Aaron, Eddie Mathews, and Joe Adcock terrorized opposing pitchers and shortstop Johnny Logan contributed in several ways.

But the Dodgers won the pennant again. This time, the Dodgers had relatively deep pitching. Ace Don Newcombe got backup when Sal Maglie was purchased early from the Indians,[5] and Clem Labine and Don Bessent gave good relief work. Roy Campanella had an off-year, but the lineup still had plenty of firepower from Duke Snider and Gil Hodges, with Jim Gilliam and Jackie Robinson providing on-base skills and exceptional defense.

1957: The Dodgers Find Pitching! But ...

AL	CHI	CLE	NY	BOS
Start	149	52	**551**	
6/1	141	223	**620**	10
7/1	261	193	**665**	
8/1	310	162	**789**	
9/1	279	131	**913**	
End	251	103	**1025**	
Spt.	1.36	1.34	**1.60**	1.04

Name	Tm	Pos	WAR	SpW	Fame
Mantle	NY	CF	11.3	18.1	6.8
McDougald	NY	SS/2B	5.8	9.3	3.5
Fox	CHI	2B	7.9	10.7	2.8
Sturdivant	NY	P	3.8	6.1	2.3
Minoso	CHI	LF	5.4	7.3	1.9
Williams	BOS	LF	9.7	10.1	0.4
Sullivan	BOS	P	6.3	6.6	0.3
Bunning	DET	P	6.3	6.3	

NL	BRO	CIN	MIL	PIT	STL	PHI
Start	531	258	297	17	44	
6/1	616	358	377		24	8
7/1	716	478	497		104	113
8/1	805	552	621		228	152
9/1	794	521	745		237	121
End	766	493	857		224	93
Spt.	1.49	1.30	**1.51**	1.02	1.18	1.09

Name	Tm	Pos	WAR	SpW	Fame
Aaron	MIL	RF/CF	8.0	12.1	4.1
Mathews	MIL	3B	7.4	11.2	3.8
Drysdale	BRO	P	6.1	9.1	3.0
Podres	BRO	P	5.8	8.6	2.8
Snider	BRO	P	5.0	7.5	2.5
Robinson	CIN	LF/CF	6.9	9.0	2.1
Mays	NY	CF	8.3	8.3	
Banks	CHI	SS	6.4	6.4	

This year, the White Sox challenged the Yankees through the end of July instead of the end of June. But Nellie Fox, Minnie Minoso, Billy Pierce, and Dick Donovan were not Mickey Mantle, with his .512 OBP (somehow only second in the league behind Ted Williams's .526). Yogi Berra had a slight down year, but Gil McDougald continued to excel, and Rookie of the Year Tony Kubek solidified the infield. Besides Mantle, the Yankees had the deepest pitching staff in the league with Whitey Ford, Tom Sturdivant, and rebounds from Bob Turley and offseason acquisition Bobby Shantz.

The NL race started similarly to 1956's. As late as July 29, the Dodgers, Braves, Reds, Cardinals, and Phillies all gained Momentum, bunched from .556 to .588 winning percentages. The Braves put the slumping Phillies and others away in a 14–1 run that left them eight games up; their own September slump let the Cardinals back in, but the Braves won ten of their last 12 games to cruise to the pennant.

Although Reds fans stuffed the All-Star Game ballot box for their lineup,[6] it neither improved their lineup nor gave them pitching. For the Cardinals, Stan Musial was joined by youngsters Don Blasingame and Joe Cunningham in the lineup and Larry Jackson on the mound. The Dodgers' lineup was reduced to Duke Snider and Gil Hodges as Jim Gilliam slumped and Jackie Robinson retired. It was a shame, since the team finally had the pitching it had dreamt of; righty Don Drysdale and lefty Johnny Podres were aces, backed by Don Newcombe and rookie Danny McDevitt.

The Braves had the league's best offense. MVP Hank Aaron, Eddie Mathews, and Johnny Logan were on their 1956 form. Trading for Giants' second baseman Red Schoendienst and calling up Bob Hazle in July addressed Joe Adcock's unavailability in July and August; Hazle hit .403. Lew Burdette wasn't as good as in 1956, but Warren Spahn was, and Bob Buhl made up the difference. Don McMahon came up at the end of June and provided an ace reliever the team had sorely lacked.

After the season, the Dodgers, who'd lost Momentum lead for the first time since 1949, and the Giants, with no Momentum at all, moved to California.

1958: Own New York, Own the World

AL	CHI	CLE	NY	BAL	WAS
Start	125	52	**513**		
6/1	103	30	**586**		
7/1	73		**706**		
8/1	42		**830**		
9/1	11		**954**		
End			**1062**		
Spt.	1.36	1.13	**1.60**	1.01	1.02

Name	Tm	Pos	WAR	SpW	Fame
Mantle	NY	CF	8.7	**13.9**	**5.2**
Siebern	NY	LF	4.8	7.7	**2.9**
Ford	NY	P	4.3	**6.9**	**2.6**
Turley	NY	P	3.6	5.8	**2.2**
Berra	NY	C/RF	3.2	5.1	**1.9**
Howard	NY	C	3.2	5.1	**1.9**
Carey	NY	3B	3.2	5.1	**1.9**
Colavito	CLE	RF	**5.8**	6.6	0.8
Lary	DET	P	**6.7**	6.7	
Kaline	DET	RF	**6.5**	6.5	
Cerv	KC	LF	**6.3**	6.3	

NL	CIN	LA	MIL	PHI	STL	CHI	PIT	SF
Start	334	518	**579**	63	151			
6/1	306	490	**671**	35	123		39	112
7/1	311	460	**791**	5	128		14	217
8/1	280	429	**915**		162	5		331
9/1	249	398	**1039**		131			300
End	222	371	**1147**		104			273
Spt.	1.26	1.40	**1.60**	1.02	1.13	1.00	1.01	1.19

Name	Tm	Pos	WAR	SpW	Fame
Aaron	MIL	RF/CF	7.3	11.7	4.4
Mathews	MIL	3B	6.4	10.2	3.8
Crandall	MIL	C	4.7	7.5	2.8
Spahn	MIL	P	4.1	6.6	2.5
Burdette	MIL	P	3.3	5.3	2.0
Mays	SF	CF	10.2	12.1	1.9
Ashburn	PHI	CF	7.1	7.2	0.1
Banks	CHI	SS	9.4	9.4	

With fast starts from the Cubs, Giants, and Pirates, from May 7 to May 25 every NL team had Momentum. The Braves and Giants emerged, but even in mid-July last place was only 6.5 games behind first. The Braves solidified their hold on the race by going 6–1 against the Dodgers and Giants from July 29 to August 3; their eventual 16–6 record against the Giants was a major reason they won the pennant.

Six NL teams gained Momentum, but not the Dodgers; Gil Hodges aged, Carl Erskine was done, and Don Newcombe went 0–6, 7.86 before being traded to the Reds. The Giants scored the most runs in the league behind Willie Mays and Rookie of the Year Orlando Cepeda, and Johnny Antonelli continued to shine on the mound with help from erstwhile journeyman Stu Miller.

The Braves still had their stars, and the supporting cast, including Johnny Logan's glove and the bats of Del Crandall, Joe Adcock, and Wes Covington, was productive. Bob Buhl was hurt midseason, but young Joey Jay filled the void, and Lew Burdette won 20 games to complement Warren Spahn's 22. An offseason trade that bought low on the Cubs' Bob Rush gave another reliable starter.

The Yankees stood alone after mid–May, due more to the league's mediocrity than their own .597 winning percentage. Tom Sturdivant was injured and ineffective, but Bob Turley won 21 games and the Cy Young Award, Whitey Ford posted a 2.01 ERA, and rookie reliever Ryne Duren was a revelation. Yogi Berra and Gil McDougald were more support for Mickey Mantle than standouts in their own right, but Andy Carey had his best season in years, Elston Howard hit .314, and Norm Siebern displayed fine on-base and defensive skills.

The 1875 National Association and the 1887 American Association had been the only league-seasons before the 1958 AL to end with a single team possessing Momentum.

1959: Giving the World Back

AL	NY	BAL	CHI	CLE	DET	KC	WAS
Start	**531**						
6/1	**502**	108	92	108			

AL	NY	BAL	CHI	CLE	DET	KC	WAS
7/1	**517**	203	212	228	54		
8/1	**496**	192	336	352	33		
9/1	**465**	161	460	431	2		
End	437	133	**572**	408			
Spt.	1.48	1.23	**1.36**	1.32	1.05	1.01	1.01

Name	Tm	Pos	WAR	SpW	Fame
Mantle	NY	CF	**6.6**	9.8	**3.2**
Fox	CHI	2B	**6.0**	8.2	**2.2**
Landis	CHI	CF	5.7	7.8	**2.1**
Berra	NY	C	3.9	5.8	**1.9**
Duren	NY	P	3.8	5.6	**1.8**
Minoso	CLE	LF	5.5	7.3	**1.8**
Wilhelm	BAL	P	**7.6**	9.3	1.7
Kaline	DET	RF	**6.0**	6.3	0.3
Pascual	WAS	P	**7.8**	7.9	0.1

NL	CIN	LA	MIL	SF	STL	PIT
Start	160	268	**829**	197	75	
6/1	190	308	**924**	272	45	
7/1	160	348	**1044**	387	15	42
8/1	129	472	**1128**	511		61
9/1	98	576	**1177**	635		30
End	69	692	**1268**	736		1
Spt.	1.20	1.43	1.50	1.37	1.04	1.06

Name	Tm	Pos	WAR	SpW	Fame
Aaron	MIL	RF	**8.6**	12.9	**4.3**
Mathews	MIL	3B	**8.2**	12.3	**4.1**
Mays	SF	CF	7.8	10.7	**2.9**
Spahn	MIL	P	5.6	8.4	**2.8**
Drysdale	LA	P	5.8	8.3	**2.5**
Boyer	STL	3B	7.4	7.7	0.3
Banks	CHI	SS	**10.2**	10.2	

The Yankees started 7–10 and the Tigers started 2–15; when they faced each other in May, the Tigers swept twice, leaving the teams tied for last on May 20. By May 26, the Indians, White Sox, and Orioles were close at the top.

The Indians went 2–11 right after, with five of those losses to the Tigers and Yankees. Almost impossibly, on June 24, the Yankees were 34–32 and only two games back, and even on August 1, the A's were in third place at 51–50, behind the Indians and White Sox. When the White Sox swept the Indians at the end of August, they stayed ahead for good. And on September 2, the White Sox passed the Yankees for Momentum lead—the first change in 12 years.

For the Yankees, Elston Howard, Gil McDougald, and Norm Siebern slumped, Bill Skowron was hurt, and Andy Carey slumped and then got hurt. Pitchers Whitey Ford and Ryne Duren were joined by a great year from Art

Ditmar, but Bob Turley was out of bullets and the rest of the rotation wasn't much better.

The Indians could hit—Minnie Minoso, Rocky Colavito, Tito Francona, and Woodie Held helped the team lead the AL in home runs—but Cal McLish and rookie Jim Perry were the only pitchers worth much. The White Sox could pitch—Cy Young winner Early Wynn and young surprise Bob Shaw had bullpen help from oldsters Gerry Staley and Turk Lown. The best position players each played up the middle, fielded well, and provided one offensive weapon—catcher Sherm Lollar (power), shortstop Luis Aparicio (speed, with 56 steals), second baseman and MVP Nellie Fox (getting on base), and centerfielder Jim Landis (also getting on base).

The NL race was a 1956-style fight among the Braves, Dodgers, and Giants. The Dodgers and Braves ended the season tied; the Dodgers beat the Braves in the playoffs to take the pennant. The Giants had a strong rotation headlined by Sam Jones, Johnny Antonelli, and Jack Sanford, with Stu Miller repeating his 1958 breakout in the bullpen. Willie Mays and Orlando Cepeda were lethal on offense, boosted by the late July callup of Willie McCovey. The Braves' offensive core was even better than normal, and Warren Spahn and Lew Burdette each won 21 games (the latter's total largely from run support). Starter Bob Buhl and reliever Don McMahon rounded out the pitching.

The Dodgers' lineup was okay, led by the extra-base power of Charlie Neal and offseason pickup Wally Moon. Don Drysdale led the pitching; the midseason callups of rookie Larry Sherry for the bullpen and organizational soldier Roger Craig worked wonders. On talent alone, the Braves and probably the Giants had an edge, but the Dodgers had enough to pull through.

1960: Return of the Yank

AL	BAL	CHI	CLE	NY	DET
Start	80	345	246	264	
6/1	154	414	325	313	
7/1	274	444	445	393	8
8/1	298	523	519	517	
9/1	422	627	488	641	
End	471	646	457	765	
Spt.	1.21	1.46	1.35	1.48	1.02

Name	Tm	Pos	WAR	SpW	Fame
Maris	NY	RF	7.5	11.1	3.6
Mantle	NY	CF	6.3	9.3	3.0
Aparicio	CHI	SS	5.6	8.2	2.6
Skowron	NY	1B	4.6	6.8	2.2

Name	Tm	Pos	WAR	SpW	Fame
Fox	CHI	2B	4.0	5.8	1.8
Bunning	DET	P	6.7	6.8	0.1
Herbert	KC	P	5.9	5.9	

NL	CIN	LA	MIL	PIT	SF
Start	36	364	668	1	388
6/1	10	338	647	105	492
7/1		308	647	225	532
8/1		277	706	349	501
9/1		246	685	473	470
End		215	654	597	439
Spt.	1.05	1.25	1.50	1.38*	1.38

Name	Tm	Pos	WAR	SpW	Fame
Aaron	MIL	RF	8.0	12.0	4.0
Mathews	MIL	3B	7.3	11.0	3.7
Mays	SF	CF	9.5	13.1	3.6
Groat	PIT	SS	6.2	8.6	2.4
Crandall	MIL	C	4.6	6.9	2.3
Drysdale	LA	P	6.9	8.6	1.7
Banks	CHI	SS	7.8	7.8	
Broglio	STL	P	7.2	7.2	

Through mid–June, the White Sox, Yankees, Indians, Orioles, and Tigers were in a clump. The White Sox faded enough to give the Indians Momentum lead on July 1; they held it for 31 days—the shortest reign since 1936—before the White Sox took it back, taking five of six from them July 6–10 and sending them into oblivion. But they held Momentum lead for only 29 days, giving it to the Yankees who, along with the Orioles, won 22 games in August. The Yankees started September slowly, keeping the Orioles in the race and bringing the White Sox back. But the Yankees swept the Orioles September 16–18 as a start to winning their last 15 games of the season and the pennant.

For the Indians, Woodie Held, Tito Francona, and Jim Perry were still good and Jim Piersall rebounded, but a frenzy of ill-advised trades left the roster thin. For the White Sox, the aging of Sherm Lollar, Early Wynn, and Turk Lown and downturn of Bob Shaw left a lot of production to replace. They largely replaced it with Roy Sievers, Minnie Minoso, and Frank Baumann, who won the ERA title after scuffling with the Red Sox, but it wasn't enough. For the Orioles, breakout star third baseman Brooks Robinson was joined in the infield by three rookies that provided defense (Marv Breeding), power (Jim Gentile), or both (Rookie of the Year Ron Hansen). The Yankees won with a full season from Bill Skowron, superb infield defense led by new third baseman Clete Boyer, Tony Kubek, and Gil McDougald, and a trade that brought Roger Maris from the A's to play right field; Maris took MVP honors in a near-tie with Mickey Mantle. The pitching, led by Whitey Ford and Art Ditmar, appreciated (and needed) the support.

In the NL, the Giants and Pirates started well, with the Braves nearby. The Giants lost 5.5 games in the standings in ten days, getting swept by the Pirates and Braves in mid-June; they never recovered. The Braves tied the Pirates for first place on July 24, but they stopped gaining Momentum 11 days later. The Cardinals gained Momentum for a single day, August 12, but the Pirates were otherwise unchallenged down the stretch.

The Dodgers gained no Momentum, having more slow starts (one) than standout hitters (zero). The Giants had downturns from Willie McCovey and their rotation, Mike McCormick's development notwithstanding. Braves' starters Warren Spahn, Lew Burdette, and Bob Buhl had high win totals, largely due to high workloads and run support from Hank Aaron, Eddie Mathews, Bill Bruton, Joe Adcock, and Del Crandall; the rest of the pitching was awful. The Pirates were a lot better in the midsection of their roster, and their frontline talent was good enough. Shortstop Dick Groat and third baseman Don Hoak were first and second in MVP voting, Roberto Clemente provided an excellent bat, catchers Smoky Burgess and Hal Smith combined for 5.5 WAR, and veteran pitchers Bob Friend and Vern Law were at the top of their games.

1961: New Team Smell

AL	BAL	CHI	CLE	NY	DET
Start	387	531	375	**628**	
6/1	359	503	372	**635**	104
7/1	329	473	442	**735**	224
8/1	298	442	411	**859**	348
9/1	267	411	380	**983**	452
End	237	381	350	**1103**	422
Spt.	1.18	1.38	1.25	**1.60**	1.18

Name	Tm	Pos	WAR	SpW	Fame
Mantle	NY	CF	**10.5**	16.8	6.3
Maris	NY	RF	**6.9**	11.0	4.1
Howard	NY	C	5.3	8.5	**3.2**
Ford	NY	P	3.8	6.1	**2.3**
Boyer	NY	3B	3.8	6.1	**2.3**
Cash	DET	1B	**9.2**	10.9	1.7
Kaline	DET	RF/CF	**8.4**	9.9	1.5
Colavito	DET	LF/RF	**7.6**	9.0	1.4

NL	LA	MIL	PIT	SF	CIN
Start	139	**422**	385	283	
6/1	249	392	**465**	393	104

NL	LA	MIL	PIT	SF	CIN
7/1	369	362	455	**473**	224
8/1	433	331	424	**442**	348
9/1	**537**	300	393	411	472
End	542	270	363	381	**592**
Spt.	1.32	1.25	1.36	1.37	**1.28**

Name	Tm	Pos	WAR	SpW	Fame
Mays	SF	CF	8.7	11.9	3.2
Aaron	MIL	CF/RF	9.4	11.8	2.4
Clemente	PIT	RF	6.4	8.7	2.3
Cepeda	SF	1B/LF	5.7	8.0	2.3
Robinson	CIN	RF/LF	7.7	9.9	2.2
Pinson	CIN	CF	7.5	9.6	2.1
Mathews	MIL	3B	7.2	9.0	1.8
Boyer	STL	3B	7.9	7.9	

New teams in the AL, the Angels and Senators (the old Senators moved to Minnesota and became the Twins), upped the odds of good teams having more free wins and therefore being separated more from the pack. On June 15, the Yankees, Indians, and Tigers were tied; the rest of the league was .500 and under. The Indians soon caved like in 1960, including losing three of four to the Tigers at the end of June; they ended the season below .500. The Tigers bowed out in September by starting it 0–8, including a Yankees' sweep that started a 13-win streak.

The Tigers scored the most runs in the league, and the rotation, led by Frank Lary, Jim Bunning, and Don Mossi, was more than capable. The Yankees' rotation, led by Whitey Ford, Ralph Terry, and sophomore Bill Stafford, was decent; reliever Luis Arroyo broke out at age 34 and rescued the team enough to win 15 games. The offense bashed 240 home runs, led by Mickey Mantle's and Roger Maris's chase at Babe Ruth's single-season record (won by Maris). Bill Skowron and all three catchers—Elston Howard, Johnny Blanchard, and Yogi Berra—cleared 20 home runs. Clete Boyer and Tony Kubek played superb defense on the left side of the infield.

The NL Momentum lead changed four times in 1961. The Braves gained no Momentum all year, ceding Momentum lead to the Pirates on May 14. Rookie Joe Torre filled in well for injured Del Crandall, and Aaron/Mathews/Adcock were still fearsome, but Warren Spahn and Don McMahon were the only remotely reliable pitchers. The Pirates took Momentum lead while in a tussle with the Giants, Dodgers, and Reds. But they lost five straight near the end of May and left the race shortly after. Vern Law was hurt and ineffective, and only Roberto Clemente, Don Hoak, and Smoky Burgess were as good as in 1960.

The Giants took Momentum lead on June 20 but disappeared after losing six straight from July 4–9. Like the Braves, the Giants had major offensive power but thin pitching besides a starter (Mike McCormick) and a reliever (Stu Miller). The Dodgers won six straight right after gaining Momentum lead on August 3. But they then lost ten straight, including three to the Reds; the Dodgers recovered, but the Reds stayed ahead, taking Momentum lead on September 22.

The Dodgers had a standout rotation, with righties Don Drysdale and Stan Williams and lefties Johnny Podres and Sandy Koufax, and the lineup had at least plugged its holes. For the Reds, Frank Robinson and Vada Pinson approximated Aaron/Mathews and veterans Wally Post and Jerry Lynch platooned for 4.7 WAR in LF. Joey Jay, acquired from the Braves in the offseason, and Jim O'Toole won 40 games between them.

So while expansion "cured" the AL's chaos, the NL was uniquely chaotic—and now it was going to expand.[7]

1962: Keeping in Touch

AL	BAL	CHI	CLE	DET	NY	LA	MIN
Start	155	250	230	277	723		
6/1	154	289	334	276	827	33	116
7/1	124	264	454	286	932	113	236
8/1	93	233	493	265	1056	177	230
9/1	62	202	462	234	1180	161	219
End	30	170	430	202	1308	129	232
Spt.	1.05	1.21	1.36	1.29	1.60	1.04	1.11

Name	Tm	Pos	WAR	SpW	Fame
Mantle	NY	CF	5.9	9.4	3.5
Ford	NY	P	5.2	8.3	3.1
Boyer	NY	3B	4.6	7.4	2.8
Tresh	NY	SS/LF	4.3	6.9	2.6
Terry	NY	P	4.0	6.4	2.4
Aguirre	DET	P	7.3	9.4	2.1
Colavito	DET	LF	5.7	7.4	1.7
Robinson	BAL	3B	6.1	6.4	0.3
Siebern	KC	1B	5.5	5.5	

NL	CIN	LA	MIL	PIT	SF	STL
Start	592	542	270	363	381	
6/1	558	593	236	334	512	2
7/1	528	713	206	304	632	
8/1	497	837	175	278	736	
9/1	476	961	144	247	770	
End	454	1089	112	215	853	
Spt.	1.36	1.47	1.10	1.20	1.46	1.00

Name	Tm	Pos	WAR	SpW	Fame
Mays	SF	CF	10.5	15.3	4.8
Robinson	CIN	RF	8.7	11.8	3.1
T. Davis	LA	LF/3B	6.0	8.8	2.8
Wills	LA	SS	6.0	8.8	2.8
W. Davis	LA	CF	5.8	8.5	2.7
Purkey	CIN	P	7.3	9.9	2.6
Aaron	MIL	CF/RF	8.5	9.4	0.9
Farrell	HOU	P	7.0	7.0	

The Reds did as well as in 1961 but finished third and only gained Momentum on four days, partly because the new Colt .45s and Mets gave out so many free wins. The Giants' 19–5 start put them ahead for all of May, but a six-loss streak starting June 6 gave the Dodgers the lead. The Dodgers swept the Giants at the end of July to pull further ahead, but the Giants swept back two weeks later. The teams traded off facing the Cardinals and Colt .45s in the last nine games of the season. The Dodgers went 2–7 while the Giants went 6–3 to force a tie; the Giants won the best-of-three playoff and took the pennant.

The Reds got strong work from newly regular shortstop Leo Cardenas and veteran Bob Purkey, while other players regressed slightly. The Dodgers had Don Drysdale and Sandy Koufax and a super reliever in Ron Perranoski, and the offense was their best in years. But Willie Mays, Orlando Cepeda, and Felipe Alou led a deeper and better Giants' offense that supported its pitchers richly.

The AL was not nearly as clear, as the second-year Angels were a contending team. As late as July 3, five teams were in the race, with the Angels and Yankees separated by a half-game. The Indians lost nine straight while the Yankees won nine straight, so the Yankees spent most of August at the top by themselves. The Angels, led by rookie pitcher Dean Chance, and the Twins, with slugger Bob Allison and pitchers Jim Kaat and Camilo Pascual, got back in it thanks to the Orioles beating the Yankees in five straight, but the Yankees led to the end.

The Yankees won with the best combination of offense and pitching. Tom Tresh was Rookie of the Year, Bobby Richardson had over 200 hits batting in front of Mickey Mantle and Roger Maris, catcher Elston Howard hit 21 home runs, and Clete Boyer scooped up everything at third base. For the pitching, Luis Arroyo was no help, but Ralph Terry won 23 games and Whitey Ford was still great.

So although recent races had involved several teams, the Yankees, Dodgers, and Giants were back atop baseball. It was like they'd never been apart.

1963: July Is When Teams Get Hot

AL	BAL	CHI	CLE	DET	LA	MIN	NY	BOS	KC
Start	22	121	306	144	92	165	932		
6/1	135	204	274	112	65	133	1015	54	88
7/1	180	324	254	82	35	158	**1135**	94	73
8/1	149	293	223	51	4	132	**1259**	63	42
9/1	118	262	192	20		101	**1383**	32	11
End	90	234	164			73	**1495**	4	
Spt.	1.14	1.33	1.34	1.04	1.02	1.15	**1.60**	1.02	1.02

Name	Tm	Pos	WAR	SpW	Fame
Howard	NY	C	5.2	8.3	3.1
Bouton	NY	P	4.8	7.7	2.9
Ford	NY	P	4.3	6.9	2.6
Tresh	NY	CF/LF	4.1	6.6	2.5
Downing	NY	P	3.8	6.1	2.3
Peters	CHI	P	**5.9**	7.9	2.0
Allison	MIN	RF	7.4	8.5	1.1
Pascual	MIN	P	**6.2**	7.1	0.9
Yastrzemski	BOS	LF	6.6	6.7	0.1
Radatz	BOS	P	5.7	5.8	0.1

NL	CIN	LA	MIL	PIT	SF	CHI	STL
Start	253	607	63	120	476		
6/1	218	672	58	140	611	12	72
7/1	243	782	28	110	731	47	192
8/1	222	**906**		79	740	31	176
9/1	191	**1030**		48	724		145
End	163	**1142**		20	696		162
Spt.	1.30	**1.60**	1.03	1.14	1.40	1.01	1.13

Name	Tm	Pos	WAR	SpW	Fame
Koufax	LA	P	10.7	17.1	6.4
Mays	SF	CF	10.6	14.8	4.2
Gilliam	LA	2B/3B	5.2	8.3	3.1
Marichal	SF	P	7.7	10.8	3.1
Perranoski	LA	P	4.5	7.2	2.7
Aaron	MIL	RF	9.1	9.4	0.3
Ellsworth	CHI	P	10.2	10.4	0.2
Callison	PHI	RF	8.1	8.1	

The AL started so oddly that the A's were in first place on May 1, with the Red Sox a game behind them. The A's bowed out at the beginning of June and the Red Sox at the end of June, leaving the Yankees, White Sox, and Twins. The Twins started July 2–9, while the Yankees started July by taking three of four from the White Sox en route to a 22–9 month. With an eight-game lead entering August, the Yankees weren't challenged again.

The Yankees' deep rotation of Whitey Ford, Ralph Terry, Jim Bouton, and Al Downing kept the team from ever losing five straight. Mickey Mantle and Roger Maris missed a season's worth of time between them; Tom Tresh moved from shortstop to cover them, while Tony Kubek came back from the military to cover shortstop. With the injuries, the team glue was now Elston Howard, who won an MVP for his steadiness and slugging.[8]

The NL had a similar pennant race. The Cardinals and Cubs surprised early, challenging the Dodgers, Giants, and Reds. But the Dodgers started July 17–3, gaining nine games in the process, to stay ahead all year. The Giants challenged in mid-August, and the Cardinals were one game back on September 15, but the Dodgers swept the Cardinals immediately afterwards to recover.

For the Dodgers, Jim Gilliam had his best season since moving to Los Angeles, Maury Wills was a leadoff pest, and Frank Howard and Tommy Davis provided thump, although Willie Davis regressed. Sandy Koufax, Don Drysdale, and reliever Ron Perranoski pitched over half the team's innings, their competence papering over a thin staff. With Koufax going 25–5, giving up zero or one run 23 times, the rest of the team only needed to be good-not-great—which is what they were.

1964: Many Things Fall Away, But the Yankees Remain

AL	BAL	BOS	CHI	CLE	MIN	NY
Start	49	2	129	91	40	825
6/1	145		205	162	101	906
7/1	265		285	132	76	951
8/1	389		385	101	45	1065
9/1	513		508	70	14	1104
End	620		610	37		1231
Spt.	1.32	1.00	1.35	1.23	1.09	**1.60**

Name	Tm	Pos	WAR	SpW	Fame
Ford	NY	P	6.7	**10.7**	4.0
Howard	NY	C	5.5	8.8	3.3
Mantle	NY	CF	4.8	7.7	2.9
Hansen	CHI	SS	7.7	10.4	2.7
Robinson	BAL	3B	8.1	**10.7**	2.6
Oliva	MIN	RF	6.8	7.4	0.6
Chance	LA	P	9.3	9.3	
Fregosi	LA	SS	7.9	7.9	

NL	CIN	LA	PIT	SF	STL	MIL	PHI
Start	83	**585**	10	356	83		
6/1	76	**558**	48	449	181	69	96
7/1	76	528	48	**569**	151	39	216
8/1	55	497	17	**693**	120	8	340

NL	CIN	LA	PIT	SF	STL	MIL	PHI
9/1	24	466		712	89		464
End	46	433		704	106		596
Spt.	1.14	1.42	1.01	1.46	1.50*	1.00	1.24

Name	Tm	Pos	WAR	SpW	Fame
Mays	SF	CF	**11.1**	16.2	5.1
W. Davis	LA	CF	**8.3**	11.8	3.5
Drysdale	LA	P	**8.0**	11.4	3.4
Koufax	LA	P	7.4	10.5	3.1
Boyer	STL	3B	6.1	9.2	3.1
Gibson	STL	P	6.0	9.0	3.0
Allen	PHI	3B	**8.8**	10.9	2.1
Santo	CHI	3B	**8.9**	8.9	

The Dodgers were 2–9 on April 25 and gained no Momentum all year; Ron Perranoski's ERA nearly doubled, and Don Drysdale, Sandy Koufax, and Willie Davis were the only players worth their keep. The Giants and Phillies pulled away from the ensuing free-for-all in mid–June; the Phillies went 5–1 against the Giants in July and pulled ahead further in mid–August. The Giants had the bats of Willie Mays, Orlando Cepeda, and rookie third baseman Jim Ray Hart, while Juan Marichal dominated on the mound. The back end of the rotation and the bullpen made up for decreased offense from Willie McCovey and the unproductive trade of Felipe Alou to the Braves. The Phillies were thin but had plenty of young upside, led by their own rookie third baseman in Dick Allen, slugging from rightfielder Johnny Callison, and great pitching from Jim Bunning and Chris Short.

The Phillies were up 6.5 games with 12 to go. But they were swept by the Reds and the Braves September 21–27, leaving the Reds, Phillies, and Cardinals separated by 1.5 games. The Cardinals, who had just swept the Pirates, swept the Phillies as well, taking first place and eliminating the Phillies. The Phillies avenged their elimination by winning their final series against the Reds, ensuring a Cardinals pennant. The Cardinals spent only three days alone in first place, but they were the right three. Bob Gibson led the pitchers, and the lineup was deep; Ken Boyer and Bill White slugged while Curt Flood and trade acquisition Lou Brock hit well in front of them.

In the AL, the Yankees, White Sox, and Orioles traded blows from mid–June forward. The Yankees looked done after a mediocre August, and the Orioles brought a narrow lead into September. But the Yankees won five straight September 4–8 and 11 straight September 16–26, enough even to survive the White Sox winning their final nine games. The three teams were only 2.5 games apart at season's end.

The Orioles and White Sox were led in large part by their shortstops, Luis Aparicio and Ron Hansen, respectively, who'd been traded for each other the year before.⁹ The White Sox had only Pete Ward and Floyd Robinson as other hitters, but Gary Peters, Joe Horlen, and Juan Pizarro made a great rotation and reliever Hoyt Wilhelm was an ageless wonder. The Orioles had the bat of Boog Powell, MVP Brooks Robinson on both sides of the ball, a decent rotation highlighted by 19-year-old Wally Bunker, and the league's best bullpen.

But the Yankees continued to be the Yankees, as Whitey Ford and Jim Bouton led the pitchers. Ralph Terry's down year was offset by August callup Mel Stottlemyre, who pitched brilliantly in his 12 starts.¹⁰ Mickey Mantle, Roger Maris, and Elston Howard were pretty much the entire offense, although Joe Pepitone hit home runs.

1965: Forget What I Said

AL	BAL	CHI	CLE	NY	CAL	DET	MIN
Start	310	305	18	616			
6/1	318	403		589	18	30	86
7/1	348	518	56	559		45	206
8/1	322	502	65	528		14	330
9/1	291	471	34	497			454
End	259	439	2	465			582
Spt.	1.28	1.37	1.09	1.49	1.02	1.02	1.33

Name	Tm	Pos	WAR	SpW	Fame
Stottlemyre	NY	P	6.8	10.1	3.3
Buford	CHI	2B/3B	7.0	9.6	2.6
Versalles	MIN	SS	7.2	9.6	2.4
Ford	NY	P	3.8	5.7	1.9
Tresh	NY	CF/LF	3.8	5.7	1.9
Oliva	MIN	RF	5.4	7.2	1.8
McDowell	CLE	P	8.1	8.8	0.7
Cash	DET	1B	5.4	5.5	0.1

NL	CIN	LA	PHI	SF	STL	HOU	MIL	PIT
Start	25	230	318	375	56			
6/1	96	336	289	351	57	16		
7/1	126	456	259	331	27		3	
8/1	240	580	238	365			14	
9/1	324	704	207	474			128	4
End	362	797	175	602			146	
Spt.	1.22	1.55	1.29	1.43	1.07	1.00	1.04	1.00

Name	Tm	Pos	WAR	SpW	Fame
Mays	SF	CF	11.2	16.0	4.8
Koufax	LA	P	8.1	12.6	4.5
Marichal	SF	P	10.3	14.7	4.4
Drysdale	LA	P/PH	5.4	8.4	3.0

Name	Tm	Pos	WAR	SpW	Fame
Wills	LA	SS	5.2	8.1	**2.9**
Bunning	PHI	P	**8.1**	**10.5**	2.4
Maloney	CIN	P	**8.1**	9.9	1.8

For the first time in 40 years, the Yankees gained no Momentum, as the lineup was toothless outside Tom Tresh and Mickey Mantle. Mantle and Roger Maris were hurt for large portions of the year, Elston Howard showed his age, and injuries drove Tony Kubek to retirement. Stottlemyre and Ford were 36–22, but lesser pitchers had no chance of winning, especially when they, like Jim Bouton (4–15), had terrible seasons.

In the Yankees' absence, the White Sox and Twins were the main teams to fight for the top. The Orioles, Indians, and Tigers were involved through June, but the Twins started July 11–1 and were unchallenged the rest of the way.

The White Sox contended off an unhittable bullpen led by Hoyt Wilhelm and Eddie Fisher and a deep, defensively sound, and dull lineup. The Twins played even better defense and scored over half a run per game more than any other AL team. MVP and Gold Glove winner Zoilo Versalles led the league in doubles, triples, and runs. Batting champion and MVP runner-up Tony Oliva joined with Jimmie Hall and Bob Allison to form the league's best-hitting outfield. .500-slugging first baseman Harmon Killebrew played some third base because of .500-slugging first baseman Don Mincher. Workhorses Jim Kaat and Mudcat Grant weren't Koufax/Drysdale, but they got plenty of support.

In Los Angeles, workhorses Sandy Koufax and Don Drysdale **were** Koufax/Drysdale, and the Dodgers started strong. A near-.500 July and August brought the Giants, Reds, and Braves into the mix, joined briefly by the Phillies and Pirates (the latter only gained Momentum on September 1). The Giants' 14-win streak in September left them 4.5 games up on September 16. But on that day the Dodgers started a 13-win streak, and by its end all that was necessary to win the pennant was for the Giants to lose one, which they did on October 1.

The Giants looked like the stronger team, as Willie Mays and Willie McCovey slugged through Orlando Cepeda's injury, and Juan Marichal, Bob Shaw, and a relief crew headed by Bobby Bolin and Frank Linzy looked fantastic. But the Giants chose to endure several bad performances; Gaylord Perry struggled mightily after a great 1964, while middle infielders Hal Lanier and Dick Schofield were automatic outs.

For the Dodgers, Claude Osteen's acquisition from the Senators for Frank Howard shored up the rotation; combined with Ron Perranoski's return to form and superb defense, the Dodgers allowed a league-low 3.2 runs/game. It was a good thing too, as the only Dodger to slug even .400 was Drysdale. Maury

Wills and Jim Gilliam got on base often enough to score, even if Wills nearly had to steal his way home, and Wills with Rookie of the Year Jim Lefebvre made an excellent double-play combo. The Dodgers didn't have much of a lineup, but everyone had a chance of contributing, and that was enough given the rotation.

1966: Orange and Black

AL	BAL	CHI	CLE	MIN	NY	DET
Start	130	220	1	**292**	233	
6/1	182	207	93	**269**	210	43
7/1	**302**	177	178	239	180	138
8/1	**426**	146	147	208	149	107
9/1	**550**	115	116	177	118	76
End	**674**	84	85	146	87	45
Spt.	**1.51**	1.17	1.16	1.44	1.33	1.06

Name	Tm	Pos	WAR	SpW	Fame
F. Robinson	BAL	RF/LF	**7.7**	**11.6**	**3.9**
Oliva	MIN	RF	**6.4**	**9.2**	**2.8**
Killebrew	MIN	3B/1B	5.9	**8.5**	**2.6**
B. Robinson	BAL	3B	4.6	6.9	**2.3**
Aparicio	BAL	SS	4.1	6.2	**2.1**
Tresh	NY	LF/3B	5.4	**7.2**	1.8
Agee	CHI	CF	**6.4**	**7.5**	1.1
McAuliffe	DET	SS	**6.0**	6.4	0.4
Wilson	2 TM	P	**6.1**	6.4	0.3

NL	ATL	CIN	LA	PHI	SF	HOU	PIT
Start	89	219	**483**	106	365		
6/1	74	189	**503**	76	485	50	
7/1	44	159	563	81	**605**	20	62
8/1	13	128	612	50	**729**		186
9/1		97	726	19	**853**		310
End		66	850		**922**		429
Spt.	1.04	1.26	**1.54**	1.14	1.46	1.01	1.15

Name	Tm	Pos	WAR	SpW	Fame
Koufax	LA	P	**10.3**	**15.9**	**5.6**
Marichal	SF	P	**9.1**	**13.3**	**4.2**
Mays	SF	CF	**9.0**	**13.1**	**4.1**
Hart	SF	3B	6.6	**9.6**	**3.0**
Lefebvre	LA	2B/3B	5.2	8.1	**2.9**
Bunning	PHI	P	**8.9**	**10.1**	1.2
Santo	CHI	3B	**8.9**	8.9	

Although the Twins finished the season in second place, they gained no Momentum, as they were a .500 team until August. The pitching improved down the roster, but the downturns of Zoilo Versalles and Jimmie Hall meant the offense was down two of its biggest threats. The Yankees didn't gain any Momentum either, starting 4–16 and ending in last place. Mel Stottlemyre lost 20, Whitey Ford's circulation issues sent him to the disabled list and then the bullpen,[11] and Mickey Mantle and Roger Maris were out for long periods again.

So on June 19, a week before going 10–1 to put away the race for good, the Orioles took Momentum lead. Offseason acquisition Frank Robinson won the Triple Crown and MVP.[12] First baseman Boog Powell, shortstop Luis Aparicio, and third baseman Brooks Robinson were the other stars, with 1965's Rookie of the Year Curt Blefary providing OBP and power if not defense. The league's youngest pitching staff had no obvious leader due to low individual innings totals; Dave McNally and Jim Palmer threw the most innings, but veteran reliever Stu Miller was more valuable than either of them.

In the NL, although the Phillies and even Astros made some early noise, the race was primarily about the Dodgers, Giants, and Pirates. The Giants were ahead most of the summer, with the same strengths and weaknesses as 1965, apart from Gaylord Perry winning 21 games while Bob Shaw aged.

The Giants' 13–16 July let the Dodgers back into the race and conceded first place to the Pirates. Pittsburgh's rotation was weak outside Bob Veale, but the team's .279 AVG was 16 points better than anybody else's. MVP Roberto Clemente, Willie Stargell, and Donn Clendenon hit for power, Matty Alou was a surprise batting champion over his Braves brother Felipe, and double-play combo Gene Alley and Bill Mazeroski contributed on both sides of the ball.

The Pirates held a narrow lead in the first week of September but cooled off as the Dodgers were heating up. Facing the Astros, Mets, and Pirates, the Dodgers won eight straight and held first place for the rest of the season.

That Sandy Koufax lost nine games in a year batters were as likely to strike out against him (317) as get a hit or walk (318) speaks volumes about the Dodgers' offense. Koufax and Don Drysdale held out at the beginning of the year, and Drysdale didn't recover from the missed training time, but Claude Osteen and rookie Don Sutton were top-ten in the league in ERA. In the bullpen, Ron Perranoski had a down year again, but Phil Regan, a washout as a Tigers starter, went 14–1, 1.62 to be the Dodgers' best pitcher behind Koufax.

After the World Series, Koufax retired at age 30, the pain of pitching too much to handle.[13]

1967: Tales of Birds and Sox

AL	BAL	CHI	CLE	DET	MIN	NY	BOS	CAL
Start	473	59	60	32	102	61		
6/1	447	153	34	136	76	35		

AL	BAL	CHI	CLE	DET	MIN	NY	BOS	CAL
7/1	417	273	4	206	46	5		
8/1	386	397		245	100		60	26
9/1	355	521		344	204		179	15
End	325	641		464	324		299	
Spt.	1.45	1.39	1.03	1.27	1.24	1.08	1.15	1.01

Name	Tm	Pos	WAR	SpW	Fame
B. Robinson	BAL	3B	7.7	11.2	3.5
Blair	BAL	CF	6.8	9.9	3.1
F. Robinson	BAL	RF/LF	5.4	7.8	2.4
Horlen	CHI	P	5.5	7.7	2.2
Kaline	DET	RF	7.5	9.5	2.0
Yastrzemski	BOS	LF	12.4	14.3	1.9
Killebrew	MIN	1B	6.4	7.9	1.5
Merritt	MIN	P	6.4	7.9	1.5

NL	CIN	LA	PIT	SF	CHI	STL
Start	33	425	215	461		
6/1	165	392	232	428		64
7/1	260	362	202	403	16	159
8/1	239	331	171	372	90	283
9/1	208	300	140	341	59	407
End	178	270	110	311	29	527
Spt.	1.22	1.37	1.19	1.47	1.02	1.33

Name	Tm	Pos	WAR	SpW	Fame
Hart	SF	3B/LF	5.8	8.5	2.7
Perry	SF	P	5.6	8.2	2.6
McCovey	SF	1B	5.0	7.4	2.4
Cepeda	STL	1B	6.8	9.0	2.2
McCormick	SF	P	4.4	6.5	2.1
Clemente	PIT	RF	8.9	10.6	1.7
Santo	CHI	3B	9.8	10.0	0.2
Aaron	ATL	RF	8.5	8.5	
Bunning	PHI	P	7.8	7.8	

Rookie Bill Singer was one of the NL's best young pitchers in 1967. But he wasn't Sandy Koufax, and the Dodgers were irrelevant all year. The Pirates' pitching was as bad as the Dodgers' hitting, and although the Giants eventually got second place, they started 1–7 and only gained Momentum on June 8. The rotation was surprisingly deep, as Juan Marichal and Gaylord Perry were joined by rebounds from former Cardinal Ray Sadecki and Mike McCormick, but 36-year-old Willie Mays wasn't his usual team-carrying self.

The Reds were 24–10 on May 17. But the pitching, led in the rotation by 19-year-old Gary Nolan and in the bullpen by veteran reclamation Ted Abernathy, could not prop up a thin offense forever, and they fell out of the race at the end of June, leaving it to the surprising Cardinals and more surprising Cubs. The Cubs, led by third baseman Ron Santo, centerfielder Adolfo Phillips, and pitcher Fergie Jenkins, followed the 14–1 run that got them in the race with a seven-loss streak; a six-loss streak at the beginning of August left the Cardinals unchallenged the rest of the season. The Cardinals were like the 1966 Orioles in that they had an MVP acquired from another team the previous year (Orlando Cepeda) and young pitching, as Nelson Briles, Steve Carlton, and Larry Jaster were all 23 or younger. Catcher Tim McCarver and outfielders Lou Brock, Curt Flood, and offseason acquisition Roger Maris were all useful hitters.

The 1967 Orioles were **not** like the 1966 Orioles, starting 9–14 and gaining no Momentum. Jim Palmer was hurt, Dave McNally was hurt and awful, and the emergence of Paul Blair wasn't enough to offset the injuries. The Tigers and White Sox were the only AL teams consistently above .500 for most of the first half; over June and July, the Twins won eight straight, the Red Sox won ten straight, and the Angels won seven straight to make a five-team race. The Twins and Red Sox swept the Angels in mid–August to knock them out, but each of the remaining four teams gained Momentum daily from August 20 forward and held first place sometime in September. The Red Sox won the pennant when the White Sox lost their last five games and the Red Sox beat the Twins in their last two games.

The White Sox had only two hitters, Pete Ward and Tommie Agee, playing aggressive small-ball highlighted by manager Eddie Stanky's extensive pinch-running. With Gary Peters and Joe Horlen in the rotation, a good bullpen, and great defense, the team allowed only 3.0 runs/game. The other teams were more obviously led by stars. Bill Freehan, Norm Cash, Dick McAuliffe, Willie Horton, and Al Kaline made a deep lineup in Detroit; the Twins had Harmon Killebrew, Jim Merritt, and Dean Chance; and the Red Sox had the Triple Crown-winning Carl Yastrzemski, the AL wins leader in Jim Lonborg, and breakouts from their young lineup, including George Scott and Rico Petrocelli.

1968: Last Year's Excitement Will Have to Do

AL	BAL	BOS	CHI	DET	MIN	CLE
Start	256	235	**504**	364	255	
6/1	356	210	474	**484**	290	79
7/1	346	180	444	**604**	260	74
8/1	315	149	413	**728**	229	43
9/1	284	118	382	**852**	198	12
End	256	90	354	**964**	170	
Spt.	1.30	1.10	1.43	**1.57**	1.20	1.02

Name	Tm	Pos	WAR	SpW	Fame
McLain	DET	P	7.4	11.6	4.2
Freehan	DET	C	6.9	10.8	3.9
Northrup	DET	RF/CF	5.9	9.3	3.4
McAuliffe	DET	2B	5.6	8.8	3.2
Horton	DET	LF	5.4	8.5	3.1
B. Robinson	BAL	3B	8.4	10.9	2.5
Yastrzemski	BOS	LF	10.5	11.6	1.1
Tiant	CLE	P	8.4	8.6	0.2

NL	CHI	CIN	LA	SF	PIT	STL	ATL	PHI
Start	19	118	178	205	72	348		
6/1		107	147	269	41	467	64	23
7/1		77	137	279	11	577	69	8
8/1		46	106	248		701	38	
9/1		15	75	217		825	7	
End			47	189		937		
Spt.	1.00	1.18	1.30	1.40	1.03	1.60	1.06	1.00

Name	Tm	Pos	WAR	SpW	Fame
Gibson	STL	P	11.2	18.0	6.8
Brock	STL	LF	5.8	9.3	3.5
McCovey	SF	1B	7.0	9.8	2.8
Mays	SF	CF	6.2	8.7	2.5
Flood	STL	CF	4.1	6.6	2.5
Aaron	ATL	RF	6.8	7.2	0.4
Clemente	PIT	RF	8.1	8.3	0.2
Seaver	NY	P	6.8	6.8	

For the first time since 1958 in the AL and 1955 in the NL, the pennant races were effectively over by mid–June. The NL result was surprising, because on May 29 the Cardinals were only a game over .500 and in fourth place. But they then won nine straight, eight of those against the Mets and Astros, gaining 6.5 games as the teams in front of them scuffled. A seven-win streak starting June 15 gave them the rest of the distance necessary to cruise to the pennant. The Tigers were already in first place entering June, and a 10–1 run starting June 4 took them from 2.5 up to 6.5 up, after which they weren't seriously challenged.

For the Cardinals, in a historically low-scoring season, giving up only 2.9 runs/game was the lowest of the low. Most of that was due to Bob Gibson, who went at least seven innings in every start and gave up more than one run only ten times. The lineup was more steady than amazing; led by Lou Brock, Curt Flood, and Mike Shannon, there were no automatic outs.

In the AL, the abundance of automatic outs in Chicago led to scoring 2.9 R/G and starting the season 0–10. The pitching was outstanding even as Gary Peters slumped; Joe Horlen and Tommy John excelled in the rotation, while knuckleballers Wilbur Wood and Hoyt Wilhelm threw over 250 bullpen innings with ERAs of 1.87 and 1.73.

The Tigers, on the other hand, led the league with 185 home runs, 52 ahead of second place; Bill Freehan, Norm Cash, Willie Horton, and Jim Northrup each hit over 20. Leadoff hitter Dick McAuliffe led the league in runs via 82 walks, 50 extra-base hits, and the sluggers behind him. Like the Cardinals, the Tigers' moundsmen were decent as a group but led by a juggernaut, in this case Denny McLain, who at age 24 went from a sometimes brilliant workhorse to a 31-game winner.

The 1969 season would bring a lowered mound to raise scoring, four expansion teams, and an East and West division for each league.[14]

12. Divisions of Labor, 1969–1981

A few notes before resuming:

First, each day of contention from 1969 to 1993 only gains three points of Momentum, because divisions create twice as many first place teams, making Momentum easier to obtain. Second, becoming the league leader in Momentum is different in divisional play, as second place in Momentum is likely to be the "other" division's first-place team. So narrative shift isn't as directly tied to the year a team takes Momentum lead. Third, a very good team in a strong division might not gain Momentum because they're too far from the division leader, making the narrative less directly tied to wins.

1969: Expect the Unexpected

	AL E	BAL	BOS	DET		
	Start	146	51	550		
	6/1	257	94	513		
	7/1	347	76	483		
	8/1	440	45	452		
	9/1	533	14	421		
	End	626		390		
	Spt.	1.51	1.04	1.44		
Name	Tm	Pos	WAR	SpW	Fame
F. Robinson	BAL	RF	7.5	11.3	3.8
Blair	BAL	CF	7.1	10.7	3.6
McLain	DET	P	8.2	11.8	3.6
Powell	BAL	1B	5.9	8.9	3.0
Petrocelli	BOS	SS	10.0	10.4	0.4

	AL W	CHI	MIN	OAK
	Start	202	97	
	6/1	165	192	96
	7/1	135	282	166

	AL W	CHI	MIN	OAK	
8/1		104	375	179	
9/1		73	468	248	
End		42	561	217	
Spt.		1.19	**1.35**	1.13	

Name	Tm	Pos	WAR	SpW	Fame
Killebrew	MIN	3B/1B	**6.2**	8.4	**2.2**
Perry	MIN	P	**6.2**	8.4	**2.2**
Carew	MIN	2B	5.6	7.6	**2.0**
Oliva	MIN	RF	5.1	6.9	**1.8**
Jackson	OAK	RF	**9.2**	10.4	1.2
Bando	OAK	3B	**8.3**	9.4	1.1

	NL E	STL	CHI	NY	PIT
Start		469			
6/1		433	108		19
7/1		403	198		
8/1		372	291		
9/1		341	**384**	2	
End		310	397	78	
Spt.		1.42	1.32	1.41*	1.01

Name	Tm	Pos	WAR	SpW	Fame
Gibson	STL	P	**10.4**	14.8	**4.4**
Seaver	NY	P	7.2	10.2	**3.0**
Carlton	STL	P	6.8	9.7	**2.9**
Jones	NY	LF	7.0	9.9	**2.9**
Hands	CHI	P	**8.4**	11.1	2.7
Jenkins	CHI	P	7.2	9.5	2.3
Clemente	PIT	RF	7.5	7.6	0.1

	NL W	LA	SF	ATL	CIN	HOU
Start		24	95			
6/1		92	123	102		
7/1		182	149	192	15	
8/1		275	210	285	9	
9/1		364	295	378	102	41
End		409	388	**471**	155	22
Spt.		1.24	1.23	**1.30**	1.02	1.00

Name	Tm	Pos	WAR	SpW	Fame
Aaron	ATL	RF	8.0	10.4	**2.4**
McCovey	SF	1B	8.1	10.0	1.9
Niekro	ATL	P	6.0	7.8	1.8
Marichal	SF	P	7.8	9.6	1.8
Dierker	HOU	P	**8.6**	8.6	

With the dominance that 1968's winners displayed, having to beat only five teams to make the playoffs would seem easy, but neither of them gained Momentum in 1969. The Tigers won 90 games and saw Mickey Lolich capitalize on his breakout World Series performance of 1968[1] to complement Denny McLain on the mound, but their home runs went down even as league offense went up.

The Red Sox started strong, but the Orioles started stronger, building an 11-game lead by the end of June and winning easily. The Orioles had good pitching in Mike Cuellar, Jim Palmer, Dave McNally, and the bullpen, and they nearly led the AL in runs while being one of the best defensive units of all time. Frank Robinson and Boog Powell hit everything while centerfielder Paul Blair, shortstop Mark Belanger, and third baseman Brooks Robinson caught everything.

In the AL West, the Twins and A's battled, with the Twins pulling conclusively ahead after the A's went 3–12 from August 27–September 10, including a series loss to the Twins (against whom they were 5–13 on the year). The A's had great offensive stars but little pitching; the Twins, meanwhile, led the league in runs and had fine pitching from 20-game winners Jim Perry and Dave Boswell and reliever Ron Perranoski.

Like the Tigers, the Cardinals ended the year well above .500, but with a limp offense and the Cubs starting 11–1 it didn't matter. With Ron Santo's bat and the sturdy pitching of Bill Hands, Fergie Jenkins, and Ken Holtzman, the Cubs hummed along with little incident, gaining Momentum lead on August 22. A couple weeks later, they lost both their division and Momentum lead by losing eight straight while their nearest competitors, the Mets, won ten straight, including two against the Cubs September 8–9. The teams both gained Momentum for a week, after which the Mets, a pitching and defense team led by youth in pitchers Tom Seaver and Jerry Koosman and outfielders Cleon Jones and Tommie Agee, stood alone from September 13 to the end of the season.

In the NL West, the Braves led most of the way but slumped in August, and as late as September 11 everybody but the new Padres gained Momentum. The Braves won the division by finishing 10–1. The Braves' success rested on stars Hank Aaron and Phil Niekro, with a deep lineup led by offseason trade acquisition Orlando Cepeda.

What little notoriety the Mets had from the regular season was made up for by beating the Orioles quickly in the World Series—just a continuation of how unexpected 1969's storylines were.

1970: Four Divisions, One Race

AL E	BAL	DET	NY
Start	313	195	
6/1	408	186	
7/1	498	156	49
8/1	591	129	18

12. Divisions of Labor

	AL E	BAL	DET	NY
	9/1	684	98	
	End	774	68	
	Spt.	**1.60**	1.30	1.03

Name	Tm	Pos	WAR	SpW	Fame
Palmer	BAL	P	6.4	**10.2**	**3.8**
Blair	BAL	CF	5.9	**9.4**	**3.5**
Powell	BAL	1B	5.1	8.2	**3.1**
F. Robinson	BAL	RF	4.8	7.7	**2.9**
White	NY	LF	**6.8**	7.0	0.2
Yastrzemski	BOS	1B/LF	**9.5**	9.5	
McDowell	CLE	P	**8.3**	8.3	
Smith	BOS	CF	**6.8**	6.8	

	AL W	CHI	MIN	OAK	CAL
	Start	21	280	109	
	6/1		371	76	99
	7/1		461	46	137
	8/1		554	15	106
	9/1		647		87
	End		737		61
	Spt.	1.01	**1.45**	1.07	1.16

Name	Tm	Pos	WAR	SpW	Fame
Oliva	MIN	RF	7.0	**10.2**	**3.2**
Killebrew	MIN	3B/1B	4.9	**7.1**	**2.2**
Hall	MIN	P	3.9	5.7	**1.8**
Perry	MIN	P	3.8	5.5	**1.7**
Fregosi	CAL	SS	**7.7**	8.9	1.2
Bando	OAK	3B	**6.1**	6.5	0.4
Harper	MIL	3B/2B	**7.4**	7.4	

	NL E	CHI	NY	STL	PIT
	Start	289	57	225	
	6/1	**376**	44	192	
	7/1	**450**	58	162	23
	8/1	**431**	151	131	116
	9/1	424	232	100	209
	End	486	282	70	299
	Spt.	1.43	1.07	1.09	**1.09**

Name	Tm	Pos	WAR	SpW	Fame
Jenkins	CHI	P	7.3	**10.4**	**3.1**
Williams	CHI	LF	6.6	**9.4**	**2.8**
Holtzman	CHI	P	6.4	**9.2**	**2.8**
Hands	CHI	P	5.2	7.4	**2.2**
Gibson	STL	P	**8.9**	9.7	0.8

	NL W	ATL	CIN	HOU	LA	SF
	Start	**343**	113	16	298	282
	6/1	306	224		261	245

NL W	ATL	CIN	HOU	LA	SF
7/1	276	314		231	215
8/1	245	407		200	184
9/1	214	**500**		169	153
End	184	**590**		139	123
Spt.	1.33	**1.39**	1.00	1.20	1.11

Name	Tm	Pos	WAR	SpW	Fame
Bench	CIN	C	**7.4**	10.3	2.9
Perez	CIN	3B	**7.2**	10.0	2.8
Tolan	CIN	CF	5.4	7.5	2.1
Carty	ATL	LF	5.8	7.7	**1.9**
Grabarkewitz	LA	3B/SS	6.5	7.8	1.3
Perry	SF	P	**7.6**	8.4	0.8
McCovey	SF	1B	**6.6**	7.3	0.7

Three divisions wrapped up without incident. The Orioles never lost more than three straight games and commanded the AL East, although the Yankees bothered them for two weeks and the Tigers gained Momentum on July 19 before finishing below .500. Jim Palmer, Mike Cuellar, and Dave McNally won 68 games, while the lineup stalwarts were joined by a breakout from outfielder Merv Rettenmund.

The Twins won the AL West with nearly the same ease. The Angels challenged them early and then pulled within three games in early September, but the Twins swept them September 4–6 to start an Angels' nine-loss streak. Rod Carew was injured for two-thirds of the year and Dave Boswell collapsed from 20 wins to three, but Jim Perry won 24 games, and the bullpen of Tom Hall, Ron Perranoski, and Stan Williams, acquired in the offseason as a starter, was effective.

In the NL West, only the Reds gained Momentum thanks to their 22–6 start. Phil Niekro's off-year, an awful bullpen, and a mediocre back of the lineup knocked the Braves out. Meanwhile, the Reds' core of Johnny Bench, Tony Perez, Pete Rose, and Bobby Tolan provided diverse offensive threats and rookie Bernie Carbo added power. The pitching was led by 22-and-younger starters Gary Nolan and Wayne Simpson and reliever Don Gullett; "veteran" 26-year-old Jim Merritt won 20 games.

In the NL East, the Cubs started 12–3. The basic strengths were the same as in 1969, but with a breakout season from veteran Jim Hickman and a return to form for Billy Williams. But a 12-loss streak in June lost them nine games in the standings, as eight of those losses were to their nearest rivals, the Mets and Pirates. On September 1 all three of them gained Momentum with winning percentages between .515 and .530. The Pirates went 6–1 against the Mets in September and pushed ahead to take the division. The Mets' rotation, led by Tom Seaver, dragged a completely average lineup behind it, while the Pirates' lineup, led by Roberto Clemente, Willie Stargell, high-average catcher Manny Sanguillen, and high-power first baseman Bob Robertson, dragged its completely average pitching into the postseason.

1971: The True West

	AL E	BAL	DET	BOS
	Start	387	34	
	6/1	473		96
	7/1	563		106
	8/1	656		115
	9/1	749		84
	End	836		55
	Spt.	1.60	1.05	1.16

Name	Tm	Pos	WAR	SpW	Fame
B. Robinson	BAL	3B	6.0	9.6	3.6
Rettenmund	BAL	RF/LF	5.8	9.3	3.5
Buford	BAL	LF	5.1	8.2	3.1
Belanger	BAL	SS	4.6	7.4	2.8
Lolich	DET	P	8.6	9.0	0.4
Nettles	CLE	3B	7.5	7.5	
White	NY	LF	6.7	6.7	
Murcer	NY	CF	6.5	6.5	

	AL W	CAL	MIN	OAK
	Start	31	369	
	6/1	25	331	114
	7/1		301	204
	8/1		270	297
	9/1		239	390
	End		210	477
	Spt.	1.08	1.36	1.34

Name	Tm	Pos	WAR	SpW	Fame
Blue	OAK	P	9.0	12.1	3.1
Blyleven	MIN	P	6.4	8.7	2.3
Jackson	OAK	RF	6.5	8.7	2.2
Bando	OAK	3B	6.4	8.6	2.2
Wood	CHI	P	11.7	11.7	

	NL E	CHI	NY	PIT	STL
	Start	381	221	234	55
	6/1	344	312	333	162
	7/1	314	350	423	176
	8/1	283	319	516	145
	9/1	252	288	609	114
	End	223	259	696	85
	Spt.	1.22	1.22	1.52	1.06

Name	Tm	Pos	WAR	SpW	Fame
Stargell	PIT	LF	7.9	12.1	4.1
Clemente	PIT	RF	7.2	10.9	3.7
Sanguillen	PIT	C	5.0	7.6	2.6
Jenkins	CHI	P	10.3	12.6	2.3
Seaver	NY	P	10.1	12.3	2.2

NL W	ATL	CIN	LA	SF
Start	144	462	109	97
6/1	107	425	72	204
7/1	77	395	42	294
8/1	46	364	11	387
9/1	15	333		480
End		304	60	567
Spt.	1.04	1.41	1.03	1.26

Name	Tm	Pos	WAR	SpW	Fame
May	CIN	1B	5.4	7.6	2.2
Rose	CIN	RF	5.1	7.2	2.1
Bonds	SF	RF/CF	6.7	8.4	1.7
Perez	CIN	3B/1B	4.1	5.8	1.7
Bench	CIN	C	4.1	5.8	1.7
Mays	SF	CF/1B	6.3	7.9	1.6
Aaron	ATL	1B/RF	7.2	7.5	0.3
Roberts	SD	P	7.4	7.4	

The basic narrative of each division remained largely the same, except that West leaders Minnesota and Cincinnati never gained Momentum and were replaced by teams actually on the West Coast. The Twins' pitching staff aged and Rod Carew was not fully back performance-wise from injury. In their place, the A's started 14–5 and were unchallenged after May, with Vida Blue winning the MVP and Cy Young awards in his first full season.

In the East, the Red Sox challenged until the end of July, but the Orioles scored the most runs in the AL and gave up the fewest. The starting pitchers were good enough to each win 20 games, with Mike Cuellar, Pat Dobson, and Jim Palmer hitting 20 on the nose and Dave McNally hitting 21.

In the NL West, the Reds started 11–20. Don Gullett successfully moved into the rotation, but Wayne Simpson's 4.76 ERA and Jim Merritt's 1–11 record more than negated the move. The Giants didn't have much pitching either—Gaylord Perry and Juan Marichal were all right—but they had a better lineup core of Willie Mays, Willie McCovey, and Bobby Bonds, and they started the season 18–5, carried a ten-game lead into June, and survived losing five times to the Dodgers in September to win the division over them by a single game.

The Reds gave up Momentum lead on June 25 to the Pirates, who had taken over first place two weeks earlier by sweeping the Cardinals over four games. By July 4, the Pirates had shaken off the Cardinals, Mets, and rest of the

East for good. The Pirates had the same strengths as in 1970, except that Willie Stargell had a spectacular season instead of his normal good ones and Steve Blass resembled an ace.

1972: August and Everything After

AL E	BAL	BOS	CLE	DET	NY
Start	418	28			
6/1	445	7	59	57	
7/1	511		29	147	
8/1	604			240	
9/1	697	17		333	63
End	764	116		432	110
Spt.	1.50	1.04	1.03	1.27	1.03

Name	Tm	Pos	WAR	SpW	Fame
Grich	BAL	SS/2B	6.0	9.0	3.0
Palmer	BAL	P	5.3	8.0	2.7
Lolich	DET	P	7.4	9.4	2.0
B. Robinson	BAL	3B	3.5	5.3	1.8
Cuellar	BAL	P	3.5	5.3	1.8
G. Perry	CLE	P	11.0	11.3	0.3
Fisk	BOS	C	7.3	7.6	0.3
Murcer	NY	CF	8.1	8.3	0.2

AL W	MIN	OAK	CHI
Start	105	239	
6/1	164	294	46
7/1	142	384	44
8/1	111	477	13
9/1	80	570	86
End	47	669	89
Spt.	1.20	1.50	1.07

Name	Tm	Pos	WAR	SpW	Fame
Rudi	OAK	LF	6.1	9.2	3.1
Bando	OAK	3B	5.6	8.4	2.8
Jackson	OAK	CF/RF	5.6	8.4	2.8
Hunter	OAK	P	5.6	8.4	2.8
Wood	CHI	P	10.7	11.5	0.8
Allen	CHI	1B	8.6	9.2	0.6
Ryan	CAL	P	6.2	6.2	

NL E	CHI	NY	PIT	STL	PHI
Start	139	161	434	53	
6/1	113	223	408	27	10
7/1	107	313	478		
8/1	76	322	571		

NL E	CHI	NY	PIT	STL	PHI
9/1	45	291	664		
End	12	258	763		
Spt.	1.05	1.29	**1.55**	1.01	1.00

Name	*Tm*	*Pos*	*WAR*	*SpW*	*Fame*
Hebner	PIT	3B	5.3	**8.2**	**2.9**
Clemente	PIT	RF	4.8	7.4	**2.6**
Blass	PIT	P	4.0	6.2	**2.2**
Stargell	PIT	1B	3.9	6.0	**2.1**
Matlack	NY	P	**6.0**	7.7	1.7
Williams	CHI	LF	**6.1**	6.4	0.3
Gibson	STL	P	**7.0**	7.1	0.1
Carlton	PHI	P	**12.1**	**12.1**	

NL W	CIN	LA	SF	HOU
Start	190	37	354	
6/1	204	111	328	69
7/1	294	157	298	147
8/1	387	126	267	168
9/1	480	95	236	137
End	579	62	203	104
Spt.	1.50*	1.06	1.29	1.06

Name	*Tm*	*Pos*	*WAR*	*SpW*	*Fame*
Morgan	CIN	2B	**9.3**	**14.0**	**4.7**
Bench	CIN	C	**8.6**	**12.9**	**4.3**
Rose	CIN	LF	6.1	9.2	**3.1**
Tolan	CIN	CF	4.9	7.4	**2.5**
Cedeno	HOU	CF	**8.0**	8.5	0.5
Sutton	LA	P	**6.6**	7.0	0.4

A players' strike shaved a few games off the schedule.[2] As July turned to August, it looked every race had wrapped up. The Mets, who started 25–7, ran out of offense and lost ground to the Pirates, who had an offense, led by veterans Willie Stargell and Roberto Clemente and youngsters Dave Cash and Richie Hebner, and bullpen, led by Dave Giusti and Ramon Hernandez, to compensate for a thin rotation. The Pirates also settled the race in the West in July by going 6–1 against the Astros but 1–5 against the Reds. And the Reds had the Astros to thank for trading Joe Morgan to them in the offseason. (The Giants aged suddenly; trading Gaylord Perry for Sam McDowell was a disaster, and Willies McCovey and Mays slumped terribly.)

In the AL, the A's led comfortably over the fast-starting Twins and resurgent White Sox. Mike Epstein, Bert Campaneris, and Sal Bando were outstanding in the infield, outfielders Reggie Jackson and Joe Rudi provided thump, and Catfish Hunter's ace performance made up for Vida Blue's collapse. Back east, the Orioles and Tigers were fighting hard for the division. The Orioles experienced slight downturns from several players and didn't fully replace the traded Frank Robinson, while the Tigers contended almost entirely on the arms of Mickey Lolich and Joe Coleman.

While the NL races concluded without fanfare, the White Sox went 15–4 in a soft part of the schedule and took over first in late August, while the Tigers' slow start to August allowed the mediocre Red Sox and Yankees to contend. The A's pulled ahead with two five-win streaks, but all four East contenders were live in the final week. In that week, the Orioles lost four straight and the Yankees lost their final five, leaving the Red Sox and Tigers to play a series in Detroit with the Sox a half-game up. The Tigers won the first two games, clinching the division because the strike let them play 156 games to Boston's 155.

1973: Oddly Designated, Oddly Playing

AL E	BAL	BOS	DET	NY	MIL
Start	468	71	264	67	
6/1	433	36	273	36	
7/1	467	6	311	122	40
8/1	552	67	324	215	9
9/1	645	80	365	256	
End	735	50	335	226	
Spt.	**1.55**	1.04	1.30	1.07	1.00

Name	Tm	Pos	WAR	SpW	Fame
Grich	BAL	2B	**8.3**	**12.9**	**4.6**
Palmer	BAL	P	6.3	**9.8**	**3.5**
Blair	BAL	CF	4.9	7.6	2.7
Hiller	DET	P	**8.1**	**10.5**	2.4
Munson	NY	C	**7.2**	7.7	0.5
Perry	CLE	P	**7.9**	7.9	

AL W	CHI	MIN	OAK	CAL	KC
Start	54	29	409		
6/1	127	9	398	35	77
7/1	217	99	436	97	143
8/1	222	116	529	106	228
9/1	191	85	622	75	289
End	161	55	712	45	259
Spt.	1.09	1.03	**1.50**	1.03	1.11

Name	Tm	Pos	WAR	SpW	Fame
Jackson	OAK	RF	**7.8**	**11.7**	**3.9**
North	OAK	CF	7.0	**10.5**	**3.5**
Bando	OAK	3B	6.5	**9.8**	**3.3**
Wood	CHI	P	**7.5**	8.2	0.7

Name	Tm	Pos	WAR	SpW	Fame
Blyleven	MIN	P	9.9	10.2	0.3
Ryan	CAL	P	7.7	7.9	0.2

NL E	CHI	NY	PIT	STL
Start	7	146	430	
6/1	105	176	400	
7/1	195	146	370	
8/1	284	115	339	54
9/1	257	84	308	131
End	227	90	298	133
Spt.	1.13	1.43*	1.45	1.03

Name	Tm	Pos	WAR	SpW	Fame
Seaver	NY	P	10.6	15.2	4.6
Stargell	PIT	LF	7.2	10.4	3.2
Koosman	NY	P	5.8	8.3	2.5
Matlack	NY	P	4.3	6.0	1.7
Reuschel	CHI	P	5.8	6.6	0.8

NL W	CIN	HOU	LA	SF
Start	326	59	35	114
6/1	372	141	57	228
7/1	342	111	139	282
8/1	311	80	232	251
9/1	356	49	325	220
End	446	19	331	190
Spt.	1.48	1.05	1.13	1.21

Name	Tm	Pos	WAR	SpW	Fame
Morgan	CIN	2B	9.2	13.6	4.4
Rose	CIN	LF	8.2	12.1	3.9
Perez	CIN	1B	5.3	7.8	2.5
Bench	CIN	C/RF	4.7	7.0	2.3
Bonds	SF	RF	7.8	9.4	1.6
Evans	ATL	3B/1B	9.0	9.0	

In a year known historically for the AL's new designated hitter,[3] the division races featured extreme mediocrity. Every team in the East had trouble breaking .500 through May; the Tigers emerged as the most believable leader, but they were overtaken as other teams got relatively hot. The West turned out not to be so great either, and as late as July 11 nine of the 12 AL teams were gaining Momentum.

On August 11, the A's started a 13–1 run that included sweeps of the Red Sox and Yankees; on August 12, the Orioles started a 14–0 run that included sweeps of the Rangers, White Sox, Twins, and Royals. Having vanquished each other's foes, the A's and Orioles won their divisions by healthy margins.

For the Orioles, Bobby Grich got on base, and rookie outfielders Al Bumbry and Rich Coggins provided high batting averages from the left side to complement veteran outfielders Paul Blair and Merv Rettenmund from the right. The top-notch defense of Blair, Grich, Mark Belanger, and Brooks Robinson was necessary for starting pitchers not named Jim Palmer. The starters were also rescued by relievers Grant Jackson (8–0, 1.90) and rookie Bob Reynolds.

The A's had three premium defenders of their own in catcher Ray Fosse, shortstop Bert Campaneris, and new centerfielder Billy North, acquired for a reliever in the offseason and given his first full-time play. North, Reggie Jackson, Sal Bando, and Gene Tenace were the offensive core, and the defense helped Catfish Hunter, Vida Blue, and Ken Holtzman obtain 20-win seasons. Reliever Rollie Fingers pitched 126 great innings.

The Cubs entered July eight games up, but a 5–27 stretch starting July 11 left them barely above .500 and the Cardinals in front. The Cardinals lost eight straight in August but were still in first on September 11, albeit at 72–72. The Pirates took first place by beating them, but the Mets went 4–1 against the Pirates September 17–21 and won two against the Cardinals to emerge as the East's alpha limper at 82–79. The Mets' rotation was legitimately great, making up for a lineup that looked like something out of spring training. The Pirates should have won—rookie rightfielder Richie Zisk ably replaced Roberto Clemente, who had died in the offseason, and Willie Stargell was spectacular—but they gave too many innings to Luke Walker (7–12, 4.65, -1 WAR) and Steve Blass (3–9, 9.85, -4 WAR), even giving Blass three starts in September.

The NL West contrasted with the other divisions by featuring good teams all year. The Astros, Dodgers, Reds, and resurgent Giants formed the early race. From mid–May to mid–June, the Dodgers went 15–7 facing East teams and then went 12–2 within the division to lead by 6.5 games entering July. While the Dodgers never tanked, the Reds went 24–7 in July and won their first five games in September to take the lead; going 4–1 against the Dodgers in September preserved it. The Dodgers' main strength was lack of weaknesses; catcher Joe Ferguson, rightfielder Willie Crawford, shortstop Bill Russell, and third baseman Ron Cey led the position players, while Don Sutton led the pitchers. The Reds were almost entirely lineup-driven, while Jack Billingham was a workhorse for the rotation and Pedro Borbon was Billingham's equivalent in the bullpen.

1974: Slow Starts and Subtle Shifts

AL E	BAL	BOS	DET	NY	CLE	MIL
Start	491	33	224	151		
6/1	483	41	200	175		39
7/1	457	131	186	145	37	45

AL E	BAL	BOS	DET	NY	CLE	MIL
8/1	534	224	171	126	130	26
9/1	507	317	140	103	139	
End	600	346	109	196	108	
Spt.	**1.48**	1.14	1.25	1.13	1.03	1.01

Name	*Tm*	*Pos*	*WAR*	*SpW*	*Fame*
Grich	BAL	2B	**7.3**	**10.8**	**3.5**
Blair	BAL	CF	5.3	**7.8**	**2.5**
Robinson	BAL	3B	5.0	7.4	**2.4**
Belanger	BAL	SS	4.5	6.7	**2.2**
Tiant	BOS	P	**7.8**	**8.9**	1.1
Maddox	NY	CF/RF	**5.4**	6.1	0.7
G. Perry	CLE	P	**8.6**	**8.9**	0.3

AL W	CAL	CHI	KC	MIN	OAK	TEX
Start	30	108	173	37	476	
6/1	18	120	161	1	**512**	9
7/1		102	143		602	
8/1		71	112		695	
9/1		40	81		788	
End		9	50		881	
Spt.	1.01	1.04	1.07	1.00	**1.57**	1.00

Name	*Tm*	*Pos*	*WAR*	*SpW*	*Fame*
Hunter	OAK	P	6.9	**10.8**	**3.9**
Jackson	OAK	RF	5.7	**8.9**	**3.2**
Campaneris	OAK	SS	5.3	**8.3**	**3.0**
Tenace	OAK	C	4.9	7.7	**2.8**
Kaat	CHI	P	**7.1**	7.4	0.3
Blyleven	MIN	P	**7.9**	**7.9**	
Jenkins	TEX	P	**7.7**	**7.7**	
Carew	MIN	2B	**7.4**	**7.4**	

NL E	CHI	NY	PIT	STL	MON	PHI
Start	184	73	243	108		
6/1	148	37	207	180	33	62
7/1	118	7	177	246	23	144
8/1	87		146	275		189
9/1	56		175	368		230
End	25		268	457		199
Spt.	1.07	1.02	**1.25**	1.26	1.01	1.09

Name	*Tm*	*Pos*	*WAR*	*SpW*	*Fame*
Smith	STL	RF	**5.5**	6.9	**1.4**
Stargell	PIT	LF	5.3	6.6	**1.3**
McGlothen	STL	P	5.0	6.3	**1.3**
Zisk	PIT	RF	5.2	6.5	**1.3**
Schmidt	PHI	3B	**9.7**	**10.6**	0.9
Matlack	NY	P	**9.1**	**9.3**	0.2
Seaver	NY	P	**6.1**	6.2	0.1

NL W	CIN	HOU	LA	SF
Start	363	15	269	155
6/1	327	15	377	123
7/1	297		467	93
8/1	266		560	62
9/1	275		653	31
End	308		746	
Spt.	1.39	1.00	1.58	1.06

Name	Tm	Pos	WAR	SpW	Fame
Wynn	LA	CF	7.7	12.2	4.5
Morgan	CIN	2B	8.6	12.0	3.4
Messersmith	LA	P	5.3	8.4	3.1
Bench	CIN	C/3B	7.8	10.8	3.0
Niekro	ATL	P	7.8	7.8	

As in 1973, the AL took a long time to get going; even in mid–June, records like the Indians' 30–28 were the fourth-best in the league. The A's opened up space for good in June and July with a Royals-Angels-Royals-Angels 15-game stretch in which they went 11–4. The lineup was six deep, as Bert Campaneris and Gene Tenace had great years to complement Sal Bando and the outfield of Joe Rudi, Billy North, and Reggie Jackson.

In the AL East, every team gained Momentum in July for at least a couple days. The Red Sox built up a seven-game lead with a week left in August, but they lost it all in two weeks, including a sweep by the Orioles, who went 28–6 at the end of the season to go from below .500 to a division title. The Yankees had taken a similar path as the Orioles up to early September; they finished two games back. The Red Sox were thin but led by big talents in Luis Tiant, Carl Yastrzemski, and Dwight Evans. Besides the Orioles' lineup mainstays, Mike Cuellar won 22 games and Reds castoff Ross Grimsley was the surprise second starter while Jim Palmer's luck was down.

In the NL East, three days in July had no teams gaining Momentum. The Cardinals' long losing streak in July gave first to the Phillies; they reclaimed it by taking five of six from them July 30–August 5. But the Pirates, who started the season 0–6 and were in last place in June, went 20–8 in August, swept the Phillies and Expos to start September, and finished the season 8–2, including a series win against the Cardinals, to win the division. The Pirates were led by their slugging outfield of Willie Stargell, Al Oliver, and Richie Zisk, while late bloomer Jim Rooker was the clear ace of a thin mound crew. The Cardinals' construction was similar, with Lynn McGlothen taking the place of Jim Rooker and an outfield of Lou Brock, Rookie of the Year Bake McBride, and Reggie Smith.

In the NL West, the Dodgers started 27–9, eliminating all suspense until late August, when back-to-back sweeps by the Mets and Pirates let the Reds into the race. Although the Reds got as close as 1.5 games during a mid–September series against the Dodgers, the Dodgers won the final game and eventually the division. The Reds were only one game worse than 1973, with a deeper lineup highlighted by shortstop Dave Concepcion's sustained progress. The Dodgers had superior pitching, behind Andy Messersmith's 292 innings as a starter and Mike Marshall's 208 as a reliever, but the surprise was the Dodgers' superior lineup; every position's starter contributed at least 3 WAR for the first time in NL history.

1975: Similar But Different

AL E	BAL	BOS	CLE	DET	NY	MIL
Start	378	218	68	69	124	
6/1	342	270	32	45	88	63
7/1	312	360	2	15	162	61
8/1	281	453			167	66
9/1	250	546			136	35
End	223	627			109	8
Spt.	1.34	**1.50***	1.01	1.03	1.19	1.02

Name	Tm	Pos	WAR	SpW	Fame
Lynn	BOS	CF	**7.4**	**11.1**	3.7
Palmer	BAL	P	**8.4**	**11.3**	2.9
Evans	BOS	RF	5.1	7.7	2.6
Grich	BAL	2B	**7.3**	**9.8**	2.5
Hunter	NY	P	**8.1**	**9.6**	1.5

AL W	CHI	KC	OAK	MIN	TEX
Start	6	32	555		
6/1		80	663	23	61
7/1		126	753		31
8/1		95	846		
9/1		64	939		
End		37	1020		
Spt.	1.00	1.08	**1.55**	1.00	1.01

Name	Tm	Pos	WAR	SpW	Fame
Jackson	OAK	RF	6.7	**10.4**	3.7
North	OAK	CF	5.7	8.8	3.1
Tenace	OAK	C/1B	5.2	8.1	2.9
Washington	OAK	LF/CF	4.9	7.6	2.7
Gossage	CHI	P	**8.2**	8.2	
Kaat	CHI	P	**7.8**	7.8	
Carew	MIN	2B	**7.4**	7.4	
Tanana	CAL	P	**7.4**	7.4	

NL E	CHI	PHI	PIT	STL	NY
Start	13	103	139	238	
6/1	97	103	163	202	11

12. Divisions of Labor

NL E	CHI	PHI	PIT	STL	NY
7/1	107	153	253	172	49
8/1	76	122	346	141	18
9/1	45	179	439	150	
End	18	152	520	123	
Spt.	1.04	1.13	**1.32**	1.24	1.01

Name	Tm	Pos	WAR	SpW	Fame
Parker	PIT	RF	**6.3**	8.3	**2.0**
Reuss	PIT	P	5.4	7.1	**1.7**
Stennett	PIT	2B	4.9	6.5	**1.6**
Sanguillen	PIT	C	4.6	6.1	**1.5**
Forsch	STL	P	**5.7**	7.1	1.4
Schmidt	PHI	3B	**7.7**	8.7	1.0
Seaver	NY	P	**7.8**	7.9	0.1

NL W	CIN	LA
Start		
6/1	160	388
7/1	184	**496**
8/1	274	**542**
9/1	367	**511**
End	460	**480**
Spt.	**541**	453
	1.48	1.48

Name	Tm	Pos	WAR	SpW	Fame
Morgan	CIN	2B	**10.9**	15.0	**4.1**
Cey	LA	3B	**6.7**	9.9	**3.2**
Messersmith	LA	P	**6.5**	9.6	**3.1**
Lopes	LA	2B/CF	5.3	7.8	**2.5**
Bench	CIN	C	6.6	9.1	**2.5**
Jones	SD	P	**7.5**	7.5	
Montefusco	SF	P	**6.8**	6.8	

The A's wrapped up the AL West in June again, with a 13–1 streak mostly at the expense of their nearest rivals, the Royals and Twins. Catfish Hunter had been granted a rare case of free agency[4] and signed with the Yankees. Hunter's departure left the rotation with issues behind Vida Blue and Ken Holtzman, but the bullpen picked up the slack; stalwarts Rollie Fingers and Paul Lindblad were joined by Jim Todd, a previously mediocre pitcher acquired just before Opening Day.

The Orioles entered June in last place, and while they eventually won 90 games, they didn't gain Momentum; the Red Sox won the East handily by winning 10 straight in July and never losing more than three straight after that. Centerfielder Fred Lynn was Rookie of the Year and MVP; teamed with fellow rookie Jim Rice, fellow outfielder Dwight Evans, and catcher Carlton Fisk when he was healthy, Lynn's contribution was the main difference between 1974's good team and 1975's great team.

In the NL West, the Reds, 20–20 on May 20, took three months to lose another 20, leading the Dodgers by over 20 games when they took Momentum lead from them on September 7. The 1974 no-weakness Dodgers saw slumps in 1975 from shortstop Bill Russell, leftfielder Bill Buckner, and closer Mike Marshall. Outside Don Gullett, the Reds didn't have pitchers as good as even the Dodgers' third starter. But the lineup matched the 1974 Dodgers' feat of all 3-WAR players, highlighted by the power of Johnny Bench, Tony Perez, and George Foster and the all-around offense of Pete Rose and unanimous MVP Joe Morgan.

In the NL East, the Pirates took the division lead in June and bumped the Cubs and Mets out of the race with sweeps at the end of the month. A 6.5-game lead in mid-July evaporated with a 4–14 start to August, letting the Phillies and the Cardinals in. But the Cardinals were as bad in September as the Pirates were in August and the Phillies lacked the talent to keep up, leaving the division to Pittsburgh. Dave Parker led the league in slugging in his first full season, while Rennie Stennett's improvement stabilized the defense. Jim Rooker wasn't quite the ace he was in 1974, but Jerry Reuss, 26 and in his sixth full season, put everything together.

At the end of 1975, Peter Seitz's arbitration decision opened the door to free agency as a way for players—and franchises—to rise and fall precipitously, although its effects for the time being were limited primarily to Dodgers ace Andy Messersmith.[5]

1976: The Reds and New Faces

AL E	BAL	BOS	MIL	NY
Start	113	317	4	55
6/1	108	292		130
7/1	78	262		220
8/1	47	231		313
9/1	16	200		**406**
End		168		**502**
Spt.	1.08	1.31	1.00	**1.45**

Name	*Tm*	*Pos*	*WAR*	*SpW*	*Fame*
Nettles	NY	3B	8.0	**11.6**	**3.6**
Rivers	NY	CF	6.4	9.2	**2.8**
White	NY	LF/CF	5.5	8.0	**2.5**
Munson	NY	C	5.3	7.7	**2.4**
Tiant	BOS	P	6.3	**8.3**	2.0
Palmer	BAL	P	**6.6**	7.1	0.5
Belanger	BAL	SS	**6.5**	7.0	0.5
Fidrych	DET	P	9.6	9.6	

12. Divisions of Labor

AL W	KC	OAK	CHI	TEX
Start	18	**516**		
6/1	85	**491**	2	75
7/1	175	**461**		113
8/1	268	**430**		86
9/1	361	**399**		55
End	457	379		23
Spt.	**1.28**	1.47	1.00	1.07

Name	Tm	Pos	WAR	SpW	Fame
Blue	OAK	P	7.7	**11.3**	3.6
Bando	OAK	3B	5.8	**8.5**	2.7
Torrez	OAK	P	5.3	**7.8**	2.5
Campaneris	OAK	SS	4.5	6.6	**2.1**
Brett	KC	3B	**7.5**	9.6	**2.1**
Tanana	CAL	P	**7.5**	7.5	
Carew	MIN	1B	**6.8**	6.8	

NL E	CHI	PHI	PIT	STL	NY
Start	9	79	268	63	
6/1		150	303	30	43
7/1		240	273		13
8/1		333	242		
9/1		426	211		
End		522	183		
Spt.	1.00	**1.34**	1.28	1.02	1.03

Name	Tm	Pos	WAR	SpW	Fame
Schmidt	PHI	3B	**8.0**	10.7	2.7
Maddox	PHI	CF	6.4	**8.6**	2.3
Johnstone	PHI	RF	4.3	**5.8**	1.5
Carlton	PHI	P	4.0	5.4	**1.4**
Seaver	NY	P	**5.5**	5.7	0.2
Burris	CHI	P	**5.2**	5.2	

NL W		CIN	LA	
Start		**279**	234	
6/1		**362**	329	
7/1		**452**	351	
8/1		**545**	320	
9/1		**638**	289	
End		**734**	257	
Spt.		**1.60**	1.34	

Name	Tm	Pos	WAR	SpW	Fame
Morgan	CIN	2B	9.6	**15.4**	5.8
Rose	CIN	3B	6.9	**11.0**	4.1
Foster	CIN	LF/CF	5.9	**9.4**	3.5
Bench	CIN	C	4.6	7.4	**2.8**
Cey	LA	3B	6.0	**8.0**	2.0
Montefusco	SF	P	**6.9**	6.9	
Niekro	ATL	P	**6.6**	6.6	

Messersmith signed with the Braves, but the Dodgers again led the race until the Reds got hot in June. The Dodgers played fantastic defense to back starters Doug Rau and Don Sutton, but Ron Cey and Steve Garvey were the only hitters of note. The Reds had no such offensive woes, as they scored 212 runs above league average and led the league in singles, doubles, triples, homers, walks, and steals. In a league with 17 4-WAR hitters, the Reds had six of them, with Ken Griffey and Dave Concepcion supporting Morgan/Rose/Foster/Bench.

In the NL East, the Phillies started 26–9 and held a 14.5-game lead in August. The Pirates beat them several times down the stretch and were three games back on September 17, but the Phillies ended the season 14–3 and finished comfortably ahead. For the Pirates, Rennie Stennett and Jerry Reuss struggled, but the outfield still slugged. The Phillies were built on their frontline talent, third baseman Mike Schmidt and centerfielder Garry Maddox. For the pitching, Steve Carlton and Jim Lonborg were on the up half of some up-and-down years, and offseason acquisition Ron Reed provided a stopper in the bullpen after several years as a back-end starter.

Owner Charlie Finley traded Reggie Jackson to the Orioles and got good short-term value from the deal in Mike Torrez and Don Baylor, but the A's started 15–23 and found themselves well behind the Rangers and Royals. The A's tried to sell their best remaining players before free agency but were blocked by commissioner Bowie Kuhn.[6] The Rangers dropped out of the race by losing 10 straight in July, leaving the Royals alone, even as a 12–19 end to the season gave the A's a chance in the last week. The Royals were led by third baseman George Brett, the bat of Hal McRae, and a deep bullpen fronted by Mark Littell.

The Red Sox gained no Momentum, returning to an assembly of decent players. Instead of them or the Orioles, the Yankees held first place alone starting in May thanks to the AL's best lineup by far. 3B Graig Nettles was superb on offense and defense, and rookie second baseman Willie Randolph was nearly Nettles's equal with the glove. Outfielders Roy White and Mickey Rivers were in the league's top three in runs scored, driven in by Nettles, first baseman Chris Chambliss, and catcher and MVP Thurman Munson. Like the Yankees of old, the offense/defense combination made the mediocre pitching, led by starters Catfish Hunter and Ed Figueroa and reliever Sparky Lyle, look good.

1977: Expansion, Chicago and the Same Endings

AL E	BOS	NY	BAL	MIL
Start	84	251		
6/1	149	348	87	9

12. Divisions of Labor

AL E	BOS	NY	BAL	MIL
7/1	239	**418**	137	
8/1	332	**511**	230	
9/1	417	**548**	283	
End	458	**641**	312	
Spt.	1.32	**1.60**	1.08	1.00

Name	Tm	Pos	WAR	SpW	Fame
Nettles	NY	3B	5.5	**8.8**	**3.3**
Rivers	NY	CF	5.3	**8.5**	**3.2**
Munson	NY	C	4.9	7.8	**2.9**
Guidry	NY	P	4.8	7.7	**2.9**
Fisk	BOS	C	**7.0**	**9.2**	2.2
Palmer	BAL	P	**7.5**	8.1	0.6
Singleton	BAL	RF	**5.7**	6.2	0.5
Rozema	DET	P	**5.7**	5.7	

AL W	KC	OAK	TEX	CHI	MIN
Start	229	190	12		
6/1	230	195	17	89	105
7/1	208	165		179	195
8/1	213	134		272	188
9/1	286	103	58	365	269
End	379	72	27	334	238
Spt.	**1.33**	1.13	1.01	1.14	1.09

Name	Tm	Pos	WAR	SpW	Fame
Brett	KC	3B	7.6	**10.1**	**2.5**
Leonard	KC	P	5.6	7.4	**1.8**
Cowens	KC	RF/CF	5.3	7.0	**1.7**
McRae	KC	DH/LF	4.8	6.4	**1.6**
Carew	MIN	1B	**9.7**	**10.6**	0.9
Tanana	CAL	P	**8.3**	8.3	
Ryan	CAL	P	**7.8**	7.8	

NL E	PHI	PIT	CHI	STL
Start	261	92		
6/1	232	179	60	72
7/1	206	185	150	74
8/1	251	190	243	43
9/1	344	199	252	12
End	437	168	221	
Spt.	**1.41**	1.15	1.14	1.03

Name	Tm	Pos	WAR	SpW	Fame
Schmidt	PHI	3B	**8.8**	**12.4**	**3.6**
Carlton	PHI	P	5.9	8.3	**2.4**
Luzinski	PHI	LF	4.2	5.9	**1.7**
Maddox	PHI	CF	3.7	5.2	**1.5**
Reuschel	CHI	P	**9.4**	**10.7**	1.3
Candelaria	PIT	P	**7.4**	**8.5**	1.1
Parker	PIT	P	**7.3**	**8.4**	1.1

NL W	CIN	LA
Start	367	128
6/1	334	227
7/1	304	317
8/1	273	410
9/1	242	503
End	211	596
Spt.	1.38	1.52

Name	Tm	Pos	WAR	SpW	Fame
Foster	CIN	LF/CF	8.4	11.6	3.2
Smith	LA	RF	6.1	9.3	3.2
Hooton	LA	P	5.5	8.4	2.9
Lopes	LA	2B	4.6	7.0	2.4
Seaver	2 TM	P	8.0	10.1	2.1
Niekro	ATL	P	8.9	8.9	

In the NL West, only the Dodgers gained Momentum, starting 22–4 and leading by 10.5 games on May 6. The Reds obtained 52 home runs from George Foster and an ace in Tom Seaver, but four pitchers had a better OPS than primary reserves Mike Lum and Bill Plummer, and the back of the rotation was terrible. The Dodgers returned to 1974's broad competence, with four 30-homer players in Steve Garvey, Reggie Smith, Dusty Baker, and Ron Cey and a superb leadoff man in Davey Lopes. Meanwhile, all five members of the starting rotation cleared 210 innings of quality work.

Even with the Reds' and Dodgers' offenses, the Phillies led the league in runs. But their offense didn't heat up until July, and the East initially was a battle among the Cardinals, Cubs, and Pirates. The Cubs, led by starter Rick Reuschel and reliever Bruce Sutter, had an 8.5-game lead in June after a 15–3 run; losing three of four to the Phillies in mid–July and four of four to them in mid–August sent the Cubs toward .500. When the Cubs disappeared, the Pirates and Phillies re-entered the race; the Phillies started August 19–2 and were unchallenged the rest of the way. June acquisition Bake McBride, .339/.392/.564 in 85 games, gave the Phillies a deep enough offense to win when Steve Carlton wasn't starting.

The expansion Mariners and Blue Jays joined the free-agency-torn A's to give AL teams free wins all year. The Royals entered June 6–2 against the expansion teams and 15–21 otherwise; at that point the White Sox and Twins, both offense-driven, were fighting for first. The Royals threatened once they hit their offensive stride. The White Sox went 22–6 in July, starting by sweeping the Twins in four and ending with three wins over the Royals, to build a good lead. But with little pitching and terrible defense the Sox gave up 6.4 runs/game in a lousy August. They and the Royals, Twins, and Rangers were viable through August, but the Royals went 35–4 from August 17 to September 25 to obliterate the division. Besides stars George Brett and Hal McRae and breakouts Al Cowens and Dennis Leonard, most Royals pitchers had better-than-average ERAs.

The Yankees, Orioles, and Red Sox fought each other all season, never falling more than 6.5 games out of first in the East. The Yankees took the division lead on August 23 and held it the rest of the way. The Orioles had rebuilt behind Ken Singleton and Jim Palmer with Rookie of the Year first baseman Eddie Murray and Doug DeCinces replacing Brooks Robinson at third base. For the Red Sox, Carlton Fisk was both productive **and** healthy, Jim Rice, Carl Yastrzemski, and George Scott provided power, and closer Bill Campbell was the team's best pitcher. For the Yankees, free agents Reggie Jackson and Don Gullett and near-rookie pitcher Ron Guidry made up for slight declines from the 1976 offensive core and Catfish Hunter's struggles. Ed Figueroa and Sparky Lyle's seasons resembled 1976's but were more valuable in 1977's higher-scoring environment.

1978: All of the Above

AL E	BAL	BOS	NY	DET
Start	181	266	**373**	
6/1	147	356	**463**	66
7/1	117	**446**	433	36
8/1	86	**539**	402	5
9/1	55	**632**	371	
End	24	**721**	444	
Spt.	1.06	1.45	**1.51**	1.01

Name	Tm	Pos	WAR	SpW	Fame
Guidry	NY	P	**9.6**	**14.5**	**4.9**
Rice	BOS	LF/DH	7.5	10.9	3.4
Eckersley	BOS	P	7.3	**10.6**	3.3
Randolph	NY	P	5.8	**8.8**	3.0
Caldwell	MIL	P	**8.1**	8.1	

AL W	CHI	KC	MIN	OAK	TEX	CAL
Start	194	220	138	42	16	
6/1	160	246	104	144	8	90
7/1	130	328	74	170	46	132
8/1	99	**405**	43	167	59	201
9/1	68	**498**	12	140	28	294
End	37	**591**		109		303
Spt.	1.08	**1.39**	1.04	1.09	1.00	1.10

Name	Tm	Pos	WAR	SpW	Fame
Otis	KC	CF	7.4	**10.3**	2.9
Brett	KC	3B	5.3	**7.4**	2.1

Name	Tm	Pos	WAR	SpW	Fame
Gura	KC	P	4.5	6.3	**1.8**
Porter	KC	C	4.2	5.8	**1.6**
Goltz	MIN	P	**6.6**	**6.9**	0.3
Smalley	MIN	SS	**5.9**	**6.1**	0.2
Matlack	TEX	P	**6.4**	**6.4**	

NL E	CHI	PHI	PIT	MON
Start	111	218	84	
6/1	141	268	54	46
7/1	227	**358**	24	68
8/1	200	**451**		37
9/1	221	**544**		6
End	190	**637**	46	
Spt.	1.17	**1.51**	1.03	1.02

Name	Tm	Pos	WAR	SpW	Fame
Schmidt	PHI	3B	**6.2**	**9.4**	**3.2**
Bowa	PHI	SS	**5.7**	**8.6**	**2.9**
Luzinski	PHI	LF	5.4	**8.2**	**2.8**
Maddox	PHI	CF	5.1	**7.7**	**2.6**
Parker	PIT	RF	**7.0**	7.2	0.2
Carter	MON	C	**5.8**	5.9	0.1

NL W	CIN	LA	SF
Start	105	**298**	
6/1	207	**372**	81
7/1	285	350	171
8/1	362	**435**	264
9/1	419	**516**	357
End	396	**609**	354
Spt.	1.29	**1.54**	1.12

Name	Tm	Pos	WAR	SpW	Fame
Cey	LA	3B	5.3	**8.2**	**2.9**
Hooton	LA	P	5.1	**7.9**	**2.8**
Lopes	LA	2B	4.8	**7.4**	**2.6**
Garvey	LA	1B	4.7	7.2	**2.5**
Knepper	SF	P	**6.3**	7.1	0.8
Clark	SF	RF	**5.9**	6.6	0.7
Blue	SF	P	**5.8**	6.5	0.7
Niekro	ATL	P	**10.0**	**10.0**	

On June 28, when the Red Sox took Momentum lead from the Yankees, they led the Brewers by 8.5 games and the Yankees by 9.5 with a red-hot offense (featuring a resurgent Fred Lynn) and better pitching than usual (featuring Dennis Eckersley, a resurgent Luis Tiant, and a blossoming Bob Stanley). But the run scoring cooled down as the Yankees' run prevention heated up, and the Yankees took the division lead by sweeping the Red Sox September 7–10 and taking two of three from them the next week. They ended tied; Mike Torrez, signed by the Red Sox after winning two World Series games for the Yankees in 1977, gave up the go-ahead home run in the tiebreaker game to light-hitting shortstop Bucky Dent.

For the Yankees, closer Goose Gossage was a great import, although erstwhile closer Sparky Lyle's relative slump made it a wash. Don Gullett and Catfish Hunter were injured for long periods, but Ed Figueroa won 20 games behind Ron Guidry (25–3), whose 1.74 ERA shone against the league's 3.76. Willie Randolph and Graig Nettles were the best position players on offense and defense.

With so many good teams in the East—the Brewers and Orioles each won at least 90 games but gained no Momentum—the West had trouble locating .500. The A's started 14–3 and went 55–90 afterward, but they still gained Momentum in August. Around them, the Royals, Angels, and Rangers stumbled together; the Royals' 15–2 run in July shook off the Rangers and their 7–0 record against the A's in September shook off the Angels. The Royals got a great year from Amos Otis to complement George Brett, offense from catcher Darrell Porter, and defense from second baseman Frank White; ace Dennis Leonard was joined by newly converted starter Larry Gura.

Like the Red Sox, the Phillies took Momentum lead on June 28, as the Dodgers were trailing the Reds, who were contending through George Foster's and Johnny Bench's hitting, and the Giants, who were contending through Bob Knepper's and Vida Blue's pitching.

The Reds left the race by losing six straight in August, while the Giants' 1–10 stretch in September, including losing four to the Dodgers, left the Dodgers as the last team standing. Their rotation was not as good as in 1977, but rookie Bob Welch was effective after a June callup, first in the bullpen and then filling in for starter Rick Rhoden. The lineup's mainstays mostly replicated their performances; Dusty Baker's decline was picked up by the bench, and Rick Monday, Lee Lacy, and Billy North provided different skills to mix and match.

The Momentum and division lead the Phillies took in late June held up, even as the Cubs threatened through August and the Pirates' 37–12 finish put them one game back on September 19. Besides Mike Schmidt's and Greg Luzinski's hitting, the Phillies won four Gold Gloves (Schmidt, Garry Maddox, Larry Bowa, and Bob Boone), every one necessary to prop up the rotation. Dick Ruthven, acquired at the June 15 trade deadline for reliever Gene Garber, gave the Phillies enough starting pitching, along with Steve Carlton, to survive.

The year 1978 is the only one in which the previous year's division winners all repeated.

1979: Rising Stars ...

AL E	BAL	BOS	NY	MIL
Start	13	375	231	
6/1	121	467	203	38
7/1	211	521	173	16
8/1	304	554	142	
9/1	397	523	111	
End	484	494	82	
Spt.	1.33*	1.49	1.13	1.01

Name	Tm	Pos	WAR	SpW	Fame
Lynn	BOS	CF	8.8	13.1	4.3
Eckersley	BOS	P	7.3	10.9	3.6
Rice	BOS	LF/DH	6.3	9.4	3.1
Burleson	BOS	SS	3.8	5.7	1.9
Guidry	NY	P	6.5	7.4	0.9

AL W	CAL	CHI	KC	OAK	MIN	TEX
Start	158	19	307	56		
6/1	234		319	20	99	52
7/1	324		365		129	86
8/1	417		338		150	151
9/1	510		335		183	124
End	597		386		178	95
Spt.	1.38	1.00	1.33	1.02	1.06	1.04

Name	Tm	Pos	WAR	SpW	Fame
Brett	KC	3B	8.6	11.4	2.8
Porter	KC	C	7.6	10.1	2.5
Grich	CAL	2B	5.9	8.1	2.2
Downing	CAL	C	5.6	7.7	2.1
Wilson	KC	LF/CF	6.3	8.4	2.1
Koosman	MIN	P	7.2	7.6	0.4
Bell	TEX	3B	6.9	7.2	0.3

NL E	CHI	PHI	PIT	MON	STL
Start	101	340	25		
6/1	67	426		88	
7/1	37	420		178	30
8/1	86	425	42	271	
9/1	55	394	135	348	
End	26	365	222	431	
Spt.	1.04	1.47	1.32*	1.13	1.00

Name	Tm	Pos	WAR	SpW	Fame
Schmidt	PHI	3B	7.9	11.6	3.7
Maddox	PHI	CF	5.0	7.4	2.4
Parker	PIT	RF	6.7	8.8	2.1
Boone	PHI	C	3.4	5.0	1.6
Carter	MON	C	5.9	6.7	0.8
Hernandez	STL	1B	7.6	7.6	

12. Divisions of Labor 237

NL W	CIN	LA	SF	HOU
Start	211	325	189	
6/1	293	291	195	102
7/1	335	261	165	192
8/1	312	230	134	285
9/1	341	199	103	378
End	428	170	74	461
Spt.	1.37	1.24	1.10	1.22

Name	Tm	Pos	WAR	SpW	Fame
Bench	CIN	C	5.6	7.7	2.1
Foster	CIN	LF	5.1	7.0	1.9
Concepcion	CIN	SS	4.9	6.7	1.8
Hume	CIN	P	3.9	5.3	1.4
Richard	HOU	P	5.6	6.8	1.2
Winfield	SD	RF	8.3	8.3	
Niekro	ATL	P	7.6	7.6	
Tenace	SD	C/1B	5.9	5.9	

Given 1978's playoff repeats, it was fitting that 1979 would be the first year in divisional play without any. And the NL was so surprising that the Astros and Expos, with 0 Momentum entering 1979, were the top two teams in Momentum by the end. The Dodgers were only over .500 for six days, hitting 35 more home runs than any other NL team but suffering from iffy defense and a bad bullpen. The Astros held a 10.5-game lead on July 4; aided by the Astrodome, their games were low-scoring on both sides through starters J.R. Richard and Joe Niekro, closer Joe Sambito, defense, and little offense outside Jose Cruz. Past July 4, the Reds allowed even fewer runs than the Astros, going 11–2 at the end of August and taking first for good by winning a two-game series against the Astros on September 11–12. Johnny Bench, George Foster, Dave Concepcion, and Tom Seaver were joined by reliever Tom Hume and third baseman Ray Knight, who replaced free agent Pete Rose.

Rose signed with the Phillies, who started 21–7. But Rose couldn't make up for the bullpen's implosion or an inconsistent Steve Carlton. Like the Astros, the Expos held a sizable lead on July 4. But the Pirates virtually tied them by going 13–1 against the West and taking three of four from the Expos on July 27–29. The Pirates went 8–1 against the Phillies in August to build a lead, survived the Expos' 17–1 run that started August 28, and went 5–1 against the Expos in September to win the East by two games. The Expos allowed one fewer run than the Astros with a deep staff headlined by starters Steve Rogers and Bill Lee and closer Elias Sosa; Gary Carter, Larry Parrish, and Andre Dawson led the offense. The Pirates scored the most runs in the NL thanks to Dave Parker, Willie Stargell, Bill Robinson, and midseason pickup Bill Madlock, with a decent rotation and a deep bullpen led by Kent Tekulve.

The AL East ended with the league's four best records, so while the Yankees weren't bad, they barely impacted the race. The Red Sox started fast while the Orioles started 3–8, but the Orioles went 15–1 right after; another 15–1 run in June and a 15–2 run in July/August left them unchallenged. The Red Sox were led by Fred Lynn, Jim Rice, and Dennis Eckersley, who were supported by Dwight Evans, Rick Burleson, and midseason acquisition Bob Watson. The Orioles' Ken Singleton and Eddie Murray weren't Lynn/Rice good, but the outstanding defense helped each pitcher record an above-average ERA, and the team allowed 3.66 runs/game to the league average of 4.67.

With so many good teams in the East, the West was bizarre. The Royals and Angels were the only teams with decent hitting, but neither could pitch and the Angels couldn't field. The Royals' 1–14 stretch, starting with a sweep by the Angels June 29–July 1, did them in; the Twins made noise in September, but the Angels won 88 games and the division. Dave Frost and Nolan Ryan were the Angels' best pitchers, but the offense was the catalyst, led by former free-agent signings Don Baylor and Bobby Grich and surprise Brian Downing. Rod Carew, acquired from the Twins in the offseason, and youngsters Willie Aikens and Carney Lansford provided extra firepower.

1980: ... Sometimes Fall Back Down

AL E	BAL	BOS	NY	TOR		
Start	276	282	47			
6/1	242	256	133	51		
7/1	212	226	223	21		
8/1	181	195	316			
9/1	222	164	409			
End	243	129	514			
Spt.	1.22	1.25	**1.28**	1.01		

Name	Tm	Pos	WAR	SpW	Fame
Randolph	NY	2B	**6.6**	**8.4**	**1.8**
May	NY	P	4.9	6.3	**1.4**
Bumbry	BAL	CF	6.1	**7.4**	**1.3**
Jackson	NY	RF/DH	4.7	6.0	**1.3**
Yount	MIL	SS	**7.1**	**7.1**	
Cooper	MIL	1B	**6.8**	**6.8**	
Oglivie	MIL	LF	**6.4**	6.4	

AL W	CAL	KC	MIN	TEX	CHI	OAK
Start	340	220	102	54		
6/1	306	270	68	100	89	87
7/1	276	**360**	38	70	71	61
8/1	245	**453**	7	39	40	30
9/1	214	**546**		8	9	

12. Divisions of Labor   239

	AL W	CAL	KC	MIN	TEX	CHI	OAK
End		179	651				
Spt.		1.37	**1.51**	1.03	1.03	1.02	1.02

Name	Tm	Pos	WAR	SpW	Fame
Brett	KC	3B	**9.4**	**14.2**	**4.8**
Wilson	KC	LF/CF	**8.4**	**12.7**	**4.3**
Gura	KC	P	6.2	**9.4**	**3.2**
Leonard	KC	P	3.7	5.6	**1.9**
Henderson	OAK	LF	**8.8**	**9.0**	0.2
Burns	CHI	P	**7.0**	7.1	0.1

	NL E	CHI	MON	PHI	PIT
Start		20	324	274	167
6/1			311	293	250
7/1			397	367	328
8/1			490	428	421
9/1			583	457	514
End			688	562	507
Spt.		1.00	1.36	**1.50***	1.15

Name	Tm	Pos	WAR	SpW	Fame
Carlton	PHI	P	**10.2**	**15.3**	**5.1**
Schmidt	PHI	3B	**8.8**	**13.2**	**4.4**
Dawson	MON	CF	**6.8**	**9.2**	**2.4**
McGraw	PHI	P	4.7	7.1	**2.4**
Carter	MON	C	6.5	**8.8**	2.3
Hernandez	STL	1B	**6.6**	6.6	

	NL W	CIN	HOU	LA	SF
Start		322	**347**	128	55
6/1		417	**430**	227	22
7/1		443	**520**	317	
8/1		412	**613**	406	
9/1		461	**706**	499	
End		450	**811**	604	
Spt.		1.23	**1.55**	1.10	1.01

Name	Tm	Pos	WAR	SpW	Fame
Puhl	HOU	RF/CF	**6.2**	**9.6**	**3.4**
Cedeno	HOU	CF	5.0	**7.8**	**2.8**
Cruz	HOU	LF	4.8	**7.4**	**2.6**
Morgan	HOU	2B	3.6	5.6	**2.0**
Sutton	LA	P	**6.3**	**6.9**	0.6
Reuss	LA	P	**5.2**	5.7	0.5
Murphy	ATL	CF/RF	**6.5**	6.5	

The Angels were nearly one-dimensional in 1979. Then Nolan Ryan signed a massive contract with the Astros and Dave Frost, Don Baylor, and Brian Downing got hurt, leaving no dimensions and 95 losses. The Royals swept the Angels over May 23–25 to take first and win easily, holding a 20-game lead entering

September. George Brett's .390/.454/.664 mark led the league in all three categories, and leadoff man Willie Wilson led the league in runs by 12 and hits by 11. For the pitchers, Larry Gura rebounded from a mediocre year to provide 280 innings with a 2.95 ERA; Dennis Leonard wasn't as good, but he provided another 280 innings and won 20 games.

The Yankees also stayed in first starting in May, but the Orioles, near last when the Yankees took first, climbed to second by the end of July, won their first ten games in August, including a sweep of the Yankees, and won a series against them a few days later. The Orioles ended the season 45–18, but the Yankees stayed ahead by starting September 15–1. For the Orioles, Steve Stone and Scott McGregor won 45 games between them, and Al Bumbry's best season in years gave Ken Singleton and Eddie Murray someone to drive in. For the Yankees, Willie Randolph excelled in the leadoff spot, and thanks to platoons and Reggie Jackson the Yankees were second in the AL in home runs. For the pitchers, Goose Gossage was his usual self as closer, Tommy John won 22 games, and 35-year-old swingman Rudy May joined the rotation in June and led the league in ERA.

Both National League races featured three teams in September. The Pirates picked up where they'd left off, buoyed by surprise contributions from Mike Easler and Lee Lacy. But the team was streaky, and the offense disappeared in September. The Expos held a narrow lead through September behind strong repeat performances from Gary Carter, Andre Dawson, and Steve Rogers, reinforced by Ellis Valentine and young starters Scott Sanderson and Bill Gullickson. But the Phillies had the league's best hitter (Mike Schmidt), starter (Steve Carlton), and reliever (Tug McGraw). The Phillies and Expos faced each other in the final series of the year; they entered it tied for first, but the Phillies won the first two games to take the division.

While the East took 161 games to sort out, the West took 163. The Reds started 8–0 and were in the race most of the year; Johnny Bench and George Foster's performances propped up struggling veterans. But the Astros and Dodgers missed only a day of Momentum apiece from Memorial Day forward. The Dodgers swept the Astros in the last series of the season to force a tiebreaker game; the Astros won it 7–1 for their first division title. Nolan Ryan was not as pivotal as his new paycheck implied[7]; instead, relievers Joe Sambito and Dave Smith and starters Vern Ruhle and J.R. Richard (the latter losing his career to a stroke in July)[8] contributed more. Crucially, the Astros' offense scored an average amount of runs instead of the fewest. The Dodgers again led the league in home runs behind Ron Cey, Dusty Baker, and Steve Garvey, and they found the pitching they'd missed in 1979 from Don Sutton, Jerry Reuss, and Rookie of the Year Steve Howe.

1981: Off from the Races

AL E	BAL	BOS	NY	CLE	DET	MIL
Start	121	64	257			
6/1	198	53	318	57		27
7/1	208	43	328	43		29
8/1	177	12	297	12		
9/1	154	2	270		9	12
End	244	64	304		111	114
Spt.	1.30	1.06	**1.58**	1.02	1.01	**1.08**

Name	Tm	Pos	WAR	SpW	Fame
Righetti	NY	P	3.4	**5.4**	**2.0**
Mumphrey	NY	CF	3.2	5.1	**1.9**
Guidry	NY	P	3.1	4.9	**1.8**
Nettles	NY	3B	2.7	4.3	**1.6**
Evans	BOS	RF	**6.7**	**7.1**	0.4
Yount	MIL	SS	**4.9**	5.3	0.4
Blyleven	CLE	P	**5.6**	**5.7**	0.1
Stieb	TOR	P	**4.5**	4.5	

AL W	CAL	KC	CHI	OAK	TEX
Start	90	326			
6/1	55	291	35	105	28
7/1	25	261	37	115	38
8/1		230	6	84	7
9/1		199		53	
End		273		79	
Spt.	1.05	**1.47**	1.01	**1.42***	1.01

Name	Tm	Pos	WAR	SpW	Fame
Henderson	OAK	LF	**6.6**	**9.4**	**2.8**
McCatty	OAK	P	4.6	**6.5**	**1.9**
Wilson	KC	LF	4.1	6.0	**1.9**
Murphy	OAK	CF	4.4	**6.2**	**1.8**
Armas	OAK	RF	4.2	6.0	**1.8**
Grich	CAL	2B	**5.4**	5.7	0.3
Bell	TEX	3B	**6.2**	**6.3**	0.1

NL E	MON	PHI	PIT	CHI	NY	STL
Start	549	448	404			
6/1	613	540	372			75
7/1	**599**	550	350			85
8/1	**568**	519	319			54
9/1	**541**	488	288	1	1	23
End	583	454	254			121
Spt.	**1.49**	**1.25**	1.10	1.00	1.00	1.02

Name	Tm	Pos	WAR	SpW	Fame
Dawson	MON	CF	**7.4**	**11.1**	**3.7**
Carter	MON	C	3.8	**5.7**	**1.9**
Schmidt	PHI	P	**7.7**	**9.6**	**1.9**

Name	Tm	Pos	WAR	SpW	Fame
Raines	MON	LF	3.5	5.2	**1.7**
Carlton	PHI	P	**5.5**	**6.6**	1.1
Hernandez	STL	1B	**4.1**	4.2	0.1

NL W	CIN	HOU	LA	ATL	SF
Start	359	646	481		
6/1	327	614	577		
7/1	321	584	587		
8/1	290	553	556		
9/1	259	534	537	9	9
End	301	**636**	575		31
Spt.	1.10	1.44	1.48*	1.00	1.00

Name	Tm	Pos	WAR	SpW	Fame
Valenzuela	LA	P	**4.8**	**7.1**	**2.3**
Ryan	HOU	P	**4.7**	**6.8**	**2.1**
Reuss	LA	P	**4.2**	**6.2**	**2.0**
Cey	LA	3B	3.5	5.2	1.7
Seaver	CIN	P	**4.0**	4.4	0.4

A third of the way through the season, the players went on a strike that lasted the next third of the season. When the strike was completed, the owners voted to declare the division leaders in the first third as winners who would face the division leaders in the upcoming third.[9] So the only part of the season that made sense was the final third, and not much happened in it.

The race had been heating up in the NL West, where the Reds were starting to challenge the Dodgers. The NL East had involved the Phillies, Expos, and Cardinals, with the Expos starting to fade. In the AL, the A's started 17–1; the Rangers and White Sox were charging behind them. In the East, the Yankees' nine-win streak put them in first place over the Orioles, while the Brewers remained in the mix. So the Dodgers, Phillies, A's, and Yankees were guaranteed playoff spots once the vote was made.

After the strike, the divisions played completely differently. The Expos finished a half-game ahead of the Cardinals thanks to an 11–4 finish. The Reds had a strong September and almost won the West, but the Astros were good in August and September and edged the Reds out.

The AL's final third saw the Royals start fast enough to survive an A's challenge. Most of the good records were in the East, where the Brewers pulled out a narrow victory over the Red Sox, Tigers, and Orioles.

While the playoffs, with their extra round due to the split season, produced some great moments, in the end the strike crushed the chances of any narrative besides itself. Whatever happened in 1982 would feel worlds away from 1980.

13. A Post-Strike World, 1982–1993

The 1980s is the hardest decade to summarize, with teams and players rising and falling abruptly due to several causes—free agency, injuries to young stars (especially pitchers), drugs, and collusion. For now, much of the popular narrative has centered by default to teams with media advantages, like the New York and Los Angeles teams, the Cubs, and the Braves. Hopefully one day these pennant races will be remembered better on their own terms.

1982: A Differently Split Season

AL E	BAL	BOS	DET	MIL	NY
Start	151	39	68	70	**187**
6/1	116	136	157	47	152
7/1	86	226	207	41	122
8/1	91	319	176	134	91
9/1	60	320	145	227	60
End	120	288	113	323	28
Spt.	1.09	1.24	1.17	**1.21***	1.15

Name	Tm	Pos	WAR	SpW	Fame
Yount	MIL	SS	**10.5**	**12.7**	**2.2**
Evans	BOS	RF	**6.4**	**7.9**	**1.5**
Molitor	MIL	3B	**6.2**	**7.5**	**1.3**
Cooper	MIL	1B	**5.6**	**6.8**	**1.2**
Stieb	TOR	P	**7.7**	**7.7**	
Harrah	CLE	3B	**6.5**	6.5	

AL W	KC	OAK	CAL	CHI
Start	168	49		
6/1	**193**	58	105	93
7/1	**283**	28	195	167
8/1	**372**		288	172
9/1	**465**		381	149
End	**545**		477	117
Spt.	1.48	1.03	**1.26**	1.08

Name	Tm	Pos	WAR	SpW	Fame
Wilson	KC	LF/CF	6.3	9.3	3.0
Brett	KC	3B	6.0	8.9	2.9
McRae	KC	DH	4.2	6.2	2.0
DeCinces	CAL	3B	7.6	9.6	2.0
Downing	CAL	LF	5.6	7.1	1.5
Henderson	OAK	LF	6.7	6.9	0.2

NL E	MON	PHI	PIT	STL	NY
Start	471	367	205	98	
6/1	452	356	170	203	27
7/1	494	362	140	293	1
8/1	479	455	137	386	
9/1	452	544	114	479	
End	440	580	82	575	
Spt.	1.38	1.32	1.06	1.26	1.00

Name	Tm	Pos	WAR	SpW	Fame
Carter	MON	C	8.6	11.9	3.3
Dawson	MON	CF	7.9	10.9	3.0
Rogers	MON	P	7.7	10.6	2.9
Schmidt	PHI	3B	7.4	9.8	2.4

NL W	CIN	HOU	LA	SF	ATL	SD
Start	243	514	465	25		
6/1	208	479	430		102	36
7/1	178	449	400		192	86
8/1	147	418	369		285	95
9/1	116	387	442		374	84
End	84	355	538	30	466	52
Spt.	1.07	1.33	1.26	1.00	1.12	1.02

Name	Tm	Pos	WAR	SpW	Fame
Niekro	HOU	P	6.8	9.0	2.2
Thon	HOU	SS	6.1	8.1	2.0
Guerrero	LA	RF/CF	6.8	8.6	1.8
Valenzuela	LA	P	5.0	6.3	1.3
Murphy	ATL	CF/LF	6.7	7.5	0.8
Soto	CIN	P	7.5	8.0	0.5

Like 1981, the second half of the season was very different from the first half, but this time it was natural. In the AL East, the Tigers challenged the Red Sox early until a 2–15 stretch in June, including six losses to the Brewers. The Brewers capitalized, taking five of seven from the Red Sox shortly after and entering the race. The Red Sox dropped out in August; the Orioles replaced them by going 17–1 in a soft spot of their schedule heading into September, and in the last series of the season the Orioles took the first three from the Brewers to tie them headed into game 162. The Brewers won the division when trade deadline acquisition Don Sutton beat Jim Palmer.

13. A Post-Strike World 245

Paul Molitor was one home run away from giving the Brewers six 20-homer players in himself, MVP Robin Yount, Ted Simmons, Cecil Cooper, Ben Oglivie, and Gorman Thomas. The Orioles were led by Eddie Murray, Jim Palmer, and Rookie of the Year Cal Ripken. And although Dwight Evans, Jim Rice, and rookie Wade Boggs gave the Red Sox good offense, it was the bullpen of Bob Stanley, Mark Clear, Tom Burgmeier, and Luis Aponte that made the team tough.

On May 6 the slumping Yankees, who'd let Reggie Jackson sign with the Angels and saw Graig Nettles age, passed Momentum lead to the Royals, who were trying to keep up with the Angels and White Sox. When the Sox slumped, the Royals caught them, but they limped badly enough at the beginning of July that even the Mariners were in contention for a week. The Royals took over first right before September, but they didn't recover from an Angels' sweep September 20–22. Many Royals had fine seasons, but Dennis Leonard's and Larry Gura's weak ones undermined the rotation. The Angels had pitching problems too, but their lineup abounded in patient sluggers, including Reggie Jackson, Don Baylor, Fred Lynn, Brian Downing, Doug DeCinces, and Bobby Grich; catcher Bob Boone gave a strong defensive presence.

In the NL West, the Astros gained no Momentum thanks to Jose Cruz's downturn and a lackluster back of the lineup and rotation. The Braves and Padres led early, the former starting 13–0 and the latter winning 11 straight after starting 1–4. The Padres left the race in July; the Braves shoved the Dodgers into contention by losing eight games to them July 30–August 8. Both teams' losing Septembers allowed the Giants, in fourth place most of the year, to have their 20–7 September matter. Going into the final series, the Braves were a game ahead of the Giants and Dodgers, who were playing each other; the Braves won the division by taking two of three from the Padres while the Giants and Dodgers split their series. For the Dodgers, young slugger Pedro Guerrero and Rookie of the Year Steve Sax joined veterans Bill Russell and Ron Cey in the lineup while Fernando Valenzuela dazzled on the mound. The Braves had talent in Dale Murphy, Bob Horner, Phil Niekro, Gene Garber, and Steve Bedrosian, but overall they looked like the .500 team they were from games 14–162.

The Expos took Momentum lead on June 20 as they tried to catch the Cardinals, who had started 13–3. The Expos tied them on June 23, but they and the Cardinals slumped, letting the Phillies and Pirates enter the race. The Phillies took Momentum lead on August 8, but they were a .500 team the rest of the way. The Phillies, Expos, and Cardinals were all live in mid-September; the Cardinals won the division with an eight-win streak including three wins against the Phillies.

The perpetually-thin Phillies were even thinner due to Tug McGraw's aging. The Expos had the two best position players in Gary Carter and Andre Dawson and the best pitcher in Steve Rogers. Veteran Al Oliver, obtained from the Rangers for Larry Parrish, had his best season in ages, while Parrish's replacement Tim Wallach had a fine season. For the speedy Cardinals, trades over the past two years for Ozzie Smith, Lonnie Smith, and starter Joaquin Andujar provided the base of the team's success. Holdover Keith Hernandez provided good offense at first base, and Bruce Sutter saved 36 games.

1983: Procrastination

AL E	BAL	BOS	DET	MIL	NY	CLE	TOR
Start	79	191	75	214	19		
6/1	177	285	41	260	12	1	70
7/1	267	283	103	238	22		140
8/1	360	252	192	247	79		233
9/1	453	221	281	328	92		286
End	**546**	190	250	297	61		255
Spt.	**1.35**	1.16	1.06	1.21	1.02	1.00	1.06

Name	Tm	Pos	WAR	SpW	Fame
Ripken	BAL	SS	**8.2**	**11.1**	**2.9**
Murray	BAL	1B	6.6	**8.9**	**2.3**
McGregor	BAL	P	5.4	7.3	**1.9**
Yount	MIL	SS	7.2	8.7	1.5
Boggs	BOS	3B	7.8	9.0	1.2
Stieb	TOR	P	7.0	7.4	0.4

AL W	CAL	CHI	KC	OAK	TEX
Start	316	78	**362**		
6/1	**418**	44	352	34	54
7/1	**508**	34	382	8	104
8/1	**545**	99	351		161
9/1	**514**	192	320		130
End	483	285	289		99
Spt.	**1.47**	**1.10**	1.36	1.00	1.04

Name	Tm	Pos	WAR	SpW	Fame
Grich	CAL	2B	4.3	**6.3**	**2.0**
Quisenberry	KC	P	**5.5**	**7.5**	**2.0**
Zahn	CAL	P	4.0	**5.9**	**1.9**
Forsch	CAL	P	3.5	5.1	**1.6**
Brett	KC	3B	4.3	5.8	1.5
Dotson	CHI	P	**5.1**	5.6	0.5
Henderson	OAK	LF	**6.9**	**6.9**	
Young	SEA	P	**5.1**	5.1	

13. A Post-Strike World 247

NL E	MON	PHI	PIT	STL
Start	373	493	70	488
6/1	424	556	37	551
7/1	510	526	7	609
8/1	547	547	32	618
9/1	576	640	125	591
End	621	733	186	592
Spt.	1.12	1.43	1.02	1.31

Name	Tm	Pos	WAR	SpW	Fame
Denny	PHI	P	7.4	10.6	3.2
Schmidt	PHI	P	6.8	9.7	2.9
Carlton	PHI	P	5.5	7.9	2.4
Holland	PHI	P	3.2	4.6	1.4
Carter	MON	C	7.1	8.0	0.9
Dawson	MON	CF	6.8	7.6	0.8

NL W	ATL	CIN	HOU	LA	SD	SF
Start	396	71	302	457	44	25
6/1	491	38	269	556	11	
7/1	537	8	239	646		
8/1	630		208	683		
9/1	723		177	696		
End	740		146	789		
Spt.	1.31	1.01	1.08	1.48	1.00	1.00

Name	Tm	Pos	WAR	SpW	Fame
Guerrero	LA	3B	5.5	8.1	2.6
Welch	LA	P	4.6	6.8	2.2
Murphy	ATL	CF/LF	7.1	9.3	2.2
Reuss	LA	P	3.7	5.5	1.8
Thon	HOU	SS	7.4	8.0	0.6
Cruz	HOU	LF	6.2	6.7	0.5
Soto	CIN	P	6.8	6.9	0.1

Although the divisions ended mostly in comfortable leads for their winners, on July 4 no eventual winner was leading. In the AL East, every team gained Momentum for at least a week, and on August 21 five teams were bunched from .554 to .574 winning percentages. The Orioles, who had scored the least runs of the quintet, scored the most by far down the stretch to pull away from the group. Cal Ripken and Eddie Murray were the main offense, and as with many Orioles teams of old, pitching was a major factor. Jim Palmer was hurt, but Scott McGregor was joined by rookie Mike Boddicker as a sterling front of the rotation, while veteran closer Tippy Martinez had his best season.

The Angels held a five-game lead on June 4, but they scuffled for the next month while the pitching-rich Rangers got hot; on June 30, the Rangers, Angels, and White Sox gained Momentum. July was a month for the West to face the East, and with so many good teams in the East the Angels went 9–20 and the Rangers went 8–20. That left the White Sox three games up entering August, and from there they went 46–15, winning the division by 20 games even though they didn't lead the division until July 18. The Angels' key contributors were almost entirely on the wrong side of 30, and it showed as Reggie Jackson hit .194 and others lost a step in the field. The White Sox lineup hit lots of home runs, but the real strength was the rotation, led by LaMarr Hoyt, Richard Dotson, and free agent Floyd Bannister.

The NL Momentum lead changed twice in 1981 and 1982; it would change thrice in 1983. The Cardinals, Expos, and Phillies started near first, but they were barely over .500; July 22 was the fifth of eight days where nobody in the East gained Momentum. The Pirates emerged first from the sludge, but even on September 8 the Cardinals' .507 winning percentage was 1.5 games back. The next day, the Phillies started a raid against all their foes, going 4–2 against the Pirates, 5–1 against the Expos, and 6–0 against the Cardinals to win the division by a surprising six games.

The Phillies' lineup was Mike Schmidt and famous ex-Reds, though of Joe Morgan, Pete Rose, and Tony Perez only Morgan mattered. In the rotation, Steve Carlton got surprising support from veteran John Denny, acquired the previous September in the middle of an awful season; in 1983, he cut 2.5 runs off his ERA and won the Cy Young.

In the West, only the Braves and Dodgers gained Momentum. After a Braves-Dodgers series that ended June 16, the Dodgers went 16–25, while the Braves went 26–17, climbing from 3.5 back to 5.5 ahead. The Dodgers had taken league Momentum lead on June 2, but their July woes gave Momentum lead to the Braves on August 15. From there to the end of the season, the Braves had the worst record in the league; the Dodgers reclaimed Momentum lead on September 18 and won the division.

Both teams shared strengths and weaknesses, although their ballparks influenced how the end stats looked. The Braves led the NL in runs behind Dale Murphy's second straight MVP season and the slugging of corner infielders Bob Horner and Chris Chambliss, while the Dodgers led the NL in home runs behind pretend third baseman Pedro Guerrero[1] and rookie first baseman Greg Brock. The Braves found the rotation they'd been missing in 1982 with young righthanders Craig McMurtry and Pascual Perez and signed reliever Terry Forster away from the Dodgers to good effect. For the Dodgers, Fernando Valenzuela's down year was compensated for by starters Bob Welch, Jerry Reuss, and young Alejandro Pena, whose relief work in 1982 hadn't signaled he'd make a good starter. Lefty reliever Steve Howe and righty reliever Tom Niedenfuer each had sub–2.00 ERAs.

1984: Plucky Upstarts

AL E	BAL	BOS	DET	MIL	NY	TOR
Start	**546**	190	250	297	61	255
6/1	507	151	347	258	22	216
7/1	477	121	437	228		186
8/1	446	90	530	197		155
9/1	415	59	623	166		124
End	386	30	710	137		95
Spt.	1.37	1.04	**1.39**	1.16	1.01	1.07

Name	Tm	Pos	WAR	SpW	Fame
Ripken	BAL	SS	**10.0**	**13.7**	3.7
Murray	BAL	1B	7.1	**9.7**	2.6
Trammell	DET	SS	6.7	**9.3**	2.6
Lemon	DET	CF	6.2	**8.6**	2.4
Stieb	TOR	P	**7.9**	8.5	0.6
Moseby	TOR	CF	**7.2**	7.7	0.5
Blyleven	CLE	P	**7.2**	7.2	

AL W	CAL	CHI	KC	TEX	MIN	OAK
Start	483	285	289	99		
6/1	**560**	246	250	60	7	23
7/1	**646**	216	220	30		
8/1	**727**	217	189		21	
9/1	**752**	190	158		114	
End	**759**	161	225		181	
Spt.	1.48	1.10	**1.14**	1.01	1.02	1.00

Name	Tm	Pos	WAR	SpW	Fame
Witt	CAL	P	4.6	**6.8**	2.2
Zahn	CAL	P	4.2	**6.2**	2.0
Lynn	CAL	CF	3.8	**5.6**	1.8
DeCinces	CAL	3B	3.3	**4.9**	1.6
Hrbek	MIN	1B	**5.5**	5.6	0.1
Bell	TEX	3B	**6.1**	**6.2**	0.1
Henderson	OAK	LF	**6.0**	**6.0**	
Davis	SEA	1B	**5.9**	5.9	

NL E	MON	PHI	PIT	STL	CHI	NY
Start	421	496	126	401		
6/1	431	550	88	363	102	86
7/1	401	640	58	341	192	160
8/1	370	**645**	27	310	265	253
9/1	339	**614**		279	358	242
End	310	**585**		250	445	213
Spt.	1.16	1.43	1.02	1.10	**1.11**	1.04

Name	Tm	Pos	WAR	SpW	Fame
Schmidt	PHI	3B	**7.0**	**10.0**	3.0
Hayes	PHI	CF/RF	4.0	5.7	**1.7**

Name	Tm	Pos	WAR	SpW	Fame
Denny	PHI	P	3.8	5.4	**1.6**
Samuel	PHI	2B	2.9	4.1	**1.2**
Carter	MON	C	7.4	8.6	**1.2**
Raines	MON	LF	**6.4**	7.4	1.0
Sandberg	CHI	2B	**8.5**	9.4	0.9

NL W	ATL	HOU	LA	CIN	SD
Start	501	99	**534**		
6/1	527	61	**648**	36	95
7/1	585	31	**658**	6	185
8/1	554		**627**		278
9/1	523		596		371
End	494		567		458
Spt.	1.31	1.01	1.45	1.00	**1.16**

Name	Tm	Pos	WAR	SpW	Fame
Pena	LA	P	5.0	7.3	**2.3**
Hershiser	LA	P	4.3	6.2	**1.9**
Murphy	ATL	CF	**5.5**	7.2	**1.7**
Valenzuela	LA	P	3.7	5.4	**1.7**
Gwynn	SD	RF	**6.3**	7.3	1.0
McReynolds	SD	CF	**5.4**	6.3	0.9
Cruz	HOU	LF	**6.3**	6.4	0.1

While Scott McGregor and Tippy Martinez struggled and the Orioles started 4–12, they ended with a better record than the AL West winner. But only the Tigers gained Momentum, because they started 35–5. The Tigers were led by their double-play tandem of Alan Trammell and Lou Whitaker as well as Kirk Gibson, Chet Lemon, and Lance Parrish. Dan Petry and Jack Morris were fine starting pitchers, but the Cy Young winner and best pitcher was lefty reliever Willie Hernandez, acquired from the Phillies during spring training. Hernandez and righty reliever Aurelio Lopez combined for 46 saves and 19 wins.

Because the East had so many good teams, the West was a carousel of mediocrity. The Angels led early, but often without gaining Momentum. While many veterans aged, Fred Lynn, Doug DeCinces, and Brian Downing still had enough to support closer Doug Corbett and starters Geoff Zahn, Mike Witt, and rookie Ron Romanick.

But the young Twins, behind Kent Hrbek and a star turn from lefty Frank Viola, took first place by sweeping the Angels July 27–29. The Twins built and dropped a 5.5-game lead; on September 6, the Angels were 69–69 and the Twins and Royals were 70–69. The Angels lost five straight starting September 22, including three to the Royals, while the Twins won five straight; but the Twins lost their final six, letting the Royals win the division. The Royals would have won more often if George Brett had been healthy; his and former ace

Larry Gura's struggles were compensated for by Willie Wilson, Frank White, Dan Quisenberry, and Bud Black.

Seven of the 12 NL teams entered 1984 with Momentum, but none of them made the playoffs. In the West, the Dodgers and Padres had great Aprils but bad Mays, allowing the slow-starting Braves to take first in early June off a nine-win streak. But they dropped their next five—three to the Dodgers and two to the Padres—and when the Dodgers swept them later that month, they bowed out. The Dodgers struggled from there, allowing the Padres a large lead the rest of the year.

With Bob Horner injured, the Braves had only two players with ten home runs, Dale Murphy and Claudell Washington; Rick Mahler's pitching was countered by young pitchers' regression. The Dodgers' strong rotation was undermined by a one-threat offense (Pedro Guerrero). Steve Howe's season-long suspension for drug abuse also left the bullpen thin, especially once Orel Hershiser joined the rotation. The Padres' capable offense was led by Alan Wiggins and outfielders Tony Gwynn, Kevin McReynolds, and rookie Carmelo Martinez. The pitching had a number of decent, interchangeable starters, and free agent Goose Gossage was a reliable closer.

In the NL East, the Phillies took first in mid–June by sweeping the Cubs, but the Cubs and Mets pushed them out with great Julys. John Denny was good again and Mike Schmidt played as though he were ageless, but Steve Carlton didn't, and closer Al Holland lost ten games. Von Hayes and rookie Juan Samuel pointed to a team that could rebuild, but Carlton was irreplaceable.

The Mets took over first despite being outscored on the season. The new young rotation was no better as a group than 1983's veterans, but 19-year-old Dwight Gooden led the league in strikeouts to win Rookie of the Year. The offense was led by 1983's Rookie of the Year, Darryl Strawberry, and first baseman Keith Hernandez. The Cubs went 7–1 against them from July 27 to August 8, giving them a 4.5-game lead that held up. The Cubs led the league in runs thanks to Leon Durham, Ron Cey, Gary Matthews, and Ryne Sandberg. The rotation was okay with Dennis Eckersley, Scott Sanderson, and Steve Trout, but it was trade deadline pickup Rick Sutcliffe's 16–1 record in 20 starts that got the attention and an easy Cy Young victory.

1985: Making Dynasties Is Hard

	AL E	BAL	BOS	DET	MIL	TOR	NY
Start	277	22	509	99	68		
6/1	343		571	65	166	4	
7/1	313		589	35	256		

AL E	BAL	BOS	DET	MIL	TOR	NY
8/1	282		578	4	349	17
9/1	251		547		442	
End	216		512		547	23
Spt.	**1.23**	1.00	1.40	1.02	**1.23**	1.00

Name	Tm	Pos	WAR	SpW	Fame
Gibson	DET	RF/CF	5.4	7.6	**2.2**
Morris	DET	P	4.9	6.9	**2.0**
Whitaker	DET	2B	4.5	6.3	**1.8**
Evans	DET	1B/DH	4.2	5.9	**1.7**
Barfield	TOR	RF	**6.8**	**8.4**	1.6
Stieb	TOR	P	**6.8**	**8.4**	1.6
Henderson	NY	CF	**9.9**	**9.9**	
Boggs	BOS	3B	**9.1**	**9.1**	

AL W	CAL	CHI	KC	MIN	OAK
Start	**545**	115	161	130	
6/1	**647**	137	195	192	
7/1	**737**	191	229	162	30
8/1	**830**	160	218	131	15
9/1	**923**	129	287	100	
End	**1028**	94	392	65	
Spt.	1.50	1.06	**1.25**	1.06	1.00

Name	Tm	Pos	WAR	SpW	Fame
Brett	KC	3B	**8.3**	**10.4**	**2.1**
Pettis	CAL	CF	3.8	5.7	**1.9**
Saberhagen	KC	P	**7.3**	**9.1**	**1.8**
Moore	CAL	P	3.6	5.4	**1.8**
Leibrandt	KC	P	**6.7**	**8.4**	1.7
Blyleven	2 TM	P	**6.7**	**6.9**	0.2

NL E	CHI	MON	NY	PHI	STL
Start	445	310	213	**585**	250
6/1	538	407	306	550	215
7/1	596	485	372	520	253
8/1	565	502	429	489	346
9/1	534	471	522	458	439
End	499	436	611	423	544
Spt.	1.27	1.10	1.10	1.20	**1.43***

Name	Tm	Pos	WAR	SpW	Fame
Tudor	STL	P	**8.1**	**11.6**	**3.5**
McGee	STL	CF	**8.1**	**11.6**	**3.5**
Smith	STL	SS	6.4	**9.2**	**2.8**
Herr	STL	2B	5.6	8.0	**2.4**
Gooden	NY	P	**12.1**	**13.3**	1.2
Raines	MON	LF	7.6	8.4	0.8

13. A Post-Strike World

NL W	ATL	LA	SD	CIN	HOU
Start	494	567	458		
6/1	459	**572**	531	36	48
7/1	429	546	**621**	50	62
8/1	398	615	**682**	19	31
9/1	367	**708**	651		
End	332	**813**	616		
Spt.	1.10	**1.48**	1.36	1.00	1.01

Name	Tm	Pos	WAR	SpW	Fame
Guerrero	LA	LF/3B	**7.9**	**11.7**	**3.8**
Hershiser	LA	P	**5.9**	**8.7**	**2.8**
Valenzuela	LA	P	**5.4**	**8.0**	**2.6**
Scioscia	LA	C	**5.4**	**8.0**	**2.6**

The Tigers started 6–0 but fell out of first after April and stopped gaining Momentum in early July. Alan Trammell and Aurelio Lopez struggled and the bench and bullpen were a mess. The Blue Jays held first place from mid–May to the end, although the Red Sox swept them in mid–June to threaten and the Yankees threated in mid–September. Although the Blue Jays had a good offense led by Jesse Barfield, George Bell, and the third base platoon of Rance Mulliniks and Garth Iorg, it was the defense, led by Barfield and shortstop Tony Fernandez, and pitching that stood out. Dave Stieb and Jimmy Key were first and fourth in league ERA; Doyle Alexander wasn't far off and won 17 games. The bullpen was deep, highlighted by Dennis Lamp's 11–0 record.

The Angels held Momentum lead all year, surviving Chicago's fast start and taking a six-game lead into the second half. But the Royals won eight straight starting September 8 and took two of three from the Angels to claim first place. In the next-to-last series of the season the Royals took three of four from the Angels to spoil their fun for the second straight year. The Angels got good offense from the outfield corners in Brian Downing and Reggie Jackson, while centerfielder Gary Pettis caught the many things ex-catcher Downing and 39-year-old Jackson couldn't. Mike Witt was the only reliable starting pitcher until midseason pickup John Candelaria; the bullpen was better, led by Donnie Moore and rookie Stew Cliburn. The Royals scored the second-fewest runs in the AL—outside George Brett, the lineup had power and nothing else—but they allowed the second-fewest behind 21-year-old Cy Young winner Bret Saberhagen, Charlie Leibrandt, and Dan Quisenberry.

NL Momentum lead changed four times. The Phillies were a nonfactor; moving Mike Schmidt to first base to make room for young Rick Schu didn't work for either player, the defense was bad, and Steve Carlton went 1–8 despite a good ERA. The Dodgers took Momentum lead on May 4 but fell below .500. On June 10, the Cubs took Momentum lead, with Ryne Sandberg still leading the offense and the rotation enjoying a full season from Rick Sutcliffe. Two days later, the Cubs started a 13-loss streak to their nearest competitors, the Mets, Expos, and Cardinals, letting the Cardinals enter the race as the Cubs exited it. On June 24, the Padres took Momentum lead, having fended off the Astros and Reds to claim first. Tony Gwynn continued to excel, Carmelo Martinez and Graig Nettles were good support, and the rotation was improved with the acquisition of LaMarr Hoyt.

The Padres stopped scoring runs in July, going 10–16, while the Dodgers went 20–7. That 9.5-game difference carried the Dodgers the rest of the way, and they reclaimed Momentum lead on August 18. Alejandro Pena was hurt and the returning Steve Howe was ineffective, but Orel Hershiser, Fernando Valenzuela, and Bob Welch led the Dodgers to a 2.96 ERA. The offense got improvements from its best three players—Pedro Guerrero, Mike Marshall, and Mike Scioscia—and Bill Madlock hit .360/.422/.447 after being acquired at the end of August.

Back in the East, the Expos hadn't kept up, leaving the race to the Cardinals and Mets. The Mets had acquired Gary Carter from the Expos in the off-season; with Carter added to Keith Hernandez and Darryl Strawberry, and with the growth of several young players, including Dwight Gooden (24–4, 1.53, 268 Ks), the team had loads of talent. But they could not catch the Cardinals, who also had a sub–2 ERA at the top of their rotation in John Tudor, a second 21-game winner in Joaquin Andujar, and an offense that led the league in runs and stole 314 bases, including Rookie of the Year Vince Coleman's 110. MVP Willie McGee, Ozzie Smith, and Tommy Herr provided strength up the middle.

1986: Sometimes Simpler Is Better

AL E	BAL	DET	NY	TOR	BOS	CLE	MIL
Start	121	287	13	306			
6/1	123	265	111	272	96	29	3
7/1	101	235	81	242	186		
8/1	70	204	62	211	279		
9/1	43	173	31	180	372		
End	9	139		146	474		
Spt.	1.05	1.22	1.03	1.32	**1.50***	1.00	1.00

Name	Tm	Pos	WAR	SpW	Fame
Clemens	BOS	P	8.9	13.4	4.5
Boggs	BOS	3B	8.0	12.0	4.0
Rice	BOS	LF	5.6	8.4	2.8
Barfield	TOR	RF	7.6	10.0	2.4
Eichhorn	TOR	P	7.4	9.8	2.4
Higuera	MIL	P	9.4	9.4	

13. A Post-Strike World

	AL W	CAL	CHI	KC	MIN	TEX
Start		575	53	219	36	
6/1		633	19	185	2	22
7/1		663		175		108
8/1		756		144		165
9/1		849		113		202
End		951		79		168
Spt.		**1.55**	1.01	1.10	1.00	1.11

Name	Tm	Pos	WAR	SpW	Fame
Witt	CAL	P	**6.2**	**9.6**	3.4
Pettis	CAL	CF	**5.1**	**7.9**	2.8
Downing	CAL	LF	4.3	**6.7**	**2.4**
McCaskill	CAL	P	4.3	**6.7**	**2.4**
Gaetti	MIN	3B	**5.8**	5.8	
Puckett	MIN	CF	**5.7**	5.7	

	NL E	CHI	MON	NY	PHI	STL
Start		499	436	611	423	544
6/1		465	426	693	389	510
7/1		435	396	**783**	359	480
8/1		404	365	**876**	328	449
9/1		373	334	**969**	297	418
End		339	300	**1071**	263	384
Spt.		1.10	1.09	**1.54**	1.08	1.19

Name	Tm	Pos	WAR	SpW	Fame
Hernandez	NY	1B	**5.5**	**8.5**	3.0
Dykstra	NY	CF	4.7	**7.2**	2.5
Ojeda	NY	P	4.7	**7.2**	2.5
Darling	NY	P	4.6	**7.1**	2.5
Smith	STL	SS	**5.6**	6.7	1.1
Raines	MON	LF	**5.5**	6.0	0.5
Schmidt	PHI	3B/1B	**6.1**	6.6	0.5
Rhoden	PIT	P	**6.6**	6.6	

	NL W	ATL	LA	SD	HOU	SF
Start		332	**813**	616		
6/1		338	**779**	642	99	98
7/1		336	**749**	636	189	188
8/1		321	**718**	665	282	257
9/1		290	**687**	634	375	226
End		256	**653**	600	477	192
Spt.		1.07	**1.44**	1.32	**1.10**	1.03

Name	Tm	Pos	WAR	SpW	Fame
Valenzuela	LA	P	**5.4**	**7.8**	2.4
Sax	LA	2B	4.8	**6.9**	2.1
Gwynn	SD	RF	**6.6**	**8.7**	2.1
Welch	LA	P	4.0	5.8	**1.8**
Scott	HOU	P	**8.4**	**9.2**	0.8
Davis	CIN	CF	**5.3**	5.3	

For the first time in divisional history, all four races concluded by September. In the NL East, the Cardinals were in last place as late as July thanks to no offense; the Mets started 20–4 and were unchallenged after May. Dwight Gooden, Ron Darling, and Bob Ojeda, a trade pickup from the Red Sox, were all top-five in ERA. The bullpen aces, righty Roger McDowell and lefty Jesse Orosco, combined to win 22 games and save 43. The offense led the league in AVG, OBP, and SLG, with Keith Hernandez, Ray Knight, and Lenny Dykstra top-ten in AVG and Darryl Strawberry and Gary Carter the home run bats.

Neither the Dodgers nor Reds, first and second in 1985, gained Momentum in 1986; the Dodgers saw Orel Hershiser and Jerry Reuss struggle, lost Pedro Guerrero to injury, and couldn't field. The Astros and Giants traded control of first place while the Braves and Padres lurked on the fringes through July; the Astros pulled permanently ahead by being the only team of the four with a winning July.

The Padres' offense, led by Tony Gwynn and Kevin McReynolds, was about as good as the Astros,' led by Kevin Bass and Glenn Davis. But the Astros allowed 569 runs—fewest in the league—while the Padres allowed 723, as the rotation after Dave Dravecky and Eric Show was unspeakably bad. Everyone who threw at least 50 innings for the Astros had better-than-average ERAs, led by Mike Scott, whose 2.22 ERA led the league by 35 points.

In the AL East, the Blue Jays started slow and gained no Momentum despite a respectable finish. The Red Sox broke away from four teams with a 15–2 stretch starting May 17, and while the Orioles approached in June and August and the Yankees approached in July, the Red Sox had a pretty easy season. The Red Sox had a good starter in Oil Can Boyd, a very good starter in Bruce Hurst, and an incredible starter in Cy Young and MVP winner Roger Clemens. In the lineup, Wade Boggs won the batting title and his .453 OBP was 48 points ahead of second place, while Jim Rice, Dwight Evans, and Don Baylor provided power to drive him in.

On June 1, the Royals and Rangers were tied for first in the AL West at 24–24, with the Angels a half-game behind. The Rangers, coming off a 99-loss season but remade with three rookie starting pitchers, won their next seven games, but the Angels swept them twice in June and took over first for good in early July, settling the race by winning seven straight in late August. For once, homegrown products—aces Mike Witt and Kirk McCaskill, defensive standouts Gary Pettis in centerfield and Dick Schofield at shortstop, and rookie first baseman and slugger Wally Joyner—were the team's strength.

1987: Last Year Means Nothing; This Summer Means Nothing

AL E	BAL	BOS	DET	TOR	MIL	NY
Start	5	241	71	74		
6/1		205	35	126	66	75
7/1		175	5	216	44	165
8/1		144	36	281	13	258
9/1		113	129	374		307
End		80	224	473		274
Spt.	1.00	1.19	**1.09**	1.34	1.02	1.15

Name	*Tm*	*Pos*	*WAR*	*SpW*	*Fame*
Key	TOR	P	**7.4**	**9.9**	**2.5**
Clemens	BOS	P	**9.4**	**11.2**	**1.8**
Fernandez	TOR	SS	5.1	6.8	**1.7**
Bell	TOR	LF	5.0	6.7	**1.7**
Clancy	TOR	P	5.0	6.7	**1.7**
Boggs	BOS	3B	**8.3**	**9.9**	1.6
Trammell	DET	SS	**8.2**	**8.9**	0.7

AL W	CAL	KC	TEX	MIN	OAK	SEA
Start	**483**	40	85			
6/1	**519**	112	49	37		28
7/1	**489**	166	19	123	49	10
8/1	**534**	203		216	142	
9/1	**531**	172		309	187	
End	**498**	147		408	194	
Spt.	1.50	1.11	1.06	**1.28***	1.04	1.01

Name	*Tm*	*Pos*	*WAR*	*SpW*	*Fame*
White	CAL	RF/CF	5.6	**8.4**	**2.8**
Viola	MIN	P	**8.1**	**10.4**	**2.3**
Joyner	CAL	1B	4.1	6.2	**2.1**
Downing	CAL	DH/LF	4.0	6.0	**2.0**
Saberhagen	KC	P	**8.0**	**8.9**	0.9
Leibrandt	KC	P	**6.0**	**6.7**	0.7
Langston	SEA	P	**5.9**	6.0	0.1

NL E	CHI	MON	NY	PHI	STL
Start	294	259	**927**	228	332
6/1	382	223	**903**	192	428
7/1	392	193	**873**	162	518
8/1	361	162	**842**	131	611
9/1	330	143	**815**	100	704
End	297	166	**858**	67	803
Spt.	1.08	1.05	1.50	1.04	**1.38**

Name	*Tm*	*Pos*	*WAR*	*SpW*	*Fame*
Strawberry	NY	RF	**6.4**	**9.6**	**3.2**
Smith	STL	SS	**6.4**	**8.6**	**2.4**

Name	Tm	Pos	WAR	SpW	Fame
Johnson	NY	3B/SS	4.3	6.5	2.2
Clark	STL	1B	5.4	7.5	2.1
Sutcliffe	CHI	P	6.1	6.6	0.5
Raines	MON	LF	6.7	7.0	0.3

NL W	ATL	HOU	LA	SD	SF	CIN
Start	221	413	565	520	166	
6/1	197	445	549	484	274	105
7/1	167	495	519	454	320	195
8/1	136	500	488	423	313	288
9/1	105	509	457	392	378	341
End	72	476	424	359	477	308
Spt.	1.04	1.24	1.29	1.16	**1.12**	1.05

Name	Tm	Pos	WAR	SpW	Fame
Welch	LA	P	7.1	9.2	2.1
Hershiser	LA	P	6.4	8.2	1.8
Scott	HOU	P	5.9	7.3	1.4
Guerrero	LA	LF/1B	4.7	6.1	1.4
Gwynn	SD	RF	8.5	9.9	1.4
Davis	CIN	CF	7.9	8.3	0.4
Murphy	ATL	RF	7.7	8.0	0.3

The Brewers started 13–0 but lost 12 straight in May, leaving the AL East to the Blue Jays and Yankees. The Tigers joined the fray in late July, and an 11–17 August doomed the Yankees, as mainstays Don Mattingly and Willie Randolph suffered from losing Rickey Henderson to injury. The Blue Jays looked like they had wrapped up entering the final week, but they gave the Tigers the division by losing their final seven games, the last three to the Tigers by a single run apiece. The Blue Jays were led defensively by Tony Fernandez and Jesse Barfield and offensively by them, George Bell, and Lloyd Moseby. Jimmy Key and Jim Clancy were top-shelf starters, while the bullpen had dual aces in Tom Henke and Mark Eichhorn. The Tigers led the league in home runs, with Darrell Evans, Alan Trammell, Kirk Gibson, Chet Lemon, and rookie catcher Matt Nokes all hitting at least 20. Jack Morris led a serviceable rotation; Doyle Alexander went 9–0 after his August trade from the Braves.

In the West, although the Twins stayed in first after June 8, they were rarely alone; on July 2, the Twins, Angels, A's, Royals, and Mariners were bunched from 40–39 to 43–36, and on August 31 the Angels were 66–66 but three games back. The Angels finished 7–21 and plummeted to the basement, and the Twins won six straight from September 18–24 to pull away from the A's. The Angels were undone by Bob Boone's and Doug DeCinces's aging and Kirk McCaskill's and Donnie Moore's injuries. The Twins' roster was dreadful after the first few names, but Frank Viola and Bert Blyleven were fine starters,

Greg Gagne excelled at shortstop, and Kent Hrbek, Gary Gaetti, Kirby Puckett, and Tom Brunansky provided power.

In the NL West, the Dodgers reclaimed their pitching dominance behind Bob Welch, Orel Hershiser, and Fernando Valenzuela, but outside Pedro Guerrero the offense was worthless. The Reds led most of the summer largely off relievers Frank Williams and John Franco and the slugging of young outfielders Eric Davis and Kal Daniels. In August, the Giants swept the Reds then won their next series, against the Astros, to take first. The Astros then went 10-1 to virtually tie the Giants on August 24, but their mediocre hitting—Nolan Ryan won an ERA title while going 8-16—vanished, and they ended 11-26 to hand the West to the Giants. For the Giants, Will Clark and Candy Maldonado were the biggest offensive threats, and a midseason trade with the Padres for third baseman Kevin Mitchell and starter Dave Dravecky did wonders. The Giants beat the flawed Dodgers and Astros with few standouts but several decent players—sort of the anti-Twins.

The Cardinals and Andre Dawson's Cubs fought until June, when the Cardinals went 6-1 against them over ten days; the Cubs finished in last. The Mets and Expos made a battle in September; the Cardinals took three of four the Expos in the season's penultimate series to moot the ultimate series against the Mets.

The Expos didn't sign Tim Raines for the first month due to the same collusion that sent Andre Dawson to the Cubs[2]; with both of them all year, they might have won the division. The Mets led the NL in runs, but Kevin McReynolds, acquired from the Padres for Kevin Mitchell and others in the offseason, was not the left field upgrade envisioned, and Gary Carter had his worst year in a decade. Outside Dwight Gooden, the rotation was hurt (Bob Ojeda), slightly worse (Sid Fernandez), or much worse (Ron Darling), and Roger McDowell and Jesse Orosco posted ERAs over 4. The Cardinals were second in runs despite the fewest home runs, thanks to walks and steals. Jack Clark hit 35 home runs and led the league in OBP, while Ozzie Smith was eighth in AVG and Vince Coleman stole 109 bases. No pitcher cleared 11 wins, but the staff avoided bad performances.

1988: No, Not You

AL E	BOS	DET	NY	TOR	CLE	MIL
Start	61	171	209	362		
6/1	60	246	316	325	108	
7/1	30	308	406	295	158	
8/1	39	401	499	264	127	

AL E	BOS	DET	NY	TOR	CLE	MIL
9/1	104	494	488	233	96	
End	197	507	457	210	65	15
Spt.	**1.08**	1.21	1.36	1.22	1.04	1.00

Name	Tm	Pos	WAR	SpW	Fame
Henderson	NY	LF	6.3	8.6	2.3
Winfield	NY	RF	5.4	7.3	**1.9**
McGriff	TOR	1B	6.2	7.6	**1.4**
Mattingly	NY	1B	3.7	5.0	**1.3**
Boggs	BOS	3B	**8.2**	**8.9**	0.7
Greenwell	BOS	LF	**7.5**	**8.1**	0.6
Clemens	BOS	P	**7.1**	**7.7**	0.6
Higuera	MIL	P	**7.4**	7.4	

AL W	CAL	KC	MIN	OAK
Start	**381**	113	312	148
6/1	**344**	84	275	259
7/1	314	54	245	349
8/1	283	23	218	442
9/1	252		187	**535**
End	221		156	**628**
Spt.	1.33	1.03	1.10	**1.38**

Name	Tm	Pos	WAR	SpW	Fame
Canseco	OAK	RF/DH	**7.2**	**9.9**	2.7
Henderson	OAK	CF	6.2	8.6	2.4
Stewart	OAK	P	4.4	6.1	**1.7**
Schofield	CAL	SS	3.7	4.9	**1.2**
Puckett	MIN	CF	**7.7**	**8.5**	0.7
Viola	MIN	P	**7.7**	**8.5**	0.7
Gubicza	KC	P	**7.7**	7.9	0.2

NL E	CHI	MON	NY	PHI	STL	PIT
Start	277	155	**801**	62	750	
6/1	241	119	**901**	26	714	45
7/1	211	89	**991**		684	15
8/1	180	58	**1084**		653	44
9/1	149	27	**1177**		622	13
End	118		**1270**		591	
Spt.	1.05	1.02	**1.55**	1.00	1.36	1.01

Name	Tm	Pos	WAR	SpW	Fame
Cone	NY	P	**5.6**	8.7	3.1
Strawberry	NY	RF	5.4	8.4	2.9
McReynolds	NY	LF	4.5	7.0	**2.5**
Smith	STL	SS	**6.6**	**9.0**	2.4
Van Slyke	PIT	CF	**6.4**	6.5	0.1
Bonds	PIT	LF	**6.2**	6.3	0.1

NL W	ATL	CIN	HOU	LA	SD	SF
Start	68	287	444	396	335	445
6/1	32	263	544	492	299	417
7/1	2	233	606	582	269	399
8/1		202	575	675	238	384
9/1		171	572	768	207	369
End		140	541	861	176	338
Spt.	1.00	1.06	1.24	**1.50***	1.06	1.13

Name	*Tm*	*Pos*	*WAR*	*SpW*	*Fame*
Hershiser	LA	P	**7.2**	**10.8**	3.6
Gibson	LA	LF	6.5	**9.8**	3.3
Tudor	2 TM	P	5.2	7.2	**2.0**
Leary	LA	P	2.8	4.2	**1.4**
Butler	SF	CF	**6.8**	7.7	0.9
Clark	SF	1B	**6.6**	7.5	0.9
Larkin	CIN	SS	**7.0**	7.4	0.4

Three of the four playoff teams in 1987 combined for 14 days of gaining Momentum in 1988. The Giants were 13 of those days, as they and the Astros bugged the Dodgers in spurts until mid–August. The Giants' lineup was effective, but the pitching was weak outside Rick Reuschel and Don Robinson. The Astros had Glenn Davis's bat and Mike Scott's pitching, but Nolan Ryan aged. The Dodgers weren't much deeper, but free agent Kirk Gibson provided power and Orel Hershiser's 59 straight scoreless innings to end the season highlighted a great year. Tim Leary and Tim Belcher were competent behind Hershiser, Jay Howell, Alejandro Pena, and Brian Holton made a deep bullpen, and—for once—the defense wasn't awful.

In the NL East, the race barely existed. The Cardinals nearly scored the fewest runs in the NL, as signing former Brave Bob Horner from Japan did not replace Jack Clark signing with the Yankees and putting Luis Alicea at second base did not replace Tom Herr (traded for Tom Brunansky). The Mets scored the most runs and allowed the fewest, which made even the Pirates' brief threat in May and July a surprise. Darryl Strawberry, Kevin McReynolds, and Howard Johnson were all top-ten in home runs, David Cone went 20–3 in his first full year, Dwight Gooden continued to excel, Ron Darling, Sid Fernandez, and Roger McDowell rebounded, and Randy Myers posted a 1.72 ERA as the new closer.

In the AL West, the Twins gained Momentum only on July 17 despite winning more games than in 1987. The Angels had a deep lineup but no pitching outside relievers Greg Minton and rookie Bryan Harvey, as Mike Witt had a rough season. The A's started 6–6 but went 18–1 after that and were unharried after May. Rookie of the Year shortstop Walt Weiss provided great defense and Jose Canseco, Dave Henderson, and Mark McGwire led the offense. Starter

Dave Stewart repeated his surprise 1987 success, backed by trade acquisition Bob Welch and reclamation project Storm Davis. Dennis Eckersley became a closer full-time and led the league with 45 saves.

In the East, the Indians started 11–2. The Yankees took first in May (and Momentum lead on June 9) after the Indians started 11–2. In June, the Tigers took first by going 6–1 against the Indians and 5–1 against the Yankees. The Yankees continued contending, as Jack Clark and Claudell Washington ably supported offensive stalwarts Don Mattingly, Rickey Henderson, and Dave Winfield, and free agent John Candelaria stabilized the rotation. The Red Sox came out of the All-Star break 19–1, and the Yankees gave up 201 runs (6.9 per game) in a 9–20 August, swapping places in the race. After the Tigers and Red Sox met in mid–August, the Tigers went 8–21 to give the Red Sox the division.

The Tigers had fine talents in Alan Trammell, Lou Whitaker, and young starter Jeff Robinson and closer Mike Henneman, but Darrell Evans got old and Kirk Gibson went to the Dodgers. Boston's farm system over the last two years had produced Mike Greenwell, Ellis Burks, and Jody Reed to join Dwight Evans and Wade Boggs. Roger Clemens was his usual self, Bruce Hurst backed him up well, and midseason acquisition Mike Boddicker gave the rotation necessary depth.

1989: Unfairly Overshadowed

AL E	BOS	CLE	DET	MIL	NY	TOR	BAL
Start	144	47	370	11	334	153	
6/1	121	8	331		295	114	14
7/1	91		301		265	84	104
8/1	60		270		234	53	197
9/1	29		239	11	203	90	290
End			209		173	180	380
Spt.	1.04	1.01	1.32	1.00	1.21	**1.10**	1.11

Name	Tm	Pos	WAR	SpW	Fame
Whitaker	DET	2B	5.3	**7.0**	**1.7**
Trammell	DET	SS	3.7	4.9	**1.2**
Tanana	DET	P	3.1	4.1	**1.0**
Sax	NY	2B	4.4	5.3	0.9
Ripken	BAL	SS	**6.6**	**7.3**	0.7
McGriff	TOR	1B	**6.6**	**7.3**	0.7
Boggs	BOS	3B	**8.4**	**8.7**	0.3
Yount	MIL	CF	5.8	5.8	

AL W	CAL	MIN	OAK	KC	TEX
Start	161	114	**458**		
6/1	250	75	**575**	47	31

13. A Post-Strike World   263

AL W	CAL	MIN	OAK	KC	TEX
7/1	328	45	**665**	101	13
8/1	421	14	**758**	98	
9/1	514		**851**	83	
End	500		**941**	77	
Spt.	1.32	1.03	**1.60**	1.03	1.01

Name	Tm	Pos	WAR	SpW	Fame
R. Henderson	2 TM	LF	**8.6**	**12.4**	**3.8**
Moore	OAK	P	5.5	**8.8**	**3.3**
Lansford	OAK	3B	4.6	7.4	**2.8**
D. Henderson	OAK	CF	4.2	6.7	**2.5**
Blyleven	CAL	P	**6.0**	**7.9**	1.9
Saberhagen	KC	P	**9.7**	**10.0**	0.3
Gubicza	KC	P	**6.3**	6.5	0.2

NL E	CHI	NY	STL	MON
Start	77	**830**	386	
6/1	144	**917**	449	19
7/1	234	**971**	455	105
8/1	287	**1004**	456	198
9/1	380	**1021**	469	275
End	470	**995**	479	269
Spt.	**1.12**	1.50	1.25	1.03

Name	Tm	Pos	WAR	SpW	Fame
Johnson	NY	3B/SS	6.9	**10.4**	**3.5**
Strawberry	NY	RF	4.7	**7.1**	**2.4**
Smith	STL	SS	7.3	**9.1**	**1.8**
Fernandez	NY	P	3.6	5.4	**1.8**
Langston	2 TM	P	**6.4**	6.6	0.2
Bonds	PIT	LF	**8.0**	**8.0**	

NL W	CIN	HOU	LA	SD	SF
Start	92	354	563	115	221
6/1	203	329	534	134	280
7/1	245	399	504	108	370
8/1	214	476	473	77	463
9/1	183	525	442	46	556
End	153	495	412	20	646
Spt.	1.05	1.25	1.30	1.03	**1.29**

Name	Tm	Pos	WAR	SpW	Fame
Clark	SF	1B	**8.6**	**11.1**	**2.5**
Hershiser	LA	P	**7.0**	**9.1**	**2.1**
Mitchell	SF	LF	6.9	**8.9**	**2.0**
Thompson	SF	2B	6.1	7.9	**1.8**
Smith	ATL	LF	**8.8**	8.8	

Pete Rose's saga that ended in his ban from baseball consumed the regular season,[3] and an earthquake affected the World Series[4]; both events obscured unusual pennant races.

The NL West had everyone but the Braves involved around the end of May. The Dodgers fell out first; acquisitions Eddie Murray and Willie Randolph did their part, and Orel Hershiser, Tim Belcher, and Jay Howell led the league's best staff, but Kirk Gibson played only half the season and centerfielder John Shelby was a disaster. The Giants went 12–2 from June 9–21 and pushed out Rose's Reds. The Astros, led by first baseman Glenn Davis on offense, third baseman Ken Caminiti on defense, and Jim Deshaies and Mike Scott on the mound, challenged through late August, and the Padres ended the season 38–19, but the Giants stayed in front. The Giants' first four hitters, Brett Butler, Robby Thompson, Will Clark, and Kevin Mitchell, provided the offense; Mitchell's .635 SLG and 47 HR were .076 and 11 ahead of the Mets' Howard Johnson in second place. Scott Garrelts converted to the rotation and won the ERA title.

In the East, first place went to the Mets in May, the Cubs in June, the Expos in July after acquiring Mark Langston, and the Cubs again in August; as late as September 8 all three, plus the Cardinals, gained Momentum. The Cardinals played great defense, led up the middle by Ozzie Smith, Jose Oquendo, and Milt Thompson and by Terry Pendleton at third base. The Mets led the NL in home runs, but Dwight Gooden got hurt, and David Cone fell to a worse-than-average ERA. Sid Fernandez and Randy Myers were good, but trading reliever Rick Aguilera and others for starter Frank Viola was a wash. Meanwhile, Ryne Sandberg and sophomore first baseman Mark Grace capably led the Cubs' offense, starters Greg Maddux and Rick Sutcliffe were joined by a breakout year from Mike Bielecki in the rotation, and callup reliever Les Lancaster went his first 20 appearances, from late June to early August, without allowing a run.[5]

AL East teams were consistently below .500 until June. The Tigers were on their way to 103 losses; 1988's 107-loss team, the Orioles, led by Cal Ripken and slugging catcher Mickey Tettleton, emerged with a 13–1 run from May 22 to June 5. A 2–12 road trip starting July 20 reduced their lead to a single game even as other teams still couldn't stay over .500. The Blue Jays, who'd fired manager Jimy Williams after a 12–24 start, and the Brewers started gaining Momentum in mid–August. The Brewers promptly lost series to the Orioles and Blue Jays; the Blue Jays took first place for good on September 1 and beat the Orioles in the last series of the season to clinch. The Blue Jays were led by the hitting of corner infielders Fred McGriff and Kelly Gruber, the defense of shortstop Tony Fernandez, and the relief pitching of Tom Henke.

In the AL West, the A's and Angels did most of the sparring, although the Royals showed up occasionally, usually after a good series against the Angels. All three teams were close as September started, but the Angels' offense and the Royals' pitching faltered, leaving the A's alone. The Angels led the AL in home runs but were twelfth in runs; when they weren't impatiently mashing, they played fine defense, led by Dick Schofield and Devon White, and the front of the rotation—Chuck Finley, Kirk McCaskill, and free agent Bert Blyleven—was strong. The A's also had fine pitching in starters Dave Stewart, Mike Moore, and Bob Welch, with Dennis Eckersley deftly handling the ninth inning. The offense was thin until trading for Rickey Henderson in late June and getting Jose Canseco back in July from a wrist injury; they were seventh in the AL in runs before Canseco returned and second after.

1990: Four Out of 12 Out of 26

	AL E	BAL	DET	NY	TOR	BOS	MIL
Start	213	117	97	101			
6/1	179	83	63	183	80		90
7/1	149	53	33	253	166		80
8/1	118	22	2	334	259		49
9/1	87			399	352		18
End	55			451	448		
Spt.	1.13	1.04		1.02	1.32	**1.22**	1.02

Name	Tm	Pos	WAR	SpW	Fame
Clemens	BOS	P	**10.6**	12.9	2.3
Stieb	TOR	P	5.8	7.7	1.9
McGriff	TOR	1B	5.2	6.9	1.7
Fernandez	TOR	SS	4.4	5.8	1.4
Boddicker	BOS	P	6.1	7.4	1.3
Ripken	BAL	SS	**7.5**	8.5	1.0
Trammell	DET	SS	**6.7**	7.0	0.3
Fielder	DET	1B	**6.5**	6.8	0.3

	AL W	CAL	KC	OAK	CHI
Start		281	43	**529**	
6/1		247	9	**627**	33
7/1		217		**717**	103
8/1		186		**810**	184
9/1		155		**903**	173
End		123		**999**	141
Spt.		1.26	1.01	**1.60**	1.08

Name	Tm	Pos	WAR	SpW	Fame
Henderson	OAK	LF	**9.9**	15.8	5.9
McGwire	OAK	1B	5.7	9.1	3.4
Canseco	OAK	RF/DH	5.4	8.6	3.2
Stewart	OAK	P	5.2	8.3	3.1
Finley	CAL	P	**7.6**	9.6	2.0
Franco	TEX	2B	**6.8**	6.8	

NL E	CHI	MON	NY	STL	PHI	PIT
Start	470	269	995	479		
6/1	436	267	961	445	48	102
7/1	406	329	971	415	22	192
8/1	375	302	1064	384		285
9/1	344	271	1133	353		378
End	312	239	1201	321		474
Spt.	1.10	1.07	1.50	1.14	1.00	1.10

Name	Tm	Pos	WAR	SpW	Fame
Viola	NY	P	6.4	9.6	3.2
Strawberry	NY	RF	6.3	9.5	3.2
Magadan	NY	1B	4.6	6.9	2.3
Cone	NY	P	3.8	5.7	1.9
Bonds	PIT	LF	9.7	10.7	1.0
Sandberg	CHI	2B	7.1	7.8	0.7
Dykstra	PHI	CF	8.9	8.9	

NL W	CIN	HOU	LA	SD	SF
Start	153	495	412	20	646
6/1	239	461	386		612
7/1	329	431	356		582
8/1	422	400	325		551
9/1	515	369	294		520
End	611	337	262		488
Spt.	1.50*	1.24	1.09	1.00	1.38

Name	Tm	Pos	WAR	SpW	Fame
Rijo	CIN	P	5.7	8.6	2.9
Larkin	CIN	SS	5.6	8.4	2.8
Sabo	CIN	3B	4.2	6.3	2.1
Browning	CIN	P	4.1	6.2	2.1
Butler	SF	CF	4.9	6.8	1.9
Whitson	SD	P	7.0	7.0	
Roberts	SD	LF/3B	5.7	5.7	

For the only time in the division era, fewer than half the teams gained Momentum. In the AL East, as the Orioles' young pitching regressed, the Brewers led through early June, but a 4–14 stretch featuring four losses to the Blue Jays left the race to the Blue Jays and Red Sox. The Red Sox went 10–3 against the Blue Jays during the season, taking first in late June by sweeping them in four games, taking three of four in late August, and—just when the Blue Jays had tied them—taking two of three in the second-to-last series of the season. The Blue Jays got a great season from Dave Stieb in the rotation and Tom Henke in the bullpen, and David Wells once he left the bullpen for the rotation in June. In the lineup, Fred McGriff, Kelly Gruber, and Tony Fernandez provided similar contributions to their 1989 selves. The Red Sox had decent performances from Jody Reed, Wade Boggs, and Ellis Burks, but their mainstays were Mike Boddicker and Roger Clemens.

The Angels' main offseason move, signing Mark Langston, was a bust, and with Bert Blyleven's aging and bad defense the Angels were never a factor. With a 22–6 start, it looked like the A's would have no trouble, but the White Sox tied them for a week after sweeping them June 22–24. As good as Carlton Fisk, sophomore southpaw Greg Hibbard, and Bobby Thigpen (on his way to a record 57 saves) were, the White Sox couldn't keep up with Oakland's depth, and they fell back in early August. Other than batting average, the A's had it all: Mark McGwire's and Jose Canseco's slugging, Walt Weiss's stellar defense, some of each in Dave Henderson, and everything in Rickey Henderson. Bob Welch won 27 games and a Cy Young; Dave Stewart got some first-place votes for 22 wins and a better ERA. All the regular relievers had ERAs under 3, led by Dennis Eckersley's 0.61.

The NL East had a four-team race again, but it didn't include the Cubs, who saw Mike Bielecki crumble and Rick Sutcliffe get hurt, or the Cardinals, who couldn't steal first base. The Phillies' offense got them through June, and the Expos' deep pitching staff got them through July. That left the Pirates, in first almost all year from a 22–9 start, and the Mets, who fired Davey Johnson after a 20–22 start and went 26–8 right after under Bud Harrelson. For the Mets, the offense led the league in runs, Frank Viola was an ace, Dwight Gooden won 19, and the bullpen, led by new closer John Franco, was sound. The Mets beat the Pirates on September 12 and 13 to get close, but the Pirates finished strong enough to clinch before the season-ending series between them. The Pirates' core—Barry Bonds, Bobby Bonilla, Andy Van Slyke, and pitcher Doug Drabek—was as good in 1990 as in 1989, but in 1990 the gaping holes in the roster got plugged, particularly on the back end of the rotation when Zane Smith was acquired from the Expos.

In the NL West, the Giants squandered their offense with a lousy rotation, and the Astros had no offense to squander. The Reds, free of Pete Rose, won their first nine games, and while the Dodgers started decently, the Reds were up seven games by May 10 and captured the division easily. The Reds were led on offense by Barry Larkin, Chris Sabo, and Eric Davis. Jose Rijo was a fine ace, but it was the bullpen that made the most impact, as the Nasty Boys—Randy Myers, Rob Dibble, and Norm Charlton—gave batters fits all year. The 1990 Reds remain the only NL team with at 3 WAR from three different relievers.

1991: Frank Viola's Legacy

AL E	BAL	BOS	TOR	DET
Start	28	224	226	
6/1		309	331	32

AL E	BAL	BOS	TOR	DET
7/1		379	421	2
8/1		348	514	
9/1		317	607	56
End		322	**712**	33
Spt.	1.00	1.29	**1.46**	1.01

Name	Tm	Pos	WAR	SpW	Fame
White	TOR	CF	6.3	**9.2**	**2.9**
Clemens	BOS	P	**7.9**	**10.2**	**2.3**
Carter	TOR	RF/LF	4.7	6.9	**2.2**
Boggs	BOS	3B	6.4	8.3	**1.9**
Candiotti	2 TM	P	7.1	**8.7**	1.6
Whitaker	DET	2B	**6.7**	6.8	0.1
Ripken	BAL	SS	**11.5**	**11.5**	

AL W	CAL	CHI	OAK	MIN	SEA	TEX
Start	61	71	**499**			
6/1	78	64	**596**	5	47	48
7/1	124	34	**650**	72	21	58
8/1	133	47	**659**	165		87
9/1	102	68	**640**	258		56
End	67	33	**605**	363		21
Spt.	1.13	1.06	1.49	**1.41***	1.01	1.02

Name	Tm	Pos	WAR	SpW	Fame
Tapani	MIN	P	6.8	**9.6**	**2.8**
D. Henderson	OAK	CF	5.4	**8.0**	**2.6**
Canseco	OAK	RF/DH	5.2	7.7	**2.5**
Moore	OAK	P	4.6	6.9	**2.3**
Abbott	CAL	P	**7.6**	**8.6**	1.0
Langston	CAL	P	**7.3**	**8.3**	1.0
Thomas	CHI	1B/DH	**6.9**	7.3	0.4
Griffey	SEA	CF	**7.1**	7.2	0.1

NL E	CHI	MON	NY	PIT	STL
Start	282	216	**1087**	429	290
6/1	248	182	**1153**	527	332
7/1	218	152	**1123**	317	302
8/1	187	121	**1124**	710	271
9/1	156	90	**1093**	803	240
End	121	55	**1058**	908	205
Spt.	1.05	1.04	1.50	**1.40**	1.07

Name	Tm	Pos	WAR	SpW	Fame
Bonds	PIT	LF	**7.9**	**11.1**	**3.2**
Cone	NY	P	4.4	**6.6**	**2.2**
Johnson	NY	3B/RF	3.4	5.1	**1.7**
Gooden	NY	P	3.2	4.8	**1.6**
Sandberg	CHI	2B	**7.1**	7.8	0.7
Smith	STL	SS	**5.0**	5.4	0.4
Martinez	MON	P	**5.8**	6.0	0.2

NL W	CIN	HOU	LA	SF	ATL	SD
Start	553	305	237	442		
6/1	547	271	287	408	67	2
7/1	529	241	377	378	93	
8/1	502	210	470	347	74	
9/1	471	179	563	316	143	
End	436	144	668	281	248	
Spt.	1.30	1.06	1.15	1.16	1.35*	1.00

Name	Tm	Pos	WAR	SpW	Fame
Glavine	ATL	P	8.5	11.5	3.0
Pendleton	ATL	3B	6.1	8.2	2.1
Smoltz	ATL	P	5.4	7.3	1.9
Larkin	CIN	SS	6.1	7.9	1.8
Gwynn	SD	RF	5.6	5.6	

The Red Sox echoed 1990 by going 9–4 against the Blue Jays, including 6–1 in August; the August games let the Red Sox and Tigers into the race. But the Tigers lost six straight starting September 15, and the Red Sox ended the season 3–11, leaving the Blue Jays, a model of consistency by going over .500 in every month, to win the division. The Blue Jays were the only team in the AL to allow under four runs/game thanks to a deep rotation, led by Jimmy Key and two June reinforcements, rookie Juan Guzman and trade pickup Tom Candiotti. Relievers Tom Henke, Duane Ward, and Mike Timlin combined for 266 innings and a 2.84 ERA. Joe Carter and Roberto Alomar, acquired together from the Padres in the offseason, joined Devon White to lead the offense.

The AL West was simple—the A's led until the Twins' 15-win streak starting June 1 took them from below .500 to first place for good. It was also complicated—five teams gained Momentum on July 10, and the A's and White Sox survived until August. The A's missed their fourth straight West title due to Mark McGwire's slump and Dave Stewart and Bob Welch dropping from 8.2 WAR to -0.8; Mike Moore and Dennis Eckersley were the only remotely reliable pitchers. The Twins, last place in 1990, signed Chili Davis and Jack Morris as free agents, saw former Rule 5 draftee rightfielder Shane Mack develop, got a great first full seasons from starter Scott Erickson and second baseman Chuck Knoblauch, and received over 9 WAR from starter Kevin Tapani and closer Rick Aguilera, returns of the 1989 Frank Viola trade.

The Mets' end of the Frank Viola trade—Viola—posted a worse-than-average ERA. They were the last team to challenge the Pirates; on July 13, their final day gaining Momentum, they had scored as many runs as the Pirates. But Darryl Strawberry's signing with the Dodgers finally caught up with them, and with only Howard Johnson as a fearsome bat, the Mets scored the fewest runs in the league from that point. The Pirates led the league in runs at season's end and won the East by 14 games; two-through-five hitters Jay Bell, Andy Van

Slyke, Bobby Bonilla, and Barry Bonds were all good, and John Smiley's 20 wins led a deep staff.

In the West, the Giants still had pitching problems, and the Reds' rotation was so thin outside Jose Rijo that 1990's closer, Randy Myers, was given 12 starts. The Dodgers had signed not only Darryl Strawberry from the Mets but also Brett Butler from the Giants; behind them and a strong rotation led by Ramon Martinez, Mike Morgan, and Tim Belcher, the Dodgers emerged from the West's slow start to lead the division uninterrupted from May to late August. The Braves, last place in 1990, challenged briefly in June and July, gained 5.5 games on the Dodgers in August, and started September a single game up. Both the Braves and the Dodgers went 22–11 down the stretch, the Braves finishing 8–1 to pass the Dodgers at the last minute. The Braves' main free agent, Terry Pendleton, surprised everyone with a batting title, .517 SLG, and MVP after seven average years. With young starters Tom Glavine, John Smoltz, and Steve Avery coming into their own and a rebuilt bullpen, the Braves allowed 177 fewer runs in 1991 than in 1990, enough improvement for Pendleton and the mix-and-match offense to win with.

1992: 96 in '92

AL E	BOS	DET	TOR	BAL	MIL	NY
Start	176	18	390			
6/1	151		501	105		41
7/1	121		591	195		11
8/1	90		684	192		
9/1	59		777	269		
End	26		876	272	23	
Spt.	1.14	1.00	1.60	1.14	1.00	1.01

Name	Tm	Pos	WAR	SpW	Fame
Alomar	TOR	2B	6.6	10.6	4.0
White	TOR	CF	6.2	9.9	3.7
Guzman	TOR	P	5.5	8.8	3.3
Cone	2 TM	P	5.2	7.8	2.6
Clemens	BOS	P	8.8	10.0	1.2
Mussina	BAL	P	8.2	9.3	1.1
Lofton	CLE	CF	6.6	6.6	

AL W	CAL	CHI	MIN	OAK	TEX
Start	37	18	199	331	11
6/1	48	93	222	434	74
7/1	18	63	288	524	108
8/1		32	381	613	77
9/1		1	398	706	46

13. A Post-Strike World

AL W	CAL	CHI	MIN	OAK	TEX
End			365	805	13
Spt.	1.02	1.02	1.30	**1.45**	1.03

Name	Tm	Pos	WAR	SpW	Fame
McGwire	OAK	1B	6.4	**9.0**	2.6
R. Henderson	OAK	LF	5.6	**8.1**	2.5
Puckett	MIN	CF	**7.1**	9.2	2.1
Mack	MIN	LF	**6.5**	8.5	2.0
Thomas	CHI	1B	**6.9**	7.0	0.1
Appier	KC	P	**8.1**	8.1	

NL E	CHI	MON	NY	PIT	STL
Start	90	41	**789**	677	153
6/1	55	6	**846**	778	198
7/1	25		832	**868**	188
8/1		28	801	**961**	157
9/1		89	770	**1054**	126
End		76	737	**1153**	93
Spt.	1.01	1.01	1.44	**1.51**	1.05

Name	Tm	Pos	WAR	SpW	Fame
Bonds	PIT	LF	**9.0**	13.1	4.1
Van Slyke	PIT	CF	6.0	8.8	2.8
Fernandez	NY	P	6.0	8.6	2.6
Drabek	PIT	P	5.2	7.6	**2.4**
Maddux	CHI	P	**9.2**	9.3	0.1
Sandberg	CHI	2B	**7.8**	7.9	0.1
Daulton	PHI	C	**6.9**	6.9	

NL W	ATL	CIN	HOU	LA	SF	SD
Start	185	325	107	498	209	
6/1	150	366	76	463	294	51
7/1	160	456	46	433	304	65
8/1	229	549	15	402	273	34
9/1	322	534		371	242	3
End	421	501		338	209	
Spt.	**1.46***	1.26	1.01	1.23	1.08	1.01

Name	Tm	Pos	WAR	SpW	Fame
Justice	ATL	RF	4.9	**7.2**	2.3
Pendleton	ATL	3B	4.9	**7.2**	2.3
Glavine	ATL	P	3.8	5.6	**1.8**
Smoltz	ATL	P	3.6	5.3	**1.7**
Larkin	CIN	SS	**5.6**	7.1	1.5
Rijo	CIN	P	**5.5**	6.9	1.4
Sheffield	SD	3B	**6.2**	6.3	0.1
Finley	HOU	CF	**5.7**	5.8	0.1

Three teams won their divisions with 96–66 records; the fourth winner finished 98–64. In the AL West, the Mariners and Royals started terribly, letting the other teams fight in May. The Rangers dropped out at the end of June, and the Twins took a series from the A's at the end of June to grab and hold first place in July. But the A's won seven straight from August 2–8 while the Twins went 2–4, wrapping things up with a ten-win streak in September. The Twins acquired John Smiley from the Pirates and got great years from regulars; for the A's, Mark McGwire rebounded to lead a versatile, walk-driven offense, Dennis Eckersley saved 51 games, and Bob Welch and Dave Stewart weren't awful.

The Blue Jays repeated 1991 by leading the AL East almost the entire way while challenged by two teams. But instead of the Red Sox and Tigers, who together brought up the rear due to no offense and pitching, respectively, the Orioles, led by outfielders Brady Anderson and Mike Devereaux, ace Mike Mussina, and a deep bullpen, gained Momentum most of the season and got to within a half-game of the Blue Jays on September 5. The Orioles scuffled in September, but the Brewers went 20–7 in September, fueled by rookies Pat Listach and Cal Eldred and veteran Paul Molitor, and entered October 2.5 games back with four to play. The Blue Jays' sweep of the Tigers kept them ahead and kept the Brewers from becoming the lowest-Momentum team ever to enter the postseason. The Jays' pitching thinned when Tom Candiotti signed with the Dodgers and Mike Timlin, Dave Stieb, and David Wells struggled, but offseason acquisition Dave Winfield, trade deadline acquisition David Cone, and first baseman John (not a Dave) Olerud offset the declines. The offense was good enough that Jack Morris won 21 games with a 4.04 ERA.

In the NL East, the Pirates started fast but slumped in May, the Mets started slowly but were contenders by May, and the Cardinals led them both for a week before slipping below .500 at the beginning of June. While the Cardinals slumped, the Pirates forced the Mets below .500 by going 6–1 against them over two series; the Mets, who'd signed Eddie Murray from the Dodgers and Bobby Bonilla from the Pirates but moved Howard Johnson to centerfield with disastrous results, finished last, with the offense and bullpen to blame. The Pirates exited June with a good lead but lost it in July to the Expos, who'd caught fire after Felipe Alou replaced Tom Runnells as manager. The Pirates won 11 straight starting July 30 to break a tie with the Expos and won seven straight starting August 29 to seal the deal. Bonilla and John Smiley were gone, but Barry Bonds and Andy Van Slyke were outstanding, and the thin pitching was strengthened by rookie knuckleballer Tim Wakefield's July callup.

The NL West started slowly again. On June 1, the Giants, Reds, and Padres were tied for first; the Dodgers were at .500 and 2.5 games behind them. The Dodgers' offense collapsed when Darryl Strawberry and free agent signee Eric Davis missed extensive time; they scored double-digit runs only once all season, and rookie Pedro Astacio's 5–5, 1.98 line spoke volumes. The Braves went 11–1 against the Padres and Dodgers at the beginning of June to enter the race, while the Giants fell below .500 permanently in the same period. The Reds led from there, having reinforced by trading prospects to the Indians for starter Greg Swindell and trading Randy Myers to the Padres for second baseman/leftfielder Bip Roberts. But the Braves won the division easily by winning 13 straight in July and their first nine in August, the latter including a sweep of the Reds. The Braves gave up the fewest runs in the league despite playing in a hitters' park; Tom Glavine won 20 games again, John Smoltz was about as good, and Pete Smith, 19-40 before 1992, went 7-0, 2.05 after an August callup.

1993: The End Before the End

AL E	BAL	BOS	MIL	TOR	DET	NY
Start	139	13	12	447		
6/1	103	57		475	105	77
7/1	73	27		553	183	127
8/1	118	80		646	212	220
9/1	123	105		739	181	313
End	139	73		835	149	349
Spt.	1.07	1.03	1.00	1.60	1.12	1.11

Name	Tm	Pos	WAR	SpW	Fame
Olerud	TOR	1B/DH	7.7	12.3	4.6
White	TOR	CF	6.2	9.9	3.7
Alomar	TOR	2B	6.1	9.8	3.7
Molitor	TOR	DH/1B	5.7	9.1	3.4
Hoiles	BAL	C	6.8	7.3	0.5
Lofton	CLE	CF	7.6	7.6	
Vaughn	MIL	LF/DH	6.7	6.7	

AL W	MIN	OAK	TEX	CAL	CHI	KC
Start	186	411	7			
6/1	150	375	79	96	97	10
7/1	120	345	49	146	179	84
8/1	89	314	78	115	272	141
9/1	58	283	51	84	365	126
End	26	251	23	52	461	94
Spt.	1.12	1.35	1.02	1.04	1.26	1.03

Name	Tm	Pos	WAR	SpW	Fame
Thomas	CHI	1B	6.2	7.8	1.6
Johnson	CHI	CF	6.1	7.7	1.6
Fernandez	CHI	P	5.4	6.8	1.4
Ventura	CHI	3B	5.3	6.7	1.4
Langston	CAL	P	8.7	9.1	0.4
Appier	KC	P	9.2	9.5	0.3
Cone	KC	P	7.2	7.4	0.2
Griffey	SEA	CF	8.7	8.7	

NL E	MON	NY	PIT	STL	PHI
Start	51	496	777	63	
6/1	13	458	739	25	105
7/1		428	709		195
8/1		397	678		288
9/1		366	647		381
End	3	334	615		477
Spt.	**1.01**	**1.34**	**1.50**	**1.01**	**1.20**

Name	*Tm*	*Pos*	*WAR*	*SpW*	*Fame*
Bell	PIT	SS	**6.2**	**9.3**	**3.1**
Merced	PIT	RF/1B	3.5	5.2	**1.7**
King	PIT	3B	3.2	4.8	**1.6**
Dykstra	PHI	CF	**6.5**	**7.8**	**1.3**
Daulton	PHI	C	5.0	**6.0**	1.0
Grissom	MON	CF	**5.2**	5.3	0.1
Wilkins	CHI	C	**6.6**	**6.6**	

NL W	ATL	CIN	LA	SF	HOU
Start	283	337	228	141	
6/1	293	299	190	251	49
7/1	263	269	160	341	19
8/1	232	238	129	434	
9/1	201	207	98	527	
End	281	175	66	611	
Spt.	**1.16**	**1.18**	**1.06**	**1.24**	**1.01**

Name	*Tm*	*Pos*	*WAR*	*SpW*	*Fame*
Bonds	SF	LF	**9.9**	**12.3**	**2.4**
Rijo	CIN	P	**9.3**	**11.0**	**1.7**
Thompson	SF	2B	6.3	**7.8**	**1.5**
Williams	SF	3B	5.8	7.2	**1.4**
Gant	ATL	LF	6.5	**7.5**	1.0
Piazza	LA	C	**7.0**	7.4	0.4

Three divisions' Momentum leaders entering the season gained none in 1993, and in two of those divisions the second-ranked team didn't gain any either. In the NL East, the Mets started 8–7 but went 13–45—a .224 pace—after that, finishing behind the expansion Marlins. The Pirates fell to fifth, as Barry Bonds and Doug Drabek left for the Giants and Astros, respectively, Andy Van Slyke missed time, and the rotation tanked. In their place, 1992's last place team, the Phillies, started 45–17 and won the division easily. The Phillies' offense, decent in 1992, improved with productive outfield platoons and having Lenny Dykstra play a full season, but the most important development was in the pitching, replacing a dozen awful performances with a healthy Tommy Greene and free agent Danny Jackson in the rotation.

In the NL West, the Reds gained no Momentum. Free agent John Smiley was a disaster replacing free agent Greg Swindell, Rob Dibble's ERA jumped to 6.48, and Barry Larkin and Bip Roberts missed time to injuries. The Giants fended off the Braves and Astros and had a ten-game lead on July 22. Signing Barry Bonds to join infielders Robby Thompson and Matt Williams and getting reliable wins from Bill Swift and John Burkett, the Giants made it look easy. But the Braves obtained first baseman Fred McGriff at the trade deadline, won nine straight in August, and went 5–1 against the Giants from August 23–September 2 to start gaining Momentum. The Giants lost their lead in September, but went 11–1 heading into game 162 to tie the Braves. In game 162, while the Dodgers beat the Giants, the Braves beat the Rockies to claim their third straight come-from-behind division title. Besides the Braves' rotation, led by free agent Greg Maddux, the bullpen was deeper than usual, and offensive stars Ron Gant and David Justice were joined by a breakout year from Jeff Blauser.

In the AL West, the A's and Twins fell from the top to the bottom. For the A's, Mark McGwire only played 27 games, Dennis Eckersley's ERA more than doubled, and Ron Darling's and Bob Welch's ERAs jumped by two runs. The Twins nearly gave up as many runs as the A's did, and all their important hitters declined. No team stepped up immediately to replace them; on June 15, the Twins were 29–31 but only three games back. The White Sox took first by sweeping the Rangers in late June and cemented it with a hot July. The White Sox allowed the fewest runs in the AL, led by a strong rotation of Cy Young winner Jack McDowell and youngsters Alex Fernandez, Wilson Alvarez, and Jason Bere.

Although the Blue Jays didn't collapse like other Momentum leaders, they weren't in first initially, as the Tigers entered June having scored more than six runs/game. But Detroit's pitching gave up six runs/game in June and July, and after the All-Star break the Tigers were barely heard from. On July 23, only a half-game separated the Blue Jays, the Yankees, who'd signed Jimmy Key from the Blue Jays and Wade Boggs from the Red Sox, and the Orioles and Red Sox, who'd been hot in June and July, respectively. Boston's thin lineup dragged them down, and the Yankees and Blue Jays traded first place while the Orioles stayed live into mid–September. The Blue Jays dispatched both rivals by winning nine straight, finishing with a seven-game lead that didn't reflect the season narrative. Dave Winfield had left in free agency, but the offense held up; replacement Paul Molitor's .332/.402/509 line was matched by Roberto Alomar's .326/.408/.492 and bested by John Olerud's .363/.473/.599. The rotation had issues, but Duane Ward led a deep bullpen.

14. Playing Your Wild Cards Right, 1994–2002

With four playoff races in each league, Momentum is only two points per day. With the addition of the wild card, teams are often fighting their division for one playoff slot and outside their division for another, making season narratives more intertwined than before. In the interest of maintaining a coherent narrative amidst the new complexity, after 1994 I will rely on the statistical tables to suffice in covering specific players.

1994: Strike While the Expos Are Hot

AL E	BAL	BOS	DET	NY	TOR
Start	91	48	98	229	**548**
6/1	135	122	61	300	**535**
7/1	186	125	31	360	**505**
8/1	233	94		422	474
End	226	84		442	464
Spt.	1.14	1.05	1.03	**1.30**	1.49

Name	Tm	Pos	WAR	SpW	Fame
Hentgen	TOR	P	**5.3**	7.9	**2.6**
Stottlemyre	TOR	P	3.6	5.4	**1.8**
Molitor	TOR	DH	3.6	5.4	**1.8**
Olerud	TOR	1B	3.2	4.8	**1.6**
Boggs	NY	3B	4.5	**5.9**	1.4
Mussina	BAL	P	**5.4**	6.2	0.8
Clemens	BOS	P	**6.1**	6.4	0.3
Phillips	DET	LF	**4.7**	4.8	0.1

AL C	CHI	KC	MIN	CLE	MIL
Start	303	62	17		
6/1	377	40		22	6
7/1	434	28	29	82	
8/1	**496**			144	

14. Playing Your Wild Cards Right 277

AL C	CHI	KC	MIN	CLE	MIL
End	**516**	14		164	
Spt.	**1.41**	1.02	1.01	**1.03**	1.00

Name	Tm	Pos	WAR	SpW	Fame
Thomas	CHI	1B	**6.3**	**8.9**	**2.6**
McDowell	CHI	P	3.8	5.4	**1.6**
Alvarez	CHI	P	3.7	5.2	**1.5**
Lofton	CLE	CF	**7.2**	**7.4**	0.2
Belle	CLE	LF	**5.7**	**5.9**	0.2
Cone	KC	P	**6.8**	**6.9**	0.1

	AL W	CAL	OAK	TEX	
	Start	34	165	15	
	6/1		128		
	7/1		98		
	8/1		67		
	End		57		
	Spt.	1.01	1.08	**1.00**	

Name	Tm	Pos	WAR	SpW	Fame
R. Henderson	OAK	LF	**3.5**	**3.8**	0.3
Javier	OAK	CF	3.4	**3.7**	0.3
Ontiveros	OAK	P	3.1	3.3	**0.2**
Steinbach	OAK	C	3.1	3.3	**0.2**
Griffey	SEA	CF	**6.9**	**6.9**	
Johnson	SEA	P	**5.5**	**5.5**	
Clark	TEX	1B	**3.6**	3.6	

NL E	ATL	MON	NY	PHI	FLA
Start	155	2	184	263	
6/1	231	68	173	225	24
7/1	291	128	143	195	
8/1	**353**	190	112	164	
End	**373**	210	102	154	
Spt.	**1.29**	**1.05**	1.10	1.19	1.00

Name	Tm	Pos	WAR	SpW	Fame
Maddux	ATL	P	**8.5**	**11.0**	**2.5**
McGriff	ATL	P	4.5	**5.8**	**1.3**
Justice	ATL	RF	3.7	**4.8**	**1.1**
Jackson	PHI	P	4.7	**5.6**	0.9
Saberhagen	NY	P	**5.5**	**6.1**	0.6
Alou	MON	LF/RF	**5.1**	**5.4**	0.3
Grissom	MON	CF	**5.1**	**5.4**	0.3

NL C	CIN	PIT	HOU	STL
Start	97	**339**		
6/1	164	328	48	50
7/1	224	298	102	62
8/1	286	267	152	31

NL C	CIN	PIT	HOU	STL
End	306	257	166	21
Spt.	1.12	1.39	1.04	1.02

Name	Tm	Pos	WAR	SpW	Fame
Bell	PIT	SS	3.4	4.7	1.3
Smith	PIT	P	3.0	4.2	1.2
Martin	PIT	LF	1.4	2.0	0.6
Larkin	CIN	SS	3.9	4.4	0.5
Bagwell	HOU	1B	8.2	8.5	0.3
Biggio	HOU	2B	4.6	4.8	0.2
Caminiti	HOU	3B	3.8	4.0	0.2

NL W	LA	SF
Start	36	337
6/1	55	335
7/1	85	305
8/1	108	274
End	104	264
Spt.	1.04	1.43

Name	Tm	Pos	WAR	SpW	Fame
Bonds	SF	LF	6.2	8.9	2.7
Williams	SF	3B	4.7	6.7	2.0
Clayton	SF	SS	2.8	4.0	1.2
Jackson	SF	P	1.7	2.4	0.7
Freeman	COL	P	4.5	4.5	
Gwynn	SD	RF	4.2	4.2	

Players went on strike August 12, cutting the season short and cancelling the postseason.[1] It was a massive failure for what was supposed to be a banner year.

With the addition of two divisions, two wild card teams, and a playoff round,[2] the Braves moved to the NL East, putting 1993's division winners together. But the Phillies weren't up to the challenge, as injuries to the offense negated improved pitching. The Braves took the early lead, with the Expos closely tracking them. The Expos were on a 20–3 run leading into the strike, opening up a six-game lead while the Braves, down a bat from Ron Gant's off-season injury, led the wild card narrowly over the Astros. The Expos got great years from their outfield of Moises Alou, Marquis Grissom, and Larry Walker, and nine of their ten regular pitchers had better-than-average ERAs.

In the NL Central, the Cardinals slumped in June and left the division for the Reds and Astros to fight over; they were separated by a half-game when the strike hit. The Pirates made noise in May but had no hitting. The Reds got healthy and effective years from Barry Larkin and 1993 acquisitions John Smiley and Kevin Mitchell; new closer Jeff Brantley and several young arms rebuilt the bullpen. The Astros's 1993 pickup of Doug Drabek paid dividends as well; he led a pitching staff that featured several off-years. The Reds and Astros were the top two run scorers in the league; despite playing in the cavernous Astrodome, Jeff Bagwell slugged .750—the best figure since Babe Ruth in 1927.

The NL West didn't have a race. Matt Williams challenged the single-season home run record; he and Barry Bonds provided more WAR than the other Giants combined. The Dodgers led the West most of the season but were 58–56 when play stopped. Sophomore catcher Mike Piazza led the offense, while the rotation, led by Ramon Martinez and Kevin Gross, was deep enough to avoid using the awful bullpen too often.

The AL West was even worse than the NL West; the division gained only one day of Momentum—the Rangers on June 10—and when play stopped its four teams had the league's four worst records. Oakland's continued decline— Mark McGwire was hurt again—was the main story, apart from Seattle's Ken Griffey also challenging the single-season home run record.

Frank Thomas **also** challenged the home run record, but he did it for a good team. The White Sox led early but fell in June to six games behind the Indians, who'd moved into the division right as their long rebuilding was wrapping up behind the electrifying Kenny Lofton, the terrifying Albert Belle, homegrown ace Charles Nagy, and imported ace Dennis Martinez. The White Sox were 18–3 after their low point, and the White Sox and Indians were a game apart when the strike hit. Thomas's .729 SLG was supplemented by free agent designated hitter Julio Franco while the rotation thrived. The Royals, with strong pitching from David Cone and Kevin Appier and slugging rookie Bob Hamelin, won 14 straight a week before the strike to climb over .500 and into contention.

The three Central contenders and the Orioles were the main candidates for the wild card. The Orioles had challenged the Yankees in the East but faded in July. The Orioles allowed the fewest runs in the AL, thanks to Mike Mussina and the league's best defense, anchored by Cal Ripken; Ripken, free agent first baseman Rafael Palmeiro, and catcher Chris Hoiles led the offense. The Yankees were a deep team led by their 1993 marquee pickups, Jimmy Key and Wade Boggs. Catcher Mike Stanley and rigthfielder Paul O'Neill provided the rest of the offense, and veteran Steve Howe put it all together for a fantastic year as closer.

1995: Late Start, Late Finish

AL E	BAL	BOS	NY	TOR
Start	119	44	233	244
6/1	103	67	229	228
7/1	73	127	199	198

AL E	BAL	BOS	NY	TOR
8/1	42	189	171	167
9/1	11	251	188	136
End		313	229	105
Spt.	1.05	1.25	1.34	1.18

Name	Tm	Pos	WAR	SpW	Fame
Williams	NY	CF	**6.4**	8.6	2.2
Valentin	BOS	SS	**8.3**	10.4	2.1
Cone	2 TM	P	**7.0**	8.7	1.7
Boggs	NY	3B	4.2	5.6	**1.4**
Leiter	TOR	P	**5.7**	6.7	1.0
Mussina	BAL	P	**6.1**	6.4	0.3

AL C	CHI	CLE	KC	MIL
Start	**271**	86	7	
6/1	**255**	109		
7/1	**225**	169	58	
8/1	194	**231**	36	9
9/1	163	**293**	11	8
End	132	**355**	13	
Spt.	1.33	1.43	1.02	1.00

Name	Tm	Pos	WAR	SpW	Fame
Belle	CLE	LF	**6.9**	9.8	2.9
Thome	CLE	3B	**5.9**	8.4	2.5
D. Martinez	CLE	P	**5.7**	8.2	2.5
Lofton	CLE	CF	4.1	5.9	**1.8**
Thomas	CHI	1B	5.3	**7.0**	1.7
Knoblauch	MIN	2B	**6.7**	6.7	

AL W	OAK	CAL	SEA	TEX
Start	30			
6/1	41	32	16	14
7/1	50	92	19	74
8/1	31	154		133
9/1		216	35	186
End		278	97	182
Spt.	1.02	1.09	1.29*	1.07

Name	Tm	Pos	WAR	SpW	Fame
Johnson	SEA	P	**8.6**	11.1	2.5
E. Martinez	SEA	DH	**7.0**	9.0	2.0
T. Martinez	SEA	1B	4.5	5.8	**1.3**
Griffey	SEA	CF	3.3	4.3	**1.0**
Salmon	CAL	RF	**6.6**	7.2	0.6
Rogers	TEX	P	**5.8**	6.2	0.4

NL E	ATL	MON	NY	PHI
Start	**298**	167	82	123
6/1	**326**	186	65	148

14. Playing Your Wild Cards Right

NL E	ATL	MON	NY	PHI
7/1	**383**	204	35	208
8/1	**445**	173	4	243
9/1	**507**	142		242
End	**569**	111		214
Spt.	**1.60**	1.09	1.02	1.16

Name	Tm	Pos	WAR	SpW	Fame
Maddux	ATL	P	**9.7**	**15.5**	**5.8**
Glavine	ATL	P	**4.8**	**7.7**	**2.9**
Smoltz	ATL	P	**4.2**	**6.7**	**2.5**
Justice	ATL	RF	3.8	**6.1**	**2.3**
P. Martinez	MON	P	**4.6**	5.0	0.4

NL C	CIN	HOU	PIT	STL	CHI
Start	244	132	205	17	
6/1	257	124	188		28
7/1	317	94	158		43
8/1	379	138	127		12
9/1	441	197	96		
End	503	247	65		
Spt.	**1.45**	1.08	1.08	1.00	1.01

Name	Tm	Pos	WAR	SpW	Fame
Sanders	CIN	RF	**6.6**	**9.6**	**3.0**
Larkin	CIN	SS	**5.9**	**8.6**	**2.7**
Schourek	CIN	P	4.1	**5.9**	**1.8**
Gant	CIN	LF	3.3	4.8	**1.5**
Biggio	HOU	2B	**6.3**	**6.8**	0.5
Wells	2 TM	P	**5.3**	5.7	0.4
Sosa	CHI	RF	**5.3**	5.4	0.1

NL W	LA	SF	COL	SD
Start	83	211		
6/1	66	209	17	
7/1	63	242	77	2
8/1	50	211	139	
9/1	103	180	201	
End	165	149	263	
Spt.	1.09	1.20	**1.12**	1.00

Name	Tm	Pos	WAR	SpW	Fame
Bonds	SF	LF	**7.5**	**9.2**	**1.7**
Williams	SF	3B	4.6	**5.5**	**0.9**
Carreon	SF	1B	2.9	3.5	**0.6**
Walker	COL	RF	4.7	**5.3**	**0.6**
Piazza	LA	C	**6.2**	**6.8**	**0.6**
Ashby	SD	P	**4.9**	4.9	
Mondesi	LA	RF	**4.8**	5.2	0.4

The strike didn't end until spring training had already started with replacement players[3]; to give the regular players time to train, the season didn't start until late April, with 18 games cut from it. This postponed the season's midpoint to around July 15. By that time, several teams had bowed out. The Blue Jays and White Sox both had pitching problems, exemplified by Juan Guzman's 4–14, 6.32 ERA for the former and Jason Bere's 8–15, 7.19 ERA for the latter. The Expos were undercut completely by finances; Marquis Grissom, starter Ken Hill, and closer John Wetteland were traded, and Larry Walker signed with the Rockies. In their place, the Indians, Red Sox, and Rockies were the only good teams in their divisions, the Braves and Reds held comfortable leads, the Phillies and Astros were fighting for the wild card, and the Angels and Rangers were virtually tied for the AL West division lead.

From there, things got weird. The Tigers, 3.5 back in the East, played .319 ball in the second half, the Rangers lost ten straight in July to give the Angels a large lead, and the Phillies played .403 ball in the second half but were in the wild card race in September thanks to the Astros' 9–20 August. On September 1, a .513 winning percentage led both wild cards—the 59–56 Royals and 60–57 Mariners in the AL and the 60–57 Astros and Rockies in the West (the Dodgers had taken first from the Rockies after the Rockies slumped in August).

The Yankees were 58–59, but they put together a 21–6 finish to take the AL wild card, though it wasn't secure until the final two weeks. The Mariners went 19–9 while the Angels had separate nine-loss streaks ending September 3 and September 23; they ended the season tied and the Mariners won the playoff game. The NL wild card race came down to the Astros, Rockies, Dodgers, with nearly identical records in September, and even the Cubs for a couple days; the Dodgers won the West and the Rockies won the wild card.

1996: 162 Games? How Novel!

AL E	BOS	NY	TOR	BAL
Start	260	190	88	
6/1	219	257	47	63
7/1	189	317	17	105
8/1	158	379		83
9/1	133	441		100
End	105	497		156
Spt.	1.12	1.50*	1.02	1.50*

Name	Tm	Pos	WAR	SpW	Fame
Anderson	BAL	CF	**6.9**	**10.4**	**3.5**
Pettitte	NY	P	5.6	**8.4**	**2.8**
Rivera	NY	P	5.0	7.5	**2.5**
Palmeiro	BAL	1B	4.4	6.6	**2.2**

14. Playing Your Wild Cards Right 283

Name	Tm	Pos	WAR	SpW	Fame
Clemens	BOS	P	7.7	8.6	0.9
Hentgen	TOR	P	8.5	8.7	0.2
Guzman	TOR	P	6.8	6.9	0.1
	AL C	CHI	CLE	KC	
	Start	110	295	11	
	6/1	186	368		
	7/1	246	428		
	8/1	308	490		
	9/1	370	552		
	End	393	608		
	Spt.	1.12	1.55	1.00	

Name	Tm	Pos	WAR	SpW	Fame
Thome	CLE	3B	7.5	11.6	4.1
Nagy	CLE	P	6.7	10.4	3.7
Belle	CLE	LF	5.6	8.7	3.1
Lofton	CLE	CF	5.5	8.5	3.0
Fernandez	CHI	P	6.4	7.2	0.8
Knoblauch	MIN	2B	8.6	8.6	
	AL W	CAL	SEA	TEX	
	Start	231	81	151	
	6/1	235	133	227	
	7/1	205	106	287	
	8/1	174	138	349	
	9/1	143	158	411	
	End	115	160	467	
	Spt.	1.17	1.07	1.28	

Name	Tm	Pos	WAR	SpW	Fame
Hill	TEX	P	6.6	8.4	1.8
I. Rodriguez	TEX	C	6.1	7.8	1.7
Greer	TEX	LF	5.3	6.8	1.5
McLemore	TEX	2B	4.4	5.6	1.2
Griffey	SEA	CF	9.7	10.4	0.7
A. Rodriguez	SEA	SS	9.4	10.1	0.7
Martinez	SEA	DH	6.5	7.0	0.5
	NL E	ATL	MON	PHI	
	Start	431	85	162	
	6/1	507	164	154	
	7/1	567	224	124	
	8/1	629	286	93	
	9/1	691	348	62	
	End	747	401	34	
	Spt.	1.60	1.24	1.06	

Name	Tm	Pos	WAR	SpW	Fame
Smoltz	ATL	P	7.3	11.7	4.4
Maddux	ATL	P	7.1	11.4	4.3

Name	Tm	Pos	WAR	SpW	Fame
C. Jones	ATL	3B/SS	6.2	9.9	3.7
Glavine	ATL	P	5.8	9.3	3.5
Gilkey	NY	LF	**8.0**	8.0	
Brown	FLA	P	**8.0**	8.0	
Johnson	NY	CF	**7.2**	7.2	

NL C	CIN	HOU	PIT	STL
Start	382	188	49	
6/1	341	150	8	
7/1	311	129		1
8/1	283	182		63
9/1	252	244		125
End	224	258		181
Spt.	1.32	1.09	1.01	1.07

Name	Tm	Pos	WAR	SpW	Fame
Larkin	CIN	SS	7.2	9.5	2.3
Smiley	CIN	P	4.5	**5.9**	1.4
Burba	CIN	P	3.4	4.5	1.2
Shaw	CIN	P	3.3	4.4	1.1
Bagwell	HOU	1B	7.5	8.2	0.7
Biggio	HOU	2B	**5.5**	6.0	0.5
Jordan	STL	RF	**5.4**	5.8	0.4

NL W	COL	LA	SF	SD
Start	200	125	113	
6/1	162	93	84	80
7/1	162	132	69	125
8/1	182	194	38	187
9/1	196	256	7	249
End	168	312		305
Spt.	1.15	1.16	1.03	1.11

Name	Tm	Pos	WAR	SpW	Fame
Burks	COL	CF	7.9	9.1	1.2
Piazza	LA	C	5.4	6.3	0.9
Caminiti	SD	3B	7.6	8.4	0.8
Mondesi	LA	RF	4.6	5.3	0.7
Astacio	LA	P	4.6	5.3	0.7
Nomo	LA	P	4.6	5.3	0.7
Valdez	LA	P	4.6	5.3	0.7
Finley	SD	CF	**5.7**	6.3	0.6
Bonds	SF	LF	**9.6**	9.9	0.3

The Red Sox started 2–12, and while they recovered enough to challenge for the wild card at the end of August, the season was a lost cause. The Yankees led the East from May forward, although their 12-game lead on July 28 dropped to 2.5 in September as the Orioles got their offense together. The Yankees took two of three from the Orioles September 18–19, keeping enough distance to win the East.

The Orioles won the wild card over the White Sox. The White Sox took three of four from the Indians July 4–7 to stay within range of first in the Central. The Indians played a little better than the White Sox over the next few weeks, opening up a seven-game lead on July 25, then turned on the jets with a 19–7 September. The White Sox lost a series to the Orioles September 10–12, including a walkoff loss; the Sox would lose four walkoff games in September, and they lost the wild card by three games.

In the AL West, the Angels were fitful. They started 5–8, progressed to 18–12, and fell to 27–32 before settling at 38–33 on June 20, tied with the Mariners and five games behind the first-place Rangers. But 14 of the Angels' wins had been by a single run, and they went 14–31 in the next stretch. The Rangers maintained their lead the entire season, but the Mariners won ten straight, including a sweep of the Rangers, to bring the lead from nine games on September 11 to one game on September 20. The Rangers had seven of their last nine games against the already-collapsed Angels, however, and getting to face them prevented their own collapse. The Mariners ended the season 2–6, taking themselves out of both the division and wild card races.

In the NL East, the Expos started best, but a rough end of May let the Braves overtake them. Although the Expos gained Momentum for the division as late as July 2, their most realistic path to the playoffs was the wild card, as they were five games ahead of every non–Braves team. The other division leaders, the Astros and Dodgers, were 44–40 at that point; the Central had spent most of the season too mediocre to gain any Momentum, with the Reds hurt by Ron Gant's signing with the Cardinals and Jose Rijo's injury. Meanwhile, all four West teams were involved after the Padres dropped a six-game lead with a 4–19 stretch in June.

On August 1, a .500 record was still only a few games back in the Central and West; the Expos led the wild card by 1.5 games. On September 1, the Astros and Cardinals were separated by 1.5 games, the Padres and Dodgers were separated by a game, and the Expos were a half-game behind the Dodgers for the wild card. With 14 games left, the Astros dropped nine straight to hand the Central to the Cardinals. The Padres won the West by sweeping the Dodgers in the season's final series, including two extra-inning games. And the Expos, who'd spent so much of the season playoff-bound, ended two games behind the Dodgers for the wild card, as they faced the Braves in nine of their last 11 games and only won two of them.

1997: East, East, West, Central

AL E	BAL	BOS	NY	TOR
Start	111	75	352	
6/1	181	40	398	24

AL E	BAL	BOS	NY	TOR
7/1	241	10	458	
8/1	303		520	
9/1	365		582	
End	419		636	
Spt.	1.17*	1.01	1.42	1.00

Name	Tm	Pos	WAR	SpW	Fame
Pettitte	NY	P	8.4	11.9	3.5
Cone	NY	P	6.8	9.7	2.9
Williams	NY	CF	5.5	7.8	2.3
Martinez	NY	1B	5.1	7.2	2.1
Clemens	TOR	P	11.9	11.9	
Thompson	DET	P	7.7	7.7	

AL C	CHI	CLE	MIL
Start	279	431	
6/1	238	432	
7/1	214	489	
8/1	195	551	2
9/1	164	613	
End	137	667	
Spt.	1.10	1.60	1.00

Name	Tm	Pos	WAR	SpW	Fame
Thome	CLE	1B	5.4	8.6	3.2
Ramirez	CLE	RF	4.6	7.4	2.8
Williams	CLE	3B	4.2	6.7	2.5
Alomar	CLE	C	3.9	6.2	2.3
Thomas	CHI	1B/DH	7.3	8.0	0.7
Knoblauch	MIN	2B	6.7	6.7	
Appier	KC	P	5.6	5.6	
Bell	KC	SS	5.4	5.4	

AL W	ANA	SEA	TEX
Start	82	113	331
6/1	83	186	404
7/1	101	246	431
8/1	127	308	400
9/1	189	370	369
End	171	424	342
Spt.	1.05	1.22	1.30

Name	Tm	Pos	WAR	SpW	Fame
Griffey	SEA	CF	9.1	11.1	2.0
I. Rodriguez	TEX	C	6.5	8.5	2.0
Johnson	SEA	P	8.0	9.8	1.8
Martinez	SEA	DH	6.2	7.6	1.4

NL E	ATL	MON	PHI	FLA	NY
Start	675	362	31		
6/1	755	352		50	4

14. Playing Your Wild Cards Right

NL E	ATL	MON	PHI	FLA	NY
7/1	815	379		110	25
8/1	877	348		172	57
9/1	939	317		234	47
End	993	290		288	20
Spt.	1.55	1.36	1.00	1.50*	1.01

Name	Tm	Pos	WAR	SpW	Fame
Maddux	ATL	P	7.8	12.1	4.3
Brown	FLA	P	7.0	10.5	3.5
Martinez	MON	P	9.0	12.2	3.2
Glavine	ATL	P	5.5	8.5	3.0
Schilling	PHI	P	6.3	6.3	

NL C	CIN	HOU	STL
Start	202	233	163
6/1	162	277	123
7/1	132	247	93
8/1	101	258	62
9/1	70	320	31
End	43	356	4
Spt.	1.05	1.25	1.04

Name	Tm	Pos	WAR	SpW	Fame
Biggio	HOU	2B	9.4	11.8	2.4
Bagwell	HOU	1B	7.7	9.6	1.9
Kile	HOU	P	5.4	6.8	1.4
Spiers	HOU	3B/SS	4.4	5.5	1.1
Lankford	STL	CF	5.2	5.4	0.2

NL W	COL	LA	SD	SF
Start	151	282	275	
6/1	222	314	235	74
7/1	243	284	205	134
8/1	212	298	174	196
9/1	181	360	143	258
End	154	414	116	312
Spt.	1.07	1.32	1.08	1.10

Name	Tm	Pos	WAR	SpW	Fame
Piazza	LA	C	8.7	11.5	2.8
Mondesi	LA	RF	5.7	7.5	1.8
Valdez	LA	P	5.3	7.0	1.7
Park	LA	P	3.5	4.6	1.1
Bonds	SF	LF	8.1	8.9	0.8
Walker	COL	RF	9.8	10.5	0.7

Both leagues had their two best records (and therefore the wild cards) from the East. The extent to which those wild-card teams were better made playoff races a lot more straightforward than in the previous few years. The Orioles entered May with a four-game lead and remained in first the entire year;

although the final margin was only two games, they would have won the wild card with no trouble. The wild card race was competitive until late June, when the Angels echoed 1996 by falling from contention to .500; that left the Yankees alone the rest of the year.

The Anaheim Angels didn't challenge the Yankees for the wild card after that, but they did win 10 straight after falling to .500 to resume challenging the Mariners in the West. The Rangers had slumped when the Angels did, but they didn't get back up, as leading lights Ken Hill, Mark McLemore, and Dean Palmer were ineffective. Neither the Angels nor Mariners took firm control in August; the Mariners won by default when the Angels' relatively soft slate to start September—the Rockies, Tigers, and Blue Jays—went 8–1 against them.

The AL Central didn't consistently gain Momentum until May 21. The Indians got ahead and stayed ahead, although the White Sox challenged in mid–July and the Brewers gained Momentum as late as September 2. It helped when the Indians called up 21-year-old Jaret Wright to solidify the rotation's past Charles Nagy and Orel Hershiser.

With Greg Maddux, John Smoltz, Tom Glavine, and 1996 trade deadline pickup Denny Neagle, the Braves had no rotation worries; starting 13–3, their lead in the East was always at least 2.5 games after April. The only suspense was the wild card, as the East on June 15 had four of the NL's six teams over .500. A month later it was still true, although the Marlins, who had signed Alex Fernandez, Moises Alou, and Bobby Bonilla as free agents, had gotten ahead slightly.

The Expos went 9–19 from July 15 to August 15 and fell to .500. That would have simplified the wild card race except that the Dodgers went 20–7 in July (six of those losses from East teams) to challenge the Giants, who had led the West most of the year, and have an outside shot at the wild card. The Mets' rough August took them out while the Dodgers were in first in the West on September 1. The Marlins' slump in late September could have cost them the wild card, but the Dodgers slumped at the same time; the Giants beat the Dodgers twice over September 17 and 18 to tie the division, after which the Rockies swept the Dodgers and the Giants took three of four from the Padres. The Marlins clinched the wild card on September 23, and the Giants clinched the West on September 27—the second-to-last day of the season.

While the East and West fought over a few slots, the Astros were fighting to gain Momentum consistently. From May 25 to July 18, the Pirates' two days of Momentum were the only ones in the Central, although the Astros had held first most of the year. On September 2, the Pirates were 69–70 but 1.5 games back. The Astros had trouble staying over .500 in September; their 7–2 finish gave them the division with an 84–78 record—which would have left them fourth in the East and third in the West.

1998: Yankees of Destiny, Marlins of Density

	AL E	BAL	NY	BOS
Start		209	318	
6/1		180	385	82
7/1		150	445	142
8/1		119	507	204
9/1		88	569	266
End		61	623	320
Spt.		1.11	**1.50**	1.15

Name	Tm	Pos	WAR	SpW	Fame
Jeter	NY	SS	7.5	**11.3**	3.8
O'Neill	NY	RF	5.8	8.7	2.9
Brosius	NY	3B	5.3	8.0	2.7
Williams	NY	CF	5.2	7.8	**2.6**
Martinez	BOS	P	**7.2**	**8.3**	1.1
Garciaparra	BOS	SS	**7.1**	**8.2**	1.1
Clemens	TOR	P	**8.1**	8.1	

	AL C	CHI	CLE	
Start		68	334	
6/1		27	413	
7/1			473	
8/1			535	
9/1			597	
End			651	
Spt.		1.01	**1.55**	

Name	Tm	Pos	WAR	SpW	Fame
Lofton	CLE	CF	**5.9**	9.1	3.2
Ramirez	CLE	RF	5.2	8.1	2.9
Colon	CLE	P	4.4	6.8	2.4
Giles	CLE	LF	3.9	6.0	2.1
Belle	CHI	LF	7.1	7.2	0.1
Ventura	CHI	3B	**5.8**	5.9	0.1
Easley	DET	2B/SS	5.6	5.6	

	AL W	ANA	SEA	TEX
Start		85	212	171
6/1		86	171	247
7/1		137	141	298
8/1		199	110	354
9/1		261	79	413
End		315	52	464
Spt.		1.08	1.08	**1.31**

Name	Tm	Pos	WAR	SpW	Fame
I. Rodriguez	TEX	C	6.4	**8.4**	2.0
Gonzalez	TEX	RF/DH	4.9	6.4	1.5
Greer	TEX	LF	3.8	5.0	1.2
Helling	TEX	P	3.7	4.8	1.1

Name	Tm	Pos	WAR	SpW	Fame
A. Rodriguez	SEA	SS	8.5	9.2	0.7
Finley	ANA	P	7.2	7.8	0.6
Griffey	SEA	CF	6.6	7.1	0.5
Rogers	OAK	P	7.5	7.5	

NL E	ATL	FLA	MON	NY
Start	682	198	199	14
6/1	763	156	157	53
7/1	823	126	127	89
8/1	885	95	96	61
9/1	947	64	65	108
End	1001	37	38	162
Spt.	1.55	1.05	1.06	1.03

Name	Tm	Pos	WAR	SpW	Fame
A. Jones	ATL	CF	7.4	11.5	4.1
C. Jones	ATL	3B	7.0	10.9	3.9
Maddux	ATL	P	6.6	10.2	3.6
Glavine	ATL	P	6.1	9.5	3.4
Guerrero	MON	RF	7.4	7.8	0.4
Olerud	NY	1B	7.6	7.8	0.2

NL C	CIN	HOU	STL	CHI	MIL
Start	29	244	3		
6/1		319	9	64	35
7/1		379		97	5
8/1		441		129	
9/1		503		191	
End		557		245	
Spt.	1.00	1.43	1.00	1.09	1.00

Name	Tm	Pos	WAR	SpW	Fame
Biggio	HOU	2B	6.5	9.3	2.8
Bagwell	HOU	1B	6.3	9.0	2.7
Alou	HOU	LF	6.2	8.9	2.7
Bell	HOU	RF	5.4	7.7	2.3
Sosa	CHI	RF	6.4	7.0	0.6
McGwire	STL	1B	7.5	7.5	
Jordan	STL	RF/CF	7.0	7.0	

NL W	COL	LA	SD	SF
Start	106	284	80	214
6/1	64	245	161	259
7/1	34	215	221	319
8/1	3	184	283	351
9/1		153	345	368
End		126	399	374
Spt.	1.02	1.18	1.50*	1.26

Name	Tm	Pos	WAR	SpW	Fame
Brown	SD	P	8.6	12.9	4.3
Vaughn	SD	LF	6.3	9.5	3.2

Name	Tm	Pos	WAR	SpW	Fame
Ashby	SD	P	4.8	7.2	2.4
Bonds	SF	LF	**8.1**	10.2	2.1
Walker	COL	RF	**5.7**	5.8	0.1

As leagues expanded again, and the Brewers moved from the AL to the NL, having a new, bad team in each league gave an opportunity for division leaders to separate from their pursuers more than normal. On May 1, five teams, the Yankees, Red Sox, Rangers, Padres, and Braves were winning over two-thirds of their games; the Brewers, tied with the Astros for the NL Central lead, were a game under that pace. The Brewers collapsed in May, but the other teams all made the playoffs. And of the other teams, only the Rangers had any obstacles, regaining first place in the final two weeks by going 5–0 against the Angels. On September 25, the Yankees broke the 1954 Indians' AL record for wins by winning their 112th game; they ended with 114, the Braves ended with 106, and the Astros ended with 102.

Although the 1998 Indians won only 89 games, they had it easy, as they were the only Central team .500 or better after April 16. That left the NL wild card race. The Marlins were decidedly out of it, as owner Wayne Huizenga gutted the team after winning the World Series; they started 1–11 and barely improved.[4] Going into the All-Star break, the Giants were three games ahead of the Cubs and five ahead of the Mets, but they came out of the break 6–14, letting the Cubs take over. The Cubs went .500 in August while the Mets went 20–12, leaving the Mets and Cubs tied on September 8 with the Giants a game behind.

None of the three teams were scheduled to face each other in September, racing in separate lanes. On September 21, the Mets were up by a game over the Cubs and 3.5 over the Giants. But the Mets lost their last five games to end the season a game behind the tied Cubs and Giants; the Cubs, led all year by Sammy Sosa's attack on Roger Maris's single-season home run record (he broke it with 66, although the Cardinals' Mark McGwire also broke it with 70), beat the Giants in a 163rd game to win the wild card.

1999: September Madness

AL E	BAL	BOS	NY	TOR
Start	31	160	312	
6/1		194	376	
7/1		254	436	
8/1		316	498	28
9/1		378	560	60
End		444	626	27
Spt.	1.00	**1.50***	**1.50**	1.01

292   Part II. Momentum: Seasons and Narratives

Name	Tm	Pos	WAR	SpW	Fame
Martinez	BOS	P	9.7	14.6	4.9
Jeter	NY	SS	8.0	12.0	4.0
Garciaparra	BOS	SS	6.6	9.9	3.3
Williams	NY	CF	5.4	8.1	2.7
Green	TOR	RF	6.4	6.5	0.1

	AL C		CLE		KC
Start			325		
6/1			392		1
7/1			452		
8/1			514		
9/1			576		
End			642		
Spt.			1.55		1.00

Name	Tm	Pos	WAR	SpW	Fame
Alomar	CLE	2B	7.4	11.5	4.1
Ramirez	CLE	RF	7.3	11.3	4.0
Vizquel	CLE	SS	6.0	9.3	3.3
Lofton	CLE	CF	5.6	8.7	3.1
Radke	MIN	P	6.5	6.5	

	AL W	ANA	SEA	TEX	OAK
Start		158	26	232	
6/1		120		299	2
7/1		90		359	
8/1		59		421	
9/1		28		483	50
End				549	32
Spt.		1.07	1.00	1.35	1.02

Name	Tm	Pos	WAR	SpW	Fame
I. Rodriguez	TEX	C	6.4	8.6	2.2
Palmeiro	TEX	DH/1B	5.2	7.0	1.8
Gonzalez	TEX	RF	3.9	5.3	1.4
Zimmerman	TEX	P	3.9	5.3	1.4
Velarde	2 TM	2B	7.0	7.4	0.4
Giambi	OAK	1B	5.9	6.0	0.1
Moyer	SEA	P	6.6	6.6	

	NL E	ATL	FLA	MON	NY	PHI
Start		557	21	21	90	
6/1		624			160	31
7/1		684			190	31
8/1		746			252	9
9/1		808			314	
End		874			380	
Spt.		1.60	1.00	1.00	1.18	1.01

14. Playing Your Wild Cards Right   293

Name	Tm	Pos	WAR	SpW	Fame
A. Jones	ATL	CF	**7.1**	**11.4**	**4.3**
C. Jones	ATL	3B	**6.9**	**11.0**	**4.1**
Millwood	ATL	P	**6.1**	9.8	3.7
Smoltz	ATL	P	4.4	7.0	**2.6**
Ventura	NY	3B	**6.7**	7.9	1.2

NL C	CHI	HOU	CIN	PIT	STL
Start	136	310			
6/1	149	377	5	2	41
7/1	167	437	56	2	11
8/1	136	499	118		
9/1	105	561	180		
End	72	627	231		
Spt.	1.06	**1.45**	1.03	1.00	1.00

Name	Tm	Pos	WAR	SpW	Fame
Bagwell	HOU	1B	**7.4**	**10.7**	**3.3**
Hampton	HOU	P	**6.6**	9.6	3.0
Everett	HOU	CF	**5.8**	8.4	2.6
Biggio	HOU	2B	5.1	7.4	2.3
Giles	PIT	CF/RF	**6.6**	6.6	

NL W	LA	SD	SF	AZ
Start	70	222	208	
6/1	110	184	284	53
7/1	80	154	344	113
8/1	49	129	406	172
9/1	18	98	378	234
End		65	345	300
Spt.	1.03	1.09	1.28	**1.10**

Name	Tm	Pos	WAR	SpW	Fame
Bonds	SF	LF	3.8	4.9	**1.1**
Kent	SF	2B	3.5	4.5	**1.0**
Johnson	AZ	P	**9.2**	**10.1**	0.9
Burks	SF	RF	2.8	3.6	0.8
Gonzalez	AZ	LF	**6.4**	7.0	0.6
Brown	LA	P	**6.2**	6.4	0.2
Astacio	COL	P	**5.9**	5.9	

The AL's playoff teams in 1998 all repeated. The Yankees didn't win 114 games, and the Red Sox occasionally challenged them for the division, but they gained Momentum all year and took the East comfortably. The Indians had no competition for the Central; the Rangers maintained at least a four-game lead after June 23. The Red Sox had led the wild card on the strength of a 20–8 May, but they were barely over .500 in April and June. A bad July let the Blue Jays, who started July under .500, take the wild card lead with a 20–5 run ending July 26. The Red Sox beat the Blue Jays in the next two games to reclaim the lead; the

A's, 51–50 after the Red Sox-Blue Jays series, got hot and overtook the Blue Jays by sweeping them August 13–15. The Rangers swept the Red Sox August 20–22 and the Blue Jays August 27–29; the Blue Jays and A's played .500 ball after that point. The Red Sox recovered from their sweep with a 21–5 run that let them coast the last two weeks of the season.

On June 15, the Braves, Astros, and second-year Diamondbacks held good leads in the NL, but six teams were within 1.5 games of each other for the wild card, as the Cubs, Giants, and Mets were joined by the Phillies, Pirates, and Reds. But the Cubs were in the middle of a 6–20 disaster, including giving up 54 runs over the first three games of July—the worst stretch in over 80 years—and they eventually finished last. The Pirates slowly sank below .500, the Phillies left the wild card chase after the All-Star break (finishing the year below .500 as well), and the Giants fell to .500 in mid–August, by which point the Diamondbacks, Mets, and Reds had gone too far past them for their recovery to matter. (The Padres had contended briefly in late July before their pitching failed them; losing Kevin Brown to the Dodgers in free agency didn't help.)

Moving into September the Diamondbacks, who'd signed Randy Johnson, Steve Finley, and several others to build an instant contender, were the safest bet in the NL to make the postseason. The Reds were 1.5 games behind the Astros for the Central lead; the Mets got hot, and with 12 games to go they were one game behind the Braves. The Mets got swept by the Braves, then by the Phillies, then lost two of three to the Braves again, putting them two games behind the tied Astros and Reds with three games to go. The Mets recovered to sweep the Pirates, the Astros took two of three from the Dodgers, and the Reds lost their series with the Brewers, forcing a 163rd game between the Reds and Mets.[5] The Mets shut the Reds out to win the wild card and avoid a full collapse for the second straight year.

2000: Trouble in Texas, Nice in New York

AL E	BOS	NY	TOR
Start	222	313	14
6/1	286	**386**	
7/1	334	**446**	40
8/1	366	**508**	93
9/1	392	**570**	80
End	398	**630**	53
Spt.	1.28	**1.59**	1.02

Name	Tm	Pos	WAR	SpW	Fame
Martinez	BOS	P	**11.7**	**15.0**	**3.3**
Posada	NY	C	5.5	8.7	**3.2**

14. Playing Your Wild Cards Right 295

Name	Tm	Pos	WAR	SpW	Fame
Williams	NY	CF	5.2	**8.1**	**2.9**
Jeter	NY	SS	4.6	7.3	**2.7**
Garciaparra	BOS	SS	**7.4**	**9.5**	2.1
Delgado	TOR	1B	**7.3**	7.4	0.1
Mussina	BAL	P	**5.6**	5.6	

	AL C	CLE	CHI	KC	
Start		321			
6/1		373	76	2	
7/1		403	136		
8/1		390	198		
9/1		422	260		
End		482	320		
Spt.		1.41	1.17	1.00	

Name	Tm	Pos	WAR	SpW	Fame
Alomar	CLE	2B	**5.6**	7.9	**2.3**
Ramirez	CLE	RF/DH	4.8	6.8	**2.0**
Colon	CLE	P	4.8	6.8	**2.0**
Thome	CLE	1B/DH	4.7	6.6	**1.9**
Thomas	CHI	DH/1B	**6.0**	7.0	1.0
Radke	MIN	P	**6.2**	6.2	
Damon	KC	CF/LF	**6.1**	6.1	

	AL W	OAK	TEX	ANA	SEA	
Start		16	275			
6/1			270	9	68	
7/1		60	258	12	128	
8/1		122	227	50	190	
9/1		184	196	25	252	
End		244	166		312	
Spt.		1.09	1.17	1.01	1.12*	

Name	Tm	Pos	WAR	SpW	Fame
A. Rodriguez	SEA	SS	**10.4**	**11.6**	**1.2**
Rogers	TEX	P	5.0	5.9	**0.9**
I. Rodriguez	TEX	C	4.8	5.6	0.8
Helling	TEX	P	4.2	4.9	0.7
Giambi	OAK	1B/DH	**7.7**	8.4	0.7
Martinez	SEA	DH	5.7	6.3	0.6
Erstad	ANA	LF/CF	**8.3**	8.4	0.1
Glaus	ANA	3B	**7.8**	7.9	0.1

	NL E	ATL	NY	FLA	MON
Start		**437**	190		
6/1		**505**	234	2	74
7/1		**565**	294		83
8/1		**627**	356		52
9/1		**689**	418		21
End		**749**	478		
Spt.		**1.55**	1.46	1.00	1.02

Name	Tm	Pos	WAR	SpW	Fame
A. Jones	ATL	CF	8.2	12.7	4.5
Maddux	ATL	P	6.6	10.2	3.6
C. Jones	ATL	3B	5.6	8.7	3.1
Alfonzo	NY	2B	6.4	9.3	2.9
Abreu	PHI	RF	6.2	6.2	

NL C	CHI	CIN	HOU	STL
Start	36	116	313	
6/1		145	273	76
7/1		148	243	136
8/1		117	212	198
9/1		86	181	260
End		56	151	320
Spt.	1.01	1.06	1.22	1.50*

Name	Tm	Pos	WAR	SpW	Fame
Edmonds	STL	CF	6.3	9.5	3.2
McGwire	STL	1B	4.2	6.3	2.1
Kile	STL	P	3.7	5.6	1.9
Drew	STL	RF/CF	3.6	5.4	1.8
Hidalgo	HOU	CF/RF	6.3	7.7	1.4
Bagwell	HOU	1B	5.4	6.6	1.2
Sosa	CHI	RF	5.7	5.8	0.1
Giles	PIT	CF/LF	6.4	6.4	

NL W	AZ	SD	SF	COL	LA
Start	150	32	173		
6/1	224		160	15	65
7/1	284		130	75	95
8/1	346		177	65	88
9/1	399		239	34	69
End	369		299	4	39
Spt.	1.24	1.00	1.14	1.02	1.03

Name	Tm	Pos	WAR	SpW	Fame
Johnson	AZ	P	8.1	10.0	1.9
Bonds	SF	LF	7.7	8.9	1.2
Gonzalez	AZ	LF	4.2	5.2	1.0
Kent	SF	2B	7.2	8.2	1.0
Helton	COL	1B	8.8	9.0	0.2

The 2000 AL was the first full-season league since the 1969 NL to have seven teams gain Momentum in September. Early on, the Yankees had the best start, the Red Sox had the best pitching, and the White Sox had the best offense. The West was a free-for-all until the Rangers' nine-loss streak from June 6–16. When the Angels fell off in August, it left the teams that would enter September in the mix: the Yankees and White Sox comfortably leading their divisions; the Indians leading the Red Sox and Blue Jays for the wild card; and the Mariners leading the A's by 2.5 games, with the loser possibly getting the wild card.

The A's knocked the Blue Jays out by taking three of four from them to start September, went 10–4 right after to keep pace with the Mariners, then delivered the finishing blow by taking three of four from the Mariners and winning six of their last seven. The Mariners finished well enough to take the wild card; the Indians went 20–12 to end the season but finished a game behind the Mariners. As for the Red Sox, they lost a series to the Yankees September 8–11 and went 11–10 afterward; had they done any better, they might have leveraged the Yankees' 5–16 finish to the season, including losing their final seven.

The NL contrasted with the AL by wrapping up its races by September, but it was no less chaotic at the start of the summer. At the start of June, the Braves and Diamondbacks were far in front of their divisions while the Mets, Expos, Cardinals, Reds, Dodgers, and Rockies had interchangeable records. (The Astros were in last, having started life in their new stadium 6–13.) The Mets pulled ahead from the wild card group with a 16–8 June; they would challenge the Braves the rest of the year for the division. The Reds were 1–11 from June 5–18, leaving the Cardinals unchallenged the rest of the year.

The Rockies lost their last seven games before the All-Star break and their first four after it. The first team they lost to in that sequence, the Giants, rode a hot July into contention; their three-game lead to start September was 8.5 by the next week thanks to the Diamondbacks' struggles. The Braves won the East by one game, the Cardinals won the Central by ten, the Giants won the West by 11, and the Mets won the wild card by eight, with a better record than every AL team except the White Sox.

2001: Strength and Weakness

AL E	BOS	NY	TOR
Start	232	367	31
6/1	310	436	70
7/1	370	496	40
8/1	432	558	9
9/1	455	620	
End	419	692	
Spt.	1.28	1.60	1.02

Name	Tm	Pos	WAR	SpW	Fame
Mussina	NY	P	7.1	11.4	4.3
Clemens	NY	P	5.6	9.0	3.4
Williams	NY	CF	5.2	8.3	3.1
Jeter	NY	SS	5.2	8.3	3.1
Ramirez	BOS	DH/LF	5.2	6.7	1.5

	AL C	CHI	CLE	MIN
	Start	187	281	
	6/1	148	350	74
	7/1	118	410	134
	8/1	87	472	196
	9/1	56	534	204
	End	20	606	168
	Spt.	1.06	1.45	1.06

Name	Tm	Pos	WAR	SpW	Fame
Alomar	CLE	2B	7.3	10.6	3.3
Thome	CLE	1B	5.6	8.1	2.5
Colon	CLE	P	4.5	6.5	2.0
Gonzalez	CLE	RF/DH	4.4	6.4	2.0
Mays	MIN	P	6.7	7.1	0.4
Koskie	MIN	3B	6.3	6.7	0.4
Beltran	KC	CF	6.4	6.4	

	AL W	OAK	SEA	TEX
	Start	142	182	97
	6/1	103	260	58
	7/1	73	320	28
	8/1	42	382	
	9/1	89	444	
	End	161	516	
	Spt.	1.10	1.26	1.02

Name	Tm	Pos	WAR	SpW	Fame
Boone	SEA	2B	8.8	11.1	2.3
Suzuki	SEA	RF	7.7	9.7	2.0
Cameron	SEA	CF	5.9	7.4	1.5
Olerud	SEA	1B	5.2	6.6	1.4
Giambi	OAK	1B	9.1	10.0	0.9
A. Rodriguez	TEX	SS	8.3	8.5	0.2

	NL E	ATL	NY	FLA	PHI
	Start	379	242		
	6/1	341	204		76
	7/1	395	174	16	136
	8/1	457	143		198
	9/1	519	112		260
	End	591	79		299
	Spt.	1.55	1.16	1.00	1.09

Name	Tm	Pos	WAR	SpW	Fame
C. Jones	ATL	3B	5.9	9.1	3.2
Maddux	ATL	P	5.1	7.9	2.8
A. Jones	ATL	CF	4.9	7.6	2.7
Burkett	ATL	P	4.8	7.4	2.6
Rolen	PHI	3B	5.5	6.0	0.5
Floyd	FLA	LF	6.6	6.6	
Vazquez	MON	P	5.7	5.7	

14. Playing Your Wild Cards Right

NL C	CIN	HOU	STL	CHI	MIL
Start	28	77	162		
6/1	23	111	196	70	53
7/1		117	232	130	41
8/1		176	201	192	10
9/1		238	203	254	
End		310	269	266	
Spt.	1.01	1.13	1.21	1.07	1.01

Name	Tm	Pos	WAR	SpW	Fame
Pujols	STL	3B/1B	**6.6**	**8.0**	**1.4**
Edmonds	STL	CF	**5.8**	**7.0**	**1.2**
Drew	STL	RF/CF	5.5	6.7	**1.2**
Kile	STL	P	4.8	5.8	**1.0**
Berkman	HOU	LF/CF	**6.5**	**7.3**	0.8
Sosa	CHI	CF	**10.3**	**11.0**	0.7

NL W	AZ	COL	LA	SF	SD
Start	187	2	20	151	
6/1	218		93	173	15
7/1	278		138	194	
8/1	340		191	175	
9/1	402		229	237	
End	474		244	309	
Spt.	1.50*	1.00	1.07	1.10	1.00

Name	Tm	Pos	WAR	SpW	Fame
Johnson	AZ	P	**10.0**	**15.0**	**5.0**
Schilling	AZ	P	**8.8**	**13.2**	**4.4**
Gonzalez	AZ	LF	**7.9**	**11.9**	**4.0**
Sanders	AZ	RF	3.2	4.8	**1.6**
Bonds	SF	LF	**11.9**	**13.1**	1.2

In 2000, seven AL teams gained Momentum in September; in 2001, only seven gained Momentum at all. Thanks in part to several bad teams (including the White Sox, whose offense had disappeared between seasons), on June 1, the Red Sox and Yankees were fighting in the East while three teams were on pace for at least 108 wins: the Indians (108); the long-terrible Twins (109); and the Mariners (125).

The A's started 6–13 but reached .500 in June; their play after June was a 125-win pace. The Twins went 0–7 against the Mariners July 20–29, presaging an 11–18 August that dropped them out of the race as surprisingly as they had entered it and gave the Central to the Indians. The Yankees won the East with ease after the Sox were swept by the A's August 7–9 and went 1–13 starting August 25, including six losses to the Yankees. The A's finished at 102 wins but only got the wild card, as the Mariners tied the all-time record for wins with 116.

The best teams in the NL only reached 93 wins, and without a clear leader

300   PART II. MOMENTUM: SEASONS AND NARRATIVES

every race was messy. The East looked like it would be the simplest, as the Phillies' 20–8 May gave them an eight-game lead over the punchless Braves. The Cubs and Diamondbacks were leading their divisions at the time; on June 19, they and the Phillies were the only teams gaining Momentum for division races, but eight teams—everyone over .500—were within two games of the wild card. The Braves went 5–1 against the Phillies from June 25–July 5, giving them a lead they would hold most of the rest of the season, even though the team wasn't good enough to expand it beyond 3.5 games, and the Mets gained Momentum on September 27 (their only day all year) with nine games to go.

It looked like the Cubs would win the Central, but the Astros took the lead with a 21–7 August. The Astros never lost the lead, but a 3–9 end to the season left them tied with the Cardinals, who won 11 straight in August and nine straight in September to leap over several teams into the wild card lead. The West's battle among the Diamondbacks, Dodgers, and Giants didn't settle until September, when the new unbalanced schedules made teams play almost entirely within their division.[6] The Dodgers lost five straight from September 8–19 (the events of September 11 delayed the season by several days),[7] then split a series with the Diamondbacks; the Diamondbacks had carried a lead into September, then followed up that series split by winning eight of their last 11, eking out the division win over the similarly hot Giants.

2002: Streaks in the West

AL E	BOS	NY
Start	210	346
6/1	279	430
7/1	339	490
8/1	401	552
9/1	409	614
End	381	670
Spt.	**1.26**	**1.55**

Name	*Tm*	*Pos*	*WAR*	*SpW*	*Fame*
Giambi	NY	1B/DH	**7.1**	**11.0**	**3.9**
Soriano	NY	2B	4.8	7.4	**2.6**
Mussina	NY	P	4.5	7.0	**2.5**
Williams	NY	CF	4.5	7.0	**2.5**
Lowe	BOS	P	**7.2**	**9.1**	1.9
Garciaparra	BOS	SS	**6.9**	**8.7**	1.8
Halladay	TOR	P	**7.4**	**7.4**	

	AL C	CHI	CLE	MIN
	Start	10	303	84
	6/1	85	276	162

14. Playing Your Wild Cards Right

	AL C	CHI	CLE	MIN		
	7/1	55	246	222		
	8/1	24	215	284		
	9/1		184	346		
	End		156	402		
	Spt.	1.02	1.20	**1.20**		
Name	*Tm*	*Pos*	*WAR*	*SpW*	*Fame*
Thome	CLE	1B	7.4	**8.9**	**1.5**
Jones	MIN	LF	5.4	**6.4**	**1.1**
Koskie	MIN	3B	4.0	4.8	**0.8**
Burks	CLE	DH	3.9	4.7	**0.8**
Ordonez	CHI	RF	**5.1**	**5.2**	0.1
Byrd	KC	P	**5.6**	**5.6**	

	AL W	OAK	SEA	ANA		
	Start	81	258			
	6/1	75	339	21		
	7/1	60	399	69		
	8/1	74	461	116		
	9/1	112	517	178		
	End	168	492	234		
	Spt.	1.10	1.38	**1.50***		
Name	*Tm*	*Pos*	*WAR*	*SpW*	*Fame*
Erstad	ANA	CF	6.4	**9.6**	**3.2**
Eckstein	ANA	SS	5.2	**7.8**	**2.6**
Anderson	ANA	LF	5.1	7.7	**2.6**
Kennedy	ANA	2B	4.7	7.1	**2.4**
Zito	OAK	P	**7.2**	**7.9**	0.7
Hudson	OAK	P	**6.9**	7.6	0.7
A. Rodriguez	TEX	SS	**8.8**	**8.8**	

	NL E	ATL	NY	PHI	FLA	MON
	Start	**380**	51	192		
	6/1	364	116	152	13	20
	7/1	424	89	122		
	8/1	486	58	91		
	9/1	548	27	60		
	End	604		32		
	Spt.	**1.48**	1.03	1.06	1.00	1.00
Name	*Tm*	*Pos*	*WAR*	*SpW*	*Fame*
A. Jones	ATL	CF	6.6	**9.8**	**3.2**
C. Jones	ATL	LF	5.7	**8.4**	**2.7**
Maddux	ATL	P	4.4	6.5	**2.1**
Sheffield	ATL	RF	4.4	6.5	**2.1**
Colon	2 TM	P	**7.1**	**8.0**	0.9
Abreu	PHI	RF	**5.8**	6.1	0.3
Guerrero	MON	RF	**7.0**	**7.0**	

NL C	CHI	HOU	STL	CIN
Start	171	199	173	
6/1	131	159	172	78
7/1	101	129	232	138
8/1	70	98	294	140
9/1	39	112	356	139
End	11	84	412	111
Spt.	1.05	1.06	1.48*	1.04

Name	Tm	Pos	WAR	SpW	Fame
Edmonds	STL	CF	6.7	9.9	3.2
Pujols	STL	LF/3B	5.5	8.1	2.6
Renteria	STL	SS	4.2	6.2	2.0
Rolen	2 TM	3B	6.5	8.0	1.5
Oswalt	HOU	P	6.9	7.3	0.4
Sosa	CHI	RF	5.7	6.0	0.3

NL W	AZ	LA	SF
Start	305	157	199
6/1	385	228	276
7/1	445	288	297
8/1	507	350	350
9/1	569	412	376
End	625	450	417
Spt.	1.53	1.19	1.43*

Name	Tm	Pos	WAR	SpW	Fame
Johnson	AZ	P	10.9	16.7	5.8
Bonds	SF	LF	11.8	16.9	5.1
Schilling	AZ	P	8.7	13.3	4.6
Kent	SF	2B	7.0	10.0	3.0

The Red Sox and Mariners cleared the 30-game mark playing .700 ball or better, but neither would make the playoffs, finishing at 93–69 but at least 10 games back. The Red Sox had trouble hitting in June; they fell out of the East race on July 20–21, when the Yankees won consecutive walkoffs against them. The Red Sox and Mariners were co-victims of Oakland's 20-win streak starting August 13 that took them from the back of the wild card race to the top of the division. The Angels went 14–6 in that time frame and 10–1 after that to tie the A's; both teams knocked the Mariners out in early September, and the Angels took the wild card with 99 wins. None of it affected the Twins, who were unchallenged after May; the White Sox couldn't put it together, and the Indians didn't hit early and didn't pitch late.

In the NL, the Braves had it as easy as the Twins did, thanks to a 21–5 June. In the Central, the Reds were the only team who started well. The Cardinals started gaining Momentum by taking three of four from the Reds May 17–20. A month later, the Cardinals took the lead for good, challenged lightly in August after a seven-loss streak. The division was won with heavy hearts, as pitcher Darryl Kile's death on June 22—four days after his win against the Angels—cast a pall over the season.[8]

The West had the 3–4–5 teams in the NL by record at season's end, and they were each in contention virtually all season. The Dodgers and Giants were booted out of the division race when the Diamondbacks went 25–5 from July 22 to August 23, nearly all the games they played between facing the Dodgers or Giants. They nearly lost the lead by losing three of four to the Giants in early September and dropping six straight before the season's final series, but they swept the Rockies to stay ahead of the charging Giants, who settled for the wild card.

15. No Change But Steroids, 2003–2011

League structure didn't change; teams weren't added; everything should have been stable in the upcoming years. Controversy over steroids became the superimposed structure of the upcoming years. But 2003 was a more halcyon time, as the Twins had avoided contraction,[1] joining teams like the A's to shake baseball from its big-market/small-market slumber.

2003: Extreme Logjams

AL E	BOS	NY	TOR
Start	190	335	
6/1	272	417	9
7/1	332	477	60
8/1	394	539	29
9/1	456	601	
End	510	655	
Spt.	1.34	1.60	1.01

Name	Tm	Pos	WAR	SpW	Fame
Mussina	NY	P	6.6	10.6	4.0
Posada	NY	C	5.9	9.4	3.5
Soriano	NY	2B	5.4	8.6	3.2
Giambi	NY	1B/DH	4.8	7.7	2.9
Martinez	BOS	P	8.0	10.7	2.7
Garciaparra	BOS	SS	6.1	8.2	2.1
Halladay	TOR	P	8.1	8.2	0.1

AL C	CLE	MIN	CHI	KC
Start	78	201		
6/1	37	232		58
7/1	7	292		76
8/1		273	8	138
9/1		308	70	200
End		362	91	191
Spt.	1.02	1.23	1.01	1.04

15. No Change but Steroids   305

Name	Tm	Pos	WAR	SpW	Fame
Pierzynski	MIN	C	4.5	5.4	**0.9**
Mientkiewicz	MIN	1B	4.2	5.0	**0.8**
Santana	MIN	P	4.2	5.0	**0.8**
Koskie	MIN	3B	4.2	5.0	**0.8**
May	KC	P	**5.9**	6.1	0.2
Beltran	KC	CF	**5.8**	6.0	0.2
Loaiza	CHI	P	**7.2**	7.3	0.1
Ordonez	CHI	RF	**5.6**	5.7	0.1

AL W	ANA	OAK	SEA
Start	117	84	246
6/1	76	163	328
7/1	46	223	388
8/1	15	264	450
9/1		326	512
End		380	536
Spt.	1.03	**1.16**	1.40

Name	Tm	Pos	WAR	SpW	Fame
Boone	SEA	2B	**5.9**	8.3	**2.4**
Suzuki	SEA	RF	5.6	7.8	**2.2**
Moyer	SEA	P	4.8	6.7	**1.9**
Cameron	SEA	CF	4.8	6.7	**1.9**
Hudson	OAK	P	**7.5**	8.7	1.2
A. Rodriguez	TEX	SS	**8.4**	8.4	
Blalock	TEX	3B	**6.4**	6.4	

NL E	ATL	PHI	FLA	MON
Start	312	17		
6/1	**394**	57		82
7/1	**454**	51		112
8/1	**516**	113	9	99
9/1	**578**	175	71	83
End	**632**	211	125	56
Spt.	**1.54**	1.04	**1.50***	1.03

Name	Tm	Pos	WAR	SpW	Fame
Giles	ATL	2B	**7.8**	12.0	**4.2**
Lopez	ATL	C	**6.8**	10.4	**3.6**
Sheffield	ATL	RF	**6.8**	10.4	**3.6**
Furcal	ATL	SS	4.9	7.5	**2.6**
Hernandez	MON	P	**6.3**	6.5	0.2

NL C	CHI	CIN	HOU	STL
Start	6	57	44	213
6/1	88	22	63	226
7/1	148		123	283
8/1	132		185	327
9/1	182		247	389
End	236		301	398
Spt.	**1.49***	1.01	1.06	1.23

Name	Tm	Pos	WAR	SpW	Fame
Prior	CHI	P	7.4	11.0	3.6
Wood	CHI	P	6.2	9.2	3.0
Zambrano	CHI	P	5.5	8.2	2.7
Pujols	STL	LF/1B	8.6	10.6	2.0
Edmonds	STL	CF	6.0	7.4	1.4

NL W	AZ	LA	SF
Start	323	232	215
6/1	282	230	294
7/1	264	278	354
8/1	305	256	416
9/1	307	237	478
End	280	219	532
Spt.	1.28	1.13	1.40

Name	Tm	Pos	WAR	SpW	Fame
Bonds	SF	LF	9.2	12.9	3.7
Schmidt	SF	P	6.7	9.4	2.7
Webb	AZ	P	6.2	7.9	1.7
Schilling	AZ	P	6.0	7.7	1.7
Helton	COL	1B	6.2	6.2	

The best starts belonged to the Yankees at 18–4, the Giants at 17–4, and ... the Royals at 16–3. The Yankees and Giants won their divisions without much competition, particularly after the All-Star break; the Royals' rollercoaster season defined the Central race. The Royals, coming off a 62–100 season, were up by 5.5 games when they were 16–3. They lost the lead to the Twins in a month, built a 7.5-game lead in the next month, lost it again as the White Sox swept the Royals in a 13–1 stretch, and stopped gaining Momentum after September 7. The White Sox stopped gaining Momentum after the Twins swept them September 16–18; the sweep was part of an 11-win streak that gave the Twins the division.

With the Central so weak, the other divisions involved a few strong teams. The Red Sox fought the Yankees hardest in the East, with the Blue Jays in the mix during interleague play in June. The Yankees won eight straight in a soft part of the September schedule; that left the wild card as Boston's only option. They had to fight the Mariners, who had led the West most of the year but had gone .500 since June while the A's, in a recurring theme, won ten straight around the end of August to take the lead. The A's won seven straight in September to put the West out of the Mariners' reach, and the Red Sox finished well enough to take the wild card.

The Giants gained ten games from June 25 to July 25, as much from their own good play as the Dodgers' dive from 44–29 to 54–55. The Braves had it even easier, unchallenged after the Expos slipped in May. That left a scramble for the Central and wild card among several decent teams—the Expos, Phillies, Dodgers, Astros, Cardinals, and Cubs. The Dodgers had started to pull away, but their collapse reopened the wild card race. When it reopened, it included the Diamondbacks, who won 12 straight, including the Astros five times. The picture looked a lot clearer after the All-Star break; on July 24, only the Braves, Astros, Giants, and Phillies gained Momentum. But the Phillies created their own competition when the Marlins swept them July 25–27; the Marlins started gaining Momentum after the end of that series for the first time all season, having replaced manager Jeff Torborg with Jack McKeon after a 16–22 start.

The Phillies lost the wild card lead with a 1–9 stretch August 19–28 against the Brewers, Cardinals, and Expos. On August 28, the Expos were 71–64, the Phillies, Marlins, Cardinals, and Astros were 70–63, the Diamondbacks were 69–64, and the Cubs and Dodgers were 68–64. The Marlins swept the Expos August 29–September 1 to make the wild card primarily about themselves and the Phillies. The Cubs started September 8–1, winning four of five against the Cardinals, to push closer to the Astros; on September 8, the Phillies, Marlins, Dodgers, Astros, and Cubs were separated by 2.5 games. The Cubs won the Central with a strong finish while the Astros slumped; the Marlins won the wild card by sweeping the Phillies September 23–25.

2004: Torrents and Torridity

	AL E	BOS	NY	BAL
Start		255	328	
6/1		321	388	23
7/1		381	448	
8/1		437	510	
9/1		499	572	
End		563	636	
Spt.		1.50*	1.55	1.00

Name	Tm	Pos	WAR	SpW	Fame
Rodriguez	NY	3B	7.6	11.8	4.2
Schilling	BOS	P	7.9	11.9	4.0
Matsui	NY	LF	5.0	7.8	2.8
Martinez	BOS	P	5.5	8.3	2.8
Tejada	BAL	SS	7.3	7.3	
Mora	BAL	3B	5.6	5.6	

	AL C	CHI	KC	MIN
Start		46	96	181
6/1		115	60	253
7/1		175	30	313
8/1		222		375

308 PART II. MOMENTUM: SEASONS AND NARRATIVES

	AL C	CHI	KC	MIN	
	9/1	191		437	
	End	159		501	
	Spt.	1.07	1.02	**1.31**	

Name	*Tm*	*Pos*	*WAR*	*SpW*	*Fame*
Santana	MIN	P	**8.6**	**11.3**	**2.7**
Radke	MIN	P	**5.8**	**7.6**	**1.8**
Ford	MIN	LF/CF	4.5	**5.9**	**1.4**
Hunter	MIN	CF	4.2	5.5	**1.3**
Rowand	CHI	CF	**5.6**	**5.9**	0.3
Hafner	CLE	DH	**5.0**	5.0	

	AL W	OAK	SEA	ANA	TEX
	Start	190	268		
	6/1	190	232	72	69
	7/1	250	202	126	129
	8/1	309	171	164	191
	9/1	371	140	223	241
	End	435	108	278	236
	Spt.	1.17	1.13	**1.10**	1.06

Name	*Tm*	*Pos*	*WAR*	*SpW*	*Fame*
Suzuki	SEA	RF	**9.1**	**10.3**	**1.2**
Chavez	OAK	3B	**5.5**	**6.4**	0.9
Kotsay	OAK	CF	4.6	**5.4**	0.8
Hudson	OAK	P	4.2	4.9	**0.7**
Guerrero	ANA	RF/DH	**5.6**	**6.2**	0.6
Drese	TEX	P	**5.0**	5.3	0.3

	NL E	ATL	FLA	MON	PHI
	Start	475	94	42	158
	6/1	**441**	165	5	184
	7/1	**411**	225		244
	8/1	**455**	218		294
	9/1	**517**	187		263
	End	**581**	173		231
	Spt.	**1.55**	1.06	1.00	1.08

Name	*Tm*	*Pos*	*WAR*	*SpW*	*Fame*
Drew	ATL	RF	**8.3**	**12.9**	**4.6**
C. Jones	ATL	3B/LF	3.9	**6.0**	**2.1**
Furcal	ATL	SS	3.3	5.1	**1.8**
Giles	ATL	2B	3.3	5.1	**1.8**
Abreu	PHI	RF	**6.5**	**7.0**	0.5
Pavano	FLA	P	**5.3**	**5.6**	0.3
Wilkerson	MON	1B/LF	**5.0**	5.0	

	NL C	CHI	HOU	STL	CIN	MIL
	Start	177	226	299		
	6/1	**248**	**294**	**313**	39	17

NL C	CHI	HOU	STL	CIN	MIL
7/1	284	312	373	99	23
8/1	343	281	435	107	10
9/1	405	250	497	76	
End	463	296	561	44	
Spt.	1.10	1.50*	1.40	1.02	1.00

Name	Tm	Pos	WAR	SpW	Fame
Rolen	STL	3B	9.1	12.7	3.6
Pujols	STL	1B	8.5	11.9	3.4
Berkman	HOU	RF/LF	6.0	9.0	3.0
Edmonds	STL	CF	7.2	10.1	2.9
Sheets	MIL	P	7.2	7.2	

NL W	AZ	LA	SF	SD
Start	210	165	400	
6/1	173	233	366	74
7/1	143	287	390	119
8/1	112	346	452	181
9/1	81	408	505	240
End	49	472	569	226
Spt.	1.05	1.15	1.40	1.04

Name	Tm	Pos	WAR	SpW	Fame
Bonds	SF	LF	10.6	14.8	4.2
Schmidt	SF	P	6.7	9.4	2.7
Beltre	LA	3B	9.5	10.9	1.4
Snow	SF	1B	3.3	4.6	1.3
Johnson	AZ	P	8.5	8.9	0.4
Helton	COL	1B	8.3	8.3	

For most of the year, the Yankees had a vast lead over the rest of the AL, ten games better than the A's on August 15. Although the Red Sox challenged them for the division title with a 40–15 finish, by that point both teams were far enough away from the league that their playoff spots were secure. In the first two-thirds of the season, the Red Sox had to fight several good teams. The White Sox challenged the Twins until the Twins swept them in late July. From late May to the end of the year, the A's, Rangers, and Angels each gained Momentum almost daily. It was difficult to separate them on any basis; in mid-August, the Rangers won eight straight, but the Angels finished August 10–3 and the A's finished August 13–1. Those finishes left the Rangers out for a couple weeks, but they gained ground despite ending the season 16–16 by sweeping the struggling A's September 21–23. The Angels hadn't been much better, but they took the division by winning the next three series of the year, against the A's, Rangers, and A's again.

The Cardinals ended the season nine games better than any other NL team, but they didn't lead the Central until June 9, as every other Central team besides the Pirates had been hovering near the top. The Cardinals demoted them to the wild card race by going 60–21 over June, July, and August; July 4 was the last day any other team gained Momentum for the division lead. At that point, the West was a three-team fight among the Dodgers, Giants, and Padres, while the East had opened up as the Phillies and Marlins wilted in June. The Phillies held first as late as July 22 but stopped gaining Momentum a week later, thanks in part to the Marlins sweeping them but in greater part to the Braves going 20–6 in July after being sub–.500 in the season's first three months; August was almost as good, and the Braves won the division by ten games.

The Dodgers' 21–7 July built a decent lead. Beneath the division leaders and their hot Julys, the wild card sublayer was crowded; on August 29, a year and a day after the eight-team wild card pileup, the Giants, Cubs, and Padres were tied for it. While all three teams had respectable finishes, none of them took the wild card. The Astros, little more than a .500 team all year, went 20–3 from August 15 to September 8, sweeping the Phillies and Reds twice each and the Cubs once. By September 8 the Astros had joined the three wild card contenders, as had the Marlins, who won nine straight ending that day.

Hurricane Frances forced the Marlins to play 30 games after that point while nobody else played more than 26; they collapsed under the load.[2] On September 10, the Giants, Cubs, and Astros were tied; the Astros' rough series against the Pirates gave the Giants and Cubs some breathing room, especially for the Giants since the Dodgers were slumping to meet them. When the Giants won their series against the Astros September 21–23, it put the Cubs and Giants a half-game apart from each other and the Astros 2.5 games behind the Cubs with nine games left. The Cubs won two of those last nine and the Giants won five, but the Astros won eight, holding the wild card alone after game 159 (September 29). The teams tied again, but the Astros won both games 161 and 162 while the Giants only won game 162. The Giants finished two games behind the Dodgers and one game behind the Astros.

2005: Not the Yankees? Not the Astros? Actually, Both

AL E	BOS	NY	BAL	TOR
Start	380	429		
6/1	426	400	76	8
7/1	474	370	136	
8/1	536	417	159	
9/1	598	440	128	
End	660	502	97	
Spt.	**1.53**	**1.38**	**1.04**	**1.00**

15. No Change but Steroids 311

Name	Tm	Pos	WAR	SpW	Fame
Rodriguez	NY	3B	9.4	13.0	3.6
Ortiz	BOS	DH	5.3	8.1	2.8
Wakefield	BOS	P	4.5	6.9	2.4
Ramirez	BOS	LF	4.4	6.7	2.3
Johnson	NY	P	5.7	7.9	2.2
Roberts	BAL	2B	7.2	7.5	0.3
Tejada	BAL	SS	5.9	6.1	0.2

	AL C	CHI	MIN	CLE
Start		107	338	
6/1		183	408	
7/1		243	468	13
8/1		305	521	21
9/1		367	490	29
End		429	459	91
Spt.		1.48*	1.35	1.01

Name	Tm	Pos	WAR	SpW	Fame
Santana	MIN	P	7.2	9.7	2.5
Buehrle	CHI	P	4.8	7.1	2.3
Garland	CHI	P	4.6	6.8	2.2
Konerko	CHI	1B	4.0	5.9	1.9
Polanco	2 TM	2B	6.1	6.2	0.1
Sizemore	CLE	CF	6.5	6.6	0.1
Hafner	CLE	DH	5.4	5.5	0.1

	AL W	LA	OAK	SEA	TEX
Start		188	294	73	159
6/1		261	256	35	181
7/1		321	226	5	208
8/1		383	228		204
9/1		445	290		173
End		507	322		142
Spt.		1.33*	1.10	1.01	1.07

Name	Tm	Pos	WAR	SpW	Fame
Guerrero	LA	RF	5.7	7.6	1.9
Lackey	LA	P	4.2	5.6	1.4
Washburn	LA	P	4.2	5.6	1.4
Colon	LA	P	4.0	5.3	1.3
Teixeira	TEX	1B	7.2	7.7	0.5
Chavez	OAK	3B	4.8	5.3	0.5
Rogers	TEX	P	4.8	5.1	0.3

	NL E	ATL	FLA	PHI	NY	WAS
Start		467	139	186		
6/1		543	212	148	12	33
7/1		585	236	184	6	93
8/1		647	214	156		155

NL E	ATL	FLA	PHI	NY	WAS
9/1	709	249	194	20	193
End	771	266	241		168
Spt.	**1.55**	1.06	1.05	1.00	1.03

Name	*Tm*	*Pos*	WAR	SpW	Fame
A. Jones	ATL	CF	**6.7**	**10.4**	**3.7**
Furcal	ATL	SS	6.4	**9.9**	**3.5**
Smoltz	ATL	P	4.9	7.6	**2.7**
C. Jones	ATL	3B	4.1	6.4	**2.3**
Willis	FLA	P	**7.2**	7.6	0.4
Utley	PHI	2B	**7.2**	7.6	0.4
Martinez	NY	P	**6.9**	6.9	

NL C	CHI	CIN	HOU	STL
Start	372	35	238	451
6/1	340		200	518
7/1	370		170	578
8/1	339		160	640
9/1	308		222	702
End	277		284	764
Spt.	1.10	1.00	**1.50***	**1.44**

Name	*Tm*	*Pos*	WAR	SpW	Fame
Clemens	HOU	P	**7.8**	**11.7**	**3.9**
Pujols	STL	1B	**8.4**	**12.1**	**3.7**
Pettitte	HOU	P	**6.8**	**10.2**	**3.4**
Ensberg	HOU	3B	6.2	9.3	**3.1**
Lee	CHI	1B	**7.2**	7.9	0.7

NL W	AZ	LA	SD	SF
Start	40	379	181	457
6/1	116	425	224	428
7/1	131	428	284	398
8/1	100	397	319	367
9/1	69	366	294	336
End	38	335	272	305
Spt.	1.03	1.27	**1.13**	1.25

Name	*Tm*	*Pos*	WAR	SpW	Fame
Lowry	SF	P	4.0	5.0	**1.0**
Kent	LA	2B	3.7	4.7	**1.0**
Alou	SF	LF/RF	3.4	4.3	0.9
Drew	LA	RF/CF	3.2	4.1	0.9
Giles	SD	RF	**4.8**	5.4	0.6
Peavy	SD	P	**4.6**	5.2	0.6
Counsell	AZ	2B	**5.5**	5.7	0.2
Webb	AZ	P	**5.0**	5.2	0.2

The lowly Orioles played six of their first 12 games against the mighty Yankees—and went 5–1 in them. Combined with an eight-win streak, on May 1

15. No Change but Steroids 313

the Orioles had a four-game lead in the East while the Yankees were 7.5 back. At that point, the Orioles, White Sox, and Twins were the teams over .600 in the AL, while the (Los Angeles) Angels (of Anaheim) barely led the mediocre West. A month later, the Rangers joined the Angels, with little else changing around the league. The Red Sox got hot in the interleague portion of June's schedule and passed the Orioles for first on June 24. From there, the Orioles disintegrated, a 9–25 stretch costing manager Lee Mazzilli his job; the Orioles finished with 74 wins.

With their exit, a flood of teams fought primarily for the wild card. The Yankees got hot enough to take first place briefly in July, but the Red Sox stayed hot enough to fight them off as August dawned. Just as importantly, as the Rangers had started to fade from the West race, the A's knocked out all the wild card contenders and tied for first in the West with a 39–10 run from June 17 to August 12. But the A's went 2–7 right after, letting the Yankees back in, along with the Indians, who had been on the wild card fringes in June and benefited greatly from a soft August schedule. The A's had a rough September and lost the division to the Angels by losing three of four to them in the season's penultimate series. On September 29, before the ultimate series, the White Sox, who led the Central the entire year, had 96 wins, the Yankees had 94, and the Red Sox and Indians had 93; each of them had their closest divisional foe to face. The Red Sox took two of three from the Yankees to tie them; the Indians gave them both a playoff spot, as the White Sox swept them.

The NL's narrative was shaped by strange talent distribution across teams. Nobody but the Cardinals gained Momentum for the Central race. The Padres' 22–6 May gave them a lead they wouldn't relinquish, although that was largely due to the West's incompetence, as the Padres' 10–17 June and 8–18 July weren't enough to stop them. After July 23, the Padres gained Momentum on only five days; the rest of the West gained none. The Padres finished 82–80—with a five-game lead.

The clarity in the Central and West created a muddle in the East and wild card. On June 4, 5, 6, and 8, the entire East gained Momentum for the division. The Braves and Nationals-nee-Expos looked the best from there, but the Nationals were giving up more runs than they scored, and their return to reality in July let the Braves go from 4.5 back to 4.5 up—a lead that nobody challenged. The Nationals' decline also created a wild card race; the Astros, who'd started 15–30 and broke .500 only on July 18, took the wild card lead on July 28. They held it until August 18, when the Phillies overtook them; they flip-flopped a little before the Phillies took hold for a few days, tied by the Marlins on August 30.

On September 5–7, the Astros swept the Phillies in Houston, opening up space in the five-team tussle. The Marlins took the lead September 12 after taking the first two games of a four-game set with the Astros, but the Astros won the final two as part of a 13–5 finish. The Phillies kept hope by sweeping the Nationals in the final series, but the Astros won the last two games of the season to make the playoffs for the second straight surprising season.

2006: Tigers, Mets and Sluggards

	AL E	BAL	BOS	NY	TOR
Start		62	419	318	
6/1		31	493	383	57
7/1		1	553	431	81
8/1			615	481	50
9/1			632	543	19
End			602	603	
Spt.		1.01	1.50	1.44	1.01

Name	Tm	Pos	WAR	SpW	Fame
Ortiz	BOS	DH	**5.7**	**8.6**	**2.9**
Schilling	BOS	P	**5.5**	**8.3**	**2.7**
Wang	NY	P	**6.0**	**8.6**	**2.6**
Papelbon	BOS	P	5.0	7.5	**2.5**
Jeter	NY	SS	5.5	**7.9**	2.4
Wells	TOR	CF	**6.2**	6.3	0.1

	AL C	CHI	CLE	MIN	DET
Start		272	58	291	
6/1		346	27	251	78
7/1		406		221	138
8/1		468		217	200
9/1		530		270	262
End		539		330	322
Spt.		1.26	1.01	**1.15**	**1.39***

Name	Tm	Pos	WAR	SpW	Fame
Guillen	DET	SS	**6.0**	**8.3**	2.3
Inge	DET	3B	4.9	6.8	**1.9**
Verlander	DET	P	4.1	5.7	**1.8**
Robertson	DET	P	3.5	4.9	**1.4**
Santana	MIN	P	**7.5**	**8.6**	1.1
Sizemore	CLE	CF	**6.6**	6.7	0.1
Hafner	CLE	DH	**5.9**	6.0	0.1

	AL W	LA	OAK	TEX	SEA
Start		321	204	90	
6/1		290	185	119	
7/1		260	212	173	3
8/1		268	274	190	

15. No Change but Steroids 315

AL W	LA	OAK	TEX	SEA
9/1	258	336	162	
End	231	396	132	
Spt.	1.18	**1.15**	1.06	1.00

Name	Tm	Pos	WAR	SpW	Fame
Weaver	LA	P	**4.8**	**5.7**	0.9
Lackey	LA	P	4.7	**5.5**	0.8
Rodriguez	LA	P	3.7	4.4	0.7
Zito	OAK	P	4.4	5.1	0.7
Matthews	TEX	CF	**5.2**	**5.5**	0.3
Beltre	SEA	3B	**5.4**	**5.4**	
Suzuki	SEA	RF/CF	**5.3**	5.3	

NL E	ATL	FLA	PHI	WAS	NY
Start	**771**	266	241	168	
6/1	747	227	244	129	76
7/1	717	197	214	99	136
8/1	686	166	183	68	198
9/1	655	135	161	37	260
End	625	108	194	7	320
Spt.	1.41	1.05	1.05	1.02	**1.28***

Name	Tm	Pos	WAR	SpW	Fame
Smoltz	ATL	P	**5.9**	**8.3**	2.4
A. Jones	ATL	CF	5.6	**7.9**	2.3
Beltran	NY	CF	**8.2**	**10.5**	2.3
McCann	ATL	C	4.3	6.1	1.8
Utley	PHI	2B	**7.3**	**7.7**	0.4
Soriano	WAS	LF	**6.1**	6.2	0.1

NL C	CHI	HOU	STL	CIN
Start	277	284	764	
6/1	256	335	**839**	78
7/1	226	317	**899**	138
8/1	195	286	**961**	188
9/1	164	255	**1023**	238
End	134	240	**1083**	208
Spt.	1.06	1.10	**1.59**	1.03

Name	Tm	Pos	WAR	SpW	Fame
Pujols	STL	1B	**8.4**	**13.4**	5.0
Rolen	STL	3B	5.8	**9.2**	3.4
Carpenter	STL	P	5.1	**8.1**	3.0
Duncan	STL	LF/RF	1.8	2.9	1.1
Berkman	HOU	1B/RF	**6.0**	6.6	0.6
Oswalt	HOU	P	**5.9**	6.5	0.6
Arroyo	CIN	P	**6.8**	7.0	0.2

NL W	AZ	LA	SD	SF	COL
Start	38	335	272	305	
6/1	89	338	287	296	61

NL W	AZ	LA	SD	SF	COL
7/1	113	395	329	293	46
8/1	112	403	391	298	36
9/1	102	450	426	267	5
End	72	510	486	246	
Spt.	1.02	1.33	1.17	1.08	1.01

Name	Tm	Pos	WAR	SpW	Fame
Lowe	LA	P	**4.8**	6.4	1.6
Furcal	LA	SS	4.3	5.7	1.4
Drew	LA	RF	4.0	5.3	1.3
Saito	LA	P	3.2	4.3	**1.1**
Webb	AZ	P	**7.0**	7.1	0.1
Jennings	COL	P	**5.0**	5.1	0.1
Atkins	COL	3B	**4.9**	4.9	

Early returns in the AL looked mostly in line with 2005's expectations, except for the Tigers, whose 44th win on June 16 eclipsed the entire total from three years before. The Tigers were in first narrowly over the White Sox; both teams were several games ahead of the East, where the Yankees, Red Sox, and Blue Jays were virtually tied, and the slow-starting West, where the A's had just taken first from the Rangers. The Red Sox won 12 straight in interleague play from June 16–29, knocking out the Blue Jays and putting the Yankees a fair amount back. But they lost ground in July, and their 9–21 August, including losing five straight to the Yankees by giving up 49 runs—gave the Yankees the division.

In the West, the Angels had taken three of four from the A's July 6–9 to become the primary challenger as the Rangers faded. But their challenge only lasted a few weeks, as the A's used a 21–6 August to pull ahead and win comfortably. That left the Central and wild card to sort out. The Tigers pulled away from the White Sox in July, largely due to the latter's slump that let the Twins' 19–1 run ending July 3 count for something. The Twins started the second half of the season 12–2, capped by sweeping the White Sox and tying them for the wild card. August changed nothing, although the Tigers lost three games of their lead. That became surprisingly relevant when the Twins took three of four from them September 7–10; after that series, the Tigers led by two games over the Twins and 3.5 over the White Sox. The White Sox stopped gaining Momentum five days later due to the A's sweeping them. The Tigers swept the Royals September 22–24 but had trouble beating anyone else; they dropped their last five games, settling for a wild card. The Twins spent only one day alone in first place—the final one.

In the NL, the Mets led the East continuously from game three and were unchallenged after May 22. The Braves had an outside chance until a 3–20 stretch that started May 29, ending history's longest consecutive postseason streak. Besides the Mets, the best early teams were all in the Central; on May

1, fifth in the Central would have led the West, as everybody but the Pirates started strong. By the end of the season, only two Central teams would finish over .500, and although the Cardinals dropped eight straight in June, eight straight again in July/August, and seven straight in the final two weeks, they held first from May 12 forward, tied occasionally by the Reds.

Like the Central, the West's end didn't match its beginning. It wasn't until July 15 that any team gained a lead better than three games (in this case the Padres), and as late as June 15 all five teams gained Momentum. The Rockies exited first with a 1–11 stretch around the All-Star break that included five losses to the Diamondbacks; at the end of that stretch the Giants were 51–47 and the Diamondbacks and Padres were 50–47. The Diamondbacks had difficulty beating non-Rockies; they fell below .500 on August 21 and didn't come back (although they were only three games behind first on August 25).

The Dodgers, who had followed a 1–13 disaster in July with a 17–1 reversal, carried a five-win streak into September and were gaining ground over the Padres. But they still were only 71–62 on August 31, and the Padres passed them permanently—albeit narrowly—in mid-September. The Giants, who'd looked done in August, crept back into the race but finished 2–13.

Complicating the mediocre West race was that it was also a wild card "race"; on September 1, the 63–69 Braves were only four games behind the wild card lead—the 68–66 Padres. The picture didn't improve much for weeks, as the Braves still had a small chance going into the final week despite being 75–80. They would have needed to go 7–0 to pass the Phillies and Dodgers, who were at 81 wins; the Dodgers made it easy for everyone by going 7–0 themselves, clinching a playoff spot on the second-to-last day of the season, and tying the Padres (who were given the division for winning their season series against the Dodgers).

2007: The Knowns and the Unknowns

AL E	BOS	NY
Start	426	427
6/1	501	388
7/1	561	358
8/1	623	330
9/1	685	380
End	745	440
Spt.	1.59	1.37

Name	Tm	Pos	WAR	SpW	Fame
Beckett	BOS	P	6.5	10.3	3.8
Ortiz	BOS	DH	6.4	10.2	3.8

Name	Tm	Pos	WAR	SpW	Fame
Rodriguez	NY	3B	**9.4**	**12.9**	**3.5**
Lowell	BOS	3B	5.0	8.0	3.0
Cano	NY	2B	**6.7**	**9.2**	2.5
Pena	TB	1B	**7.2**	7.2	

AL C	CHI	DET	MIN	CLE
Start	381	228	234	
6/1	354	303	228	72
7/1	324	363	198	132
8/1	293	425	167	194
9/1	262	472	136	256
End	232	442	106	316
Spt.	1.18	1.26	1.08	**1.32***

Name	Tm	Pos	WAR	SpW	Fame
Sabathia	CLE	P	**6.3**	**8.3**	2.0
Hernandez	CLE	P	**6.2**	**8.2**	2.0
Granderson	DET	CF	**7.6**	**9.6**	2.0
Ordonez	DET	RF	**7.3**	**9.2**	1.9
Vazquez	CHI	P	**6.2**	7.3	1.1

AL W	LA	OAK	TEX	SEA
Start	164	280	94	
6/1	230	256	55	
7/1	290	262	25	20
8/1	352	231		61
9/1	414	200		123
End	474	170		102
Spt.	**1.20**	1.10	1.01	1.02

Name	Tm	Pos	WAR	SpW	Fame
Lackey	LA	P	**6.3**	7.6	1.3
Escobar	LA	P	4.9	5.9	1.0
Guerrero	LA	RF/DH	4.6	**5.5**	0.9
Cabrera	LA	SS	4.2	5.0	0.8
Ellis	OAK	2B	**4.8**	5.3	0.5
Suzuki	SEA	CF	**5.8**	5.9	0.1

NL E	ATL	FLA	NY	PHI	WAS
Start	493	85	253	153	6
6/1	571	46	328	114	
7/1	595	16	388	129	
8/1	636		450	113	
9/1	668		512	154	
End	638		572	187	
Spt.	**1.39**	1.01	1.10	**1.09**	1.00

Name	Tm	Pos	WAR	SpW	Fame
C. Jones	ATL	3B	**7.6**	**10.6**	3.0
Hudson	ATL	P	4.7	**6.5**	1.8

15. No Change but Steroids

Name	Tm	Pos	WAR	SpW	Fame
Smoltz	ATL	P	4.6	6.4	**1.8**
Renteria	ATL	SS	4.1	5.7	**1.6**
Wright	NY	3B	**8.3**	**9.1**	0.8
Utley	PHI	2B	**7.8**	**8.5**	0.7
Rollins	PHI	SS	**6.0**	**6.5**	0.5

NL C	CHI	CIN	HOU	STL	MIL
Start	106	164	189	**854**	
6/1	67	125	150	**815**	78
7/1	37	95	120	**785**	138
8/1	45	64	89	**754**	200
9/1	104	33	58	**723**	238
End	164	3	28	**693**	292
Spt.	**1.07**	1.03	1.03	1.50	1.04

Name	Tm	Pos	WAR	SpW	Fame
Pujols	STL	1B	**8.7**	**13.1**	**4.4**
Wainwright	STL	P	2.8	4.2	**1.4**
Molina	STL	C	2.1	3.2	**1.1**
Rolen	STL	3B	1.8	2.7	0.9
Ramirez	CHI	3B	**5.2**	**5.6**	0.4
Oswalt	HOU	P	**6.7**	**6.9**	0.2
Harang	CIN	P	**6.0**	**6.2**	0.2

NL W	AZ	LA	SD	SF	COL
Start	56	402	384	194	
6/1	101	480	441	194	
7/1	161	540	501	164	
8/1	184	602	563	133	
9/1	246	595	625	102	
End	306	577	685	72	18
Spt.	**1.09**	1.28	1.23	1.04	**1.10**

Name	Tm	Pos	WAR	SpW	Fame
Penny	LA	P	5.9	**7.6**	**1.7**
Martin	LA	C	5.6	**7.2**	**1.6**
Peavy	SD	P	**6.2**	**7.6**	**1.4**
Billingsley	LA	P	3.6	4.6	**1.0**
Tulowitzki	COL	SS	**6.8**	**7.5**	0.7
Holliday	COL	LF	**6.0**	**6.6**	0.6
Webb	AZ	P	**6.4**	**7.0**	0.6

In the AL, the four teams in the playoffs were ranked 1–2–3–5 in Momentum by the end of the season. The Red Sox and Angels led their divisions every day after April. The Mariners got within a game of the Angels in July but then lost seven straight; they recovered and were a game behind in August but then lost nine straight. The Red Sox were only challenged at the end by the Yankees, who didn't pass .500 permanently until after the All-Star break and didn't gain Momentum until August 1; they secured the wild card after the Mariners'

August losing streak. By the end of the season, the Yankees were far enough ahead for the wild card that the Red Sox nearly losing their division lead was irrelevant.

In the Central, the Tigers were pursued not by the customary Twins (who ran out of offense) but by the Indians. The Indians led for most of the first half; the Tigers took first by winning a series against them July 3–5. The Tigers lost the lead with a rough end to August that, when combined with the Indians' 11–1 streak starting August 25 and the Yankees' ascendancy, took them out of the Central and wild card races for good.

In the NL, the four teams in the playoffs were ranked 6–7–8–12 in Momentum by the end of the season. Never before had a league's top five teams by Momentum failed to make the playoffs. Initially, most things seemed clear; the Cardinals' pitching woes let the Brewers start strong and unopposed, the Braves and Mets were the only relevant teams in the East, and the West was up for grabs by anyone except the Rockies. The Phillies became relevant by sweeping the Mets June 5–7, right before interleague play started and not long after the Giants had left the West race. The Mets swept the Phillies at the end of June to send them back out, but they returned in July.

The Brewers blew a 7.5-game lead over July, letting the surging Cubs into the race. By that point no team was particularly good; on August 1 only the Mets were on pace for even 90 wins. The Braves' middling August sent them packing. The Cubs went 12–16 in August but the Brewers went 9–18, so the Cubs gained 2.5 games. The Rockies flickered in and out of the wild card race in August, as did everyone over .500. On September 1, the Mets, Diamondbacks, and Padres were tied at a 90-win pace (although the Diamondbacks had been outscored on the year), and the rest was mediocrity. Even the Cardinals' 66–66 record left them only two games back in the Central. Not much changed in the next two weeks; on September 13, the Mets held a 6.5-game lead, the Diamondbacks held a four-game lead, and the Padres were up 1.5 games for the wild card.

The Cubs finished strong enough to take the Central, but the stories in the other divisions covered the Central race over completely. The Phillies swept the Mets September 14–16. That would not have meant much, but the Phillies didn't lose a series the rest of the season while the Mets lost six of their final seven games; the Phillies won the East by a single game, taking the lead only in the last series. The Padres struggled in the first part of September, then won seven straight. The Rockies swept them September 21–23 as part of a 13–1 end to the season; when the Padres lost their final two games, it left the two teams tied for the wild card, a game behind the Diamondbacks. The Rockies won the tiebreaker game in 13 innings to claim a playoff spot with only 18 points of Momentum—the lowest in history.

2008: The Tampa Connection

AL E	BOS	NY	BAL	TB	TOR
Start	**493**	291			
6/1	**579**	251	19	59	2
7/1	**639**	221		119	
8/1	**701**	214		181	
9/1	**763**	183		243	
End	**821**	154		301	
Spt.	**1.55**	1.19	1.00	**1.50***	1.00

Name	Tm	Pos	WAR	SpW	Fame
Pedroia	BOS	2B	**6.9**	**10.7**	**3.8**
Youkilis	BOS	3B/1B	**6.3**	**9.8**	**3.5**
Lester	BOS	P	**6.1**	**9.5**	**3.4**
Matsuzaka	BOS	P	5.3	**8.2**	**2.9**
Rodriguez	NY	3B	**6.8**	8.1	1.3
Markakis	BAL	RF	**7.4**	7.4	
Halladay	TOR	P	**6.2**	6.2	

AL C	CHI	CLE	DET	MIN
Start	154	209	292	70
6/1	186	175	249	60
7/1	246	145	219	75
8/1	308	114	188	128
9/1	370	83	157	190
End	428	54	128	248
Spt.	1.22	1.06	1.13	1.05

Name	Tm	Pos	WAR	SpW	Fame
Danks	CHI	P	**6.4**	7.8	**1.4**
Quentin	CHI	LF	5.3	**6.5**	**1.2**
Buehrle	CHI	P	4.4	5.4	**1.0**
Floyd	CHI	P	3.4	4.1	0.7
Lee	CLE	P	**6.9**	7.3	0.4
Sizemore	CLE	CF	**5.9**	6.3	0.4
Mauer	MIN	C	**5.6**	5.9	0.3

AL W	LA	OAK	SEA
Start	313	113	67
6/1	399	190	24
7/1	459	175	
8/1	521	144	
9/1	583	113	
End	641	84	
Spt.	1.45	1.06	1.01

Name	Tm	Pos	WAR	SpW	Fame
Teixeira	2 TM	1B	**7.8**	**10.6**	**2.8**
Santana	LA	P	5.0	7.3	**2.3**
Saunders	LA	P	4.6	6.7	**2.1**
Hunter	LA	CF	3.5	5.1	**1.6**

Name	Tm	Pos	WAR	SpW	Fame
Beltre	SEA	3B	**5.6**	**5.7**	0.1
Suzuki	SEA	RF/CF	**5.3**	5.4	0.1
Hamilton	TEX	CF/RF	**5.4**	5.4	

NL E	ATL	NY	PHI	FLA	
Start	462	414	135		
6/1	465	435	207	82	
7/1	435	405	267	124	
8/1	404	449	329	180	
9/1	373	511	391	188	
End	344	569	446	159	
Spt.	1.27	1.27	**1.17**	1.03	

Name	Tm	Pos	WAR	SpW	Fame
C. Jones	ATL	3B	7.3	9.3	2.0
Santana	NY	P	7.1	9.0	1.9
Beltran	NY	CF	6.9	8.8	1.9
Wright	NY	3B	6.8	8.6	1.8
Utley	PHI	2B	**9.0**	**10.5**	1.5

NL C	CHI	CIN	HOU	MIL	STL
Start	118	2	20	211	**502**
6/1	199		44	205	**586**
7/1	259		14	205	**646**
8/1	321			261	**699**
9/1	383			323	**701**
End	441			378	**672**
Spt.	**1.12**	1.00	1.00	**1.12**	1.50

Name	Tm	Pos	WAR	SpW	Fame
Pujols	STL	1B	**9.2**	**13.8**	4.6
Ludwick	STL	RF/LF	5.5	**8.3**	2.8
Glaus	STL	3B	4.4	6.6	2.2
Lohse	STL	P	2.8	4.2	1.4
Dempster	CHI	P	**7.0**	**7.8**	0.8
Sabathia	2 TM	P	**6.8**	**7.5**	0.7
Berkman	HOU	1B	**6.8**	6.8	

NL W	AZ	COL	LA	SD	SF
Start	222	13	418	496	52
6/1	303		412	454	10
7/1	342		382	424	
8/1	326		351	393	
9/1	385		350	362	
End	386		396	333	
Spt.	1.09	1.00	**1.15**	1.25	1.00

Name	Tm	Pos	WAR	SpW	Fame
Ramirez	2 TM	LF/DH	**5.9**	**7.9**	2.0
Giles	SD	RF	4.8	6.0	1.2

15. No Change but Steroids   323

Name	Tm	Pos	WAR	SpW	Fame
Peavy	SD	P	3.9	4.9	**1.0**
Gonzalez	SD	1B	3.5	4.4	**0.9**
Haren	AZ	P	**6.1**	**6.6**	0.5
Webb	AZ	P	**5.8**	**6.3**	0.5
Lincecum	SF	P	**7.9**	**7.9**	

The Yankees, in their longtime spring training home of Tampa, went 14–12 in spring training. The newly named Tampa Bay Rays,[3] in their final year training in St. Petersburg, went 18–8 in spring training. Every year before 2008, the Yankees would make the playoffs while the (Devil) Rays would wander aimlessly near the bottom of the East. But in 2008, the magic of Tampa didn't go north with the Yankees, as they started slowly and the Rays, Red Sox, and Orioles spent the first two months in contention. The Orioles couldn't keep up, and although an eight-win streak at the end of July put the Yankees in contention for a week, they couldn't overtake the Rays and Red Sox. The Rays took first for good on July 18, the first day after the All-Star break. The Red Sox went 18–9 in August; they still lost ground to the 21–7 Rays, but it distanced them enough from the rest of the league to take the wild card easily.

The primary competition for the wild card had been from the Twins-White Sox race in the Central. The entire Central started slowly, heating up when the White Sox swept the Twins in four games June 6–9. The Twins responded by winning ten straight in interleague play; as that streak was ending, the White Sox started a seven-win streak. The teams stayed close the rest of the season; the Twins took over first in the penultimate series by sweeping the White Sox, but the Sox evened it up and won a tiebreaker game 1–0 to win the Central.

As tough as the Central was, the West was easy. The Angels pulled away from the A's in mid-June, sealing it by winning a series against them just before the All-Star break, then starting the second half 18–5, eventually winning the West by 21 games.

In the NL, the Cubs had the easiest time, their eight-win streak starting May 26 giving them a good hold of first over the Brewers and Cardinals. Both the Cubs and Brewers won 20 games in August to eliminate the Cardinals. The Brewers started September 4–15, allowing the Astros, in last place on July 26, to challenge for the wild card in mid-September with a 14–1 run. But the Brewers won six of their last seven games to keep the Astros away.

The Brewers had to win that much to keep the Mets and Phillies away as well. The East race initially involved everyone but the Nationals; the Marlins led in April and May, giving way to the Phillies in June and July. The Mets went 5–1 against the Phillies in July and took over first place in mid-August. On

September 10, the Mets led the Phillies by 3.5 games, but in an echo of 2007, they didn't win a series after that, while the Phillies finished the season 13–3. The Mets and Brewers were tied for the wild card going into the final game, but the Brewers beat the Cubs while the Mets lost to the Marlins.

The Mets, Phillies, and four Central teams had good enough records to win the West at the end. It didn't look like that would be the case when the Diamondbacks' 20–8 April gave them a 5.5-game lead. They remained in first until September 5, but a .393 May and a .407 June meant first place was often below .500. The Dodgers tied the Diamondbacks intermittently in July and August; they tied again on August 17 but went 1–9 after it to leave them 3.5 back before facing the Diamondbacks on August 29–31. The Dodgers lost the first game but recovered to win the series. They then swept the Padres, swept the Diamondbacks again, and won the three series after that to clinch the division in the final week.

2009: The Underdog Yankees

AL E	BOS	NY	TB	TOR
Start	516	97	189	
6/1	584	120	152	74
7/1	644	180	152	113
8/1	706	242	124	82
9/1	768	304	99	51
End	838	374	64	16
Spt.	1.55	1.40*	1.07	1.03

Name	Tm	Pos	WAR	SpW	Fame
Youkilis	BOS	1B/3B	6.6	10.2	3.6
Lester	BOS	P	6.3	9.8	3.5
Pedroia	BOS	2B	5.6	8.7	3.1
Beckett	BOS	P	5.1	7.9	2.8
Jeter	NY	SS	6.5	9.1	2.6
Zobrist	TB	2B/RF	8.6	9.2	0.6
Longoria	TB	3B	7.0	7.5	0.5
Halladay	TOR	P	6.9	7.1	0.2

AL C	CHI	CLE	DET	MIN	KC
Start	269	34	81	156	
6/1	235	131	119		21
7/1	208	191	92		
8/1	243	253	94		
9/1	266	315	63		
End	231	385	85		
Spt.	1.22	1.00	1.18	1.10	1.00

15. No Change but Steroids

Name	Tm	Pos	WAR	SpW	Fame
Buehrle	CHI	P	5.3	6.5	1.2
Danks	CHI	P	5.0	6.1	1.1
Verlander	DET	P	5.6	6.6	1.0
Cabrera	DET	1B	5.1	6.0	0.9
Mauer	MIN	C/DH	7.8	8.6	0.8
Greinke	KC	P	10.4	10.4	
Choo	CLE	RF/LF	5.5	5.5	

	AL W	LA	OAK	SEA	TEX
Start		403	53		
6/1		405	16		56
7/1		432		2	116
8/1		494			163
9/1		556			195
End		626			178
Spt.		1.50*	1.01	1.00	1.05

Name	Tm	Pos	WAR	SpW	Fame
Figgins	LA	3B	7.7	11.6	3.9
Hunter	LA	CF	5.2	7.8	2.6
Morales	LA	1B	4.3	6.5	2.2
Rivera	LA	LF	3.8	5.7	1.9
Kinsler	TEX	2B	6.0	6.3	0.3
Gutierrez	SEA	CF	6.6	6.6	
Hernandez	SEA	P	6.0	6.0	

	NL E	ATL	FLA	NY	PHI
Start		344	159	569	446
6/1		317	162	608	497
7/1		287	138	647	557
8/1		256	137	616	619
9/1		225	124	585	681
End		193	89	550	751
Spt.		1.06	1.03	1.33	1.44

Name	Tm	Pos	WAR	SpW	Fame
Utley	PHI	2B	8.2	11.8	3.6
Werth	PHI	RF	4.5	6.5	2.0
Happ	PHI	P	4.2	6.0	1.8
Howard	PHI	1B	3.8	5.5	1.7
Ramirez	FLA	SS	7.3	7.5	0.2
Johnson	FLA	P	6.6	6.8	0.2
Zimmerman	WAS	3B	7.3	7.3	

	NL C	CHI	MIL	STL	CIN	HOU
Start		441	378	672		
6/1		462	432	744	43	
7/1		453	492	804	49	
8/1		473	518	866	18	9
9/1		472	487	928		

NL C	CHI	MIL	STL	CIN	HOU
End	437	452	998		
Spt.	1.10	1.10	**1.55**	1.00	1.00

Name	Tm	Pos	WAR	SpW	Fame
Pujols	STL	1B	9.7	15.0	5.3
Carpenter	STL	P	6.5	10.1	3.6
Wainwright	STL	P	6.2	9.6	3.4
Ryan	STL	SS	4.5	7.0	2.5
Fielder	MIL	1B	6.3	6.9	0.6

NL W	AZ	LA	SD	COL	SF
Start	386	396	333		
6/1	350	468	300		
7/1	320	528	270	18	54
8/1	289	590	239	77	116
9/1	258	652	208	139	163
End	223	722	173	209	146
Spt.	1.07	**1.50***	1.06	**1.06**	1.02

Name	Tm	Pos	WAR	SpW	Fame
Kemp	LA	CF	4.8	7.2	2.4
Kershaw	LA	P	4.7	7.1	2.4
Blake	LA	3B	4.6	6.9	2.3
Hudson	LA	2B	4.1	6.2	2.1
Haren	AZ	P	6.5	7.0	0.5
Tulowitzki	COL	SS	6.5	6.9	0.4
Gonzalez	SD	1B	6.9	7.1	0.2
Lincecum	SF	P	7.5	7.7	0.2

The Yankees entered 2009 sixth in AL Momentum—their lowest ranking since July 1993—but they won the East with ease. The Blue Jays led early but left first place after losing nine straight in May and left the wild card race with some rough patches in June. The Red Sox took over first place but lost five straight right after the All-Star break; when the Yankees swept them in four games August 6–9 as part of a 21-win August, the Red Sox stopped gaining Momentum for the East. That left the Sox fighting for the wild card with the Rays and the Rangers. The Rangers had lost the West lead to the Angels after the Angels thrived in June's interleague play and won six straight July series. The Angels swept the Rays August 10–12 to cut off their contention; the Red Sox pulled out the wild card by winning seven straight in early September.

The AL Central featured lower-caliber teams but a surprisingly tight race. The Royals started 18–11 to lead the division but went 5–20 after, giving the lead to the Tigers. The Tigers were good, not great, holding first through the summer mostly by default. On July 23, the White Sox tied them at five games over .500; the Twins were 2.5 back at .500. A month later, the White Sox had fallen back slightly, giving the Tigers some room. The Tigers won their first six games of September, giving them a five-game lead, but they lost their next five to shrink the lead to five games. Over the next three weeks, the Tigers went .500, but the Twins went 16–4, coming from below .500 to tie the Tigers on the last two days of the season. The Twins played a tiebreaker game for the second straight year; this time, they won, beating the Tigers in 12 innings to take a division they'd barely led all year.

In the NL, the Phillies had the easiest time. The Mets challenged them early; neither team's June was productive, allowing the slow-starting Marlins to enter the race. The Phillies swept the Mets and Marlins in July amid a 14–1 stretch; the Marlins gained Momentum for the wild card as late as August 18, but nobody approached the Phillies for the division lead.

Although the end-of-season records didn't indicate competition in the Central, the Cardinals had difficulty winning it. The Brewers and Cardinals entered their series starting May 16 tied, with the Cubs and Reds within a game of them; the Brewers swept to take control of first. All four teams were streaky; on June 15, the last-place Astros at 29–33 were only five games out of first. The Astros surged and got within a game of first by sweeping the Cardinals July 20–22, as the Reds and Brewers were showing themselves out the door. The Cubs and Cardinals won series against the Astros the next week to send them below .500; they wouldn't get back above it. But what looked like a Cubs-Cardinals race the rest of the way was surprisingly wrapped up a couple weeks later as the Cubs' pitching slumped and the Cardinals won 20 games in August, turning a half-game lead into a ten-game lead.

The Dodgers started 21–8, led by 9.5 games on June 2, and were only challenged slightly in September. The Giants and Rockies, slow starters in part because they faced the Dodgers frequently in April, became wild card contenders in June; the Rockies fired manager Clint Hurdle after an 18–28 start and then went 17–1 starting in new manager Jim Tracy's second week. As the Central collapsed, they became the primary wild card contenders.

A sweep by the Giants left the teams tied entering September. The Rockies started September 10–1, enough to eliminate the Giants and put the division lead in play. The Rockies stumbled, giving the Dodgers breathing room, but the Dodgers also stumbled and lost most of their lead in a week. Meanwhile, the Braves had closed most of the gap between them and the Rockies with two seven-win streaks on the month. This would have left the Dodgers and Rockies sweating bullets as they entered the last series of the season pitted against each other, but the Braves lost their last six games to send both West teams to the playoffs.

2010: AL's Early Leaders Hold Up; NL's Early Leaders Struggle

AL E	BOS	NY	TB	TOR
Start	499	223	38	10
6/1	479	290	108	28
7/1	506	350	168	1
8/1	493	412	230	
9/1	462	474	292	
End	430	538	356	
Spt.	1.48	1.39	1.13	1.00

Name	Tm	Pos	WAR	SpW	Fame
Beltre	BOS	3B	7.8	11.5	3.7
Cano	NY	2B	8.1	11.3	3.2
Gardner	NY	LF/CF	7.3	10.1	2.8
Buchholz	BOS	P	5.6	8.3	2.7
Longoria	TB	3B	8.1	9.2	1.1

AL C	CHI	DET	MIN
Start	138	229	51
6/1	100	281	124
7/1	94	311	184
8/1	156	352	222
9/1	170	321	284
End	138	289	348
Spt.	1.06	1.23	1.13

Name	Tm	Pos	WAR	SpW	Fame
Cabrera	DET	1B	6.4	7.9	1.5
Jackson	DET	CF	5.1	6.3	1.2
Verlander	DET	P	4.3	5.3	1.0
Mauer	MIN	C/DH	5.9	6.7	0.8
Ramirez	CHI	SS	5.6	5.9	0.3
Choo	CLE	RF	5.9	5.9	

AL W	LA	TEX	OAK
Start	373	106	
6/1	335	149	12
7/1	350	209	
8/1	319	271	
9/1	288	333	
End	256	397	
Spt.	1.26	1.34*	1.00

Name	Tm	Pos	WAR	SpW	Fame
Hamilton	TEX	LF/CF	8.7	11.7	3.0
Wilson	TEX	P	4.4	5.9	1.5
Weaver	LA	P	5.4	6.8	1.4
Cruz	TEX	RF	4.1	5.5	1.4
Hernandez	SEA	P	7.1	7.1	
Barton	OAK	1B	5.5	5.5	

15. No Change but Steroids

NL E	ATL	FLA	NY	PHI	WAS
Start	140	65	399	546	
6/1	133	46	413	617	10
7/1	193	16	461	641	
8/1	255		481	646	
9/1	317		450	708	
End	381		418	772	
Spt.	**1.10**	1.01	1.20	**1.45**	1.00

Name	Tm	Pos	WAR	SpW	Fame
Halladay	PHI	P	**8.3**	**12.0**	**3.7**
Utley	PHI	2B	5.8	**8.4**	**2.6**
Hamels	PHI	P	5.4	7.8	**2.4**
Werth	PHI	RF/CF	4.5	6.5	**2.0**
Heyward	ATL	RF	**6.4**	7.0	0.6
Johnson	FLA	P	**7.2**	7.3	0.1
Zimmerman	WAS	3B	**6.2**	6.2	

NL C	CHI	MIL	STL	CIN	
Start	318	329	**725**		
6/1	281	282	**796**	46	
7/1	251	262	**856**	106	
8/1	220	231	**918**	168	
9/1	189	200	**965**	230	
End	157	168	**933**	294	
Spt.	1.06	1.06	1.50	**1.08**	

Name	Tm	Pos	WAR	SpW	Fame
Pujols	STL	1B	**7.5**	**11.3**	**3.8**
Wainwright	STL	P	**6.3**	**9.5**	**3.2**
Holliday	STL	LF	**5.9**	**8.9**	**3.0**
Rasmus	STL	CF	3.6	5.4	1.8
Votto	CIN	1B	**6.9**	7.5	0.8

NL W	AZ	COL	LA	SD	SF
Start	162	152	525	125	106
6/1	125	130	542	196	165
7/1	95	109	593	256	204
8/1	64	141	616	318	242
9/1	33	110	585	380	304
End	1	114	553	444	368
Spt.	1.02	1.03	1.30	1.06	**1.40***

Name	Tm	Pos	WAR	SpW	Fame
Huff	SF	1B/LF	**5.7**	**8.0**	**2.3**
Torres	SF	CF/RF	5.3	7.4	**2.1**
Cain	SF	P	4.5	6.3	1.8
Kershaw	LA	P	5.5	7.2	1.7
Jimenez	COL	P	**7.5**	7.7	0.2
Tulowitzki	COL	SS	**6.7**	6.9	0.2
Gonzalez	COL	LF/CF	**5.9**	6.1	0.2

In the AL, everything wrapped up in mid–August. The West started slowly; the Rangers went 13–2 in June's interleague play, opening up a 4.5-game lead and never getting challenged again. The Twins led the Central most of the way but were out of first from July 6 to August 8, due less to their own struggles and more to others' winning streaks. The Tigers led for a week, including a series win against the Twins just before the All-Star break, but they started the second half 6–21. The White Sox won 11 straight in June and took first from the Tigers by winning nine straight in July. But they lost three series to the Twins over July and August, and the Twins built a 12-game lead from there, clinching with two weeks left.

When the White Sox left the Central race, they also left the wild card race. That left the wild card and the East a formality, as the Rays and Yankees were enough in front to have secured both spots. The Rays led early, and the Yankees took over in late June. The Rays fell to four games back, but they swept the Red Sox July 5–7 to remove their remaining non–Yankee competition. The Rays and Yankees spent eight days tied at the end of August; both teams were mediocre in September, and the Rays won the division by a game.

In the NL, the Central was simple and the East and West were complicated. The Cardinals built a five-game lead by starting 18–8, and they were 12–6 against the Reds—their most wins against any team. But the Reds were good against everybody else, and apart from a few weeks around the Cardinals' eight-win streak in July, the Reds led from May to the end of the season, cementing their lead with a 14–4 run from July 31 to August 20 (three losses were to the Cardinals).

The East involved all five teams at various points. The Phillies led in May but got swept by the Mets May 25–27 and the Braves May 31–June 2; that gave first to the Braves, who held a seven-game lead on July 22. The Mets were fading, but the Phillies won eight straight to re-enter the conversation. The Braves could have gained ground when the Phillies were swept by the Astros August 23–26, but the Braves were getting swept by the Rockies at the same time. After that sweep, the Phillies finished 27–8, including 5–1 against the Braves in the final two weeks, to take first for good.

That left the Braves to fight for the wild card with the Giants and Padres, who were also battling for the West. The Padres started 3–6 but won eight straight after that to take first. They held the lead through the summer and built up a six-game lead in August; the Dodgers and Rockies stayed close until late July, and the Giants were in the wild card mix. Then the Padres lost ten straight August 26–September 5, reducing their lead to a single game. The Rockies were the Padres' eighth through tenth losses of that streak, starting a ten-win streak for them; on September 18, the Rockies, Giants, and Padres were separated by a game. But the Rockies finished 1–13. The Giants and Padres faced each other in the final series of the year; the Padres won the first two games to enter the final game at 90–71 while the Giants were 91–70 and the Braves were also 90–71. The Giants four-hit the Padres while the Braves won their game by a run; the Braves and Padres spent most of the year in first, but only the Braves moved on to October.

2011: What an Attractive Cliff

	AL E	BOS	NY	TB		
	Start	331	414	274		
	6/1	335	481	338		
	7/1	395	541	359		
	8/1	457	603	328		
	9/1	519	665	297		
	End	573	719	297		
	Spt.	1.31	1.55	1.22		
Name	Tm	Pos	WAR	SpW	Fame	
Sabathia	NY	P	7.5	11.6	4.1	
Cano	NY	2B	5.7	8.8	3.1	
Granderson	NY	CF	5.7	8.8	3.1	
Ellsbury	BOS	CF	8.1	10.6	2.5	
Pedroia	BOS	2B	7.9	10.3	2.4	
Zobrist	TB	2B/RF	8.7	10.6	1.9	
Bautista	TOR	RF/3B	8.1	8.1		

	AL C	CHI	DET	MIN	CLE	KC
	Start	106	222	267		
	6/1	65	223	226	80	7
	7/1	35	283	196	140	
	8/1	4	345	165	196	
	9/1		407	134	192	
	End		461	107	165	
	Spt.	1.02	1.50*	1.08	1.04	1.00
Name	Tm	Pos	WAR	SpW	Fame	
Verlander	DET	P	8.4	12.6	4.2	
Cabrera	DET	1B	7.5	11.3	3.8	
Avila	DET	C	5.1	7.7	2.6	
Jackson	DET	CF	4.9	7.4	2.5	
Fister	2 TM	P	5.2	6.5	1.3	
Gordon	KC	LF	7.2	7.2		

AL W	LA	TEX	SEA
Start	197	305	
6/1	234	357	1
7/1	213	417	4

AL W	LA	TEX	SEA
8/1	257	479	
9/1	277	541	
End	277	595	
Spt.	1.09	**1.48**	1.00

Name	Tm	Pos	WAR	SpW	Fame
Kinsler	TEX	2B	**7.1**	**10.5**	**3.4**
Beltre	TEX	3B	**5.8**	**8.6**	**2.8**
Napoli	TEX	C/1B	**5.4**	**8.0**	**2.6**
Wilson	TEX	P	4.9	**7.3**	**2.4**
Weaver	LA	P	**7.0**	**7.6**	0.6

NL E	ATL	NY	PHI	FLA
Start	269	295	545	
6/1	288	254	624	78
7/1	348	224	684	66
8/1	410	193	746	35
9/1	472	162	808	4
End	526	135	862	
Spt.	1.15	1.06	**1.46**	1.01

Name	Tm	Pos	WAR	SpW	Fame
Halladay	PHI	P	**8.9**	**13.0**	**4.1**
Lee	PHI	P	**8.6**	**12.6**	**4.0**
Hamels	PHI	P	**6.6**	**9.6**	**3.0**
Victorino	PHI	CF	5.4	**7.9**	**2.5**
Pence	2 TM	RF	**5.6**	6.7	1.1

NL C	CHI	CIN	MIL	STL	PIT
Start	111	207	118	658	
6/1	70	214	98	**734**	
7/1	40	223	158	**794**	2
8/1	9	192	220	**853**	52
9/1		161	282	**840**	21
End		134	336	834	
Spt.	1.01	1.05	**1.10**	**1.59**	1.00

Name	Tm	Pos	WAR	SpW	Fame
Pujols	STL	1B	**5.3**	**8.4**	**3.1**
Holliday	STL	LF	3.9	**6.2**	**2.3**
Berkman	STL	RF/1B	3.5	**5.4**	**1.9**
Carpenter	STL	P	3.5	**5.4**	**1.9**
Braun	MIL	LF	**7.8**	**8.6**	0.8
Votto	CIN	1B	**6.3**	**6.6**	0.3
McCutchen	PIT	CF	**5.7**	5.7	

NL W	AZ	COL	LA	SD	SF
Start	1	80	390	314	260
6/1	14	126	349	273	294
7/1	74	96	319	243	354

NL W	AZ	COL	LA	SD	SF
8/1	94	65	288	212	416
9/1	156	34	257	181	460
End	210	7	230	154	433
Spt.	**1.07**	1.02	1.17	1.07	1.18

Name	Tm	Pos	WAR	SpW	Fame
Kemp	LA	CF	**8.2**	9.6	1.4
Kershaw	LA	P	**6.5**	7.6	1.1
Sandoval	SF	3B	**6.1**	7.2	1.1
Lincecum	SF	P	4.2	5.0	**0.8**
Upton	AZ	RF	**6.1**	6.5	0.4
Tulowitzki	COL	SS	**6.1**	6.2	0.1

Most of the races were straightforward—or seemingly so. The Rays and Red Sox got off to terrible starts but caught up to compete with the Yankees; the Red Sox took first in June after a seven-win streak in May and a nine-win streak in June, sweeping the Yankees in both streaks. The lead never extended beyond three games, as the Yankees stayed close, and the teams were far ahead of the rest of the league, making the wild card seemingly unreachable for everyone else. The Indians built up a seven-game lead in May, but the next two months were rough, and the Tigers took the lead by default, building some distance by sweeping the Indians August 19–21. The West didn't gain Momentum consistently until May 28; the Rangers and Mariners were the best early teams, joined by the Angels after interleague play. The Rangers won 12 straight starting July 4, and the Mariners lost 17 straight starting July 6; the Angels got close occasionally, but the Rangers led the rest of the way.

The National League settled most of its races entering September. The Phillies, Marlins, and Rockies had the strongest starts. But the Rockies lost five straight series, centered around the Giants sweeping them May 6–8, and they didn't gain Momentum the rest of the year. The Giants picked up the lead but struggled through August; the Diamondbacks, who'd hung in since a 15–2 run in the second half of May, won seven straight in August to gain a 3.5-game lead, lost six straight to go down to a one-game lead, then won nine straight to enter September with a six-game lead, which they maintained to the end of the season. The Marlins had long since exited the race, two games back entering June but starting the month 1–19 to thud into last place and stay there most of the year. The Phillies were challenged briefly by the Braves, but the Phillies went 18–4 from July 19 to August 10, the Braves settled for a large wild card lead.

In the Central, the Brewers were the last team. The Reds took first on May 14 but lost six straight the next week; the Cardinals took first from them but lost seven straight June 10–17, leaving them tied the new few weeks with the Brewers. The Pirates took sole possession of first on July 18, but they lost ten straight July 29–August 7. While the Pirates were losing, the Brewers went 22–3 from July 26 to August 21, 18 of those 25 games against the Central, to build an untouchable lead.

As September dawned, the Yankees were 1.5 games behind the Red Sox and led the wild card race by 7.5 games, and the Braves led the wild card race by 8.5 games. The Tigers won 12 straight in September, but the bigger news was the collapse of the Red Sox **and** Braves. The Yankees started September 6–0 while the Red Sox started 2–4, putting the Yankees up by 2.5 games. On September 10, the Red Sox and Braves still held 4.5- and 5.5-game leads; the Braves were struggling but not amazingly so. Both teams' closest competition, the Rays and Cardinals, swept them September 9–11; when the Rays took three of four from the Sox September 15–18, a race was suddenly on. The Red Sox, falling apart internally,[4] went 2–5 over the next week and the Braves went 2–4 while the Cardinals were hot.

Going into game 162, the Red Sox and Rays were tied; so were the Braves and Cardinals. The Cardinals beat the lowly Astros 8–0; the Orioles beat the Red Sox with a walkoff single. The Braves led going into the ninth inning, but the Phillies scored a run; the Rays were down by a run going into the ninth inning but scored a run. Both games went to extra innings. The Rays won in the twelfth and the Braves lost in the thirteenth. The Rays and Cardinals were the league's wild cards, stunning everyone—possibly even themselves.

16. The Last (?) Changes, 2012–2015

Given the drama of 2011's wild card races, it was curious timing when, in March 2012, a second wild card was added to each league; the first and second wild cards were to play a one-game playoff against each other for the right to enter the Division Series.[1] So five teams in each league would gain Momentum every day of the season, complicating Spotlight but ideally giving more teams hope as well.

Seasons after the end of this book are covered, along with other commentary, on baseballspotlight.com.

2012: Kerplunk

AL E	BOS	NY	TB	BAL	TOR
Start	375	470	194		
6/1	345	494	266	72	47
7/1	336	554	320	132	35
8/1	308	616	316	170	4
9/1	277	678	363	229	
End	245	742	364	293	
Spt.	1.22	**1.55**	1.21	**1.10**	1.01

Name	Tm	Pos	WAR	SpW	Fame
Cano	NY	2B	**8.4**	**13.0**	4.6
Kuroda	NY	P	**5.5**	**8.5**	3.0
Swisher	NY	RF/1B	3.8	5.7	**1.9**
Teixeira	NY	1B	3.8	5.7	**1.9**
Price	TB	P	**6.9**	**8.3**	1.4
Zobrist	TB	RF/2B	5.7	6.9	1.2

AL C	CLE	DET	MIN	CHI
Start	108	302	70	
6/1	171	266	34	16
7/1	213	236	4	76
8/1	227	256		138

AL C	CLE	DET	MIN	CHI
9/1	196	318		200
End	164	382		264
Spt.	1.07	1.50*	1.01	1.03

Name	Tm	Pos	WAR	SpW	Fame
Verlander	DET	P	7.8	11.7	3.9
Cabrera	DET	3B	7.2	10.8	3.6
Jackson	DET	CF	5.4	8.1	2.7
Fielder	DET	1B	4.7	7.1	2.4
Sale	CHI	P	5.9	6.1	0.2
Gordon	KC	LF	6.3	6.3	

AL W	LA	TEX	OAK
Start	181	389	
6/1	145	461	
7/1	163	521	
8/1	225	583	28
9/1	224	645	84
End	192	709	148
Spt.	1.07	1.42	1.06

Name	Tm	Pos	WAR	SpW	Fame
Beltre	TEX	3B/DH	7.2	10.2	3.0
Harrison	TEX	P	6.1	8.7	2.6
Andrus	TEX	SS	4.0	5.7	1.7
Darvish	TEX	P	3.9	5.5	1.6
Trout	LA	CF/LF	10.8	11.6	0.8
Hunter	LA	RF	5.7	6.1	0.4

NL E	ATL	NY	PHI	MIA	WAS
Start	365	94	598		
6/1	437	151	577	31	72
7/1	494	199	547	28	132
8/1	550	204	516		194
9/1	612	173	485		173
End	676	141	453		320
Spt.	1.36	1.05	1.36	1.00	1.09

Name	Tm	Pos	WAR	SpW	Fame
Bourn	ATL	CF	6.1	8.3	2.2
Heyward	ATL	RF	5.8	7.9	2.1
Prado	ATL	LF/3B	5.5	7.5	2.0
Hamels	PHI	P	4.6	6.3	1.7
Wright	NY	3B	7.0	7.4	0.4
Dickey	NY	P	5.8	6.1	0.3

NL C	CIN	MIL	STL	PIT
Start	93	234	579	
6/1	111	198	651	
7/1	171	168	654	45

NL C	CIN	MIL	STL	PIT
8/1	233	137	**659**	107
9/1	295	106	**664**	136
End	359	74	**728**	104
Spt.	1.11	1.05	**1.54**	1.02

Name	Tm	Pos	WAR	SpW	Fame
Molina	STL	C	**6.9**	**10.6**	**3.7**
Lohse	STL	P	4.3	**6.6**	**2.3**
Holliday	STL	LF	4.0	**6.2**	**2.2**
Beltran	STL	RF	3.9	**6.0**	**2.1**
Votto	CIN	1B	**5.9**	6.5	0.6
Braun	MIL	LF	**6.9**	**7.2**	0.3
McCutchen	PIT	CF	**7.0**	**7.1**	0.1

NL W	AZ	COL	LA	SD	SF
Start	146	5	160	107	301
6/1	113		232	71	298
7/1	83		292	41	358
8/1	55		354	10	420
9/1	33		401		482
End	1		372		546
Spt.	1.03	1.00	1.09	1.02	**1.49***

Name	Tm	Pos	WAR	SpW	Fame
Posey	SF	C/1B	**7.3**	**10.9**	**3.6**
Cabrera	SF	LF	4.7	**7.0**	**2.3**
Pagan	SF	CF	4.0	**6.0**	**2.0**
Cain	SF	P	3.9	5.8	**1.9**
Kershaw	LA	P	**6.2**	**6.8**	0.6
Hill	AZ	2B	**5.0**	5.2	0.2
Headley	SD	3B	**6.3**	**6.4**	0.1

The funny thing about the second wild card is how little excitement it added in its debut. The NL was the simpler league, though it took awhile to settle out. The Dodgers started 9–1 and built a 7.5-game lead by May 27. They lost their lead by going 1–11 starting June 19; the Giants swept them in that freefall and took the lead. The Dodgers swept the Giants July 27–29, but the Giants swept them back August 20–22 and put the race away in mid–September.

The East and Central races wrapped up in the first week of August. In the Central, the Cardinals started fast, but the Reds went 8–1 at the end of May to take first. The Pirates kicked into gear in June; the Reds stayed mostly ahead by going 22–3 from July 6 to August 4. They lost five straight after that, but the Pirates fell apart, going 20–39 from August 1 on. When the Pirates slid downward, the Cardinals took second place, and after a brief mid–September challenge from the Dodgers, the Cardinals stayed steady for the second wild card.

The first wild card went to the Braves, who had been the Nationals' last competition in the East. All five teams gained Momentum for the division May 30 through June 1; the Nationals pulled away by winning their first six games of interleague play in June, going 5–1 against the Mets in July (as the Mets went from wild card contender to below .500), and winning eight straight in August.

The AL looked normal for awhile. The Indians were the only team in the Central with a good start; the White Sox passed them by finishing May with a 12–1 rush, including a sweep of the Indians. In the West, the Rangers started 12–2, and from April to July the Angels were the only team to come within three games of them (although they were in wild card contention after a 25–8 run starting May 22). The East had been tumultuous; the Orioles and Rays started the best, but like the NL East all five teams gained Momentum at the end of May. The Yankees started June 14–2 to take first and built a ten-game lead in mid-July, thanks to the Orioles' and Rays' June struggles.

The Tigers went 13–2 from July 4–22 to take the Central lead briefly. The A's entered July under .500 but started July 16–2 and started to gain Momentum on July 19; on that date eight teams were within three games of each other, from the Indians at 47–45 to the White Sox at 50–42. What happened from there could not have been predicted by the first half. The Red Sox were swept by the Blue Jays July 20–22, and went 16–42 after July. A week after the Blue Jays swept, they went 5–21. Meanwhile, the Indians went 8–33 starting July 19. On August 10, the Yankees and Rangers were virtually tied, while six teams were 4.5 to 6.5 games behind the Yankees. The Angels lost four of five series to start August (their win was against the Indians); they recovered, but the race moved on without them.

And it moved surprisingly. The White Sox swept the Yankees August 20–22; combined with the A's ending August 13–2, the Yankees were vulnerable. The A's swept the Red Sox, got swept by the Angels, swept the Mariners, then took the first three games of their series against the Angels, cutting the Rangers' division lead to three games; their surge meant all seven AL teams gaining Momentum were fighting for a division title. The Rays were swept by the Orioles September 11–13 (including two walkoff losses) and lost the next series to the Yankees, taking them out of the race despite a 12–2 finish to the season. That left the Orioles, Yankees, Tigers, White Sox, A's, and Rangers.

After the White Sox and Tigers played a makeup game on September 17, the White Sox lost four straight series, letting the Tigers get ahead after they swept the Royals September 24–27. The Yankees won their series against the A's September 21–23 (including two walkoff wins) as part of a seven-win streak; the Orioles tied them going into the final series thanks to sweeping the Red Sox, but the Yankees won because they also got to sweep the Red Sox.

16. The Last (?) Changes

The A's entered their last ten games four behind the Rangers for the West and one behind the Orioles for the wild card; they were slated to play four games against the Rangers, three against the Mariners, and three against the Rangers again. They split the first series; the A's swept the Mariners to enter the last series two games back. They needed to sweep the Rangers to win the division—and they did it. The Rangers were never more than one game back all year, but they had to settle for the first wild card while the Orioles took the second one and the Yankees, Tigers, and A's won their divisions.

2013: 15–15

AL E	BAL	BOS	NY	TB
Start	227	190	576	283
6/1	279	269	652	254
7/1	333	329	694	236
8/1	371	391	669	283
9/1	346	453	638	345
End	326	511	609	403
Spt.	1.12	1.50*	1.45	1.14

Name	Tm	Pos	WAR	SpW	Fame
Cano	NY	2B	7.8	11.3	3.5
Pedroia	BOS	2B	6.3	9.5	3.2
Victorino	BOS	RF	6.1	9.2	3.1
Ellsbury	BOS	CF	5.7	8.6	2.9
Machado	BAL	3B	6.7	7.5	0.8
Davis	BAL	1B	6.5	7.3	0.8

AL C	CHI	CLE	DET	KC
Start	205	127	296	
6/1	164	164	363	27
7/1	134	167	423	
8/1	103	214	485	
9/1	72	192	547	
End	43	214	605	
Spt.	1.04	1.07	1.35	

Name	Tm	Pos	WAR	SpW	Fame
Cabrera	DET	3B	7.3	9.9	2.6
Scherzer	DET	P	6.7	9.0	2.3
Sanchez	DET	P	6.3	8.5	2.2
Verlander	DET	P	4.6	6.2	1.6
Sale	CHI	P	6.9	7.2	0.3

AL W	LA	OAK	TEX
Start	149	115	550
6/1	108	137	629

	AL W	LA	OAK	TEX
7/1		78	197	689
8/1		47	259	**730**
9/1		16	321	**789**
End			379	**847**
Spt.		1.03	**1.11**	**1.15**

Name	Tm	Pos	WAR	SpW	Fame
Darvish	TEX	P	**5.8**	**8.4**	**2.6**
Beltre	TEX	3B	**5.6**	**8.1**	**2.5**
Kinsler	TEX	2B	**5.0**	7.3	**2.3**
Andrus	TEX	SS	4.3	6.2	**1.9**
Donaldson	OAK	3B	**7.7**	**8.5**	0.8
Trout	LA	CF/LF	**9.3**	**9.6**	0.3
Iwakuma	SEA	P	**7.0**	7.0	

	NL E	ATL	NY	PHI	WAS
Start		417	87	279	197
6/1		496	46	238	204
7/1		556	16	208	174
8/1		618		177	143
9/1		680		146	112
End		738		117	83
Spt.		**1.45**	1.01	1.08	1.06

Name	Tm	Pos	WAR	SpW	Fame
Simmons	ATL	SS	**7.0**	**10.2**	**3.2**
Freeman	ATL	1B	**5.7**	**8.3**	**2.6**
Heyward	ATL	RF/CF	3.7	5.4	**1.7**
Kimbrel	ATL	P	3.3	4.8	**1.5**
Lee	PHI	P	**7.3**	7.9	0.6
Wright	NY	3B	**5.9**	6.0	0.1
Fernandez	MIA	P	**6.3**	6.3	

	NL C	CIN	MIL	PIT	STL
Start		221	45	64	449
6/1		294	22	143	**528**
7/1		354		203	**588**
8/1		416		265	**650**
9/1		478		327	**712**
End		536		385	**770**
Spt.		1.22	1.01	1.12	**1.60**

Name	Tm	Pos	WAR	SpW	Fame
Carpenter	STL	2B/3B	**6.4**	**10.2**	**3.8**
Wainwright	STL	P	**6.2**	**9.9**	**3.7**
Molina	STL	C	**5.6**	**9.0**	**3.4**
Miller	STL	P	3.4	5.4	**2.0**
Votto	CIN	1B	**6.6**	8.1	1.5
McCutchen	PIT	CF	**8.1**	**9.1**	1.0
Gomez	MIL	CF	**8.5**	8.6	0.1

16. The Last (?) Changes

NL W	AZ	LA	SF	COL
Start	1	229	336	
6/1	74	188	415	74
7/1	134	158	439	95
8/1	187	166	408	64
9/1	156	228	377	33
End	127	286	348	4
Spt.	1.03	**1.40***	1.26	1.02

Name	Tm	Pos	WAR	SpW	Fame
Kershaw	LA	P	**7.8**	10.9	3.1
Ramirez	LA	SS	5.4	7.6	2.2
Puig	LA	RF	4.9	6.9	2.0
Uribe	LA	3B	4.1	5.7	1.6
Goldschmidt	AZ	1B	**7.1**	7.3	0.2
Parra	AZ	RF/CF	**6.1**	6.3	0.2
Chacin	COL	P	**5.8**	5.9	0.1

The sale of the awful Houston Astros was conditioned on the prospective owner's consent to switch leagues, putting them in the AL West, creating 15 teams in each league and necessitating an interleague game every day.[2] NL teams missed the Astros' free win supply, but the Marlins filled the role well. The best starts belonged to the Cardinals, Reds, and Pirates, all in the Central. The Rockies started 13–4 but fell into a mix with the Giants and Diamondbacks. The Braves and Nationals were the best in the East headed into May.

The Braves pulled ahead with three stretches: eight straight wins starting May 17, series wins against the Nationals and Pirates May 31–June 5, and 14 straight wins starting July 26. The Cardinals, Reds, and Pirates never led by more than four games. All of them gained Momentum for the division into the final week, settled only when the Reds lost their last five games, including a sweep by the Pirates. The Cardinals won their last six games, including a sweep of the Nationals, who had become the only challenger to the second wild card. That gave the Cardinals the division, the Pirates the first wild card, and the Reds the second wild card. The West had enough troubles that on July 2 nobody gained Momentum, although the Diamondbacks had a 1.5-game lead, about as good as they'd had all season. The Dodgers had started 30–42 but were 9–1 going into July 2; three weeks later, they were in first for good as that 9–1 turned into 42–8—an .840 clip.

The Astros moving to the AL helped the Rangers build a seven-game lead by May 15. But that was the largest they would get all year, as the A's went 18–3 after that to take first. The Rangers fell out of division and wild card contention, but they went 13–1 starting July 29 to reclaim first. Their two-game lead entering September eroded to 6.5 games back in two weeks as they went 1–5 against the A's.

342 PART II. MOMENTUM: SEASONS AND NARRATIVES

In the Central, the Indians had gained Momentum for the division most of the year but spent only a week in first, as the Tigers kept beating them at critical moments (they'd go 15–4 against them over the year). The Tigers won 12 straight starting July 26, capping it with a sweep of the Indians, to seemingly settle the division.

The East took awhile to sort out. The Red Sox recovered from 2012 to lead most of the way, challenged by the Orioles and Yankees early. The Yankees had two five-loss streaks in June; the Rays took away the Yankees' chance to recover with a 21–3 run starting June 29 that put the Rays in first. The Rays stumbled at the beginning of August, reclaimed a piece of first on August 20, and then stumbled again, giving the division to the Red Sox.

Entering September, it looked like the wild cards would be the Rays and whoever lost the West, which looked like the Rangers. When the Rangers kept losing, it put the Rays in the mix for both wild cards and let the Orioles and Indians in as well. On September 19, the Rangers and Rays were tied for the wild card lead, the Indians were a half-game back, and the Orioles were two back. The Rays swept the Orioles as a part of a 9–2 finish to the season, and the Indians finished 10–0 as part of a 21–6 September. But those stellar performances weren't enough to settle anything, as the Rangers recovered to finish the season 7–0. The Indians finished a game ahead of the Rays and Rangers, who had to play a tiebreaker game; the Rays won it to secure the second wild card.

2014: A Few Ups, Many Downs

AL E	BAL	BOS	NY	TB	TOR
Start	178	278	331	219	
6/1	202	236	397	177	26
7/1	244	206	424	147	86
8/1	306	175	411	116	118
9/1	368	144	380	85	102
End	422	117	353	58	75
Spt.	**1.43***	1.08	1.32	1.06	1.02

Name	*Tm*	*Pos*	*WAR*	*SpW*	*Fame*
Pearce	BAL	1B/LF	**5.9**	**8.4**	**2.5**
Jones	BAL	CF	4.8	**6.9**	**2.1**
Cruz	BAL	DH/LF	4.6	**6.6**	**2.0**
Hardy	BAL	SS	3.3	4.7	**1.4**
Pedroia	BOS	2B	**4.9**	5.3	0.4
Zobrist	TB	2B/LF	**4.9**	5.2	0.3
Bautista	TOR	RF	**6.1**	**6.2**	0.1

16. The Last (?) Changes

AL C	CHI	CLE	DET	KC
Start	23	117	330	
6/1		75	402	
7/1		48	**462**	17
8/1		17	**524**	
9/1			**586**	52
End			**640**	106
Spt.	1.00	1.02	**1.48**	**1.11**

Name	Tm	Pos	WAR	SpW	Fame
Scherzer	DET	P	6.0	**8.9**	**2.9**
Kinsler	DET	2B	5.7	**8.4**	**2.7**
Martinez	DET	DH/1B	5.4	**8.0**	**2.6**
Cabrera	DET	1B/DH	5.0	7.4	**2.4**
Gordon	KC	LF	**6.6**	7.3	0.7
Kluber	CLE	P	**7.4**	**7.5**	0.1
Brantley	CLE	LF/CF	**6.8**	6.9	0.1
Sale	CHI	P	**6.6**	6.6	

AL W	OAK	TEX	LA	SEA
Start	206	**461**		
6/1	287	**467**	41	
7/1	347	437	101	43
8/1	409	406	163	78
9/1	471	375	225	86
End	525	348	279	104
Spt.	**1.25**	1.36	**1.09**	1.02

Name	Tm	Pos	WAR	SpW	Fame
Beltre	TEX	3B	7.0	**9.5**	**2.5**
Donaldson	OAK	3B	7.3	**9.1**	**1.8**
Martin	TEX	CF	4.6	6.3	**1.7**
Darvish	TEX	P	3.2	4.4	**1.2**
Trout	LA	CF	**7.9**	**8.6**	0.7
Hernandez	SEA	P	**6.8**	**6.9**	0.1

NL E	ATL	PHI	WAS	MIA
Start	452	72	51	
6/1	**533**	30	90	17
7/1	**584**		141	26
8/1	**646**		203	
9/1	636		265	
End	615		319	
Spt.	1.46	1.01	**1.11**	1.00

Name	Tm	Pos	WAR	SpW	Fame
Heyward	ATL	RF	6.2	**9.1**	**2.9**
Teheran	ATL	P	3.9	5.7	**1.8**
Wood	ATL	P	3.7	5.4	**1.7**
Simmons	ATL	SS	3.3	4.8	**1.5**
Rendon	WAS	3B/2B	**6.6**	7.3	0.7
Hamels	PHI	P	**6.6**	6.7	0.1
Stanton	MIA	RF	**6.5**	6.5	

NL C	CIN	PIT	STL	MIL
Start	329	236	**471**	
6/1	287	194	495	84
7/1	260	164	537	144
8/1	268	193	596	206
9/1	237	219	**658**	268
End	210	258	**712**	256
Spt.	1.16	1.10	**1.49**	1.05

Name	Tm	Pos	WAR	SpW	Fame
Wainwright	STL	P	6.1	**9.1**	**3.0**
Peralta	STL	SS	5.7	**8.5**	**2.8**
Lynn	STL	P	3.7	5.5	**1.8**
Holliday	STL	LF	3.3	4.9	**1.6**
Cueto	CIN	P	**6.4**	7.4	1.0
McCutchen	PIT	CF	**6.3**	6.9	0.6
Lucroy	MIL	C	**6.7**	7.0	0.3

NL W	AZ	COL	LA	SF
Start	77	2	175	213
6/1	35	68	241	294
7/1	5	38	292	354
8/1		7	354	416
9/1			416	478
End			470	532
Spt.	1.01	1.01	1.18	**1.44***

Name	Tm	Pos	WAR	SpW	Fame
Posey	SF	C/1B	**5.3**	**7.6**	**2.3**
Bumgarner	SF	P	4.0	**5.8**	**1.8**
Pence	SF	RF	3.7	5.3	**1.6**
Sandoval	SF	3B	3.4	4.9	**1.5**
Kershaw	LA	P	**7.5**	**8.9**	1.4
Puig	LA	RF	**5.3**	6.3	1.0
Tulowitzki	COL	SS	**5.5**	5.6	0.1

As the alpha team in the AL, the Rangers' 14–8 record through April 23 looked perfectly normal. At that point, they and the A's, Tigers, Yankees, and Blue Jays were the league's only teams over .500. It took 36 days for the Rangers win another 14 games … and another 60 days to win the next 14. As they tanked, there weren't always five teams to gain Momentum. The Blue Jays clarified things by going 20–4 starting May 12, building a six-game lead in June. The streaky Mariners entered the wild card race in June; the Royals won ten straight, including three against the Tigers, to take first in the Central for three days before leaving the race quickly. The Yankees swept the Blue Jays June 17–19 to re-open the East to themselves and the Orioles. The Blue Jays continued to struggle; entering the All-Star break, the only teams gaining Momentum were the Orioles, Tigers, A's, Angels, and Mariners.

16. The Last (?) Changes 345

The Blue Jays started the second half 11–3 to dispatch the Yankees. A week after their streak, the Jays were out of the race for good, leaving the Orioles unchallenged the rest of the year. Early August changed the race for everyone else. The Royals had gone back under .500 but took first in the Central with a 22–5 run from July 22 to August 19. They won two series against the A's in that run, giving the Angels a chance to catch the A's; the Angels rose to the occasion by going 25–6 from August 12 to September 13, breaking away by sweeping the A's in the last four games of August. The A's continued to slide, letting the Mariners back into the wild card race. In September, the Tigers won both their series against the Royals to win the Central. Although the A's faltered down the stretch, the Mariners let them get away with it by losing five straight, giving the A's and Royals the wild cards.

The NL narrative was formed by the Brewers; they started 18–6 and carried a 5.5-game lead into May while the Cardinals hovered around .500. The Braves started almost as well, but a slump to start May created a race with the Marlins and Nationals. The Giants went 20–9 in May to demote the Dodgers and Rockies to the wild card race (which the Rockies left permanently after May). The Giants built a ten-game lead on June 8 but lost it all in a month. While they and the Dodgers were tied on July 3, the Braves and Nationals were separated by a half-game, the Brewers were up by five games, and the Nationals and Cardinals were close for the second wild card.

The Brewers started July 1–10, giving the Pirates and Reds a chance to enter the race. The Reds stayed in it for a week before getting swept by the Yankees and Brewers; the Pirates stayed in it for the next month. The Dodgers and Giants exchanged the lead in July until the Dodgers swept the Giants and the Braves starting July 25; their new lead turned out to be permanent. For the Braves, that sweep started an eight-loss streak that put them four games behind the Nationals. The Braves then won a series against the Nationals, but the Nationals won ten straight, holding a seven-game lead on August 21. Three of those ten wins were a sweep against the Pirates, causing the Pirates to leave the Central and wild card races; on August 17, the Nationals, Brewers, Cardinals, Dodgers, and Giants were the only teams gaining Momentum.

From there, the races sorted out surprisingly and with ease. The Brewers, who hadn't had a winning month since June, were still only a half-game behind the Nationals for the league's best record, but they only won one of their remaining 12 series. The Cardinals tied them for first on August 31 and seized the lead by taking three of four from the Brewers September 4–7. The Pirates challenged down the stretch and were a game behind going into the final game of the season; they settled for a wild card, as did the Giants. The Giants were outscored in September—but their only remaining competition, the Braves, scored only 59 runs in 25 September games, going 7–18 to finish below .500. In the end, every team over the Brewers' 82 wins made the postseason.

2015: Exports to the East

AL E	BAL	BOS	NY	TB	TOR
Start	284	79	238	39	51
6/1	248	52	295	75	15
7/1	260	22	355	132	45
8/1	253		417	113	26
9/1	243		479	82	88
End	210		545	49	154
Spt.	1.19	1.01	1.39	1.03	1.09*

Name	Tm	Pos	WAR	SpW	Fame
Price	2 TM	P	6.0	7.8	1.8
Teixeira	NY	1B	3.9	5.4	1.5
Betances	NY	P	3.7	5.1	1.4
Machado	BAL	3B	7.1	8.4	1.3
Donaldson	TOR	3B	8.8	9.6	0.8
Kiermaier	TB	CF	7.4	7.6	0.2

AL C	DET	KC	MIN
Start	431	71	
6/1	503	140	55
7/1	521	200	115
8/1	499	262	177
9/1	468	324	158
End	435	390	125
Spt.	1.48	1.22	1.04

Name	Tm	Pos	WAR	SpW	Fame
Kinsler	DET	2B	6.0	8.9	2.9
Cabrera	DET	1B	5.2	7.7	2.5
Martinez	DET	RF	5.0	7.4	2.4
Cain	KC	CF	7.2	8.8	1.6

AL W	LA	OAK	SEA	TEX	HOU
Start	188	354	70	235	
6/1	158	318	34	199	70
7/1	146	288	4	226	130
8/1	208	257		198	192
9/1	234	226		200	254
End	222	193		266	320
Spt.	1.08	1.24	1.01	1.14	1.10

Name	Tm	Pos	WAR	SpW	Fame
Gray	OAK	P	5.8	7.2	1.4
Reddick	OAK	RF	3.5	4.3	0.8

16. The Last (?) Changes

Name	Tm	Pos	WAR	SpW	Fame
Vogt	OAK	C/1B	3.5	4.3	0.8
Beltre	TEX	3B	**5.8**	**6.6**	0.8
Trout	LA	CF	**9.4**	**10.2**	0.8
Keuchel	HOU	P	**7.2**	**7.9**	0.7

	NL E	ATL	WAS	NY	
	Start	307	159		
	6/1	270	191	72	
	7/1	240	245	105	
	8/1	209	307	146	
	9/1	178	306	208	
	End	145	273	274	
	Spt.	1.16	1.14	**1.36***	

Name	Tm	Pos	WAR	SpW	Fame
Cespedes	2 TM	LF/CF	**6.3**	**9.0**	2.7
Granderson	NY	RF	**5.1**	**6.9**	**1.8**
deGrom	NY	P	4.7	**6.4**	**1.7**
Harvey	NY	P	4.3	5.8	**1.5**
Harper	WAS	RF	**9.9**	**11.3**	1.4
Scherzer	WAS	P	**7.0**	**8.0**	1.0

	NL C	CIN	MIL	PIT	STL	CHI
	Start	105	128	129	**356**	
	6/1	68	91	104	**421**	44
	7/1	38	61	164	**481**	92
	8/1	7	30	226	**543**	127
	9/1			288	**605**	186
	End			354	**671**	252
	Spt.	1.02	1.03	**1.11**	**1.55**	**1.50***

Name	Tm	Pos	WAR	SpW	Fame
Arrieta	CHI	P	**8.6**	**12.9**	**4.3**
Heyward	STL	RF	**6.5**	**10.1**	**3.6**
Rizzo	CHI	1B	**6.3**	**9.5**	**3.2**
Lackey	STL	P	5.6	**8.7**	**3.1**
Bryant	CHI	3B	5.9	**8.9**	3.0
Votto	CIN	1B	**7.6**	7.8	0.2

	NL W	LA	SF
	Start	235	266
	6/1	303	277
	7/1	363	334
	8/1	425	345
	9/1	487	392
	End	553	359
	Spt.	**1.41**	1.29

Name	Tm	Pos	WAR	SpW	Fame
Greinke	LA	P	9.3	13.1	3.8
Kershaw	LA	P	7.5	10.6	3.1
Posey	SF	C/1B	6.1	7.9	1.8
Crawford	SF	SS	5.6	7.2	1.6
Goldschmidt	AZ	1B	**8.8**	8.8	
Pollock	AZ	CF	**7.4**	7.4	

The most famous players in the AL East and NL East were, when the season started, Detroit Tigers. Although comparatively few teams were seriously involved in the races, the narrative twisted and turned enough to be a unique season. From May 15 forward, only seven NL teams gained Momentum. The Mets started fast and the Nationals started slow, but the teams were a half-game apart on May 15. The Dodgers had a five-game lead over the .500 Giants, while the Cardinals had a four-game lead over the Cubs.

In the next two weeks, the Giants went 13–2, including a sweep of the Dodgers, to claim first. But they lost five straight after that; the Pirates swept them in that time for their own 12–2 run that brought them into the wild card race. The Nationals took the East lead when the Mets lost seven straight June 17–24 and dropped below .500. On July 1, the Cardinals had a seven-game lead over the Pirates, who were the second-best team in the league; the Dodgers, Nationals, Cubs, and Giants were in a clump behind them.

The Giants fell to .500 by losing their first six games of July. The Pirates took three out of four from the Cardinals July 9–12, with back-to-back extra-inning walkoff wins, to threaten for the division while the Cubs took the Giants' place atop the second wild card. The Giants reversed it with a 12–1 run that also put them back in the division race. The Nationals' offense struggled in July, and on July 30, the 52–50 Mets were only three games out.

The Mets had made trades for made players, but acquiring the Tigers' Yoenis Cespedes on July 31 was a marker that the narrative favored immediately. The Mets swept the Nationals July 31–August 2; a few sweeps later, the Mets had built a permanent lead and the Nationals stopped gaining Momentum. The Cardinals and Pirates were fairly secure for playoff spots while the Dodgers, Giants, and Cubs fought for the West and second wild card. The Cubs decided the wild card by going 21–4 starting July 29. Five of those wins were against the Giants; when the Giants were swept by the Dodgers August 31–September 2 in the middle of a seven-loss streak, the playoff spots were settled. The Pirates had a shot at overtaking the Cardinals for the division, but the Cubs and Cardinals took series from them in the last three weeks of the season. The Cardinals ended with 100 wins, the Pirates ended with 98, and the Cubs ended with 97.

16. The Last (?) Changes

In the AL, the Royals surprised everyone by following up their 2014 late-season rush with a strong start. But the greatest surprise was the Astros, who led the West by seven games on May 3. The Tigers joined the Royals atop the Central, trailed by the Twins, while the rest of the league struggled. In the East, the Yankees led early, but nobody gained Momentum on May 29 and 31. The Royals swept the Twins June 8–10 to gain permanent ground over them; the Tigers were under .500 in May and June and started to leave the race. The Tigers' plight was made worse by the Blue Jays, who won ten straight at the start of June, and the Orioles, who went 18–5 starting June 4; both streaks brought the teams into the East race. The Rangers approached the Astros in June but fell away with six straight losses starting June 20.

July changed several fortunes. The Yankees were the only East team to start July well; the Rays fell below .500 on July 8 and were done for the season. The Angels surged out of .500 by going 17–3 from June 27 to July 22. They took first in that streak when the Astros lost six straight, but the Astros tied it up again and swept the Angels July 28–30.

Meanwhile, the wild card races were a mess; the Twins led the second wild card, but the sub–.500 White Sox and Rays were still only 2.5 games back. With so many teams in the mix and the Royals having built a secure division lead, the Tigers stunned the world by packing it in, trading Yoenis Cespedes to the Mets and ace David Price to the Blue Jays, who also obtained Rockies' star shortstop Troy Tulowitzki and several other players.

Stripped of stars, the Tigers crashed to last place by the end of August. The Blue Jays swept the Twins August 3–6; the Twins were .500 after that series, and while they were on the fringes of the second wild card, they ultimately fell short. After the Blue Jays swept the Twins, they swept the Yankees and the A's, winning 11 straight and taking first from the Yankees on August 12. The Yankees reclaimed first by winning a series against the Blue Jays August 14–16 and sweeping the Twins, but the Blue Jays went 13–5, took first again on August 23, and won both September series against the Yankees to win the East.

The Orioles were in the wild card mix until they went 1–12 starting August 19. That included sweeps by the Twins and Rangers; as the Astros broke even and the Angels slumped, the Rangers used the Orioles sweep to gain Momentum for the West lead. September saw the Astros, Rangers, Yankees, and Twins fighting for three playoff spots. Only the Rangers played well; when they swept the Astros September 14–17, they took first and managed to hold it narrowly. The Angels jumped from 76–74 to 83–74 from September 20–29; at the end of it, the Angels held second place and the Astros fell to third after leading the West almost the entire year. The Yankees stayed ahead enough to take the first wild card despite ending the season 1–6. The Rangers and Angels split their four-game series to end the season, while the Astros won their penultimate series against the Mariners and their ultimate series against the Diamondbacks. With only 86 wins, the Astros won the second wild card, capping a rollercoaster season for them and all of baseball.

17. Modern Playoffs: Better for Fans, Worse for Everyone Else

Craig Calcaterra is fond of commenting on every article that can be summarized as "baseball is dying, you guys."[1] Normally, this type of article is written by a sportswriter comparing baseball's national popularity to other sports, like football or old-timey baseball, to pronounce the changes baseball must make to keep competitive, like a doctor convinced he knows the panacea diet.

The easiest counterpoint to such articles normally is the record amounts of money MLB is getting, from TV deals to high attendance and everything in between. For some reason, these vital signs are ignored in the articles, picking diseased cherries for comparison instead. How does such a major disconnect occur? Writer stupidity is an easy answer, but that might not explain **all** the articles.

I think the answer lies in the difference between productivity and fame illustrated throughout this book and how each is noticed. In particular, the ways in which a sport increases excitement are, as a group, antithetical to building a sport that's easy for non-fans to understand. Bud Selig, for all his flaws, knew how to make the on-field product more exciting for everyone who cared about it—and most of those decisions made baseball harder to follow for the non-fan, like many sportswriters.

How are those two things in tension? Take any movie with a complicated, twisting plot. The things that make it creative—depth of story, abundance of characters, and so forth—also make it harder to follow. By contrast, Disney films tend to be very simple, since they're geared to a young audience. Good and evil are clearly marked and unchanging, and plots are linear. This can make fine product, but that simplicity also can get dull after awhile.

A playoff system that's only one layer deep puts only two teams into the playoffs, and letting teams at the top dominate the resources ups the odds that it will be the same two teams for awhile. 1950s baseball was the Disney movie of baseball history—the Yankees and Dodgers were the only major characters, making the narrative followable even if you weren't paying much attention. With such repetition, it was easy for Mickey Mantle, Yogi Berra, Jackie Robinson, and Duke Snider to be part of the mainstream culture. Baseball was sending the same few players out for attention every year.

The amateur draft, divisions, and wild cards are all efforts to get more teams regularly involved in the season narrative. This is important for the health of baseball, since enough teams have to be alive for the sport to survive. But those structures add characters to the plot through playoff upsets, a more regularly rotating cast in the World Series, and so forth. Deeper and more inherently interesting, yes. More complicated, also yes.

And part of that complication is that even the best team in each league by win-loss record has only a one-in-four chance in the abstract of making the World Series. The 2007 Rockies weren't anyone's idea of a marquee team; neither were the 2014 Royals. They were exciting, but mostly to the intrepid baseball fan. The non-fan wonders why it's them in the playoffs instead of the Cardinals or Tigers or Yankees or somebody. Who are these new characters? Why can't it just be simple like it used to be?

From my statistics' perspective, the extra playoffs do a couple things. First, they up the odds that the alpha team won't make it to the World Series. This makes great theater but to a non-fan looks like the deserving team lost. Second, they bring more non-famous teams into October. Not every matchup can be premier, and even as the chances increase for an upset that catapults a team into a brighter Spotlight, there are also going to be some teams that get to the World Series beating none of the teams the public knows anything about.

And third, it makes team and player reputations more tied to playoff success, as it's often the only time some players will get that sort of exposure. That inconsistency of team narrative dissipates fame across several teams, making it generally harder for any one player to collect loads of it. The Yankees, Braves, and Cardinals of my lifetime have offered that opportunity at different times, but the system is now designed against them doing that.

So baseball's moves to produce more for its fans have made it produce less for its non-fans. This is usually the correct move. Baseball doesn't need to make itself simple to follow; it needs to sustain excitement for a majority of the year, and based on attendance and revenue figures it's doing that just fine. But the non-fan doesn't understand this fundamental tension, how the stars of the 1950s often shine brighter than today's stars because baseball was more set up to push a couple teams at the other teams' expense. It's like calling someone grumpy for being introverted—just because they didn't greet **you** with what you consider enough enthusiasm doesn't mean they were unkind. You were just expecting the wrong thing.

So the next time you see a football writer or a cranky baseball writer moan about the death of baseball, remember that they're asking for a Disney movie to follow and understand without any effort. And then be thankful that baseball is presently set up to give your favorite team a chance of doing something you'll remember. As the history of baseball narrative shows, you can't serve both ends, and I'd much rather my favorite game tweaked its structure toward me than toward the cranky guy who doesn't even like the game.

Chapter Notes

Acknowledgments

1. Calcaterra, Craig, "Who Is the Next Face of Baseball?" http://mlb.nbcsports.com/2014/07/21/who-is-the-next-face-of-baseball. NBC Sports, 21 July 2014. Web. 22 December 2015. Calcaterra, Craig, "Derek Jeter: The Last Face of Baseball." http://mlb.nbcsports.com/2014/08/05/derek-jeter-the-last-face-of-baseball. NBC Sports, 5 August 2014. Web. 22 December 2015.
2. Isleib, Brandon, "Sir Bert the Obscure." http://www.hardballtimes.com/sir-bert-the-obscure. *Hardball Times*, 20 March 2008. Web. 22 December 2015.

Introduction

1. Blyleven, Bert. "Re: Thank you for your support." Message to Brandon Isleib. 23 March 2008. Email.
2. "Scott Sanderson (baseball)." https://en.wikipedia.org/wiki/Scott_Sanderson_(baseball). Wikipedia, n.d. Web. 22 December 2015.

Chapter 1

1. All six ESPN experts previewing the 2014 wild card game picked the A's to win. Granted, the A's had a vastly better run differential than the Royals, but the Royals had the better record, the better second half, and a 5–2 record against the A's during the season. "2014 ALWC: Oakland Athletics vs. Kansas City Royals." http://espn.go.com/mlb/playoffs/2014/matchup/_/teams/oak-kan. ESPN, n.d. Web. 23 December 2015.

Chapter 3

1. "Baseball-Reference.com WAR Explained." http://www.baseball-reference.com/about/war_explained.shtml. Baseball-reference.com, n.d. Web. 24 January 2016.
2. Although the Mets won 100 games, the Mets-Orioles World Series was billed as "a classic confrontation between logic and mysticism or perhaps logic and reality." "[T]he Orioles... are accepted on all sides as one of the more powerful teams of all baseball history." Koppett, Leonard, "Orioles Rated 'Logical' Favorites Over Mets as World Series Opens Today." *New York Times*, 11 October 1969: 47. *ProQuest Historical Newspapers: The New York Times*. Web. 23 December 2015.
3. "Oddsmakers have rated the Mets second choice behind the St. Louis Cardinals in the National League East and even with the Chicago Cubs." Momentum ranking for those teams entering 1970 was Cubs-Cardinals-Mets. The article, a UPI wire story repeated in several papers, also summarizes the Mets' 1969 as featuring "zany heroics" that would be difficult to repeat. Griffin, John G., "Another Miracle in '70? Hard to Say." *Logan Herald Journal* 20 March 1970: 7. *NewspaperARCHIVE*. Web. 23 December 2015.
4. Of 88 ESPN experts polled before the 2015 season on who would win the Central, 43 chose

the 0-point Indians (dark horses are often misevaluated), 25 chose the Tigers, 17 chose the White Sox, three chose the Royals, and none chose the Twins. Ranking the teams by Momentum (and 0-point teams by fewest-to-most consecutive seasons ending with 0 points), the order entering 2015 was Tigers-Royals-Indians-White Sox-Twins. The final real-life standings were Royals-Twins-Indians-White Sox-Tigers. "ESPN Forecast: Expert Team Predictions for the 2015 MLB season." http://espn.go.com/mlb/preview15/story/_/id/12588378/expert-team-predictions-2015-mlb-season. ESPN, 4 April 2015. Web. 23 December 2015.

5. For a fairly responsible version of the lament, see Mahler, Jonathan and Bill Carter, "Series Is On, and Everybody's Watching ... Football." http://www.nytimes.com/2014/10/24/sports/baseball/world-series-2014-baseball-is-no-longer-center-of-attention-in-new-landscape.html?_r=1. *New York Times*, 23 October 2014. Web. 23 December 2015.

Chapter 4

1. Jaffe, Jay, "Jaffe WAR Score system (JAWS)." http://www.baseball-reference.com/about/jaws.shtml. Baseball-reference.com, n.d. Web. 24 December 2015.

2. This was acknowledged during Sandberg's prime. "A very unselfish, unassuming player, Ryne Sandberg blossomed into The Franchise on national television in 1984." This is the first sentence of a Sandberg profile before the 1985 season, on page 406 of Matthews, Denny, et al. *The Scouting Report: 1985* (New York: Harper & Row, 1985). Print.

Chapter 5

1. Paul Simon chose DiMaggio because he was "really famous" and fit the syllables, unlike Mickey Mantle. Johnson, Richard, "Paul Simon Clears Up Mystery behind Joe DiMaggio Lyric." http://pagesix.com/2014/03/07/paul-simon-clears-mystery-behind-joe-dimaggio-lyric/. Page Six, 7 March 2014. Web. 25 December 2015.

2. "Hall of Fame Announces Change to BBWAA Voting Electorate." http://baseballhall.org/news/hall-of-fame-announces-change-to-bbwaa-voting-electorate. National Baseball Hall of Fame, 28 July 2015. Web. 25 December 2015.

3. Fred Lynn ended with 17.8 Fame, more than Rice or Evans, but his Hall of Fame case never got off the ground. It might be that my system overrates the reputation of the mid-'80s Angels. It might also be that switching teams should be measured as a penalty to Fame for disrupting the narrative, bringing Lynn, who played on several teams at the end of his career, behind a one-team player like Rice.

4. "Dishonest Base-Ball Players." *New York Times*, 3 November 1877: 2. ProQuest Historical Newspapers. Web. 26 December 2015. For Devlin's side of the story, see "Devlin's Confessions." *St. Louis Globe-Democrat*, 13 November 1877: 3. *19th Century U.S. Newspapers*. Web. 26 December 2015.

5. A 1915 article exclusively about John's career asserted he had "a winning record which was as great as any made by a Chicago pitcher and as great as any ever made for any club," noting further that his and King Kelly's sale to Boston was of great importance in its day. "New Style Pitching Made Clarkson." *New York Times*, 7 March 1915: S3. *ProQuest Historical Newspapers: The New York Times.* Web. 25 December 2015. A 1916 article discussing the all-time greats mentioned Clarkson prominently, again linked to Kelly. "Baseball, Too, Has Its Hall of Fame." *New York Times*, 6 February 1916: S3. *ProQuest Historical Newspapers: The New York Times.* Web. 25 December 2015.

6. Regarding the history of Dahlen's case, see Womack, Graham, "Why Has Bill Dahlen's Hall of Fame Induction Taken So Long?" http://www.sportingnews.com/mlb-news/4658077-bill-dahlen-hall-of-fame-chances-stats-chicago-colts-orphans-brooklyn. *Sporting News*, 13 October 2015. Web. 24 January 2016.

7. Stein, Fred. "Frankie Frisch." http://sabr.org/bioproj/person/0bbf3136. Society for American Baseball Research, n.d. Web. 24 January 2016.

8. "Rogers Hornsby, the Hall of Fame slugger, who also had been a contemporary of Ruth, said in the passion of the day: 'Maris has no right to break Ruth's record.'... [M]aris was considered an upstart in the House That Ruth built, and the house that Mantle dominated." Durso, Joseph,

"Roger Maris Is Dead at 51, Set Record Home Runs." *New York Times*, 15 December 1985: 52. *ProQuest Historical Newspapers: The New York Times*. Web. 26 December 2015.

9. "A Money Store official said the lender decided to change spokesmen because the new generation of customers that it wants to court will identify more readily with Palmer." "Palmer now pitching for Rizzuto." *The Day* (New London, CT), 3 March 1993: B7. *NewspaperARCHIVE*. Web. 26 December 2015.

10. If so, it would be in contrast to long balls. Gardner, Dakota, "Greg Maddux and Tom Glavine Reveal 'Chicks Dig the Long Ball' Was Their Idea." http://m.mlb.com/cutfour/2014/08/07/88415190/video-greg-maddux-and-tom-glavine-reveal-chicks-dig-the-long-ball-was-their-idea. MLB, 7 August 2014. Web. 26 December 2015.

11. "Chipper Jones' Retirement Gifts." http://www.si.com/mlb/photos/2012/10/01chipper-jones-retirement-gifts. Sports Illustrated, 1 October 2012. Web. 26 December 2015.

12. Lapointe, Joe, "Pettitte Apologizes to Yankees and His Fans." http://www.nytimes.com/2008/02/19/sports/baseball/19yankees.html. *New York Times*, 19 February 2008. Web. 26 December 2015.

Chapter 6

1. Gammons, Peter, "Gordon Beckham and His Wedding Invitation List." http://www.gammonsdaily.com/gordon-beckham-and-his-wedding-invitation-list. *Gammons Daily*, 9 September 2013. Web. 26 December 2015.

Chapter 7

1. For a summary of Asa's career, particularly his fame coming into the National Association, see McKenna, Brian, "Asa Brainard." http://sabr.org/bioproj/person/a151ac94. Society for Baseball Research: n.d. Web. 11 January 2016.

2. The rest of the season had to be played elsewhere. On October 30, Chicago and Philadelphia played in Brooklyn. "The Athletics of Philadelphia Defeated the White Stockings of Chicago." *Lowell Daily Citizen and News*, 31 October 1871: n.p. *19th Century U.S. Newspapers*. Web. 26 December 2015.

3. For a good discussion of the problems, see "Base Ball in 1876." *Boston Daily Advertiser*, 6 November 1875, n.p. *19th Century U.S. Newspapers*. Web. 26 December 2015. The particulars of the agreement to form the National League were received enthusiastically. "The Diamond Squared." *St. Louis Globe-Democrat*, 5 February 1876: 4. *19th Century U.S. Newspapers*. Web. 26 December 2015.

4. "Sporting." *The Cleveland Herald*, 14 November 1881: 3. *19th Century U.S. Newspapers*. Web. 26 December 2015.

5. St. Louis owner Chris Von der Ahe expressed doubt about the capabilities of the new teams but noted that "They want to come in, and the best thing we can do is to receive them. We will have to admit them to sustain ourselves." Given the threat of the Union Association, it would seem that the necessity to which Von der Ahe referred would be financial. "Sporting." *St. Louis Globe-Democrat*, 27 November 1883: 8. *19th Century U.S. Newspapers*. Web. 26 December 2015.

6. The damage had been done the previous year, as the most important players were transferred in mid-September but didn't play for Detroit until 1886. Some decisions appear to have been made on the fly; originally it was thought they might play for Detroit in 1885, but at the end of the season there was talk that the league might force them back to Buffalo or that the key players would be free agents instead. "No ... There." *Milwaukee Sentinel*, 19 September 1885, n.p. *19th Century U.S. Newspapers*. Web. 29 December 2015. "Sporting." *St. Louis Globe-Democrat*, 25 October 1885: 9. *19th Century U.S. Newspapers*. Web. 29 December 2015. "Last of the List." *Rocky Mountain News* (Denver, CO), 26 October 1885: 2. *19th Century U.S. Newspapers*. Web. 29 December 2015.

7. "Base Ball Matters." *Atchison Daily Champion*, 15 November 1887: n.p. *19th Century U.S. Newspapers*. Web. 29 December 2015.

8. After several players prized players were sold around the league, the rest of the team was sold to Cleveland. "Base-Ball." *Los Angeles Times*, 15 October 1888: 4. *19th Century U.S. Newspapers*. Web. 29 December 2015.

9. It escalated very quickly in the offseason as a response to in-season grievances. "John M. Ward Talks." *Daily Inter Ocean*, 22 October 1889: 2. *19th Century U.S. Newspapers*. Web. 29 December 2015. "War to the Knife." *The North American* (Philadelphia, PA), 24 October 1889: n.p. *19th Century U.S. Newspapers*. Web. 29 December 2015. "Plans of the Brotherhood." *Daily Inter Ocean* (Chicago, IL), 31 October 1889: 2. *19th Century U.S. Newspapers*. Web. 29 December 2015. "Ball Men Meet." *The Milwaukee Sentinel*, 14 November 1889: 2. *19th Century U.S. Newspapers*. Web. 29 December 2015.

10. "One of the Philadelphia Base-Ball Clubs Is Said to Be Bankrupt." *Daily Evening Bulletin* (San Francisco, CA), 12 September 1890: 4. *19th Century U.S. Newspapers*. Web. 29 December 2015. A few months earlier, the club had been sued by a carpenter for $103, an implication that "[t]heir finances must be pretty low." "Called to Time." *Milwaukee Sentinel*, 30 June 1890: 8. *19th Century U.S. Newspapers*. Web. 29 December 2015.

11. "The World's Championship Series." *News and Observer* (Raleigh, NC), 29 October 1890: n.p. *19th Century U.S. Newspapers*. Web. 29 December 2015.

12. For the progression of rumors and happenings, read these in order:
"For an Eight Club Circuit." *Milwaukee Journal*, 23 October 1891: n.p. *19th Century U.S. Newspapers*. Web. 29 December 2015.
"Chicago is Admitted." *Milwaukee Sentinel*, 23 October 1891: 2. *19th Century U.S. Newspapers*. Web. 29 December 2015.
"New Plan of the League." *Milwaukee Journal*, 5 November 1891: 7. *19th Century U.S. Newspapers*. Web. 29 December 2015.
"In the League's Maw." *Milwaukee Sentinel*, 16 December 1891: 2. *19th Century U.S. Newspapers*. Web. 29 December 2015.
"Baseball Fight Is Ended." *Milwaukee Journal*, 18 December 1891: 2. *19th Century U.S. Newspapers*. Web. 29 December 2015.

13. This was done "in consequence of the increased number of clubs in the new organization." "Ready for Play." *Daily Inter Ocean* (Chicago, IL), 4 March 1892: 6. *19th Century U.S. Newspapers*. Web. 13 January 2016.

14. "The New Base-Ball Rules." *North American* (Philadelphia, PA), 16 March 1893: 2. *19th Century U.S. Newspapers*. Web. 30 December 2015. There was also a proposal to increase the distance between bases from 90 to 93 feet. "Base-Ball Rules." *The Daily Inter Ocean* (Chicago, IL), 14 February 1893: n.p. *19th Century U.S. Newspapers*. Web. 30 December 2015.

15. "Colonels Lose Their Best Men." *North American* (Philadelphia, PA), 9 December 1899: 11. *19th Century U.S. Newspapers*. Web. 30 December 2015.

16. "A Ten-Club Circuit." *Milwaukee Sentinel*, 14 December 1899: 7. *19th Century U.S. Newspapers*. Web. 30 December 2015.

17. "Events of a Day in the Field of Sport." *New York Times*, 9 March 1900: 9. *ProQuest Historical Newspapers: The New York Times*. Web. 30 December 2015.

Chapter 8

1. "Big Leaguers Amazed." *Milwaukee Sentinel*, 24 November 1899: 7. *19th Century U.S. Newspapers*. Web. 31 December 2015.

2. "American League Organized." *New York Times*, 30 January 1901: 7. *ProQuest Historical Newspapers: The New York Times*. Web. 31 December 2015.

3. "American League Team in St. Louis." *New York Times*, 10 October 1901: 7. *ProQuest Historical Newspapers: The New York Times*. Web. 31 December 2015.

4. "Three Struck Out." *Boston Daily Globe*, 29 April 1902: 5. *NewspaperARCHIVE*. Web. 31 December 2015.

5. "Lajoie and Bernhard." *Boston Daily Globe*, 31 May 1902: 50. *NewspaperARCHIVE*. Web. 31 December 2015. Cleveland made two visits to Philadelphia over the rest of the season; in the latter series, the enjoined players visited Lajoie's hometown and played for the Woonsocket team. "The Big Three." *Boston Daily Globe*, 24 August 1902: 73. *NewspaperARCHIVE*. Web. 31 December 2015.

6. "Sheckard Jumps Again." *Boston Daily Globe*, 29 April 1902: 5. *NewspaperARCHIVE*. Web. 31 December 2015.

7. "McGraw Accuses Ban Johnson." *New York Times*, 3 July 1902: 6. *ProQuest Historical Newspapers: The New York Times.* Web. 31 December 2015.
8. "M'Graw at Polo Grounds." *New York Times*, 18 July 1902: 6. *ProQuest Historical Newspapers: The New York Times.* Web. 31 December 2015.
9. The text of the agreement is reprinted at "1903 AL-NL Peace Agreement." http://bizofbaseball.com/index.php?option=com_content&view=article&id=54:1903-al-nl-peace-agreement&catid=37:1900-1960&Itemid=47. The Biz of Baseball, 29 November 1999. Web. 1 January 2016.
10. "American League Teams." *New York Times*, 26 October 1902: 9. *NewspaperARCHIVE.* Web. 31 December 2015.
11. "Easy Victory for Giants." *New York Times*, 18 September 1906: 7. *NewspaperARCHIVE.* Web. 1 January 2016. See also "Mike Donlin Disabled, Transformed to a Fan." *Des Moines Daily News*, 21 July 1906: 6. *NewspaperARCHIVE.* Web. 1 January 2016.
12. "Donlin Signs a $5,000 Contract." *New York Times*, 27 November 1907: 8. *ProQuest Historical Newspapers: The New York Times.* Web. 1 January 2016. Nine days earlier with his theater act, he was reported to be "not much interested in baseball right now." "Great Baseball Player in City." *Connersville Evening News*, 18 November 1907: 1. *NewspaperARCHIVE.* Web. 1 January 2016.
13. At least one paper called it a "nervous prostration." "Evers to Return on Sunday to Old Job." *Hammond Lake County Times*, 1 July 1911: 3. *NewspaperARCHIVE.* Web. 1 January 2016.
14. "Waivers Are Asked on Mordecai Brown." *Reno Evening Gazette*, 30 September 1912: 9. *NewspaperARCHIVE.* Web. 1 January 2016. Brown was listed with some retirees in November. "Father Time Was Very Busy During Past Year." *East Liverpool Evening Review*, 30 November 1912: 13. *NewspaperARCHIVE.* Web. 1 January 2016. And at least one doctor Brown consulted told him never to play again. "Star Is Barred from Game." *Silver Lake Record*, 12 December 1912: 10. *Newspaper ARCHIVE.* Web. 1 January 2016.
15. It started a couple weeks after the World Series and was leaked by Tigers' manager Hughie Jennings, much to Mack's consternation. "Bender, Plank, and Coombs to Go." *New York Times*, 1 November 1914: S1. *ProQuest Historical Newspapers: The New York Times.* Web. 1 January 2016.
16. "Koney Jumps to Feds to Escape Jinx on Pirates." *Muskogee Times Democrat*, 9 December 1914: 9. *NewspaperARCHIVE.* Web. 1 January 2016.
17. For an excellent and well-sourced discussion of the financial conditions of the Federal League, see Ruzzo, Bob, "Fate and the Federal League: Were the Federals Incompetent, Outmaneuvered, or Just Unlucky?" http://sabr.org/research/fate-and-federal-league-were-federals-incompetent-outmaneuvered-or-just-unlucky. Society for American Baseball Research: Fall 2013. Web. 1 January 2016.
18. "Tris Speaker Sold to Cleveland Club." *New York Times*, 9 April 1916: S1. *ProQuest Historical Newspapers: The New York Times.* Web. 1 January 2016.

Chapter 9

1. To get the sense of the matter as it developed over time, see the following four articles: "Baseball May Stop If New Order Stands." *New York Times*, 24 May 1918: 14. *ProQuest Historical Newspapers: The New York Times.* Web. 3 January 2016.
"Baseball Teams Must Go to Work." *New York Times*, 20 July 1918: 7. *ProQuest Historical Newspapers: The New York Times.* Web. 3 January 2016.
"Postpone Baseball Decision." *New York Times*, 24 July 1918: 12. *ProQuest Historical Newspapers: The New York Times.* Web. 3 January 2016.
"Crowder Sanctions Series." *New York Times*, 29 August 1918: 8. *ProQuest Historical Newspapers: The New York Times.* Web. 3 January 2016.
2. Chastain, Bill, "Mixup Forces Rays to Bat Sonnanstine." http://m.mlb.com/news/article/4783714. MLB, 17 May 2009. Web. 3 January 2016.
3. "Want Baseball Season to Open on May 1." *New York Times*, 13 December 1918: 12. *ProQuest Historical Newspapers: The New York Times.* Web. 3 January 2016.
4. A "temporary indisposition" turned into a season-long problem. "Red Sox Start on Wednesday." *Boston Sunday Post*, 20 April 1919: 15. *NewspaperARCHIVE.* Web. 3 January 2016. "Joe Bush Through for Rest of Year." *New Castle News*, 15 August 1919: 30. *NewspaperARCHIVE.* Web. 3 January 2016.

5. In "a series of articles dealing with big league gossip," Christy Mathewson wrote a week after the World Series that "if ball players on a world's series team found fellows trying to toss one off they would kill the guilty ones." Mathewson, Christy, "Baseball Is Not Crooked." *New York Times*, 16 October 1919: 26. *ProQuest Historical Newspapers: The New York Times.* Web. 3 January 2016. Some Reds stated after the indictment that they had no suspicion of thrown games. "Mystery to the Reds." *New York Times*, 1 October 1920: 2. *ProQuest Historical Newspapers: The New York Times.* Web. 3 January 2016.

6. At the time, Ruth was sometimes called the "Colossus of Swat" rather than the Sultan moniker more popularly known today. "Babe Ruth Accepts Terms of Yankees." *New York Times*, 7 January 1920: 22. *ProQuest Historical Newspapers: The New York Times.* Web. 3 January 2016.

7. As a bonus, the Yankees were nicknamed for manager Miller Huggins as the "Hugmen" in the recap. "Babe Sets Record, Then Adds Another." *New York Times*, 20 July 1920: 14. *ProQuest Historical Newspapers: The New York Times.* Web. 3 January 2016.

8. "Severe Blow to Baseball." *Boston Post*, 18 August 1920: 1. *NewspaperARCHIVE.* Web. 3 January 2016.

9. "Eight White Sox Players Are Indicted on Charge of Fixing 1919 World Series." *New York Times*, 29 September 1920: 1. *ProQuest Historical Newspapers: The New York Times.* Web. 3 January 2016.

10. When Roush finally signed a contract, possible tension with Groh was cited as a reason for the holdout. "Rumored Roush Would Not Play with Groh on Cincy Team." *Hamilton Evening Journal*, 27 April 1921: 8. *NewspaperARCHIVE.* Web. 3 January 2016.

11. Lynch, Mike, "Phil Douglas." http://sabr.org/bioproj/person/3db5329e. Society for American Baseball Research: n.d. Web. 3 January 2016.

12. "Ruth Is Suspended; Fined Series Money." *New York Times*, 6 December 1921: 25. *ProQuest Historical Newspapers: The New York Times.* Web. 3 January 2016.

13. Isleib, Brandon, "Hughie Jennings and Hack Wilson." http://www.hardballtimes.com/hughie-jennings-and-hack-wilson. *Hardball Times*, 28 January 2010. Web. 3 January 2016.

14. Isleib, Brandon, "Portrait of a Reliever: Firpo Marberry, 1925." http://www.hardballtimes.com/portrait-of-a-reliever-firpo-marberry-1925. *Hardball Times*, 24 September 2009. Web. 3 January 2016.

15. The Associated Press write-up noted all the offensive records Ruth set in that World Series and gave credit to Pete Alexander for his relief work in the seventh game, barely mentioning Ruth's blunder at all. To the extent it was given any description, it was described as "a hit-and-run play [that] went wrong." Vidmer, Richards, "Valiant Alexander Turns Back Threats." *New York Times*, 11 October 1926: 24. *ProQuest Historical Newspapers: The New York Times.* Web. 3 January 2016. Wilbert Robinson's write-up of the game mentions several "critical errors" on the Yankees' part, but doesn't mention Ruth's running. Robinson, Wilbert, "Thevenow Was Key,' Asserts Robinson." 11 October 1926: 25. *ProQuest Historical Newspapers: The New York Times.* Web. 3 January 2016. And those who have particularly looked for contemporary evidence blaming Ruth haven't found any. Costa, Father Gabe, "By the Numbers: Judging Babe Ruth's Attempted Steal in the 1926 World Series." http://newyork.cbslocal.com/2011/07/29/by-the-numbers-judging-babe-ruth%E2%80%99s-attempted-steal-of-second-base-in-the-1926-world-series. CBS, 29 July 2011. Web. 3 January 2016.

16. It was immediately hailed as "the biggest deal of modern baseball history." Harrison, James R., "Giants Get Hornsby; Trade Big Surprise." *New York Times*, 21 December 1926: 1. *ProQuest Historical Newspapers: The New York Times.* Web. 3 January 2016.

17. Cardinals owner Sam Breadon had cared too much about the World Series loss in 1928 and sent McKechnie to manage the Rochester minor league team, promoting Southworth. The July change swapped them again. "M'Kechnie Back as Card Pilot; Southworth Out" and "Gets St. Louis Job Back." *Berkeley Daily Gazette*, 23 July 1929: 11. *NewspaperARCHIVE.* Web. 4 January 2016. For a good history of Cardinals owner-manager relations in this period, see Corbett, Warren, "Bill McKechnie." http://sabr.org/bioproj/person/8bb2437d. Society for American Baseball Research: n.d. Web. 4 January 2016.

18. "Donie Bush Resigns as Manager of Pirate Club; Jewel Ens to Fill Post." *Titusville Herald*, 29 August 1929: 10. *NewspaperARCHIVE.* Web. 4 January 2016.

19. "Hornsby Dropped; Grimm Cubs' Pilot." *New York Times*, 3 August 1932: 18. *ProQuest Historical Newspapers: The New York Times.* Web. 4 January 2016.

20. "[Mack] declined to say whether the deal presaged a break-up of the Athletics machine...."

Baseball observers figured, however, that even with depression prices, at least $150,000 must have changed hands." Simmons had been rumored to want out of Philadelphia as it was, wanting to be closer to home in the Midwest. "Simmons and Haas Sold to White Sox" and "Philadelphia Fans Surprised." *New York Times*, 29 September 1932: 26. *ProQuest Historical Newspapers: The New York Times*. Web. 4 January 2016.

21. "Breadon said the change was made because 'we want to win the pennant.'" The Cardinals were 46–45 and eight games back at the time. *Laredo Times*, 25 July 1933: 7. *NewspaperARCHIVE*. Web. 5 January 2016.

22. Hurst hit .199/.239/.291 for the Cubs—labeled a "decided batting slump" in August by an understating columnist. McCormick, Henry, "No Foolin' Now." *Madison Wisconsin State Journal* (Madison, WI), 2 August 1934: 11. *NewspaperARCHIVE*. Web. 5 January 2016. The Cubs sent first base prospect Dolph Camilli to the Phillies to obtain Hurst; Giants' manager Bill Terry said in August that he would have offered a lot more for Camilli if he'd had the opportunity. "Cubs Outwitted in Player Swap." *Lincoln Star*, 6 August 1934: 6. *NewspaperARCHIVE*. Web. 5 January 2016.

23. Cochrane was sold on the same day George Earnshaw went to the White Sox and Lefty Grove, Max Bishop, and Rube Walberg went to the Red Sox. "Mack Sells Grove and 4 Other Stars." *New York Times*, 13 December 1933: 32. *ProQuest Historical Newspapers: The New York Times*. Web. 5 January 2016.

Chapter 10

1. "Ruth, Seeking Managerial Career, Insists Playing Career Is Over." *New York Times*, 9 October 1934: 23. *ProQuest Historical Newspapers: The New York Times*. Web. 6 January 2016.

2. "No Place Open in Major Leagues for Ruth, Poll of Clubs Reveals." *New York Times*, 4 June 1935: 27. *ProQuest Historical Newspapers: The New York Times*. Web. 6 January 2016.

3. It was due to bone chips in his elbow; the ensuing surgery was the beginning of the end. For a good summary and analysis of the surgery's impacts, see Corbett, Warren, "Hubbell's Elbow: Don't Blame the Screwball." http://sabr.org/research/hubbell-s-elbow-don-t-blame-screwball. Society for American Baseball Research: Fall 2011. Web. 6 January 2016.

4. Dean was injured early in the year, then came back with severely diminished stuff, because the Cubs' owner ordered him back to pitch and was antsy to fire manager Charlie Grimm, which he did. "'Dizzy' Dean Is Back at Work Again" and Snider, Steve, "Dean Uses Foxy, Slow Stuff Instead of Fireball." *Wisconsin State Journal* (Madison, WI), 18 July 1938: 17. *NewspaperARCHIVE*. Web. 6 January 2016.

5. "The deal with the Giants was the Cubs' first move to rebuild for their new manager, Gabby Hartnett." McGowen, Roscoe, "Giants Get Jurges, O'Dea and Demaree in Deal with Cubs." *New York Times*, 7 December 1938: 29. *ProQuest Historical Newspapers: The New York Times*. Web. 6 January 2016.

6. "Roger Peckinpaugh, Tribal manager, said he knew Trosky had been bothered by headaches for several seasons but that he was surprised they were so serious and frequent." "Trosky Suffers from Severe Headaches." *Ogden Standard Examiner*, 13 July 1941. *NewspaperARCHIVE*. Web. 7 January 2016.

7. MacPhail became a lieutenant colonel and Rickey's contract with the Cardinals was expiring at the end of the year. Rickey's son was already in the Dodgers' front office, so it was a logical enough transition. "Rickey Conference Permitted Dodgers." *New York Times*, 4 October 1942: S9. *ProQuest Historical Newspapers: The New York Times*. Web. 7 January 2016. "Rickey said it was a pleasure to be 'with a rich club' in Brooklyn, even as he was the 'father of chain-store baseball.'" McGowen, Roscoe, "Rickey Named Dodger President and General Manager for Five Years." *New York Times*, 30 October 1942: 24. *ProQuest Historical Newspapers: The New York Times*. Web. 7 January 2016.

8. Cooper and his brother Walker were upset because, according to them, Cardinals owner Sam Breadon pledged they would be the highest-paid players of the Cardinals, then raised MVP Marty Marion's salary above theirs. At the time, the trade gave pundits reason to believe in Boston, while the Cardinals were considered to have waved a white flag. Cuddy, Jack. "Mort Cooper Due to Report to Boston Braves Tomorrow." and Hand, Jack, "Braves Counted Into Race Now That Cooper's Signed." *Lowell Sun*, 24 May 1945: 47. *NewspaperARCHIVE*. Web. 9 January 2016.

9. Schreiber had been the Yankees' batting practice pitcher for about nine years; it was said that he had "served up more home-run balls than any pitcher in the history of baseball" in that capacity. Initially, even he couldn't remember when how far back his last major league games had been. Daley, Arthur, "The Kid Makes Good." *New York Times*, 6 September 1945: 19. *ProQuest Historical Newspapers: The New York Times*. Web. 9 January 2016.

10. The preseason oddsmakers put the Yankees as the favorites at 7–5 and the Tigers and Red Sox next behind them at 2–1. So the Red Sox were expected, but not completely so—and certainly not expected to dominate as they did. "Yankees and Cards Pennant Favorites." *New York Times*, 3 March 1946: S1. *ProQuest Historical Newspapers: The New York Times*. Web. 9 January 2016.

11. The Mexican League "had a briefcase full of money" to offer. Lanier got his first year of salary and his signing bonus before he even went down to Mexico, making the offer very attractive. "Interview with Max Lanier, June 26, 1987." http://www.nunncenter.org/OHMS-Viewer/viewer.php?cachefile=1987oh092_chan104_lanier_ohm.xml. Baseball Commissioner Oral History Project, n.d. Web. 9 January 2016.

12. The MVP voting was considered a "wide open race." "The writers' chief difficulty with Brooklyn was in settling on any one or two of an imposing list of 'valuables.'" Jackie Robinson was fifth in the voting, right behind Edwards; as the Associated Press noted dryly, Robinson was "the first Negro ever to appear in any such vote." "Elliott of Braves Most Valuable in National League Last Season." *New York Times*, 21 November 1947: 38. *ProQuest Historical Newspapers: The New York Times*. Web. 9 January 2016.

13. If that sounds confusing, it is. And it was immediately controversial, as Durocher was "a stormy petrel all through his diamond career." "Fans Here Are Stunned by Sudden Shift; Reaction on Durocher Varied and Violent." *New York Times*, 17 July 1948: 9. *ProQuest Historical Newspapers: The New York Times*. Web. 9 January 2016.

14. To get a fuller picture of the Robinson-Walker relationship, see Spatz, Lyle, "Dixie Walker." http://sabr.org/bioproj/person/74909ba3. Society for American Baseball Research: n.d. Web. 9 January 2016.

15. Heath was a controversial figure in his day, to say the least, as shown by the mixed reactions to his injury right after it happened. Sargent, Frank. "Vern Stephens Sorry to Hear About Jeff Heath's Accident." *Lowell Sun*, 30 September 1948: 52. *NewspaperARCHIVE*. Web. 9 January 2016.

16. Konstanty also won the Associated Press's Athlete of the Year. The write-up for his MVP and Athlete of the Year awards mentioned his 74 relief appearances, the modern record at the time; that plus his team's success would make Konstanty's award the precursor to Mike Marshall's 1974 Cy Young award for 106 relief appearances. Other high totals for baseball players in the Athlete of the Year voting included Phil Rizzuto, Eddie Ford (i.e., Whitey), Billy Goodman, Walt Dropo, and Stan Musial. "Konstanty, Phillies' Star, Chosen Most Valuable Player in League." *New York Times*, 3 November 1950: 34. *ProQuest Historical Newspapers: The New York Times*. Web. 10 January 2016. "Konstanty Named Athlete of Year." *New York Times*, 10 January 1951. *ProQuest Historical Newspapers: The New York Times*. Web. 10 January 2016.

17. Lost in the usual retelling of Thomson's home run is that it was redemption for his running into an out at second base because there was already a runner on second. Dawson, James P., "Game-Winning Homer Wiped Out Stigma of Play-Off Hero's Boner on Bases." *New York Times*, 4 October 1951: 42. *ProQuest Historical Newspapers: The New York Times*. Web. 10 January 2016.

Chapter 11

1. Among other things, DiMaggio blamed night baseball for "shorten[ing] his career by at least two years." Drebinger, John. "DiMaggio Retires as Players but Expects to Remain in Yankee Organization." *New York Times*, 12 December 1951: 63. *ProQuest Historical Newspapers: The New York Times*. Web. 10 January 2016.

2. Feller was well aware of it: "It seems every time I went out there I made the whole club tighten up." "Bob Feller Says He Jinxed Team." *Cumberland Evening Times*, 26 September 1952: 15. *NewspaperARCHIVE*. Web. 10 January 2016. (Incidentally, Feller that year credited the length of his career in part to skipping minor league baseball's night games, "agreeing with many major league stars that night baseball shortens careers." Snider, Steve, "Bob Feller Flays Night Baseball." *Arizona Republic*, 7 June 1952: 26. *NewspaperARCHIVE*. Web. 10 January 2016.)

Notes. Chapter 11

3. As it happened in spring training 1953 mid-game, the history surrounding the move is unusual. Brady, Bob, "The Sad Last Spring of Boston's Braves." http://bostonbaseballhistory.com/the-sad-last-spring-of-bostons-braves. 27 February 2013. N.p., 27 February 2013. Web. 10 January 2016.

4. Although the name change was official in 1953 and lasted a few years, the team had been called the Redlegs at different times before that and continued to be called the Reds occasionally after that. Much like how the Washington AL team was officially the Nationals for many years but called the Senators, I have chosen to leave the Redlegs as the Reds throughout my 1950s summaries, as there are no good lines of demarcation to draw between the Redlegs and Reds era in print media of the decade.

5. Maglie was well-known at the time as a Dodger killer. "The center of many a Dodger-Giant hassle because of his use of brush-back pitches to discourage the plate-crowding right-handed sluggers of the Brooks, ... [i]t will be a strange sight indeed to see him at Ebbets Field in a home uniform." "Maglie, Ex-Nemesis of Dodgers, Bought by Brooks from Indians." *New York Times*, 16 May 1956: 41. *ProQuest Historical Newspapers: The New York Times*. Web. 10 January 2016.

6. When Commissioner Ford Frick intervened, it was possible all eight starters in the All-Star Game would be Reds by popular vote. "Redlegs All-Star Votes Bring Action by Ford Frick." *Beckley Post Herald*, 29 June 1957: 23. *NewspaperARCHIVE*. Web. 11 January 2016.

7. For coverage of the inaugural expansion drafts for the AL and the NL, see:
McCue, Andy, and Eric Thompson, "Mis-Management 101: The American League Expansion for 1961." http://sabr.org/research/mis-management-101-american-league-expansion-1961. Society for American Baseball Research: n.d. Web. 11 January 2016.
Boren, Stephen, and Eric Thompson, "The Colt .45s and the 1961 Expansion Draft." http://sabr.org/research/colt-45s-and-1961-expansion-draft. Society for American Baseball Research: n.d. Web. 11 January 2016.

8. Manager Ralph Houk stated it after he won the MVP: "With both Mantle and Maris out for long stretches, it was Howard who kept us going with his hitting. And when our pitching started to wobble at the start and we had to make changes it was Ellie's skillful handling of the young pitchers—Bouton and Downing—that again saved the day for us." Drebinger, John, "Howard of Yanks Named American League's Most Valuable Player." *New York Times*, 8 November 1963: 50. *ProQuest Historical Newspapers: The New York Times*. Web. 13 January 2016.

9. "Orioles Trade Four to Chisox for Smith, Aparicio." *Frederick News Post*, 15 January 1963: 6. *NewspaperARCHIVE*. Web. 13 January 2016.

10. For a large story written about him as a hot shot in the World Series, see "Stottlemyre Reaches High Point of Short Career by Keeping Pitches Low." *New York Times*, 9 October 1964: 47. *ProQuest Historical Newspapers: The New York Times*. Web. 13 January 2016.

11. Early in the year it was thought to be an elbow problem; Ford eventually got a vein transplant. "Ford to Undergo Tests." *New York Times*, 5 June 1966: 219. *ProQuest Historical Newspapers: The New York Times*. Web. 14 January 2016. Koppett, Leonard, "Ford Undergoes 2d Operation on Shoulder; A Full Cure Seen." *New York Times*, 26 August 1966: 23. *ProQuest Historical Newspapers: The New York Times*. Web. 14 January 2016.

12. The day after the trade, Reds' owner Bill DeWitt called Robinson "the third best ballplayer in the National League" behind Hank Aaron and Willie Mays. He called pitcher Milt Pappas, acquired in the trade, "the sixth most effective pitcher in the American League," referring to his 1965 ERA. This quotation was an example of the article's assertion that "Like any good businessman, DeWitt obtains all the possible information he can on a prospective employee before he takes him into the organization." Richman, Milton, "Today's Parade." *Ames Daily Tribune*, 11 December 1965: 14. *NewspaperARCHIVE*. Web. 14 January 2016.

13. For the Dodgers' perspective on the retirement and holdout, the general manager wrote about it in 1967. Bavasi, Buzzie, "The Great Holdout." http://www.si.com/vault/1967/05/15/610695/the-great-holdout. *Sports Illustrated*, 15 May 1967. Web. 14 January 2016.

14. Minor leagues were going to try different types of pinch-hitting as well, including a Texas League experiment for a designated pinch hitter to appear as frequently as once an inning and a New York-Pennsylvania League experiment for a "pinch-hitting specialist" to "bat twice for anyone in the line-up without actually displacing the regular player in the field." Durso, Joseph, "Baseball Scene in '69: New Commissioner, Format Changes and Experiments." *New York Times*, 16 February 1969: S1. *ProQuest Historical Newspapers: The New York Times*. Web. 14 January 2016.

Chapter 12

1. "Mickey Lolich of the Tigers, whose three victories made him the star of the World Series, did not receive any votes [for the end-of-season All-Star team] on the basis of somewhat erratic season during which he had a 17–9 record." "McLain Out-Polls Gibson on AP All-Star Team." *Pacific Stars and Stripes* (Washington, DC), 14 October 1968: 17. *NewspaperARCHIVE*. Web. 15 January 2016.

2. For the reasons behind the strike, see Koppett, Leonard. "Owners' Meeting: $500,000 Later, 'Hawks' Finally Yield to 'Doves.'" *New York Times*, 14 April 1972: 30. *ProQuest Historical Newspapers: The New York Times*. Web. 15 January 2016. For the reaction to the owners' decision not to make up missed games, see Chass, Murray. "Owners Throw Players a Curve by Shortening Season." *New York Times*, 14 April 1972: 30. *ProQuest Historical Newspapers: The New York Times*. Web. 15 January 2016.

3. The plan initially was a three-year experiment. Interleague play was also considered at the same meeting and assigned to a committee. Durso, Joseph. "American League to Let Pitcher Have a Pinch-Hitter and Stay In." *New York Times*, 12 January 1973: 69. *ProQuest Historical Newspapers: The New York Times*. Web. 15 January 2016.

4. "Neither complicated nor controversial legal issues were involved, nor did his case affect any other player or any part of baseball's established structure." Koppett, Leonard. "Real Hunter Fuss Is on Bidding." *New York Times*, 17 December 1974: 45. *ProQuest Historical Newspapers: The New York Times*. Web. 18 January 2016.

5. Smith, Red. "Christmas Spirit." *New York Times*, 24 December 1975: 15. *ProQuest Historical Newspapers: The New York Times*. Web. 18 January 2016.

6. Among his statements, Kuhn said, "Nor can I persuade myself that the spectacle of the Yankees and Red Sox buying contracts of star players in the prime of their careers for cash sums totaling $3.5 million is anything but devastating to baseball's reputation for integrity and to public confidence in the game." It's nice to know Kuhn stopped that from ever happening again. "Kuhn Blocks Sale; Court Battle Ahead." *Lakeland Ledger*, 19 June 1976: 9A. *Google News*. Web. 18 January 2016.

7. Ryan's agent, Dick Moss, said at the time of the signing, "We feel that there are 10 players in the league that before their careers are over will be more higher paid. But he (Ryan) has certainly reached the pinnacle of his profession." Sherrington, Kevin. "Nolan Ryan Signs Multi-Million Dollar Astro Contract." *Galveston Daily News*, 20 November 1979: B1. *NewspaperARCHIVE*. Web. 18 January 2016.

8. Richard's autobiography vividly recalls how far away 1980's sports culture was from that of the 21st century in terms of understanding medical issues and setting reasonable player expectations. Richard, J.R., and Lew Freedman. "J.R. Richard Details Stroke That Ended MLB Career When He Was Dominating." http://www.thepostgame.com/blog/throwback/201507/jr-richard-still-throwing-heat-houston-astros-pitcher-stroke-strikeouts. ThePostGame, 20 July 2015. Web. 18 January 2016.

9. Durso, Joseph. "Owners Approve a Plan to Split Baseball Season." *New York Times*, 7 August 1981: A15. *ProQuest Historical Newspapers: The New York Times*. Web. 18 January 2016.

Chapter 13

1. A Dodgers fan described Guerrero's fielding at third base as "a wedge of Swiss cheese, with lots of holes.... The Dodgers should do what every other major league team has [done] with a power hitter who can't field: Play him at first base, trade him for a quality third baseman or wish you had the designated hitter rule." Fournier, Thomas D. "Pedro Guerrero at Third? On Second Thought, Play Him at First." http://articles.latimes.com/1988-02-13/sports/sp-10690_1_power-hitter-pedro-guerrero-base. *Los Angeles Times*, 13 February 1988. Web. 19 January 2016.

2. The owners denied it vehemently, but years later they settled several claims with affected players. Spitz, Bob. "Is Collusion the Name of the Game?" http://www.nytimes.com/1987/07/12/magazine/is-collusion-the-name-of-the-game.html?pagewanted=all. *New York Times*, 12 July 1987. Web. 20 January 2016. Chass, Murray. "Baseball; Big Collusion Winners: Clark, Parrish, Dawson." http://www.nytimes.com/1992/12/15/sports/baseball-big-collusion-winners-clark-parrish-dawson.html. *New York Times*, 15 December 1992. Web. 20 January 2016.

3. The ordeal lasted from February to August. Weinberg, Rick. "5: Pete Rose Banned from Baseball." http://espn.go.com/espn/espn25/story?page=moments/5. ESPN, 4 September 2004. Web. 20 January 2016.
4. For an oral history of that World Series, see Curtis, Bryan and Patricia Lee. "Rocked." http://grantland.com/features/the-1989-world-series-earthquake-oral-history. Grantland, 30 October 2013. Web. 20 January 2016.
5. The streak was broken by the Phillies, who won 16–13 after being behind 10–3. One Chicago write-up understated drastically by stating that Lancaster had, along with Steve Wilson, been "usually reliable." How much more reliable could Lancaster have been to that point? Nordlund, Jeff. "Cubs' Big Lead Blown Away." *Daily Herald* (Chicago, IL): Section 3, Page 1. *NewspaperARCHIVE*. Web. 18 January 2016.

Chapter 14

1. To promote *Ken Griffey Jr. Presents Major League Baseball*, Nintendo had a contest in 1994 in which the winner would go to the World Series. "We don't know who'll be playing.... We don't know where the games will be.... We DO know that one lucky winner will be in the crowd!" The contest entry form asked, "Do you like the new Major League Baseball divisions and playoff structure?" The winner of the contest was to be selected "On or about August 15, 1994." No record appears to exist as to what became of this contest. I believe I entered the contest. "Player's Poll Contest." *Nintendo Power* July 1994: 98–99. Print.
2. The only owner to vote against the plan was George W. Bush, saying "'I represent the silent voices of baseball purists.... History will prove I was right." Newhan, Ross. "Baseball Owners Approve New League Lineup." *Los Angeles Times*, 10 September 1993: 1. *National Newspapers Core*. Web. 23 January 2016. Several early returns from the media agreed with Bush. "Baseball will never be quite as good again.... In time, we will get used to baseball wild cards, as we accommodate ourselves to all new horrors." Boswell, Thomas. "Wild Card's a Joker." *Washington Post*, 11 September 1993: G01. *National Newspapers Core*. Web. 23 January 2016. The excitement of the Braves/Giants race of 1993 was invoked to show how terrible the new idea was. "By late August, both would have been ensured playoff spots. It is important to understand how big a blunder this is." Krauthammer, Charles. "How to Save Baseball." *Washington Post*, 15 October 1993: A25. *National Newspapers Core*. Web. 23 January 2016.
3. "The Yankees replacement team was so bad, it took batting practice for three days at Coors Field in Denver and didn't hit a ball over the fence." Kurkjian, Tim. "The Replacements." http://espn.go.com/magazine/kurkjian_20020829.html. *ESPN: The Magazine*, 29 August 2002. Web. 23 January 2016.
4. For a detailed explanation of the financial impetus behind Huizenga's actions, see Zimbalist, Andrew. "The Capitalist; A Miami Fish Story." http://www.nytimes.com/1998/10/18/magazine/the-capitalist-a-miami-fish-story.html?pagewanted=all. *New York Times*, 18 October 1998. Web. 24 January 2016.
5. If the Astros had lost game 162, there would have been a three-way tie. Only the Central would be sorted out, because the loser of their 163rd game would have a worse record than the Mets. Most final day scenarios—three out of five—involved an extra game. Haft, Chris. "Win or Else." http://reds.enquirer.com/1999/10/03/red_win_or_else.html. *Cincinnati Enquirer*, 3 October 1999. Web. 24 January 2016.
6. The unbalanced schedule had significant history in divisional play. Johnson, Chuck. "Hot Races on Baseball Schedule." *USA Today*, 23 January 2001: C1. *National Newspapers Core*. Web. 24 January 2016.
7. "Games Postponed in Wake of Terror." http://m.mlb.com/news/article/24147644. MLB.com, 11 September 2001. Web. 24 January 2016.
8. Ten years later, it still made an impact on the organization, as the Cardinals continued not to stay in the Chicago hotel in which Kile died. Strauss, Joe. "Kile's Death Still Shakes Those Who Were Close to Him." http://www.stltoday.com/sports/baseball/professional/kile-s-death-still-shakes-those-who-were-close-to/article_a2340214-c63a-517e-8a48-c827ac0baf48.html. *St. Louis Post-Dispatch*, 18 June 2012. Web. 24 January 2016.

Chapter 15

1. For a retrospective discussing how the Twins' contention is widely considered to have saved Minnesota baseball, see Nightengale, Bob. "Twins Go from Near Contraction to All-Star Host." http://www.usatoday.com/story/sports/mlb/2014/07/13/harry-crump-judge-who-saved-minnesota-twins/12607399. *USA Today*, 14 July 2014. Web. 24 January 2016.

2. O'Connell, Jack. "Marlins' Schedule Taken by Storm." http://articles.courant.com/2004-09-12/sports/0409120193_1_marlins-hurricane-frances-expos. *Hartford Courant*, 12 September 2004. Web. 25 January 2016.

3. Owner Stuart Sternberg said, "We were tied to the past, and the past wasn't necessarily something we wanted to be known for." "D-Rays Drop Devil from Name, Now Just Rays." http://espn.go.com/mlb/news/story?id=3101213. ESPN, 8 November 2007. Web. 26 January 2016.

4. The legacy of the collapse was pitchers Josh Beckett, Jon Lester, and John Lackey relaxing with fried chicken and beer between starts. Hohler, Bob. "Inside the Collapse." http://www.boston.com/sports/baseball/redsox/articles/2011/10/12/red_sox_unity_dedication_dissolved_during_epic_late_season_collapse/?page=1. *Boston Globe*, 12 October 2011. Web. 27 January 2016. Even in 2016, a Web search for fried chicken and beer can turn up the 2011 Red Sox on the first page of results. https://www.google.com/search?q=fried+chicken+beer&biw=1600&bih=782&ei=LpWpVrjYC8b8jwOxvrkI&start=0&sa=N. Google, n.d. Web. 27 January 2016.

Chapter 16

1. Bloom, Barry M. "Addition of Wild Card Berths Finalized for 2012." http://m.mlb.com/news/article/26927024. MLB, 2 March 2012. Web. 27 January 2016.

2. Bloom, Barry M. "Astros Sale to Crane, Move to AL Approved." http://m.mlb.com/news/article/25992120. MLB, 17 November 2011. Web. 28 January 2016.

Chapter 17

1. Calcaterra, Craig, "Baseball Is Dying, You Guys." http://mlb.nbcsports.com/2014/11/03/baseball-is-dying-you-guys-6. NBC Sports, 3 November 2014. Web. 26 December 2015.

Index

Aaron, Hank 30, 55–56, 190–94, 196–99, 200–01, 208, 210, 213–14, 218
Abbott, Jim 268
Abernathy, Ted 208
Abreu, Bobby 296, 301, 308
Adams, Babe 113–14, 116, 119, 130, 134
Adams, Buster 172
Adcock, Joe 190, 192–93, 197–98
Agee, Tommie 206, 209, 214
Aguilera, Rick 264, 269
Aguirre, Hank 199
Aikens, Willie 238
Aldridge, Vic 140
Alexander, Doyle 253, 258
Alexander, Pete 30, 46–48, 54, 63, 116–18, 120, 122–23, 125–27, 129, 130–31, 143, 145, 360n15
Alfonzo, Edgardo 296
Alicea, Luis 261
Allen, Dick 203, 219
Allen, Frank 123
Allen, Johnny 150, 157, 167
Alley, Gene 207
Allison, Bob 200–01, 205
Alomar, Roberto 28, 31, 62–63, 269–70, 273, 275, 292, 296, 298
Alomar, Sandy 286
Alou, Felipe 200, 203, 207, 272
Alou, Matty 207
Alou, Moises 277, 288, 290, 312
Altrock, Nick 107
Alvarez, Wilson 275, 277
Ames, Red 113, 116
Amole, Doc 97
Anderson, Brady 272, 282
Anderson, Fred 127
Anderson, Garret 301
Anderson, Sparky 68
Andrus, Elvis 336, 340
Andujar, Joaquin 254
Anson, Cap 30, 39–43, 77–78, 81, 83–84, 87, 90–91
Antonelli, Johnny 187, 193, 195
Aparicio, Luis 32, 195, 203, 206–07
Aponte, Luis 245

Appier, Kevin 271, 273, 279, 286
Appling, Luke 28–29, 32, 51–52, 66, 168
Armas, Tony 241
Arrieta, Jake 23, 347
Arroyo, Bronson 315
Arroyo, Luis 198, 200
Ashburn, Richie 32, 188, 193
Ashby, Andy 281, 291
Astacio, Pedro 272, 284, 293
Atkins, Garrett 316
Averill, Earl 33, 160
Avery, Steve 270
Avila, Alex 331
Avila, Bobby 184, 186–87

Baerga, Carlos 68
Bagby, Jim 126, 131–32, 134
Bagwell, Jeff 69, 278–79, 284, 287, 290, 293, 296
Bailey, Ed 190
Baker, Dusty 232, 235, 240
Baker, Frank 31, 46–47, 61, 113, 115, 117–19, 123
Baldwin, Lady 83
Baldwin, Mark 89
Bancroft, Dave 33, 123, 127, 132–38
Bando, Sal 213, 215, 217, 219–21, 223, 229
Banks, Ernie 28–30, 33, 66, 188, 191, 193–94, 196
Bannister, Floyd 248
Barfield, Jesse 251, 253–54, 258
Barnes, Jesse 131–32
Barnes, Ross 37–39, 73–76
Barrett, Red 171
Barry, Jack 115, 118–19, 123
Bartell, Dick 157–58, 160, 162
Barton, Daric 328
Bass, Kevin 256
Bassler, Johnny 138
Bauer, Hank 184–86, 188
Baumann, Frank 196
Bautista, Jose 70, 331, 342
Bavasi, Buzzie 363n13
Baylor, Don 230, 238–39, 245, 256
Bearden, Gene 177
Beaumont, Ginger 102

367

Beazley, Johnny 167–68
Beckett, Josh 317, 324, 366n4
Beckham, Gordon 357ch6n1
Beckley, Jake 33, 44, 98
Bedient, Hugh 118
Bedrosian, Steve 245
Belanger, Mark 214, 217, 223–24, 228
Belcher, Tim 261, 264, 270
Bell, Buddy 236, 241, 249
Bell, Derek 290
Bell, George 253, 257–58
Bell, Gus 190
Bell, Jay 269, 274, 278, 286
Bell, Les 141–142
Belle, Albert 277, 279–80, 283, 289
Beltran, Carlos 65, 298, 305, 315, 322, 337
Beltre, Adrian 65, 309, 315, 322, 328, 332, 336, 340, 343, 347
Bench, Johnny 31, 57–58, 216, 218, 220, 222, 225, 227–30, 235, 237, 240
Bender, Chief 33, 69, 109, 114–15, 121, 125, 127, 359n15
Benes, Andy 70
Benge, Ray 149
Bennett, Charlie 79
Bentley, Jack 140
Benton, Larry 144–45
Bere, Jason 275, 282
Berger, Wally 149, 152
Berkman, Lance 299, 309, 315, 322, 332
Bernhard, Bill 102
Berra, Yogi 24, 27, 31, 53–55, 61, 177, 179–186, 188–89, 192–94, 198, 352
Bessent, Don 190
Betances, Dellin 346
Bielecki, Mike 264, 267
Bierbauer, Lou 89
Bigbee, Carson 135
Biggio, Craig 25, 32, 66, 69, 278, 281, 284, 287, 290, 293
Billingham, Jack 223
Billingsley, Chad 319
Bishop, Max 148–49, 361n23
Black, Bud 251
Black, Joe 184, 186
Blackwell, Ewell 175, 180
Blair, Paul 57, 207, 209, 212, 214–15, 221, 223–24
Blake, Casey 326
Blake, Sheriff 145
Blalock, Hank 305
Blanchard, Johnny 198
Blanton, Cy 156
Blasingame, Don 191
Blass, Steve 219–20, 223
Blauser, Jeff 275
Blefary, Curt 207
Blue, Lu 138
Blue, Vida 217–18, 220, 223, 227, 229, 234–35
Blyleven, Bert vii, 2, 7, 28–29, 31, 46, 58–60,
217, 222, 224, 241, 249, 252, 258, 263, 265, 267
Boddicker, Mike 247, 262, 265–66
Boggs, Wade 30, 61–62, 245–46, 251, 254, 256–57, 260, 262, 266, 268, 275–76, 279–80
Bolin, Bobby 205
Bond, Tommy 38–40, 74–76
Bonds, Barry 40, 57, 61–64, 134, 260, 263, 266–68, 270–72, 274–75, 278–79, 281, 284, 287, 291, 293, 296, 299, 302, 306, 309
Bonds, Bobby 218, 222
Bonham, Tiny 166–68
Bonilla, Bobby 267, 270, 272, 288
Boone, Bob 235–36, 245, 258
Boone, Bret 298, 305
Boone, Ray 185
Borbon, Pedro 223
Borowy, Hank 167, 171–72
Bosio, Chris 70
Boswell, Dave 214, 216
Bottomley, Jim 34, 142, 144
Boudreau, Lou 32, 52, 163–65, 168–69, 174, 176–77
Bourn, Michael 336
Bouton, Jim 201, 204–05, 363n8
Bowa, Larry 234–35
Boyd, Oil Can 256
Boyer, Clete 196–200
Boyer, Ken 190, 194, 198, 203
Bradley, Bill 103
Bradley, George 75, 80
Brainard, Asa 72
Branca, Ralph 175, 182
Brandt, Ed 70
Brantley, Jeff 278
Brantley, Michael 343
Braun, Ryan 70, 332, 337
Brazle, Al 175, 178
Breadon, Sam 360n17, 360n21, 361n8
Brecheen, Harry 171, 173–77
Breeding, Marv 196
Breitenstein, Ted 43, 93–97
Brennan, Ad 119
Bresnahan, Roger 33, 104
Bressler, Rube 121, 141
Brett, George 30, 59–60, 229–31, 233, 235–36, 239–40, 244, 246, 250, 252–53
Bridges, Tommy 154, 164
Briles, Nelson 209
Brock, Greg 248
Brock, Lou 33, 203, 209–10, 225
Brodie, Steve 94
Broglio, Ernie 196
Brosius, Scott 289
Brouthers, Dan 31, 41–44, 83, 85, 87, 89–90, 92–95
Brown, Bobby 177
Brown, Jimmy 166–67
Brown, Kevin 284, 287, 290, 293–94
Brown, Mace 160

Brown, Mordecai 32, 45, 108–109, 111–15, 117, 124
Browning, Pete 79
Browning, Tom 266
Brunansky, Tom 259, 261
Bryant, Clay 160–61
Bryant, Kris 23, 347
Buchholz, Clay 328
Buckner, Bill 228
Buehrle, Mark 311, 321, 325
Buffinton, Charlie 81, 85, 87, 90–91
Buford, Don 204, 217
Buhl, Bob 192–93, 195, 197
Bumbry, Al 222–23, 238, 240
Bumgarner, Madison 344
Bunker, Wally 204
Bunning, Jim 33, 191, 196, 198, 203, 205–06, 208
Burba, Dave 284
Burdette, Lew 190, 192–93, 195, 197
Burdock, Jack 80–81
Burgess, Smoky 197–98
Burgmeier, Tom 245
Burkett, Jesse 33, 44, 98
Burkett, John 275, 298
Burkhart, Ken 171
Burks, Ellis 262, 266, 284, 293, 301
Burleson, Rick 236, 238
Burns, Britt 239
Burns, George 120–21, 126–27, 129–31
Burns, Oyster 87, 89
Burris, Ray 229
Bush, Donie 112–13, 123, 146
Bush, George W. 365n2
Bush, Guy 146–147
Bush, Joe 121, 128–30, 135–37
Butler, Brett 261, 264, 266, 270
Byrd, Paul 301
Byrne, Bobby 114

Cabrera, Melky 337
Cabrera, Miguel 65, 325, 328, 331, 336, 339, 343, 346
Cabrera, Orlando 318
Cadore, Leon 127, 130
Cain, Lorenzo 23, 346
Cain, Matt 329, 337
Caldwell, Mike 233
Callahan, Jimmy 100
Callison, Johnny 201, 203
Cameron, Mike 298, 305
Camilli, Dolph 159, 162, 165–67, 361n22
Caminiti, Ken 264, 278, 284
Camnitz, Howie 113
Campanella, Roy 27, 34, 179–81, 185, 187–88, 190
Campaneris, Bert 220, 223–25, 229
Campbell, Bill 233
Canavan, Jim 92
Candelaria, John 231, 253, 262

Candiotti, Tom 268–69, 272
Cano, Robinson 65, 318, 328, 331, 335, 339
Canseco, Jose 68, 260–61, 265, 267–68
Carbo, Bernie 216
Carew, Rod 31, 213, 216, 218, 224, 226, 229, 231, 238
Carey, Andy 187, 192–94
Carey, Max 33, 134–35, 137, 139–140
Carleton, Tex 152
Carlson, Hal 141
Carlton, Steve 30, 58–59, 209, 213, 220, 229–32, 235, 237, 239–40, 242, 247–48, 251, 253
Carpenter, Chris 315, 326, 332
Carpenter, Hick 79
Carpenter, Matt 340
Carrasquel, Chico 189
Carreon, Mark 281
Carroll, Fred 66–67
Carter, Gary 31, 60, 234, 236–37, 239–41, 244, 246–47, 250, 254, 256, 259
Carter, Joe 268–69
Carty, Rico 216
Caruthers, Bob 41–42, 61, 82–87, 89–90
Casey, Dan 84
Casey, Hugh 174
Cash, Dave 220
Cash, Norm 197, 204, 209, 211
Cavarretta, Phil 171–72
Cedeno, Cesar 220, 239
Cepeda, Orlando 33, 68, 193, 195, 198, 200, 203, 205, 208–09, 214
Cerv, Bob 192
Cespedes, Yoenis 23, 347–49
Cey, Ron 223, 227, 229–30, 232, 234, 240, 242, 245, 251
Chacin, Jhoulys 341
Chamberlain, Ice Box 86–87
Chambliss, Chris 230, 248
Chance, Dean 200, 202, 209
Chance, Frank 33, 104–05, 108
Chandler, Spud 167–68, 170, 173
Chapman, Ben 150
Chapman, Ray 132
Charlton, Norm 267
Chase, Hal 108
Chavez, Eric 308, 311
Cheney, Larry 117
Chesbro, Jack 34, 102, 104–05
Childs, Cupid 92, 98
Choo, Shin-Soo 325, 328
Christensen, Cuckoo 141
Cicotte, Eddie 126–27, 130
Clancy, Jim 257–58
Clark, Jack 234, 258–59, 261–62, 364n2
Clark, Watty 149
Clark, Will 259, 261, 263–64, 277
Clarke, Fred 31, 102, 113–14, 116
Clarkson, Dad 95
Clarkson, John 30, 41–42, 82–83, 86–90, 92, 95
Clayton, Royce 278

Clear, Mark 245
Clemens, Roger 57, 62–64, 70, 254, 256–57, 260, 262, 265–66, 268, 270, 276, 283, 286, 289, 292, 312
Clemente, Roberto 30, 46, 55–56, 197–98, 207–08, 210, 213, 217–18, 220, 223
Clendenon, Donn 207
Cliburn, Stew 253
Clift, Harlond 159
Cobb, Ty 30, 45–48, 54, 68, 109–10, 112–18, 122–24, 126–28, 138
Cochrane, Mickey 32, 146–49, 154–57
Coggins, Rich 223
Colavito, Rocky 192, 195, 197, 199
Cole, King 114–15, 117
Coleman, Joe 221
Coleman, Vince 254, 259
Collins, Eddie 30, 45–48, 52, 54, 61, 112–15, 117–19, 122–23, 127, 130–32
Collins, Hub 89
Collins, Jimmy 32, 44–45, 96–97, 100, 103–04
Collins, Ray 118
Collins, Ripper 153–54, 156
Colon, Bartolo 289, 295, 298, 301, 311
Combs, Earle 33, 142, 150
Comiskey, Charlie 91–92, 100
Concepcion, Dave 226, 230, 237
Cone, David 61–62, 260–61, 264, 266, 268, 270, 272–73, 277, 279–80, 286
Connolly, Joe 121
Connor, Roger 31, 41–43, 82–83, 86
Conway, Pete 85
Coombs, Jack 114–16, 359n15
Cooney, Jimmy 91–92
Cooper, Cecil 238, 243, 245
Cooper, Mort 166–69, 171
Cooper, Walker 169, 361n8
Cooper, Wilbur 126, 134–35, 140
Corbett, Doug 250
Corbett, Joe 97
Corcoran, Larry 39–40, 77–78, 80
Counsell, Craig 312
Coveleski, Harry 123–24
Coveleski, Stan 31, 126, 128, 130–33, 135, 139–40
Covington, Wes 193
Cowens, Al 231, 233
Craig, Roger 195
Crandall, Del 193, 196–98
Crandall, Doc 116
Crane, Jim 366ch16n2
Cravath, Gavvy 119, 122–23, 126–27
Crawford, Brandon 23, 348
Crawford, Sam 31, 110, 112–13, 116, 119, 123, 125
Crawford, Willie 223
Crespi, Creepy 166
Critz, Hughie 141
Cronin, Joe 32, 51, 147–48, 151–52, 159–60, 164

Crosetti, Frankie 157, 160, 162, 165
Crowder, General 148, 152
Cruz, Jose 237, 239, 245, 247, 250
Cruz, Nelson 328, 342
Cuellar, Mike 214, 216, 218–19, 225
Cueto, Johnny 344
Cullenbine, Roy 171–72
Cummings, Candy 37–38, 73–74
Cunningham, Joe 191
Cuppy, Nig 92, 96, 98
Cuyler, Kiki 33, 139–140, 146–47, 154

Dahlen, Bill 44–45, 91–92, 98, 105–06
Daily, Hugh 80
Dalrymple, Abner 78, 83
Daly, Tom 98
Damon, Johnny 295
Danforth, Dave 127
Daniels, Kal 259
Danks, John 321, 325
Dark, Al 177–78, 182
Darling, Ron 255–56, 259, 261, 275
Darvish, Yu 336, 340, 343
Daubert, Jake 125
Daulton, Darren 271, 274
Dauss, Hooks 122–23, 125
Davenport, Dave 123
Davis, Alvin 249
Davis, Chili 269
Davis, Chris 339
Davis, Curt 153, 156, 167
Davis, Eric 255, 259, 267, 272
Davis, George 31, 44–45, 94, 102, 104, 106–07, 109
Davis, Glenn 256, 261, 264
Davis, Harry 107, 116
Davis, Storm 262
Davis, Tommy 200, 202
Davis, Willie 200, 202–203
Dawson, Andre 32, 60, 237, 239–41, 244, 246–47, 259
Dean, Dizzy 33, 150–54, 156–57, 161
Dean, Paul 154, 156, 158
DeCinces, Doug 233, 244–45, 249–50, 258
deGrom, Jacob 347
Delahanty, Ed 32, 43–44, 93–94, 98–99, 102
Delgado, Carlos 295
Demaree, Al 119
Demaree, Frank 157, 159, 162
DeMontreville, Gene 97
Dempster, Ryan 322
Denny, John 247–48, 250–51
Dent, Bucky 235
Derby, George 78
Derringer, Paul 149, 162, 165
Deshaies, Jim 264
Devereaux, Mike 272
Devlin, Art 105, 108
Devlin, Jim 38, 75–76
DeWitt, Bill 363n12

Dibble, Rob 267, 274
Dickey, Bill 27, 31, 50–51, 146, 157–59, 161–62, 164–65, 173
Dickey, R.A. 336
Dickson, Murry 175
Dierker, Larry 69, 213
DiMaggio, Dom 173, 179
DiMaggio, Joe 27, 30, 35, 48, 50–52, 61, 157–59, 161–66, 168, 173–74, 176–80, 183
Dinneen, Bill 99, 101–03, 105
Ditmar, Art 194–95, 197
Dobson, Joe 174–75, 177
Dobson, Pat 218
Doby, Larry 33, 177, 179–81, 183–84, 186–87
Doerr, Bobby 33, 173, 177, 179
Donahue, Jiggs 107
Donaldson, Josh 23, 340, 343, 346
Donlin, Mike 106–08, 112
Donovan, Bill 101, 110
Donovan, Dick 191
Dotson, Rich 246, 248
Dougherty, Patsy 104
Douglas, Phil 129, 136
Downing, Al 201–202, 363n8
Downing, Brian 236, 238–39, 244–45, 250, 253, 255, 257
Doyle, Jack 94, 97
Doyle, Jim 116
Doyle, Larry 115, 117, 122, 131
Drabek, Doug 267, 271, 274, 278
Dravecky, Dave 256, 259
Drese, Ryan 308
Drew, J.D. 296, 299, 308, 312, 316
Dreyfuss, Barney 99
Driscoll, Denny 79
Dropo, Walt 180, 362n16
Drucke, Louis 115
Drysdale, Don 28, 31, 55, 69, 191–92, 194–96, 199–200, 202–05, 207
Dubuc, Jean 117–18
Duffy, Hugh 33, 42–44, 91–96
Duncan, Chris 315
Dundon, Gus 107
Dunlap, Fred 80
Dunn, Adam 66
Dunn, Jack 98
Duren, Ryne 193–94
Durham, Leon 251
Durocher, Leo 176
Duryea, Jesse 87
Dwyer, Frank 96–97
Dykes, Jimmie 151
Dykstra, Lenny 255–56, 266, 274

Earnshaw, George 146, 148–50, 361n23
Easler, Mike 240
Easley, Damion 289
Eckersley, Dennis 25, 32, 60–62, 65, 233–34, 236, 238, 251, 262, 265, 267, 269, 272, 275
Eckstein, David 301

Edmonds, Jim 296, 299, 302, 306, 309
Edwards, Bruce 175
Ehmke, Howard 138
Ehret, Red 89, 96
Eichhorn, Mark 254, 258
Elberfeld, Kid 108
Eldred, Cal 272
Elliott, Bob 175–77, 362n12
Ellis, Mark 318
Ellsbury, Jacoby 331, 339
Ellsworth, Dick 201
English, Woody 147, 149, 151
Ennis, Del 180
Ens, Jewel 360n18
Ensberg, Morgan 312
Epstein, Mike 220
Erickson, Scott 269
Erskine, Carl 184, 186, 193
Erstad, Darin 295, 301
Escobar, Kelvim 318
Esper, Duke 94–95
Esterbrook, Dude 82–83
Etten, Nick 169, 172
Evans, Darrell 222, 252, 258
Evans, Dwight 2, 35–37, 225–27, 238, 241, 243, 245, 256, 262
Everett, Carl 293
Evers, Johnny 33, 108–09, 111–12, 115–17, 120
Ewing, Bob 70, 109
Ewing, Buck 33, 86

Faber, Red 32, 48–49, 127, 132–33, 135
Falkenberg, Cy 120–21
Farrell, Duke 91
Farrell, Jack 80
Farrell, Turk 200
Feller, Bob 32, 52–53, 160–61, 163–65, 173, 177, 184
Felsch, Happy 127, 132
Ferguson, Bob 76
Ferguson, Charlie 83–84
Ferguson, Joe 223
Fernandez, Alex 273, 275, 283, 288
Fernandez, Jose 340
Fernandez, Sid 259, 261, 263–64, 271
Fernandez, Tony 253, 257–58, 264–66
Ferrell, Rick 34
Ferrell, Wes 40, 147–48, 155, 157
Fidrych, Mark 228
Fielder, Cecil 265
Fielder, Prince 326, 336
Figgins, Chone 325
Figueroa, Ed 230, 233, 235
Fingers, Rollie 7, 34, 223, 227
Finley, Charlie 7, 230
Finley, Chuck 265, 290
Finley, Steve 271, 284, 294
Fischer, William 122
Fisher, Cherokee 37
Fisher, Eddie 205

Fisk, Carlton 32, 219, 227, 231, 233, 267
Fister, Doug 331
Flack, Max 122
Flaherty, Patsy 105, 112
Fletcher, Art 46–47, 118, 125–27, 129–32
Fletcher, Scott 67
Flick, Elmer 33, 99, 102, 107
Flint, Silver 77
Flood, Curt 203, 209–10
Floyd, Cliff 298
Floyd, Gavin 321
Fogarty, Jim 68
Force, Davy 72–73
Ford, Lew 308
Ford, Russ 69, 114, 120
Ford, Whitey 27–28, 31, 54–55, 61, 180, 186, 189–94, 197–202, 204–05, 207, 362n16
Forsch, Bob 227
Forsch, Ken 246
Forster, Terry 248
Fosse, Ray 223
Foster, George 228–30, 232, 235, 237, 240
Foster, Rube 123
Fournier, Jack 123, 138
Foutz, Dave 82–87, 89
Fox, Nellie 25, 33, 182, 189, 191, 194–95
Fox, Pete 156
Foxx, Jimmie 30, 49–51, 145, 147–51, 153, 155, 159–61, 164
Franco, John 259, 267
Franco, Julio 265, 279
Francona, Tito 195–96
Freehan, Bill 209–211
Freeman, Freddie 340
Freeman, Marvin 278
Fregosi, Jim 202, 215
French, Larry 156, 167–68
Frey, Lonny 161–63
Frick, Ford 363n6
Friend, Bob 197
Frisch, Frankie 24, 27, 31, 48–49, 133–39, 142–43, 147, 149, 152
Frost, Dave 238–39
Furcal, Rafael 65, 305, 308, 312, 316
Furillo, Carl 174, 182, 186, 188

Gaetti, Gary 255, 259
Gagne, Greg 259
Galan, Augie 156, 168, 171
Galvin, Pud 31, 39–41, 77–78, 80–81
Gant, Ron 274–75, 278, 281, 285
Garber, Gene 235, 245
Garcia, Mike 184, 187
Garciaparra, Nomar 289, 292, 295, 300, 304
Gardner, Brett 328
Gardner, Larry 118, 127
Garland, Jon 311
Garrelts, Scott 264
Garver, Ned 69, 179, 181
Garvey, Steve 62, 230, 232, 234, 240

Gehrig, Lou 8, 27, 30, 48–52, 56, 61–62, 140, 142–43, 145, 147–48, 150–51, 153–59, 162
Gehringer, Charlie 31, 50, 151, 153–57, 164
Gelbert, Charlie 149
Gentile, Jim 196
Getzien, Pretzels 89, 91
Giambi, Jason 292, 295, 298, 300, 304
Gibson, Bob 31, 56, 203, 210, 213, 215, 220, 364n1
Gibson, George 116, 134
Gibson, Kirk 250, 252, 258, 261–62, 264
Gibson, Norwood 105
Giles, Brian 289, 293, 296, 312, 322
Giles, Marcus 305, 308
Gilkey, Bernard 284
Gilliam, Jim 186, 188–89, 192, 201–02, 206
Giusti, Dave 220
Glasscock, Jack 42, 87
Glaus, Troy 295, 322
Glaviano, Tommy 180
Glavine, Tom 31, 62–63, 269–71, 273, 281, 284, 287–88, 290
Glazner, Whitey 133–134, 136
Gleason, Bill 79
Gleason, Jack 79
Gleason, Kid 88, 94
Goldschmidt, Paul 23, 341, 348
Goldsmith, Fred 78–79
Goltz, Dave 234
Gomez, Carlos 340
Gomez, Lefty 33, 50, 150, 152–54, 156–59, 164
Gomez, Ruben 187
Gonzalez, Adrian 323, 326
Gonzalez, Carlos 329
Gonzalez, Juan 289, 292, 298
Gonzalez, Luis 293, 296, 299
Gooden, Dwight 41, 61, 251–52, 254, 256, 259, 261, 264, 267–68
Goodman, Billy 362n16
Goodman, Ival 160–62
Gordon, Alex 331, 336, 343
Gordon, Joe 32, 51–52, 160–61, 163, 165–66, 168, 170, 174, 176–77
Gore, George 40, 77–78, 83, 85, 87
Goslin, Goose 31, 138–41, 144, 148, 152, 156
Gossage, Goose 34, 226, 235, 240, 251
Grabarkewitz, Billy 216
Grace, Mark 264
Granderson, Curtis 318, 331, 347
Grant, Mudcat 205
Grantham, George 138, 140, 146
Gray, Sam 140
Gray, Sonny 23, 346
Green, Shawn 292
Greenberg, Hank 32, 154–59, 163–64, 172–73
Greene, Tommy 274
Greenwell, Mike 260, 262
Greer, Rusty 283, 289
Gregg, Hal 169
Gregg, Vean 115

Greinke, Zack 23, 325, 348
Grich, Bobby 44, 58–59, 219, 221–22, 224–25, 236, 238, 241, 245–46
Griffey, Ken, Jr. 28–29, 31, 64, 268, 273, 277, 279–80, 283, 286, 290
Griffey, Ken, Sr. 230
Griffith, Clark 97, 100–01
Grim, Bob 187
Grimes, Burleigh 33, 129, 132–133, 144, 146, 148
Grimes, Oscar 172
Grimes, Ray 135
Grimm, Charlie 140, 151, 361n4
Grimsley, Ross 225
Grissom, Marquis 274, 277, 282
Grissom, Marv 187
Groat, Dick 196–97
Groh, Heinie 126, 130–31, 134, 137–38
Gross, Kevin 279
Grove, Lefty 30, 49–50, 141, 144–51, 155, 157–58, 160–61, 164, 361n23
Gruber, Kelly 264, 26
Gubicza, Mark 260, 263
Guerrero, Pedro 244–45, 247–48, 251, 253–54, 256, 258–59
Guerrero, Vladimir 290, 301, 308, 311, 318
Guidry, Ron 29, 231, 233, 235–36, 241
Guillen, Carlos 314
Gullett, Don 216, 218, 228, 233, 235
Gullickson, Bill 240
Gura, Larry 234–35, 239–40, 245, 251
Gutierrez, Franklin 325
Guzman, Juan 269–70, 282–83
Gwynn, Tony 32, 250–51, 254–56, 258, 269, 278

Haas, Mule 151
Hack, Stan 160, 171–72
Haddock, George 90–92
Hadley, Bump 148, 151
Hafey, Chick 34, 144–45, 147, 149, 151
Hafner, Travis 308, 311, 314
Hahn, Ed 110
Hahn, Noodles 98–99, 101–03, 105
Haines, Jesse 34, 146
Hall, Jimmie 205–06
Hall, Tom 215–16
Halladay, Roy 300, 304, 321, 324, 329, 332
Hallahan, Bill 149
Hamelin, Bob 279
Hamels, Cole 329, 332, 336, 343
Hamilton, Billy 24, 32, 43, 93–94, 96
Hamilton, Earl 134
Hamilton, Josh 322, 328
Hampton, Mike 293
Hands, Bill 213–15
Hanlon, Ned 94, 96, 98
Hansen, Ron 196, 202–03
Happ, J.A. 325
Harang, Aaron 319
Harder, Mel 153, 160
Hardy, J.J. 342

Haren, Dan 323, 326
Hargrave, Bubbles 141
Hargrove, Mike 67
Harper, Bryce 23, 347
Harper, Jack 105
Harper, Tommy 215
Harrah, Toby 67, 243
Harrelson, Bud 267
Harris, Bucky 140
Harris, Joe 143
Harris, Lenny 68
Harrison, Matt 336
Harriss, Slim 140
Hart, Jim Ray 203, 206, 208
Hartnett, Gabby 32, 138, 145, 147, 154, 156, 159–60, 361n5
Hartsel, Topsy 107
Harvey, Bryan 261
Harvey, Matt 347
Hatten, Joe 174
Hawley, Pink 95–97
Hayes, Von 249, 251
Hazle, Bob 192
Headley, Chase 337
Healy, Egyptian 88
Hearn, Jim 175
Heath, Jeff 165, 177–78
Hebner, Richie 220
Hecker, Guy 81–82
Heilmann, Harry 28–29, 32, 48, 136, 138–39, 142
Held, Woodie 195–96
Helling, Rick 289, 295
Helton, Todd 67, 296, 306, 309
Hemming, George 95
Hemus, Solly 184
Henderson, Dave 260–61, 263, 267–68
Henderson, Hardie 82
Henderson, Rickey 30, 59–63, 239, 241, 244, 246, 249, 251, 258, 260, 262–63, 265, 267, 271, 277
Hendrix, Claude 120–21
Henke, Tom 258, 264, 266, 269
Henneman, Mike 262
Henrich, Tommy 160, 165, 168, 174, 176–79
Hentgen, Pat 276, 283
Herbert, Ray 196
Herman, Babe 147, 150, 152, 154, 156
Herman, Billy 32, 51, 150–51, 156, 159, 161, 166, 168
Hernandez, Felix 69–70, 325, 328, 343
Hernandez, Keith 236, 239, 242, 246, 251, 254–56
Hernandez, Livan 305
Hernandez, Ramon 220
Hernandez, Roberto 318
Hernandez, Willie 250
Herr, Tommy 252, 254, 261
Hershiser, Orel 61–62, 250–51, 253–54, 256, 258–59, 261, 263–64, 288

Herzog, Whitey 60
Hess, Otto 108
Heyward, Jason 23, 65, 329, 336, 340, 343, 347
Hibbard, Greg 267
Hickman, Jim 216
Hidalgo, Richard 296
Higbe, Kirby 174
Higginson, Bobby 68
Higuera, Teddy 69–70, 254, 260
Hill, Aaron 337
Hill, Carmen 143
Hill, Ken 282–83, 288
Hiller, John 221
Hines, Paul 77, 80–81
Hoak, Don 188, 197–98
Hodges, Gil 181, 184, 186, 190, 192–93
Hoffer, Bill 95–96
Hofman, Solly 114
Hoiles, Chris 273, 279
Holland, Al 247, 251
Holliday, Matt 319, 329, 332, 337, 344
Hollocher, Charlie 129
Holmes, Tommy 171
Holton, Brian 261
Holtzman, Ken 214–15, 223, 227, 236
Hooper, Harry 33, 127–28
Hooton, Burt 232, 234
Hopp, Johnny 170
Horlen, Joe 204, 208–10
Horner, Bob 245, 248, 251, 261
Hornsby, Rogers 30, 46, 48–49, 126, 129, 130, 132–133, 135, 137–39, 141–46, 149, 151, 173, 356n8
Horton, Willie 209–11
Houk, Ralph 363n8
Houtteman, Art 179–180
Howard, Elston 192–94, 197–98, 200–02, 204–05
Howard, Frank 202, 205
Howard, Ryan 66, 325
Howe, Steve 240, 248, 251, 254, 279
Howell, Jay 261, 264
Hoy, Dummy 100
Hoyt, LaMarr 248, 254
Hoyt, Waite 32, 48–49, 134, 137, 142–144
Hrbek, Kent 249–50, 259
Hubbell, Carl 31, 50, 150, 152–53, 156–60
Hudson, Nat 86
Hudson, Orlando 326
Hudson, Tim 28, 301, 305, 308, 318
Huff, Aubrey 329
Huggins, Miller 67
Hughes, Jim 98
Hughes, Mickey 86
Hughson, Tex 166, 173, 175
Huizenga, Wayne 291
Hume, Tom 237
Hunter, Billy 189
Hunter, Catfish 7, 34, 219–20, 223–25, 227, 230, 233, 235

Hunter, Torii 308, 321, 325, 336
Hurdle, Clint 327
Hurst, Bruce 256, 262
Hurst, Don 154
Hutchinson, Bill 90, 92

Inge, Brandon 314
Iorg, Garth 253
Irvin, Monte 182
Irwin, Arthur 80
Isbell, Frank 107
Iwakuma, Hisashi 340

Jacklitsch, Fred 121
Jackson, Austin 328, 331, 336
Jackson, Danny 274, 277
Jackson, Grant 223
Jackson, Joe 115, 117, 124, 126–27, 129–33
Jackson, Larry 191
Jackson, Mike 278
Jackson, Reggie 31, 57–59, 213, 217, 219–21, 223–26, 230, 233, 238, 240, 245, 248, 253
Jackson, Travis 33, 137–38, 140, 154
James, Bill 120, 123
Jansen, Larry 175, 182
Jaster, Larry 209
Javier, Stan 277
Jay, Joey 193, 199
Jenkins, Fergie 31, 53, 209, 213–15, 218, 224
Jennings, Hughie 33, 43–44, 94–98, 116, 138, 359n15
Jennings, Jason 316
Jeter, Derek 7–8, 64–65, 289, 292, 295, 297, 314, 324
Jimenez, Ubaldo 329
John, Tommy 59, 210, 240
Johnson, Ban 100, 359n7
Johnson, Bob 169
Johnson, Charles 68
Johnson, Davey 267
Johnson, Howard 258, 261, 263–64, 268–69, 272
Johnson, Josh 325, 329
Johnson, Lance 273, 284
Johnson, Randy 30, 63–64, 277, 280, 286, 293–94, 296, 299, 302, 309, 311
Johnson, Walter 28–30, 40, 45–48, 58, 114–15, 117–19, 122, 124, 128, 130, 137–40
Johnstone, Jay 229
Jones, Adam 342
Jones, Andruw 58, 63–64, 290, 293, 296, 298, 301, 312, 315
Jones, Charley 76–77
Jones, Chipper 63–64, 284, 290, 293, 296, 298, 301, 308, 312, 318, 322
Jones, Cleon 213–14
Jones, Davy 110
Jones, Fielder 107, 110, 112
Jones, Jacque 301
Jones, Randy 227
Jones, Sam (RHP, 1914–35) 133

Jones, Sam (RHP, 1951–64) 195
Joost, Eddie 163, 178, 181
Jordan, Brian 284, 290
Joss, Addie 33, 108–10
Joyce, Bill 92
Joyner, Wally 256–57
Judge, Joe 138, 148
Jurges, Billy 151–52, 161–62
Justice, David 271, 275, 277, 281

Kaat, Jim 200, 205, 224, 226
Kaline, Al 31, 55–56, 188–89, 192, 194–95, 208–09
Karger, Ed 109
Kauff, Benny 120, 123, 127
Keefe, Tim 31, 39–42, 80–83, 85–86
Keeler, Willie 25, 32, 43–45, 94–98, 104–05
Kell, George 34, 180
Keller, Charlie 51–52, 163, 165–66, 168, 170, 173
Kelley, Joe 33, 43–44, 94–99, 102, 105
Kelly, George 34, 134–36, 138–39
Kelly, King 33, 68, 78, 81, 83, 85, 89, 355ch5n5
Keltner, Ken 165, 177
Kemp, Matt 326, 333
Kendall, Jason 66–67
Kennedy, Adam 301
Kennedy, Brickyard 93, 98–99
Kent, Jeff 293, 296, 302, 312
Kershaw, Clayton 23, 65, 326, 329, 333, 337, 341, 344, 348
Keuchel, Dallas 23, 347
Key, Jimmy 253, 257–58, 269, 275, 279
Kiermaier, Kevin 23, 346
Kilduff, Pete 132
Kile, Darryl 287, 296, 299, 303
Killebrew, Harmon 32, 205–06, 208–09, 213, 215
Killen, Frank 93, 96
Killian, Ed 106, 109–10, 113
Kilroy, Matt 85
Kimbrel, Craig 340
Kinder, Ellis 179
Kiner, Ralph 28–29, 34, 175, 177–78, 181
King, Jeff 274
King, Silver 41, 43, 85–87, 89, 91
Kinsler, Ian 23, 325, 332, 340, 343, 346
Kitson, Frank 98
Klein, Chuck 34, 147, 152, 154
Klein, Lou 168
Kluber, Corey 343
Kluszewski, Ted 187, 190
Knepper, Bob 234–35
Knight, Ray 237, 256
Knoblauch, Chuck 269, 280, 283, 286
Konerko, Paul 311
Konetchy, Ed 122, 124
Konstanty, Jim 180
Koosman, Jerry 214, 222
Koskie, Corey 298, 301, 305
Kotsay, Mark 308
Koufax, Sandy 27, 32, 55, 199–207

Kramer, Jack 169–70
Krause, Harry 113
Kremer, Ray 140–42, 144, 146
Krock, Gus 85–87
Kubek, Tony 191, 196, 198, 202, 205
Kucks, Johnny 190
Kuhel, Joe 172
Kuhn, Bowie 230
Kuroda, Hiroki 335
Kurowski, Whitey 171–75

Labine, Clem 186, 190
Lackey, John 23, 311, 315, 318, 347, 366n4
Lacy, Lee 235, 240
Lajoie, Nap 30, 44–46, 99–104, 107, 109–10, 112
Lake, Eddie 171
Lamp, Dennis 253
Lancaster, Les 264
Landis, Jim 194–95
Langston, Mark 257, 263–64, 267–68, 273
Lanier, Hal 205
Lanier, Max 167–68, 174
Lankford, Ray 287
Lansford, Carney 238, 263
Lapp, Jack 116
Larkin, Barry 24, 32, 261, 266–67, 269, 271, 275, 278, 281, 284
Larkin, Terry 76–77
Larsen, Don 189–90
Lary, Frank 192, 198
Latham, Arlie 82, 84, 86–87
Law, Vern 197–98
Lazzeri, Tony 32, 49–50, 142, 145, 150, 157, 160
Leach, Tommy 102
Leary, Tim 261
Lee, Bill (LHP) 237
Lee, Bill (RHP) 160–61
Lee, Carlos 68
Lee, Cliff 321, 332, 340
Lee, Derrek 312
Lee, Thornton 165
Leever, Sam 103–05
Lefebvre, Jim 205–06
Leiber, Hank 156, 162
Leibrandt, Charlie 252–53, 257
Leifield, Lefty 116
Leiter, Al 280
Lemon, Bob 33, 176–78, 184, 187, 189
Lemon, Chet 249–50, 258
Leonard, Dennis 231, 233, 235, 239–40, 245
Leonard, Dutch (LHP) 119, 123–24, 127
Leonard, Dutch (RHP) 172
Lester, Jon 65, 321, 324, 366n4
Lewis, Duffy 127
Lewis, Fred 82
Lewis, Ted 97
Lincecum, Tim 323, 326, 333
Lindblad, Paul 227
Lindell, Johnny 169, 172
Lindstrom, Freddie 34, 144

Linzy, Frank 205
Listach, Pat 272
Littell, Mark 230
Loaiza, Esteban 305
Lobert, Hans 116, 123
Loes, Billy 184
Lofton, Kenny 270, 273, 277, 279–80, 283, 289, 292
Logan, Johnny 190, 192–93
Lohse, Kyle 322, 337
Lolich, Mickey 213, 217, 219, 221
Lollar, Sherm 195–96
Lombardi, Ernie 34, 162–63, 171
Lombardi, Vic 174
Lonborg, Jim 209, 230
Long, Herman 44, 91, 93, 97
Longoria, Evan 324, 328
Lopat, Eddie 174, 177, 181, 186
Lopes, Davey 227, 232, 234
Lopez, Aurelio 250, 253
Lopez, Javy 305
Lord, Bris 116
Lowe, Bobby 97
Lowe, Derek 300, 316
Lowell, Mike 318
Lown, Turk 195–96
Lowry, Noah 312
Lucas, Red 143, 146
Lucroy, Jonathan 344
Luderus, Fred 116, 122–23
Ludwick, Ryan 322
Lum, Mike 232
Lundgren, Carl 109
Luque, Dolf 133, 137, 139
Luzinski, Greg 231, 234–35
Lyle, Sparky 230, 233, 235
Lynch, Jack 82
Lynch, Jerry 199
Lynn, Fred 36, 59–60, 226–27, 234, 236–38, 245, 249–50
Lynn, Lance 344
Lyons, Ted 28–29, 32, 51, 142

Machado, Manny 23, 339, 346
Mack, Connie 123, 151
Mack, Ray 164
Mack, Shane 269–70
MacPhail, Larry 167
Maddox, Elliott 224
Maddox, Garry 229–31, 234–36
Maddux, Greg 30, 62–64, 264, 271, 275, 277, 281, 283, 287–88, 290, 296, 298, 301
Madlock, Bill 237, 254
Magadan, Dave 266
Magee, Sherry 109, 114, 116, 123
Maglie, Sal 182, 187, 189–90
Mahler, Rick 251
Mails, Duster 134
Maisel, Fritz 68
Maldonado, Candy 259

Malone, Pat 145–46
Maloney, Jim 205
Mamaux, Al 122
Mancuso, Gus 162
Manfred, Rob 57
Mann, Les 122
Mantle, Mickey 27, 30, 51, 53–55, 61, 183–86, 188–95, 197–200, 202, 204–05, 207, 352, 356ch5n1
Manush, Heinie 33, 144, 148
Maranville, Rabbit 34, 120, 134, 140
Marberry, Firpo 140
Marichal, Juan 31, 55–56, 201, 203–06, 208, 213, 218
Marion, Marty 166–67, 169, 361n8
Maris, Roger 54, 56, 195–98, 200, 202, 204–05, 207, 209, 291
Markakis, Nick 321
Marquard, Rube 34, 113, 115–19, 123, 125
Marshall, Mike (RF) 254
Marshall, Mike (RHP) 226, 228, 362n16
Martin, Al 278
Martin, Billy 184
Martin, Leonys 343
Martin, Pepper 152
Martin, Russell 319
Martinez, Carmelo 251, 254
Martinez, Dennis 268, 279–80
Martinez, Edgar 24, 280, 283, 286, 295
Martinez, J.D. 346
Martinez, Pedro 1, 25, 30, 63–64, 281, 287, 289, 292, 294, 304, 307, 312
Martinez, Ramon 270, 279
Martinez, Tino 280, 286
Martinez, Tippy 247, 250
Martinez, Victor 343
Mathews, Bobby 37–41, 73–74, 80
Mathews, Eddie 25, 30, 54–55, 185, 187–88, 190–94, 196–99
Mathewson, Christy 30, 45–46, 101, 103–09, 111–19, 123, 131, 360n5
Matlack, Jon 220, 222, 224, 234
Matsui, Hideki 307
Matsuzaka, Daisuke 321
Matthews, Gary, Jr. 315
Matthews, Gary, Sr. 251
Mattingly, Don 29, 258, 260, 262
Mauer, Joe 321, 325, 328
Maul, Al 97
May, Darrell 305
May, Lee 218
May, Rudy 238, 240
Mayo, Eddie 171–72
Mays, Carl 126–28, 132, 134
Mays, Joe 298
Mays, Willie 30, 51, 54–56, 182, 184, 186–88, 190–91, 193–96, 198, 200–01, 203–06, 208, 210, 218, 220
Mazeroski, Bill 34, 207
Mazzilli, Lee 313

McAuliffe, Dick 206, 209–11
McBride, Bake 225, 232
McBride, Dick 37–38, 40, 72–74
McCann, Brian 315
McCarthy, Joe 155, 177
McCarthy, Tommy 34, 86, 88, 93
McCarver, Tim 209
McCaskill, Kirk 255–56, 258, 265
McCatty, Steve 241
McConnell, George 124
McCormick, Frank 161–63, 166
McCormick, Harry 79
McCormick, Jim 39–41, 77–80, 83
McCormick, Mike (CF) 166
McCormick, Mike (LHP) 197, 199, 208
McCosky, Barney 164
McCovey, Willie 31, 56, 195, 197, 203, 205, 208, 210, 213, 216, 218, 220
McCutchen, Andrew 70, 332, 337, 340, 344
McDevitt, Danny 192
McDougald, Gil 181–82, 184, 188–89, 191, 193–94, 196
McDowell, Jack 275, 277
McDowell, Roger 256, 259, 261
McDowell, Sam 204, 215, 220
McGann, Dan 97, 105–06
McGee, Willie 252, 254
McGinnis, Jumbo 80
McGinnity, Joe 24, 32, 98–100, 103–05
McGlothen, Lynn 224–25
McGraw, John 94, 97–98, 101–02, 117, 119, 134, 138, 153
McGraw, Tug 240, 246
McGregor, Scott 240, 246–47, 250
McGriff, Fred 260, 262, 264–66, 275, 277
McGwire, Mark 62, 261, 265, 267, 269, 271–72, 275, 279, 290–91, 296
McInnis, Stuffy 116, 118
McIntyre, Matty 112
McJames, Doc 97–98
McKechnie, Bill 146
McKeon, Jack 307
McLain, Denny 210–13, 364n1
McLemore, Mark 283, 288
McLish, Cal 169, 195
McMahon, Don 192, 195, 198
McMahon, Sadie 88–90, 95
McMurtry, Craig 248
McNally, Dave 207, 209, 214, 216, 218
McPhee, Bid 33, 43
McQuillan, George 111
McQuinn, George 170, 174
McRae, Hal 230–31, 233, 244
McReynolds, Kevin 250–51, 256, 259–61
McVey, Cal 38–40, 73–76
Meadows, Lee 140, 142, 144
Medwick, Joe 25, 32, 51, 152, 154, 156–58, 166
Meekin, Jouett 94–95
Melton, Cliff 158–60
Merced, Orlando 274

Merrill, Stump 7
Merritt, Jim 208–09, 216, 218
Mertes, Sam 105
Messersmith, Andy 225–28, 230
Meusel, Bob 134, 136
Meusel, Irish 136
Meyerle, Levi 37, 72
Meyers, Chief 116–17
Mientkiewicz, Doug 305
Miller, Dots 113–14
Miller, Roscoe 100
Miller, Shelby 340
Miller, Stu 193, 195, 199, 207
Milligan, Jocko 87
Millwood, Kevin 293
Milnar, Al 164
Mincher, Don 205
Minoso, Minnie 181, 186, 189, 191, 194–96
Minton, Greg 261
Mitchell, Clarence 145–46
Mitchell, Kevin 259, 263–64, 278
Mize, Johnny 31, 51–52, 158, 160, 162–63, 166–67, 173, 175–76
Mogridge, George 133
Molina, Yadier 65, 319, 337, 340
Molitor, Paul 28–29, 31, 243, 245, 272–73, 275–76
Monday, Rick 235
Mondesi, Raul 68, 281, 284, 287
Montefusco, John 227, 229
Moon, Wally 195
Moore, Donnie 252–53, 258
Moore, Earl 114
Moore, Mike 263, 265, 268–69
Moore, Wilcy 142–143
Mora, Melvin 307
Morales, Kendrys 325
Moran, Pat 131
Morgan, Cy 112
Morgan, Joe 30, 56–58, 220, 222, 225, 227–230, 239, 248
Morgan, Mike 270
Morrill, John 80–81
Morris, Ed 68–69, 81–82, 84
Morris, Jack 2, 60, 250, 252, 258, 269, 272
Morrison, Johnny 134–35
Morton, Guy 122
Moseby, Lloyd 249, 258
Moss, Dick 364n7
Mossi, Don 187, 198
Moyer, Jamie 292, 305
Moynahan, Mike 80
Mullane, Tony 79–81
Mullin, George 113, 116
Mulliniks, Rance 253
Mumphrey, Jerry 241
Munger, Red 175
Mungo, Van 171
Munson, Thurman 221, 228, 230–31
Murcer, Bobby 7, 217, 219

Murphy, Dale 239, 244–45, 247–48, 250–51, 258
Murphy, Danny 107, 115
Murphy, Dwayne 241
Murphy, Eddie 32, 123, 233, 238, 240, 245–47, 249, 264, 272
Murphy, Johnny 154
Murray, Eddie 32
Musial, Stan 30, 48, 51–54, 61, 167–69, 171, 173–78, 180–81, 184–85, 191, 362n16
Mussina, Mike 270, 272, 276, 279–80, 295, 297, 300, 304
Myer, Buddy 152
Myers, Billy 162–63
Myers, Hi 132
Myers, Randy 261, 264, 267, 270, 273

Nabors, Jack 125
Nagy, Charles 279, 283, 288
Napoli, Mike 332
Narleski, Ray 187
Nash, Billy 89, 93
Neagle, Denny 288
Neal, Charlie 195
Nelson, Candy 82
Nettles, Graig 217, 228, 230–31, 235, 241, 245, 254
Newcombe, Don 178–80, 184, 187–90, 192–93
Newhouser, Hal 32, 52–53, 169–70, 172–74
Newsom, Bobo 161, 163–64
Nichols, Kid 30, 42–44, 47, 56, 88, 90, 92–98, 105
Nichols, Tricky 76
Nicholson, Bill 167–68
Niedenfuer, Tom 248
Niekro, Joe 237
Niekro, Phil 28, 29, 31, 46, 57–59, 213–14, 216, 225, 229, 232, 234, 237, 244–45
Nokes, Matt 258
Nolan, Gary 208, 216
Nomo, Hideo 284
Nops, Jerry 97
Noren, Irv 187
North, Billy 221, 223, 225–26, 235
Northrup, Jim 210–11

Oakes, Rebel 124
O'Brien, Buck 118
O'Brien, Cinders 91
O'Brien, Darby 87, 89
O'Brien, Jack 79–80
O'Dea, Ken 162
O'Doul, Lefty 146, 153
O'Farrell, Bob 142
Oglivie, Ben 238, 245
Ojeda, Bob 255–56, 259
Oldring, Rube 115–16
Olerud, John 272–73, 275–76, 290, 298
Oliva, Tony 202, 204–05, 213, 215
Oliver, Al 225, 246
Olson, Ivy 132

O'Neill, Paul 279, 288
O'Neill, Tip 84–87, 91–92
Ontiveros, Steve 277
Oquendo, Jose 264
Ordonez, Magglio 301, 305, 318
Orosco, Jesse 256, 259
O'Rourke, Jim 33, 39, 44, 76–77
O'Rourke, John 77
Orr, Dave 81–83, 89
Orth, Al 101, 107–108
Ortiz, David 65, 311, 314, 317
Osteen, Claude 205, 207
Oswalt, Roy 302, 315, 319
Otis, Amos 233, 235
O'Toole, Jim 199
Ott, Mel 30, 49–52, 145, 149–50, 152–53, 156–58, 160–61, 167, 171
Overall, Orval 109, 113

Pafko, Andy 172
Pagan, Angel 337
Page, Joe 175, 178–79
Paige, Satchel 177
Palica, Erv 180
Palmeiro, Rafael 279, 282, 292
Palmer, Dean 288
Palmer, Jim 31, 57, 207, 209, 214–16, 218–19, 221, 223, 225–26, 228, 231, 233, 244–45, 247
Papelbon, Jonathan 314
Parent, Freddy 101, 103–04, 106, 112
Park, Chan Ho 287
Parker, Dave 227, 231, 234, 236–37
Parnell, Mel 177–80
Parra, Gerardo 341
Parrish, Lance 250, 364n2
Parrish, Larry 237, 246
Pascual, Camilo 194, 200–01
Passeau, Claude 161, 163, 171
Patterson, Roy 102
Pavano, Carl 308
Pearce, Steve 342
Pearson, Monte 157
Peavy, Jake 312, 319, 323
Peckinpaugh, Roger 138, 361n6
Pedroia, Dustin 65, 321, 324, 331, 339, 342
Pena, Alejandro 248, 250, 254, 261
Pena, Carlos 318
Pence, Hunter 332, 344
Pendleton, Terry 264, 269–71
Pennock, Herb 28, 33, 48–49, 121, 136–37, 139, 144
Penny, Brad 319
Pepitone, Joe 204
Peralta, Jhonny 344
Perez, Pascual 248
Perez, Tony 33, 216, 218, 222, 228, 248
Perranoski, Ron 200–03, 205, 207, 214, 216
Perritt, Pol 123
Perry, Gaylord 31, 46, 56–58, 205, 207–08, 216, 218–21, 224

Perry, Jim 195–96, 213–16
Perry, Scott 128
Pesky, Johnny 173, 177, 179
Peters, Gary 201, 204, 209–10
Petrocelli, Rico 209, 211
Petry, Dan 250
Pettis, Gary 252–53, 255–56
Pettitte, Andy 64–65, 282, 286, 312
Petty, Jesse 141
Pfeffer, Fred 91–92
Pfeffer, Jeff 120, 122, 125
Pfiester, Jack 108–09
Phillippe, Deacon 103–05
Phillips, Adolfo 208
Phillips, Tony 276
Piazza, Mike 33, 274, 279, 281, 284, 287
Pierce, Billy 182–83, 185, 188–89, 191
Piersall, Jim 196
Pierzynski, A.J. 305
Pike, Lip 73
Pinkney, George 89
Pinson, Vada 198–99
Pipgras, George 144
Pipp, Wally 136
Pittinger, Togie 102
Pizarro, Juan 204
Plank, Eddie 30, 45–46, 61, 101–04, 106–07, 109–10, 112, 115, 117, 121, 123, 359n15
Plummer, Bill 232
Podres, Johnny 191–92, 199
Polanco, Placido 311
Pollet, Howie 173–75, 178
Pollock, A.J. 23, 348
Porter, Darrell 234–36
Posada, Jorge 293, 304
Posey, Buster 23, 65, 337, 344, 348
Post, Wally 190, 199
Potter, Nels 169–70
Powell, Boog 204, 206, 212, 214–15
Prado, Martin 336
Price, David 23, 335, 346, 349
Prim, Ray 171
Prior, Mark 306
Puckett, Kirby 33, 60, 255, 259–60, 271
Puhl, Terry 239
Puig, Yasiel 341, 344
Pujols, Albert 64–65, 299, 302, 306, 309, 312, 315, 319, 322, 326, 329, 332
Purkey, Bob 200

Quentin, Carlos 321
Quinn, Jack 120–21
Quisenberry, Dan 246, 251, 253

Radatz, Dick 201
Radbourn, Old Hoss 31, 39–41, 78–82, 87, 89
Radford, Paul 91
Radke, Brad 295, 308
Raffensberger, Ken 69
Raines, Tim 24, 242, 250, 252, 255, 258–59

Ramirez, Alexei 328
Ramirez, Aramis 319
Ramirez, Hanley 325, 341
Ramirez, Manny 64, 286, 289, 292, 295, 297, 307, 311, 322
Ramsey, Toad 84–85
Randolph, Willie 2, 29, 60, 230, 233, 235, 238, 240, 258, 264
Raschi, Vic 177, 179, 182, 186
Rasmus, Colby 329
Rath, Morrie 131
Rau, Doug 230
Reddick, Josh 346
Reed, Jody 262, 266
Reed, Ron 230
Reese, Pee Wee 31, 52–53, 61, 167–68, 173–75, 178, 180–81, 184–86, 188
Regan, Phil 207
Reilly, John 86
Reiser, Pete 165, 167–68, 174
Reitz, Heinie 97
Rendon, Anthony 343
Renteria, Edgar 302, 319
Rettenmund, Merv 216, 218, 223
Reulbach, Ed 106, 108, 111, 113, 117
Reuschel, Rick 222, 231–32, 261
Reuss, Jerry 227–28, 230, 239–40, 242, 247–48, 256
Reynolds, Allie 179, 181, 183–84
Reynolds, Bob 223
Rhines, Billy 88, 96–97
Rhoads, Bob 108
Rhoden, Rick 235, 255
Rice, Jim 2, 33, 35–37, 227, 233, 236, 238, 245, 254, 256
Rice, Sam 33, 138, 148
Richard, J.R. 237, 240
Richardson, Bobby 200
Richardson, Hardy 87, 89, 91
Richmond, Lee 77
Rickey, Branch 68, 167–68, 178
Riddle, Elmer 165–66
Righetti, Dave 241
Rigney, Topper 138
Rijo, Jose 266–67, 270–71, 274, 285
Ring, Jimmy 137
Ripken, Cal 30, 46, 60–63, 245–47, 249, 262, 264–65, 268, 279
Rivera, Juan 325
Rivera, Mariano 65, 282
Rivers, Mickey 228, 230–31
Rixey, Eppa 32, 125, 127, 133, 137, 139
Rizzo, Anthony 23, 347
Rizzo, Johnny 160
Rizzuto, Phil 25, 33, 52, 57, 165–66, 168, 179–84, 186, 362n16
Roberts, Bip 266, 273, 275
Roberts, Brian 311
Roberts, Dave 218
Roberts, Robin 31, 53–55, 180–81, 184–85, 187

Robertson, Bob 217
Robertson, Nate 314
Robinson, Bill 237
Robinson, Brooks 30, 55–57, 61, 196, 199, 202, 204, 206–08, 210, 214, 218–19, 223–24, 233
Robinson, Don 261
Robinson, Floyd 204
Robinson, Frank 30, 52, 55–56, 61, 190–91, 198–200, 206–08, 212, 214–15, 221
Robinson, Jackie 27, 31, 52–53, 61, 175–76, 178, 180–81, 184–86, 189–90, 192, 352
Robinson, Jeff 262
Robinson, Wilbert 94–95, 132, 360n15
Robinson, Yank 84, 86–87
Rodriguez, Alex 51, 57, 63–65, 283, 290, 295, 298, 301, 305, 307, 311, 318, 321
Rodriguez, Francisco 315
Rodriguez, Ivan 283, 286, 289, 292, 295
Roe, Preacher 171, 177–81, 184, 187
Rogell, Billy 154–55
Rogers, Kenny 280, 290, 295, 311
Rogers, Steve 237, 240, 244, 246
Rolen, Scott 298, 302, 309, 315, 319
Rolfe, Red 156–57, 161–62, 165
Rollins, Jimmy 319
Romanick, Ron 250
Rommel, Eddie 135, 140
Rooker, Jim 225, 228
Root, Charlie 141, 146, 161
Rose, Pete 7, 18, 40, 56–59, 216, 218, 220, 222, 228–30, 237, 248, 263–64, 267
Rosen, Al 179–80, 183–85, 187–88
Rosen, Goody 171
Rossman, Claude 112
Roush, Edd 33, 131, 134
Rowand, Aaron 308
Rowe, Schoolboy 153–54, 164, 168
Rozema, Dave 231
Rucker, Nap 113–14, 116–17
Rudi, Joe 219–20, 225
Rudolph, Dick 120
Rueter, Kirk 68
Ruether, Dutch 132, 140
Ruffing, Red 28, 31, 40, 50–51, 150, 157–59, 162, 168, 173
Ruhle, Vern 240
Runnells, Tom 272
Rush, Bob 193
Rusie, Amos 32, 43, 88, 90, 92–96
Russell, Bill 223, 228, 245
Russell, Reb 118, 127, 136
Ruth, Babe 8, 27, 30, 47–49, 51–52, 54, 56, 61–63, 123–40, 142–43, 145, 147–48, 150–51, 153–56, 183, 198, 279
Ruthven, Dick 235
Ryan, Brendan 326
Ryan, Jimmy 85
Ryan, Nolan 28–29, 31, 58–60, 219, 222, 231, 238–40, 242, 259, 261
Ryan, Rosy 136

Sabathia, CC 318, 322, 331
Saberhagen, Bret 252–53, 257, 263, 277
Sabo, Chris 266–67
Sadecki, Ray 208
Sain, Johnny 173, 176–78, 186
Saito, Takashi 316
Sale, Chris 336, 339, 343
Sallee, Slim 119, 131–32
Salmon, Tim 280
Sambito, Joe 237, 240
Samuel, Juan 250–51
Sanchez, Anibal 339
Sandberg, Ryne 28–30, 32, 60, 250–51, 253, 264, 266, 268, 271
Sanders, Ben 85, 87
Sanders, Reggie 281, 299
Sanderson, Scott 7, 240, 251
Sandoval, Pablo 333, 344
Sanford, Jack 195
Sanguillen, Manny 217–18, 227
Santana, Ervin 321
Santana, Johan 305, 308, 311, 314, 322
Santo, Ron 32, 203, 206, 208, 214
Saunders, Joe 321
Sax, Steve 255, 262
Schalk, Ray 34, 143
Schang, Wally 119, 129, 134, 136
Scherzer, Max 23, 65, 339, 343, 347
Schilling, Curt 287, 299, 302, 306–07, 314
Schmidt, Jason 306, 309
Schmidt, Mike 30, 58–59, 224, 227, 229–31, 234–36, 239–41, 244, 247–49, 251, 253, 255
Schoendienst, Red 33, 192
Schofield, Dick (SS, 1953–71) 205
Schofield, Dick (SS, 1983–96) 256, 260, 265
Schourek, Pete 281
Schreiber, Paul 172
Schu, Rick 253
Schulte, Frank 115–16
Schulte, Fred 152
Schumacher, Hal 153
Schupp, Ferdie 127, 129
Scioscia, Mike 253–54
Score, Herb 188–89
Scott, Everett 61–62
Scott, George 209, 233
Scott, Jack 139–140
Scott, Jim 122, 127
Scott, Mike 255–56, 258, 261, 264
Seaton, Tom 118–19
Seaver, Tom 30, 46, 57–59, 210, 213–14, 216, 218, 222, 224, 227, 229, 232, 237, 242
Seitz, Peter 228
Selee, Frank 96
Selig, Bud 351
Selkirk, George 156, 161–62
Seminick, Andy 180
Seward, Ed 86
Sewell, Joe 33, 133, 136
Seybold, Socks 107

Seymour, Cy 102, 105–07
Shannon, Mike 210
Shantz, Bobby 183, 191
Shaw, Bob 195–96, 205, 207
Shaw, Jeff 284
Shawkey, Bob 123, 132, 135–37
Sheckard, Jimmy 99, 101–03, 115–16
Sheets, Ben 70, 309
Sheffield, Gary 271, 301, 305
Shelby, John 264
Sherdel, Bill 144–46
Sherry, Larry 195
Shocker, Urban 133, 135–36, 139, 141
Shore, Ernie 123
Short, Chris 203
Shotton, Burt 68, 176
Show, Eric 256
Siebern, Norm 192–94, 199
Siever, Ed 110
Sievers, Roy 196
Simmons, Al 25, 31, 50–51, 140, 145, 147–49, 151
Simmons, Andrelton 340, 343
Simmons, Curt 180–81
Simmons, Ted 245
Simpson, Wayne 216, 218
Singer, Bill 208
Singleton, Jonathan 19
Singleton, Ken 231, 233, 238, 240
Sisler, George 29, 33, 128–29, 131, 135–37
Sizemore, Grady 311, 314, 321
Skowron, Bill 187, 190, 194–96
Slaughter, Enos 32, 166–68, 173–75, 178, 180–81
Smalley, Roy 234
Smiley, John 270, 272, 274, 278, 284
Smith, Al 187, 363n9
Smith, Dave 240
Smith, Earl 134
Smith, Frank 112
Smith, Hal 197
Smith, Lonnie 246, 263
Smith, Mike 85, 97
Smith, Ozzie 25, 31, 58, 61, 246, 252, 254–55, 257, 259–60, 263–64, 268
Smith, Pete 273
Smith, Reggie 215, 224–25, 232
Smith, Zane 267, 278
Smoltz, John 28, 31, 60, 64, 269–71, 273, 281, 283, 288, 293, 312, 315, 319
Snider, Duke 27, 31, 53–54, 61, 178–80, 182, 184–86, 188–92, 352
Snow, J.T. 309
Snyder, Frank 134
Snyder, Pop 79
Sonnanstine, Andy 129
Soriano, Alfonso 300, 304, 315
Sosa, Elias 237
Sosa, Sammy 62, 281, 290–91, 296, 299, 302
Sothoron, Allan 134
Soto, Mario 244, 247

Southworth, Billy 138, 146
Spahn, Warren 30, 53–55, 175, 177, 181, 184–85, 190, 192–95, 197–98
Spalding, Al 37–39, 72–76
Speaker, Tris 30, 46–48, 54, 117–19, 122–25, 131–33, 135–36
Spiers, Bill 287
Stafford, Bill 198
Stahl, Chick 96, 98
Staley, Gerry 178, 180, 195
Staley, Harry 90–92
Stanky, Eddie 173–77, 180, 182, 209
Stanley, Bob 234, 245
Stanley, Mike 279
Stanton, Giancarlo 343
Stargell, Willie 32, 207, 217–20, 222–25, 237
Start, Joe 76–77
Stein, Ed 92–93
Steinbach, Terry 277
Steinfeldt, Harry 108–09
Stengel, Casey 53, 182
Stennett, Rennie 227–28, 230
Stenzel, Jake 97
Stephens, Vern 169–70, 177–179, 362n15
Stephenson, Riggs 146, 150
Sternberg, Stuart 366n3
Stewart, Dave 260, 262, 265, 267, 269, 272
Stewart, Lefty 152
Stieb, Dave 241, 243, 246, 249, 251, 253, 265–66, 272
Stirnweiss, Snuffy 169–70, 172
Stivetts, Jack 42–43, 87–88, 90, 92–94
Stock, Milt 127
Stone, George 107
Stone, Steve 240
Stottlemyre, Mel 204–05, 207
Stottlemyre, Todd 70, 276
Stovey, Harry 80, 86, 89, 91–82
Stratton, Scott 88
Strawberry, Darryl 61, 251, 254, 256–57, 260–61, 263, 266, 269–70, 272
Stroud, Sailor 123
Strunk, Amos 129
Sturdivant, Tom 190–91, 193
Suggs, George 120–21
Suhr, Gus 160
Sullivan, Billy 113
Sullivan, Frank 191
Sullivan, Marty 85
Summers, Ed 113
Sutcliffe, Rick 251, 253, 258, 264, 267
Sutter, Bruce 28–29, 34, 60, 232, 246
Sutton, Don 31, 59, 207, 220, 223, 230, 239–40, 244
Sutton, Ezra 81
Suzuki, Ichiro 298, 305, 308, 315, 318, 322
Sweeney, Charlie 81
Swift, Bill 275
Swindell, Greg 273–74
Swisher, Nick 335

Tanana, Frank 226, 229, 231, 262
Tannehill, Jesse 104–106
Tannehill, Lee 107
Tapani, Kevin 268–69
Taylor, Billy 81
Taylor, Harry (1B) 89
Taylor, Harry (RHP) 175
Taylor, Jack 102, 104
Tebeau, Patsy 98
Teheran, Julio 343
Teixeira, Mark 311, 321, 335, 346
Tejada, Miguel 67, 307, 311
Tekulve, Kent 237
Tenace, Gene 223–26, 237
Tenney, Fred 96, 98
Terry, Bill 33, 147, 149–50, 153, 156, 361n22
Terry, Ralph 198–201, 204
Tesreau, Jeff 117–19, 121–22, 127
Tettleton, Mickey 264
Thevenow, Tommy 142, 360n15
Thigpen, Bobby 267
Thomas, Frank 30, 32, 60, 268, 271, 277, 279–80, 286, 295
Thomas, Gorman 245
Thomas, Ira 116
Thomas, Tommy 142
Thome, Jim 64, 280, 283, 286, 295, 298, 301
Thompson, Hank 187
Thompson, Justin 286
Thompson, Milt 264
Thompson, Robby 263–64, 274–75
Thompson, Sam 34, 85, 93
Thomson, Bobby 182
Thon, Dickie 244, 247
Tiant, Luis 210, 224–25, 228, 234
Tiernan, Mike 86
Timlin, Mike 269, 272
Tinker, Joe 32, 108, 111–12, 114–16, 121
Titcomb, Cannonball 86
Todd, Jim 227
Tolan, Bobby 216, 220
Tomney, Phil 89
Toney, Fred 122, 131–32
Torborg, Jeff 307
Torre, Joe 198
Torres, Andres 329
Torrez, Mike 229–30, 234–35
Tracy, Jim 327
Trammell, Alan 24, 60, 249–50, 253, 257–58, 262, 265
Traynor, Pie 34
Tresh, Tom 199–202, 204–06
Trosky, Hal 164–65
Trout, Dizzy 169, 173
Trout, Mike 23, 336, 340, 343, 347
Trout, Steve 251
Trucks, Virgil 173, 178, 185
Tudor, John 252, 254, 261
Tulowitzki, Troy 70, 319, 326, 329, 333, 344, 349
Turley, Bob 189–93, 195

Turner, Terry 107
Tyler, Lefty 129

Uggla, Dan 19
Uhle, George 134, 136, 141
Upton, Justin 333
Upton, Melvin, Jr. 19
Uribe, Juan 341
Utley, Chase 65, 312, 315, 319, 322, 325, 329

Valdez, Ismael 284, 287
Valentin, John 280
Valentine, Ellis 240
Valenzuela, Fernando 242, 244–45, 248, 250, 253–55, 259
Vance, Dazzy 28–29, 33, 48, 138–39, 143–44, 147
Vander Meer, Johnny 165–66
Van Slyke, Andy 260, 267, 269–72, 274
Vaughan, Arky 30–31, 50–51, 152–53, 156–57, 160, 162–63, 168
Vaughn, Greg 273, 290
Vaughn, Hippo 125–26, 129–30
Vazquez, Javier 298, 318
Veach, Bobby 122–24, 127, 130
Veale, Bob 207
Velarde, Randy 292
Ventura, Robin 273, 289, 293
Vergez, Johnny 153
Verlander, Justin 65, 314, 325, 328, 331, 336, 339
Vernon, Mickey 185
Versalles, Zoilo 204–06
Vickers, Rube 110
Victorino, Shane 332, 339
Viola, Frank 250, 257–58, 260, 264, 266–67, 269
Virtue, Jake 92
Vitt, Ossie 123
Vizquel, Omar 292
Vogt, Stephen 347
Von der Ahe, Chris 357n5
Votto, Joey 23, 329, 332, 337, 340, 347

Waddell, Rube 32, 102–04, 106–07
Wagner, Honus 30, 44–46, 99, 101–09, 111–17, 146
Wainwright, Adam 65, 319, 326, 329, 340, 344
Wakefield, Tim 272, 311
Walberg, Rube 145–46, 148–50, 361n23
Walker, Curt 141
Walker, Dixie 165–66, 171, 174–76
Walker, Larry 24, 278, 281–82, 287, 291
Walker, Luke 223
Walker, Tom 105
Wallace, Bobby 32, 45–46, 98, 101
Wallach, Tim 246
Walsh, Ed 31, 45–46, 108–10, 112, 114–15, 117
Walters, Bucky 161–63, 165
Waner, Lloyd 34, 143, 146, 162
Waner, Paul 31, 50–51, 141–44, 146, 150, 162
Wang, Chien-Ming 314

Ward, Duane 269, 275
Ward, Monte 32, 76–77, 89–90, 94, 358n9
Ward, Pete 204, 209
Warneke, Lon 150–52, 154, 156, 166
Washburn, Jarrod 311
Washington, Claudell 226, 251, 262
Watson, Bob 238
Weaver, Buck 133
Weaver, Jered 315, 328, 332
Weaver, Sam 76, 79
Webb, Brandon 306, 312, 316, 319, 323
Weidman, Stump 79
Weimer, Jake 104–05, 108
Weiss, Walt 261, 267
Welch, Bob 59–61, 235, 247–48, 254–55, 258–59, 262, 265, 267, 269, 272, 275
Welch, Mickey 32, 41, 81–83, 85–87
Wells, David 266, 272, 281
Wells, Vernon 314
Werber, Billy 162–63
Werth, Jayson 325, 329
Wertz, Vic 180
Wetteland, John 282
Weyhing, Gus 89–90
Wheat, Zack 32, 125, 132, 138
Whitaker, Lou 2, 60–61, 250, 252, 262, 268
White, Bill 203
White, Deacon 33, 38–39, 73–76, 79
White, Devon 60–62, 257, 265, 268–70, 273
White, Doc 104, 107–08, 113
White, Ernie 166
White, Frank 235, 251
White, Roy 7, 215, 217, 228, 230
White, Will 39–40, 76, 79–80
Whitehead, Burgess 158
Whitehill, Earl 152
Whitney, Jim 78, 80–81, 84
Whitson, Ed 266
Wickland, Al 121
Wiggins, Alan 251
Wilhelm, Hoyt 24, 33, 187, 194, 204–05, 210
Wilkerson, Brad 308
Wilkins, Rick 274
Wilks, Ted 169, 174
Williams, Bernie 25, 280, 286, 288, 292, 295, 297, 300
Williams, Billy 28–29, 32, 215–16, 220
Williams, Frank 259
Williams, Jimmy 108
Williams, Jimy 264
Williams, Ken 135–36
Williams, Lefty 130
Williams, Matt 274–75, 278–79, 281, 286
Williams, Stan 199, 216
Williams, Ted 30, 35, 51–53, 164–67, 173–81, 186, 188, 191
Williamson, Ned 40–41, 77–78, 83
Willis, Dontrelle 312

Willis, Vic 32, 97–99, 101–02, 108, 113
Wills, Maury 200, 202, 205–06
Wilson, Art 116, 120–22, 124
Wilson, C.J. 328, 332
Wilson, Earl 206
Wilson, Hack 34, 138, 141, 143, 145–47, 149
Wilson, Steve 365n5
Wilson, Willie 61, 236, 239–41, 244, 251
Wiltse, Hooks 112
Winfield, Dave 28–29, 32, 237, 260, 262, 272, 275
Winter, George 105
Witt, Mike 249–50, 253, 255–56, 261
Wolf, Chicken 89
Wolff, Roger 171–72
Wolters, Rynie 37, 72
Wood, Alex 343
Wood, Jimmy 37
Wood, Joe 117–18, 123
Wood, Kerry 306
Wood, Wilbur 210, 217, 219, 221
Woodling, Gene 184–87
Wright, David 319, 322, 336, 340
Wright, George 37–39, 73–75, 77, 79
Wright, Glenn 140
Wright, Harry 72, 75, 79
Wright, Jaret 288
Wyatt, Whit 165, 168
Wyckoff, Weldon 121
Wynn, Early 33, 184, 186–89, 195–96
Wynn, Jim 225
Wyse, Hank 171

Yastrzemski, Carl 31, 46, 56–58, 201, 208–10, 215, 225, 233
York, Rudy 164
Youkilis, Kevin 321, 324
Young, Cy 30, 43–45, 56, 92–96, 98–100, 102, 103–06, 109–10
Young, Irv 106
Young, Matt 246
Young, Pep 160
Youngs, Ross 34, 129, 131–32, 134, 136–38, 140–141
Yount, Robin 28–29, 32, 60, 238, 241, 243, 245–46, 262

Zachary, Tom 138, 146
Zahn, Geoff 246, 249–50
Zambrano, Carlos 306
Zettlein, George 37–38, 40, 72–73
Zimmer, Chief 92
Zimmerman, Heinie 116–17, 126–27
Zimmerman, Jeff 292
Zimmerman, Ryan 325, 329
Zisk, Richie 223–25
Zito, Barry 301, 315
Zobrist, Ben 324, 331, 335, 342
Zwilling, Dutch 120–22, 124

www.ingramcontent.com/pod-product-compliance
Lightning Source LLC
Chambersburg PA
CBHW051205300426
44116CB00006B/440